CW01337071

THE

Lay Folks Mass Book

OR

THE MANNER OF HEARING MASS

WITH RUBRICS AND DEVOTIONS FOR THE PEOPLE

IN FOUR TEXTS

AND

Offices in English

ACCORDING TO THE USE OF YORK

FROM MANUSCRIPTS OF THE Xth TO THE XVth CENTURY

WITH

Appendix, Notes, and Glossary

BY

THOMAS FREDERICK SIMMONS, M.A.

CANON OF YORK, RECTOR OF DALTON HOLME

DISCARDED

LONDON

PUBLISHED FOR THE EARLY ENGLISH TEXT SOCIETY

BY N. TRÜBNER & CO., 57 & 59, LUDGATE HILL

MDCCCLXXIX

Printing Statement:

Due to the very old age and scarcity of this book, many of the pages may be hard to read due to the blurring of the original text, possible missing pages, missing text, dark backgrounds and other issues beyond our control.

Because this is such an important and rare work, we believe it is best to reproduce this book regardless of its original condition.

Thank you for your understanding.

CONTENTS.

THE EDITOR'S PREFACE

The Early English Text Society.

THE early English treatise on the Mass, which has for some years appeared among the intended publications of this Society as the Lay-Folks Mass-Book—a title adopted to indicate its purpose—is at length placed in the hands of the members. It has been so long delayed from various unforeseen causes, and chiefly in the hope of finding the needful manuscripts.

I have altogether failed in the search for a copy of the original treatise, and our earliest and best text (B) is a transcript of the English translation, which has been subjected to systematic verbal alterations at the hands of a midland scribe of the fourteenth century. From a comparison with text E, which is an independent transcript by a west-midland scribe of a hundred years later, there do not appear to be any variations that leave us in doubt as to the tenour of the original translation. With the help of text C, though that, like texts A, D, and F, has undergone a ritual revision, it would not be difficult to restore the verbal forms, if a *textus restitutus* were the object of the Society.

My attention was in the first instance drawn to the British Museum MS. (our text B) by Mr. Maskell's extracts from it in the notes to his Ancient English Liturgies. It was one of the first books I asked for on my next visit to the Reading-room, and, besides its curious ritual information, I was much struck by the fact that it was the only document I had met with that enables us to know the prayers which the unlearned of our forefathers used at mass, and by the light it threw upon

their inner religious life from a point of view different from
that afforded by the many mediæval sermons(*) that have
come down to us. I made as many extracts as I had time for,
and there my concern with it might have ended, but that some
ten or twelve years afterwards I was asked to help in the
work of this Society. When I agreed to edit this manuscript,
which was all I originally undertook to do, I had very little
idea of the time it would be hanging about, nor of the inroad
which it would make on my leisure, but having undertaken
it, I have been unwilling to put it forth in an incomplete
condition. That I have done so, has not been from any
sparing of trouble on my part. When I went through the
transcript, which Mr. E. Brock had made for the Society,
with close attention, as a man does who has undertaken the
task of editor, I found not only what I had forgotten or had
not observed when I had examined the manuscript, that it
was a translation, but also that it was the work of a scribe
who was not familiar with the northern dialect in which, as I
hope to prove to the satisfaction of the reader, the translation
had been originally written.

I was unwilling to send it to the press without an attempt
to procure copies of this, and of the original from which it
had been translated. I circulated a print of the British
Museum MS. in the hope of getting the needful information,
and I am almost ashamed to think of the time I have myself

---

* NOTE.—Besides the series of mediæval sermons, the E. E. T. Society
has already printed Myrc's *Duties of a Parish Priest*, edited by
Mr. Peacock, and *Oure Ladyes Myroure*, edited by Revd J. H. Blunt.
The present editor has undertaken Archbishop Thoresby's *Catechism
in English*, with the Latin as agreed on in the Convocation of York,
A.D. 1357, both from the authentic copy inserted in this Arch-
bishop's register, and a Lollard paraphrase from a MS. in the
Lambeth Library to be printed on the opposite page. This with
the few pieces in this volume will complete the extant authorized
English formularies of the Northern province.

The Committee propose to continue this series by the Festival
from the MSS. or Caxton's edition, the *Oculus Sacerdotis* in English
verse, and some English Primers and Offices in English for the
Southern province, which are known to exist in larger numbers
than those hitherto found in the North.

spent, as I had opportunity, in hunting through manuscripts and searching catalogues; and I am sorry to have to add, what is of more consequence, the trouble I have given to my friends, and to others whose help I could only claim on the score of their being able to assist in the enquiry.

After all, the result has been that, not to mention other libraries at home and abroad, I have had to give up the hope of finding the missing MSS. in the British Museum, the Bodleian, the University Library at Cambridge, the public libraries at Paris and Edinburgh, the Lambeth Library, the libraries at Durham, Lincoln, and other cathedrals in this country, at Ushaw and other Roman Catholic colleges, or in the libraries at Rouen and Caen, where, from the Norman origin of the treatise, it seemed not impossible that a copy may have found its way at the revolution among the spoils of some Norman monastery or manor house.

I did, however, succeed in getting to know of other MSS., which, though later than the Museum MS., are interesting as showing the changes that were afterwards introduced. Mr. Furnivall told me of the fragment printed from the Advocate's Library at Edinburgh (*Text* A); and also of the MS. in the University Library at Cambridge (*MS.* D), which Mr. Bradshaw, the librarian, had been good enough to mention to him. Professor Skeat placed at my disposal his own transcript of our text F. I venture to offer to these gentlemen the thanks of the Society and my own for their kindness in helping me; and equally to those also, who though unsuccessful, were not less ready in giving their time and trouble for the search. I had myself noticed the mention of our text C (*Corpus Library, Oxford*) and text E (*Gonville and Caius College, Cambridge*) in Barnard's *Catalogus Librorum MSS. Angliæ et Hiberniæ*, a book which at the end of nearly two hundred years remains without a second edition, invaluable as that would be, if it were brought down to the present time.

A transcript of the Oxford MS. I obtained without any difficulty, but I did not receive our E text until the texts B, C, and F had been arranged and printed in a three-text form.

It appeared to Mr. Furnivall and the committee to be of such dialectic interest that it has been added as a fourth text. Although it is late, and written by a very illiterate scribe—perhaps from that very circumstance—it has retained what I am disposed to think will be found to be the wording of the original, if that should ever be recovered; and it justifies my conjectural insertions in text B, where there were holes in the vellum of the MS.

In the course of the enquiry I obtained transcripts of several MSS. relating to the mass, which had not been published. Three of them are printed *in extenso* in the Appendix, and I have quoted largely from some of the others in the notes.

It may have been disappointing not to find the originals of which we were in search, but it is hardly to be wondered at, when we consider the wear and tear of small books in constant use, and the risk of their being "defaced and abolished" in times of religious persecution, when the narrow bigotry which destroyed the service-books would not have spared books of private devotion. The Book of Common Prayer is a much larger book, and must have existed in a far greater number of copies, and yet how few are known of the early editions. Of those in the time of Edward the Sixth no doubt great numbers were brought in and burnt in the time of Queen Mary; but take the case of the many editions known to have been printed in the long reign of Elizabeth,—how rare they are. No doubt many were destroyed when churches and parsonages were "rabbled" in the civil wars; but the puritans, when they got the upper hand, did not pretend to do this under colour of written law, even when they so far prevailed that a third conviction of using the Common Prayer was followed by a year's imprisonment.

The Bidding Prayers according to the use of York are added as the complement of the private prayers of the people at the mass, and as being the only devotions in English which were used publicly in our churches before the reformation. The series is not complete, only four MS. York Manuals being known to have escaped the ravages of time and the system-

atic destruction to which they were exposed in common with
other service-books. The Hours of the Cross from the unique
MS. *Horæ* in the York Minster Library make up our scanty
array of liturgical forms in the mother tongue, but they are
all that are known to have been used in the Northern
province.(1)

The ordinary of the mass is given in the Appendix, as the
four texts obviously suggest a reference to the service to
which they were subsidiary; and there must be members of
the Society who have not a missal within reach, and most
certainly not a missal of an English use of the period of the
MSS. I have appended a mass according to the use of
York, not so much because I could do so with least trouble
from having made a transcript of it many years since, but
because it was the one used in the greater part of the north
of England, where the translation appears to have been made;
and also because, whilst equally answering the purpose of
those who do not care to investigate the specific differences
of particular uses, it may be very acceptable to others who
have had their attention drawn to the study of comparative
liturgiology, from the extreme rarity of missals of the
York use,(2) and the silence of liturgiologists as to its
peculiarities.(3)

In the translation, as my object was simply to convey to
the English reader the grammatical force of the Latin, I have
not been tempted to make a vain effort to emulate the
rythmical flow of the revisers of our old service-books, which
is essential to any translation for liturgical use; but I have
used the prayer-book rendering of the parts which they
retained.

(1) There are many prayers for personal use in the *Horæ*. See
Notes, p. 248, &c.

(2) When the Appendix was stereotyped, now more than four years
ago, Mr. Maskell's Ancient Liturgies was the only work where the
student could find the York Mass. He there gave the ordinary of the
mass from the printed edition of 1517; but Dr. Henderson's edition
of the York Missal was soon after published for the Surtees Society, and
for this he collated all the known MSS. and editions. He gives (Vol.
II. p. 358) a list of the manuscripts, seven in number, and of twenty-
four copies of the five editions known to be extant.

(3) See Notes, p. 353(3) and p. 355(10).

Dogmatic decrees and other synodal decisions in Latin as to the doctrine of the Eucharist were very numerous; but so far as I have observed, the only English authorized statements that were put forth in the middle ages are those in Appendix II. The piece in Appendix III does not treat of the manner of celebrating or hearing mass, and has little of antiquarian or linguistic interest; but I make no apology for including it in this collection, as it may prove—even to those of us who may not accept the doctrinal opinions that underlie it— that there were some among our forefathers who approached the subject in a devout and humble spirit, that was in strong contrast with the tone of many of their contemporaries.

The pieces in Appendix IV and V are of a very different character. There is much more to interest the antiquarian, and they serve to bring before us an aspect of the religion of the time, which has to be considered in forming an opinion on the subject.

In these and the other pieces here brought together, as in all monuments of the religious life and feeling of our forefathers, there is much to be noted from a theological point of view. This is altogether beyond the scope of the Society, but it will be readily understood that in any attempt to illustrate the text, it would be impossible to avoid ritual and doctrinal questions. These it has been my object to discuss —to use a well-drawn distinction—not δογματικῶς, but διηγη- ματικῶς, placing facts and quotations that bear upon them before my readers, and leaving it to those, who care to do so, to form their own conclusions.

Some of these questions bear upon certain doctrines and practices that were received or allowed in the Church of England when the manuscripts were written, and were after- wards either formally rejected or advisedly put away : but the circumstance that I am a clergyman of the reformed Church, and that I am one of those " who according to the order of " our Holy Reformation have deliberately and with good reason " renounced the errors, corruptions, and superstitions, as " well as the Papal Tyranny, which once here prevailed,"(1)

(1) Instead of using my own words, I have adopted the above from

has not appeared to me to be a reason why I should accompany the notes with the running comment of a controversialist. It is from no failure in loyalty in this matter, but because it is due to the E. E. T. Society—and the list will show that there are members who do not belong to the Church of England—that I have been careful to avoid the expression of my own opinion upon points which are the subject of religious controversy; and I have done this,—not because I had not formed opinions in respect to them, but because I had long arrived at very definite conclusions, and I thought I had no right to obtrude them upon my fellow members, who had not joined the Society in the expectation of any such encounter.

In the Glossary will be found all the noticeable words and forms in the B text of the Mass Book, and the references there given will serve for the corresponding places in the other texts. It also includes some of the less usual words and the more peculiar forms in those texts, and in the Appendix and notes. In it, and the notes, I have added illustrative quotations to some few words, for the most part when I have given a meaning that differs from that in some other glossary.

In printing the texts and direct quotations from English MSS., every care has been taken to reproduce the original, except that the punctuation has not uniformly been retained unless when it is so expressly noted. The use of capital letters has been followed; and where contractions are printed at length, the words or letters so expanded are shewn in *italic*. All additions are printed in *italic* within brackets— [broad-faced] where there is a hole in the MS., or when the surface of the vellum has been worn away; and [ordinary type] when they supply what is supposed to be an omission of the scribe. Glosses or verbal explanations are printed in

the " Form of Prayer " which is still used " at the opening of each day's session in both houses of [*the northern*] Convocation." As, for this once, I have allowed myself to give utterance to my own view of one side of the teaching of the Church of England, I venture to add the remaining words of this prayer, which equally express my feeling as to the other: " so " that we may all constantly hold fast the Apostolical and truly " Catholic Faith, and may duly serve Thee without fear, and with a " pure worship."

xvi   PREFACE.

(*italic*) in a parenthesis. Rubrics or words written in red
are printed in **Clarendon**.

Having given some account of my work as editor, it
remains for me to acknowledge the friendly assistance I have
received in the course of it. I have already mentioned the
kindness of the Reverend W. W. Skeat, Professor of Anglo-
Saxon at Cambridge, in respect to our Text F. The thanks
of the Society are also due to the Reverend W. G. Henderson,
D.C.L., Head Master of the Leeds Grammar-School, for a
similar kindness in allowing me to print his own transcript of
the Bidding Prayer in Sir John Lawson's Manual. It would
have been a pleasure to me to have taken this opportunity of
publicly thanking many friends, and others to whom I was
personally unknown, for their valuable help—I have acknowledged the services of some of them in the notes—but I
must now only single out Mr. Edward Maunde Thompson,
Keeper of the MSS. in the British Museum. His scholar-like
knowledge of the treasures in his custody is only equalled by his
kindness in imparting it.—I should have often been at a stand-
still without it, and I never found him at fault at a bad place
in a manuscript, where I could neither read nor construe.

The Very Reverend Hugh Mc. Neile, D.D., then Dean, and
the Chapter of Ripon were good enough to grant me the
loan of their unique service-books according to the use of York;
and I cannot forbear to mention the readiness with which my
brethren the Dean and Chapter of York allowed me to take
away the Manual and other manuscripts ordinarily confined
to the Minster Library.

I venture to add that I shall be much obliged by a note
of any additional MSS. of the texts of the Mass-Book now
printed, or any information as to the French original, or the
author.

T. F. SIMMONS.

Dalton Holme, Yorkshire,
  6th December, 1878.

INTRODUCTION

TO THE FOUR TEXTS OF THE MASS BOOK.

THE publications of the Early English Text Society do far more than fulfil their primary purpose of illustrating the course of the English language. Many of them are no less available for the study of history, where it is not confined to political events, which are most prominent in ordinary histories. A comparison of the four texts will supply an additional opportunity of examining the peculiarities of their several dialects; and the texts themselves,—apart from their liturgical interest, as showing the changes in the ritual, and more especially as to the part which the people were expected to take in the service,—will open a fresh page to the historical student who recognizes the religious condition of the people, or of any particular class, as an important element in the national life.

It is assumed as an axiom that the *lex orandi* at any period in the history of a church is also its *lex credendi;* and if the common prayers may be accepted as the best evidence of the creed of a church, the private prayers of our forefathers, if they were known, would be equally important in an estimate of their personal belief and spiritual condition.

Very little of this kind has come down to us. At all events, with the exception of incidental notices in contemporary documents, and the English primer of about the year 1400,(1) there is nothing, as

---

(1) It is printed in his *Monumenta Ritualia* (vol. II. 1—242) with a valuable preliminary dissertation by Mr Maskell, who has opened the way for the study of the English devotions in the Church of England before the reformation, as he has for that of the comparative liturgiology of the several English uses, both by the information he has actually embodied in his liturgical works, and by his having drawn attention to the sources from which further information was to be gained.

yet(1) within the reach of the ordinary student, till we come to the time immediately preceding the reformation.

It must, however, be remembered that a primer in English, though understood by those who used it, was the translation of a service-book, the use of which was enjoined by the Church; whereas the *Lay Folks Mass Book*, as possessing no ecclesiastical authority, is, on that very account, more satisfactory evidence both as to the private prayers and as to the personal feelings, not only of the author of the devotions, but of those of his readers who made them their own by adopting them.

But prior to the enquiry as to the time when, and the class for whom, the book was written, and the extent to which it was used; or before forming an opinion as to how far the work of Dan Jeremy has fulfilled its purpose, and justifies the name of *Lay Folks Mass Book* here given to it,(2) we must take into account: first, that the people did not understand the Latin of the missal service when it was written; and next, that the form in which it was cast was very probably due to the previous practice of the Church in having appointed simultaneous but separate devotions for the priest and people.

Whether the change commends itself to our judgment or the contrary, we must class the persistent retention of Latin as the language of the Latin rite, as one of many examples where rigid adherence to outward form has brought about a marked change in the original institution. There can be no question that, when the Eucharist was first celebrated in Latin—most probably when the main features of the liturgy, and almost the very words of the canon were stereotyped by Pope Gregory the Great,—it was a congregational service in which the lay people took their part in their own tongue.

Nor was this the case at Rome only. Latin, though falling very far below the classical standard, had spread through all the countries where the Roman empire had extended: in some of them it had displaced the native language; and throughout the West, except in Britain, it maintained its ground in various Romance forms, not-withstanding successive Teutonic invasions.

(1) See Note under Preface, *ante*, p. x.   (2) Notes, p. 155, 156.

In proportion as the several dialects branched off from the common stock, the service must have grown harder to be understood by the people. The passing of the canon requiring them to join with the clerks and "the virgins vowed to God" in answering the priest *consona voce*,(1) may be due to this greater difference between the written Latin and the spoken language.

In the Gallican Church the laity gradually ceased to take their appointed part. In the eighth century the forcing of the Roman rite upon a reluctant church was found to have hastened this change—probably by interrupting the traditional responses to which the people had been used in their Gallican liturgy. We gather from Dan Jeremy's rubrics that in the twelfth century the laity did not join in the Nicene creed, and that there were but few answers expected in Normandy, or from French speaking worshippers in England; though it is curious to observe, as an instance of the tenacity of custom in opposition to ritual changes, that one of these answers was also made in the Eastern Church, and in all likelihood a survival, after nearly four centuries, from that very Gallican liturgy which the ecclesiastical power at Rome and the civil power at the Frankish court had combined to suppress.(2)

The modifications in the English translation of Dan Jeremy's work that were made in the fifteenth century,(3) prove that the people were no longer required to answer aloud in the Church of England, if indeed any, except literates,(4) had ever done so, except at the *Orate* in the offertory, possibly at the *Sanctus*,(5) and in the *Paternoster* at the end of the canon. We must not forget that St Augustine and his Latin missionaries brought the Latin offices to a people who had not been subject to the Roman empire, and were never in the way of acquiring the Latin language, except in their minster schools; and therefore it is most probable that as respects the lay folk, there never had been that answering the priest as with one voice of which we read in countries where Latin, or what passed for Latin, had been the common tongue.

Be this as it may, we know that for years before the reformation

(1) Note, p. 256(3).   (2) Page 24. Note, p. 260.
(3) Notes, p. 255, 257, 310.   (4) Note, p. 200-201.   (5) Note, p. 271.

neither the unlearned, nor—unless they were members of a religious foundation, or were in minor or holy orders,—those

"Who of the letter could,"(1)

had taken any audible part in the service when they "heard mass" as their share in it, very fittingly came to be called. In the reign of Queen Mary it was argued by a learned and temperate apologist for the papal system, that instead of its being an advantage for Englishmen to understand the common service of the church, it was a hindrance to their being occupied with their own prayers.(2) Very much in the same sense Lyndwood,(3) more than a hundred years before, quoting from Johannes Andreas, the great authority of the canon law in the earlier half of the fourteenth century, had already given "*Ne impediatur populus orare*," as one of his reasons for the canon being said in silence.

This we may fairly class among the *a posteriori* arguments that are apt to grow up around whatever is *de facto* established, but a publication of the Early English Text Society is not the place to discuss the character of the primitive practice or of the developed theory. In our present enquiry we have to consider the change, only in so far as Dan Jeremy had to deal with it, when he wrote the *Lay Folks Mass Book;* and the fact that the Latin was not understood by the people, much as it had to do with the form in which he has cast their devotions, does not altogether account for it.

If the difference of language had alone to have been taken into account, it would have been enough to have translated the appointed service of the mass, whereas he translates only a few parts, and does not draw the remainder from the missal.

We know that afterwards, as, for example, among the brethren of the common life,(4) who were especially devoted to the religious instruction of the laity, a scruple was felt as to translating the missal. In the treatise from the Vernon MS. in the appendix,(5) it is expressly said that certain parts are "out taken" as being what—

(1) Page 14, C 83.
(2) Note, p. 364. See also a quotation from Romsée, as the modern rule in the Church of Rome, *post*, p. 201.
(3) Lib. I, Tit. 10. *Ut archidiaconi (a).*
(4) Note, p. 387.   (5) Page 146, line 666.—Note, p. 386-7.

"No man but a priest should read."

In the middle of the seventeenth century this feeling was fully developed, and a papal bull denounced the translation of the mass into French as a rash attempt to expose the dignity of the holy mysteries to the vulgar;(1) nor has this become a dead letter, for at the beginning of this present half century the congregation of rites at Rome guarded against the translation of the ordinary of the mass into the vulgar tongue.(2)

There may have been something of this exclusive sacerdotal feeling in an undeveloped form when Dan Jeremy wrote, but whenever and however it did originate—and no one has argued that it was the custom of the primitive church to have public prayers or to minister the sacraments in a tongue not understanded of the people—there must have been some other cause to account for the form of these devotions. It has occurred to me that we may explain it upon the supposition, that before the difficulty from the difference of language had assumed its later proportions, the people were accustomed to separate devotions in the time of the divine service, simultaneous with, but not led by, the devotions of the officiating priest; and if I do not mistake, we may trace the origin of this custom in the practice of the church as early as the fourth century.

The nineteenth canon of the council of Laodicæa directs that the first prayer of the faithful, after the withdrawal of the penitents, shall be διὰ σιωπῆς; and this appears to be rightly explained by Bingham(3) as meaning, that the communion service began with private confessions, and "that they were not only made by the people in silence by themselves, but by the minister in private also."(4)

---

(1) Note, p. 388. (2) Note, p. 389.
(3) *Antiquities*, Book XV, ch. i, *sec.* 1.
(4) The Apostolical Constitutions describe the silent or private prayer in this place as being said kneeling at the bidding of the deacon: "All we of the faithful, let us bend the knee." (*Cons. Apost.*, VIII, 9.) The prayer ended, the people were bidden to stand, and the principal or presiding priest (ὁ ἀρχιερεύς) resumed the common service. (*Ib.*, c. 10.)
Cassian in his *Instituta Cœnobiorum* speaks of this as being the established practice in the beginning of the fifth century, not only at the celebration of the liturgy, but also at the canonical hours. He suggests that those, who were in haste to kneel, did so, not so much to pray, as for a pretext to rest

I may add, in confirmation of this explanation, that the prayer in this place in the modern *Euchologium* is rubricated, "First prayer of the faithful," and is said *in silence*, as μυστικῶς is generally translated, though perhaps *in an undertone* might more correctly convey its meaning.(1) A rubric for the simultaneous prayers of the priest within the sanctuary, and of the people led by the deacon without, was to be found in the earliest printed editions of the *Euchologium*,(2) and the practice survives, though this rubric is expunged. There still remain directions for the continuance of the service of the people in other parts of the liturgy, when the priest is engaged in private devotion. For example, there is a prayer appointed for the priest to say secretly, whilst the cherubic hymn is being sung,(3) and it is very easy to understand, that by a reverse process, the people, especially

(*obtentu refectionis*) when weary with long standing; and then lays down the rule as follows : "Cum autem is qui orationem collecturus est e terra surrexit, omnes pariter eriguntur; ita ut nullus, nec antequam inclinetur ille, genuflectere, nec cum e terra surrexerit, remorari præsumat." This was subject to the exception of the custom of not kneeling on Sundays, and in Quinquagesima or the fifty days between Easter and Whitsunday, mentioned by him in a subsequent chapter (*Lib.* II, c. 18), as by other writers, both before and after him, and enforced by an express canon of the council of Nice.

It did not occur to me, when I wrote the note, p. 319(5), some years ago ; but I take this opportunity of drawing attention to the early custom of kneeling in the time of public worship, when engaged in personal prayer, as contrasted with that of standing when joining in the common prayer of the church, because it seems not improbable that in it we may find the true explanation of the people kneeling more and more at mass, in proportion as they used other devotions and ceased to join in the service; until they ended, by kneeling throughout,—a gradual change, which may be very plainly traced in the later revisions of our treatise.

(1) In the liturgy of St Chrysostom, when the deacon calls upon the priest to bless (*sign with cross*) the consecrated bread, he must clearly speak so as to be heard. The rubric is worded λέγει μυστικῶς.—Goar, p. 77 ; *Euchol.* 60. So also in the liturgy of St Basil.—Goar, 169 ; *Euchol.* 84.

(2) Goar (p. 65) gives the following rubric from the liturgy of St Chrysostom at the beginning of the service : Τοῦ ἱερέως λέγοντος τὴν εὐχὴν μυστικῶς ἐν τῷ βήματι, ἐν τῷ αὐτῷ καιρῷ ὁ διάκονος λέγει ἔξω τοῦ βήματος τὰ εἰρηνικά. (Whilst the priest is saying the prayer in an under tone in the sanctuary, at the same time the deacon says the Eirenica (*Litany with the people*) outside the sanctuary.)

He notes (p. 90) that this rubric had been changed in later Venice editions, which he quotes ; and it has been again altered, as appears by the present Euchologion (Venice, 1854), p. 46.

(3) Goar, 72. *Euchol.* 76. And so too the Mechitarist (*Uniate Armenian*) liturgy, Venice, 1826—"Whilst the clerks sing the 'Agiologia' (*as the cherubic hymn is called in the Italian translation*), the priest, bowing towards the altar, prays secretly."

when they did not understand the spoken words, might have contracted the corresponding habit of offering their private prayers
instead of hearkening to the priest.

To whatever extent this may actually be the case in the Eastern
Church, we know that in the Roman Catholic communion, the
laity, as a rule, do not habitually use the missal or follow the prayers
of the liturgy. They have devotions provided for them, by episcopal
authority or "*permissu superiorum*," in various manuals in their own
languages, but these for the most part are not nearly so system-
atically adapted to the Latin office as our mediæval Mass Book.

Now, however widely established this state of things may have
become, we cannot assume that it was ever authoritatively substituted
for a congregational service at any definite time. It is far more easy
to suppose, that at first in the Latin Church, priest and people were
in the habit of using private prayers at prescribed times in the public
service, as was appointed by the Laodicæan canon, and as still the rule
of the ordinal of the Church of England at the ordering of priests.

There may be no direct proof that such private prayer was the
rule—and I do not remember to have seen the question (1) raised—

(1) The offertory of the Roman mass still begins with "*Oremus*," though
no interval is allowed for prayer, and the offertory anthem is forthwith sung.
(Cf. York Use, *post*, p. 98, l. 21.) This is precisely that part of the Latin rite
to which the Laodicæan canon would apply: and if we suppose that the
faithful did at one time engage in private prayer when they were apart
(*secreti*) from those who were not admitted to communion (*Note*, p. 267);
and that this direction was then inserted in the service books; it will supply
a reason for the "*Oremus*" in this place, for which, in its present isolated
position, Roman Catholic commentators have found a difficulty in accounting.
In the same way, namely, that the invitation to private prayer has been
allowed to remain, after the custom had been discontinued, we may explain
the "*Oremus. Flectamus genua. Levate.*" (Let us pray. Let us bow our
knees. Rise up), which, according to the existing rubric of the Roman Missal,
has become simply a direction for a transient genuflection ("*sine mora*,"
Rit. Celeb. Miss. V, 4)—the call to kneel being made by the deacon, and that
to rise by the subdeacon, lest, as explained by Romsée (*Tom.* IV, 9, viii), if both
these calls were made by the deacon, as of old, and without any pause, he
might contradict himself—"*contraria videatur proferre.*"
This form continued to be used at the Ember seasons, and in Lent, and
especially after the *Orationes solemnes* on Good Friday, except the one for the
Jews, several mediæval rubrics assigning as a reason for the exception, that
the Jews bowed their knees before our Lord and mocked him, the history
in the gospel notwithstanding, which records this of the soldiers of the
Roman governor.
Now, no doubt, in the course of time, the people knelt throughout when

but whether it was used or not there is sufficient ground for con-
cluding that in the West there were at one time simultaneous
devotions, which may be supposed, as in the case of the Greek
Church, to have taken their rise in these private prayers of priest
and people. I do not refer to the overlapping of the several parts
of the service. This, as resorted to in their own day, was animad-
verted on by French ritualists of the seventeenth century. For
example, the priest began the *secreta* during the singing of the
offertory; or the canon before the *Sanctus* had been sung, which
last was forbidden as early as the ninth century. It is enjoined by
the sixteenth of the *Capitula* of Archbishop Herardus of Tours
(A.D. 858). "Ut secreta presbyteri non inchoent antequam *Sanctus*
finiatur, sed cum populo *Sanctus* cantent."

The *preces in prostratione* of the Sarum use, and the psalms and
prayers that were sung or said in other uses during the canon,
indirectly prove the existence of earlier simultaneous devotions by
this resort to them when it became the rule that the canon should
be said *secrete*. There can, however, be little doubt that at the first
part of the service was carried on by the congregation, whilst the

hearing mass, except at the gospel, as is the existing rule of the Roman
Missal in respect to those who are present at low mass, "*etiam tempore
paschali*" (*Rubr. Gen.* xvii. 2)—but bearing in mind the fact that at the
first the people stood, or rather stood *inclinati*, that is, bowing down, when
joining in the common prayer of the church, kneeling only for their private
prayers, and not then on Sundays and between Easter and Whitsunday—it
does not seem a very violent supposition, that instead of a momentary genuflection, the *Oremus, Flectamus genua* referred both to clergy and people, and
called on them to add their silent prayers in furtherance of the petition which
was bidden, and then stand whilst the priest "*collected*" their several devotions
in the prayer, to which they added their Amen.

I am confirmed in this view by a rubric in the Sherborne Missal, from
which, by the kind permission of the Duke of Northumberland, I have given
other rubrics in the notes. The rubric at the *Preces solemnes* (p. 205) is as
follows, and proves that in the xivth century, an interval for private prayer
was allowed before the word was given to stand—and this whether we understand the saying of Psalm (51) l. to be a measure of time, as in the phrases,
"for the space of five paternosters" and so forth; or the Spanish *en un credo,
en dos credos* (in one, in two creeds, in a trice); or that the psalm itself was
intended to be said as a prescribed form of private prayer: "*Flectamus genua
diutissime donec dicatur Psalmus.* Miserere mei, Deus. *Levate.*" Marteno
(IV, 137) gives a somewhat similar rubric from a "very old" Corby service
book: "*Dicat Sacerdos* Oremus *et diaconus* Flectamus genua *et orent
diutissime usque dum dicat diaconus* Levate."

priest was engaged in private prayer, very much as was done in the Eastern Church. It has been supposed by learned Roman Catholic ritualists, that the office or introit, and other devotions at the beginning of mass, were not said by the celebrant until the fourteenth century.(1) Until the several parts of the mass were written together in a *Missale plenarium*, probably not sooner than the twelfth century,(2) these portions were contained in the antiphoner, or more commonly in this country in the grayle ;(3) and this appears to prove that they were the part of the choir and people. The old sacramentaries and the earliest missals, intended for the priest, have nothing before the *oratio* or collect,(4) but they not infrequently contain prayers for the priest, in some cases headed *apologia* or *accusatio sacerdotis*. For the most part, there are no rubrics as to when these prayers were to be said—and, indeed, in the oldest manuscript service-books there never are any rubrical directions— but I give the following rubrics from forms printed by Martene, which will suffice to show when the same or similar prayers in MSS. without rubrics were intended to be said.

First, from the well-known *Missa Illyrici* :—" *Has orationes interim dicat* (sacerdos) *donec cantentur Versus ad introitum, Kyrie Eleison, et deinde Carmen Angelorum.*" " *Finita angelica laude*" (The *Gloria in excelsis*) " *missalem orationem dicat sacerdos.*"

The next rubric is from a sacramentary which was given by the Abbot of St Benignus at Dijon, to the Bishop of Paris, in the year 1036 :—" *Interim quando Gloria in excelsis Deo canitur dicat has orationes.*(5) The following is from a MS. of which Martene does not give the date ——" *Post hanc* " (kissing the gospels on the altar) *sequentur hæ orationes interim dum* Kyrie Eleison et Gloria in excelsis Deo *canitur in quantum ei a Deo conceditur.*(6)

Nor was this saying of simultaneous devotions confined to the Continent, as we may see by the following rubric from a Sarum missal, which was given by the Lord Prior of Worcester Cathedral

(1) Gerbert, *Diss.* I, 293.   (2) Note (1), page 155.
(3) Note (1), page 156. See also the article of enquiry in Regino: "10. Si missalem, psalterium, lectionarium, et antiphonarium habeat. Nam sine his missa perfecte non celebratur."
(4) *Post*, page 94, line 25.   (5) Martene, I, 209.   (6) *Ib.*, 211.

to the church of Bromesgrove, in the year 1511, though the last clause of the rubric shows that the practice was dying out:—
"*Oratio sancti Augustini dicenda a sacerdote in missa dum canitur Officium et* Kyrie *et* Gloria in excelsis *et* Credo in unum : *vel tota dicitur ante Missam quod melius est.*"(1)

There is no occasion to multiply quotations, or to bring examples of a similar kind in other parts of the mass. These parallel devotions may be strange to the notions of those of us who are used to the common prayer of priest and people in a common tongue, and the continuous arrangement of offices, alternating between priest and people in the reformed church of England; but it will be evident that Dan Jeremy did but adopt the principle of an example which had been set by the church in very early times. In the application of this principle, the fact that the Latin of the common service was no longer understood by the people, accounts for the private devotions being assigned to them, instead of to the officiating priest, as they were in the liturgies both of the Eastern and of the Western Church.

In the present day, as has been already remarked, handbooks of the same general character are to be found in the languages of all Roman Catholic countries. In German, too, there was a Messbüchlein, dating from the time of the reformation; and in English there were similar manuals for the Roman Catholic laymen, before the penal laws had ceased to inspire caution—the earlier editions bearing the imprint of Paris or Antwerp, though not impossibly the production of unlicensed presses in this country.

In some of the later English *Horæ* and primers before the reformation, and of the reign of Queen Mary, there were added some or all of the following forms, sometimes in Latin with an English rubric, as Ebor, "When the priest him turneth after the lavatory;" or Sarum, "When he saith *Orate pro me ;*" at other times in Latin with a Latin rubric; or in English with a Latin rubric; or English and Latin, in the primers Latin and English, viz. : at the *Orate*, the elevation, the giving of *Pax* before receiving the sacrament, and after receiving it. There is no attempt at supplying devotions for every part of the mass resembling those which are now general in

(1) *Miss. Sar.* 567.

the Roman communion. In this, Dan Jeremy appears to have stood alone—in this country, to say the least.

Any man who is acquainted with mediæval theology, or has run through a catalogue of mediæval manuscripts, must have observed that the mass was a very favourite topic; but our good Norman's "treatise" is in signal contrast with the greater number of the ritual and devotional works on this subject that have come down to us from the middle ages. There were many painstaking and devout commentaries, in which the words and ceremonies are minutely explained and devoutly "moralized," but as a rule they ignore the presence of the people, or at most are content with the direction, that all stand at the gospel, or that none depart before the end of the service. This silence as to the lay people extends to the rubrics of the mass, which almost exclusively refer to the officiating priest (*executor officii*) and the assistant minister and clerks, at least after the "*responsio populi*" had been assigned to the clergy or a clerk.

The *Instructions for Parish Priests* and the *Myroure of our Lady* are no exception—most valuable, almost indispensable as they are in the study of the religious life of our forefathers. Myre's "*work*," as he himself styles it after what sounds like a more modern fashion, was intended for the "priest curatour," who was "not great clerk;" and the *Myroure* was written for the nuns of Syon with reference to their peculiar conventual offices.

Numerous tales and doctrinal books were indeed written for the layman. For the most part, they merely insist upon the obligation of hearing mass, or set forth the advantages, spiritual and temporal, of so doing, or of procuring a mass to be said with some specified intention; but they do not profess to furnish the reader with suitable devotions, or to give him instruction as to his part in the service.

This was indeed the purpose of both Lydgate's *Merita Missæ* and the "*Treatise*" from the Vernon MS. printed in the Appendix; but they differ from the Mass-book in having been intended for recitation

"To the lewd that cannot read."(1)

Our Mass Book was written for a more educated class. It was designed at the first for those who heard mass in the chapels and

(1) *Post*, p. 148, l. 3.

oratories of the great, though, as time went on, it was adapted, as in text F, for general use; or, as in text C, for the members of a monastic foundation when not ministering at the altar. It was intended to be read rather than heard, as is evident from references to what is "written above," "written in black letter," and so forth; and from the suggestion to "look at the rubrics" from time to time and get the prayers off by heart.

As already pointed out, the devotions are not a translation from the missal. The only parts that are retained in the translation are the general confession, the *Gloria in excelsis*, the answer at the *Orate*, and the Lord's Prayer. There is a version of the Apostles' Creed instead of the Nicene Creed, which was known as the mass-creed from being said in the mass. Nothing is said of the houselling, or administration of the sacrament—an omission which is very significant, as proving how completely the celebration of the mass had been dissociated from the communion of the laity. With this exception, rubrics and devotions are provided for the whole of the mass; these devotions being analogous to the parallel form which was being used by the clergy, though in some cases bearing traces of the still surviving influence of the proscribed Gallican liturgy.

A few of the shorter forms may serve to give some idea of the general character of the whole; and I modernize them for the ease of any who may find the facsimile texts uncouth from not being used to them.

AT THE GOSPEL (p. 18, 19).

Ihesu, my Lord, grant me Thy grace,
And of amendment might and space,
Thy word to keep and do thy will.
The good to choose and leave the ill:
And that it may be so,
Good Ihesu, grant it me.   Amen.

AT THE SANCTUS (p. 28).

In world of worlds (*to all ages*) with out ending
Thanked be Thou, Ihesu, my king.
All my heart I give it Thee.
Great right is it that it so be;
With all my will I worship Thee,
Iesu, blessed mayst Thou be.

> With all my heart I thankë Thee
> The good that Thou hast done to me;
> Sweet Iesu, grant me now this,
> That I may come unto thy bliss,
> There with angels for to sing
> The sweet song of thy praising:
> *Sanctus: Sanctus: Sanctus.*
> Iesu, grant that it be thus. Amen.

AT THE ELEVATION OF THE HOST (p. 40).

> Praised be Thou, King,
> And blessed be Thou, King,
>   Of all Thy giftës good
> And thanked be Thou, King.
> Iesu, all my joying,
>   That for me spilt Thy blood
>   And died upon the rood,
> Thou give me grace to sing
> The song of Thy praising.

It may be noticed that, so far as these words are concerned, there is nothing in them to prevent their being used by those who protest against the doctrine of transubstantiation or any local presence of "whole Christ" upon the altar; but it is very evident that this hymn was not intended to be so used, from the fact that concomitance is elsewhere taught in the same text.(1) The devotion substituted for it in the later texts is more definite:

> Welcome, Lord, in form of bread,
> For me Thou suffred hard deed.
> As Thou (*didst*) bear the crown of thorn
> Suffer me not to be forlorn.

PRAYER AFTER THE ELEVATION (p. 40).

> Lord, as Thou canst and as Thou will
> Have mercy on me that has done ill,
> For whatsoever Thou will me do,
> I hold me paid to stand thereto,
> Thy mercy, Iesu, would I have.
> And (*if*) I for ferdness (*fear*) durst it crave,
> But Thou bidst ask, and we shall have,
> Sweet Iesu, make me save (*safe*),
> And give me wit and wisdom right
> To love Thee, Lord, with all my might.

In the longer devotions we have prayers for all conditions of men, for deliverance from evils spiritual and temporal, and for grace

(1) Page 20, B 235-6; page 38, notes, p. 225, 286.

to live according to God's will and in charity with all men. Whatever difference of opinion there may be as to points of ritual or
doctrine, the view that they give us of the religious character of the
author is that of a God-fearing Christian man, of humble and devout
mind, with a trustful love for his Saviour, and a single-hearted
desire for the soul's health of those whom he sought to instruct. He
would have sovereign and subject, priest and people, learned and
lewed of all ranks to do their duty,

> " To his estate and his degree ; "

or, in our more modern phrase, according to, or in, that state of life
to which it hath pleased God to call them. He mentions tenants,
servants, and inferiors, and so enforces the duty of kindness and
consideration upon the class for whom he wrote ; and though they
were in the enjoyment of the lands from which Englishmen had been
ousted, he did not shrink from specifying the disherited. Not only
so, but from first to last there is an entire absence of that

> " Preching the people for profit of themselven,"(1)

or of that appeal to their superstition or cupidity, which was a painful
feature in many mediæval books for the layman, and furnished a
frequent subject for contemporary satirists. When treating of the
offertory there is not one word

> "That profiteth to purseward."(2)

No exhortation to go up to the priest, and

> " Let him not his offering ask ; "(3)

no urging that the mass-penny will be well-spent money ; no swear-
ing by Saint Christopher, that

> " Of sins it will make thee to cease,
> And thy chattel also encrease
> Of silver in thy coffer."(4)

On the contrary, in all simplicity he says,

> " Offer or stay, whether thee list—
> How thou should pray I would thou wist."(5)

---

(1) *Piers the Plowman*, Skeat, B-text, I, 50.   (2) *Ib.*, C-text, Pass. I, 101.
(3) *Post*, Vernon MS., page 142.   (4) Page 142, lines 518—520.
(5) Page 22, B. 214-5.

And this seems to have been his desire throughout—how they should pray—to furnish those with devotions, who but for them would have been hearing—when they did (1) hear—prayers in a language they did not understand, or else "jangling at the mass,"(2) when they were not reciting paternosters, or, as time went on, paternosters and aves, as all that was required of them in the ordinary practice of the Church.(3)

In short, we may well believe that the author deserved the character which his translator has given him of

"A devout man and(4) religious."

This character he may have drawn merely from an estimate of the work before him ; but if we identify the Jeremy of our treatise with the Jeremy who held the dignity of archdeacon of Cleveland in the Cathedral Church of York, it is by no means improbable that the translator, writing little more than a hundred years after his death in the northern dialect, and therefore most probably within the diocese of York, may have been influenced by some tradition as to the author of a book in daily use; or may—in addition to the few words from Hugh the Chantor, which are all I shall be able to lay before the reader(5)—have had access to more ample materials for forming an estimate of his character.

The treatise tells us nothing in direct terms of the author. His name was, no doubt, Jeremy or Jeremias, though in Texts C and D the scribes with the preference for a well-known or venerated name, which was not unusual,(6) have substituted that of St. Jerome.(7) As to who he was and when he wrote, we have no definite information.

(1)   "When the priest prays in privity
           Time of prayer then is to thee."—B. 29, 30.

(2) Page 4, line 22 ; page 136, line 282 ; Note, p. 169-170.

(3) Note, p. 202.

(4) This is the reading of C and E. Text B (p. 4, l. 19) reads "a religyus," and D "a relygius." The insertion of the article adds a superfluous syllable to the metre, which is regular in C and E—an insertion, nevertheless, not unlikely to have been made by a scribe, who was familiar with the use of "religious" as a substantive. (*See note*, p. 169.) If our Jeremy was the friend of Archbishop Thurstan of York (*see post*, p. xli), he was not a regular or religious in this sense, but a canon of Rouen and the first archdeacon of Cleveland, of whom we have any record.

(5) *Post*, p. xli.   (6) Notes, p. 366, 369(2), 378(3).

(7) Note, p. 172.

There was indeed a Jeremy in the Middle Ages, who had a high character for learning among his contemporaries—Hieremias, Archbishop of Sens in the beginning of the ninth century. There are still extant letters that passed between him and Amalarius, as to the proper spelling and pronunciation of the name JESUS ;(1) and if he had written on the mass, we should in all probability have found some allusion to it in some of Amalarius's works. This silence is not by itself conclusive—still if we assume that the translation does in the main represent the original, the archbishop can hardly have been the author, for he lived more than two hundred years before the Berengarian controversy, and the consequent introduction of the elevation of the host.(2) Even if we suppose that the mention of the ceremony was interpolated by a transcriber of the original or by the translator, we have no reason to think that the ritual peculiarities which we can identify with the use of Rouen,(3) were also to be found in that of Sens; and it does not seem too much to assume that the archbishop would have adapted the treatise to the use of his own church, if he had been the author.

As our Jeremy was not the Archbishop of Sens, and I could not meet with any other of the name in the wonderfully complete literary history of the Middle Ages, which we owe to the industry of foreign antiquarians of the seventeenth and early eighteenth centuries, and specially to the French Benedictines, I had to fall back upon the internal evidence of the treatise itself; and, if I am not mistaken, it will justify the following conclusions:

First—That the original was written in French.

Second—That the author was a Norman, or, if not a Norman born, that he wrote with reference to the liturgic use of Rouen, which was that of the province of Normandy, of which the Archbishop of Rouen was metropolitan.

Third—That he wrote towards the middle of the twelfth century.

I. Our treatise, as we have it, is not an original, but (B 32) "drawn into English." The translator does not tell us from what language; but there can be no doubt it was either from French or Latin; and

(1) Dacherii *Spicileg.* VII, 164.
(2) *Post*, p. 38, 40.   Notes, p. 281-2.   (3) *Post*, p. xxxv.

hardly from the latter. We find the Latin contrasted with the vulgar, whether French in the original, or English in the translation (B. 494-5) : the treatise expressly contemplates the instruction of the "lewed" (B. 173) or unlearned, in the sense of not being literate or understanding Latin ; and, moreover, if it had been in Latin, any one who could have understood it, would have been able to understand the Latin order of mass, and therefore would not have required it.

II. But because Dan Jeremy wrote in French, it by no means follows that he may not have been himself an Englishman, and have written for readers of English birth, if not of English descent, or who at all events had made this country their home. It was for this class that, in the middle of the twelfth century, about which time I suppose our treatise to have been written, Wace—but he was a Jersey-man —wrote in French, or, as he himself tells us, "translated" the Brut from the Latin, as it would seem, of Geoffry of Monmouth. In the next century Grosseteste, himself a native-born Englishman, stood out among the bishops of his day for his zeal in requiring the clergy of his diocese of Lincoln to instruct the people every Sunday in the vulgar tongue (*in idiomate communi*) ; and braved the displeasure of the Pope by resisting the intrusion of Italian clerks into English benefices, mainly on the score of their ignorance of the language of their flock. But in the same practical spirit he recognised the fact that there was another class, who were to be reached, if at all, through French, and he wrote his *Chasteau d'Amour*

> " En Romanz
> Por ceus ki ne seuent mie
> Ne lettrure ne clergie."(1)

Later still, not to mention other examples of Englishmen writing in French, we have Peter Langtoft, and William of Waddington, whose works were translated into English by Robert of Brunne. The former an Austin canon of the Priory of that order at Bridlington in Yorkshire, and very probably a native of Langtoft in the East Riding,

> "On Frankis style his storie he wrote of Inglis Kinges."(2)

---

(1) C. L., Note, p. 3. In a Latin Preface, he apologizes to the clergy for writing in French : "Quamvis lingua Romana (*Romance*) coram clericis saporem suavitatis non habet, tamen pro laicis, qui minus intelligunt, opusculum illud aptum est."—Warton, *English Poetry*, I. 78.

(2) Hearne, Preface, p. cvi.

The latter apologizing for his French at the end of his *Manuel des Pechiez*, explains—

> " De le franceis, ne del rimer,
> Ne me dait nuls hom blamer,
> Kar en engletere fu ne,
> Et nourri, ordine, et aleue." (1)

In the case of our treatise, therefore, it does not follow that it may not have been the work of an English ecclesiastic, because it was written in French. But an examination of the liturgic use which the author had in view leads altogether to the contrary conclusion, unless we suppose that he was an Englishman anxious to propitiate the stranger—designedly introducing the foreign use, and carefully on his guard against a reference to insular peculiarities.(2)

The main features of the mass were the same in both countries ; and in a treatise of this kind we cannot expect to find many of those

(1) M. P., p. 413, l. 12736-9.

(2) Not only at the conquest was the greater part of the land granted to Norman or French-speaking strangers, but from that time till Normandy was separated from the crown all the higher positions in the Church were filled exclusively by foreign ecclesiastics. In many cases the same men held preferment on both sides of the channel, and there was a constant transfer between this country and Normandy, the intruders returning to an archbishoprick, or bishoprick, or other preferment among their own countrymen.

Nor was the process of de-nationalizing the Church of England confined to this systematic slighting of the native clergy. Even if there were no formal attempt to assimilate the insular ritual to that of Normandy, it is easy to understand that the foreign prelates would have felt a preference for the manner of conducting the services to which they had been accustomed. If we do not hear of any change in the Ebor use, it is not improbably due to the fact that the northern province under the guidance of Alcuin (*post*, p. 353) had already followed in the wake of the Frankish court. St Osmund reformed the use of Sarum ; and we meet with other instances of this Normanizing movement. Remigius, who had been a monk at Fécamp, when he transferred the see of Dorchester to Lincoln, ordained, as we learn from the statutes, first printed by his present successor, Bishop Christopher Wordsworth, that the services should be " juxta ritum ecclesiæ Rothomagensis, quæ est totius Normanniæ metropolis."—*Statuta Ecclesiæ Cathedralis Lincolniensis*, 1873, p. 3. Mr Freeman (*Norman Conquest*, IV. 394), in the story of an outrage at Glastonbury, has drawn attention to the fact that these innovations were not always tamely submitted to in the reign of the Conqueror. The chroniclers tell how the Norman Thurstan, a monk of Caen, who had displaced the English Abbot, called in his Norman retainers to overawe the English monks, who were ill-pleased that he required them to give up the Gregorian use, or *cantus*,—which is technically used for the order as well as the melody of a service—and took refuge in the church, where they were shot down by archers from the up-floor or triforium, as they crowded about, and under, the altar, Thurstan himself spearing one monk who was clinging to it, and putting another to death who

minor diversities which constitute a diocesan or provincial use ; but, as it happens, there is quite enough to determine the use to which it was adapted. Assuming that the longer texts (B and E) more or less accurately reproduce the original—and it is evident that if any alterations were made by the English translator, they would have been in an Anglican direction, as was actually the case in the alterations and omissions of the later revisions—we find that the use of the treatise was that of Rouen. It agrees with it in points where that use differed from any English use ; some of these points being where the Rouen differed from other continental uses, or rather from all of a considerable number which I have examined.

As the agreement of the treatise with the early Rouen missal printed by Martene is pointed out in the notes on the several passages, there will be no occasion to repeat my remarks in this place, merely drawing attention to the observation that it is only by the accumulation of small coincidences that, in the absence of direct evidence, we can arrive at any conclusion as to what, to the writer, must have been a matter of course.

1. The peculiar rubric as to the vesting of the celebrant is translated almost word for word, B 35-8. Note, p. 179. Contrast the English usages, p. 164.

2. The identity of the form of confession in the treatise (B 65-82) with the earlier Rouen form, and this—if we allow C 46 as preserving the reading of the original—in a point where the Rouen use appears to have been peculiar. Notes, p. 186-188.

3. In B 86 there is a verbal translation of a Rouen rubric, where the grammatical construction of the Latin is peculiar. Note, p. 190.

4. In B 163-6 we have what may be an allusion to a Rouen peculiarity in reading the gospel in the vernacular. Note, p. 210.

5. In B 275 we have the early Rouen answer to the *Orate*—as I venture to think I have proved in the notes, p. 258-264 ; as also

was lying wounded with the arrows at its foot. In the next century we find a clerk of the Bishop of Exeter going to Lisieux, " ut divinis informaretur officiis " (Launoy *de Scholis celebrioribus*, quoted, Wiltsh, *Handbuch*, § 372).

If, therefore, Norman ritual found its way into existing foundations, or those which were intended for all, high and low, English and French alike, it is not too much to assume that it was retained in the baronial households of the foreigners who had established themselves in this country.

that it was itself a survival from the Gallican Liturgy, and probably
derived from an eastern source.

6. The retention of the eastern Στῶμεν καλῶς in B 303 (Note,
p. 270) may possibly represent a Rouen usage, in like manner to
be traced to the Gallican Liturgy.(1)

III. The question as to date can be answered only in the same
way as that as to use, by what may be described as the unconscious
evidence of the original, which we have to gather from incidental
allusions.

I need not stop to point out that the general structure of the
treatise proves that it must have been written in the later centuries
of the middle ages, because the evidence on particular points seems
to be sufficient to fix the date within a few years earlier or later than
the middle of the twelfth century. I quite admit that if the original
did enjoin the use of the Ave-Maria, it would be a strong reason for
placing the date a hundred years later; but I think we shall all be
disposed to allow, that (though the incidental reference to the existence
of customs, which afterwards became obsolete, is a test of age) the
mention of some later practice in a transcript, or in a translation,
does not necessarily prove a later date. A very cursory collation of
English manuscripts of this character will show the force of this
observation; and we have only to read Brunne's *Handlyng Synne*,
as edited by Mr Furnivall for the Roxburghe Club with the French
in a parallel column, to see how much fresh matter a translator felt
himself at liberty to introduce. For myself I have no doubt that
the mention of the Ave-Maria in text B (*lines* 59, 60) was first
inserted in the English translation, as I have attempted to prove in
p. 183.

I now refer the reader to the remarks I have made on those notes
of time which we can have no hesitation in tracing to the original:

1. The direct personal address to the Blessed Virgin in the form
of general confession in the treatise (C 46) has already been pointed
out (2) as a peculiarity of the Rouen use, and it is in so far evidence

(1) Other indications of an eastern influence are pointed out in the notes,
pp. 193, 206, 280, 301, 312.
(2) Page xxxv, 2 ; Notes, p. 187.   See also as to *kissing* the *Pax*, p. 295.

for the earlier date I have suggested for the original, that this peculiarity disappears in the later Rouen missals.

2. In B 236 there is a distinct expression of the doctrine of the presence of both the flesh and the blood of Christ, under one species, from which, as stated in the note, p. 225, I infer that the original was not earlier than the twelfth century.

3. In B 274 the people are supposed to answer the *Orate* " in hie," that is, with a loud voice. The answer is assigned to the " clerks " (1) in the thirteenth century Rouen missal ; hence we may argue that our original was written not later than the twelfth century, for the abrogation of the ancient custom must have been well-established, before it was formulated in a rubric.

4. The retention of the early eastern answer to the *Orate* is in like manner an argument for the original having been written before other answers were introduced in the later Rouen missals.(2)

5. The manner in which the rubric speaks of the ringing of the bell at the elevation (B 401), especially when compared with the wording of the same rubric in the later revisions, argues that the practice had not as yet become general ; and from this I infer (p. 282) that Dan Jeremy did not write later than the middle of the twelfth century.

6. The same inference may be drawn from the manner in which the author speaks of the doctrine of a real presence (B 403-415). The argumentative tone, as I have endeavoured to show in the notes, p. 282, reveals the fact that the doctrine was not generally accepted, and points to a time when there were still traces of the Berengarian controversy.

7. In the notes, p. 303, will be found evidence that the mention of rinsing in B 576 is not inconsistent with the date here assigned to the original.

IV. There is a fourth inference as to the author which, though resting on less substantial grounds, seems not to be improbable, namely :

That he was writing—not for the whole population, nor yet for all of the " lewed " (3) who would read his treatise, as they might have done, if the language had been that of the country in which

(1) " Clerici respondeant." Note, p. 255.
(2) Note (5), p. 258.   (3) Page 16, B 174.

he wrote — but for those who had tenants, servants,(1) and subjects (2); who could hear mass on days besides high "festivals and
holy days" (3); and on Sundays not in the parish church (4); and
consequently that he may have been writing for Norman barons, and
French-speaking grantees of the lands of "disherited" (5) English
in this country, who had chaplains and clerks,(6) and heard mass
daily,(7) in their consecrated chapels and private oratories, or in

(1) Page 34, B 369. (2) Page 52, B 554.

(3) When the *Gloria in Excelsis* was sung or said (p. 14, B 115), or the
Nicene Creed (p. 18, B 198) was said.

(4) The ritual contemplated by the treatise was founded, as we have seen,
on the use of Rouen cathedral, but it is not adapted for a large church nor for
such a "chapel" as that of which in later times we find the details in the
Northumberland Household Book. There was not merely a parish clerk, but
clerks confessed their (*plural*) sins (B 46). The gospel was read by deacon or
priest (B 153), and a clerk flits the book to the south end when the rinsing is
done at the end of mass (B 576-9); but there is no reference to the bidding of
the bedes in parish and conventual masses on the Sunday, which from being in
the mother tongue, was especially a devotion for the layman, and—as will be
readily seen on comparison—embodied many of the petitions which Dan
Jeremy has assigned to the silence of the canon.

(5) It would perhaps be far-fetched to find in Dan Jeremy's reference to the
"disherited" (B 379) a confirmation of my suggestion that he was writing for
his countrymen in England; for in those troublous days they might have
found many that had been deprived of their possessions without leaving their
own country; but the fact that he does refer to them is—to say the least—
not inconsistent with the supposition.

(6) "Lordes þat haue prestes at wyl,
Me þenketh þey trespas ful yl
Þat any day ete, are þey here messe
But ȝyf hit be þurghe harder dystresse."—H. S. 7312-15.

(7) The decrees of councils and the formal injunctions of the canon law
required every one to hear mass every day, whether holy day or not, with
exception of "the common people," who from being necessarily employed in
labour or otherwise were obliged to do so only on Sundays and high days.
("Populares qui celebrationi missarum non valent quotidie interesse."—
Provinc. II. Tit. 23, *In elevatione* (q), p. 231.) But it is more to the point,
as proving that this was the ordinary practice of the class for which the mass-
book was intended, to give a few extracts from books that were intended for
popular use.

Thus Andrew Borde in his "Regyment":

"And than" (after rising and dressing) "great and noble men doth use
to hear masse & other men that can not do so, but muste applye theyr
busynes, doth serue god with some prayers, surrenderynge thankes to hym for
hys manyfolde goodnes, with askynge mercye for theyr offences."—*Babees
Book*, E. E. T. S., Furnivall, p. 246-7.

In a MS. of about the year 1500, the young child is taught after rising
from his bed, and asking God's grace to "help him in all his works:"

"Than go to þe chyrche & here A messe,
And aske mersy fore þi trespasse."—*Babees Book*, p. 17.

In Wynkyn de Worde's *Boke of Keruynge* the chamberlain is instructed

their dining-halls, it may be, with circumstances that when a more exact discipline was attempted (1) were not allowed as convenient

"at morne" to "go to the chyrche or chapell to your soueraynes closet & laye carpentes & cuysshens & lay downe his boke of prayers / than drawe the curtynes."—*Babees Book*, p. 283—where note the book of prayers, and the curtained pew of the great man.

So too Robert of Gloucester of William the Conqueror :—

> "In chyrche he was deuout ynou, for hym non day abyde
> Þat he ne hurde masse & matyns, & euenson[g] & eche tyde."
>
> <div align="right">Hearne, <i>reprint</i>, 1810, p. 369.</div>

But that the rule of the church was not a dead letter is perhaps most unmistakably shown by the matter-of-course way in which hearing mass before breaking their fast is introduced as an incident in the every day life of knights and other personages in works of fiction, which nevertheless in their details were no doubt true to the ordinary habits of the class they intended to portray, and that was the very class which Dan Jeremy had in view.

For example, in *Sir Gawayne and the Green Knight* (ed. Morris, E. E. T. S. 1864), Gawayne, after the lady has kissed him,—

> "dos hir forth at þe dore, with outen dyn more,
> *And* he ryches him to ryse, & rapes hym sone,
> Clepes to his chamberlayn, choses his wede,
> Boȝeȝ forth, quen he watȝ boun, blyþely to masse,
> *And* þenne he meued to his mete, þat menskly hym keped."
>
> ll. 1308-12.

And so again Gawayne—

> "ryses to þe masse,
> *And* siþen hor diner watȝ dyȝt & derely serued."—ll. 1558-9.

The Lord of the castle hears mass before he eats and goes hunting at daybreak :—

> "Ete a sop hastyly, when he hade herde masse,
> With bugle to bent felde he buskeȝ by-lyue ;
> By þat þat any day-lyȝt lemed vpon erþe,
> He with his haþeles on hyȝe horsses weren."—ll. 1135-8.

And so again (l. 1691)—

> "After messe a morsel he & his men token."

(1) In the year 1238 we find Bishop Grossteste citing the Earl of Warren and his chaplain to appear because mass was celebrated in the Earl's hall at Graham (*Grantham in Lincolnshire*), which was an unconsecrated place and otherwise unfit.—*Roberti Grosseteste Epistolæ*, Luard, 1861, p. 171.

In 1251 Pope Innocent IV. on the petition of the Countess of Lincoln required Archbishop Gray, of York, to grant her a license to have a portable altar where she might have divine offices celebrated for her and her family.—*Archbishop Gray's Register*, Raine, 209.

At the provincial council held by Archbishop Stratford in 1342 a constitution was passed for the suspension *ipso facto* for one month of priests celebrating mass in unconsecrated chapels, oratories, or houses, or elsewhere without the licence of the diocesan : and forbidding the bishops of the province of Canterbury to grant this licence except under certain conditions to great and noble men — *magnatibus seu nobilibus* — this last term being explained to include knights, and esquire holding dignified office.—*Provinc.*, III, *Tit.* 23, *Quam sit inhonestum* (n.), p. 234.

—and therefore he wrote in French, as he was writing for them as a class, and that was the language which they spoke among themselves.

IDENTIFICATION OF THE AUTHOR.

We gather nothing definite as to the author from our manuscripts, except his name (1); and as my search for any reference to a Jeremy who had written on the mass has been altogether without result,(2) I had made up my mind to rest content with the inferences above given, when the mention of a Jeremias as being at Rome with Archbishop Thurstan of York in 1123,(3) set me on a fresh search. I do not pretend to have obtained conclusive evidence, but at the least I have found a Jeremy, who, if not the Jeremy of our mass-book, might very well have been the author.

This is a mere guess, I am ready to admit, and I cannot tell how far those of my readers, who do not look upon enquiries of this kind as a waste of time, may be disposed to agree with me, when, in the absence of proof to the contrary, I have assumed the identity of our "Dan Jeremy" and Archdeacon Jeremias. Obviously, when we are concerned with a man, who lived more than seven hundred years ago, whose name is brought forward by a local chronicler, only in connection with the controversy of the English metropolitans as to

(1) Page xxxi. (2) Page xxxii.
(3) "Jeremias, Archdeacon of Rouen"—Raine, *Fasti Eboracenses*, I. 193. This is not quoted from Hugh the Chantor, and it would seem that there may have been some inaccuracy in the authority here relied upon. Jeremy could hardly have been archdeacon of Rouen in 1123 without some proof of it having been met with by Rouen antiquarians. In 1120 a Richard held that office and witnessed the gift of the church of St Leu to the abbey of St Martin of Pontoise (Pommeraye, *Histoire des Archevéques de Rouen*, p. 308). Fulbert was archdeacon in 1124 (Pommeraye, *Histoire de l'Église Cathédrale de Rouen*, 302). He became the fifth Dean, but retained his office of archdeacon. About the year 1128, on the approach of death, he became a monk at St Ouen; and his monument in the cloister of that abbey records:

"metropolitanus fuit archidiaconus iste."—*Gallia Christiana*, XI. p. 115.

It is possible that though not Archdeacon of Rouen, in the sense of "metropolitan" or "grand" archdeacon, he may have been a Rouen archdeacon in the sense of holding one of the six archdeaconries into which the diocese was divided, although his name does not occur in the local histories. But it is far more probable that he was so styled in reference to his being a York archdeacon, and holding the archdeaconry of Cleveland; and that the fact of his having originally come from Rouen may have given occasion for the mention of him as "of Rouen" in the Fasti.

the precedence of their respective sees, we cannot expect to discover many facts respecting him : but in the few that I have been able to meet with, there is nothing inconsistent with my supposition. On the contrary, they will be found to tally most exactly with the particulars which we gather from the treatise itself :

1. Name ; and the name, it may be observed, was most unusual.

2. Time.—About the middle of the twelfth century.

3. As a canon of Rouen, Jeremias must have been familiar with the use of his own cathedral.

4. And as archdeacon of Cleveland, the duties of his office would have directed his attention to the spiritual requirements of his fellow-countrymen, who were cut off from the ministrations of their English parish-priests by the difference of language.

Hugh the Chantor elsewhere incidentally speaks of Jeremy in reference to his presence at Rome, where Henry II had directed him to remain after the Lateran council (18th March—5th April, 1123), but I confine my quotation from the manuscript(1) to one passage, which gives us some notion of the man himself. Hugh is relating a discussion(2) which was closed by the Pope (Calixtus II) desiring Archbishop Thurstan and his followers to retire to their hostel. "There," he says, " was our archbishop (*Thurstan*) with his people, and Jeremias, a canon of the Church of Rouen, whom the king (*Henry I*) had caused to await the archbishops (*William de Corbeil of Canterbury and Thurstan of York*); who, though small of stature, was little neither in sense, nor learning, nor eloquence ;

(1) The lives of the first Norman archbishops of York by Hugh Sotevagina, precentor and archdeacon of York, otherwise " Hugh the Chantor," are prefixed to the "Great White Register " in the custody of the Dean and Chapter of York (Raine, *Fasti Ebor.* I. 147 n. ; Id. *Northern Registers*, p. xv), and are now in the course of publication in the Master of the Rolls Series.

Stubbs in the *Chronica Pontificum Ecclesiæ Ebor.* quotes largely from Hugh, and thus speaks of him : " Thomæ Seniori, Gerardo, Thomæ Juniori et Thurstino necessarius tam in divinis quam in humanis tractatibus conciliarius, multo tempore conversatus est . . . . . . ad mortem comes adhæsit individuus."—*Scriptores Decem.*, Twysden, p. 1705.

(2) The story of the archbishops going to Rome, but too late to attend the Lateran council, and of their contention as to their relative hierarchical position, is very well told, with all the advantage of access to fresh authorities, in the *Life of Archbishop Thurstan*, by Canon Raine, *Fasti Ebor.* I, 193-4.

and greatly he loved our archbishop and his friends and was beloved."(1)

Jeremy cannot at this time have been much more than four or five and twenty,(2) though it is not improbable that he had already played a conspicuous part in the cause of the Archbishop Thurstan,(3)

(1) "Apostolicus... Thurstinum cum suis ad hospitium secedere præcepit. Erat ibi archiepiscopus noster cum suis et Jeremias Rotomagensis ecclesiæ canonicus, quem rex archiepiscopos expectare fecerat, qui licet statura brevis, nec sensu, nec scientia, nec loquentia erat exilis (MS. ex illis) ; Et ipse valde archiepiscopum nostrum et suos diligebat et diligebatur."—*Registrum Magnum Album (Ebor.)*, fol. 27.

(2) In reference to what is here said, it may be necessary to explain that though to us modern Englishmen the idea of a canon suggests priest's orders as of necessity and a man of a certain age in ordinary cases, it was very different in continental cathedrals, and in our own in the middle ages. Not only might a proportion of the canonries be held by deacons and subdeacons, but canonries were given to boys of fourteen. Borbosa, the best authority on these questions (*De Canonicis*, Lugduni 1658, cap. xiii. § 9), referring to the canonists, says that while some held fourteen to be necessary, some held seven years to be sufficient—"ad canonicatum ecclesiæ cathedralis, olim quidam septennium completum." In 1563 the Council of Trent (Sess. xxiv. *De Reformatione*, c. 12) decreed that cathedral canons must at least take subdeacon's orders within a limited time, and so intended the minimum age to be not under twenty-one years. But, to judge from later constitutions and decisions in this matter, this was not held to operate against papal provisions or dispensations for age, or, in some cases, the privileges of noble birth ; and the abuse seems to have gone on as before. To give one example. At Orleans in 1582 the chapter refused to admit a nephew of the bishop because he was under age ; and in 1638 they ordained that canons, who were scholars studying at Orleans (*Chanoines écoliers étudians à Orleans*), should be mulct if absent from the church on festivals and Sundays.—*Voyages Liturgiques*, 190, 191.

We have an example of the early age at which ecclesiastical patronage was conferred in England on children with good interest, in the case of Geoffrey Plantagenet, afterwards treasurer, and eventually Archbishop of York, who was Archdeacon of Lincoln, though a mere child, when Jeremy was Archdeacon of Cleveland, and was elected and confirmed Bishop of Lincoln in 1173 when only fourteen. He visited the papal court in 1174, but the Pope deferred his consecration for three years, and even then he would have been only eighteen. *Fast. Ebor.*, 252-3.

(3) More than three years before this, when Thurstan, then Archbishop-elect of York, had not yet induced Pope Calixtus to consecrate him, Hugh the Chantor tells us : "Veniente papa ad Blesense (*of Blois*) castellum, duo archidiaconi nostri (*of York*) et scholasticus qui cum electo nostro venierunt, voce et litteris petitionem fecerunt ad dominum papam ut eum consecraret ; at ille benigne respondet se fratribus suis inde collocuturum." *Regist. Magnum Album*, fol. 17. *Fast. Ebor.* I, 181. When Hugh is in print, the reader, who cares to do so, will be easily able to satisfy himself, whether Jeremy is here referred to. The editor having examined the MS. once in the fruitless search for a passage, as to the existence of which he had been misinformed (*ante*, page lx, *n*. (3)), does not feel himself bound to do so again

or otherwise he must have been of very advanced age, when we find him with Archbishop Roger at Rouen, which might have been as much as fifty-two years afterwards, if we assign the latest date of 1175 to the charters which he witnessed. In the mean time he had been preferred to the archdeaconry of Cleveland, within the metropolitical Church of York. When he was admitted to this dignity I have been unable to discover, but nothing is more likely than that Archbishop Thurstan should have promoted his Norman adherent. All that Le Neve found to say of him is that he was Archdeacon of Cleveland "about 1170" (1); and Torre does not give the year: "A.D. 11 · ·, Jeremia was admitted to this Archdeaconry of Clyveland. This Jeremiah, Archdeacon of Clyveland subscribed to William de Somerville's charter to the Knights Hospitallers of Land and common of pasture in the town of Secroft."(2)

It was nothing unusual for benefices in Normandy and this country to be held in plurality, and it had occurred to me that Jeremy, the canon of Rouen, and Jeremy, Archdeacon of Cleveland, were the same man, but I had nothing to go upon except that they were contemporaries, that the name was uncommon, and that the canon of Rouen, by an authority, which however I could not verify,(3) was styled archdeacon. At the last moment, after the preface and the preceding sheet of this introduction had been printed, I am enabled to lay before the reader what appears to be conclusive proof that I was right in my conjecture.

For this information the thanks of the Society are due to Monsieur de Beaurepaire, Keeper of the Records (*Archiviste*) of the

for this purpose, as it does not help to identify the author or to illustrate his work. This much, however, is very evident, that if Jeremy did not on this, he must have recommended himself to Thurstan, on some other occasion, or otherwise the king would not have held out his remaining at Rome as an inducement to the archbishop to defer his visit till after the council.

(1) *Ed.* Hardy, III, 145. The name is not found in the Dodsworth MSS.

(2) Torre's MSS. (York Minster), p. 715. Seacroft is a township and chepelry in the parish of Whitkirk in Skyrack wapentake and the West Riding of York. *Inter alia* William de Somerville *al.* Summervil gave a mill at Seacroft to Bolton Percy, an evident misprint for Bolton Priory (Thoresby, *Loidis & Elmete*, 1816, p. 135. Cf. Burton, *Mon. Ebor.*, 119); and also gave seven acres at Seacroft to Kirkstall Abbey (Burton, *u. s.*, p. 296); but I have not been able to ascertain the date in the twelfth century when these gifts were made.

(3) See note (3), *ante*, p. xl.

Department of the Lower Seine (at Rouen), and Member of the
Academy *des Inscriptions et Belles-lettres.* He not only furnished
me, at the instance of a friend of our Society, with transcripts of the
charters with Dan Jeremy's witness, which were all the more valuable, as their correctness was guaranteed by being copied with his
own hand; but he also with the greatest kindness permitted me to
avail myself of his special learning and local information in my
further enquiries.

I have added some notes to these charters(1) which will assist us
when we endeavour to fix their date: "Notum sit presentibus et
"futuris quod Tustanus le Macon et Bona uxor sua vendiderunt
"Rogero de Waruuic capellano Dom*i*ni Regis mansuram suam
"in vico S*anc*ti Dionisii quam jure hereditario tenebant de feodo
"archiepiscopi Eboracensis que est inter mansuram Richardi Monachi
"et Dominicum prefati archiepiscopi cum gardino et tota terra a vico
"usque ad murum castelli cum omnibus pertinenciis suis in latum et
"longum sicut se proportat a turre ejusdem muri usque ad antiquum
"murum civitatis versus Rodobeccam pro septem libris andegav
ensibus.   .   .   .   .(2)

"Factum fuit hoc in plena communia coram Bartholomeo Fer-
"gant * (3) tunc majore Rothomagi et sigillo communie confirmatum.
"Testibus his Gaufrido* decano Rothom*agensi.* Radulfo de Wane-
"villa* sacrista. Jeremia*. Rad*ulpho* filio Tehardi. Willelmo de
"Ripa. canonicis Rothom*agensibus.* Reinaudo de Gerpunvilla*.
"Willelmo de Malapalude*. Johanne * filio Luce. Hugone filio vice-
"com*itis.* Ganfrido * fratre suo. Rad*ulpho* Waspal. Henrico filio
"suo. Waltero* filio Geroldi. Guidone * parvo. Hugone Wastal.
"Nicholao Gronnet. Rogero* de Bello monte. Bartholomeo Batalle*.
"Ricardo * filio Benedicti et pluribus aliis." [Seal lost.]

It will be observed that the sale of this messuage was executed
before the mayor at an open meeting of the commonalty, and was

(1) The two charters and a third connected with them are in the same
file : "*Archives de la Département de la Seine Inférieure,* G. 4278."—M. de
Beaurepaire.
(2) Here follows a provision for the archbishop's reserved rent.
(3) The witnesses marked (*) also appear as attesting the charter of confirmation.

witnessed amongst others by the dean and sacrist of the cathedral
church, and by three of the canons, Jeremiah being the senior of
them. But it required the confirmation of the Archbishop of York, in
whose fee the messuage was situate; and this was granted, most
probably on the same day, as no less than twelve of the witnesses
are the same :

"Omnibus ad quos presens scriptum pervenerit! Rogerus(1) dei
"gratia Eboracensis archiepiscopus! Salutem in domino. Notum esse
"volumus universis. quod Rogerus de Waruuic capellanus domini
"Regis. emit quandam mansuram apud Rothomagum de feondo nostro
"in vico Sancti Dionisii de Bona uxore Tustani Cementarii. pro septem
"libris andegavensibus de consensu nostro et permissione. quam de
"nobis jure hereditario tenebat cum gardino et tota terra de retro
"supra fossatum a dextris et a sinistris sicut terra se extendit a turre-
"nula muri castelli. usque ad antiquum murum Civitatis. versus
"Rodobeccam libere ac. quiete jure hereditario tenendum (sic) de
"nobis et heredibus(2) nostris. ei et heredibus suis. reddendo inde

---

(1) Roger de Pont l'Évesque was consecrated Archbishop of York at
Westminster on the 10th October, 1154, and died at York on 22nd November,
1181.

(2) It does not appear whether the archbishop held this fee in right of his
archbishoprick, or as his private property. From the use of *hæredes* and not
successores, or some similar term, it would seem that it was the latter. In
1195 it is described as the "feodum Thome de Ponte-Episcopi,"—this Thomas
from the name being apparently of the same family. In either case it must
have passed into his hands by having been alienated by the archbishop in
his lifetime, as at his death the king seized all his property.—*Fast. Ebor,*
I, 249. I here quote a third document which is in the file with the charters
given in the text, from the "*analyse,*" given by M. de Beaurepaire in his *Archives du Département de la Seine Inférieure, Série* G (*Clergé Seculier*), Tom.
III, p. 325. In this deed Roger of Warwick, who is described as Canon of Rouen
(Henry II being dead), conveys all his property at Rouen to his nephew
Elias, and among the rest the messuage he had purchased in Rue Saint Denis,
which in those charters is described as belonging to the Archbishop of York,
but in this, in the words above quoted, as that of Thomas de Pont l'Évêque.
For these curious particulars, which will be new to those who take an
interest in the history of our Norman archbishops, I am indebted to the personal kindness of the learned Editor of the *Archives.* M. de Beaurepaire, with
the same readiness to help an absolute stranger, that gave me the information
I was anxious to obtain as to our author, and anticipated my enquiries—as
only those can who are thoroughly masters of their subject and know how
much in these matters turns upon details—has been kind enough to favour me,
unasked, with the sight of a proof sheet of the third volume which is still in the
press.

" nobis vel heredibus nostris per annum duos solidos usualis monete
" et sex denarios. pro omni servitio a se vel ab heredibus suis.

. . . .(1)

" Hujus autem concessionis nostre et confirmationis. Testes sunt.
" Gaufridus * Rothom*agensis*(2) Decanus. Radulphus de Wan-
" nevilla*. Thesaurarius (3) Eboracensis. Jeremias * Archid*iaco-*

(1) The original here goes on to confirm the alienation to the same Roger
of another messuage within the archbishop's fief by his bailiff and by his
direction.

(2) A Geoffry was the sixth dean of Rouen in 1123 (*Gallia Christiana*,
XI, 116) ; and another, or the same again, from 1130 to 1135 (compare the
Gallia, u. s. and Pommeraye, *Église Cathédrale de Rouen*, p. 303), but he
cannot be the dean here mentioned, as he did not hold that office whilst
Roger was Archbishop, or Ralph de Wanneville was Treasurer of York.

The *Gallia Christiana* (XI, 116) gives Geoffry III as dean from 1148 to
1175, and Robert de Callot as succeeding him in that year ; but Dom Pommeraye gives Geoffry as dean from 1155 till 1163 only, when an Ives appears
as dean. He supposes Geoffry was again elected dean. The last document in
which he is mentioned, as referred to both in the *Gallia* and by the local
historian, being dated in 1175. (Pommeraye, *u. s.*, p. 304.)

If Ralph de Wanneville immediately followed John as treasurer of York,
when John was made Bishop of Poictiers, he may have signed this in 1163, but
we have no proof that he did so succeed him, or that Archbishop Roger was
in Normandy in that year, and it is far more probable that the charters date
from Geoffry's second period of office.

(3) Ralph de Warneville was sacrist or treasurer of Rouen, signing himself,
or being described as one or the other, as early as 1150 (*Gallia Christiana*,
XI, Instrumenta, col. 24, 25, 26), but, as mentioned in the last note, we have
no evidence as to when he was appointed treasurer of York. In Le Neve
(*Fasti*, III. p. 158) he follows a John, who "succeeded to this dignity, 1154,"
and was made Bishop of Poictiers, as stated by Le Neve, following R. de Diceto,
in 1163 ; but R. de Monte places his becoming bishop under the year 1162,
and this date is given in the *Gallia Christiana*, II. 1180. Be this as it
may, we find no mention of Ralph as treasurer until 1173, when he was made
Chancellor of England. He may have held the treasurership for some years
before this, and probably continued to hold it until he was succeeded by Geoffry
Plantagenet, who, according to Le Neve, held it in 1181. As proved by the
following quotations, he certainly was succeeded by him as chancellor in 1182.

"Anno gratiæ 1173 . . . . Illo etiam anno Rudulphus de Warnevilla,
sacrista Rothomagensis, et thesaurarius Ebor. constitutus est Angliæ cancellarius."—Matt. Westmonast., *Flores Hist.* Francof. 1601, p. 250. And so
Matthew Paris, *Hist.*, *ad ann.* 1173, p. 88.

We have the same in R. de Diceto in his *Imagines Historiarum*, but he
further informs us that Ralph appointed Walter of Coutances to take his
place at the king's court—this Walter, who was afterwards Archbishop of
Rouen, being at this time a Canon of Rouen, and, like Jeremy, holding an
English archdeaconry, that of Oxford. This information enables us to assume
that Ralph may have remained at Rouen after he was made chancellor, and
so may have witnessed the charters in 1175, as well as in 1170. "1173 Adulphus
de Warnevilla Rotomagensis Sacrista, Thesaurarius Eboracensis, constitutus

"*nus.*(1) Magister Vacarius. Magister Ausgotus. Rad*ulphus* prior(2) "de Gloecestria. Godardus de Vallibus. Reginaldus de Gerpunvilla*. "Willelmus(3) de mala palude*. Bartholomeus Fergant*. tunc(4) "major communie Rothom*agi*. Johannes * filius Luce. Bartholomeus

est Angliæ cancellarius : qui modum vivendi parum a privato dissimilem, quem prius semper habuerat, non immutavit, malens Waltero de Constantiis Canonico Rotomagensi vices in curia Regis committere, quam circa latus Principis militantes, expensis profusioribus, lautioribus mensis, ad sui gloriam nominis propagandum per dies singulos invitare."—R. de Diceto, in *Recueil des Historiens des Gaules et de la France*, XIII. 191.

He resigned his chancellorship in 1182, when he would seem to have been no longer sacrist at Rouen : "Radulfus de Venneuilla (*sic*) Archidiaconus Rothomagensis renunciavit Cancellariæ Regis et Rex dedit ei terras magnorum reddituum."—R. de Monte, Paris, 1651, p. 804.

In the same year he was made Bishop of Lisieux, which fact seems to have escaped the notice of Lord Campbell in his *Lives of the Lord Chancellors* (vol. I. p. 100) : "Arnulfus Episcopus . . . . renuntiavit episcopatum . . . . . Adulfus de Venneuilla (*sic*), Archidiaconus Rothomagensis, qui fuerat Cancellarius Regis, electus est ad prædictam Episcopatum." — R. de Monte, p. 805.

(1) *Eboracensis* is not repeated after his name, as in the first charter (p. xliv) *Rothomagensi* is not repeated after the name of the treasurer, the name of the church having been specified after that of the dean. It may be observed that repetitions of this kind are not usual in charters of this date.

(2) Hameline was abbot of Gloucester from 1148 till 1179, and was succeeded by Thomas Carbonel or Carbonach, who died in the beginning of the thirteenth century. (Rutter, *History of Gloucester*, 216—218, Dugdale, *Monasticon*, I. 532-3.) I do not find any list of priors in the local histories ; but in reference to the prior attesting the charter by the Archbishop of York, it may be observed that Gloucester Abbey at this time owed honorary subjection to the northern metropolitan. The abbey had been granted to Archbishop Thomas in 1093 by William Rufus (Raine, *Fast. Ebor.*, I. 151), but in 1157 Archbishop Roger, in consideration of certain lands having been given by the abbey to the archbishoprick to prevent future controversy, with the assent of his chapter and a general synod renounced all claim to the other estates.—Rutter, *u. s.*, 217. Dugdale, I, 533. See as to Archbishop Roger's action in behalf of his abbey, *post*, p. xlix.

(3) M. de Beaurepaire informs me that Malpalu (*Mala palus*) was formerly the name of a quarter at Rouen, and that there is still a very old street of that name. The name frequently occurs in Rouen charters as the name of several families ; and we cannot therefore ascribe the signature of W. de Mala Palude to any connection with the Archbishop, though the name is met with in contemporary documents in the north of England. Pommeraye (*Église*, 306), in reference to a Richard de Malpalu who was dean of Rouen in 1200, mentions that he and others of the name, who were Mayors of Rouen, were of the same family as Odin de Malpalu, Painter of Henry II.

(4) The name of Bartholomew Fergant occurs as mayor in a dated document of 1182, after Archbishop Roger was dead ; but, as remarked by M. de Beaurepaire, there is no reason why he may not have held the office, which was annual, in previous years—and it follows that he may have been Mayor of Rouen at the date here assigned to the charter.

" Bataille*. Gaufridus* filius(1) vicecomitisse. Walterus* filius
" Giroldi. Guido* parvus. Rogerus* de Bello munte. Ricardus*
" filius Benedicti. Rogerus Dorgoil. Bernardus pistor. et multi alii."

Now in this charter we may observe first that it was executed at
Rouen, after the sale had been completed before the civic authorities,
and in all likelihood on the same day—no less than twelve of the
witnesses being the same as in the previous charter,—some inhabit-
ants of Rouen—and we cannot suppose that they could have transferred themselves in a body to the Archbishop's court, if it had been
held elsewhere than in their own home.

Next we may observe that, there being no mention of any
bailiff(2) or other representative of the archbishop, we may infer that
he was himself present at Rouen.

Lastly—and what is more to our present purpose of proving the
identity of Jeremy of Rouen, and Jeremy of Cleveland, both he and
Ralph de Wanneville,—who, when attesting the sale before the
mayor of Rouen, are described by their local titles in the cathedral,
the one as sacrist, the other as canon,—now, before the Archbishop of
York, to whom they owed canonical obedience, are designated by the
offices they held in his cathedral, Ralph as treasurer and Jeremy as
archdeacon : and thus the charters establish a fact in the history of
our author, which cannot have been without its influence upon the
character of his work, and, but for them, would have been merely a
matter of conjecture.

The exact date of the charter does not directly bear upon our
present enquiry. It might perhaps be arrived at more nearly, with
access to a library containing the necessary authorities, and specially
if the year of the earlier mayoralty of Fergant(3) could be ascer-
tained. It would seem from an examination of the dates which are

(1) This Geoffry appears among the witnesses to the deed of sale as the
brother of Hugh, the son of the sheriff : here as the son of the sheriff's wife—
no doubt his step-son. I draw attention to this trifling matter because, like
the change in the description of Ralph de Warneville, and our Jeremy, it is an
instance of the precision of ancient records in these matters, which was in strong
contrast with the uncertainty of their orthography. For an instance we need
only compare these two documents, most probably executed on the same day,
the one drawn up by the town-clerk, the other by an officer of the archbishop.
(2) Note (1), *ante*, p. xlvi.   (3) Note (4), p. xlvii.

given in the notes, that it will be found to be somewhere between 20th November, St Andrew's day, 1170, and the year 1175. About the first of these dates Roger passed into Normandy,(1) and remained there until after St Nicolas' day (6th Dec.) in the year 1171 ;(2) but we do not know that Geoffry had been re-elected Dean of Rouen at that time. And as to the later date, though Geoffry was known to have been dean in 1175,(3) I do not find, and I do not stop the press whilst I go in search of any notice of Roger being in Normandy in that year, though there is no reason to think he might not have been there. In the autumn of 1174 Richard, Archbishop of Canterbury, sharply rebuked the monks at Gloucester for pleading exemption from his jurisdiction.(4) In the May of 1175, Roger gave notice by his clerks at a synod, held by the Archbishop of Canterbury at Westminster, of an appeal to Rome against a sentence of excommunication which he had passed against the monks of Gloucester,(5) their abbey belonging to York, for refusing to pay him obedience.(6) If we suppose the prior of Gloucester to have resorted to Archbishop Roger on business connected with this dispute, his attestation to the charter is, in so far, an argument for the later date ; nor is the fact that R. de Warneville was made chancellor in 1173 any argument against the likelihood of his having been a witness at Rouen after that date, for, as noticed in a note above,(7) he appointed a deputy for the discharge of his office about the court of the king : and with this suggestion to any of my readers who may be at the pains to investigate the question of date more thoroughly, I go on to the next question in our enquiry.

TRANSLATION INTO ENGLISH.

In the middle of the twelfth century a book of prayers in English would have been of small use, even if the very notion had not been offensive, to the stranger lords of the new-built castles and crenclated manors, and their foreign retainers. Some eighty years had passed since the Normans had invaded this country, but their successors

---

(1) R. de Diceto, *ed.* Stevenson, p. 332. (2) Mat. Paris, *ed.* 1644, p. 87.
    (3) Note (2), p. xlvi. (4) R. de Diceto, *u. s.*, 334.
  (5) Note (2), p. xlvii. (6) *Fasti Ebor.* I. 242. (7) Page xlvii.
  MASS-BOOK. *d*

were still in the position of an army cantoned among a subject population, rather than the fellow-countrymen of their English vassals.
They may have picked up some knowledge of the language, and in
their intercourse with their native dependents may have grafted some
of their own French words upon the old stock, but English was not
what they spoke among themselves, nor what they would have used
when they desired to pray to God in the silence of their hearts.

Before the end of the next century a very different state of things
had grown into existence. The mere lapse of time, and the fact that
men of the two races had to act together in military and political
emergencies, had much to do with this, but would hardly have been
sufficient if Normandy had still been held with the crown of England.
When the chief patronage was no longer in the same hands there
was less opportunity for the interchange of ecclesiastical benefices in
this country and Normandy, and there was no more of the intrusion of
Normans into every high place in the Church of England. Dating
from 1244 a still more effectual stop was put to the constant passing
backwards and forwards between the two countries. In this year
Lewis IX. of France required his subjects who had lands beyond sea,
to choose between allegiance to him or to the King of England; and
Henry III. hearing of this, went farther, and instead of leaving them
a choice, gave orders for all, who held under the crown of France,
especially those who were Normans, to be desseized of their English
estates.(1) We can easily understand how, fifty years after this, the
descendants of the Normans who remained in this country, though
they may have prided themselves upon their Norman ancestry, had
become English in feeling, and were proud to call themselves
Englishmen.(2)

French was indeed still used for formal documents, and in the
courts of law; and it was habitually spoken at court, and, very
possibly, in the families of those who were about the court; but there

---

(1) Matt. Paris, *ad ann.* 1244, p. 416. "Rex Angliæ omnes de regno
Franciæ, præcipue Normannos, jussit terris suis, quas in Anglia habuerunt,
disseisiri."

(2) We are so in the habit of speaking of the Normans, that we are apt to
forget that, at the conquest and long afterwards, they spoke of themselves as
French, and were so described in formal documents.

can be no doubt that the class for whom our treatise was written now spoke English as a rule, and had not only learnt to speak it, but think and pray in it, as their mother tongue; though they may have looked upon French as a mark of good breeding, or brought it forth like their best robe, as a homage to fashion, much as French was spoken in the last century at all the German courts; and as, until within these few years, if it is not so now, it used to be the language of society in Russia and Poland.

The very reasons, therefore, which made it expedient for Dan Jeremy to write in French at the close of the thirteenth century, pointed to the translation of his work into English. And there may perhaps have been other causes at work; the growth of a middle class, who could read English; and the revived care of the Church for the spiritual instruction of her more humble members in their own tongue.(1) It is at this time, or, to be more precise, in the last half of the reign of Edward the First, that I should have been disposed to place the date of the translation upon the antecedent grounds, here pointed out; the grammar and vocabulary are consistent with the suggestion that it was made at this time, that is, contemporaneously with Robert Mannyng; some years later than the metrical version of the psalms, often referred to in the following notes ; (2) and rather earlier than another northern writer, Richard Rolle of Hampole.(3)

(1) The domination of foreigners in all the higher places in the Church had no doubt tended to the greater neglect of the canons of the Anglo-Saxon Church in that behalf; and we must admit that the first attempt at amendment was made, also from abroad, by the introduction of the black and grey friars shortly before the beginning of the second quarter of this century. Grosseteste and other home-born prelates lent them willing help, and the synod at Lambeth in 1281 was presided over by Archbishop Peckham, who affected to call himself Friar John after he was raised to the see of Canterbury, and their constitutions for the systematic teaching of the elements of religious knowledge by the parish priest (*Provinc*, Lib. I, Tit. xi, Cap. 4, *Ignorantia sacerdotum*) may perhaps be traced to the early friar spirit, when the high purpose of their founders had not ceased to animate the mendicant orders, and they had not become a byword for the satirist, and a scandal to the name of religion.

(2) *Anglo-Saxon and Early English Psalter*, Surtees Society, *Ed.* Stevenson, 1843. The MS. from which the metrical psalms are printed is about the year 1316 or 1317, but the original is supposed to have been written soon after the middle of the thirteenth century.

(3) It must not be forgotten when forming an estimate as to the age of an early English work that in the north the inflexions of the older language were, for the most part, early cast aside, whilst they continued to characterize the

But we are not left to mere conjectures, however well founded, for the British Museum manuscript (our B text), though it is some eighty, or possibly only seventy years later than the translation itself, and has been subjected to dialectical alteration throughout, nevertheless, if I do not mistake, has preserved a note of time which enables us to fix the date still more definitely. It will be seen that in the prayers for the state of the Church in this text (*page* 32), the clergy are prayed for as follows : "and the bishops, priests, and clerks," the pope not being mentioned; and that in the other four texts, there given, no two introduce the mention of the pope in the same way.

From this I infer that the pope was not specified in the original translation; and hence that the papal see was vacant (1) when it was made. The variations in the other texts may be explained by supposing that the scribes who wrote them, or those they copied, noticing the omission when the see was full, each for himself, as it occurred to him, and more or less awkwardly as it happened, inserted the mention of the pope, this being what they were used to in the canon of the mass, and other devotions of the church, when the clergy in their several degrees were publicly prayed for.(2)

There were two occasions during the period here indicated when there was an interval, between the death of one pope and the election of his successor, sufficiently long to be marked in the list of popes : the first of *two years and three months,* from the death of Nicholas

---

southern dialects to a later period. This will account for what may seem a less archaic character in our text, which we ought to compare, not with the *Ayenbite of Inwyt,* the *Ancren Riwle,* or other works of a later date in a southern dialect, but with works, such as those of the Lincolnshire *Mannyng,* or the Yorkshire Hermit, to which I have referred, that were written in the north, and though of an earlier date, are more like the common English of modern times.

(1) The fact of there being a pope, or of the see being vacant, must have been necessarily known to scribes in general and specially to those in the scriptorium of a religious house, or who acted as notaries. A great number of documents, and specially those issued by ecclesiastical authorities, bear the date of the year of the pope's pontificate, in addition to and sometimes without the regnal year of the prince.

(2) See the canon of the mass, *post,* 124/22; the bidding prayers, 62/7, 64/6, 68/10, 74/5, and 75/10. In the Litany, Sarum, and Ebor, we have "Ut domnum Apostolicum et omnes gradus ecclesiæ in sancta religione conservare digneris."

IV. on the 4th of April, 1292, to the election of Celistine V. on the 5th of July, 1294, and it is here that our date may more probably be found, both because the interval was longer, and because it was nearer the time, when on other grounds it would seem that the translation was made. The other was an interval of only eleven months, between the election of Clement V. on the 15th June, 1305, and the 6th or 7th of July, 1304, when his predecessor Benedict was poisoned.(1)

Verbal changes of this kind were no doubt made by the scribe according to his knowledge of the facts of the case ; but the translator, in his " drawing into English " (2) would seem to have kept very close to the original. It is possible that by a sort of afterthought, as already remarked,(3) he may have interpolated the halting couplet as to the use of the Ave-Maria (B 59-60) ; and the reader may perhaps be disposed to accept the alternative suggestion which I have offered,(4) that he may have added the two lines (B 277-8), to represent what may have been the alternative answer of the earlier Rouen use to the *Orate* of the priest, as it was afterwards the layman's answer in both provinces (5) in this country : but with the exception of the interpolated couplet, above specified, there is nothing that Dan Jeremy may not have himself written in the twelfth century, and the retention—in some cases the retention of the very words— of a foreign use is a strong proof that the translator faithfully rendered his original without making alterations to adapt it to the existing English ritual, as subsequent transcribers did not hesitate to do in respect to his own version.

(1) There were two similar intervals, during which the translation might have been made—one of *two years and nine months* before the election of Gregory X. in 1271, but this would seem too early ; and the other, after the papal see was transferred to Avignon, of *two years and three months* before the election of John by a conclave at Lyons in 1316. This perhaps is rather late ; and in any case is the latest date, when the translation could have been made, if my suggestion is rightly founded, as there is no subsequent interregnum of exceptional length.

(2) Page 2, line 4.   (3) Page xxxvi. Note, p. 183.
(4) Page 263.   (5) Page 264.

DIALECT OF THE TRANSLATION AND VARIATIONS BY SCRIBES.

Dr Morris has described the Lay Folks Mass Book as a "specimen of the East Midland dialect."(1) He had before him the print of our text B, which, as mentioned in the preface,(2) was circulated when the transcript first came into my hands; and as I had come to the conclusion that this particular MS. was the work of a Midland scribe, I was very pleased to have my opinion confirmed by a philologist in every way entitled to speak with authority on any question connected with English dialect.

It is mainly to Dr Morris' systematic classification of their grammatical forms that I am indebted for most of what little I know of our old English dialects—always excepting the northern, which, from having been an East Riding clergyman for more than thirty years, I have had ample opportunities of studying as a living language; —and therefore an attempt to modify a judgment of his, *obiter dictum* though it be, may seem presumptuous : but I venture to think that the original was translated into a northern dialect, however much the manuscripts may have been altered by successive scribes in the process of copying, in order to adapt them to the language of their own time and district—texts E and F, as well as text B, being examples of a Midland dialect, and text C of a northern dialect, though of a hundred and fifty years later, when many older northern forms and words were passing out of use.

Nor were the alterations made by the scribes merely grammatical, or confined to the alteration of a word which was unknown or distasteful to them. Instead of reproducing the copy before them, they seem to have held themselves at liberty, and especially where it was a question of religion, to exercise the functions of revisers. In some cases, they may have thought they were carrying out the wishes of the author in making what seemed to be amendments and improvements. Hampole, at the end of his *Prick of Conscience*, not only bespeaks excuse for defaults of rhyme, but invites the correction of the learned in the matter of his treatise. He says,

(1) *Alliterative Poems*, Revised Edition, Preface, p. xxviii, note 1.
(2) Page x.

> " I rek noght, þogh þe ryme be rude,
> If þe maters þarof be gude.
> And if any man þat es clerk,
> Can fynde any errour in þis werk,
> I pray hym do me þat favour,
> þat he wille amende þat errour ;
> For if men may here any errour se,
> Or if any defaut in þis tretice be,
> I make here a protestacion,
> þat I wil staud til þe correccion
> Of ilka rightwyse lered man,
> þat my defaut here correcte can."(1)

The worthy old hermit's desire was to stir lewed men to the love and fear of God, and he recked nothing as to shape in which his message might come to them. Chaucer, on the other hand, was quite alive to the risks to which his highly-wrought verse was exposed. In his *Troilus and Cryseyde*, he thus addresses his " litel boke " :

> " And for ther is so grete diversite
> In Englissh, and in writynge of our tongue,
> So preye I to God, that non myswrite the
> Ne the mys-metre for defaute of tongue ! "(2)

This diversity is so great that we find a northern scribe describing his work as a translation, and his fellow north countrymen as unable to read other English :

> " In other Inglis was it drawin
> And turnid Ic haue it til ur awin
> Language of the Northin lede,
> That can na nother Inglis rede "(3)

In our texts it is the turning of a northern poem into midland, though from being a case of neighbouring dialects, the contrast, especially in B, is not so great ; and the original northern, in many of its peculiarities, would have been uncouth rather than unintelligible. The invention of printing has tended more than anything else to the formation of a common language, and the fixing of its spelling ;

(1) P. C. 9585—9596.

(2) Quoted, Ellis, *Early English Pronunciation*, I, 249. We find an appeal of the same character in the *Ormulum*, and the *Preambulum* of the *Promptorium Parvulorum*.

(3) *The Embassy of Helis*, MS. Edinburgh, quoted, Small, E. M. H., Preface, p. xxii. The caution in the *Promptorium* referred to in the last note speaks of a different dialect as being " *alterius patriæ* " ; much as here we have another "lede." One of the examples given is *hande* and *honde*, an alteration which occurs in our texts : " Non scribat HONDE pro HANDE, nec NOSE pro NESE, nec KAYE pro KEYE, et sic de aliis."—P. P. I, 4.

but it may not be uninteresting to see how Caxton at the first dealt with his copy. He is speaking of Trevisa's translation of the *Poly-chronicon*, which had not been written a hundred years—it was finished in 1387 :

"I William Caxton . . . . . somewhat have chaunged the rude and old Englysh, that is to wete certayn wordes which in these days [1482] be neither vsed ne understanden."(1)

And now to the examination(2) of our text B. At first sight it has an un-northern look. The scribe has written þo for þe, *hom* and *hor* for þam and þair, *shal* and *shulde* for *sal* and *suld* or *soulde*; and not only are these forms constantly recurring from the words being necessarily in such constant use, but there are many other words which he has written according to his Midland spelling (3) :

alone	*and not*	al ane
among	,, ,,	amang
boke	,, ,,	buke
bos	,, ,,	bus
con (*to get by heart*)	,, ,,	cun (4)
,, (*to be able*)	,, ,,	kan
felouse	,, ,,	felawes
fro	,, ,,	fra
foundyng (*temptation*)	,, ,,	fanding
gode	,, ,,	gude
home	,, ,,	hame
knowe	,, ,,	knawe
loke	,, ,,	luke
mone	,, ,,	mun (*must*)
mony	,, ,,	many
monyfold	,, ,,	manyfalde
moo	,, ,,	ma (*more*)

(1) *Polychronicon* Ranulphi Higden, *ed.* Babington, 1865, I, p. lxiii.

(2) If it should occur to any of my readers that the circumstance of the answer of the York missal not being used (lines 275-8) is an argument for the text having been written in the southern province, I beg to refer to the note, page 263.

(3) The use of " o " in this text is almost as marked a feature as the perpetual upsilonism of our West-Midland text E. See note, p. 185.

(4) See notes, p. 293, 312.

most	*and not* masto
no	,, ,, na
none	,, ,, nane (1)
opon	,, ,, upon
owe	,, ,, awe
so, soo	,, ,, swa
soule	,, ,, saule
þoo	,, ,, þes *or* þas (*those*)
world	,, ,, werld

On the other hand, there are a few northern words :

flytte	mirk
heþen (*hence*)	sere (*several*)
ilk	swilk, swylk
ill	þirre
kirk, kyrc	þiþin (*thence*)
michel, mychel	til (*to*)

I lay no great stress on the occurrence of these words, because northern words may have found, and in many cases did find their way into neighbouring dialects.

What is more to the point, not only do we find northern grammatical flexions as I shall proceed to show, but we find the words in the following list both in the Northern and the Midland forms :

| *aght | *and* owe |
| ane(2) [name, 18] | ,, one |

(1) The scribe (E 141) evidently did not understand the northern *nane*, but writes *name*, which points to it.

(2) Our Midland scribe seems to have been quite at fault with the northern *a* or *ane* (one). In line 11 he has let *ane* pass for the sake of the rhyme. In line 157 *a* may very well have been the article as in line 19, though it may have been used of *one* in contrast to the several crosses, which are sometimes directed to be made. In line 173 *a* is used in contrasting *one* with *the other ;* but the scribe most likely let it pass as the indefinite article ; and in line 180, probably for the same reason, though here it was intended of the oneness of the Trinity (see note, p. 215-16). In line 561 he has written *ay* (=ever) instead of *a* (=one), though this is clearly a better reading, and has been retained in C. (See note, p. 300.)

In lines 424 and 425, from not being used to "ane," and from the Aue-Maria being an established devotion when he wrote, he has made utter nonsense, by writing *ave ;* though the usually blundering scribe of our E text has rightly translated the *ane* into *on.* See note, p. 183.

*awen   *and* owne

bandes [handes, 404]   „ bondes

behalde [salde, 406]   „ biholde

ere (er) [were (*noun subs.*), 588] ⎫
here (er)(1) [prayere, 460]   ⎬ „ are

es (2 *sing.*) [les, 125]   ⎫
es (3 *sing.*) [mes, 118]   ⎬ „ is

esse (es, 3 *plur.*) [mes, 462]   „ are

gast [hast, 213]   ⎫
gastly(2) [largely, 67]   ⎬ „ gost [most, 144]

haly [Mary, 75]   ⎫
  „ [specialy, 375]   ⎬ „ holy
heli (haly) [mercy, 474]   ⎭

*hald   „ hold

hande(3) (*sing.*) [lyvande, 140]   ⎫
  „   [offrande, 241]   ⎬ „ honde

handes [bandes, 405]   ⎫
hende(4) [ende, 35]   ⎬ „ hondes [stondes, 40]
  „   [amende, 284]   ⎭

man [þan, 330]   „ mon [con, 613]

*many   „ mony

mare [þare, 42]   ⎫
  „ [care, 478]   ⎬ „ more

*namely   „ nomely

stande [goande, 592]   „ stondes [hondes, 39]

þan [man, 330]   „ þen

*thank   „ thonk

*thanked   „ thonked

þare [mare, 42]   „ þere

untille [wille, 121]   „ unto

Now except those words which are marked with an * asterisk, where the northern form may have been copied mechanically by the scribe, although midlandized in other cases, it will be observed that the northern forms occur in rhymes, where both words did not admit

(1) Note, p. 288.   (2) Note, p. 223.   (3) Note, p. 199.
               (4) Note, p. 179.

of a ready alteration to a Midland form. I add the intractable rhyme
and the number of the line within brackets ; and I cannot help thinking, that it makes very strongly for my suggestion of the original
manuscript being northern, that the scribe has altered it to Midland,
whenever he could do so without " mismetering "(1) his copy.

In addition to these northern rhymes which have been retained, I
may add the following rhymes which are much improved by restoring,
or—not to beg the question—by substituting northern forms :

son es	*for* son is [endles, 206]	
fles(2)	„ flesshe [forgyfnes, 237]	
haly(3)	„ hely [mercy, 474]	
blis(4) ⎱	„ blesse ⎱	618-19
his ⎰	„ hesse ⎰	

But strong as is the presumption in favour of a northern original
from the use of northern orthography, the evidence of grammatical
forms is still more important in a question of dialect ; and I venture
to think that what we gather from an examination of text B in this
point of view tells no less strongly in the same direction—most certainly the occasional use of " -en " at the termination of the plural of
the present tense is no proof the original was Midland. The northern
translator might have written " -en " sometimes(5) ; and the only
question is, when the scribe has written so many "-en" s,(6) why he
did not do his work more thoroughly, and should have left a single

(1) See quotation from Chaucer, *ante*, p. lv. The West Midland scribe
of text E has had no scruple of this kind in altering the northern reading.
He writes " is—lasse," 125 ; " gost—chas," 213 ; " londe—mayntenande,"
361 ; " specially—holy," 371, and so forth.
(2) Note, p. 228.
(3) This, it will be observed, is an assonant rhyme, if we give *mercy* the
French pronunciation, as it may have had like *prayere, grace, place, conscience*, and other words in our text, at least, so far as accent is concerned.
Perhaps the alteration to *hely* may point to our modern pronunciation of
mercy, when text B was written (in 1375).
(4) The Midland scribe distinguishes between the substantive *bliss* and the
verb *bless*, as in modern English. To the north of Humber, *blis* did for both.
(5) Dr. Morris remarks on the conjugation of the present tense of the
Northumbrian verb, " We have occasionally (thai) *loven* instead of (thai)
loves."—*Pricke of Conscience*, Preface, p. xviii. There are examples in the
northern MS. he prints.
(6) Sometimes to the injury of the metre. See *lyuen*, line 293, and note,
p. 269.

northern "-es" to serve as mint mark; and the only explanation is that he wrote mechanically and sometimes copied what was before him, without being on the alert to correct the "other English" "of the Northern lede" as in other places, where it presented no difficulty, according to the Midland standard of spelling and pronunciation, with which he was familiar.

There is perhaps nothing distinctive in the use of the northern plural *brether* in a North-Midland MS., and the same remarks may perhaps apply to "-es" in the singular, as (*second person*) þou has, bids, sittes, is, es,(1) &c, and (*third person*) men(2) singes or sayes, standes, es, &c. But the "-es" in the plural stands on quite another footing. Dr Morris speaks of it as "a test by which Northumbrian may be distinguished from other dialects of the North of England."(3) When we come to apply this test to our text we find the tell-tale termination in the following places: *dos*, lines 16 and 44; *askes*, line 46; *heres*,(4) line 105; *has*, line 164, and *prayes*, line 420.(5)

(1) "is" and "es" in the second person occur in B only with the relative, or quasi-relative, als es, 125; þat is, 496.

(2) The indefinite "men" (see Glossary) is here followed by verbs which might be either singular or plural; but (line 167) the scribe has written in good Northern "men aght," which is unmistakably in the singular. The next time he comes upon the word (line 197) he writes "men oen" in the plural —not impossibly because his Midland proprieties may have been shocked by the uncouthness of what, if I am right in my suggestion above, he had written mechanically, and he had meantime bethought himself of the meaning of the phrase.

(3) *Pricke of Conscience*, Preface, p. xviii. I cannot lay my hand on the passage, but I well recollect that in some of Dr Morris' works I first met with the remark, which I took possession of at once, and have used as my touch-stone ever since, that plurals in -es, -en, and -eth, were respectively marks of Northern, Midland or Southern dialect. Mr. Oliphant (*Standard English*, p. 62) makes a remark to the same effect. He adds: "Another Shibboleth of English dialects is the Active Participle. In the north this ended in *ande*, the Norse form. In the Midland it became *ende*, the Old English form, though in Lincolnshire and East Anglia this was often supplanted by the Danish *ande*." It will be noticed that the participle in our text invariably ends in -*ande*, but this shibboleth will not help us in deciding between the northern dialect, and that of the border-land south of Humber.

In one instance the scribe has got rid of the northern participial ending, not so much apparently for dialectic reason as from having missed the meaning. See note on *passed* (B 112), p. 193.

(4) Note, p. 194.

(5) A northern reading in text F (p. 27, l. 119), which the scribe very probably retained only because he construed it wrong, adds one more to these examples of -es in the third person plural, viz. *lyres*, where our text B (line 293) reads *lyven*. See note, p. 269.

There is this to be remarked in reference to the escape of these
northern plurals from the Midlandizing process, which gives us
saien (line 63) and *heren* (line 173), that only *has* in line 164 and
prayes in line 420 have a substantive in the plural immediately before
them as their nominative. In other cases the nominative is a relative,
as in lines 16 and 105 ; or it follows, as in line 44 ; or is at a distance
of two lines, as before *askes* in line 46 ; and so may have thrown the
scribe off his guard. In this last example it is not unlikely that he
wrote the "dos" before it struck him that the nominative was plural,
and then wrote "clerk" in the singular, by way of making it good
Midland, and went on to write *hom* and *hor*, where he found *þam*
and *þaire*, without observing that his Midland equivalents remained
to bear witness to the alteration, and thus, at the end of five
hundred years, have served as one of a number of proofs that,
although a high authority did pronounce "*the poem never was
northern*," the editor had sufficient grounds for suggesting that Dan
Jeremy's treatise was originally translated into the northern dialect,
the language, as it happens, of his own archdeaconry of Cleveland.

RITUAL REVISION OF TRANSLATION.

It would seem that our texts B and E in the main, and apart
from dialectical alterations, reproduce the English version of the
translator; and that he, for his part, if we may judge by his retaining
the foreign ritual, appears, as already remarked, to have kept closely
to his original without an attempt to adapt it to an English use. But
for the Mass Book to serve the same purpose for Englishmen in
general, as it did for the French speaking baronage and their retainers,
when it was written, it had to be revised in reference to the Rouen
use, and the changed conditions under which, as time went on, mass
came to be celebrated—from a common service in which the people
joined with the priest, standing when they were "bidden," and
"answering on high" when it was their appointed part — to an
exclusively clerical function by the priest and clerks, or by the priest
alone, the people being supposed to remain on their knees, and to
be engaged in private devotion.

In this point of view the changes in the rubrics, as to standing and answering, are something more than the regulation of an indifferent ceremony.(1) I must not discuss the question in this place, but will proceed to point out as briefly as I can, first, the alterations that were made, after the translation of Dan Jeremy's work, to adapt it to the existing practice(2) of ordinary English congregations; and then, some further changes when it was intended for the use of members of a monastic foundation.

The first alteration is made because by the Rouen rubric the priest was ready vested at the beginning of mass except his chasuble, and in England he vested at the altar. With the reference to the foreign use, the explanation of the mutual confession of priest and people is also struck out,(3) though the form was, as it is to this day, retained in the missal.

Instead of merely leaving out the lines that were inapplicable, text F provides a prayer (*lines* 16-38) " whilst the priest does on his vestments," using for that purpose a prayer that had been appointed to be said after the confession.

Text B (*line* 41) notes that whilst the people are kneeling at the confession, the priest stands, and (B 61, 83) directs the people to stand when he begins the office—the later texts omitting this direction —and they continue to stand till after the *Gloria in Excelsis* (B 150), when they kneel until the gospel,(4) during which they stand (B 153) ; and they are also directed to stand when saying the prayer at the offertory (B 214), and to continue standing whilst " the priest is washing " (B 261) and until he begins the *secreta*, when the people " kneel down " (B 281) and pray for the acceptance of the sacrifice

(1) See note, p. 257.

(2) The more definite character of the hymn at the elevation has been noticed, p. xxix.

(3) B 33-58. See the notes there, and on the other places in the B text that are referred to.

(4) The remarks before the direction to make the sign of the gospel (B 152-174) are left out in the later texts, either because a reference to what might have been a Rouen custom (*see* note, p. 210), which would have been natural in one, who, as Dan Jeremy, might have been used to the reading of the gospel in French, would have been out of place ; or because, if retained, it might have seemed to countenance Lollard opinions as to the scripture in an unknown tongue, which may have already aroused jealousy, when the text was revised in the fourteenth century.

that has been offered. Then they stand up "as men them bid"(1) during the preface and *sanctus*, and at the beginning of the canon the layman is taught (B 328) to kneel down

> "And that with good devotion."

At the elevation, text B (*line* 405) desires the layman still "kneeling, to hold up both his hands," the later texts (C 225, F 201) adding the "inclination of the body." The later texts also (C 243, F 220) insert a reference to the Anglican ceremony of the priest spreading his arms cross-wise at the oblation of the consecrated bread and wine.(2) These texts have no direction to stand, but in B, when the priest has said *Per omnia sæcula* aloud at the end of the canon, the layman (*line* 483) is counselled, rather than directed — "I would "—to stand upright, whilst answering *Sed libera nos a malo. Amen*, and whilst the priest is making the fraction.

He is to "stand still" (B 507) at the *Agnus Dei*, but to kneel (B 515) at the *Pax*, and until "the priest has rinsing done," and then (B 577) he is—

> "Upon his feet to stand up soon,"

and after saying a prayer, corresponding to the postcommon of the priest, to "kneel down" (B 600) and continue saying paternosters till mass is done ; and when it is done, still to say a prayer of thanksgiving, before "wending his way."

It will be noticed that except to introduce the "inclination of the body" at the elevation, there is no mention of the posture of the layman in the later texts ; and if the reader will compare the places in the parallel texts where the original makes mention of standing, he will at once see, more readily than from any remarks without the texts before him, that the alterations were made of purpose aforethought, and so made, we must conclude, because kneeling throughout was already the approved practice.

The same may be said as to the change in answering aloud. In B 274 there is a plain direction to "answer the priest aloud ; " and this is changed in the later texts (C 127, F 107) to a wish. ("I would ") that a prayer should be used. There is indeed in the later

(1) B 303. See note, p. 270.   (2) See note, p. 288.

texts (C 86, F 66) a previous direction to answer with good will,
or with an alternative of "reading in a book." We find that the
answering with good will, contemplated in these texts, might be made
silently. It was to be "loud or still" (C 274, F 250): and this
explanation is inserted at the answer in the Lord's Prayer after the
canon, where the original text (B 490) gives the direction to answer,
quite in an apologetic strain, because those who "know not this, are
lewed men."

Text C was written, as we shall see, for the Cistercian monastery
of Rievaulx in the Archdeaconry of Cleveland towards the middle of
the fifteenth century,(1) and some further changes were introduced
into the later text to adapt it for monastic use. Many of the monks
were in holy orders, and others knew Latin, hence (C 31) they are
told, if they could, to translate the service book into English, as the
preferable alternative to using Dan Jeremy's English devotions, as no
doubt he would have himself thought.

In C 73 is a various reading which seems to have been due to the
mass being said in a conventual church, which was not frequented
by strangers.(2) In the other five MSS. the prayer is that the mass
should be for the souls' health of all *who heard it*, here for " our soul-
hele," that is, of all members of the order.(3)

Except that this text (C 351) supposes that the reader may
minister as deacon at mass,(4) there is only one other ritual variation,
but that is very significant of its conventual origin. In MSS. C, D,
F, the priest is said to make an "end of his service" at the end of
the mass: and in all four others, the worshipper wends his way home
after his final prayer; but in C 346 we have "that service," of the

(1) *Post*, p. lxviii.
(2) This would apply to Cistercian churches in general, and not merely to
Rievaulx on account of its solitary situation. It was forbidden to have a font
or to baptize in a Cistercian church (Mart. I. 6). Women especially were
excluded; and so rigidly, it would seem, as to require a papal dispensation for
the relaxation of the rule. On the 2nd September, 1251, about a hundred
years before this manuscript was written, Pope Innocent IV. allowed the
Countess of Lincoln, "accompanied by three or five honest matrons to enter
and hear service in the Cistercian monasteries in England."—Raine, *Archbishop Gray's Register*, S. S. p. 209.
(3) As to C 89-90, see note, p. 216; and as to " sugettes," C 188, see note,
p. 278.
(4) Note, p. 310.

priest, for another is to follow, and in C 356 the monk is directed to remain "God to pay," by taking part in the service for the hour which followed without an interval.(1)

THE MANUSCRIPTS.

The Mass Book has come down to us in three separate forms :—

I. As in texts B and E, which, as we have seen, keep closely to the original.

II. A, C, and D are in a revised form. The references to foreign ritual, and the translation of the *Gloria in Excelsis*, the Apostles' Creed and the Lord's Prayer have been left out : and the rubrics have been modified, as has been already specified; as have also the additional alterations to adapt text C for use in a monastery.

III. Text F has been further adapted for English use by appointing a prayer to be said whilst the priest is vesting.

The manuscripts agree in speaking of the directions as rubrics, and the devotions as written in black letter, though as a matter of fact the rubrics are marked as such, only in texts B and F. They are written in the first person singular, and the reader is addressed as "Thou," except in an altered rubric in C (line 127), where the second person plural is substituted, evidently by a slip, which does not occur in other later manuscripts.

All the rubrics and the greater part of the devotions are written in rhyming couplets of four feet or accents,—some few of three only, and some three or four of the rhymes being only assonant.

The general confession is in the ordinary cowee, as the piece from the Vernon MS. in the Appendix, except that there we have the double cowee of twelve lines, instead of six, as here.(2) It will be seen that in text F an attempt has been made to change it into the more usual couplets, but with sorry success.

The creed is written in four-line staves with alternating rhymes. The first and third lines of four accents rhyme together, as do the second and fourth of two feet, or accents. In the prayer at the elevation in B and E, we have nine verses in an interwoven stave of one of the many arrangements of the rhyme, which were founded on

(1) Note, p. 312.   (2) See as to this metre, note, p. 361.

Romance models, and are often to be met with in the English verse of the thirteenth and fourteenth centuries.

MS. A.

Our MS. A is a fragment of 130 lines of the revised form of the Mass Book. Mr W. B. D. D. Turnbull, then an advocate at the Scotch bar,(1) well known for his antiquarian pursuits, and the founder and for many years the secretary of a kindred society, the Abbotsford Club, has already printed it under the title of "The Masse" with other pieces from the same MS.(2) This manuscript, he tells us in his introduction (p. vi), "is a small 4to volume of the 15th century, preserved in the Advocates' Library (Jac. v. 7. 27), consisting of 216 folios. It was from the same MS. that Mr. Weber printed the 'Huntyng of the Hare' in his collection of Metrical Romances."

The Reverend T. Milville Raven was good enough to give me a transcript for this edition, which had the advantage of being examined by Mr. Cosmo Innes.(3) I afterwards obtained copies of complete manuscripts, and consequently have not printed it at length, for it is both late and corrupt.

TEXT B.

This text is from the MS. in the King's Library, now in the British Museum, where it is catalogued as "Royal MS. 17 B. xvii." It is quoted by Mr. Maskell in his *Ancient English Liturgies* as the Museum manuscript.

The volume in which it is contained is described in Casley's *Catalogue of the MSS. of the King's Library*, 4to, London, p. 263,

(1) Some years later Mr Turnbull was called to the English bar, and edited *The Buik of the Cronicles of Scotland* for the Rolls Series in 1858. He was afterwards employed to calendar State Papers (Foreign Series) of the reigns of Edward VI and Mary, but gave up his appointment, though the highest testimony was borne to the fairness and ability with which he had done his work, in consequence of exceptions that were taken against the employment of a man, who had become a Roman Catholic, in calendaring papers so much mixed up with the reformation. He died in 1863 in the fifty-second year of his age.

(2) *The Visions of Tundale, together with Metrical Moralizations and other fragments of early poetry, hitherto unedited.* 8vo. Edinburgh, 1843. The impression was restricted to one hundred and five copies.

(3) Note, page 245(1).

but by a singular carelessness, this piece is not specified, though it stands first in the volume, the first entry being " 1. *Speculum Utile istius Mundi*, An English Poem, XV." [century], which we may account for, by our text having no title prefixed to it, and by the above title appearing in the colophon of the piece that follows it.

The volume was bound after the catalogue was printed, as appears by the date on the cover, "G. II. R. 1757." It had at one time belonged to John, Lord Lumley,(1) and his autograph, " Lumley," is on a blank leaf (*fol.* 1), but there is no other remaining clue to what might have been the history of the book.

There are nine other pieces ; one of them, the last in the volume, seems to have been written by the same scribe, and in this there does not appear to be any trace of a northern dialect, which I mention, as a proof, if proof were wanting, that the northernisms in that text were not due to the scribe.(2)

The MS. is on vellum 7½ by 5½ inches, and is very neatly written. Date about 1375.

The rubrics are in a smaller character than the "black letter," but are not written in red, being only underlined in red throughout, except lines 520—523, 536—539, and 546—549, which are properly rubrics, and are so written in text F, but in this MS. are left unmarked.

The rubrics are further distinguished from the devotions by the initials being only two-line letters, except the capital thorn letter at the beginning ; whereas the initials in the black letter devotions are all three-line, except the I (line 205) and two or three others as shown in the print.(3)

---

(1) His library was "noted for a choice collection of books " (Surtees' *Durham*, II. 159). He succeeded his grandfather John Lord Lumley in his estates, but not in his title, his father Sir George Lumley having been attainted and executed at Tyburn in 1537 for his share in Aske's rising. He was restored to the peerage in the first year of Edward VI ; made a Knight of the Bath in the first year of Philip and Mary, and High Steward of the University of Oxford in 1558. He was himself a Cambridge man, and gave presents of books to both universities. He died in 1609 without issue, leaving his estates to his kinsman Richard Lumley, ancestor of the present Earl of Scarborough.

(2) *Ante*, page lvii—lxi.

(3) The number of lines for the size of the "great" letters was a matter of express stipulation. See note (3), page 401.

The MS. was copied for the Society by Mr E. Brock, and the proof-sheets were collated with it by the editor, who, in any doubtful case, had the advantage of the opinions of Mr Thompson, now Keeper of the Manuscripts.

TEXT C.

This text is the last but one of sixteen pieces in a vellum MS. now in the library of Corpus Christi College, Oxford (C. C. C. MS. 155). It was written for the Cistercian Abbey of Rieval or Rievaulx, in the valley of the Rye, in the North Riding of Yorkshire; and is inscribed both at the beginning and the end as follows: " Liber beate Marie de Rieualle ex procuracione domini Willelmi Spenser, Abbatis eiusdem."

This inscription, taken in connection with the omission of the prayer for the queen, shows that the manuscript was written, probably in the scriptorium of the abbey, when it was added to the library— one of those rich monastic libraries of which there remains a catalogue, and that of the previous century, to prove how much has been lost.(1)

In line 183 the king and the lords of the land are prayed for; and as all the other manuscripts insert a prayer for the queen in this place, we can have no hesitation in explaining the omission by the fact of there being neither a queen consort nor a queen dowager at the time when the MS. was written. There was an interval of more than seven years, during the minority of Henry VI. and until his marriage with Margaret of Anjou in 1445, when there was no queen, Joan of Navarre, widow of Henry IV, having died in 1437, and his own mother, if she were still prayed for as queen after the exposure of her marriage with Owen Tudor, having died six months before her.

I have not succeeded in my search for the date of Abbot William Spenser's appointment. His predecessor was Henry Burton, a monk of Salley, who was confirmed on the 18th November, 1423; and he was succeeded by John Inkelay. His " free and voluntary resignation " is dated the 4th April, 1449,—Inkelay subscribing his " obedience " to the Archbishop of York on the 8th of the same month,(2)

(1) This is preserved in a 14th-century MS. in the library of Jesus College, Cambridge. N. B. 17, pp. 180—189. "Hi sunt libri sancte Marie Rievallensis." It is printed in Edward's *Memoirs of Libraries*, I. 333.

(2) Archbishop Kempe's *Register*, fcl. 420*b*.

—so that he may very well have been abbot during the time there was no queen to be prayed for.

The ritual changes that were made in this manuscript to adapt it for use in the monastery have been pointed out.(1) In respect to the dialect, as might have been expected in a Yorkshire Abbey, it is unquestionably northern as to the verbal and participial endings, though there are many indications of the change that was taking place in northern literary English by the adoption of southern forms. For example, though we have *at* (C 278), the preposition *to*(2) sometimes replaces *till*, *fro* is used as well as *fra*, *gode* and *gude*; *boke* and *buke*, *oon* and *noon*(3) as well as *a*, *ane*, and *nane*; *so* and *also*, with *swa* and *alswa*. *Sere* is retained for the rhyme, though *many* replaces it in the middle of the line, as *ever* does *ay*, but both words were perhaps becoming obsolete.

Mr George Parker of the Bodleian copied this text from the manuscript and also collated the proofs with it.

MS. D.

This MS, Gg. 5. 31, No. 1 of the University Library, Cambridge, is a 4to. on parchment, and the handwriting is said to be of the earlier part of the sixteenth century. It is of the revised form and generally agrees with our text C, except in respect to what I have described as the monastic modifications, but the dialect is a purer northern, or rather, not modernized as that is, though written more than fifty years later.(4)

Text E.

This text is copied from a MS. which is one of several on paper and parchment that are bound up in a folio volume in the library of Gonville and Caius College, Cambridge, and catalogued MS. 84(2). This is on paper, pages 173—179 of the volume, two columns on a page, badly written in a hand of the middle of the fifteenth century; and that it is so, is confirmed by an entry (page 195 of the volume) in a

(1) *Ante*, p. lxiii.
(2) The scribe overdoes his adaptation by writing *to* (C 91) for *till* or *until*.
(3) Note, p. 400.
(4) In places it preserves the true reading, where it has been changed in text B. See note (2), page 53.

calendar in the same handwriting : " This Kalender hath his begynnyng in the yere of oure Lorde *Jhesu* a Mill cccc · xl. and iij."(1)

This MS. contains the same matter as text B, but is derived from
an independent transcript of the original ; and in some cases preserves
evidence of the original reading where it has been lost in B. The
dialect is West Midland of a very broad type.

The scribe has made many mistakes, some of which are pointed
out in the notes, from ignorance of northern or archaic forms. He
has also made the most unaccountable transpositions,—not at the
beginning of a page, for there are catch-words throughout—and
apparently without any suspicion on his part that they are utterly
destructive of the sense. For the sake of comparison I have arranged
the text according to the proper order as in B, but it is written as
follows, the references being to the corresponding lines in B as numbered in the print. 1—4, 39—48, 5—38, 49—260, 336—397, 261
—337, 398—621, and this is followed by the last line (E 615, as
printed), which is not found in text B.

Text F.

This text is from a manuscript the property of Mr. Henry Yates
Thompson of Thingwall, Liverpool, Vice-President of the Holbein
Society, and was copied by Professor Skeat. He not only placed his
transcript at my disposal, as I have already mentioned in the preface,
but also corrected the proof of the text. He informs me that it is
written on eleven blank pages at the end of the MS. of *Piers Plowman*, which he has collated for the text B of his edition. He considers that the *Piers Plowman* was written early in the fifteenth century, and the *Mass Poem* in a later hand of about the year 1450.(2)
The rubrics are written in red, and it is the only one of our texts
which has them complete.

It is of the later revised form, but differs from the other copies by
transferring the prayer (F 15—38) which in them occurs after the

(1) For this information I am indebted to the Revd Dennis Hall, of the
University Library, who procured the transcript for the Society and collated
the proof with the manuscript.

(2) See also his description of the manuscript. *Piers the Plowman*, Text
B, p. xiv.

mutual confession of priest and people to the beginning, in order to be used whilst the priest is vesting.(1) It also, to the damage of the meaning, trans-metres the confession (F 43—60) from *versus caudati*, or cowee to rhyming couplets.

The scribe was West-Midland, and uses Southern forms to a very great extent, though it is not difficult to read the northern original between the lines ; and like the scribe in B, he often leaves it unmutilated for the rhyme.(2) He uses *fyndest, ert* (2 sing.), *maketh, doth on* (3 sing.), *hereth, lasteth, beth* (3 plur.), and so forth.

Sometimes he is tolerably successful in his attempt to get rid of unwelcome rhymes :

> " And gif thame grace to laste and lende
> In þy servyce to þere *last* ende."—C 206-7.

> " Grace euere-lasting thu ham sende
> In thi seruice to here laste ende."—F 183-4.

> " Fra alle pyne and fra alle kare
> Into þe joye þat lastes eueremare."—C 267-8.

> " Fram alle paynes to heuuene blis,
> With angeles to dwelle euere endeles."—F 245-6.

but for the most part he alters very much for the worse.

The following are some of the northern or archaic words which the scribe has got rid of ; *kyd, lende, loute, mot, þir, wissed.* He changes the following words :

folk	*to*	pepil	pyne	*to*	payne
gude	„	welfare	sere	„	many
hele	„	helthe	sirly	„	diversli
hethen	„	hennes	sib men	„	kinnes men
ilk	„	eche	skille	„	resoun
kirk	„	chirche	swilke	„	sucche
lese	„	loose			

He is not, however, equally successful in every instance. He renders *halowes here* (army of saints) by *halwes dere* ; *sere* by *i-fere* in one place (F 236) ; and he has entirely missed the meaning of *fremd*, a word still in every-day use here in the north, and, instead of it, writes *frend*.

(1) See Note, p. lxii. (2) *Ante*, p. lviii.

The Lay-Folks Mass-Book.

FOUR TEXTS.

B. British Museum—Royal MS. 17 B. *XVII.*

C (Rievaulx). Corpus Christi College, Oxford—MS. 155.

E. Gonville and Caius College, Cambridge—MS. 84 (2).

F. MS. in Library of Henry Yates Thompson, Esq.

WITH VARIOUS READINGS FROM

A. MS. Advocates' Library, Edinburgh—19, 3, 1. Art. 7.

D. MS. University Library, Cambridge—Gg. 5. 31. No. 1.

The Lay-Folks Mass-Book,

TEXT B.
[fol. 3]
Of things on
earth, the mass is
of most worth;

its praises have
been told in
church books at
all times,

but authors,
however learned,
could not tell the
fifth part of
them,

Þo worthyest þing, most of godnesse,
    In al þis world, [hit] is þo messe.
    In alle þo bokes of holy kyrc,
    þate holy men, þat tyme, con wyrc,   4
    þo m[esse is p]raysed mony-folde ;
    þo [vertus mi]ght neuer be [t]olde,
    for if [thousand] clerkes d[id nogh]t ellis,
    After þat [þo boke] tellis,   8
    bot tolde [þo vertus of] messe syngynge,
and þo [profet of m]esse herynge,
ȝit shuld þa[i never þo] fift parte
for al þaire wit & alle þaire arte,   12
telle þo vertu [me]des & pardoun
to hom þat [with devocyo]un

TEXT C.
[fol. 250 b.]

(Incip. Præmia Missæ.)

THe worthyest thynge, þe maste of gudnes,
    In alle þe werlde, þan is the mes.
In alle þe bokes of haly kyrke,
þat haly men, þat tyme, gone wyrke,   4
þe messe is praysed many falde ;
þe vertues may neuere be talde ;
For if a M¹ clerkes did noght els,
After þat þe boke tels,   8
Bot talde þe vertus of messe singynge,
And þe profet of the messe herynge,
ȝitte soulde thay neuere fifte parte
For alle þere crafte and þere arte,   12
Telle þe vertus, medes, [and] pardone
To þame þat with deuocyon

or Manner of Hearing Mass.

A Worthy þyng, moste of godnesse,
In aH þe world, hit is þe messe.
In al bokus of holy kyrke,
þat holy tyme men coþ wyrke   4
þe messe is preysud mony-folde ;
þe vertuus may neuer be tolde.
þaf a Mᵗᵉ clerkus dyd noght ellus,
But after as þis boke tellus,   8
But told þe vertuus of messyngynge,
And þe profettus of messe herynge,
3yt schuld þei neuer telle þe fyfte parte,
ffor aH hore wytte and aH artte   12
Telle þe vertuus medus and pardoþ
To honþ þat haþ deuociþ

TEXT E.
[page 173]

[page 173]

---

m   an or woman þat wol lere,
A masse deuou[t]ly for to here,
Gode entent þou 3eue þereto,
And as þis boke techeth, so þow do,   4
For hit is wretyn what þou schalt say,
Whane þow schalt rest, whane þou schalt pray
Bothe for þe quyke and for þe dede ;
As þow fyndest wryte, so make thy bede.   8
Whiles the prest maketh hym boune,
Vpon thi knees sette the doune ;
And hew vp thyn herte wyt gode entente,
The whiles he doth on his westemente,   12
To god thu pray on þis manere,
As next thu fyndest wrytyn here.
Now lord god, for thi godenesse,
At the begynnynge of this messe,   16
Thou graunte to alle that hit schal here,

TEXT F.
Adapted to the
practice of
smaller churches
and chapels in
England, where
the priest vested
before the people.

A prayer whilst
the priest is
vesting ;

In clennes [*and in gode ent*]ent

where men of a
clear conscience
are minded to
reverence it
aright.
dos worship [*to*] þis sacrament.   16

In boke fynde I [*wryten*] of ane,

dam Ieremy was his name,(1)

a deuoute mon & a religyus,

In his boke he spekis þus ;   20

he saies, þou shulde gode tent take,

þat þou at þo messe no ianglyng make ;

grett sau*m*pel he settis þer-to,

whi hit is ful ille to do ;   24

als-so he telles þo manere,

and directions
for hearing it,
whether sung or
said,
how þou shulde þi messe here.

when þo pr*e*ste saies he, or if he singe,

to hi*m* þou gyue gode herknynge ;   28

when þo. pr*e*ste pr*a*ies i*n* pr*i*nete,

tyme of pr*a*yere is þen to þe.

In clennes and gode entente

Dos worschyp to þat sacr*a*mente.   16

In boke fynde I writen of ane,

Saynte Ierome was his name,(1)

A deuoute man *and* religyous,

In his buke he spekes thus :   20

He says þou soulde gude entent take

þat þou at þe mes na Iangelynge make ;

Grete ensaumple he sett*es* þere-to

Why it is full*e* yll*e* to do ;   24

Als swa he telles how

þou soulde þe mes þat þou heris now.

¶ When the priest sayes, or if he synge,

To hym þou gif gude herkenynge.   28

When the prieste prayes in pr*i*uate,

Tyme of prayer*e* than is to þe.

(1) In a boke fynd I of a man
þ*at* Jeremye was his name.—A.

In bukes fynd I of ane
Sayne Jerome was hys name.—D.

In clannes *and in* gud entent   TEXT E.
Dos worschyp to þe Sac*r*ament.   16
In a boke fynde I of o*n*,
Dane Ieremi was his nome,(1)
A deuowte mo*n and* religyus,
In hys boke he tellus þus :   20
þat þou schalt gud tent take,
At þe messe no yangully*ng* make.
Grete sampul he sett*us* þer to,
Why h*i*t is ful hely to do :   24
Also he tellus þo maner*e*
How þ*o*u schalt þo messe here.
Whe*n* þe preyst says, or yf he syng,
To hy*m* þou gyf gud herkenyng :   28
Whe*n* he pr*e*yus in pr*í*uyte,
Tyme of pr*e*ying is þe*n* to þe.

That in concience thei may be clere ;   TEXT F.
Lord, thu saue the prest, þat hit schal say,   which in the
                                                  other forms is
Fram gret temptacioun this ilke day,   20 appointed to be
                                                  said at the Office.
That he be clene in dede and thought,
That yuel spirit noy him nought
To fulfylle this sacrament
With clene herte and gode entent ;   24
First princypaly to thyn honour*e*,
That souereyn ert and socour*e*,
And to thy moder*e*, maiden clene,
And to thyne seyntes alle bi-dene,   28
And all*e* that hit hereth to here soules helthe,
Thu help hem with thi grace and thi welthe,
And all*e* that we haue in mynde,
'Sib or any frend bi any kynde ;   32
And, lorde, graunt ham for this messe,
Of all*e* har*e* synnes forgifnesse,
And rest and pes that lasteth ay,
To cristene soules that beth passyd away ;   36
And bryng us to ioie with-outen ende
And to us all*e* thi socour*e* sende.   Ame*n*.

TEXT β.	when I vp-on þo boke know hit,	[fol. 3 b.]
which I English.	In-til englishe þus I draw hit.	32
	when þo auter is al dight,	
The priest fully vested, except the chasuble, takes it from off the altar.	& þo preste is reuysht right,	
	þen [he] takes in bothe his hende	
	a clothe o-pon þo auter ende,	36
	and comes obac a litel doune,	
	dos hit o-pon him al a-boune.	
	alle men knelen, bot he stondes,	
	and haldes to god vp bothe his hondes;	40
He stands to make his confession to the people,	þere, or he þo messe bi-gynne,	
	wil he meke him for his synne;	
	til alle þo folk he shryues him þare	
	of alle his synnes lesse & mare:	44
and the clerks confess to him.	so dos þo clerk a-gayn to him	
	shryuen hom þere of al hor synn,	
	and askes god forgyuenes,	
	or þai bigynne to here þo mes.	48
He pronounces absolution to literate and lay, who are willing to confess,	þo preste assoyles hom þere belyue,	
	lered & lewed þat wil hom shryue,	
	& knowe to god þat þai are ille,	
	wheþer hit be in loude or stille.	52
	þerfore knelande on þi knese,	
	als þou bisyde þe oþer sese,	
wherefore do thou confess thy sins; and that thou mayest receive the benefit, add a Hail-mary to Pater-noster,	shryue þe þere of alle þi synnes,	
	bigynnande þus when he bigynnes,	56
	als next binethe þis robrik standes,	
	and þer-with ioyntly hold þi handes;	
	and þat hit so may be	
	eke to pater and* aue,	60

TEXT C.	If þou apon the boke kan knawe it,	
Readers who may be able to construe Latin may translate for themselves.	Into Inglische þou drawe it.	32
	¶ When þe priest hym revistis, *and* þe messe bigynnes,	
	And mekes hym to god for his synnes,(1)	

[* *read* an]

When he oponowt þe boke me kneu hyt   TEXT E.
In to englys he turneth hyt.   32
When þe awter is aH dyght,
And þe prest is re-wesshut ryght,
þen he takus in bothe is hondus
A chesepuH cloth on þe awter hongus,   36
And komus a lytul downe,
And dows hyt al a-poune.
AH men knelun, bot he stondus   [page 173]
And holdyt vp both hys hondus: 40
þer, or he þe messe be-gynnus,
Wel he makunhyt hym of aH hys synnus;
To aH þe folke he schryues hym ȝare
Of aH hys synnus lesse and mare.   44
So dos þe clerke a-ȝeyn to hym
Schryuet hym þere of aH hys syn,
And askut god for-ȝyfnes,
Or þey be-gynne to here þo messe.   48
þe prest asoylus hem þer blyue,
lerud and lewd þat wyl hem schryue
And know to god, þat harowd helle,
Wheþur hit be lowde or stylle.   52
þer fore kneland on þi kneus,
As þou be-syde oþer seus,
Schryue þe þer of aH þi synnus,
By-gynnand þus as þou bygynnus,   56
As nexte þis rubrych stondus
And þer wyht iountly hald þi hondus;
And, þat hit so may be,
Eke þerto say pater noster and aue,   60

Whanne the prest is reuest and begynnes,   TEXT F.
Whan he marketh him for his synnes,(1)   40

(1) When þo prest revestis hym mass to be-gyn
  and mekis hym to God for his syn.—A.
  When the prest revest mess by-gynnys
  and mekes hym to god for hys synnys.—D.

[fol. 4]

TEXT B.
and also a Creed.

and, or þou ryse, þou saie þi crede,

al þo better may þou spede.

many saien confiteor (1);

were als gode saie þis þer-for.   64

A general con-
fession in English
to God, the
Blessed Virgin,
the whole host of
saints, and the
priest.

I know [to Go]d, ful of myght,

    & [to his] modir mayden bright,

      & [to alle h]alouse here,

    & [to þe, fa]dre gastly,   68

    þat I [have s]ynned largely.

      In mony synnes sere :

In thoght, in speche, & in delite,

In worde, & werk I am to wite   72

    and worth to blame ;

Pray for the
prayers of St
Mary and all
saints, and the
priest,

þer-fore I praie saynt mary

and alle halouse haly,

    In gods name,   76

and þo preste to praye for me,

TEXT C.

þan say þou with hym þy Confiteor,

Or elles on ynglische þus þer-fore.   36

I knawe to god fulle of myght,

And to his moder, mayden bryght,

    And to alle halowes here,

And to þe, fader gastly,   40

þat I haue synned largely

[fol. 251 b.]   In many synnes sere.

In thoghte, in speche, and in delyte,

In worde, in werke, I am to wyte   44

    And worthy forto blame.

þerfore I praye the, marye,

And thy halowes haly,

    In goddes haly name,   48

And þe priest to praye for me,

(1) MS. corfiteor.

And or we say þe crede, TEXT E.
Al þe bettur we may spede.
Mony sayn) *confiteor*,
Were als gud say þis *per*-for : 64
I know to god ful of myght,
And to hys mod*ur*, mary mayd bryght,
   And to all halows here,
And to þe fad*ur* gostely, 68
I haue sy*n*nud largely,
   In mony sy*nnus* sere,
In þowthg, i*n* speche, *and in* delyte,
In word, i*n* werke, I am to wyte, 72
   And worthy for to blame.
þe*r*for I pray sent Mari
And all þe halows holly,
   here i*n* godd*us* name, 76
And þe prest to pray for me,

Thanne say thu with him confiteor,(2) TEXT F.
Or in englisch*e* thus therfore.

I know to god ful of myght,
And to his moder, mayde bright, 44
And to all*e* his halwes der*e*,
In many synnes of diuerse maner*e*,
And to the, fader gostely,
That I haw synned largely. 48
In thought, in speche, in delite,
In worde, in werke, I am to wite,(3)
And worthi I am to blame,
For falsly I haw take goddys name. 52
There-fore I pray seynte mari
And alle halwes specialy,
And the preste [*to*] pray for me,

       (2) MS. confiteore.   (3) MS. witte.

TEXT B.   þat god haue merci & pyte,

that Christ, in
that He has taken
our nature,
would pity and
forgive.
    for his manhede,

of my wreched synfulnes,   80

& gyue me grace & forgyuenes

    of my mys-dede. Pater. aue. credo.

After confession
the people stand
and the priest
finds his places
and begins the
Office.
When þou þi crede þus has done,

  vp-on þi fete þou stande vp sone,   84

for bi þis tyme, als I gesse,

þo prest bigynnes office of messe ;

or ellis he standes turnande his boke

  at þo south auter noke.   88

euen þen so stondande,

wolde I þat þou were þis sayande.

[fol. 4 b.]
A prayer to be
said, still stand-
ing, that all
present may be
well prepared,
and that the
priest be kept
this day
God, for þi godnes,

  at þo bigynnyng of þis mes,   92

  graunt alle, þate hit shal here,

of conscience be clene & clere ;

lord, saue þo prest þat hit shal say

fro temptacions to day,   96

TEXT C.   þat god haue mercy and pite

    for his grete mede

Of my wricchyd synfulnes,   52

And gif me grace of forgifnes

    Of my mysdede. Amen.

¶ When þou þere þy confiteor has done,

Say a pater-noster and an Aue fast þereon :   56

þan with-owten any tariynge

On þis wise be saiynge :

¶ God, for þi gudnes,

At the beginnynge of þis mes,   60

Graunte alle þat it salle here

Of þere synnes þat þay be clere ;

Lorde, saue the priest, þat it salle saye,

Fra temptacyon þis ilke daye,   64

þat god haue mercy *and* pete, TEXT E.
  ffor his moŋ-hedde,
Of my wrecched synfulnes, 80
And gyf me grace of for-ȝyfnes
  Of aH my mysdede. pat*er* nost*er* Aue *and* Crede
When þou þ*us* þi crede has done,
Vp-oŋ þi fete stond vp sone, 84
ffor be this tyme, as I gesse, [page 174]
þe preyst begynn*us* þe offys of þe messe,
Or ell*us* he stond*us* t*ur*nand his boke
At þe sowt awter noke. 88
Anoŋ so stondande,
Wold I þat þu were seyande :
Lord, for þi godnesse,
Let hy*m* bygynne þo offesse of þe messe. 92
Grawnt aH þat h*i*t schaH here,
Of conciens gud *and* clere.
Lord saue þe preyst þ*at* h*i*t schaH say
ffro aH temtacioŋ to day, 96

That god haw merci and pitte 56 TEXT F.
Of mi mysdede þat mochel is,
For his manhode and his godnys,
And of me wreche that synful is,
And ȝew me grace of for-ȝeuenys. 60

The prayer, in F. 15—38, is here again inserted for
comparison.

[Now lord god, for thi godenesse,
At the begynnyng*e* of this messe, 16
Thou graunte to alle that hit schal her*e*,
That in concience thei may be clere ;
Lord, thu saue the prest, þat hit schal say,
Fram gret temptacioun this ilke day, 20

þ*at* he be clene i*n* dede & þoght,
þ*at* yuel spiritis noy hi*m* noght,
þat he fulfille þis sacr*a*ment
w*ith* clene he*r*t & gode entent,   100
first heghly to þin honoure,
þ*at* soucrayne is of al socoure ;
& to þi modir, mayden clene,
& to þi halouse alle bi-dene ;   104
& to alle þ*at* heres hit, soul hele,
helpe & grace & al kyns wele ;
and to alle þate we haue i*n* mynde,
sib [*or fre*]mde bi ony kynde,   108
go[*d lo*]rd gra*u*nt ho*m* for þis messe
of alle hore synnes forgyfnesse ;
And rest & pese þ*at* lastis ay
to c*r*isten soules passed away ;   112
and til vs alle þi socoure sende,
& bring vs to ioy w*ith*-oute*n* ende. Amen.

þ*at* he be clene of will*e and* thoght,
þ*at* þe ill*e* wild spirite noy hym noght,
þ*at* he fulfille this sacrame*n*te
With clene herte *and* gude entent ;   68
Firste hyghly to þe hono*ur*,
þ*at* suffrayne is of alle soco*ur*,
And to þe, moder, mayden clene,
And to thy halowes all*e* be-dene,   72
þ*at* this mes be till*e* o*u*re sawll*e* hele,
Helpe *and* grace in allekyns wele ;
and to all*e* þ*at* we have in mynde,
Syb and fremd be any kynde,   76
Gode lorde, grau*n*te for this mes
Of þere synnes forgifnes,
And reste and pes þ*at* lastes aye
To cristenyd sawlles passyd awaye ;   80
And to vs all*e* thy soco*ur* sende
And brynge vs all*e* to þy ioy w*ith*-outen ende.   Amen.

þat he be clene in dede and þowght,   TEXT E.
þat hille spiritus nye hym noght,
þat he fulfylle þe sacramente
Wyt clene hert and gud entente,   100
ffurst heley to goddus honowre,
þat sufreɳ art of aꝉ socowre,
And to þi modur, maydoɳ clene,
And to þi halows aꝉ by-dene ;   104
And to aꝉ þat heruɳ hit sowle hele,
Helpe, and grace of aꝉ kynnus wele ;
And to aꝉ þat we haue in mynde,
Syb or fremde or any kynde,   108
God grawnt honɳ for þis messe
Of aꝉ hor synnus for-ȝyfnesse ;
And reste and pes þat last-het ay
To crystoɳ sowlus passe and way ;   112
And to vs aꝉ þi socur sende,
And brynge vs aꝉ to gud ende.

That he be clene in dede and thought,   TEXT F.
That yuel spirit noy him nought
To fulfylle this sacrament
With clene herte and gode entent ;   24
First princypaly to thyn honoure,
That souereyn ert and socoure,
And to thy modere, maiden clene,
And to thyne seyntes alle bi-dene,   28
And alle that hit hereth to here soules helthe,
Thu help hem with thi grace and thi welthe,
And alle that we haue in mynde,
Sib or any frend bi any kynde ;   32
And, lorde, graunt ham for this messe,
Of alle hare synnes forgifnesse,
And rest and pes that lasteth ay,
To cristene soules that beth passyd away ;   36
And bryng us to ioie with-outen ende
And to us alle thi socoure sende.   Amen.]

14 THE LAY-FOLKS MASS-BOOK.

TEXT B.

On high days,
when the Angels'
song is ap-
pointed,

do thou say it as
here written,
with a farce in
English.

[fol. 5]

On hegh festis, or on haly dayes,
  when-so men outher synges or sayes
gloria in excelsis in hor mes,
saie þou þen als here wryten es.

Ioy be vnto god in heuen,
  with alkyns myrthe, þat men may neuen;
  and pese in erthe, alle men vntille,
þat rightwis are, & of gode wille.
we loue þe, lord god almyghty,
and als we blesse þe bisyly,
we worsh[ip þe], als worthi es,
& makes [ioy to] þe more & les;
we than[k þe go]d of al þi grace,
for þo g[rete ioy] þat þou hase,
oure lord, [oure] god, oure king heuenly,
oure god, oure fadir almyghty.
oure lord, þo son of god of heuen,
Ihesu crist, comly to neuen,
oure lord, lamb of god, name we þe,
& son of god, þi fadir fre.
þou þat wostis þo worlds synne,
haue mercie on vs, more & mynne;
þou þat wostis þo worlds wrake,
oure praiere in þis tyme þou take;
þou þat sittes on þi fadir right hande,
with merci help vs here lyuande,
for þou art holly, made of none,
bot of þi selue, & lord alone.
þou art þo heghest, of wisdam most,
Ihesu crist with þo holy gost,
wonand with þo fadre of heuen,
In more ioy þen mon may neuen;
vnto þat ioy, ihesu, vs ken
thorght prayere of þi modre, amen.

116

120

124

128

132

136

140

144

148

TEXT C.
If literate,

¶ If þou of letter kan,
To þe priest herken þan

84

On Sunday or onꝺ holi dayus,   TEXT E.
Wheþur-so menꝺ syngus or sayus,   116
Gloria in excelsis in hor messe,
Say þou þenꝺ as here wrytonꝺ is :
Ioy be on-to God in hewonꝺ,
Wyt aꝇ kynnus myrthe, þat monꝺ may newonꝺ   120
And pees in herthe aꝇ menꝺ to teꝇ
    [A line left out in MS.]
We loue þe, lorde aꝇ-myȝthy,
And also we blessunꝺ þe bysyly ;   124
We Worschyp þe, as worthy is,
And makunꝺ to þe joy more and lasse ;
We þonkunꝺ þe, lord, of aꝇ þi grace
ffor þe grete joy þat þou hase,   128
Howre lord owre god kyng lelly,
Owre god, owre almyȝthy,
Owre lord of hewonꝺ,
Ihesu criste, comely to newnꝺ,   132
Owre lord, lombe of god, neme we þe,
And sunꝺ of god, þ[i] fadur fre.
þou þat wastus þe wordus synne,
Haue mercy onꝺ vs, more and mynne ;   136
þou þat wastus þo wordus wrake
Owre preyer in þis þou take ;
þou þat syttus onꝺ þi fadur ryght hande,
With þi mercy helpus here lyuande,   140
ffor þou art holy, made of name,
But of þi self, lord al onne.
þou art he of wysdam moste,
Ihesu criste wyt holy goste,   144
Wonnying with þe fadur of heunꝺ,
In more joy þenꝺ monꝺ may neunꝺ.
Wnꝺto þat joy, ihesu, vs kenne
Wyt þe preyere of modur, amenꝺ.   148

───

Whanne confiteor thus is done,   TEXT F.
Pater-noster folweth sone.
To the prest herkyn than,
ȝefe thu ought of the lettre can,   64

TEXT B.

Then kneel and
say pater-nosters
[fol. 5 b.]
all through the
collects and
epistle.

A nd when þou has þis al done,
knele doun on þi knese sone ;
If þai singe messe, or if þai saie,
þi pater-noster reherce al-waie,   152
til deken or prest þo gospel rede.
stonde vp þen & take gode hede ;

The priest moves
the book to the
north end of the
altar ; he makes
crosses, as
directed in the
rubric.

for þen þo prest flyttes his boke
north to þat oþer auter noke,   156
And makes a cros vpon þo letter
with his thoume, he spedes þo bette[r],
and sithen an oþer open his face ;

He has need of
grace in reading
God's word ; and

for he has mikel nede of grace,   160
for þen an erthly mon shal neuen
þo wordes of ihesu crist, gods son of heuen.

both readers and
hearers need
teaching,

bothe þo reders & þo herers
has mykil nede, me þenk, of lerers,   164
how þai shulde rede, & þai shulde here
þo wordes of god, so leue & dere
Men aght to haue ful mikel drede,
when þai shuld here or els hit rede ;   168
and loue als-so vnto þat swete
þat with þoo wordes oure bale wold bete

but our present
concern is hear-
ing,

bot syn oure matir is of hering
þer-of newe shal be oure lering.   172
Clerkes heren on a manere,
bot lewed men bos anoþer lere.

TEXT C.

then make the
responses, or
read the Latin :

Hys office, prayere, and pistille,
And answere þere-to with gude wille,
Or on a boke þy-selfe it rede.
I wate þerfore nane vnspede (1)   88

if not, say pater-
noster ; thy want
of learning will
not hinder thy
prayer.

If þou kan noghte rede ne saye ·
þy pater-noster rehers alwaye
To Dekyn or preste þe gospelle salle rede

[fol. 252 b.]

þere-tille þou take righte gude hede ;   92

(1) I wat thar-off na noye bede.—D.

And when þou hast all done,   TEXT E.
Knele downe on þi kneus sone ;
If þay synge, or þay say,
þi pater noster rehers alway.   152
When þo decun or þe prest þo gospel rede,
Stonde vp þen, and take gud hede,
ffor þen flyttu is his boke
Northe to þe awter noke,   156
And makud a ✠ on þe lettur
With his þowmb he speduth þe bettur,
And sech a noþur on his face,
ffor he hase nede of goddus grace,   160
ffor þen a hertly mon schal neun
þe blessud wordus of Ihesu of heun.
Both herersse and redersse
haue muche nede of lerersse,   164
how þay schul rede and here
þo wordus of goddus lawus dere.
Men auhȝt to haue mycul drede,
When þay schul hit here or hit rede,   168
And lowe to þat suete,
þat with þe wordus owre bale wolde bete.
But sethun owre mater his vp hereyng
þer-of schal be owre leryng.   172
Clercus herun on o manere,
But lewed men be-howus anoþer to lere.   [page 175]

The office, the orison, and the pistil,   TEXT F.
And answere him wel with gode wil,
Or on the bok thi-self hit rede,(2)
There-to take thu wel gode hede.   68
Ȝef thu can noght rede, ne say,
Thi pater-noster reherse alway,
Til the decon or þe prest the gospel rede,
There-to thu take wel gode hede ;   72

(2) MS. redde.

MASS-BOOK.   2

TEXT B.

Sign thyself with
a cross, and
standing up,

At þo bigynnyng tent þou take,
a large cros on þe þou make,   176
stonde & saye on þis manere,
als þou may se wryten here.

pray in the name
of the Trinity
in Unity, that
thou mayest
gladly receive
God's word.

In þo name of fadre, & son, & þo holi gost,
   a sothfast god of mightes most ;   180
   Bi* gods worde welcome to me ;   [* MS. bi; *read* be]
Ioy & louyng, lord, be to þe.

At the Gospel
meditate on thy
Redeemer, and

Whils hit is red, speke þou noght,
   bot þenk on him þat dere þe boght,   184
sayande þus in þi mynde,
als þou shalt after wryten fynde.

pray for His
grace and strength
to do His will.

Ihesu, myne, graunt me þi grace,
   and of amendment might & space,   188
   þi word to kepe & do þi wille,
þo gode to chese & leeue þo ille,

[fol. 6]

and þat hit so may be,
Gode ihesu, graunt hit me. Amen.   192

Repeat this to
thyself, and at
end of the gospel
make a cross and
kiss it.

Reherce þis oft in þi þoght,
   to þo gosple be don for-gete hit noght ;
Som-where bisyde, when hit is done,
þou make a cros, and kys hit sone.   196

When the mass-
creed is said,
say the Apostles'
creed in English,
but not else.

Men oen to saie þo crede som tyme,
when þai saie hore, loke þou saie þine ;
þis þat folouse in englishe letter,
I wold þou sayde hit for þo better.   200
bot þai say hore, say þou non ellis,
bot do forthe after, als þis boke tellis.

TEXT C.

At the biginnynge tente þou take
A large crosse on þe þou make,
Saiand þus on this manere,
Als þou may se writen here :   96
¶ þe name of the fader *and* sone *and* haly gaste,
And† sothfast god of myghtes maste,[† *Sic* MS. *Read* a = one.]
Goddes wordes be welcome vnto me,
Ioy and lonuynge, lorde, to þe.   100

At þe begynnyng gud tente þou take,
A large �֍ on) þe þou make, 176
Stonde *and* say on þis manere,
As þou may see wryton) here :
In þe name of þe fad*ur and* þe sonne *and* þe holy goste,
On stydfast god of myghtt*us* moste, 180
Be godd*us* worde welcu*m* to me,
Ay ioy *and* luf be to the.
Whyl he hyt rede, speke þou noghte,
But þynke on hym) þat þe dere bogthe, 184
Sayande þ*us in* þi mynde,
As þou aft*ur* schal wryton) fynde
Ihe*su*, my lorde, grawnte me grace
Of amendmente myghte *and* space, 188
þi worde to kepe, *and* al þi wylle,
þe gud to chese, *and* leue þe ylle.
And þat hi*t* so may be,
Eke "Ihe*su* lord, grawnt hi*t* me." 192
Rehersse hyt i*n* þi þowghte,
Tyl þe gospelł be don) forgete hi*t* noghte.
Sone besyde when) hyt is done
þou make a ✤ *and* kus hyt sone. 196
Men) owght to say þe crede su*m* tyme,
When) men) herun) hyt, say þou þine.
þis þat folows i*n* englys lett*ur*
I wold þou sayd hyt for þi bett*ur* ; 200
But qwen) þay sayn), say þou not ell*us*,
But do as þo boke þe tell*us*.

TEXT E.

"Glory be to
Thee, O Lord."

And at the begynnyng*e* **tent thu take,**
A large cros on the thu make,
Seyeng*e* **thus in this maner***e*
As thu maist se writen her*e.* 76
In the name of the fadir, the sone, and þe holigost,
On sothfast god of myghtes most,
Wel-come, lorde, thi worde to me,
As, ihe*su*, lowynge be to the. 80

TEXT F.

TEXT B.

The Apostles'
creed with a
farsure in
English.

[fol. 6 b.]

The Body and
Blood of Christ
both in form of
bread.

TEXT C.

here to loke þou take gode hede,

for here is wryten þin englyshe crede. 204

Trow in god, fader of might,

þat alle has wroght,

heuen & erthe, day & night,

And alle of noght. 208

And in ihesu þat gods son is

al-onely,

bothe god & mon, lord endles,

In him trow I ; 212

thurgh mekenes of þo holy gast,

þat was so milde,

he lyght in mary mayden chast,

be-come a childe ; 216

vnder pounce pilat pyned he was,

vs forto saue,

done on cros & deed he was,

layde in his graue ; 220

þo soul of him went in-to helle,

þo sothe to say ;

vp he rose in flesshe & felle

þo thryd day ; 224

he stegh til heuen with woundis wide,

thurgh his pouste ;

Now sittes opon his fader right syde,

In mageste ; 228

þeþin shal he come vs alle to deme

In his manhede,

qwyk & ded, alle þat has ben

In adam sede. 232

wel I trow in þo holi gost,

And holi kirc þat is so gode ;

And so I trow þat housel es

bothe flesshe & blode ; 236

After þe gospelle ay whil þe crede.

þe tyme is nere with-owten drede

Hereto loke þou take gud hede,

ffor here is wrytun) þe englys crede 204

 I beleue in god, ful of myȝhte,

  þat al has wroghte,

 Heun) and erthe,

  and al of noghte. 208

And in Ihesu, þat goddus son) is, .

 al holly,

Both god and mon), endles,

 in hym trowe I ; 212

þoro þe mekenes of þe holy gost,

 þat was so mylde,

He lyȝhte in to mari maidon) chas

 to cum a chylde. 216

Vndur pownse pilate pynnd was he,

 vs to saue

Down) on þe ✚ and ded he was,

 and leyd in his graue. .220

þo soule of hym wente to helle,

 þo sothe to say,

Vp he ros as fel

 vp-on) þe thryd day ; 224

Vp he ros with his wondus

 þoro his pouste ;

Now syttus he on his fadur ryȝhte honde

 in maieste. 228

Ȝyt schal he kum vs al to deme

 in hys monhedde

Quyk and ded and al þat haue bene

 of adam sede. 232

Wole I trowe in þo holy gost,

 and holy kyrke þat is gode ;

And so I trow þat howful is

 bothe flesche and blode ; 236

After the gospel whiles he seyth the crede.

The time is nei whit-oute drede

TEXT B. of my synnes*, forgyfnes,   [* MS. fynnes]
          If I wil mende ;
vp-risyng als-so of my flesshe,
          and lyf *with*-outen ende.   240

[fol. 7]
Then go up with
a mass penny,
or else remain in
thy place.

A fter þat, fast at hande,
     Comes þo tyme of offrande ;
Offer or leeue, wheþer þe lyst,
how þou shulde pr*a*ye, I wold þou wyst.   244

Either way, say
this prayer:

I-whyls þou stondes, I rede þou saye,
als next is wryten, god to paye.(1)

As with the Magi,
so may Christ
receive our
prayers to His
praise,

I hesu, þat was i*n* bethlem borne,
     And thre kynges come þe by-forne,   248
     þai offerd gold ensense & myrre,
     and þou forsoke none of þirre,
bot wissed hom wele alle thre
home a-gayne to hor contre.   252

Right so oure offrandes þat we offer,
and oure pr*a*ieres þat we pr*o*fer,
þou take, lorde, to þi louyng,
& be oure helpe i*n* alkyn thyng,   256

_____

TEXT C. þat men soulde pr*o*fer þere offrandes,
Or the priest take water to his handes.   104
Offer or leve, whether þe liste ;
How þou soulde praye I walde þou wyste.
Als nexte is writen, I rede þou saye,
On this man*er*e, god to paye.(1)   108
Ihe*su*, þat was in bedlem borne,
And thre kynges come þe biforne ;
þere thay offerd þe golde, ensens, *and* myrre,
And þou forsoke noon of þir,   112
Bot wyssed(2) þame wele all*e* three
Hame agayne to þere cuntre.
Right so *oure* offrandes þat we offyr,
And *oure* prayers þat we pr*o*fere,   116
[fol. 253] þou take, lorde, to thy lowynge,
And be *oure* helpe in alkyn thynge,

          (1) pey.—A. (prey.—*Turnbull*). pray.—D.

And of my synn*us* for-ȝyfnes, TEXT E.
  if I wold a-mende ;
Vp-rysynge also of my flesche,
  and lyfe w*ith* owtu*n* ende. 240
Aft*ur* þat, faste on honde,
Cometh tyme of offeronde ;
Offur wheþur þe luste,
How þou schuld pray, I wold þou wyste. 244
And whyl þou stond*us*, I rede þou say,
As is wrytu*n*, god to pay : (1)
Ih*es*u, þat was i*n* bethlem) borne,
And iij kyng*us* come þe beforne, 248
þey offurud-don) gold, sensse, *and* myrre,
þ*ou* forsoke non) of hem) þere,
But wyssud (2) he*m* þi wyl aꝉ thre
Whom) a-ȝeyne i*n*to hore cuntre. 252
Ryȝꝉt so þe offeryng þat we offur,
And owre preyowr*us* þat we p*ro*fur,
þ*ou* take, lord, to þi lonynge,
And be owre lord of aꝉ kynn*us* þinge, 256

That men schulle profre her*e* offrendes, TEXT F.
Or the prest tak water to his handis. 84
Offer*e* or lete, whether*e* thu list ;
How thow schalt pray, I wolde thu wist.
As next is wryten, I rede thu say,
On this maner*e*, god to pay.(1) 88
Ih*es*u, that in bedlem was borne,
And thre kynges come the biforne,
Thei offred gold, mirre, and encense,
And thu forsoke not here presense, 92
Bot blessede (2) hem alle thre,
Aȝen thei wente to here contre ;
Right so, lorde, offrynge that we offre,
And oure prayeris that we here profere, 96
Thu take ham, lorde, to thyn lowynge,
And be oure help in alle thynge,
    (2) wende.—A. wylled.—D.

TEXT B.

þat alle per̄els be for-done ;

fulfil our good desires, and be our help in time of need.

oure gode ӡernynges þou gra*u*nt vs sone,

of al oure mys þou vs amende,

In al oure nede vs socoure sende. amen. 260

Be saying pater-nosters, whilst the priest is washing. Then he bows before the altar

Saye pater-noster, ӡit vp-standande
 al þo tyme þo pr*e*st is wasshande,

Til aft*er* wasshing þo pr*e*ste wil loute

þo aut*er*, & sithen turne aboute.(1) 264

and turns to ask thy prayers :

þen he askes w*ith* stille steuen,

Ilk mo*n*nes pr*a*yers to god of heuen.

Take gode kepe vnto þo pr*e*st,

do thou smite on thy breast and pray aloud:

when he hi*m* turnes, knoc on þi brest, 268

And þenk þen, for þi sy*n*n

þou art noght worthe to pray for hy*m*m,

bot when þou pr*a*yes, god lokes þi wille,

[fol. 7 b.]

If hit be gode, forgetis þin ille. 272

for-þi w*ith* hope i*n* his mercie,

Answere þo prest w*ith* þis i*n* hie.

that the Holy Ghost may come upon him and rule his heart.

Po holi gost i*n* þe light,
 & sende i*n*-to þe right,(2) 276
 Reule þi hert & þi speking

to gods worship & his louyng.

TEXT C.

þa*t* all*e* per̄ils before* done, [* *Sic* in MS. *Read* be for-done.]

Oure gode ӡernynge þou grau*n*te vs sone, 120

Of all*e* oure mys þou vs amende,

In all*e* oure nedes vs soco*ur* sende. Amen.

After the waschynge, þe priest will*e* loute

þe awter, and sithen turne hym aboute ; (1) 124

þa*t* he askes with stille steven

Ilke man prayers to god of heuene.

Swilke prayers I walde ӡe toke

Als nexte folowes on the buke. 128

¶ The haly gaste in þe light,

And sende grace into þe righte (2)

To rewle thy herte and þy spekynge

To god*es* worschep *and* his lovynge. 132

  (1) Aft*er* þo weschyng þo pr*y*st wyl lowte
    Þo awter kyste and storne hym a-bowte.—A.
  (2) Þo holy goste þat is on hyght
    Send hus grace to leue ryght. Explicit.—A.

þat aH perelus beyn) for-don) : TEXT E.
Owre lord, of for-gyfnes grawntus son),
Of aH owre mysdedus þou vs a-mende,
In aH owre nede vs sokowre sende. 260
Sey pater noster ryght upstondyng, [page 176]
Al tyme þe preyste is wassyng,
þen aftur þe wassyng þo preyste wyl lowte
To þo awter & syt turne hym) abowte.(1) 264
þen he hasket with stylle stewon)
Ilke monnus prayere to god of hewon).
Take gud kepe vn)-to þo preyste,
When) he turnus, knoke on) þi breste, 268
And thynke þen) for þi synne
þow art ioynud to pray for hyme.
When) þou prayuste, god locus on) þi wylle,
If hit be gud, he for-3euus þo ille. 272
ffor-þi with hope in his mercy,
Onswere þo preste with in þis hoy : [read þis in]
þo holy gost in-to þe lyghte,
And sende in-to þe ryghte 276
To rule þi herte & þi spekyng
To goddus worschyp & his lonyng.

That alle pereiles be fro vs don, TEXT F.
Oure gode desire thu graunt vs son ; 100
Off all oure mis-dedis thu us amende,
And in alle oure nede socour thu vs sende.
Aftir wasschynge, the prest wol lowte
To the auter, and torne him abowte (1) ; 104
Thanne he asketh wyth gode steu[e]ne
Al men praeris to god of heuene.
Suche praiere I wolde thu toke
As next folweth in the boke. 108
The holi gost in the lyght,
And sende his grace vn-to the right,
He ruwele thyn herte and thi spekynge
To godis worschepe and his lowynge. 112

(2) *The* haly gast in *the* lyght
   And send hys *grace* vnto *the* right.
   Rewle *thi* hert and *thi* spekyn
   To goddes wyrscype an louynge.—D.

When the priest
is praying,
do thou kneel,

Þen þo prest gos to his boke
his priuey prayers for to loke,   280
knele þou doun, & say þen þis,
þat next in blak wryten is:
hit wil þi prayere mykel amende,

If þou wil holde vp bothe þi hende   284
to god with gode deuocioun,
when þou sayes þis [o]resoun,

to receive the
sacrifice of the
priest and all
present,

God resayue þi seruyce
And þis solempne sacrifice,   288
for þo prest & for vs alle,
þat now are here, or here be shalle,
þis messe to here or worship do,
þo sakring to se, or pray þer-to;   292
And for alle þat lyuen in gods name,

for help to the
living, and eternal
rest to the dead.

þat þai haue helpe fro synne & shame,
And for þo soules þat hethen are past,
þat þai haue rest þat ay shal last.   amen.   296
Pater noster: Aue maria: Credo.

Loke pater-noster þou be sayande,
I-whils þo preste is priuey prayande;
þo prest wil after in þat place   300
Remow him a litel space,

[fol. 8]
The priest comes
to the midst of
the altar; then
lift up heart and
body,

To he come til þo auter myddis.
stande vp þou, als men þe biddis,
hert & body & ilk a dele,   304
take gode kepe & here him wele,

God resceyf thy servyce,
And this solempne sacrifice
For the priest, and for vs alle,
þat now er here, or [here] be salle,   136
this mes to here, or worschep do,
þis sacrynge to se, or praye þere-to;
And for alle, þat leves in goddes name,
þat thay be kepyd fra synne and schame;   140
And for the saulles, þat er past,
þat thay have reste þat euere salle laste.

þo preyste gos to þo boke
His pryuey *preyure* for to loke : 280
Knele þou downe & say þeɴ) þis
As nexte *in* blac wrytuɴ) is :
H*i*t wil þi *preiur* mycul amendus,
If þou wolt holde vp þi hondus 284
To god w*ith* gud deuocyoɴ),
Wheɴ) þou sayst þis orisoɴ).
God receywe þi *seruyse*
And þis solenne sac*ri*fyse 288
ffor þo preste & for vs alle,
þat here now aru*n* or here be schalle,
þis messe [*to*] here or worschyp do,
þo sacryng to see, or pray þ*er*-to ; 292

And for þo sowl*us*, þat hensse beɴ) passud,
þat þai haue rest þat ew*ur* lastus.

Loce pat*er* nost*er* þou be sayand
Whyl he is *preuele preyand* ; 296
þo preyste wyl aft*ur* iɴ) þat place
Remo hym) a lytul space,
Tyl he cu*m* to þo awt*er* mydd*us* :
Stond þen, aꝉ meɴ) he bydd*us*, 300
Hert & body & ylka dele :
Take gud kepe, & here hy*m* weꝉ,

God reherse thyn seruyse,
And solempne this sacrifise
For the prest, and for vs alle,
That now ben here, or her*e* be schal, 116
This masse to her*e*, or worschepe do,
The sacryng to se, or pray there-to ;
And for alle, the lyues in godes nam,
That thei haue help fram synne and scham ; 120
And for the soules, that hennes be past,
That thei haw rest that ay schal last.

TEXT B.
when the priest
has ended the
secreta and begun
the preface aloud.

þen he bygynnes per omnia,
And sithen sursum corda.
At þo ende [he] sayes sanctus thryese,   308
In excelsis he neuens twyese.
Als fast als euer þat he has done,
loke þat þou be redy sone,

Then say this
prayer;

and saye þese wordis with stille steuen   312
priuely to god of heuen.

In world of worlds with outen endyng
þanked be ihesu, my kyng.

yielding a thank-
ful heart unto the
Lord, and praying

    Al my hert I gyue hit þe,   316
    grete right hit is þat hit so be;
with al my wille I worship þe,
Ihesu, blessid mot þou be.

with al my hert I þank hit þe,   320
þo gode þat þou has don to me;
swete ihesu, graunt me now þis,

that thou mayest
evermore praise
him with angels
in the bliss of
heaven.

þat I may come vn-to þi blis,
þere with aungels for to syng   324
þis swete song of þi louyng,
sanctus: sanctus: sanctus.
Ihesu graunt þat hit be þus. Amen.

Kneel when the
Canon begins,
and offer thy
thanksgivings

When þis is sayde, knele þou doune,   328
    and þat wyth gode deuocioune;
Of al gode þou thonk god þan,
And pray als-so for ilk a man (1)

TEXT C.
[fol. 253 b.]

¶ The priest wille than in þat place
Sethen bigynne the preface,   144
þat begynnes with per omnia,
And sethen with sursum corda;
And at the ende says sanctus thryes,
In excelsis he newen bot twys.   148
Of alle gude þou thankes god þan,
And praye also [for] euere ilke aman (1)

þen) he begynnus per omnia,   TEXT E.
And siþun sursum corda.   304
And sanctus he says thryus,
In excelcis he nomus twyus.
As fast as he has done,
Loke þat þou be redy sone,   308
And say þus wyt stylle stewon)   [page 177]
Priuely to god of hewon) :
In word, in werke, with owtun) endyng,
þonkud be Ihesu, my soucreyn) kyng.   312
And al herto I ȝif hyt þe,
Grete & ryche hit is ryghte þat hit so be.
With aH my wyH I worschyp þe,
Ihesu, blessud mot þu be :   316
With al my hert I þonke þe,
AH þe gud þou haste don to me.
Swete Ihesu, graunte me now þis,
þat I may com to þi blis,   320
þer with angels for to synge
þo swete song of lowynge.
Sanctus.   Sanctus.   Sanctus.
God grawnte þat hit be þus.   324
When þis is seyd, knele a-don),
And wyt gud deuocion),
Of aH gode þou þonke god þen),
And als so for aH men) (1)   328

The prest wil sone, in that plase,   TEXT F.
Swythe begynne the prefacе,   124
That begynneth with per omnia,
And afterward sursum corda.
Of alle gode thu thanke god than,
And pray also for eche man,(1)   128

(1) And pray alswa for ilk a man.—D.

TEXT B.
[fol. 8 b.]
and intercessions
for all estates of
men.

Of ilk [a]state, and ilk degre,   332
so wil þo law of charite ;
for-þi wíth-outen taryinge
on þis wise be þi sayinge.

Act of thanks-
giving for good
gifts ;

L ord,(1) honourd mot þou be,   336
    wíth al my hert I worship þe ;
    I þonk þe, lord, als me wele owe,
Of more gode þen I con knowe,

talents of nature,

þat I haue of þe resayued,   340
Syn þo tyme I was consayued :
My lyue, my lymmes þou has me lent,

right mind,

my right witt þou has me sent,

and grace
in divers perils.

þou has me keped of þi grace   344
fro sere perils in mony place.

All these are the
gifts of our
Redeemer.

Al my lyue & al my lyuynge
holly haue I of þi gyuynge ; (2)
þou boght me dere wíth þi blode,   348
and dyed for me o-pon þo rode ;

TEXT C.

Of ilke a-state and ilke degre,
So wille the lawe of charite ;   152
þer-fore begynne this prayere sone,
When þe preste the preface has doone :
Oure lorde,(1) honourde þou be ;
With alle my herte and my degre   156
I thanke the, lorde, as me wele awe,
Of mare gude, than I kan knawe,
þat I haue of þe resceyved
Sen the tyme I was consauyd ;   160
My lyfe, my lyms, þou has me lente,
My righte witte þou hase me sente ;
þou has me kepid of thy grace
Fro many perils in many place ;   164
Alle my helpe and my levynge,
Haly hafe [I] of thy givynge. (2)
þou boghte me dere wíth thy blode,

[fol. 254]

And dyed for me opon the rode ;   168

(1) Loverd God.—D.

Of state & of ilke degre,　　　　　　　　　　　TEXT E.
So wolde þe lawe of charyte.
ffor-þi w*ith*-owtoɴ tariyng
On þis wyse þou be saiyng.　　　　　332
Lord,(1) anowryd mot þou be,　　　　　[page 175]
With al my hert I worschyp þe ;
I þonke þe, lord, as I wel owe,
Of more gud þen I coɴ knowe,　　　　336
Syth þe tyme þat I was co*n*sewud,
þat I haue of þe recewud :
My lyfe, my lymm*us* þou haste me lente,
My rygh̄t wytte þou haste me sentte,　　340
þ*o*u hast me kepte al of þi grace
ffro sere p*er*ell*us* i*n* mony place.
Aꞁ my lyf *and* al my lykynge,
Wholly haue I of þi gou*er*nynge.(2)　　344
þou boȝte me dere w*ith* þi blode,
And dede for me oɴ þe rode.

For eche astat, and eche degre,　　　　　　TEXT F.
So wol the law of cherite ;
And therfore begynne this p*r*ayer*e* sone,
Whanne the prest hath his preface done.　132
Lord god,(1) honoured thu be,
With alle myn herte I worschepe the.
I thanke the, lorde, as I wel owe,
Of mi godnesse, that I can wel knowe,　136
That I haw of the resceyued
Setthe tyme that I was conceyued ;
Mi lyfe, my lymes, thu hast me sent,
Mi rigth witte thu hast me lent ;　　　140
Thu hast kept me of thi grace
Fro many perel in many place ;
Alle myn helthe and alle my lyuyng*e*,
Holi haw I of thi gyuyng*e*.(2)　　　144
Thu bought me dere with thi blode,
And deiede Fore me on the rode :
　　(2) Haly I have of *th*i gyfyng.—D.

TEXT B.

I haue done a-gaynes þi wille
synnes mony, grete & ille ;

And He is ready to forgive our sins.

þou art redy, of þi godnesse,   352
for to graunt me forgyuenesse

Thanksgiving for good gifts;

Of [þes] godes,(1) and mony moo
I þonk þe, lord, I *pra*ye als-soo

prayer for pardon of past sins,

þat al my gylt þou me forgyue,   356
and be my helpe whils I shal lyue ;

strength in the future, and a good will to do God's will.

And gyue me grace for to etchewe
to do þat þing þat me shulde rewe ;
And gyue me wille ay wel to wirk.   360

Intercessions for Church, king, and nobility.

Lord, þenk on þo state of holy kirk,
And þo bishops, *pr*estes & clerkes,(2)
þat þai be keped i*n* alle gode werkes,
þo kyng, þo quene(3), þo lordes of þo lande,   364
þat þai be wele mayntenande
hore states i*n*(4) alle godnesse,

TEXT C.

I have done agayne thy will*e*
Synnes many, grete and ill*e* ;
þou erte redy of thy gudnes
Forto graun*te* me forgifnes.   172
Of this gude (1) and many ma
I thanke the, lorde, *and* prayes alswa
þat alle my gilte þou me forgif,
And be my helpe whils I sall*e* lyf.   176
Gif me grace forto eschewe
To do þat me sall*e* rewe,
And gif me will*e* aye forto wyrke.
Lorde, thynke of state of haly kyrke,   180
Of the pape, byschope, priestes, clerk*es*,(2)
þat þay be kepyd in alle gude werk*es* ;
the kynge,(3) the lordes of the lande,
þat thay be wele mayñtennand   184
þere states and(4) alle gudnes,

(1) thes gud.—D.   (2) pape, bischopes & clerkes.—D.

I haue doŋ, a-ȝeynus þi wylle,

Synnus mony, grete *and* grylle. 348

þou arte redy of þi godnes

ffor to grawnt vs for-gyfnes.

Of þis godnes (1) *and* mony moo

I thonke þe, lord, *and* pray also, 352

þat my gylt þou me for-gyffe,

And be my help whyl I schal lyfe ;

[page 176]

And gyf me grace to eschwe

To do þat þinge, þat schuld me rewe, 356

And ȝyf vs ay wylle to wyrke ;

And þinke oŋ þe state of þe kyrke,

þo pope, þo byschopus, preystus, *and* clerkus,(2)

þat þay be keptte iŋ gode werkus ; 360

þo kynge, þo qwene,(3) þo lordus of þe londe,

þat þai be wel mayntonande

Her statu*s* iŋ (4) aH godnes,

I haw done, aȝen thi wille,

Synnes diuers, bothe foule and ille, 148

And ȝut art thu redi of thi godenes

To graunt me ay forȝefnesse.

Of thes godys, and many mo,

I thanke the, lord, and pray also, 152

And alle mi gult thu me forȝeue,

And be myn help the whiles I leue.

Thu graunt me grace for to enchiwe

To do that thynge, that me schold rywe, 156

And ȝeue me wil ay wel to worche.

Swet lorde, thenke on the state of holi chirche,

On the pope, bisschopes, and* clerkes,(2)

[* MS. ad]

That thei be bysi in alle gode werkes ; 160

The kynge, the queene,(3) the lordes of the londe,

That thei be in wile of gode meyntenande

Here state in (4) alle godenes,

(3) *the* qwene—*ins.* D.   (4) in.—D.

TEXT B.

For kinsmen, friends, tenants, and servants;

all of every age and station;

for all living in sin or sorrow;

for the sick and captive, the poor, banished, and dispossessed;

for such as stand,

and reule þo folk in rightwisnesse ;

Oure sib men, and oure wele-willandes,(1)   368

Oure frendes, tenandes,(2) & sernandes,

Olde men, childer & alle wymmen,(3)

marchandes, men of craft, & tilmen,

Riche men, & pore, grete & smalle,   372

I pray þe, lord, for hom alle,

þat þai be keped specialy

In gode hele & lyue haly.

To hom þat are in ille lyue,   376

In sclaunder, myscounforth, or in stryue,

seke or prisonde, or o-pon þo see,

pore, exilde, deserit,(4) if þer be,

til alle hom, þou sende socoure,   380

to þi worship and þin honoure.(5)

Alle þat are in gode lyue to day,

TEXT C.

[fol. 254 b.]

And rewle the folke in rightwisnes ;

Oure sybmen and (1) oure wele-willandes,(1)

Oure frendes, sugettes(2) and servandes.   188

Pater noster. Aue. Credo et cetera

Alle thy childer and wymmen,(3)

Merchaundes, men of craftes, and tilmen,

Ryche and pore, grete and smalle,   192

I pray the, lorde, for thame alle

þat thay be kepyd specially

In gode hele, and lyfe haly ;

To thame þat er in ille lyfe,   196

In sclaunder, myscomforth, or in stryfe,

Seke men, or prisoned ; or apon þe se,

Pore or exsilyd, disheryd(4) if thay be,

To alle this, þou sende socoure,   200

To hym worschep and hym honoure.(5)

Alle þat er in gude lyfe to daye,

(1) & well lyfand.—D.   (2) tenundes.—D.
(3) Ald men, childer, and women.—D.
(4) disheryd] om.—D, F.

And rewle þe folke in ryghtwyues ;   364   TEXT E.
Owre syb men), oure wyl wyllande,(1)
Oure fryndus, oure seruandus and tenandus,(2)
Olde men), chyldurn), and aH wymmen),(3)
Marchandus, men) of crafte, and tylmen),   368
Ryche men), and pore, grete and smalle,
I pray þe, lord, for hom) alle,
þat þai be kepte specyally
In gud lyfe and in holy ;   372
ffor hem) þat are in heuy lyfe,
I[n] sclawndure, mys-conforde, or in stryfe,
Seke or presund, or on þe see,
Pore, exylde, dysesud,(4) if þai be,   376
To hem) aH sende socure,
ffor þi worschyp and þin) onowre.(5)
AH þat are in gud lyfe to day,

And rewele here pepil in rightwisnesse.   164   TEXT F.
Oure sibbe, and oure wel-willynge,(1)
Frendes, tenauntes,(2) and vs seruynge,
Olde men, children, and wymmen,(3)
Marchaunte, men of crafte, and tilme[n].   168
Riche men, poure, and smale,
I pray to the, god, for hem bi tale,
That thei be kepe specialy
In gode helthe, and life holi ;   172
To alle that ben in wikete lyfe,
In sclandere, miscomfort, or strife,
Sike, in prisone, or vppon the see,
Poure, or exiled this lond, thow thei be,   176
To alle thes, thu sende socoure,
To þin worschepe,(5) and (6) þin honore.
Alle that ben in gode lif to-day,

(5) To thi wyrscepe and thine honour.—D.
(6) Here the MS. has to inserted above the line ; but it is
not wanted.—Mr Skeat.

TEXT B.

& clenly lyuen to þi pay,

and please Thee, the grace of perseverance;

kepe hom, lord, fro alle foly,   384

and fro alle synne for þi mercy,

And gyue hom grace to last & lende,

In þi seruyce to hor [*last*] ende.(1)

order the course of this world for our good;

þis world þat turnes mony wayes,   388

make gode til vs in alle oure dayes;

send weather that we may receive the fruits of the earth; [fol. 9 b.]

þo weders (2) grete & vnstable,

lord make gode & sesonable;

þo froytes of þo erthe make plenteuus,   392

als þou sees best, ordayn for vs,

ordain for us as seemeth best for our everlasting glory.

swilk grace til vs þou sende,

þat in oure last day, at oure ende,

when þis worlde & we shal seuer,   396

Bring vs til ioy þat lastis euer. Amen.

Loke pater-noster þou be sayande,
to þo chalyce he be saynande:

At the ringing

þen tyme is nere of sakring,(3)   400

TEXT C.

And clene lyues to þy paye,

kepe thame, lorde, fro alle foly,   204

And fro alle synne for thy mercy;

And gif thame grace to laste and lende

In þy servyce to þere ende.(1)

þis werlde, þat turnes many ways,   208

Make gude to vs in alle [*oure*] days;

The wedders (2) grete and vnstabille,

lorde, make gude and sesonabille;

þe frute of the erthe make plentevous;   212

As þou seys best, ordan for vs,

Swilke grace to vs þou sende,

þat on oure laste daye at *oure* laste ende,

When this werlde and wee salle seu*ere*.   216

Bri*n*ge vs to þat ioye þat lastes eu*ere*.   Amen.

Pater noster. Aue maria *et cetera*.

¶ Than is the tyme nere of þe sacrynge,(3)

(1) unto *th*air ende.—D.
(2) wedirs.—D.

And lelly beꝺ þe to pay, 380   TEXT E.
Kepe hem), lord, fro aH foly,
And fro aH synn*us* for þi mercy ;
And gyf *grace* to laste *and* lende
In þi ser*uise* to here ende.(1) 384
In þis worde, *þat* t*ur*nus mony wayus,
Make hyt gud to vs i*n* oure dayus ;
þo word is (2) grete & vꝺ-stabuH,
Lord, make h*i*t gud & sencybuaH ; 388
þe frut*us* oꝺ þe erthe make plentuus,
As þou sees best, ordeꝺ for vs ;
Suche *grace* to vs þou sende,
þ*at* at i*n* owr*e* laste ende, 392
Wheꝺ þis word & we schal seuure,
Bryng vs to þ*at* ioye þ*at* lastny euur*e*.
Loke p*ater* *noster* þou be seyande,   [page 17]
To þo chales be vp-heuande ; 396
þen tyme is of þe sacrynge,(3)

And clenli leuen vn-to thi pay, 180   TEXT F.
Thu kepe ham, lord, fram alle folie,
And fram alle schame fore thi mercy.
Grace euer*e*-lastyng*e* thu ham sende
In thi ser*uice* to her*e* laste ende.(1) 184
This worlde, that torneth many wayes,
Be gode to vs in alle our*e* days ;
Wedres (3) grete, that ben vnstable,
Lord make ham gode, and sesenable ; 188
The frutes on þe erthe make plenteouse,
As thu seist best, ordeyne for ouse,
Sucche grace to vs, swete god, þu sende,
That [*in*] our*e* laste day and laste ende, 192
Whanne this worlde and we schulle seuere,
Thu bryng*e* vs to ioy that lasteth euere.

Thanne is time ney of sacryng*e*,

    (3) *Than* es tyme ner*e* *the* sakering
      A litill bell me*n* use to rynge.— D.

TEXT B.   A litel belle men oyse to ryng.

of the sacring bell   þen shal þou do reuerence
do reverence to
the presence of   to ihesu crist awen presence,
Christ,
             þat may lese alle baleful bandes;   404
             knelande holde vp bothe þi handes,(1)
             And so þo leuacioun þou be-halde,
             for þat is he þat iudas salde,
             and sithen was scourged & don on rode,   408
our Redeemer   and for mankynde þere shad his blode,
             and dyed & ros & went to heuen,
and our Judge.   and ȝit shal come to deme vs euen,
             Ilk mon aftur he has done,   412
             þat same es he þou lokes opone.
Warning against   þis is þo trouthe of holy kirk,
disbelief,
             who trowes noght þis mone sitt ful myrk;
and advice to   for-þi I rede with gode entent   416
behold the mys-
tery with good   þat þou biholde þis sacrament.
purpose and
to use some   swilk prayere þen þou make,
prayer at each
one's liking.   als lykes best þe to take.
             sondry men prayes sere,(2)   420
             Ilk mon on his best manere.
[fol. 10]   Short (3) prayere shulde be with-outen drede,

TEXT C.   A litille belle men is to rynge :   220
[fol. 255]
             þan is skille to do reuerence
             To ihesu criste awghen presence,
             þat may lese alle bandes ;
             Kneland halde vp thy handes,(1)   224
             And with inclinacyon
             Behalde þe Eleuacyon.
             Swylke prayere þan þou take,
             As the likes best forto make.   228
             Many men prayes sere,(2)
             Ilke man prayes on his manere.
             Schorte (3) prayer soulde be with-owten drede.

                   (1) Knele downe & hald up bath handys.—D.
                     (2) Sundyrer men prayers serer.—D.

A lytul belł men vsuþ to rynge.   TEXT E.
þen schal þou do reuerensse,
To Ihesu crist owne presensse,   400
þat may lese alle baful bondus ;
Knele & holde vp botħ þi hondus (1)
And so þou þo leuacion beholde,
ffor þat is he þat iudas solde   404
And Sythun schowrgut, on þo rode
ffor mon-kynde sched hys blode,
And ded, & rose & went to hewon,
And ȝit schal come to demus ewon,   408
Ilke man aftur þat he hase don.
þo same is he þou locus upon,
Hyt is þo feythe of holy kyrke :
Who trowe þis not schal sytte wel marke ;   412
ffor-þi I rede with gud entente
þat þou be-holde þe sacramente.
Suche prayer þen schal þou make,
As lieus beste to þe þu take.   416
Dyuerse men preyus sere,(2)
Ilke mon on his beste manere.
Schort (3) prayer schuld be with-owtun drede,

A litil belle he wol to vs rynge.   196   TEXT F.
Thanne is resoune that we do reuerence
To ihesu criste presence,
That may loose of alle balful bondes ;
Therefore knelynge, hold vp thyn hondes,(1)   200
And with inclinacion of thi bodi,
Be-hold the leuacioun reuerently.
Sucche praere there thanne thu make,
As liketh the best for to take.   204
Sum men * maketh here praierys (2)   [* MS. Sumen]
In here best manerys,
For (3) praieris scholde be thanne wyt-out drede,
                (3) Swylk.—D.

TEXT B. and þer-wíth pater-noster & þo crede.

A prayer is set
down, if no other
is preferred, If þou of aue* be vn-puruayde, [* *sic* in MS. *Read* ane] 424

I set here aue* þat may be sayde; (1)

þof I merk hit here in lettir.

þou may chaun[g]e hit for a bettir.

lauding and
blessing Christ,
for all His good
gifts. Loued be þou, kyng;   428
   & blessid be þou, kyng;
    of alle þi gyftes gode,
   & þanked be þou, kyng;
   ihesu, al my ioying,   432
    þat for me spilt þi blode,
    and dyed opon þo rode,
   þou gyue me grace to sing
   þo song of þi louing.   436

pater noster; aue maria; Credo.

When þou has sayde al þi crede,
   þis short prayere I rede þou rede,
þat next is wryten in blak letter,   440
ful mykel shal þou fare þo better.

A short prayer
after the levation
for mercy; Lord, als þou con, & als þou wille,
   haue mercie of me, þat has don ille;
   for what-so þou with me wil do,   444
I holde me payde to stonde þer-to;

TEXT C. And þere-with a pater-noster and crede.   232

[† *Read* a *or* ane] I set here and† may be sayde,

Prayer to Christ
present in form
of bread. If þou be vnpuruayde; (1)

If I merke it here in letter,

þou may schewe (2) it for a better.   236

¶ Welcome, lorde, in fourme of brede

For me þou sufferde herd deede;

Als þou bare the crowne of thorne

[‡ MS. beforlorne] þou suffer me noghte be forlorne ‡   240

(1) I set here *that* may be sayd
   If *thu* of ane and be vnpurwayde.—D.
    (2) chaunce.—D.

And þere with pater-noster, aue & crede.   420   TEXT E.
If þou of any be vn-purueyde,
I set þe here on) þat be seyde.(1)
If I make hit for þo bettur,
þou may teH hit here in lettur :   424
   Lowod be þou, kyng,
   And blessud be þou, kyng,
     Of aH þi gyftus gode ;
   And þonkud be þou kyng,   428
   Ihesu all my Ioyng
     þat for me spylt þi blode,
     And dede for me vpon) þo rode.
   þou gyf me grace to synge   432
   þo songe of þi louynge.
       [Pater-noster; Ave-Mary; Crede]
When) þou hast don) al þi crede,
þis schalte þen) þou rede,
As nexte is wryton in blac lettur,   436
fful mycul schal þou fare þo bettur.
Lord as þou kon), & as þou wylle,
Haue mercy on) me, þat hase don) ille,
ffor what-so þou wolt with me do,   440
I holde me payud to stonde þer-to.

And there-with-al þe pater-noster and þe crede. 208   TEXT F.
I sette here oyn that may be sayd,
Ʒef of oyn thu be vn-purueyd ; (1)
Thu maist hit chaunge (2) for a bettere,
Thow I make hit here in lettere.*   212 [* MS. mlettere]
Welcome, lord, in fourme of brede,
For me thu tholedest a pyneful dede ;
As thu suffredest the coroune of thorne,
Graunt me grace, lorde, I be nought lorne. 216
Or elles thus in latyn speche,
Thu maist hym pray and be-seche.   218
Aue ihesu christe. &c. &c.
     [Here follow Latin hymns, see Notes.]

TEXT B.

þi merci, ihesu, wold I haue,

and I for ferdnes durst hit craue,

for Christ has
said, Ask, and ye
shall have.

bot þou bids aske, & we shal haue ;   448

swete ihesu make me saue,

And gyue me witt & wisdame right,

to loue þe, lord, with al my might.

When þou has made þis orison,   452
   þen shal þow with deuocion

Then after the
sacring, pray for
the dead,

Make þi prayeres in þat stede

for alle þi frendes, þat are dede,

[fol. 10 b.]

And for alle cristen soules sake,   456

swilk prayere shal þou make.

Lord, for þi holy grace,
   here oure prayers in þis place,

that they may
have part in the
mass,

   graunt now, lord, for oure prayere,   460

þat cristen soules, þate passed here (2)

fro þis lyue, þat synful esse,

þat ilk one haue part of þis messe ;

for hore soules, I pray derly,   464

þate I shal neuen serly,(3)

TEXT C.

When the preste the eleuacyon has made,

The priest spreads
his arms abroad
to form a cross,
and then brings
them to their
former position.

He wille sprede his armes on-brade,

Sethen dres ðam* in þe firste stede ;(1)   [* MS. dresdam]

þan is tyme to praye for þe dede,   244

For alle cristen saulles sake,

[fol. 255 b.]

Swilke [prayere], as þou wille take.

God, for thy haly grace,

Here oure prayere here in this place.   248

Graunte vs, lorde, for oure prayere,

þat cristen men, þat passed er (2)

Fra this life, þat synfulle es,

þat ilke an have parte of this messe ;   252

For þere saulles I praye derly,

þat I salle neven sekirly,(3)

(1) He wyll sprede his armes o-brade
    Sethen dresse thaim in thaier friste stede.—D.

þi mercy, Ihesu, wold I haue, TEXT E.
And I for ferdnes durste hit craue;
But þou byddus aske & haue. 444
Swete Ihesu, make aH saue
And gyf me wytte & wysdam ryghte,
To lowe þe, lord, with al my myghte.
When þou hase made þis orison, 448
þeiɔ schal þou with deuocioɔ
Make þi preyer in þat stede
ffor þi fryndus, þat are dede;
And for aH sowlus sake 452
Suche a preyer schal þou make.
Lord, for þi holy grace,
Here owre preyurs in þis place,
Grawnt now, lord, for owre preyere, 456
þat cristoɔ sowlus, þat passud are (2)
ffro þis lyfe, þat synful is,
þat ilke one haue parte of þi blysse.
ffor hore sowlus I prey derly, 460
þat I schal prey fore serly, (3)

Whanne the prest hath the leuacioun made, TEXT F.
He spredeth his handes thanne abrade, 220
Setthen he dresseth him in þe ferst stede, (1)
Thanne is tyme to pray for the dede;
For alle cristene sowles sake
Suche praere I rede thu take. 224
Gode lord, for thyu holi grace,
Thu here oure praierys in this place.
Graunt vs, lord, for this praiere,
That cristene sowles that passeth the aiere (2) 228
Fro this lif, that synful is,
That eche of hem haw part of þis messe;
And fore here soules I pray inwardli,
That I schal neuene dyuersli, (3) 232

> (2) Graunt vs lord for oure prayeres
> That cristen saules that passed es.—D.
> (3) neuen serly.—D.

TEXT B.

þat þis messe may be hore mede,

helpe & hele fro alkyns drede,

specially for parents, kinsmen, well-wishers, and benefactors,

fader soule, moder soule, breþer dere,   468

Sisters soules, sib men & oþer sere,

þate vs gode wolde, or vs gode did,

or ony kyndnes vntil vs kid;

and all souls in purgatory,

and til alle in purgatory pyne,   472

þis messe be mede & medicyne;

til alle cristen soules hely

graunt þi grace & þi mercy;

forgyue hom alle hor trespasse,   476

for their release and everlasting glory.

lese hore bondes, & let hom passe,

fro al-kyns pyne and [fro] al care,

In-til þo ioy þat lastis euer-mare. amen.

Continue thy prayers till the priest concludes his,

Loke pater-noster þou be prayande,   480

Ay to þou here þo preste be sayande

per omnia secula al on hight,(1)

þen I wold þou stode vp-right,

TEXT C.

þat þis may be þam mede,

Helpe and hele fro alkyn drede;   256

For fader saulles, moder and brother dere,

Syster saulles, sybmen and other sere,

þat vs gode wolde, or vs gude dydde,

Or any kyndenes vnto vs kydde,   260

And to alle in purgatory pyne,

þis messe be mede and medecyne;

To alle cristen saulles haly

Graunte þy grace and thy mercy,   264

Forgif thame alle þere trespase,

lese thame of þere bandes, and lat thame passe

Fra alle pyne and fra alle kare,

Into þe ioye þat lastes eueremare.   268

[* MS. for þe]

¶ When þe preste forþe* righte

Says Per omnia alle on heghte,(1)

þat þis masse may be hore mede,
Help & hele to al kynnus drede,
ffadur sowle, & modur sowle, brodur sowle dere   464
Sustur sowle sybmennus sowlus & oþur sowlus sere,
þat vs gud wold, or vs gud dyd,
Or any kyndnes to vs haue kyd ;
And to hom all þat byn in purgatory pyne,   468
þo messe be to hom mede & medicyne.
To all cryston sowlus holly [page 176]
Grawnt þi grace & þi mercy ;
ffor-ȝyf hom all hore trespas,   472
Vnloke hor bondus, & let hom passe,
ffro all pyne & all care,
Into þo ioy lastyng euurmare.
Loce pater-noster þou be preyande   476
Ay tyl þo tyme þo preyst be seyande
Per omnia secula al on heyghte.(1)
þen I wold þou stode preyng hyt,

That this messe be hem to mede,
Socoure, and help, in al here nede ;
Fadir and modire, and brothere sowles so dere,
Soster and sibbe men, and othere ifere,   236
That vs gode wolde, or vs gode do,
Or any kyndenesse to vs haw ido,
And to alle tho, þat in purgatori haue payne,
Lord, this messe be mede and medecyne.   240
And to alle cristene sowles holi,
Swet lord, thu graunt thi mercy,
For-ȝew hem alle here trespasse,
Lowse here bondes, and lete ham passe   244
Fram alle paynes to heuuene blis,
With angeles to dwelle euere endeles.

(1) *than the* prest furt ryght
    Says *per omnia* al on heght
    We will saye *with* heghe steuen
    Pater noster gude to neuen.—D.

TEXT B.
[fol. 11]

and says the
Lord's prayer
aloud,

with the response
of the people,

for he wil saie w*ith* hegh steuen   484
pat*er*-nost*er* to god of heuen ;
herken hi*m* w*ith* gode wille,
and whils he saies, hold þe stille,
bot answere at temptac*i*onem   488
set libera nos a malo, amen.
hit were no nede þe þis to ken,
for who con not þis are lewed men.
when þis is done, saye p*r*iuely(1)   492
other prayer none þe*r*-by.
pat*er*-nost*er* first i*n* laten,
and sithen i*n* englishe als here is wryten.

The Lord's
Prayer in
English.

Fader oure, þat is i*n* heuen,   496
    blessid be þi name to neuen.
    Come to vs þi kyngdome.
In heuen & erthe þi wille be done.
oure ilk day bred gr*au*nt vs to day.   500
and oure mysdedes forgyue vs ay,
als we do hom þ*at* trespas us,
right so haue merci vp-on vs.
and lede vs i*n* no foundynge,   504
bot shild vs fro al wicked þinge. Amen.

When the priest
continues, listen
to him.

þen eft-sone þo p*r*este wil saye,
    stande stille & herken hi*m* al-waye.
he saies agnus thryse or he cese,(2)   508
þo last worde he spekis of pese.

TEXT C.
[fol. 256]

He will*e* saye with hygh steven
his pat*er*-nost*er* to god of hevene ;   272
Herken hy*m* w*ith* gode wille,
And answere hym, lowde or still*e*,
And saye it priualy (1)
Other prayer noon þe*r*e by.   276
Eftsones the prieste on-heght will*e* saye
Be redy at answere hym all*e*waye
Herken how he spekes on pes,
Says agnus thryes or he ses.(2)   280

(1) And *sethen* th*u* say it p*r*iuely.—D.

ffor þer he wyl pray wi*th* he stewoꝛ,   480   TEXT E.
Pater-noster to god of hewoꝛ.
he[r]koꝛ hy*m* wi*th* gud wylle,
And whyl he says holde þe stylle,
But vnswere at *temtacion*em   484
Or *libera nos a malo.* ameꝛ.
Hyt were nede þeꝛ þus to kenne,
But qwoso kenneþ not þis is leude me*n*.
Wheꝛ þis is done, sey pri*uely* (1)   488
Oꝛ preyer anoþer þerby
Pater-noster & furste i*n* latyne
And syþuꝛ i*n* englys as here is wrytoꝛ.
Owre fad*ur*, þat art i*n* hewoꝛ,   492
Blessud be þi name to newoꝛ.
Cum to vs þi kyndome,
In hewoꝛ & erthe þi wyl be done.
Owre ilke dayus bred grawnt vs to day,   496
And owre mysded*us* for-ȝyf vs ay,
As we do hoꝛ þat to vs trespas,
Ryght so haue me*r*cy vp-oꝛ vs,
And lede vs i*n*to no fowndyng,   500
But schyld vs fro alł wyceud þing.
þen aft þo preyst wyl say,
Stond stylł, & herkuꝛ hy*m* al-way.
He seys *agn*us thryus or he ses,(2)   504
þo laste word he spek*us* of pes.

Thanne the prest seith with hie steu[*e*]ne   TEXT F.
The pater-noster to god of heuene,   248
Herkene him with gode wile,
And answer*e* him, loude or sti[*l*]le ;
And sethen thu sey hit pryueli,(1)
For beter praeier*e* may thu non sey.   252
Efte-sone the prest wol somwhat say,
Be redi and answer*e* him alway,
Herkyn hym how he speketh of pes,
And says agnus thries or he ses.(2)   256
                    (2) lese.—D.

TEXT B.   In þe þat pese may noght be,

Thou canst not be
at peace, if not in
charity;   If þou be oute of charyte.

þen is gode of god to craue,   512

þat þou charyte may haue.

þere when þo prest [þo] pax wil kis,

knele þou & praye þen þis.

[fol. 11 b.]
therefore at the
Pax, pray for
peace and charity.   Gods lamb, þat best may   516

do þo synne of þis world a-way,

of vs haue merci & pite,

and graunt vs pese & charite.

Charity is three-
fold: for in charyte are thre kyns loues,   520

þat to parfite pese nedlyng behoues.

þo first loue is certenly

first to love God;   to loue þo lord souerenly.

þer-fore I pray þe, god of myght,   524

þou make my loue, both day & nyght,

sykerly sett euer-ilk dele

soueranly to loue þe wele,

TEXT C.   In þe þat pes may [þou] noght be

If þou owte of charite be ;

than is gude on god to craue,

þat þou charite may haue.   284

Wharfore when the priest þe pax wille kysse,

loke þat þou be sayand this :

Goddes lambe, þat best maye,

Do the synne of þis werlde awaye,   288

Of vs haue mercy and pite,

And graunte vs pes and charite.

For in charite er thre kynde loues,

þat perfet* pes nedlynges behoues   [* MS. profet]   292

The firste luf is certanly

To thy lorde souerandly.

þerfore I praye the, god of myghte,

þou make me lowe bothe daye and nyghte   296

[fol. 256 b.]   Be sikirly set euerilke a dele

Soueranly to luf þe wele;

In þo laste pes may þou not be,
If þou be owte of charite,
þen is gud of god to craue, 508
þat charite þou may haue.
þere qwen) þo preyst þo pax wil kusse,
Knele þen) down) & say þou þus.
Godd*us* lowmpe, þat best may, 512
Do þo synn*us* of þo word away ;
On vs haue m*er*cy & pyte,
And grawnt vs pes & charite.
ffor i*n* charite ar thre kynn*us* low*us*, 516
þat þo p*er*fet pes nedely be-how*us*.
þo furste loue is c*er*tenley
To luf þi lord so wortely.
þere-of I prey god of his myghte 520
To make me to luf þe, day & nyghte,
Sicurly to sette ow*ur* ilke a delle
Souerenly to luf þe welle.

_____

Bot in that pes may thu nogth be,
ȝef thu be out of cherite ;
Ther*e*fore of god I rede thu craue,
That thu charite of hym may haue. 260
Therfore þe prest whanne þe pax schal kysse,
Loke that þu be seiende this.
Godes lombe, that best may,
Do the synne of þis worlde away, 264
On vs thu haue mercy and pité,
And graunt vs pes and charité.
Sut (1) in charité beth thre maner*e* of loues,
That to parfite pes be-houes ; 268
The first loue * is certeynly,
To lowe thi lord souereynly ;
Therefore I pray god, ful of myght,
To make me loue, bothe day and nyght, 272
Sikerliche þe, lord, eueridel
Souereynli to low wel,

(1) *Sic* in MS. *Read* Suth = since.—*Mr Skeat.*

TEXT B.   þat be þi myght & gouernynge,   528
I be euer in [þi] ʒernynge,
soueranly þe to pay,
In al þat euer I con or may ;
and prest be I, erly & late,   532
to my degre & myn a-state,
alle gode dedes to fulfylle,
& to eschewe alle þat are ille.

Secondly, to love thyself; þo secunde is a priue loue,   536
þat is nedeful to my behoue,

so that there may be peace between the spirit and the flesh. þo whilk loue is propirly
by-twix my soule & my body.
þerfore make þou, gode lorde,   540
my body & my soule of one a-corde,
þat ayther part by one assent
serue þe with gode entent.
Let neuer my body do þat ille,   544
þat hit may my soule spille.

TEXT C.   þat be thy myghte and gouernynge,
I be euere in thy ʒernynge,   300
Soueranly þe to paye
In alle þat euere I kan or maye ;
And pyrst be, arly and late,
To my degre and myne astate,   304
Alle gude dedes to fulfille
And to eschewe [alle] þat er ille.
¶ þe secunde is a priuay luf,
þat nedfulle is to my behoue,   308
Whilke loue is propirly
Betwix the saule and þe body.
þere make þou, gude lorde,
My body and my saulle accorde,   312
þat ayther be of oon assente
To saryf the with gude entente,
And lat neuere my body do þat ille,
þat it may my saulle spylle.   316

TEXT E.

Soucrenly þe to pay   524
In aH þat ewur I conv or may;
And to þe preyste erly & late,
To my degre & mynv astate,
AH gode dedus to fulfylle,   528
To eschew þo þat are ylle.
þo secund is a priucy lowe
þat is nedeful to my be-howe,
þo whylke luf is propurly   532
be-twyx my sowle & my body.
þerfore make þenv, god lorde,
My body & my sowle on a-corde,
þat eyþur part, be of onv a-sente   536
To serue the with gud entente.
Let my body newur do þat ille,
þat I may newur my sowle spyH.

That bi thi myght and thi gouernynge,   TEXT F.
That I be euere at thyn ȝernynge,   276
Soucrenli the to pay,
In alle that euere I can and may;
And redi be, erli and late,
To myn degre and myn estate,   280
And gode dedes al to fulfille,
And to enchewe alle that ben ille.
The secunde is priue loue,
That nedeful is to mi be-houe,   284
The whiche is properli
Bitwixe mi soule and my bodi;
Therfore make thu, gode lord,
Mi bodi and soule of on acord,   288
That eythere parte, by on asent,
Serue the, lord, whit alle entent;
And late neuere my bodi to do þat ille
That by any way may my soule spille.   292

TEXT B.
[fol. 12]
The third is
external, or
peace between
man and man
in the love of thy
neighbour,

þo thrid loue is *with*-outen (1)

to loue ilk neghtbur me aboute[*n*],(2)

and of þat loue for no þing cese,   548

þerfore I p*ra*y þe, p*r*ince of pese,

þat þou wil make, als þou may best,

my hert to be i*n* pese & rest,

& redy to loue alle man*er* of men,   552

My sib men namely, þen

Neghtburs, seruandes, & ilk sugete,

felouse, frendes, none to forgete,

bot loue ilk-one, bothe fer & nere,   556

als my-selue w*ith* hert[*e*] clere,

and turne hore hertis so to me,

þat we may fully frendis be,

·þat I of hor gode, & þai of myne.   560

haue ay ioy w*ith* hert[*e*] fyne.

TEXT C.   ¶ þe thyrde luf is w*ith* owten doute,

To luf thy neghbur the aboute,(2)

And of þat luf for no thynge þou ses

þerfore I praye the, prynce of pes,   320

[fol. 257]

þat þou will*e* [*make*], as þou may best,

Mikell*e* to be in pes and reste,

And redy to luf all*e* man*er*e of men,

My sybmen namely, than   324

Neghburs, seruau*nt*ȝ, *and* ilke suget,

Felawes, frendes, nane.forget,

Bot luf ilkane fer and nere

Als my self*e* w*ith* herte clere,   328

And turne þere herte swa to me

þat wee fully frendes be,

þat I of þer*e* gude, *and* thay of myne,

Have a ioye w*ith* herte fyne.   332

(1) MS. *adds* doute.

þo thryd luf is with-owte dowte,   540   TEXT E.
To luf yche neghtbur all abowte,(2)
And of þat luf no þinge sese,
þerfore I pray þe, furste of pes,
þat þou wylt make, as þou may beste,   544
My hert to be in pes & reste,
And redely to luf all maner of men,
And my tylmen nomly þen,
Neghtburs & seruandus & ilke soget,   548
ffelows, fryndus, non to for-ȝete,
But luf ilkone, fer & nere,
As my selfe wyt herte clere.
And turne hor hertus so to me,   552
þat we may fully fryndus be,
And þat I of hor godus, & þei of myne,
Haue ay ioy, with herte fyne.

The thred loue is with-oute doute,   TEXT F.
To low eche cristen man aboute,(2)
And of þat loue neuere ces;
Therefore I pray the, prince of pes,   296

That thu wilt make, as þu may best,
Myn herte to loue in pes and rest,
And redi to loue alle manere of men,
And speciali myne kynnesmen,   300
Neighbores, seruantes, and subiectes,
Frendes and foes, and for-ȝectes,
To loue echon, fere and nere,
As my-self with hert[e] clere;   304
And turne here hertes so to me,
That we fulli frendes be,
That I of here wel-fare, and þey of myne,
Haw cherité with herte fyne.   308

     (2) Þe thirde luf es with-outene
       To ilk a neghbur me a-butene.—D.

TEXT B.

als I pray for my selue here,
graunt so til oþer on selue manere,

that so in love
and charity with
all men and with
God,

so þat ilk mon loue wele othere,   564
as he were his owne broþere.(1)
swilk loue among vs be,
þat we be wel loued of þe ;

by the mass and
presence of the
sacrament,

þat be þis holy sacrament,   568
þat now is here in present,
and be þo vertu of þis messe,

we may obtain
forgiveness and
grace.

we mot haue forgyuenesse
of al oure gilt & al oure mys,   572
& be þi help come to þis blis. Amen.

Loke pater-noster þou be sayande,
I-whils þo preste is rynsande.

After the rinsing
the priest goes on
with his service;

when þo preste has rinsynge done,   [fol. 12 b.]   576
opon þi fete þou stonde vp sone.

the mass-book
being brought
again to the
south end, as at
the office.

þen þo clerk flyttis þo boke
agayne to þo south auter noke,
þo preste turnes til his seruyce   580
and saies(2) forthe more of his office.

─────────────────────────────────

TEXT C.

Als I praye for my selfe here,
Graunte so to other on this manere,
So þat ilke man luf wel other
Als he ware his awen brother,(1)   336
And amange vs, be þat sacramente
þat now is in presente,
And be vertue of this messe,
Wee mowght have forgifnesse   340
Of oure gilte and oure mys,
þat wee may come vnto thy blysse.
¶ When the preste hase [rynsyng] done,
He wille speke (2) on-heghte sone   344
More forthe of his offys,
And sethen make ende of þat servyce.

                    (1) And swylk lufe o-mang vs be
                        þat we be wel lufed of þe.
                        þat by þis haly sacrament.—D.

As I prey for my selfe here,   556
Grawnte tyl oþur ben) þat on) þo same manere,
So þat ilke mon) luf oþur,
As he were hys owne broþur.(1)
Suche luf amungus be,   560
þat we be wel lowyd of þe,
And be þis holy sacramente,
þat now is here in presente,
And be þo vertu of þo messe,   564
þat we may haue for3yfnesse
Of aH owre gylte, of aH owre mysse,   [page 179]
And be þi help cum to blysse.
Loke pater-noster þou be seyande,   568
WhyH þo preste is receyuande.
When) þo preyste has receuyng done,
Opon) þi fete þou stonde vp sone.
þen) þe clerke flyttuþ his boke   572
Ageyn) to þo sowthe awter noke :
þo preyste turnus to his offys,
And says(2) forthe of his seruys.

Right as I pray for my-self here,
I pray the, graunt to othere þe same manere,
That eche man loue wel othere,
As eche of vs were otheres brothere.(1)   312
Suche loue, lord, among vs be,
That we be loued of the,
That therwe the vertu of the messe
Thu graunte vs, lord, for-3ewnesse   316
Of alle oure gylt and alle oure mysse,
And thorw thyn help [we] come to blysse.

Whanne the prest hath the rensynge don,
He wol make an ende son ;   320
He seith(2) forth of his offis,
Sithe he maketh ende of his seruis.

(2) say.—D.

TEXT B.

Then do thou say
this prayer to
Christ for pro-
tection in all
dangers;

þen with-outen tarying
on þis wyse be þi saying.

Jhesu, my king, I pray to þe,　　　584
　　bow doun þin eren of pyte,
　　And here my prayer in þis place.
　　gode lord, for þi holi grace
　　for me & alle þate here ere,　　　588
　　þat þou vs kepe fro alkyns were,
þat may byfalle on ony way,
In oure dedes do to day,
wheþer we ryde, or be goande,　　　592
lyg, or sitt, or if we stande ;

and that, if pre-
vented by sudden
death, hearing
this mass may
avail instead of
absolution and
the viaticum.

what sodan chaunce þat comes vs tille,
oþerwayse þen were oure wille,
we praye þis messe vs stande in stede　　　596
of shrift, & als of housel-brede.
And, ihesu, for þi woundes fyue,
wys vs þo waye of rightwis lyue. Amen.

When þis is saide, knele doun sone,　　　600
　　saye pater-noster til messe be done,

Keep repeating
paternosters till
the mass is done,

for þo messe is noght sest,
or tyme of ite, misa est.
þen when þou heris say ite,　　　604
or benedicamus,(2) if hit be,.
þen is þo messe al done ;

and then say this
prayer,

bot ʒit þis prayere þou make right sone ;

TEXT C.
[fol. 257 b.]

Euere þou gif gude herkenynge,
lowde or stille aye answerynge,　　　348
For þe mes is noght sest,
Or þe tyme of ite(1) missa est.
When þou has saide Ite,
Or benedicamus,(2) wheder it be,　　　352
þan is the messe alle done ;
Bot ʒitte this prayer þou saye sone.

　　　　　(1) MS. ita.

þer wiþ-owtoñ taryinge   576
On þis wyse þou be seyinge.
Iheſu my kynge I prey þe
Bowe downe þi nere of pyte,
And here my preyer in þis place.   580
God lord, for þi holy grace,
ffor me & aH þat here are
þu vs kepe fro aH kynnus kare,
þat may be-falle in any way,   584
In owre dedus to do or say,
Where we ryde, or we be goand,
Lyg or sytte, or we stond ;
What sodeñ schamce coñ vs tyllc,   588
Oþur-weyus þeñ were owre wylle,
We preyuñ þis messe stond vs in-stede
Of schryfte & of howsul bred.
And, Iheſu criste, for þi woundus fyue,   592
Wyssus vs þe wey of ryȝtwes lyue.
Wheñ þis is seyd, knele þou downe sone,
Sey pater-noster tyl þe messe be done,
ffor þe messe is not cest,   596
Or tyme of *ite missa est*
þen þou heruste *ite*
Or *benedicam*us,(2) if þat hit be,
þen is þe messe al done,   600
But ȝit a preyer þou make sone ;

There-to ȝew thu gode herkenynge,
Lowde or stil ay answerynge,   324
For the masse is noght cest,
Or the tyme of ite, missa est.
Bot whanne the prest seith it*e***,**
Or ben e dicamus,(2) wether hit be,   328
Thanne is the masse alle do ;
But ȝet this praiere thu say also,

      (2) or *requiescant in pace.*—D.

TEXT B.   after hit, welc þou may   608
before leaving. In gods name wende þi way.(1)

Thank God,   God be þonked of alle his werkes,
                 God be þonked of prestes & clerkes,
                 God be þonked of ilk a mon,   612
                 and I þonke god als I con.
                 I thonk god of his godnesse,
specially for this   And nomely now of þis messe,
mass,
and pray for its   and of alle þo prayers þat here are prayde,   616
acceptance.   pray I to god þat he be payde.

Crossing thyself,   In mynde of god here I me blesse,
in memory of
Christ, ask the   with my blessyng god sende me hesse.
blessing of the
Blessed.   In nomine patris & filii & spiritus sancti. Amen 620
                     Pater noster. Aue maria. Credo.

Here ends my   How þou at þo messe þi tym shuld spende
treatise.
The rubric is good   haue I told : now wil I ende.
to refer to, and
the prayers to   þo robryk is gode vm while to loke,   624
learn by heart.   þo praiers to con with-outen boke.

TEXT C.   After þat wele þou maye
                 In goddes name lyve to paye.(1)   356
                 God be thanked of alle his werkes,
                 God be thanked of priestes and clerkes,
                 God be thanked of ilke a man,
                 And I thanke hym in þat I kan;   360
                 I thanke god of his gudnes,
                 And alswa of this mes;
                 And of alle the prayers, þat here er prayed,
                 I pray hym þat he be payed.   364
                 In mynde of god here I me blysse,
                 With my blissynge god sende me hys.
                 How tyme of the messe is spendyd,
                 Have(2) I talde : now wille I endyd.   368
                 þe rubryke is gude vmwhile to luke,
                 þe prayers to cun with-owten buke.

             (1) ga thi way.—D.   (2) MS. How.

Aft*ur* hyt wyl þou may   TEXT E.
In godd*us* name wynde þi way.(1)
God be þonkud i*n* aH owr*e* werk*us*,   604
God be þonkud of preyst*us* & clerk*us*,

I þonke god as I con),
I þonke god of his godnes,
And namly of þis messe.   608
Of aH þo preyurs þat now be preyud,
I pray god þat he be payud.
In mynde of god I her*e* me blesse,
Wyt my blessyng god sende me hys.   612
In nomine patris et *filii* et *spiritus sancti.* Amen.
Pat*er*-noster aue-mary & credo.
God send vs to owr*e* mede. Amen).

And aftir for sothe wel þu may,   TEXT F.
In godis name, go hom thi way.(1)   332
God be thanked of all*e* his werkes,
And thankede of prestes and clerkys ;
God be thankede of eche man,
I thanke my lord, as hertly as I can ;   336
I thanke him hertli of his kyndenesse,
And nameli now of this holi messe ;
Of all*e* the praierys that her*e* ben praied,
I pray my swete lord that he be paied.   340
In mynde of god I me blesse,
With my blessyng*e* god sende me his.

How thu at the masse thi tyme schal spende,
I haw tolde now wel to þe ende.   344
The ribrusch * I rede thu loke somdel,   [* *Sic* in MS.]
The praierys þu record with-oute boke wel ;

TEXT B.

It is doubtless reason to honour the mass, for I have shown it worth more than all besides.

hit is skille w*ith*-outen doute,
þat ilk mon [þe] messe loue & loute,
for of alle i*n* þis world, þen is þo messe   628
þo worthiest þing, most of godnesse.

      Explicit. Amen. fiat.

TEXT C.

It is swilke w*ith*-owten doute
þat ilke man þe mes luff*es* and loute,   372
For of alle thinges i*n* þis werlde is þe mes

[fol. 258]

The worthyest and maste of gudnes.   374

      Expliciunt p*r*emia misse !

TEXT F.

For hit is suche with-oute doute,
That cristene her*e* har*e* masse, stil or loude,   348
For [*of*] all*e* that in this world is,
Most worthi thyng*e* I hold the messe.
Whoso wol vse this deuocioun,
I pray him of his benisoun,   352

The writer beseeches the reader's prayers,

In eche a masse that he schal this her*e*,
Sey a pater-noster for the writer*e*,
And an aue-maria, ȝef he may ;
For godis low sey noght nay.   356

and may God reward him.

And that hey holi god he queyte the thi mede,
Of whom we spek of when we say our*e* crede.   358

    Gratias. God, that his brede brake
      at his maw[*n*]de whanne he sate
       Among*e* his postyllis twelue,
     He bles our*e* brede and our*e* ayl
     þat we haw and haw schal,
      and be with vs him-selwe.

Bidding Prayers

ACCORDING TO THE USE OF YORK.

BIDDING PRAYER, I.

(Before the Conquest.)

✝ Wutan we gebiddan god ealmiti*g*ne heofena heah
cyning 7 *sancta* marian 7 calle godes halgan · *þaet*
we moton godes ælmihtiges willan gewyrcan · þa hwil
4 þe we on þyssan lænan life wunian · *þaet* hy ûs
gehealdan 7 gescyldan· wið ealra feonda costnunga
gesenelicra 7 ungesenelicra, Pat*er* no*st*er;
    Wutan we gebiddan· for urne papan on rome·
8 7 for urne cyning· 7 forne arceb*isceop* 7 forne eald-
orman· 7 for eallê þa þe us gehealdað frið 7 freondscype on feower healfe into þysse halgan stowe· 7 for
ealle þa þe ûs fore gebiddað binnan angelcynne 7
12 butan angelcynne · pat*er* no*st*er·

Wutan we gebiddan for ure godsybbas· 7 for ure
cumpeðran 7 for ure gildan · 7 gildsweostran 7 ealles
þæs folces gebed þe þas halgan stowe mid ælmesan
16 seceð· mid lihte 7 mid tigeðinge· 7 for ealle þa þe we
æfre heora ælmessan befonde wæron ær life and æfter
life· pat*er* [*nost*]er

    Bidde we _____ _____
20 _____
    _____

For þor[*fe*]rþes saule bidde we pa*t*er no*st*er. 7 for
mi*c*el mere saule 7 for ealle þa saula þe fulluht under-
fengan· 7 on crist gelyfdan fram adames dæge to
25 þisu*m* dæge· pat*er* no*st*er·

THE OLD ENGLISH MODERNIZED.

(*The inversions are retained.*)

Let us pray God Almighty, heavens' high King, and Saint Mary and all God's saints, that we may God Almighty's will work, the while that we in this transitory life continue; that they us uphold and shield against all enemies' temptations, visible and invisible: Our Father.

Prayer to do God's will, and for support and protection against the craft and subtilty of the devil or man.

Let us pray for our Pope in (*at*) Rome, and for our King, and for the Archbishop, and for the Alderman; and for all those that to (*with*) us hold (*maintain*) peace and friendship on the four sides towards (*of*) this holy place; and for all those that us for pray within the English nation, or without the English nation: Our Father.

For the Pope, King, Archbishop of York, the Alderman (or Senior of the Minster clergy); for plighted friends within the Minster bounds; and prayer-fellows of English or other race.

Let us pray for our gossips (*God-mothers*) and for our God-fathers, and for our gild-fellows and gild-sisters; and [*let us pray for*] all those people's prayer, who this holy place with alms seek, with light, and with tithe; and for all those whom we ever their alms receiving were before (*during their*) life and after life: Our Father.

For God-parents, gild-fellows, gild-sisters, and for the obtaining of the petitions of all benefactors to the Minster, by offerings or personal or testamentary gifts.

Pray we. (*The remainder of the line and the two following lines, are ruled and left blank in the manuscript.*) For Thorferth's soul pray we a Pater-noster; and for many more souls, and for all the souls that baptism have undertaken and in Christ believed from Adam's day to this day: Our Father.

For souls whose names are recited from the bede-roll, and other souls, and all the souls that have received baptism, or seen the day of Christ afar off.

BIDDING PRAYER, II.

From *MS. Manual:* A.D. 1405.   (Sir J. LAWSON, Bart.)

PRO PRECIBUS DOMINICALIBUS.

Prayers are
bidden

Deprecemur Deum Patrem omnipotentem pro pace et
stabilitate sanctæ matris ecclesiæ.

for the whole
state of Christ's
Church.

ʒe sal mak your prayers specially till our lord god
almighti *and* til his blessyd moder mary and till' all'
5 *th*e haly court of heuen for *th*e state *and th*e stabilnes

For the Pope
and other bishops.

of al halykirk. For *th*e pape of Rome and al his car-
di*n*als and for *th*e archebishop of York and for al
8 ercebischops *and* bischops and for al men *and* women

For all "re-
ligious."
For the rector
and clergy of the
parish church,
and for all ordin-
aries,

of religion and for *th*e person of *th*is kirke *th*at has
your saules to kepe *and* for all' *th*e prestes and clerkes
*th*at has serued or serues in *th*is kirk or in any other.

12 And for al p*re*lates *and* ordiners and al *th*at halykirk

that God grant
(lend) them grace
to govern the
people committed
to their charge,
and for example
to set them.

reules *and* gouerns *th*at god len *th*aim grace so for to
reuel *th*e popil *and* swilk ensaumpil for to tak or scheu
*th*aim and *th*aim for to do *th*are-after. *th*at it may be
16 louing unto god and saluacyon of *th*aire saules.

For the good
estate of the
realm, the king,
queen, and all the
nobility;

Also ʒe sal p*ra*y specially for *th*e gode state of *th*is
reume for *th*e kyng *and th*e quene and for al *th*e peris
19 *and th*e lordes of *th*is lande *th*at God send loue *and*

and God's
grace for the
government of
the kingdom to
His glory and the
benefit of the
commons.

charite *th*aim oma*n*g and gif *th*aim grace so for to reule
it and gouern it in pes *th*at it be louing to God and
*th*e comons un-to profet.

23

And for them that
loyally pay
church dues,
and for amend-
ment to those who
do otherwise.

Also ʒe sal pray specially for *th*a *th*at lely and trwly
payes *th*are tendes and *th*air offerandes til God and
halykirk *and* for al *th*at other does *th*at God *th*aim
amende.

Also ȝe sal pray specialy for thaim that this kirk For the founders and maintainers of the church, first biggid and edefied and al that it up-haldes and for all that thar-in findes boke or chales vestiment lyght and those who find the things necessary for divine service, or towell' or any other anourment whare-wit godes scruys es sustend and for thaim that halybred gaf to and provide holy-bread. this kirk to day and for thaim that first began and 6 langest haldis on. And for al land tilland and for al For husbandmen, mariners, seasonable weather, see farand and for the wedir and for the fruyt that es and for the fruits of the earth on erthe. that the erthe may bring forthe his fruyt to the enjoyment of man. cristen men to profet. And for al pilgrymes and palm- For pilgrims and palmers, ers and for al that any gode gates has gane or sal ga. 11 and for thaim that brigges and stretes makes and and those who make or repair bridges or highways; and the imputation of all good works. amendes that god grant us parte of thare gode dedes and thaim of oures. Also ȝe sal pray for all' our For fellow-parishioners. parischyns whar-so thai be on land or on water that god saue thaim fra al missaunters and for all wymen 16 that er with chield in this parische or in any other. That women labouring of child may have safe deliverance and the child baptism. that God delyuer thaim with joy and gife the child For the sick and afflicted. cristendom and thaim purificacion. and for al that er sek and sary that god al-mighthi conforth thaim and For strength to such as do stand; and for deliverance to the debtor, the sinner, and the prisoner. thaim that er in gode lyfe that God hald thaim thare-in. for tham that er in dette or in dedly synne or in prison that God bring tham out thare-of. 23

for tham and for us and for al cristen folke for charite says a Pater-noster and a aue.

Psalmus.

Deus misereatur nostri et cetera Ps. (67) 66, and the doxology.
Gloria Patri.
Kyrie eleyson. Christe eleyson. Kyrie eleyson. 29
Pater noster.
   Et ne nos. The priest aloud. THE SUFFRAGES.
Saluos fac servos tuos, et ancillas tuas, Deus meus.
   Sperantes [in te.]
Esto eis Domine turris fortitudinis.
   A facie inimici. 35

MASS-BOOK. 5

Suffrages at
length.
(*Page* 77, *l.* 27.)
Domine, Deus virtutum.

Et ostende faciem.

Domine exaudi orationem:

Dominus vobiscum.

5   Ecclesiæ tuæ preces, Domine.

Oratio.

Prayer.
(*Page* 78.)
Deus, qui caritatis.

Oratio.

Prayer.
(*Page* 78.)
Deus a quo sancta desideria.

Prayer to the
Virgin-mother
for her advocacy
with her Son.
¶ Also ȝe sal pray specialy til oure lady saynt
mary *that* sche becum oure auoket and at sche pray for

12   hus specially till' hir' dere son.

For the brethren
and sisters of the
three Minsters in
Yorkshire;
for all to whom
beholden, and
that God would
have prayed for.
And also ȝe sal pray specialy for *the* breder' *and*
the sisters of saynt petir minster of york and of sant
jon of beuerlay and of saynt wilfryde of rypon *and* for
al *that* ȝe er halden un-to and for al *that* God wald

17   ȝe prayed for says a Pater noster and ave.

Ant*iphona*.

Anthem.
(*Page* 79.)
Ave regina cælorum.

In tempore.   Paschali.   Ant*iphona*.

At Easter-tide.
(*Page* 79.)
Regina cæli, lætare.

22   **Versiculus.**

Versicle.
(*Page* 72.)
Post partum virgo.

Oratio.

Prayer.
(*Page* 79.)
Famulorum tuorum.

For the souls of
relations natural
and spiritual,
Also ȝe sal pray specialy for oure fader' saules and
oure moder saules and for oure god-fader saules and

28   oure god-moder saules and for oure brether saules and
oure sister saules and for oure eldir saules and for al

and of those
buried in the
parish,
and in purgatory,
the saules of whame *the* bodis es berid *in* *th*is kirk or
in *th*is kirk-ȝerde and for al saules *that* in purgatori
godis mercy abydes and for al cristen saules of whame

we have had any god of says specialy a Pater-noster and benefactors. and Ave.

Psalmus.

De profundis. Ps. (130) 122.

Kyrie eleyson. Christe eleyson. Kyrie eleyson. 5

Pater noster.

Et ne nos.

Requiem æternam.

A porta inferi. Suffrages.

Credo videre bona Domini. (Page 73.) 10

Requiescant in pace. Amen.

Fidelium, Deus, omnium cond*itor* et rede*mptor* Prayer for remission of sins to animabus famu*lorum*. quick and dead. (Page 73.)

BIDDING PRAYER, III.

From MS. Manual, York Minster Library.

[* p. 172]

'Deprecacio pro pace ecclesie et regni in diebus dominicis.

Prayers are bidden

Deprecemur deum patrem omnipotentem pro statu et stabilitate sancte matris ecclesie et pro pace
5 regis et regni.

We sall make a speciall' prayer unto god all'

[* p. 173]
for the whole state of Christ's church,
myghty'. and to þe glorius uirgin his moder 'ouer lady sante mary. and to al þe fare felichyp of heuen. ffor alle þe state and þe stabilite of all' haly kirke. specially
10 for our haly fader þe pope of rome. and for alle hys trewe cardinals. for þe patriark of ierusalem. and spe-

and the recovery of the Holy Cross.
cially for þe haly crose. þat god was done opon. þat god for hys mercy. bringe itt oute of hethen men handes.
14 into cristen menes kepyng.

For the arch-bishop, bishop, and all "re-ligious."
¶ Also we sall pray specially for our haly fader þe archbyschop of þis See. and for alle other archbischopes & byschopes ande for all maner of men and women of relygion. þat god gyfe þame grace perseverance in onest
19 and clene relygyon kepinge.

For the curate and all pastors;
¶ We sall pray specially. for þe person or for þe vikar of þis kirke þat hase ȝoure saules for to kepe. and for alle þase þat cure has tane of cristenmen saules. þat god gyf þame grace so well for to teche þare sugettis
24 ilke curet in his degre. ande þe sugettes so weill to

wyrke efter heylfull teching þat bothe þe techers and 1
þe sugettes may com [to] þe blys þat aye sall last.

¶ We sall pray specially for all prestes & clerkes and other clergy of all orders.
þat redis or singes. in þis kirke or in any other and for
all other thurgh whame goddes servys es maintened 5
or uphalden

¶ We sal prey specially for oure kynge and þe For the King, Royal Family,
queyn and all' þe kynges childer and for þe peris and Lords, Commons, and Council.
þe lordes and þe ˙gode communers of þe lande. and [* p. 174]
specially for all þas þat hafes. þe gude counsale of þe 10
lande for to kepe þat god gef þame grase swilk coun-
selle to take & orden and for to do þare efter þat itt
may be louyng to god allmyghty. profet and weillfare
to þe rem and schame and senchyp to ouer enmyse.
gaynstanding and restrenyng of þare power & þare 15
males.

¶ We sall pray especially for þe meer[,] þe xij[,] For the mayor and corporation
þe schirriues and þe xxiiij. and for all gode communers of York.
of þis cite. and for þame þat has þis cite for to govern.
þat god gife þame grace so weil to rewle itt þat may be 20
to god louyng & sauing to þe Citè[1] and profet & help [¹ Citè sic in MS.]
to þe communers.

¶ We sall pray specially for all oure gode parechens For fellow-parish-ioners that travel
whare so euer þai be. on land or on water. þat god by land or water.
almyghty saue þame fra all maner of parels & bring 25
þam whar þai walde be inquart[2] & heill both of body [² Read in quart]
& of saule.

¶ We sall pray specially for all þase þat lely and For those that duly pay tithe;
trewly pays þer tendes & þer offerandes to god & to and amendment to defaulters.
haly kirke. þat god do þame meid in þe blise of heuen.
and þai þat dose noght so. þat god brynge þame sone 31
till amendment.

¶ We sall pray also for all trewe pilgrams & palm- For pilgrims and benefit of
ers whare so euer þai be on lande or on water. þat god their pilgrimage.
of his gudenes ˙graunt þame parte of our gode prayers [* p. 175]
& us of þare gode gates. 36

For prosperity to husbandmen, and safety to seafaring people.

¶ Allso we sall pray specially for all lande tyllande þat god for his godenes and his he grace and thurgh our gude prayers. maynteyn þame so. þat þai may be

4 upstandand. and for all þe see farand þat god all-myghtty saue þame fra all maner of parels & brynge þame and þer gudes in quart whare þaie walde be.

For deliverance from the bands of sins,

¶ We sall pray specially for all þaes þat er bun in dette or in dedely syn. þat god for hys mercy bryng

9 þam sone oute þer of. And for all þase þat er in gode lyfe þat god maynten þame þare in and gif þame gode

and for perseverance in well-doing; and pray each one for this.

perseuerance in þer gudenes. And þat þis prayer may be harde and sped þe titter thurgh ȝour praier. ilk a man & woman þat here is helpes hartly with a pater

14 noster and a Ave.

Ps. (67) 66.

Deus miseriatur nostri et cetera cum Gloria patri.
Kyrieleeson. Christeleeson. Kyrieleeson.

Priest secretly.

Pater noster [&c].

Priest aloud.

Sacerdos sine nota Et ne nos [inducas in tempta-

19 tionem.]

People answer.

[Sed libera nos a malo. Amen.]

Suffrages.

Sacerdotes tui [induantur justitiam
Et sancti tui exultent.]

23   **D**omine salvum fac regem.
[Et exaudi nos in die qua invocaverimus te]
Saluum fac populum tuum domine [et benedic hære-
ditati tuæ]

27   [Et rege nos et extolle illos usque in æternum.]
Domine fiat pax [in virtute tua]
[Et abundantia in turribus tuis]
Exurge domine [, adjuva nos.]

31   [Et libera nos propter nomen tuum.]
Domine deus virtutum [converte nos]
[Et ostende faciem tuam et salvi erimus.]
Domine exaudi [orationem meam]
[Et clamor meus ad te veniat.]
Dominus uobiscum

37   [Et cum spiritu tuo]

Orem*us*. **Or***acio* 1

Ecclesie tue qu*esumu*s dom*ine* pre*ces* placatus ad- Prayer for the church.
mitte ut destructis adu*er*sitatib*us* & errorib*us*
nniv*er*sis. secura tibi seruiat libertate. 4

Or*atio*

Deus a quo s*ancta* desideria. Prayer.
(*Page* 78.)

Or*atio*

Deus qui caritatis. Prayer.
(*Page* 78.)

¶ We sall*e* make a speciall pr*a*yer to ou*r* lady 9
saynt mary. and to all þe feir falychyp ˙þat is in heuen [* p. 176]
for all þe brether & sistirs of ou*r* moder kirke saynt For the four
Minsters in the
Petyr house of ʒorke. saynt Iohn' house of Beuerlay. diocese of York;
saynt Wilfride of Rypon. and saynt Mary of Suthwell. 13
and specially for all þaes þ*at* ar seik in þis parych or i*n* and for the sick.
any other. þ*at* god of his godhede relese þame of þare
panes & seknes and turne þame to þat way þat is maste
to goddes louyng & heill of þare saules. 17

¶ We sal pr*a*y specially for all þaes þ*at* wirchips For those that
honour the church
þ*is* kirke owther w*ith* buke or bell nestment or chales, by gifts of ornaments.
awterclath or towel. or any other anourment þurgh
qwilk haly kirke is or may be more honorde or wir- 21
chipt.

¶ We sal pray also specialy for all þase þ*at* gifes. For those that
give or bequeath
or sends or i*n* testment wytes. any gode i*n* mayntenyng for church work,
of þ*is* kirk or kirkwarke. And for all þaes þat fyndes or find light in
honour of God or
any lyght i*n* þ*is* kirke. as torche. serge. or lampe i*n* His saints.
wirchyping of god or any of his halouse. 27

¶ We sall pr*a*y also for all women þat er bun w*ith* For women with
child.
childer i*n* þis parichin or i*n* any other þ*at* god comforth
þame and delyuer þame w*ith* ioy˙ & send þare childer
cristendom & þe moders puryfying of holy kirk. and 31
relese of payn i*n* þare trauelyng.

¶ We sall*e* also pray for þame þat þis day gafe brede For those that
give the holy
to þ*is* kirk haly brede to be made of. for þame it first bread.

For these and all,
hail the Blessed
Virgin with five
Aves.
[* p. 177]
began and langest haldes opon. ffor þamc & for us and
for all oþer þat neid has of prayer. in wirchyp of our
lady saynt mary ˙ilk man and woman hayls oure lady
4 with v. Aues.

antifona.

Anthem.

Aue regina cclorum ·
7   aue domina angelorum

V*er.*

Verse.

Post partum [*virgo inviolata permansisti*]
[*Dei genetrix, intercede pro nobis.*]

O*ratio.*

Prayer.
(*Page* 79.)

Famulorum tuorum
13   tempore paschali antifona.

Anthem.
(*Page* 79.)

Regina celi

V*er.*

Verse repeated.

Post partum [&c]
17   O*racio.*

Prayer.
(*Page* 80.)
For the souls of
relatives, natural
and spiritual,

Gra*ti*am tuam
¶ We sal make a speciall*e* prayer for oure faders
saules moder saules oure godfader saules godmoder
saules. brether saules. sisters saules. and (for ellwill) all
22 oure euenkyn saules. and for all our gudefrendes saules.

and those here
buried,
and for all þe saules whas banes er berryd in þis kirke.
or in þis kirk ȝerd. or in any other & specialy for all

and of all in
purgatory.
þe saules þat abydes þe mercy of god in þe paynes of
purgatory. þat god for his mykill mercy relese þame of
27 þare payns if itt be his will.   And þat oure prayers

With this inten-
tion say a pater-
nqster and ave.
myght sumwhat stand þame in stede ilk man and
woman helpes hertly with a pater noster and a ave.

P*salmus.*

Ps. (130) 129.
De profundis.
Kyrieleeson. *Christeleeson.* Kyrielson.
pater noster
34   Et ne nos inducas.

Requiem eternam [*dona eis, Domine.*]   [York Horæ, fo cxxxliii.]
   [*Et lux perpetua luceat eis.*]
Credo uidere [*bona domini*
   In terra viuentium.]   4
A porta inferi.
   [*Erue domine animas eorum.*]
Dominus uo*biscum.*
   [*Et cum spiritu tuo.*]   8
Orem*us.*

Oracio.

Fidelium de*us* omn*ium* [*conditor et redemptor ani-* Prayer. [York Horæ, fo. xcvii.]
mabus omnium famulorum famularumque tuarum re-
missionem cunctorum tribue peccatorum ut indulgentiam 13
quam semper optauerunt piis supplicationibus conse-
quantur.]

Requiescant i*n* pace ffidelium anime per misericordiam [*dei. Amen.*]   17

BIDDING PRAYER, IV.

Added in MS. York Manual, York Minster Library.

[* p. 178]

Der frendes. ye sall make a speciall prayer unto
2 gode allmyghty and to þat gloryes Virgyn [*his moder*]
saynt mary and to all þᵉ fayre fellischyp of heven ffor

For the state of Holy Church, the pope,
þe peas and þe stabylnes óf all haly kyrke for our haly
fadyr yᵉ pape of rome wyth all his trew cardynallys.

6 And in generall for all men & women of relygyon.

regulars, and parochial clergy.
and specially for all þaes whilk has taken charge or
cure of cristynmen sallys. þat gode gif þaim gras so for
to do þʳ charges yᵗ it may be plesyng to gode & salva-
10 cyon to all crystynmen sallys. Also ye sall pray for

For the Realm, King, and his council.
yᵉ prosperite & wallfare of yˢ Reygne for yᵉ kyng &
his counsell yᵗ god sende hym gude counsell & wytt &
gras so for do yerafter yat it may be plesyng to gode,
14 profet wyrchyp & salvacyon to yᵉ reygne. And for all

For nobility, gentlefolks, and commonalty. For fellow parishioners.
yᵉ lordys gentylles & comynerrys and specially for all
our pareschynges yat Gode of his marcy wyll keype
ycm for all moner of parellys of body & sall : also ye

For all souls,
sall pray for all crysten sallys yt er in ye paynes of
19 purgotory yer ye mercy of gode abydyng. And spe-

especially the friendless.
cially for all yos sallys yᵗ has moste nyde to be prayed
for and fewest frendes has For ye . . . . . res and all

Say three paters and two aves, and obtain a blessing.
oyer whilk gode walde haue prayed for & [n]ow ilk
man and woman say iij pater noster & ji ave m̄a and
haue goddes blyssyng & our ladys & all haly kyrks.

BIDDING PRAYER, V.

From "*Manuale secundum usum matris ecclesie Eboracensis*," W. de Worde, 1509.

Preces pro diebus Dominicis.

[fol. 100 b.]

Preces in dominicis dicende. Deprecemur deum patrem omnipotentem pro stabilitate sancte matris ecclesie et pro pace terre. ¶ we shall make a specyall prayer unto god almighty : And to the gloryous virgyn his moder our Lady saynt mary : and to all the gloryous company of heven. For the state of all holy chirche/ and for the peas of the royalme. And for all that are Trewe to the Kynge *and* to the crowne. Specyally for our holy Fader the [pope of Rome][1] and all his trewe Cardynals. And specially for the holy crosse that god was done upon that god for his merci bringe it out of the hethen ˙mennes handes into cristen mennes kepynge. ¶ we shall pray specyally for our holy fader the Archebisshop of this See. and for all other archebysshops *and* bysshops Abbottes Pryors˙ Monkes Chanons. *and* for all maner of men *and* women of relygion that god gyue them good perseuerance in honest and clene relygious lyuynge. ¶ we shall pray specially for the person of this chirche that hathe cure of mannes sowles : that god gyve them grace well for to teche theyr subgettes every curat in his degre : *and* the subgettes so well to worke after helefull techynge that bothe the techers *and* the subgets come to the blys everlastinge. ¶ we shall pray also for all prestes *and* clerkes that redys or singes in this chirche or in any other : and for all other thrughe whome goddis

Marginal notes:

Prayers are bidden

4

for the whole church, and the peace of the kingdom, and all loyal subjects,

[1 Struck out.] the Pope and Cardinals, and the recovery of the holy cross.
[* fol. 101]

14

For bishops and regulars,

19

and for the rector of the parish,

24

and all other clergy.

1 service is in holy chirche mayntayned *and* upholden.

For the King,
Queen, Lords,
and Commons.

¶ we shall pray specyally for the kynge *and* the quene *and* the peers *and* lords and all the good com*m*eners of this londe. *and* specyally for all those that hathe the

5 good counsayle of the londe to gouerne : that God gyue them grace such cou*n*sayle to take and ordeyne and so for to worke therafter that it may be louinge to god almighty *and* profite *and* welfare to the royalme : *and*

9 gaynstandi*n*ge *and* refrayni*n*ge of our enmyes power

For benefactors
of the church,
in ornaments,

and malice ¶ we shall pray especially for all those that worshippes this chirche or any other with boke belle vestimente chalice auterclothe or towell : or any other

· [* fol. 101 b.]
[¹ nat *sic*]

ornament thrugh the whiche holy chirche ˙is or may be in any poynte nat¹ honowred or worshipped. ¶ we

gifts,

shall pray also specyally for al that giues or sendes in

bequests,

testame*n*t any good to the right mayntenau*n*ce *and* up-

17 holdinge of the worke of this chirche. *and* for all

or light.

theym that fyndes any lyght in this chirche : as in torche taper lampe in worshippynge of god or of our

For parishioners,

lady or of any of his sayntes. ¶ we shal also pray

21 specially for all our good parisshens wheresover they

in their bodies,
souls, and pro-
perty.

be / on water or on londe. that god of his goodnes saue theim frome all maner of peryls and bringe them safe where they wolde be in helthe of body *and* sowle *and*

For unassoiled
sinners,

also of goodes. ¶ we shal pray specyally for all those that are in dette or in dedely synne : that god for his

27 great mercy brynge them sone therof. *and* for al those

and good livers,

that are in good lyvynge / that god maynten them *and* gyue them good perseuerau*n*ce in their goodnes. *and* that these prayers may be herd *and* sped the soner

pray heartily a
pater and ave.

thrughe your prayers, euery man and woman that here is helpe the*m* hertely with a. Pater noster and an Ave

33 maria. &c.

Ps. (67) 66.

DEus misereat*ur* nostri, et ben*e*dicat nobis : illuminet vultu*m* suu*m* sup*er* nos *et* misereat*ur*
nostri.

Ut cognoscemus in terra viam tuam : *in* omni*bus* 1
gentibus salutare tuum.

Confiteantur tibi populi deus : confiteantur tibi
populi omnes.

Lete*ntur* et exultent gentes : quoniam iudicas popu- 5
lor in equitate et gentes in terra dirigis.

Confiteantur tibi populi deus : confiteantur tibi
populi om*nes : terra dedit fructum suu*m*.   [* fol. 102]

Benedicat nos deus deus noster b*e*nedicat nos deus :
et metuant eum omnes fines terre.   10

Gloria patri.

Kyrieleyso*n*. *Christ*eleyson. Kyrieleyson.

Pater noster.   Priest secretly.

Et ne nos in.

Sed libera nos   15

Sacerdotes tui induantur iustitiam.   Suffrages.

Et sancti tui exultent.   The priest aloud.

Domine saluu*m* fac regem.   The people
                                                    answer.
Et exaudi nos in die qua inuocauerimus te.

Saluum fac populu*m* tuum domine et benedic 20
hereditati tue.

Et rege nos *et* extolle illos vsq*ue* in eternum.

Domine fiat pax in virtute tua.

Et habundantia in turribus tuis.

Exurge domine adiuva nos.   25

Et libera nos propter nomen tuu*m*.

Domine deus virtutum converte nos.

Et oste*n*de faciem tuam et salui erimus.

Domine exaudi orationem meam.

Et clamor meus ad te veniat.   30

Domin*us* vobiscu*m*.

Et c*um* spiritu tuo.

Oremus.

Oracio

ECclesie tue quesumus domine preces placatus ad- Prayer for church.
mitte : ut destructis aduersitatibus et erroribus 36
universis secura tibi serviat libertate.

1   O*racio*

Collect for health
of mind and body. **D**Eus q*ui* caritatis dona per gr*ati*am s*a*ncti sp*iritus*
            tuor*um* cordibus fidelium infundisti : da famulis
        et famulab*us* tuis pro q*ui*bus tuam deprecamur cl*e*men-
    5   ti*am* salut*em* m*e*ntis *et* corporis : ut te tota *vir*tute.
        diligant : *et* q*ue* tibi placita su*n*t tota dilecti*one* p*er*fi-
        ciant.

                             O*racio*

Collect for peace. **D**Eus a quo s*a*ncta desideria recta *con*silia *et* justa
    10   su*n*t op*er*a da sc*r*uis tuis illam qua*m* mu*n*dus
        dare no*n* potest pacem : ut et corda nostra ma*n*dat*is*
        tuis dedita : *et* hostiu*m* sublata formidine, tempora
[¹ *sic*] sint tua protecti*one* ¹transqu*i*lla¹: per *ch*ristu*m*.

    14   ¶ ye shall knele downe deuoutly on your knese *and*
[* fol. 102 *b*.] *make a specyall praer unto our blessed lady saint Mary
For the four
Minsters in the
diocese of York. *and* to all the felawshyp of heuen/ for all the brethcren
        and sisters of our moder chirch saynt Peter of yorke.
    18 saynt Johñ of Beuerlay. saynt wilfred of Ryppon :
For the sick. *and* saint Mary of Suthwell. and specially for all those
        that be seke in this parisshe or in any other that god
        of his goodnes / releas them of their peynes in theyr
    22 sekenes and turne them to the way that is moste to
        goddes plesure *and* welfare of theyre soules. vve shall
For those who
"pay their
duties," praye for all those that duely *and* truly payes theyr
        tendes and theyr offerynges to god and to the holy
    26 Chirche that god do them mede in the blisse of heven
and amendment
to those who fail
herein. that euer shall last : *and* they that dose nat so : that
        god of his mercy brynge theym sone to amendemente.
For pilgrims
and mutual
imputation of
good works. vve shall pray also for all true pylgrymes *and* palmers
        vvheresoeuer they be on vvater or on londe that god of
        his goodnes gra*un*t them parte of our good prayers *and*
    32 us parte of theyr good pylgrimages. we shall also praye
For husbandmen, for all lande tylla*n*d, that god for his goodnes *and* for
        his grace *and* through our good prayers may[*n*]teyne
fair weather, them that they may be saued frome all euyll wyndes
    36 and weders *and* from all dredfull stormes that god

sende us corne *and* catell for to lyue upon to goddes and good produce.
pleasu[r]e and the welfare of our sowles. we shall 2
pray also for all women that be with chylde in this For women
parysshe or any other, that god conforte them and labouring with child.
sende the chil[*de*][1] ·Christendom and the moder Purifi- [1 *at end of line*]
cacion of holy chirche / and releacynge of peyne·in [* fol. 103]
theyr trauelynge. ¶ we shall pray specyally for theym For those who
that this daye gave brede to this chirche : for to be find the holy loaf.
made holy brede of. For them that it began and 9
lengest upholdes. For them *and* for us and for all
them that nede hathe of good prayers. In worshyp of Prayer in honour
our lady saynt Mary and of her .v. Ioyes. Every man of the Blessed Virgin.
and woman say in the honoure of hir .v. tymes Ave 13
maria

Ant*iphona.*

Ave regina celor*um*   Anthem.
   mater regis angelorum   17
     O maria flos virginu*m*
   velut rosa vel lilium
   funde preces ad filium
     pro salute fidelium.   21

V*ersus.*

Post partum virgo i*n*uio.   Verse.
(*Page* 72.)

Oremus. Or*acio.*   Collect.

FAmulorum tuorum quesum*us* domi*ne* delictis ig- 25
nosce : ut qui tibi placere de actibus nostris non
valemus genitricis filii tui d*o*mi*ni* dei n*ost*ri interces-
sione saluemur. Per eunde*m* *christum* domi*num* nos-
tru*m*.   29
   Hec an*tiphona* dicet*ur* tempore paschali.   At Easter-tide,

Regina celi letare   alleluya :   Anthem.
quia que*m* meruisti portare all*eluy*a :
resurrexit sicut dixit   all*eluy*a :   33
ora pro nobis deum   alleluya.

Versus.

Verse repeated.

2 Post partum virgo inuio.

Oremus. Oracio.

Collect.

G Ratiam tuam quesumus domine mentibus nostris
infunde : ut qui angelo nunciante Christi filii
6 tui incarnationem cognouimus : per passionem eius et
crucem ad resurrectionis gloriam perducamur. Per
eundem christum dominum nostrum. Amen.

For the dead,
kneeling,

¶ ye shall make a speciall prayer for your faders
sowles : for your moders sowles : godfaders sowles and
11 godmothers sowles : broders sowles and sisters sowles :
[* fol. 103 b.] and for all your elders sowles : and for all the ˙sowles
that ye or I be bownde to praye for. and specyally for
all the sowles whose bones are buryed in this chirche
15 or in this chirche yerde : or in any other holy place.
and in especyall for all the sowles that bydes the great
mercy of almighty god in the bytter peynes of Purgatory : that god for his great mercy releas them of theyr
19 peyne if it be his blessyd wyll. And that our prayers

say a pater and
ave.

may sumwhat stande them in stede : Every man and
woman of your charite / helpe them with a Pater noster
and an Ave maria.

Ps. (130) 129.

Psalmus. De profundis. etc.
24 Kyrieleyson. Christeleyson. Kyrieleyson.
Pater noster.
Et ne nos.

(Page 73.)

Requiem eternam.
Credo videre.
29 A porta inferi.
Dominus uobiscum.
Et cum spiritu tuo.
Oremus.

Oracio.

Prayer.
(Page 73.)

Fidelium Deus omnium conditor, etc.
Fidelium anime per misericordiam dei in pace
36 requiescant. AMEN.

York Hours of the Cross.

YORK HOURS OF THE CROSS.

[fol. 1]
MATINS.

Lorde un-do my lyppis, iesu, heuen kyng,
    And my mouthe sall say þi loueyng.
Domine labia mea apperies, et os meum: et cetera.

God þu be my help at my begynnyng,   4
And me to help þu þe hy, at my endyng.
Deus in adiutorium meum intende. Domine ad, et
                                                    cetera.

Ioy un-to fadyr and þe sonn and þe haly gast in heuen
þat was at þe begynnyng and euer es in heuen.   8
Gloria patri et filio et spiritui sancto: sicut erat et
                                                    cetera.

The Memory.   lord iesu cryste, I pray þe here my steuenen.
              for þi swete modyr sak, þat es qwhen of heuen;
Anthem.   þi wysdome of þe fadyr, þe god ryghtwesnes.   12
              God and man, at morne tyde, taken he es,
              for-sakyne of hys frendes & left—witoutyn les.
His Betrayal. Be-trayede to þe jewys & dampnyde sackles.
              lord for þat ylk payn þu suffyrde at morne tyde   16
              Iat neuer my saule· on domis day be forlorne.
Patris sapiencia veritas diuina. Deus homo et cetera.

Versicle.   We wyrchyppe þe cryste iesu, god son.
Answer.   For wit þi holy cros: þis world haues þu won.   20
[fol. 1 b.]
Read Adoramus. Adorarus te Christe et benedicimus tibi: Quia per
                                                crucem et cetera

HORÆ DE SANCTA CRUCE SECUNDUM USUM EBORACEN.

Ad Matutinas.

[fol. 2 b.]

Domine labia mea aperies :   Ps. (51) 50, 15.
Et os meum annunciabit laudem tuam.

Deus in adiutorium meum intende :   Ps. (70) 69, 1.
Domine ad adiuvandum me festina.   4

Gloria patri et filio et spiritui *sancto* :
Sicut erat in 'principio et nunc et semp*er* et in   [* fol. 3]
*secu*la *seculorum*.   Amen.

(Antiphona)

Patris sapiencia, veritas diuina,   8   [fol. 13]
    Deus homo captus est hora matutina,
A notis discipulis cito derelictus,
A iudeis traditus, venditus, afflictus.

(Versus)

Adoramus te *Christe* et benedicimus tibi :   12

(Responsorium)

Qui[a] per sanctam crucem tuam redimisti mundum.

The Prayer.

lorde iesu cryste, leuand god sone,
þu set þi deyd, þi cros, and þi passione,
Be-twix þi dome, & my saul, for deyd þat I haue don,   24
Now [and] at my endyng þat I be noght fordon.
And graunte us mercy, & grace whyls we er on lyue
Un-to þi kyrke, un-to þi rewme, for þi wondys fiue ;
forgyuenes & reste to þaim þat to ded ere dryue,   28
joy to al synful : þis graunt us be-liue.
þu þat liues, þu þat reynnes, god wit-owtyn ende
in werld of werles wit ioy þat euer sal lende.
Dne ihu *Christe* fili dei uiui pone passione*m*. et ce*tera*.

PRIME.
His Mocking.

At p*r*ime led was iesu unto Pilate   33
yai (*sic*) band hym as a thefe, and sor hy*m* smate ;
many fals witnes, þai wryed hym many gate,
þai spytted ie*su*ys face, þe light of heuens yate.   36

lord for þat ilk shame· þu soffird at prime,
lat neu*er* my saul on domesday mystime.

[fol. 2] **Hora prima ductus est** ı*esu*s **ad pilatu***m* **et ce***tera*.

TIERCE.
His Scourging.

At þe tyme of oundron þai gun cry & call,   40
For hethyng þai hy*m* cled i*n* purper & in pall,
þai set on his heyde a cron of thorn w*it*-all,
and gerte hy*m* bere on his bak þe cros to þe pynstal.

lord for þat ilk shame, þu sofyrd in þat place,   44
of deydly synne me to shryue, þu gyue grace.
Crucefige clamitan*t* **hora terciarum. et ce***tera*.

SEXT.
His Crucifixion.

At þe tyme of myd-day þai dyd hy*m* on þe rode
Betwix two theues þat had spylt manys blode ;   48
for þe panys he threstyd il· þai gaue hi*m* dry*n*k ungod,
Bytt*er* gall [. . . . .] he wald noght of þat fod.

lord for þat ilk shame þat was þi body neghe
Scheld me fro my il fays, þe world, fend & fleshe   52
Hora sexta ie*su*s **est cruci conclavatus et ce***tera*.

(Oracio) Orem*us.*

D*omine* ie*su* *Christe*, fili dei uiui, pone passione*m*
 cruce*m* *et* morte*m* tuam inter iudicium tuu*m* et
a*n*imas nostras, nunc et in hora mortis nostre, et largiri 16
digneris uiuis mi*sericordi*am et gra*ti*am, defunctis ve-
niam et requie*m*, ecclesie regnoq*ue* pacem et concordiam,
infirmis sanitate*m*, et nobis peccatoribus vitam et gloriam sempiternam. Qui vivis et regnas [de*us*, Per From printed
Horæ, fo. xlii.
om*n*ia secula seculorum. Amen].

(Versus)

Gloriosa passio d*o*mini n*os*tri ie*su* *chri*st*i* perducat 22
nos *ad uera gaudia paradisi : Amen.   [* fol. 13 b.]

. (Ad Primam)

Hora prima d*o*m*i*n*u*m ducu*n*t ad *pilatu*m*,   [fol. 16]
Falsis testimoniis multum accusatum
In collo p*er*cutiu*n*t, manib*us* ligatu*m*,   26
Vultum dei conspuu*n*t, lumen deo gratu*m*.
Adoramus te *Christe*. Quia p*er*. [ut supra]

[Ad Terciam]

Crucifige clamita*n*t hora terciaru*m*,   [fol. 17 b.]
Illusus induitur veste purpuraru*m* :   30
Caput ei*us* pu*n*gitu*r* corona spinaru*m*,
Cruce*m* portat humeris ad loca penaru*m*.
Adoram*us*. Qu*i*a. [ut supra]

[Ad Sextam]

Hora sexta ie*sus* est cruci conclavatus,   [fol. 19]
Et est cu*m* latronib*us* pende*n*s deputatus :
Pre tormentis s[*i*]cie*n*s felle satur[*at*]us,   36
Agnus crimen diluit sic ludificatus.
Adoramus te *Chri*ste. Quia p*er*.

NONES.
His Death.

At þe tyme of none iesu gun cry;
he wytte his saul to his fadyr, [Eli].
A knyght smat him to þe hert, had he no mercy;   56
þe sone be-gane to wax myrk qwen iesu gun dy.

[fol. 2 b.]

lord out of þi syd ran a ful fayre flude
As clere as well water our rannson be þi blode.
Hora nona dominus iesus expirauit: Et cetera.   60

EVENSONG.
His taking from
the Cross.

At þe tyme of ouen-sang þai tok hym fro þe rod
his myght was in his godhede, so gracius & god,
þe meydcyne of his paynes, þe schedyng his blod,
Be noryschyng to us of or gastly fod.   64

lord for þat ilk schame þat þu doun was tane
lat neuer my saul wit deydly syn be sclayne.
De cruce deponitur hora uespertina. Et cetera.

COMPLINE.
His Burial.
[Cambridge MS.
Maskell M. R. 2,
70.]

[At our of comepelyn, thei leiden hym in graue,   68
The noble bodi of Iesu, that mankind schal saue :
With spicerie he was biried, hooli writ to fulfille,
Thenke we sadli on his deeth, that schal saue us from
                 helle.]

From the Prymer
of 1543.
Maskell M. R. 2,
p. xvii.

[O blessed chryst these houres canonycall,   72
To thee I offer with meke deuocyon :
For us thou hast suffered those paynes all,
In thy greuous agony by lyke reason,
So by the remembraunce of thy passyon,   76
Make me accordyng to my busynes,
Partaker of thy crowne and glory endles.]

[Ad Nonam]

Hora nona *dominus iesus* expirauit,   [fol. 20 b.]

Heli clamans *animam patri* commendauit :   40

Lat*us* eius lancea miles *per*forauit ;

Terra tunc contremuit, et sol obscurauit.

[Versus]

Adoramus te *Christe.* Quia *per*

[Ad Vesperas de cruce.]

De cruce deponitur hora uespertina,   [fol. 22]

Fortitudo latuit in mente diuina :

Talem mortem subiit vite medicina,   46

Heu corona glorie iacuit supina.

Adoramus te *Christe.* Quia per *sanctam.*

(Ad Completorium)

H ora completorii datur sepulture   [fol. 24]

    Corpus *Christi* nobile, spes vite future ;   50

Conditor aromate, complentur scripture,   Frag. Conditur.

Jugis sit memoria mortis michi cure.(1)

[Recommendatio]

Has horas canonicas cum devotione   Title from Horæ, 1536.
    [fol. 24 b.]

Christe tibi recolo pie racione,   Frag. "pia."

Tu, q*ui* pro me passus es amoris ardore,

Sis michi solacium mortis in agone.   56

Ve*rsus.*

Adoramus te, *Christe* et benedicimus tibi :   Verse.

    quia per sanctam crucem tuam redimisti mundum   Response.

Qui passus es *pro* nobis

Domine miserere nobis.   60

    Oratio.   Domine iesu. Amen.   Prayer. (*Page* 85.)

(1) Jugi sit memoria mors hec michi cure. . . . . . Printed
Hours and Fragment (*York*); Horæ 1536 (*Lincoln Cathedral Library*).

Appendix.

APPENDIX I.

ORDO MISSÆ
IN FESTO SANCTÆ TRINITATIS
SECUNDUM USUM MATRIS ECCLESIÆ
EBORACENSIS.

(From *MS.*, *York Minster Library*, xvi. A. 9.)

5 **Quando presbyter lavat manus ante missam dicat hanc orationem sequentem.**

Largire sensibus nostris, omnipotens pater, ut sic[*ut*] hic abluuntur inquinamenta manuum : ita a te mundentur pollutiones mentium, et crescat in nobis augmentum
10 sanctarum virtutum ; Per *Christum Dominum.*

Antiphona.

Introibo ad altare Dei, ad Deum qui lætificat iuventutem meam.

Psalmus. Judica me, Deus.

15 Gloria patri.

Kyrie eleyson.

Christe eleyson.

Kyrie eleyson

Pater noster.

20 **Sacerdos introeat ad Altare, præcedentibus in ordine ministris.**

Dicat :

Confitemini Domino quoniam bonus :

Quoniam in sæculum misericordia ejus.

25 Confiteor Deo, beatæ Mariæ, et omnibus sanctis eius et vobis, fratres, quia ego peccator peccavi nimis corde, ore, opere, omissione, mea culpa : ideo precor gloriosam dei genetricem Mariam et omnes sanctos Dei
29 et vos orare pro me.

A VERBAL RENDERING

OF THE

ORDINARY OF THE MASS,
WITH THE SERVICE OF TRINITY SUNDAY,
ACCORDING TO THE USE OF YORK.

When the presbyter washes his hands before mass, The Priest, before
let him say the prayer here following. Mass.

Grant to our understandings, Almighty Father, that
like as the filth of our hands is here washed away, so
the defilement of our minds may be cleansed by Thee,
and the growth of holy virtues may increase in us;
through Christ our Lord.

Anthem.

I will go in unto the altar. [*From* Ps. (43) xlii, 4.] On entering the
Psalm (43) xlii, and *Gloria Patri.* Church.

Lord, have mercy upon us.

Christ, have mercy upon us.

Lord, have mercy upon us.

Our Father, &c.

*Let the priest go in to the altar, the ministers going
in order before him.*

Let him say [the Versicle].

O give thanks unto the Lord, for he is gracious:
for his mercy endureth for ever. [Ps. (118) cxvii, 1.]

I confess to God, Blessed Mary and all His saints, The Confession
and to you, brethren, that, sinner, I have sinned ex- of the Priest.
ceedingly in heart, in mouth, in things done, in things *Page* 6, B. 42-3.
left undone, by my fault; wherefore I beseech Mary,
the glorious mother of God, and all the saints of God,
and you, to pray for me.

1   Misereatur vestri omnipotens Deus, et dimittat
vobis omnia peccata vestra; liberet vos ab omni malo,
conservet et confirmet in omni opere bono, et perducat
vos ad vitam æternam.
5   Amen.

Absolutionem et remissionem omnium peccatorum
vestrorum, spatium veræ pænitentiæ, emendationem
vitæ, gratiam et consolationem sancti Spiritus, tribuat
vobis omnipotens et misericors Deus.
10   **Chorus.** Amen.
**Factaque ante gradus altaris confessione, ascen-
dat ad altare dicens.**
Deus, tu conversus vivificabis nos.
Et plebs tua lætabitur in te.
15   Ostende nobis, Domine, misericordiam tuam.
Et salutare tuum da nobis.
Sacerdotes tui induantur justitiam.
Et sancti tui exultent.
Domine Deus virtutum converte nos.
20   Et ostende faciem tuam, [*et salvi erimus.*]
Domine exaudi orationem meam.
Et clamor meus ad [*te veniat*].
Dominus vobiscum.
Et cum spiritu tuo.
25   **Inclinatus ad altare dicat** Oremus.

Oratio.
Aufer a nobis, Domine, iniquitates nostras, ut ad
sancta sanctorum mereamur puris mentibus introire.
Per Dominum nostrum.
30   ¶. **Erectus signet se, et in dextro cornu altaris
dicat officium et cætera.**

[**In Festo sanctæ Trinitatis.   Officium.**
Benedicta sit sancta Trinitas atque indivisa Unitas:

(*The answer of the ministers and people and their confession are not inserted in the Manuscript.*) Confiteor in English. Page 8—10.

Almighty God have mercy upon you, and forgive you all your sins, deliver you from all evil, preserve and strengthen you in all goodness, and bring you to everlasting life. (*The Answer.*) Amen. The answer of the priest to the confession of the ministers and people.

[*The priest.*] Almighty and merciful God grant unto you absolution and remission of all your sins, space for true repentance, amendment of life, and the grace and consolation of the Holy Spirit. *The Choir.* Amen. The General Absolution. Page 6, B. 48.

And the confession ended before the altar step, let him go up to the altar, saying:

O God, when thou art turned again, thou wilt quicken
And thy people shall rejoice in thee.   [us.
Show us thy mercy, O Lord.
And grant us thy salvation. [Ps. (85) lxxxiv, 6 & 7.]
Let thy priests be clothed with righteousness.
And let thy saints rejoice.   [Ps. (132) cxxxi, 9.]
Turn us again, thou God of hosts.
And show the light of thy countenance, and we shall be whole. [Ps. (80) lxxix. 7.]
Lord hear my prayer.
And let my cry come unto thee. [Ps. (102) ci, 1.]
The Lord be with you.
And with thy spirit.

"*Inclining afore*" *the altar, let him say,* Let us pray.
Orison.

Take away from us, O Lord, our iniquities, that, with pure minds, we may be worthy to enter into the holy of holies; through Christ our Lord. The Orison.

Standing upright let him sign himself (with the cross), and at the right corner of the altar let him say the Office with Gloria Patri, *and* Kyrie eleyson, &c. The Office. Page 10, B. 8S, and Kyries.

The Office of Trinity Sunday.

Blessed be the Holy Trinity and the undivided

1 confitebimur ei quia fecit nobiscum misericordiam
   suam.

Psalmus.

Benedicamus Patri et Filio : cum Spiritu Sancto.]

5   **Et postea incenset altare.**
       In medio altaris erectis manibus incipiat Gloria
       in excelsis.
       Gloria in excelsis Deo. Et in terra pax hominibus
       bonæ voluntatis. Laudamus te, Benedicimus te, Ado-
10   ramus te, Glorificamus te. Gratias agimus tibi propter
       magnam gloriam tuam. Domine Deus, Rex cœlestis,
       Deus Pater omnipotens.
       Domine Fili unigenite, Jesu Christe. Domine Deus,
       Agnus Dei, Filius Patris, Qui tollis peccata mundi,(1)
15   suscipe deprecationem nostram. Qui sedes ad dexteram
       Patris, miserere nobis.
       Quoniam tu solus sanctus, Tu solus Dominus, Tu
       solus altissimus, Jesu Christe cum Sancto Spiritu, In
       gloria Dei Patris. Amen.
20   **Postea conversus sacerdos ad populum dicat:**
       Dominus vobiscum.
       [*Et cum spiritu tuo.*]
       Et reversus dicat Oremus. **cum collecta.**

[Oratio

25   Omnipotens sempiterne Deus, qui dedisti nobis
       famulis tuis, in confessione veræ fidei, æternæ Trinitatis
       gloriam agnoscere : et in potentia maiestatis adorare
       Unitatem, quæsumus, ut eiusdem fidei firmitate ab om-
       nibus semper muniamur adversis. In qua vivis et
30   regnas Deus. *per omnia sæcula sæculorum. Amen.*]

       Notandum quod ad missam juxta Romanum ordi

(1) The MS. does not insert *Qui tollis peccata mundi, miserere nobis.*

Unity : we will praise Him, for He hath wrought His merciful kindness upon us.

Psalm.

Let us bless the Father and the Son with the Holy Ghost.

And afterward let him cense the altar.

In the midst of the altar, with uplifted hands, let him begin the Gloria in Excelsis.

On high days. *Page 14, B. 115.*

Glory be to God on high, And in earth peace, towards men of goodwill. We praise thee, We bless thee, We worship thee, We glorify thee, We give thanks to thee for thy great glory, O Lord God, Heavenly King, God the Father Almighty.

The Gloria in Excelsis, or Angelic Hymn.

O Lord, the only-begotten Son Jesu Christ ; O Lord God, Lamb of God, Son of the Father, That takest away the sins of the world, receive our prayer. Thou that sittest at the right hand of the Father, have mercy upon us.

For thou only art holy ; Thou only art the Lord ; Thou only, O Christ Jesus, with the Holy Ghost, art most high in the glory of God the Father. Amen.

Afterwards let the priest turn to the people and say :

The Lord be with you.

Answer. And with thy spirit.

And let him turn to the altar again and say, Let us pray, *with the collect.*

The Collect of Trinity Sunday.

The Collect for the day.

Almighty and everlasting God, who hast given unto us, thy servants, grace by the confession of the true faith to acknowledge the glory of the eternal Trinity, and in the power of thy majesty to worship the Unity : We beseech thee that by stedfastness in this faith, we may evermore be defended from all adversities, in which [*Unity*] thou livest and reignest one God, world without end. Amen.

It is to be noted that at mass, according to the

1 nem una collecta dicitur propter unitatis sacramentum : et tres exemplo Domini, qui ter ante passionem
orasse legitur, vel propter Trinitatis mysterium :
quinque propter quinquepartitam Domini passionem,
5 in cuius commemoratione eadem celebrantur officia :
septem, quia septem dominicæ orationis petitiones ad
consecrationem eorum mysteriorum apostoli frequen-
tasse leguntur, vel ad impetranda (1) septem dona
Spiritus sancti : quem numerum (2) nemo excedere
10 ulla ratione permittitur.(3)

Dum legitur Epistola et canitur Gradale et Alleluya vel Tractus vel Tropus, sedeat cum ministris ad
legendum evangelium.
[Lectio libri apocalypsis beati Iohannis apostoli.
15 In diebus illis . . . . . in sæcula sæculorum.]

Dum petit diaconus benedictionem, respondeat
sacerdos :
Dominus aperiat tibi os ad legendum et nobis aures
ad intelligendum sanctum evangelium pacis. In nomine
20 Patris et Filii et Spiritus Sancti. Amen.

Et vicarius
Da mihi, Domine, sermonem rectum et benesonantem in os meum, ut placeant tibi verba mea ; et omnibus
audientibus propter nomen tuum in vitam æternam.

25   [Gradale
Benedictus es, Domine, qui intueris abyssos et sedes
super cherubim.
Versus.
Benedicite Deum cœli : quia fecit nobiscum miseri-
30 cordiam suam.
Alleluya.

(1) impetrandam—MS.   (2) numeros—MS.

Roman Order, one collect is said on account of the
sacrament of Unity: and three after the example of our
Lord, who is read to have prayed thrice before his pas-
sion, or on account of the mystery of the Trinity: five
on account of the fivefold passion of the Lord, in com-
memoration of whom these same offices are celebrated:
seven because the apostles are read to have repeated the
seven petitions of the Lord's prayer for the consecration
of the mysteries, or for the obtaining of the seven gifts
of the Holy Spirit, and this number no one is on any
account allowed to exceed.

At the reading of the epistle, and the singing of the
gradual and alleluya, or the tract or trope, let (the priest)
sit with the ministers until the gospel is to be read.

The portion of scripture appointed for the epistle is [*Chapter* iv. *vv.* 1—10] of the Book of the Revelation of Saint John.

When the deacon asks a blessing, let the priest *answer:*

The Lord open thy mouth to read, and our ears to understand the holy gospel of peace. In the name of the Father, and of the Son, and of the Holy Ghost. Amen.

And let the vicar[-choral answer]

Give me, O Lord, unto my mouth, speech, right and well-sounding, that my words may be pleasing unto thee; and for thy name's sake [*may they be*] to all that hear them unto everlasting life.

The Gradual of Trinity Sunday.

Blessed art thou that beholdest the depths, and sittest upon the cherubims. [Dan. (*Apocr.*) iii, 32.]

Verse of Gradual.

Bless ye God, ye heavens, for he hath wrought his merciful kindness upon us.

Alleluya.

(3) The long rubric as to the ending of the collects is given in the notes.

1   **Versus**
     Benedictus es Domine Deus patrum nostrorum : et
laudabilis in sæcula.

             Sequentia.
5   Benedicta [*sit beata Trinitas . . . . a iudice præmia.*]
             Evangelium
     In illo tempore . . . . . . eternam.]
     Post lectum evangelium dicat sacerdos : (1)
     Benedictus qui venit in nomine Domini.
10   **Postea osculetur textum.**
     Statim sacerdos in medio altaris incipiat excelsa
voce :
     Credo in unum Deum . . . . . venturi sæculi. Amen.
     ¶. **Notandum est quod** Credo **dicitur generaliter**
15 **omnibus dominicis diebus per totum annum** . . . (&c)
     Dum canitur . Credo **subdiaconus cum textu et**
acolytus cum thuribulo chorum circumeant.   Post
conversus sacerdos ad populum dicat :
     Dominus vobiscum.
20   **Et reversus dicat :**
     Oremus.
     Et canat cum suis ministris offertorium.

             [Offertorium
     Benedictus sit Deus Pater, Unigenitusque Dei
25 Filius, Sanctus quoque Spiritus, quia fecit nobiscum
misericordiam suam.] (2)   •
     Et componat hostiam super corporales pannos
et dicat :
     Suscipe, Sancta Trinitas, hanc oblationem, quam
30 ego miser indignus peccator offero in honore tuo, et
beatæ Mariæ et omnium sanctorum tuorum, pro peccatis
et offensionibus meis, et pro salute vivorum et requie·

     (1) The Rouen edition of the Missal (1517) and other
editions here add "*secrete.*"

Verse of the Alleluya.

Blessed art thou, O Lord God of our fathers, and worthy to be praised for evermore. [*From* Dan. (*Apocr.*] iii, 3.)

The Sequence of Trinity Sunday.   The Sequence.

Blessed be the Holy Trinity, &c.

The Gospel. Trinity Sunday.

[St John, iii, 1—15.]   Reading the Gospel. Page 16, B. 153.

After the Gospel is read, let the priest say :

Blessed is he who cometh in the name of the Lord.

Then let him kiss the book of the gospels.

Forthwith let the priest in the midst of the altar begin with a loud voice :

[The Nicene Creed, known as the "Mass-Creed."]   The Creed. Page 18, B. 195.

It is to be noted that the Creed is said without exception on all Sundays throughout the year, &c. &c.

Whilst the Creed is in singing let the subdeacon with the book of the gospels and the acolyte with the censer go about the quire. Afterwards let the priest turn to the people and say :

The Lord be with you.

And let him turn again (to the altar) and say :

Let us pray.

And let him sing the Offertory with his ministers.   Offertory.

The Offertory. Trinity Sunday.

Blessed be God the Father, and the Only-begotten   Page 22, B. 241-4
Son of God, and also the Holy Spirit, who hath wrought His loving-kindness upon us.(2)

And let him lay in order the host upon the corporas-   Presenting the Oblations, or *cloths and say :*   Sacrifice.

Accept, O Holy Trinity, this oblation which, miserable, unworthy sinner, I offer in honour of thee and blessed Mary and all thy saints ; for mine own sins and offences, for the salvation of the living and the repose

(2) After the Offertory in parish churches on Sundays came the Bidding of Prayer in the vulgar tongue.—*Pages* 62—80.

1 fidelium defunctorum. In nomine Patris et Filii et
Spiritus Sancti.

Item calicem cum vino et aqua et tunc dicat:

Acceptum sit sacrificium istud omnipotenti Deo.

5 **Lavet manus et dicat:**

Lavabo inter innocentes manus meas: et circum-
dabo altare tuam, Domine.

Hymnus.

Veni creator spiritus **& cætera**

10 **Postea ante medium altare inclinatus dicat:**

In spiritu humilitatis et animo contrito suspiciamur
Domine, a te, et sic fiat sacrificium nostrum in con-
spectu tuo, ut a te suscipiatur hodie: et placeat tibi,
Domine Deus meus.

15 **Et ingrediendo osculetur altare, et signet sacrificium dicendo**

Sit signa✠tum ordi✠natum et sancti✠ficatum hoc
sacrificium nostrum.

Post versus ad populum dicat.

20 Orate, fratres et sorores, pro me peccatore ut meum
pariterque vestrum Domino Deo acceptum sit sacrificium.

Chorus (1) respondeat

Exaudiat te Dominus in die tribulationis

25 **usque** Memor sit omnis sacrificii tui.

Post versus ad altare dicat secretas:

[Secreta.

28 Sanctifica quæsumus Domine Deus noster per sancti

(1) The Rouen edition of 1517 and other printed Missals
insert "*secrete*"—a very significant alteration.

of the faithful departed, in the name of the Father and of the Son and of the Holy Ghost.

And the chalice also with wine and water, and then let him say:

May this sacrifice be acceptable to Almighty God.

Let him wash his hands and say:

I will wash my hands among the innocent (*in innocency*): and I will compass thine altar, O Lord. [Ps. (26) xxv, 6.] *The Washing. Page 24, C. 123.*

The Hymn.

" Come, Holy Ghost, our souls inspire."

Afterwards let him bow before the midst of the altar and say:

In a spirit of humility and with a contrite mind may we be accepted of Thee, O Lord, and may our sacrifice be so offered in thy sight that it may be accepted of Thee this day, and may be pleasing to Thee, O Lord, my God. *Prayer for acceptance of the Sacrifice.*

And let him go up to and kiss the altar, and sign the sacrifice (with the sign of the cross), saying: *Page 24, B. 263.*

May this our sacrifice be signed, " set in order " (*Exodus* xl, 23), and sanctified. *The old form of Oblation.*

Afterwards, turning to the people, let him say:

Pray, brethren and sisters, for me a sinner, that the sacrifice, mine and yours not less, may be accepted by the Lord our God. *The priest asks the people's prayers. Page 24, B. 265.*

Let the choir answer:

The Lord hear thee in the day of trouble : the Name of the God of Jacob defend thee ; *Answer. Page 24, B. 274.*

Send thee help from the sanctuary : and strengthen thee out of Sion ;

Remember all thy offerings. [Ps. (20) xix, 1—3.]

Afterwards turning to the altar, let him say his secret prayers. *The priest prays secretly. Page 26, B. 280.*

For Trinity Sunday.

Sanctify, we beseech Thee, O Lord our God, the

1 tui nominis invocationem et per Unigeniti tui virtutem
huius oblationis hostiam, et cooperante Spiritu Sancto,
per eam nosmet ipsos tibi perfice munus æternum.
Qui in Trinitatis perfectione]

5   **Et concludat.**

Per Dominum nostrum Jesum Christum filium
tuum : qui tecum vivit et regnat.
Et dicat
Per omnia sæcula sæculorum.   **Cum alta voce.**
10   **Et sequatur præfatio quæ pertinet ad diem.**
**Subnotatur. Pelagius [papa] constituit cantari
has ix præfationes : I. de Nativitate ; II. de Appari-
tione ; III. de Quadragesima ; IIII. de Passione et de
Cruce ; V. de Pascha ; VI. [de] Ascensione ; VII. de
15 Pentecoste ; VIII. de Trinitate ; IX. de Apostolis
Petro et Paulo, et etiam de pluribus apostolis dicitur.
Gregorius [papa] decimam adiecit de sancto Andrea
apostolo, et etiam Urbanus [papa] (1) undecimam de
Sancta Maria addidit.**
20   Per omnia sæcula sæculorum.
[Amen]
Dominus vobiscum
[Et cum spiritu tuo]
Sursum corda.
25   Habemus ad Dominum.
Gratias agamus Domino Deo nostro
Vere dignum et iustum est, æquum et salutare, nos
tibi semper et ubique gratias agere, Domine, Sancte
Pater, Omnipotens,
30   **[Præfatio in die Trinitatis et in dominicis diebus
quando de dominica agitur, a festo sanctæ Trinitatis
usque ad Adventum.**
Æterne Deus, Qui cum unigenito Filio tuo et
Spiritu Sancto unus es Deus, unus es Dominus : non
35 in unius singularitate personæ, sed in unius Trinitate
substantiæ.   Quod enim de tua gloria, revelante te,
credimus, hoc de Filio tuo, hoc de Spiritu Sancto, sine

(1) "*Papa*," erased.

sacrifice now being offered by the invocation of thy holy name, and by the power of thy Only-begotten; and do Thou, the Holy Ghost working therewith, by it perfect us, even us, for an everlasting offering unto Thee, who livest and reignest in the perfection of the Trinity.

And let him end (except when another ending is appointed, as on Trinity Sunday).

Through Jesus Christ thy Son, who liveth and reigneth with Thee.

And say For ever and ever *with a loud voice.*
Then let there follow the preface for the day.

The priest ends the *secreta* and

NOTE. Pope Pelagius appointed these nine prefaces to be sung: The first, [at masses] of the Nativity; the second, of the Epiphany; the third, of Lent; the fourth, of the Passion, and [festivals of] the Cross; the fifth, of Easter-tide; the sixth, of the Ascension; the seventh, of Whitsuntide; the eighth, of Trinity; the ninth, is said [at masses] of the apostles Peter and Paul, and also of many apostles. Pope Gregory added a tenth of Saint Andrew, the apostle; and, moreover, Pope Urban added an eleventh [for masses] of Saint Mary.

For ever and ever. [The ending of the *Secreta.*]

Amen.

begins the preface with these words. *Page* 28, C. 145.

The Lord be with you.

And with thy spirit.

Lift up your hearts.

Page 28, B. 307.

Answer. We lift them up unto the Lord.

Let us give thanks unto our Lord God.

It is very meet and right, just and salutary that we should at all times and in all places give thanks unto thee, O Lord, Holy Father, Almighty,

The constant beginning of the Preface,

(*Proper Preface for Trinity.*) Everlasting God, who with thy only begotten Son and the Holy Ghost art one God, and one Lord: not in the singleness of one Person, but in the Trinity of one substance. For what we believe of thy glory, as thou dost reveal, the same do we think of the Son, the same of the Holy

continued as appointed for Trinity Sunday.

1 differentiæ discretione sentimus. Ut in confessione
veræ sempiternæque Deitatis, et in Personis proprietas,
et in essentia unitas, et in Maiestate adoretur æqualitas.
Quam laudant angeli atque archangeli cherubyn quoque
5 ac seraphyn, qui non cessant clamare una voce, di-
centes :]

Sanctus, Sanctus, Sanctus, Dominus Deus Sabaoth,
pleni sunt cæli et terra gloria tua : Hosanna in excelsis.
Benedictus qui venit in [*nomine*] Domini ; Hosanna in
10 excelsis.

[CANON MISSÆ.]
Junctis manibus sacerdos inclinet se dicens :

Te igitur clementissime Pater, per Iesum Christum
Filium tuum Dominum nostrum supplices roga-
15 mus ac petimus :

**Hic erigat se et osculetur altare, faciendo signum
super calicem.**

Uti accepta habeas et benedicas hæc ✠ dona, hæc ✠
munera, hæc ✠ sancta sacrificia illibata, In primis quæ
20 tibi offerimus pro ecclesia tua sancta catholica, quam
pacificare, custodire, adunare, et regere digneris toto
orbe terrarum, [una cum famulo tuo Papa nostro *N.*](1)
et antistite nostro *N.* et rege nostro *N.* et omnibus
orthodoxis, atque catholicæ et apostolicæ fidei cul-
25 toribus.

Hic commemoratio vivorum.

Memento, Domine, famulorum famularumque tuarum *N.* et omnium circumstantium atque omnium fidelium Christianorum quorum tibi fides cognita est et
30 nota devotio ; pro quibus tibi offerimus vel qui tibi
offerunt hoc sacrificium laudis, pro se suisque omnibus,
pro redemptione animarum suarum, pro spe salutis et
incolumitatis suæ, tibique reddunt vota sua æterno Deo,
34 vivo et vero.

(1) Mention of Pope erased in MS.

Ghost, without distinction of difference ; so that in the confession of the true and everlasting Godhead there may be adored a property in the Persons, a unity in the essence, and an equality in the majesty : Which Angels and Archangels are praising, Cherubim also and Seraphim, who cease not to cry with one voice, saying :

Holy, Holy, Holy, Lord God of hosts, heaven and earth are full of thy glory; Hosanna in the highest. Blessed is he that cometh in the name of the Lord; Hosanna in the highest. *The Sanctus. Page 28, B. 308.*

CANON OF THE MASS.

Let the priest with his hands together bow himself and say :

Thee therefore most merciful Father, through Jesus Christ, thy Son, our Lord, we humbly pray and beseech : *Renewed prayer for acceptance of the Oblations.*

Here let him raise himself and kiss the altar, and making a cross over the chalice (let him say) :

That thou wouldest hold accepted and bless these gifts, these offerings, these holy undefiled sacrifices, which first of all we offer to thee for thy holy catholic church, which do thou vouchsafe to keep in peace, to watch over, to knit together and govern, throughout the whole world, together with thy servant our Pope, and our Bishop N, and our King N, and all right believers, and maintainers of the Catholic and Apostolic faith. *Prayers for the whole Church, the King, and Faithful,* *Page 28, B. 331.*

Here the Commemoration of the living.

Remember, O Lord, thy servants and handmaidens, N and all here standing around, and all faithful Christians, whose faith is known and devotion noted by thee ; for whom we offer unto thee, or who are offering unto thee, this sacrifice of praise, for themselves and all theirs, for the redemption of their souls, for the hope of their salvation and safety, and unto thee, eternal God, living and true, are rendering their vows. *with special mention of the congregation, in the name of all whom the sacrifice is offered in thanksgiving for redemption and for the hope of glory.*

1   Communicantes et memoriam venerantes: In primis, gloriosæ et semper virginis Mariæ, genetricis Dei et Domini nostri Jesu Christi, sed et beatorum apostolorum ac martyrum tuorum, Petri, Pauli, Andreæ, 5 Jacobi, Johannis, Thomæ, Jacobi, Philippi, Bartholomæi, Matthæi, Simonis et Thaddæi, Lini, Cleti, Clementis, Sixti, Cornelii, Cypriani, Laurentii, Grisogoni, Johannis et Pauli, Cosmæ et Damiani, et omnium sanctorum tuorum: quorum meritis precibusque concedas, ut in omnibus protectionis tuæ muniamur auxilio. 10 Per eundem Christum Dominum nostrum.

Eugenius septem(1) instituit. Et cum dicat, parum tangat calicem, dicens:

Hanc igitur oblationem servitutis nostræ, sed et 15 cunctæ familiæ tuæ, quæsumus, Domine, ut placatus accipias, diesque nostros in tua pace disponas, atque ab æterna damnatione nos eripi, et in electorum tuorum jubeas grege numerari. Per Christum Dominum nostrum. Amen.

20   Quam oblationem tu Deus omnipotens, in omnibus, quæsumus, bene✠dictam, adscrip✠tam, ra✠tam, rationabilem, acceptabilemque facere digneris, ut nobis cor✠pus et san✠guis fiat dilectissimi Filii tui Domini nostri Jesu Christi.

25   **Alexander papa instituit. Inclinato capite, super linteamina,(2) hostiam accipiendo:**

Qui pridie quam pateretur, accepit panem in sanctas et venerabiles manus suas, **Hic elevet oculos** et elevatis oculis suis in cœlum, ad te Deum Patrem suum omni- 30 potentem, tibi gratias agens, bene✠dixit, ac **Hic tangat hostiam** fregit deditque discipulis suis dicens: Accipite et manducate ex hoc omnes, Hoc est enim(3) corpus meum. Simili modo posteaquam cœnatum est, accipiens et hunc præclarum calicem in sanctas et venera-

34

       (1) VII—MS.   (2) linthiamina—MS.

In communion with and venerating the memory, first *Communion with saints departed,* of all, of the glorious and ever-virgin Mary, the mother of our God and Lord Jesus Christ, as also of thy blessed apostles and martyrs, Peter, Paul, Andrew, James, John, Thomas, James, Philip, Bartholomew, Matthew, Simon, and Thaddæus, Linus, Cletus, Clement, Sixtus, Cornelius, Cyprian, Laurence, Grisogonus, John and Paul, Cosmas and Damian, and of all thy saints: To whose merits and prayers grant that we may *and prayer for their intercession.* in all things be defended by the help of thy protection, through the same Jesus Christ, our Lord.

Eugenius appointed the seven [words *or* crosses]. *And whilst speaking, let him somewhat touch the chalice, and say:*

This oblation therefore of our service as also of thy *Renewed presentation of the oblations,* whole household, we beseech thee, O Lord, that having been reconciled thou wouldest accept; and wouldest order our days in thy peace, and ordain that we be delivered from eternal damnation and numbered with the flock of thine elect; through Christ our Lord. Amen.

Which oblation, do thou, we beseech thee, O God *Page 36, B. 399. and prayer that God would accept them for the purpose of the Sacrament.* Almighty, vouchsafe to render altogether blessed, counted, reckoned, reasonable and acceptable, that it may be made unto us the Body and Blood of thy most beloved Son, our Lord Jesus Christ.

Pope Alexander appointed [*the* Qui pridie]. *With head bowed over the linen cloths* (*let him say*) *at taking up the host:*

Who on the day before he suffered took bread into *The Institution.* his holy and most honoured hands, (*Here let him raise his eyes*) and with his eyes raised up towards heaven, unto Thee, O God, his Father almighty, giving thanks to Thee, he blessed and (*Here let him touch the host*) brake and gave to his disciples, saying, Take and eat ye all of this, for this is my Body. In like manner after supper, taking also this most excellent cup into his holy and most

(3) Without capital letter in MS.

1 biles manus suas, item tibi gratias agens, bene✠dixit
dcditque discipulis suis, dicens : Accipite et bibite ex
eo omnes, Hic est enim calix sanguinis mei,(1) novi et
æterni testamenti, mysterium fidei, [*here in MS. is a*
5 *space of two half lines as if for a rubric*] qui pro vobis
et pro multis effundetur in remissionem peccatorum,
Hic superponit corporalia.

Hæc quotiescunque feceritis, in mei memoriam
facietis.
10 **Hic extendit brachia ad modum crucis**

Unde et memores, Domine, nos tui servi, sed et
plebs tua sancta ejusdem Christi Filii tui Domini Dei
nostri tam beatæ passionis, necnon et ab inferis resurrectionis, sed et in cælos gloriosæ ascensionis, offerimus
15 præclaræ maiestati tuæ de tuis donis ac datis

Hic retrahat brachia et faciat signum crucis.
           ✠   ✠   ✠
Hostiam puram, hostiam sanctam, hostiam imma-
          ✠   ✠
culatam, panem sanctum vitæ æternæ, et calicem salutis
perpetuæ.(2)
20 Supra quæ propitio ac sereno vultu respicere digneris, et accepta habere sicut accepta habere dignatus
es munera pueri tui justi Abel, et sacrificium patri-
archæ nostri Abrahæ, et quod tibi obtulit summus
sacerdos tuus Melchisedech, sanctum sacrificium, im-
25 maculatam hostiam.

Supplices te rogamus, omnipotens Deus, jube hæc
perferri per manus sancti angeli tui in sublime altare
tuum, in conspectu divinæ majestatis tuæ, ut quotquot
ex hac altaris participatione, sacrosanctum Filii tui
30 Cor✠pus et san✠guinem(3) sumpserimus omni bene✠

(1) Without capital letter in MS.
(2) In the MS. these crosses are inserted above the line in
very pale red ink—apparently *secundâ manu.*

honoured hands, and likewise giving thanks unto Thee,
he blessed and gave to his disciples, saying, Take and
drink ye all of this, for this is the cup of my Blood,
of the new and everlasting covenant, a mystery of faith,
which shall be shed for you and for many for the
remission of sins :

Here the priest covers the chalice with the corporasses.

As often as ye do (*or* offer) these˟ things; ye shall
do them in memory of me.

Here the priest spreadeth abroad his arms after the Page 42, C. 242.
manner of a cross.

Wherefore also we thy servants, O Lord, and also
thy holy people, in memory as well of the blessed
passion of the same Christ, thy Son, our Lord, as of
his resurrection from the dead, and also of his glorious
ascension into the heavens do offer unto thy excellent
majesty, of thine own gifts, albeit given unto us,

Continued presentation, in remembrance of Christ, of the oblations given to God, His own of His own.

Here let him draw back his arms and make the sign Page 42, C. 243.
of the cross
a pure, a holy, an undefiled sacrifice, the holy bread of
eternal life, and the cup of everlasting salvation ;

Upon which do thou vouchsafe to look with favourable and gracious countenance, and hold them accepted,
as thou didst vouchsafe to hold accepted the offerings
of thy righteous servant Abel, and the sacrifice of our
forefather Abraham, and that holy sacrifice, the pure
offering, which thy high priest Melchizedek did offer
unto thee.

Still is their acceptance prayed for,

We humbly beseech thee, Almighty God, Command
that these things be carried by the hands of thy holy
Angel, to thy altar on high in the sight of thy divine
majesty, that as many of us as of this partaking of the
altar shall have received the most sacred Body and
Blood of thy Son, may be fulfilled with all heavenly

and that all who eat of the altar may be partakers of the benefits of the Sacrament.

(3) Without capital letter in MS.

1 dictione cœlesti et gratia repleamur, Per eundem
Christum Dominum nostrum. Amen.

Memento etiam, Domine, famulorum famularumque
tuarum N. qui nos præcesserunt cum signo fidei, et
5 dormiunt in somno pacis ; ipsis, Domine, et omnibus in
Christo quiescentibus locum refrigerii, lucis, et pacis ut
indulgeas deprecamur. Per eundem Christum, Dominum nostrum. Amen.

Nobis quoque peccatoribus, famulis tuis, de multi-
10 tudine miserationum tuarum sperantibus, partem ali-
quam et societatem donare digneris, cum tuis sanctis
Apostolis et Martyribus, cum Johanne, Stephano, Mat-
thia, Barnaba, Ignatio, Alexandro, Marcellino, Petro,
Felicitate, Perpetua, Agatha, Lucia, Agnete, Cæcilia,
15 Anastasia, et cum omnibus sanctis tuis, intra quorum
nos consortium, non æstimator meriti, sed veniæ, quæsumus, largitor admitte. Per Christum, Dominum
nostrum, [*space in MS.*] per quem hæc omnia, Domine,
semper bona creas, sancti✠ficas, vivi✠ficas, bene✠dicis,
20 et præstas nobis.

Per ip✠sum, et cum ip✠so, et in ip✠so est tibi
Dèo Patri omnipotenti in unitate Spiritus sancti omnis
honor et gloria,

Per omnia sæcula sæculorum.
25   Amen.

Oremus. Præceptis salutaribus moniti, et divina
institutione formati audemus dicere :

Pater noster, qui es in cœlis, sanctificetur nomen
tuum. Adveniat regnum tuum. Fiat voluntas tua
30 sicut in cœlo, sic in terra. Panem nostrum quotidia-
num da nobis hodie : et dimitte nobis debita nostra,
sicut ut nos dimittimus debitoribus nostris : et ne nos
inducas in tentationem,
34   Sed libera nos a malo. Amen.

benediction and grace, through the same Jesus Christ our Lord. Amen.

Remember also, O Lord, thy servants and handmaidens N, who have gone before us with the sign of faith, and sleep the sleep of peace ; unto them, O Lord, and to all that rest in Christ, we entreat that thou wouldest grant a place of refreshing, light, and peace ; through the same Christ, our Lord. Amen.

The Second Memento, or prayer for the faithful departed, Page 42, B. 454.

Unto us sinners also, thy servants, that hope in the multitude of thy mercies, vouchsafe to grant some part and fellowship with thy holy apostles and martyrs, with John, Stephen, Matthias, Barnabas, Ignatius, Alexander, Marcellinus, Peter, Felicity, Perpetua, Agatha, Lucy, Agnes, Cecilia, Anastasia, and with all thy saints, unto whose company do thou admit us, not weighing our merits, but freely granting pardon, we beseech thee; through Christ, our Lord, by whom all these good (*creatures*) thou, O Lord, ever createst, sanctifiest, fillest with life, blessest, and bestowest upon us.

and for fellowship with them.

Through him and with him, and in him is unto thee, God the Father almighty, in the unity of the Holy Ghost, all honour and glory, world without end. Amen.

"The second Sacring."

Page 44, B. 482.

[HERE ENDS THE CANON.]

Let us pray. Admonished by healthful precepts and informed by the divine instruction, we are bold to say :

Our Father, which art in heaven, Hallowed be thy Name. Thy kingdom come. Thy will be done, As in heaven, so in earth. Give us this day our daily bread. And forgive us our debts, As we forgive our debtors. And lead us not into temptation ;

The Lord's Prayer. Page 46, B. 484.

The people. But deliver us from evil.
The Priest. Amen.

Page 46, B. 488.

1   Libera nos, quæsumus, Domine, ab omnibus malis,
praeteritis, praesentibus, et futuris: et intercedente pro
nobis beata et gloriosa semper virgine Dei genetrice
Maria, et beatis Apostolis tuis Petro et Paulo atque
5 Andrea, cum omnibus Sanctis tuis.

**Hic accipiat patenam et osculetur istam : signat
eadem in facie ✠ pectore ✠ a capitis vertice (1)
usque ad pectus ✠ ad dextram usque ad sinistram,
dicendo :**

10   Da propitius pacem in diebus nostris ; ut ope misericordiæ tuæ adiuti, et a peccato simus semper liberi, et
ab omni purturbatione securi.

Et dicat

Per eundem Dominum nostrum

15   **Et frangat corpus in tres partes**

Jesum Christum Filium tuum qui tecum regnat in
unitate spiritus Sancti, Deus, Per omnia saecula saecu-
lorum

Pax Do✠mini sit sem✠per vo✠biscum.

20   Et cum spiritu tuo.

Agnus Dei, qui tollis [*peccata mundi, miserere nobis.*

Agnus Dei, qui tollis peccata mundi, miserere nobis

*Agnus Dei, qui tollis peccata mundi, dona nobis
pacem.*]

25   **Tertiam partem in sanguinem et dicat:**

Hæc sacrosancta commixtio corporis et sanguinis
Domini nostri Jesu Christi, fiat nobis et omnibus su-
mentibus salus mentis et corporis ; et ad vitam æternam
capessendam præparatio salutaris.   Per eundem Chris-
30 tum Dominum nostrum.   Amen.

**Det osculari calicem et corporalia et [? *ut*] postea
erectus dare[*t*] pacem ministris, dicens :**

(1) a capite *uertite*—MS.

Deliver us, we beseech thee, O Lord, from all evils *Page 46, B. 406-7.*
past, present and to come; and inasmuch as there is
interceding for us the blessed and glorious ever-virgin
mother of God, Mary, and thy blessed apostles Peter
and Paul and Andrew, with all thy saints.

*Here let him take the paten and kiss it: he makes
a cross therewith on his face, [and] breast: from the
crown of the head down to the breast, on the right across
to the left, saying:*

Favourably give peace in our days, that we, being
succoured by the help of thy merciful kindness, may
both be free from sin, and safe from troubles;

And let him say:

Through the same, our Lord,

And let him break the Body into three pieces.   The Fraction.

Jesus Christ thy Son, who liveth and reigneth with
thee, in the unity of the Holy Ghost, God, world without end. Amen.

The peace of God be with you always.

And with thy spirit.

O Lamb of God, that takest away the sins of the   The Agnus.
world, have mercy upon us.   *Page 46, B. 508.*

O Lamb of God, that takest away the sins of the
world, have mercy upon us.

O Lamb of God, that takest away the sins of the
world, grant us thy peace.

Let him put the third piece into the Blood and say: The Commixture.

May this all-holy mingling of the Body and Blood
of our Lord Jesus Christ be unto us and to all that
receive, health of mind and body, and a healthful preparation for laying hold on eternal life, through the
same Christ our Lord. Amen.

Let him give (to himself) *to kiss the chalice and
the corporasses, and* (that), *risen up, he might give the* The Pax.
Pax *to the ministers, saying:*   *Page 48, B. 513.*

MASS-BOOK.   8

1   Habete vinculum pacis et caritatis ut apti sitis
sacrosanctis mysteriis Dei.

Oremus.

Domine, sancte Pater, omnipotens æterne Deus, da
5 nobis hoc corpus et sanguinem Filii tui Domini Dei
nostri ita sumere ut mereamur per hoc remissionem
omnium peccatorum nostrorum accipere et tuo Sancto
Spiritu repleri ; quia tu es Deus et præter te non est
alius, nisi tu solus ; Qui vivis et regnas Deus per
10 omnia sæcula sæculorum. Amen.

Perceptio corporis et sanguinis tui, Domine Jesu
Christe, quam ego indignus sumere præsumo, non mihi
veniat ad judicium nec ad condemnationem, sed pro
tua pietate prosit mihi ad tutamentum animæ et cor-
15 poris ; Qui cum Deo Patre et Spiritu Sancto vivis et
regnas Deus, per omnia sæcula sæculorum. Amen.

Domine Jesu Christe, Fili Dei vivi, qui ex volun-
tate Patris, cooperante Spiritu Sancto, per mortem tuam
mundum vivificasti ; libera me, per hoc sacrum corpus
20 et sanguinem tuum ab omnibus iniquitatibus meis et
universis malis meis ; et fac me tuis obedire præceptis,
et a te nunquam in perpetuum separari permittas ; Qui
cum Deo Patre et eodem Spiritu Sancto vivis et regnas
Deus per omnia sæcula [sæculorum.]   Amen.

25   **Ad corpus**
Corpus Domini nostri Jesu Christi sit mihi remedium sempiternum in vitam æternam.   Amen.

Ad sanguinem.

Sanguis Domini nostri Jesu Christi conservet me
30 in vitam æternam.   Amen.

Ad corpus et sanguinem.

Corpus et sanguis Domini nostri Jesu Christi cus-
todiat corpus meum et animam meam in vitam æternam.
34 Amen.

Receive the bond of peace and charity that ye may be meet for the most holy mysteries of God.

Let us pray.

O Lord, holy Father, Almighty everlasting God, grant us so to receive this Body and Blood of thy Son the Lord, our God, that we may be worthy thereby to obtain remission of all our sins and to be replenished by thy Holy Spirit; for thou art God, and beside thee, there is none other, but thou only, Who livest and reignest God, world without end. Amen.

Prayer for worthy reception by priest and people.

The Priest for himself.

May the partaking of thy Body and Blood, O Lord Jesu Christ, which I unworthy, am daring to receive, come upon me neither unto judgment nor unto condemnation, but for thy pity's sake may it be profitable unto me for defence of soul and body; who with God the Father and the Holy Ghost livest and reignest God, world without end. Amen.

Prayer at reception by priest.

O Lord Jesu Christ, Son of the living God, who of the will of the Father, and with the co-operation of the Holy Ghost, hast by thy death given life to the world; Deliver me by this thy holy Body and Blood from all my iniquities, and from all that is evil in me; and make me to be obedient to thy commandments, and never suffer me to be for ever separated from thee; who with God the Father and the same Holy Spirit livest and reignest God, world without end. Amen.

At taking the Body.

The Body of our Lord Jesus Christ be unto me an everlasting medicine unto eternal life. Amen.

At receiving the Blood.

The Blood of our Lord Jesus Christ preserve me unto everlasting life. Amen.

At receiving the Body and Blood.

The Body and the Blood of our Lord Jesus Christ preserve my body and my soul unto everlasting life. Amen.

1   [" *Resinceret sacerdos manus suas.*"—Rubr. Missalis
Sarum.]

Quod ore sumpsimus, Domine, pura mente capia-
mus : et de munere temporali fiat nobis remedium
5 sempiternum in vitam eternam. Amen.

Hæc nos, Domine, communio purget a crimine, et
cœlestis remedii faciat esse consortes. Per Christum
Dominum nostrum. Amen.

[Communio.

10   Benedicimus Deum cœli et coram omnibus viventi-
bus confitebimur ei :

Quia fecit nobiscum misericordiam suam.]

[Postcommunio

Proficiat nobis ad salutem corporis et animæ, Do-
15 mine Deus, huius sacramenti perceptio et sempiternæ
Sanctæ Trinitatis ciusdemque individuæ Unitatis con-
fessio. In qua vivis et regnas Deus, per omnia sæcula
sæculorum.]

[" *Deinde diaconus.*

20   (e.g. In Festo S. Trinitatis.)   Benedicamus Domino
In alio vero tempore.

Ite, missa est."—*Rubr. Missalis Sarum.*]

When the priest has rinsing done.

Page 54, B. 576.

What we have taken with our mouth, O Lord, may Prayer in the name of the communicants we receive with a pure mind ; and from a temporal gift (2 Cor. iv, 18) may it be made unto us an everlasting remedy unto eternal life. Amen.

May this communion, O Lord, cleanse us from guilt, and make us to be partakers of the heavenly remedy, through Christ, our Lord. Amen.

The Communion-Anthem for Trinity Sunday. at the south end. *Page* 54, B. 581.

We bless the God of heaven, and will praise him in the sight of all that live ; for he hath wrought his merciful kindness upon us. [*From* Tobit xii, 6.]

The Postcommon or Prayer after the Communion.

May the receiving of this sacrament, O Lord God, be profitable unto us for the health of body and soul; and also the confession of the eternal Holy Trinity, and of the same undivided Unity, in which Thou livest and reignest, for ever and ever.

The deacon. Let us bless the Lord.

At other times. Depart, the congregation is dis- *Page* 56, B. 604. missed. ["Go ye, Mass is done."—*Myroure* (E. E. T. S.), 332.]

After *Ite, missa est*, the priest standeth in the midst of the altar and so blesseth the people. (*Meditacyons, f.* 25.)

The missal appoints the prayer *Placeat tibi* to be *Page* 56, B. 607. said by the priest, and adds other devotions for priest and clerks, beginning with the canticle *Benedicite omnia opera* (the Song of the Three Children), as an anthem, and ending with the collect, *Deus qui tribus pueris.*

APPENDIX II.

AUTHORIZED EXPOSITIONS

OF THE

DOCTRINE OF THE EUCHARIST PUT FORTH IN ENGLISH,
CONTEMPORARY WITH THE MSS. OF THE
LAY MASS BOOK.

1. EXTRACT FROM THE CATECHISM OF JOHN THORESBY, ARCHBISHOP OF YORK,

A.D. 1357.   *Put forth with the advice of his clergy, the 25th Nov.*, 1357.

(From the authentic MS., Thoresby's Register, *fol.* 296 *b.*)

THE SEVEN SACRAMENTS.

[*The Sacrament of the Altar.*]

Every man and woman, that is come to age,

The ferthe is the sacrement of the auter,
cristes owen bodi in likeness of brede,
als hale as he toke it of that blessed maiden ;
whilk ilk man *and* woman, that of eld is,   4

ought to receive the Body of Christ at Easter,

aught forto resceyve anes in the yhere,
that is at sai, at paskes, als hali kirke uses,
when thai er clensed of syn thurgh penaunce,

on pain of excommunication, unless a reasonable cause be shown.

of payne of doyng + out of hali kirke.   8
bot if thai forbere it be skilwise cause,
that aught to be knawen to thaim that sal gif it,
for he that takes it worthili, takes his salvation,
and who-so unworthili, takes his dampnation.   12

The corresponding Paragraph, from the original
Latin, as approved by the clergy of the diocese of York

in Synod, and by the clergy of the northern province 1
in Convocation, and entered in Archbishop Thoresby's
Register, *fol.* 298 *b.*:—

¶ **Eucharistia** est unum corpus Christi, et illud,
si digne sumatur, sumenti proficit ad vitam æternam; 5
si indigne, ædificat ad gehennam.

2. JUDICIAL DETERMINATION AT THE TRIAL OF   A.D. 1414.
     SIR JOHN OLDCASTLE, LORD COBHAM.

(From the "*Processus magnus domini* Thomæ Arundel *Archie-*   F. Z. p. 450.
*piscopi Cantuarensis contra Johannem Oldcastel, militem,
sed hereticum.*"—Fasciculi Zizaniorum (*ed.* Shirley). Master of Rolls Series, 1858.)

On the 23rd September, 1413, Sir John Oldcastle
appeared before the Archbishop of Canterbury and the
bishops his assessors, in charge of the Keeper of the
Tower, when he produced and read the following 10
schedule :—

"I Johan Oldcastell knygt, lord of Cobham, wole   F. Z. p. 438.
"that alle crysten men wyte and understonde, that y   He declares his desire to hold
"clepe Almyghty God in to wytnesse that it hath be,   rightly the sacra-ments ordained of
"now is, and ever, with the help of God, schal be myn   Christ;
"entent and my wylle, to beleve, feythfully and fully, 16
"alle the sacramentys that ever God ordeyned to be do
"in holy chirche.

    "And more over for to declare me in these foure   and his belief as to the sacrament
"poyntys, I beleve that the moost worshipful sacra-   of the altar.
"ment of the auter is Crystis body in fourme of bred; 21
"the same body that was born of the blessyd virgyne
"oure lady seynt Mary, doon on the crosse, deed &
"beryed, the thrydde day roos fro deth to lyve, the   F. Z. p. 439.
"whyche body is now glorefyed in hevene."

    (Here follow articles on penance, images, and pil- 26
grimages.)

    It was intimated to him that his statement con-   This was held insufficient,
tained some things sufficiently catholic, but savoured of

and his further
answer was re-
quired to certain
determinations,
sent to him in
Latin with an
English transla-
tion.
heresy in others. He constantly refused to give any
further answer, and the bishops therefore sent him
certain determinations in Latin, "*pro leviori intellectu
ejusdem in Anglicum translatis,*" and required him to
give his answer fully and clearly. The tenor is as

6 follows :—

F. Z. p. 441.
The tenor of the
article as to the
Eucharist,
"The feyth, and the determinacion of holy chyrche
"towchyng the blysful sacrament of the auter, is thys :
"that after the sacramental wordys ben seyd be a prest
"in hys masse, the materyall bred that was before is
"turnyd into Chrystys verray body ; and the materyal
12 "wyn that was before, is turnyd into Chrystys veray
"blood, and so there levyth in the auter no materyal
F. Z. p. 442.
and more particu-
larly as to the
desition of the
material elements.
"bred, ne materyal wyn, the whyche were there before
"the seyinge of the sacramental wordys. How leeve
"ȝe thys article ?"

(Here follow determinations as to confession, the
18 authority of the pope and clergy, and pilgrimages.)

F. Z. p. 443.
On the 25th September he again appeared, and
answered thus :—

To which the ac-
cused answered
in explanation,
"Quod sicut Christus hic in terra degens habuit in
se divinitatem et humanitatem, divinitatem tamen vela-
F. Z. p. 444.
tam et invisibilem sub humanitate, quæ in eo aperta
24 et visibilis fuerat, sic in sacramento altaris est verum
corpus et verus panis ; panis videlicet quem videmus, et
corpus Christi sub eodem velatum, quod non videmus."
He denied that the determination of the Roman church
which had been sent him could be or was the deter-
29 mination of the primitive church.

and, being excom-
municate, was
burnt as a heretic.
Persisting in his answer, he was excommunicated
as a heretic, more especially as to the sacraments of
Eucharist and penance, by sentence, dated 10th December, 1413, and, although he escaped from the Tower,
34 he was eventually burned in pursuance thereof.

3. THE SACRAMENT OF THE ALTAR.

A.D. 1515.

(From the *Festyvale*, W. de Worde, 1515, fol. 169 *b*.)

The fourth is the holy sacrament of the awter, the whiche is crystes owne body, his flesshe *and* blode in fourme of brede : the same that was borne of *the* virgyn Mary, and done on the rode, this is made thrugh the vertue of goddes wordes of *the* priest that hath power, which power neyther aungel ne archaungel hath, but only man in my*n*de of hymselfe. This sacrament is every man *and* woman bounde by the lawe ones a yere as at eester, yf he be xiiii yeres of aege, *and* haue dyscrecyon to receyue it, wha*n* they ben with shryft and penau*n*ce made clene of theyr synnes, and elles to be put out of the chyrche, and of cryste*n* buryelles, but yf it be for sikenesse, or for some reasonable cause, whiche cause he must certefy his curate of. For he that unworthely receyueth this sacrament receyueth his dampnacyon.

The Festival furnishes a popular statement of the doctrine, similar to that in Thoresby's Catechism (page 118) without the scholastic subtleties which cost Lord Cobham his life,

8

and specifying the age, more generally referred to in the older document. (Page 188, l. 4.)

16

4. EXTRACT—EXHORTATION BEFORE COMMUNION.

(From *Festyvale, In die Pasche*, fol. 38.)

"I charge you in goddes name that none of you come thus to goddes borde but yf ye be i*n* perfyte loue and charite, and be clene shryue*n* *and* in full purpose to leve your syn*n*e."

Men must come to the Lord's table holy and clean, and in love and charity with their neighbours.

APPENDIX III.

[*Ashm. MS.*, 1286, *fol.* 223.]

Here sueþ a preciouse mater. how a man schal make
hym cleer *and* perfite clene bifore þe resseyuynge
of þe sacramente of þe auter.

BIfore þe resceyuynge of cristis body syxe þingis þer
ben to concidere.

¶ The firste is þat a man knowe by vertu of dis-
cressioun. what he schal resceyue. and what he is þat
8 resseyueþ it.   ¶ Lo ! lo ! what schal he resceyue ?
soþely ihesu crist—sooþfaste god and man, þat made
alle þing of nouȝtte, And sooþfaste man þat dyed for vs
on þe crosse—in forme of breed. what is he þat re-
12 sceyueþ it ? soþely a man and no beeste, ne feende, þerfore alle feendis malice. and alle beestelynesse of synne
he owiþ to caste 'from hym.

¶ þe secunde is deuocioun of herte ; for he schal
concidere, þat whom he resseyueþ he shal resseyue it in
17 as myche holinesse as he may : *and* loke he þat he
here-wiþ putte awey from hym bittirnesse and blynde-
nesse of herte, wiþ compassioun of teeris and þorouȝ
besynesse of preyers.

with reverence
at drawing near
to One so great,
¶ þe þridde is wiþ reuerence of herte. þat suche a
vyle creature and a wrecchid synner be aferde to
23 neiȝ hem suche a lord ; For if a man were dipped alle
in stynke, vnworþi he were to stonde in presence of þe
kyng   ¶ I preye þee þenne—how myche more vnworþi
is eny man, as of hym silf, for to resceyue crist in þe
preciouse sacramente.   For whi alle oure good deedis.
ben as vnclennesse in his siȝtte, what ben oure synnes
29 þenne ? trewely nouȝt.   ¶ But not wiþstandande alle

þat, his goodnesse and his pitee is more þenne al oure but trusting in his mercy, we wreechidnesse ; and þer-fore do we þat is in vs. and in triste of hym wiþ reuerente drede goo we to hym, For whi his worþinesse schal maken vs worþi to do hym seruise.   5

¶ þe fourþe is loue and desyre of herte. wherfore a man owiþ to be war þat he go not to þis sacramente rechelesly, ne wiþ heuinesse, ne wiþ irkynge of herte, but loke he do it deuoutely and gladdely. and wiþ greet desyre, wherfore it semiþ myche wondir to me 10 þat euery man in resceyuynge of þis worþi sacramente meltiþ [*not*] al in-to loue.

¶ þe conciderynge of cristis passyoun and of his loue vn-to vs is souereyne meene to steere a mannes affeccioun to deuoute resceyuyng of þis hooly and blessydful sacramente.   16

¶ The fy3fte is a meke deuoute preyere. For whi for þat encheson amonge oþur was þe sacramente ordeyned. so þat a man þorou3 offrynge and takynge of it schulde aske for3euenesse of synnes ·and grace of good lijf.

¶ þe sixte is þat he be a preste þat schulde mynistre þis sacramente. so þat he do alle his diligence aboute it. in þat, þat in him is. ¶ For siþen a man is besy. to serue an eerþely man. or a lord wiþ al his diligence abouten hym, miche more schulde he ben besy. for to 25 serue to oure lord god. ¶ And þerfore alle maner of men of moste honeste. and of sobrenesse. and of good continuaunce. and here-wiþ to ben wel avysed. is þenne moste nedeful to ministre þis moste worschipeful sacra- mente ¶ And so þat a preeste may þe bettir do þis worþi ocupacioun. I counceyle hym þat he absteyne 31 hym from alle þingis tymely þat my3tte fylen his soule þat is þe wonyinge of crist. þe heuenly kyng. so þat he may bere(1) myche more stiffeloker groundyd in goddis seruise. 3e, 3e, myche more þenne eny oþur seculer man. 35

(1) *Read* ben.—*Compare* ben, *l.* 25.

Marginal notes:

but trusting in his mercy, we come to him, and he will enable us to serve him truly.

With a loving and glad heart,

which is most of all moved by considering Christ's love in dying for us.

With devout prayer for pardon and grace.

[* fol. 224]

Considerations if he be the priest that has to administer this sacrament.

He should abstain from things of this world,

and especially
when going to
mass.
and namely þenne whenne he schal go to masse. þat he
hym redily speede.

A man must with-
draw into him-
self,
¶ The seuenþe is þat he wiþdrawe his mynde from
alle outward þingis. and gadre hym silf al hool in-to
5 hym silf, if he may, so enteerly. þat neiþir he be
scatered by bodily witte ne wiþ veyneglorie. ¶ And
and search and
examine his own
conscience,
þenne ransake his owne concience. and þat þat he
fyndeþ vncleene. loke þat he wasche hem awey wiþ
and go to con-
fession.
teeris of conpunccioun. þenne bihoueþ him go to his
confessoure. and caste out wiþ meke schrifte alle venym
11 of synne.

In all humility he
must think of
the meekness of
God
¶ And whenne he haþ doon þus. þenne muste hym
lifte vp his herte wiþ alle maner of þe moste humilite.
and concidere þe mekenesse of god. and þe wrecchid
and his own
frailty;
freyelte of his owne fleische. ¶ How myche and how
worþi þat god is and how litle and how vnworþi hym
17 silf is / and þus schal he of hym silf make nouȝtte and
[* fol. 224 b.]
magnifye god. þat he ˙may be turned in-to god. so þat
he se noon oþur þing. ne feele but god ¶ þenne if he
suffre þus mekely and pacientely. in alle tymes. he may
myche þe liȝtteloker. and þe more suloker þenke on þe
of the great love
of our Lord;
greet loue of oure lord ihesu crist. þat wolde of hym
silf þat is so worþi ȝeue his lijf to distroye þe syneful
24 lijf of mankynde ¶ þenne may he wel þenke vp-on þe
poyntis of cristis passioun. and ouere þat for to wondre.
in dying for us,
and offering him-
self to us in this
sacrament.
of his wondirful charite. þat not oonly wolde offre hym
silf to vs on þe crosse. but he offriþ hym silf to vs in
þe sacramente of þe auter for to be fully with vs ¶ ȝe
ȝe and ȝit þerto ful myche more. for he ȝeueþ hym silf
30 to vs. for to be ful surely groundyd in oure hertis.
¶ A ! good and graciouse swete lord. who may suffyse
for to þenke þe leste sparkele of þi wondirful sweete
loue—soþely no man.
Devotion for a
priest before
receiving;
¶ þerfore byfore þe resseyuynge of þis worþi and
moste hooly sacramente. a preeste may seye þus ful per-
36 fitely in his herte ¶ I haue a tyme, lord. I knowe

wel þat alle werkis and desertis of men, be þei neuere 1
so hooly, þei ben vnworþi for to resceyue þee, lord. So
worþi. So myȝtty. So benynge. So mercyful as þou
art in alle neede. ¶ A! a! soþefast merciful lord.
how myche more þenne am I vnworþi þat euery day 5
synne. and as a man vncorrigible dwelle þer-in stylle
¶ A! good lord, whi do I suche dispite to þee. to caste acknowledging his vileness;
þee my lord god so preciouse in-to so foule a pitte of
my concience, For soþely my sweete and graciouse
souereyne lord. I knoweleche to þe þat þer nys no 10
goonge more stynkynge þenne my soule is. ¶ A!
lord, lord, þat art so humble. and so meke. what schal
I do wiþ þee, kyndely lord, whi, what schal I leye þee
lord in þat foule place, soþely lord I durste not. but þat 14
I ‘hope to þi mercy ¶ But souereyne myȝtteful lord, [* fol. 225]
I trowe þat þi mercy is eendeles more þenne alle myn but trusting in the mercy of Christ,
orible and foule wreechid synne, þerfore I am al trist-
ynge in þi goodnesse, merciful lord. ¶ I aventure me 18
to resceyue þee, swete lord, as a syke man resseyueþ a
medcyne. ¶ þou art a sooþfaste leche, lord, and soþely who is the true physician.
I am syke. þerfore I take þee. for to be maad hool
þorouȝ þee. ¶ And þe syker þat I am, by so myche I 22
wolde ben maad hool bi þee, my swete lord; and þe
more nede þat I haue of þee, þe more ententely and
bisili schulde I þenke to calle vp-on þee ¶ For whi
lord in helynge of my deedly sykenesse schal wel be 26
schewyd and commendyd þe michilheed of þi goodnesse.

        ¶ And þenne aftir þis whenne he haþ resceyued þat Thoughts after receiving, as to the vanity of the world;
myȝtteful and blessydful sacramente he may þenne
þenke þus ¶ I wole not now aftir þis moste worþi
mete. fede me wiþ myche of þe wordely vanite / nouþir
I wole not aftir suche goostely sauoure delyte me 32
fleischely in eny creature. ¶ Neuereþeles if it be so.
þat a man feele not goostely affeccioun. ne ȝit in de-
uoute sterynge þorouȝ goostely encentynge of herte in or when there has been an absence of spiritual affections.
tyme of his resseyuynge. it is good þat he þenke þenne.

1 þat it is a tokene of greet sykenesse of synne. or ellis
of greet deeþ. or ellis it is suffraunce of god for to meke

A man should
always recognize
his short comings,

a man. ¶ But a man schal euere conceyue in his owne
concience. þat he is continuelly in defaute aȝen þat
myȝtteful lord *and* þerfore schulde he ful mekely. and
6 obeschauntely seye to hym þus. ¶ A! lord, lord, now
ful mercyful lord, what schal I do. I haue putte fyre
in my bosum, and I feele noon heete of it. ¶ Lo! lo!

[* fol. 225 b.]

lord euereful mercyful to 'synneful wrecchis. I haue
put hony in my mouþ, and I fele no maner swetnesse

and plead for
mercy.

þer-of. ¶ A! good lord ihesu crist, rue vp-on me, þe
moste vnkynde and frowarde wrecche, for I haue re-
13 sceyued a souereyne medcyne, and ȝit I feele neuere þe
more heele.

Thus should a
man humble him-
self before Christ,

¶ þus schal a man lowely and debonerly meke hym
silf wiþ dreede *and* loue þat he schulde haue, and euere
owiþ to haue, to þat worþi lord in þe sacramente of þe
18 auter in forme of breed, þe whiche is crist ihesu.
¶ And þenne anoon þorouȝ þis deuoute drede and loue,

and so amend.

he schal amende his lijf and turne to bettir. ¶ For
alle if a man may not anoon feele swetnesse and gostely
22 sauoure in þis worþi sacramente. he schal not þerfore
dispeyre. but abyde mekely and paciently þe grace of

Where the virtue
of the sacrament
has not been felt,

god. and do þat in hym is for to haue it ¶ For whenne
a syke man resceyueþ a medcyne he is not anoon hool.
26 but ȝit he hopiþ þorouȝ it to ben hool / And þerfore he
kepiþ him warly from alle þingis þat is contrarie to his

still its benefits
should be patient-
ly waited for.

medcyne. and suffriþ pacientely dissese. vn-to þe tyme
þat þe medcyne haue wrouȝtte in hym. and restored
30 hym wel aȝen. ¶ þus schulden we þat ben syke in
synne resseyue þe heelful medcyne of þis preciouse
sacramente

Where the benefits
have been experi-
enced,

¶ Neuerþeles if a man þorouȝ eny goostely feelynge
feele hym silf wel, it is good þat he þenke not þat it
comeþ of hym silf, but of þe goodnesse of god. þat
36 fediþ of his grace. boþe good man and badde / and wel

may he þenne þenke þus ¶ Lo! lo! eu*ery* synneful 1
creature. þis dooþ oure merciful and graciouse lord to
me for to schewe to me my wickidnesse. and for to
ouerecome my wrecchidnesse wiþ plente of his goodnesse ¶ Lo! lo! wel may I be Ioyeful for he makiþ
me, a deed man. for to feele lijf / And me a styn*k*ynge 6
worme for to taste 'heuenly delyte ¶ A! a! siþen
oure lord is so curteyse to me. þat alwey lyue in synne.
what trowe I þat he wole do to me. ȝif I fully offre me
to hym soþely mych bettir þenne I can seye. or eny 10
herte may þenke.

    ¶ Preye we to god wiþ good entente. þat we mowne
to his plesaunce resceyue þe sacramente.   Amen.

they must be received with acknowledgments of unworthiness.

[* fol. 226]

Prayer for due reception.

APPENDIX IV.

A TREATISE OF THE MANNER AND MEDE
OF THE MASS.

(From the Vernon MS., Bodleian Library.)

[fol. 302 b., col. 1] **Her techeþ þys tretys þenne,**

This treatise teaches how people should hear their mass, and is needful to high and low.
Hou mon scholde here hys masse:
Hit is ful nedful to alle menne,
To more and eke to lasse.   4

Hearing mass, good for all baptized Christians.
Ȝong *and* olde · More and lasse,
Ful god hit is · to here A Masse.
þat Cristendam · haþ tan.

It was made for soul's health, and the Lord's Prayer,
Hit was mad · for soule hele,   8
þe Pater noster · wiþ dedes fele
And deprofundis · Is on.

prayer of price, with others, many and diverse.
þe Pater noster · Is pris preyere
Wiþ oþer orisons · mony and sere.   12
Holdeþ ow stille as ston,

Silence bespoken,
And ȝe schul here · þe beste þing
þat euer ȝe herde · of Olde or ȝyng
As wyde · as mon haþ gon.   16

¶ Lustneþ here · *and* ȝe wol lyþe,

for a discourse full of comfort,
Of a talkyng · I wol ȝou kiþe,
Cumfort · to al Mon-kynde,

viz. The merits of the mass.
þat is þe Meedes · of þe Masse.   20
Eueri mon · boþe more and lasse,

All should know how to take part
Schulde haue hit · in his mynde,

Hou þat ȝe scholde · ȝor seruise seye,

And priueliche · ȝor preyers preye   24

   To him þat may · vn-bynde,

In saluyng · of ȝor synnes seuene

To þe mihtful kyng · of heuene

   Vr Fader · þat we schal fynde.   28

¶ And hou vr Fader · schal be founde

To veche a mon · þat is I-bounde

   In sunne · as I ow say.

His suffrance · we may se   32

Hou þat he suffreþ · þe and me

   Wiþ miht · al þat he may,

And euere is redi · vr bales to bete,

To loke what tyme · þat we wol leete   36

   In-to vr laste day,

Ȝif we ben in wille · to leue vr synne,

He techeþ vs wel · hou we schal wynne

   To heuene · þe heiȝe way.   40

¶ What mon wolde now · suffre so,

His sone I-slayen · and hedde no mo,

   But ȝif he miȝte · lyue a-ȝeyn.

Ȝif he for traytrie · weore take,   44

Sone he schulde · be forsake,

   Or elles · soþli slayn.

Whon þou dost · a dedly synne,

Al þe while · þat þou dwellest þer-Inne,   48

   þou puttest · to his payn,

þe same he suffred · for vr sake.

þen most merci · a-mendes make

   Boþe wiþ miht · and mayn.   52

¶ þorw his Merci · and his miht

He reweþ of vs · a-ȝeynes þe riht,

   As Rihtwysnes · wol rede.

Rihtwysnes · wolde assone   56

As we dedly synne · haue done

   To dampne vs · to þe dede.

MASS-BOOK.   9

Side notes:

in common prayer, and use of private devotion;

and how they may turn to God.

His longsuffering and readiness to help.

If we have a good will, he teaches the way to heaven.

No man in the like case would be so longsuffering,

and we by sin crucify the Lord afresh,

but his mercy clears us.

He grieves for us,

where justice would condemn us to death.

Therefore, mercy, stand us in stead,

þen most Merci · be Mayster most,

þorw þe miht · of þe holy gost,   60

and remain with us till prayer has freed us from that sentence of death.

   And stonde wiþ vs · in stede ;

And lenge wiþ vs · in leo and lede

Til we beo don · out of þat dede

   þorw bone · of holy bede.   64

Now I begin to put you in mind of the Mass, and it is a good subject for my verse-making.

¶ Wiþ ȝor leue · I wol be-gynne

Of A Mater · for to mynne,

   A good þing · for to make,

On þe hexte þing hit is,   68

þat euer was mad · þat is þe Mes,

   Monnes sunnes · to slake.

Thou mayest see the Body of Christ, who died for thee,

Eueri day · þou maiȝt se

þe same bodi · þat diȝed for þe,   72

   Tent · ȝif þou wolt take,

in figure, and in form of bread, as He gave it before His death.

In figure · and in fourme of Bred,

þat Iesus dalte · er he weore ded,

   For his disciples · sake.   76

High as it is,

On þe hexte þing · to here,

It is easy for the unlearned to learn

And þe lihtest · for to lere,

   For lewed men · In lare.

when to join in the service, and [Fol. 302 b., col. 2] when to pray by themselves,

Hou þat ȝe schul · ȝor seruise say,   80

And priueliche · ȝor preyers pray,

   In churche · whon þat ȝe are.

   do ow wel to witen · wiþ-outen drede,

for the Mass is for all.

þe Masse was mad · for monnes nede,   84

   For al folk lasse and mare.

All ought to pray as the priest, if they knew what he said.

As þe prest seiþ · his preyere,

So schulde vche mon · þat him gon here,

   And þei wuste · what hit ware.   88

I do not speak of myself, without warrant of holy writ,

¶ Ȝif I seide þis word · wiþ my wit

Wiþ-outen witnesse · of holi writ,

   Wisdam weore hit non :

þerfore I wole þat ȝe hit witen,   92

Hou þat we · fynde hit writen

   Wiþ Auctours · mony on.

Of Austin, Ambrose · Bernard, and Bede

ȝit heore Resons · wol I rede   96   and so I give the reasons of St Augustine, &c.,

  A-Mong ȝow · euerichon.

þei make muynde · of mony a mede   who put on record the merits of the Mass.

þat we schul haue · for vre good dede,

  To churche · whon þat we gon.   100

What tyme · þat þow biginnest to go,   Every step to and from hearing Mass is noted by the guardian angel.

  Ouþer · to þe churche or fro,

  To here A Masse · ȝif þou may,

Eueri fote · þat þou gas,   104

þyn Angel poynteþ hit · vch a pas

  þe Prince of heuene · to pay.

þat day schalt þou elde nouȝt,   That day a man does not age,

ȝif þou beo studefast in þi þouht   108

  On God · þat is verray.

Not Blynt þat day · schalt þou not be,   nor become blind:

þat þou þi sauiour · hast se,

  þorw him þat mihtes · may.   112

¶ A Fair grace · God haþ þe ȝiuen   he has God's pardon, if he goes to confession;

Of þi sunnes · and þou be schriuen

  þat day · þou hast god se.

ȝif þou be ded · þe same day,   116   and if he die, it avails as the viaticum.

þou schalt be founden · I þe fay,

  Hoseled · as þou hed be.

Baldely maiȝt þou · swete and swynke   It makes work to be without annoyance or trouble,

For to wynne þe · Mete and drinke   120

  Wiþ-outen tray · or tene.

And ȝif þou be · in eny drede,   and helps to cure sharp sorrows.

Al þe better · schalt þou spede

  To keuere of cares kene.   124

¶ ȝif þou haue eny · wey to wende,   Before a journey hear early Mass,

I rede þou here · a masse to ende

  In þe Morennynge · ȝif þow may :

And ȝif þou may not · do so,   128

I rede beo vnderne · ar þou go,   or ad tertiam,

  Or elles · be heiȝ midday.   or ad sextam.

Serteynliche · wiþ-outen fayle,

It will not hinder your journey.
þou schalt not leose · of þi trauayle

Not half a foote · of way.

O þi bodi · þou schalt be lihtore,

And þi weyes · wende þe Rihtore,

þorwh him · þat mihtes may.   136

Be not kept away by any priest.
þOuh he be nouȝt · at þi lykynge

þe prest þat schal þy masse synge,

þerfore lette þou nouht :

His unworthiness cannot hinder the Sacrament;
His Masse schal be · as good to heere,   140

As Monk, Chanoun · Hermyte, or Frere.

þus þenk hit · in þy þouht.

þauȝ his preyere · and his bone

Bi-fore God · come not so sone,   144

As he þat neuer synne wrouȝt.

and his Master, Christ, will judge him.
Ihesu crist · souereyn of al

He may deeme · boþe gret and smal.

þus Doctours · han I-souht.   148

St Ambrose says
¶ Seynt Ambrose seiþ · hose redeþ riht,

þe Masse · Is of so muche miht,

þer nys no mon · þat May,

Wheþer þat he · be old or ȝonge,   152

þe tenþe part · telle wiþ tonge,

þeiȝ he schulde · liue for ay.

the subject is inexhaustible by time or skill.
þe Exposission · is so expres

Wiþ al þe priuete of þe Mes   156

Serteyn · wiþ-oute delay

þat couþe a mon neuere · so muche of art

He mihte not telle · þe tenþe part,

þauȝ he hedde þouȝt to say.   160

[Fol. 302 b., col. 3]
St Jerome cited for the necessity for a mass for every several soul.
¶ Seynt Ierom seiþ · for soules sere

þauh a Mon wolde · a þousent ȝere

Do a Masse · for to synge,

[¹ read Hit]
His¹ is nouþer more ne las,   164

But vch a soule · schal haue a mas—

Hit is so heiȝ · a þinge.

ʒit I Rede ow · go to chirche,

Godes werkes · for to worche,   168

     In-to vr laste · endynge.

Haue we no doute · of vr dole,

Vch soule schal haue · a masse al hole,

     þorw help · of heuene kynge.   172

Ful hard hit were · to vre bi-houe

Vch a prouerbe · for to proue

     Of þeos Auctours · alle :

Serteynliche · wiþ-outen lees   176

Of sum of hem · þen wol I sees

     For þing · þat may be-falle

ʒif I drouʒ hem · on lengþe,

I trou no mon · schulde haue þe strengþe   180

     To stonde · and heere hem alle.

Lewed men · and ʒe wol list,

Ful fayn I wolde · þat ʒe hit wist,

     On Crist · whon ʒe schulde calle.   184

¶ To calle on Crist · with mylde chere,

Lewed Men · I schal ʒou lere

     Whon þat þe prest · bi-ginnes,

Whon he seiþ · his Confiteore,   188

Feire he louteþ · þe Auter bi-fore

     To schriue him of his synnes.

Serteynly · wiþ-oute delay

And ʒe for þe prest pray,   192

     And he atte Masse ʒou mynne,

Sikerli · I dar wel say,

þer nis no tonge · þat telle may

     What Mede · þat ʒe may wynne.   196

¶ But ʒit I telle ʒou sikerly,

And ʒe preye · but only

     For ʒor owne · hele,

I do ʒow to witen · with-outen drede,   200

ʒe beo not worþ · so muche meede,

     Not be þe haluendele,

Glosses (right margin):

Still go to church and be doing God's work.

Every soul shall have a separate Mass.

Hard to prove all this by all these authors;

for I foresee if I only cited some at length,

no man could stand it out;

but I shall be glad for you to know when to call on Christ.

You are ignorant, and I will teach you.

When the priest says his Confiteor, bowing before the altar,

and you pray for him, if he remembers you in the *memento,* how great is your reward.

But if you only pray for yourself, it is not half what your fallen nature demands from you,

As þi kuynde · puttes þe to,

since it inclines
you to evil.
To don vuele · he biddes þe do :   204

3if þou wol wone · in weole,

Where there is this
mutual prayer,
there is true
praise.
Prey for þe prest · and he for þe.

þat Is a preyere · of charite,

þen maiȝt þou synge · of loue lele.   208

¶ Loue is trewe · in vche a leede

"Ill deed, ill
speed."
ȝif þou do ille · vuel schalt þou spede

For al þe craftes · þat þou con.

Whon þat þou comest · þe chirche with-Inne   212

Whilst the priest
is vesting,
And þou sest · þe prest bi-gynne

Take his vestimens · on,

Loke þou do · as I sey þe :

kneel and be still,
Knele a-doun · vppon þi kne,   216

Noyse · þat þow make non.

then stand and do
your service,
Seþþe stond vp · at þi seruise

And serue god · on þis wyse,

all of you.
Al folk · euerichon.   220

Say thy *Domine in
multitudine*, &c.,
and place thyself
under the safe-
guard of the
Blessed Virgin ;
¶ þou schalt say · þi drihten,

And deore god almihten,

And In Marie · I me a-seure,

þat heo saue vs alle,   224

Boþe grete · and smalle,—

and pray for
shrift of sins
Of sunnes · we beþ vn-pure—

And þat I may me schriue

Of al my wikked lyue,   228

To Prest · þat bereþ þe cure,

þat I haue I-wrouȝt,

in deed and
thought against
man's better
nature.
And in herte · I-þouȝt,

As vnkuynde · creature.   232

A Form of Con-
fession.
¶ I was vn-kuynde,

And was þenne · blynde,

To worche · a-ȝeynes his wille,

þat furst me wrouȝt,   236

And seþþe me bouȝt,

Fro peynes · he was put to ille,

þer-fore · we pray
To þe · to-day,   240
   þat knowes boþe good · and ille,   [Fol. 303, col. 1]
Graunt vs lyue,   Prayer to live to complete penance.
We may vs schriue,
   Vr penaunce · to folfille.   244

¶ We schal preyȝe *Iesus*   Prayer to Christ for forgiveness,
þat he forȝiue vs
   Vr sunnes · þat we may synge,
þat we may pray,   248
þe Prince · to-day,
   Schop eorþe · and alle þinge ;
þat in Clannesse,   for purity, and for benefit
We may þe Messe,   252 from the Mass.
   þorw miht · of heuene kynge,
So deorliche · to do,
To torne þe to
   Vs alle · to good endynge.   256

¶ Certes sires · ful good hit is   It is no doubt good to stand and say a word of prayer at the Mass;
To stonde stille · at þe Mes,
   Sum good word · for-to say,
Whuche þat ȝe wole preye fore,   260 you may pray for scores,
þauh ȝe do · for mony a score
   At a Masse ȝe may,
Alle þo · þat ȝe nempne nouȝt,   either naming them or thinking
But only þenke · in ȝor þouȝt   264 of them,
   þat ȝe wolde · fore pray.
I do ow to wite · *with*-outen doute,   and every soul of them has a Mass, if not lost in hell for ever.
þer nis no soule · a Masse wiþ-oute,
   But he haue helle for ay.   268

¶ Wust I my Fader · in flesch and felle   If my father was in hell,
Weore holliche · I-holden in helle,
   þer weore · non hope of hele.
To preye for hi*m* · I couþe no Red,   272 I would no more pray for him than for a dead dog;
No more · þen for A Dogge were ded,
   But let hem wiþ him · dele.

Ȝit I rede · we go to chirche
Godes werkes for-to worche   276
Ȝif we wole wone · in wele.

but still, as this is
not known, we
pray for all the
faithful.
Seþþe hit is · vnknowe to vs,
We schul preye for alle · Fidelibus
To Rewe soules · þat beþ lele.   280

Now take care
you don't talk
with any man,
Ȝit I bidde ȝou · takeþ good tent
þat ȝe holde · no parlyment
Wiþ no cristen mon
Whon ȝe come · þe Churche with-Inne,   284

after the priest
begins to vest,
And ȝe seo · þe prest bi-ginne
Take · þe vestimens on.

or the Devil will
write all you say,
þe foule fend · so fel is.
He writ ȝor wordes · I-wis   288
On A Rolle · euerichon.

as witness Saint
Angustine of
England.
Also witnesseþ · seynt Austine,
þat furst wit · in Engelond gan lene
And preched · þe treuþe bi-gon.   292

¶ Ar seynt Austin · In Engelond come,

When he was at
Rome, he was one
day called to
minister as deacon
by Saint Gregory
the Great,
Wiþ [1]Pope Gregori · of Rome   [1 scratched out]
Ful long tyme · gon he dwelle.
Vppon a day · for worschupefulnesse   296
þe [1]Pope wolde · synge A Messe,
As him ful fayre · bi-felle.

He made a signe · to seynt Austyne,
For he schulde ben · his dekne digne   300
To Rede · þe gospelle,

and he saw two
women talking
together, whilst
he read the
gospel,
And as he radde · þen sauh he þen
Two wyues · as ȝe may witen,
Tales þen gonne þei telle.   304

¶ Seynt Austin · herde þis wordes alle,
In A wyndow · on þe walle,
þer · bi-fore his face

and he saw a
devil also (so God
gave him grace),
who wrote what
they said,
A foul fend · he sauȝ þer-In   308
Wiþ penne · and enke. and parchemin
As God ȝaf him þe grace

He wrot so faste · til þat he want,

For his parchemyn skin · was so scant,   312   but soon used his parchment,

    To speken · þei hedde such space.

Wiþ his teeþ · he gon hit togge,   so he tugged it with his teeth,

And so radli · he gon hit Rogge,   till it stretched,

    þat al þe Rolle · gon race.   316

¶ So harde raced · he þat Rolle,

þat he chopped · his Cholle,   and he knocked his head against

    A-ȝeyn þe Marbel-ston.   the wall.

Al þe folk · I þe chirche A-bout   320

Was a-stoneid · of þat clout,   [Fol. 303, col. 2]

    And herden hit · euerichone.   Every one heard the blow,

Seynt Austin seiȝ · hou faste he drouh,   and St Austin burst out laugh-

He barst on lauhtre · and loude louh ;   324   ing,

    þe [¹Pope] ful sore · gon grone   [¹ erased]   to the great grief of the Pope,

For serwe · neiȝ þe ¹Pope wept.   who remonstrated with him after

After masse · Austyn he met   Mass,

    And Mekely · made his mone.   328

¶ He made his mone · wiþ mylde mod,

Whi weore þou · so wikked and wod

    For to do · þat dede,   charging him with madness for what

A worse dede · miht þou neuer done.   332   he had done;

Austin onswerde · him ful sone—

    þer-of he hedde · gret drede—

Lord, greue ȝe nouȝt · til þat ȝe wite ;   but he asked him not to grieve till

A foul fend · I say site—   336   he knew all,

    Serwe · mot ben his mede—

Two wyues · sat ȝonder, langare,   and told him the story of the

Alle heore wordes · wrot he þare   women and the fiend,

    Vppon a Rolle · to rede.   340

¶ þei tok no tent · til heore Mas,

Al heore wordes · more and las

    He wrot hem · euerichon.   who wrote all they said,

For to speke · þei hedde such space,   344

þe fend wrot · wiþ a foul face,

    Til his Parchemyn · was al gon.

and how in
stretching the
parchment,
Whon his parchemyn · was al spende,

He rauhte þe Rolle · bi þe onde   348

Wiþ his teth · a-non

He logged · þat al in synder gon lasch

*he dashed his
head against the
marble,*
And wiþ his hed · he ȝaf a dasch

A-ȝeyn þe Marbel-ston.   352

*and that cut the
saint short in his
reading.*
¶ Lord greue ȝe not · for þat dunt

He stoneyd me · and made me stunt

Stille out of my steuene.

*He said as he saw,
without a lie,*
I wol sigge · as I seȝe,   356

For a word · wol I not lyȝe

Be Mihtful kyng · of heuene.

*and led the Pope
to the window,*
He ladde him forþ · as I trowe,

Til he com · to þe wynt-douwe   360

þat I be-fore · gon nemene.

*and there they
found black filth
on the asblar.*
Foul þei fond · þer I-sched

As blac as pich · was I-spred

Vppon þe Aschelers · euene.   364

*This is a miracle,
no doubt, for
devils have no
blood, but it was
allowed for cor-
rection sake.*
¶ þis is wonder-þing · with-outen drede—

þer was neuer fend · blod mihte blede,

He haþ nouþer · flesch ne bon,

But god wolde · þat hit were so   368

To chastise hem · and oþer mo

þat to churche · gun gon.

*Till Mass is ended,
a man should be
stone-still,*
Til a Masse · was seid to ende.

A Mon schulde talke · with fo nor frende,   372

But holde him stille · as ston.

*for it is the house
of prayer to Jesus
and His mother.*
þat hous was mad · for preyere

To Iesu · and to his Moder dere

To þonke hem · al heore lon.   376

*The women had
much unseemly
talk,*
At þe wyues · gon þei witen

What þei seiden · whon þei siten

Seynt Austyn · hem bi-syde,

Bi heore onswere · þei wuste ful wel,   380

*and would fain
have kept it
secret;*
þat þei hedde spoken · muchel vncel,

And in heore hertes · gun hyde.

þerfore sires · I rede ȝe loke,
God tent · I wolde ȝe toke, 384 so do you take
care,
   For þing · þat may bi-tyde,
þat ȝe mesure ȝou · þe mare
Of speche · þat ȝe ow spare and moderate
your loquacity at
   At Masse · whon þat ȝe byde. 388 Mass.

¶ þe ¹ Pope greued him · wel þe lasse, [¹ *erased*] The Pope com-
manded that the
He let comaunden · at þe Masse miracle should be
borne in mind,
   Of þat Miracle · to mynne,
And also bad · wiþ ful good wille 392
þat eueri Mon · schulde stonde stille, and that every
one should be
   Whon he comeþ · þe churche with-Inne. silent at Mass.
And þenne hou wel · þat god may wreke Think of God's
anger.
Euerich a word · þat we speke, 396 A word might
hinder the priest
   We do ful muche synne ; in his Mass,
A Prest miȝt be let · of his mes,
Al þis world · miȝt fare þe wers, and the whole
world might suf-
   Vs alle to wo · to wynne. 400 fer for it.

¶ Vr Fader vre · al weldyng is, [Fol. 303, col. 3]
God let vs neuere · his murþes mis. Here follows a
paraphrase of the
   Lord halwed · be þi name. Lord's Prayer
with a *Farsura*.
In heuene and eorþe · þi wille 404
Be don · and þat is skille,
   Or elles we ben · to blame.
Vr vche dayes bred · ȝif vs to-day,
þat we may trustily · whon we schul a-way, 408
   To come · to þi kyndame
God kepe vs · to vre laste endynge
Let neuer þe fend · with fals fondynge
   Cumbre vs · in no schame. 412

¶ þis pater noster · schulde ben vsed The Paternoster
should be put
And for non orison · beo refused— aside for no
prayer,
   I schal ȝow telle · for whi.
Of his Mouþ · hit was maad 416 for it was He made
it who redeemed
þat al þis world · long and braad the world from
woe.
   Out of Bale · gan buyȝe.

Believe the Lord's Prayer, Leeue hit wel · and not wene hit,
þe pater noster · contened   420
Alle þing · hollye,

as none other comprises all we need in this world and the next. þat vs neodeþ · and non oþer,
Boþe for þis world · and þat oþer,
Quik · whon we schal dye.   424

Stand at the gospel; ¶ At the gospel · were ful good,
Studefastliche · þat ȝe stod,
For no þing · þat ȝe stured hit.
Al ȝor lykyng · þer-on leiþ   428
To wite what þe prest seiþ,
Holliche · þat ȝe here hit.

you may understand none of it, but it is what Christ wrought, and it is wisdom in the unlearned to honour His work. þauȝ ȝe vnderstonde · hit nouȝt,
ȝe may wel wite · þat god hit wrouȝt,   432
And þerfore · wisdam were hit
For to worschupe · al godes werkes
To lewed men · þat ben none clerkes:

Now learn that, þis lesson · now go lere hit.   436

¶ And whi ȝe schulde · þis lessun lere
exemplum. Herkneþ alle · and ȝe may here.
And here's a reason. þer a Neddre · hauntes
ȝe may wel fynde · and ȝe wol seche.   440

The adder understands not a word of thy charm, He[o] vnderstond · no þing þi speche,
Whon þou hire · enchauntes,

but she knows thy meaning. Neuerþeles · heo wot ful wel
What is þi menynge · eueri-del   444
Whon þat þou hire · endauntes.

So, when not understood, the power of God's word still avails, So fareþ · þer vnderstondyng fayles,
þe verrey vertu · ȝow alle a-vayles
þorw grace · þat god ȝow grauntes.   448

After the Gospel WHon þe gospel · is I-don,
ȝit wolde I, gode men · euerichon,
comes the Creed. þat ȝe couþe · ȝor crede,

Would that you knew it, and could say it with the priest, What tyme · þat þe prest say,   452
þat ȝe miȝte · ȝor-self pray,
Forsoþe · hit were gret nede.

And seþþe trewely · trouwe þer-Inne,

And fulliche · out of ȝor mouþ hit mynne,   456

    þer-to liht · muche mede.

And ȝif ȝe trowe · and wol not telle,

So dude þe fend · þat from heuene felle,

    And doþ hit nouht · in dede.   460

¶ þouȝ þou neuere · so trewely trowe,

Wiþ-oute dede[1] · ful luytel hit douwe,   [1 MS. drede]

    So doþ þe deuel · þat dredes.

But seynt Jacob · Josepes broþer   464

Seiþ þat we schal · don non oþer

    In his pistel · whose redes.

Such þing as þou seyst and doos

þi Neiȝebor wol þer-of · make Roos   468

    What lyf · þat þow lede.

Wiþ-In a storie · in þat stede

He seiþ · þat trouþe is but dede,

    But hit be don · in dede.   472

¶ Ȝit beo þer mo men · lyuing in lede,

þat I wolde · couþe heore crede,

    And whon þei couþe ken hit.

I haue I-seid · as I con: 476

Ȝif þer beo euer · eny mon,

    þat seiþ he con a-mende hit,

Faute þer-Inne · ȝif þat he fynde,

Mak no scornynge · me be-hynde,   480

    But a-ȝeyn to me · he sende hit,

Or elles help · þat I may here hit.

þus an Englisch · as I lernde hit,   483

    I haue I-þouht · to ende hit.[2]   [2 The MS. does not insert the Creed.]

¶ A Resun · I schal reden ow riht,

Whi þe day · bi-fore þe niht

    Was ordeynt · for-to be.

For Adam · of þe Appel eete,   488

Iesu Crist · vr bales con beete,

    þat dyed · vppon þe Tre.

Marginal glosses:

and believed it, as well as said it, for therein is great reward;

but believing without doing is devil's deed.

To believe without works is nothing; the devil believes and trembles;

and man's praise is according to the life you lead.

"Faith without works is dead," (Ja. ii. 20,)

still I would more men, that live in the world, knew their creed.

I have done my best to English it—If there is a fault, do not turn me into ridicule behind my back, but let me know of it.

[Fol. 303 b., col. 1]

The reason why day precedes the night.

Adam sinned.

Christ betters our woe.

Adam for his sin became the prisoner of hell,	Out of liht · þat he was Inne In-to helle · for his sinne Holliche · þer was he, He was banischt · out of blis In-to helle · boþe he and his,	492
though at first so free.	Bi-foren · þat was so fre.	496
Another reason—why night before day.	¶ Ȝit a Resun · I schal ȝou say, Whi þe niht · bi-fore þe day Was ordeynt · I schal ȝou telle.	
Christ suffered and harrowed hell, and then rose again out of darkness:	For Iesus suffred · woundes fyue, And siþþe a-Ros · fro deþ to lyue, And after · herwede helle, Out of þesternes · þorw his miht,	500
He restored Adam to the light of paradise.	A-ȝeyn he put him · to þe liht, Whuch · þat he fro felle, And dude him a-ȝeyn · in paradis, þat he hedde lost · boþe he and his, Wiþ speche · as I ow spelle.	504 508
Before the washing, don't wait for the priest to ask for the mass-penny, but go up and offer:	A luytel bi-fore · þe prest wasch, let him not · his offryng asch, Ȝif þou þenke · for-to offre. Whon he torneþ · a-non þe tille, Go vp to him · with ful good-wille, And þi peny · him profre,	512
though there is no obligation, it is well bestowed,	þauȝ þou be not · þer-to in dette, þou schalt þinke hit · ful wel bi-set,	516
for it will keep you from sin,	I swere bi seynt Cristofre. Of sinnes · hit wol make þe to sese,	
and make thy chattel increase in thy strong box.	And þi catel · also encrese Of seluer · in þi Cofre.	520
Devotion to be said at the offering to God,	But fayn I wolde · þat þou þus seide, Whon þou · in his hond hit leide, Or þenk hit · in þi þouht:	
that was born in Bethlehem,	God þat was · In Bethleem bore, þreo kynges kneled · þe beó-fore, And heore offryng · brouȝt.	524

þou tok heore offryng · of alle þre,

So receyue · þis of me   528

     And for-ȝete me · nouȝt

þat I may euere · wiþ þe wone

And kuyndelich clepe þe · godes sone

     On þe Roode · as þou me bouȝt.   532

and accepted the gifts of the Magi to receive thine, and that thou mayest dwell with Him.

¶ Whon he haþ waschen · þen he walkes

Priueliche · and stille he stalkes

     To his Auter · a-ȝeyn.

þe furste þing he doþ · *with*-oute doute   536

To his weuede · þen wol he loute—

     þe soþe is nouȝt to leyn.

Seþþe he stondeþ · vp-riht

His hondes heueþ · vppon hiht   540

     Him-self · for-to sayn.

After washing the priest returns to the altar,

when he bows before it,

and crosses him-self,

þenne he torneþ · him to ȝow ;

Cristene men · herkeneþ now

     And preyeþ · wiþ al ȝor mayn.   544

and turns towards the people to ask their prayers.

¶ þen he bi-ginnes · his secre

A-doun þenne · knele ȝe

     A luyte while way,

Til þat he seþ p*er* omnia,   548

And seþþe · Sursum corda.

     What is þat · to say,

Hit is a nedful note to nemen :

Hef vp ȝor hertes · in-to heuen   552

     To him · þat al mihtes may.

Seþþe schul ȝe · þonke him þus

Of bodi and soule · has ȝiuen vs,

     And þus maner · schul ȝe pray.   556

Then he says his secreta, the people kneel-ing,

until the Sursum corda ;

Heave (lift) up your hearts.

¶ Lustneþ alle · to þis þing—

Bi-twene þe *sanctus* · and þe sakeryng.

     ȝe schal preye · stondynge.

Hit semes wel · in þat whyle   560

þat god · in his Exyle

     In þis world · was wonynge.

From the Sanctus to the consecra-tion, the people stand,

but then kneel and meditate of Christ's passion,

Seþþe schul ȝe · knele a-doun
And þenke · vppon his passioun   564
þat he hedde heer · suffrande—
Hou þat he suffrede · woundes fyue
And seþþe he ros · from depe to lyue
And nou has heuene · in hande.   568

though before the bell rings they may pray as they will.

¶ Ȝit schul ȝe preye · for eny þing
Bi-twene þe sanctus · and þe sakeryng,
Til þat þe belle knelle :
Ȝif eny mon haþ scorn · to here hit,   572

A warning against scorn of the doctrine— go home, ye scorners!

Be my trouþe · wisdam weore hit,
·þat he heolde · him stille.
þe same mon · ȝe lauȝwhe to scorn,
Was of A Mayden · in Bethleem born,   576
Me þinke · ȝe don ful ille.
Whose has hoker · gas hame :
To telle hit ȝou · me þinkes no schame,
I preue hit bi a Bille .   580

At the elevation of the body and also of the blood,

¶ Godes Flesch · he reiseth o-lofte,
And his blod · feir and softe
In þe chalis · wiþ-Inne ;

kneel and say a prayer.

þen schul ȝe knele a-doun,   584
And sey a luyte · orisoun,
For no þing · þat ȝe blynne.
God þat on þe Rode · was slon,

Both the species and the crucified are but one.

þo two and he · beoþ boþe on   588
þat dyed · for al monnes synne.

Then the priest spreads his arms cross-wise.

After, þe prest · his Armes spredes he
In toknynge · he dyed vppon þe tre
For me · and al mon-kunne.   592

After the Lord's prayer follows the Agnus Dei.

¶ Whon þe pater noster · is don,
To þe Agnus dei · he goþ ful son,
(Herkneþ hende · in halle)
Godes lomb · hit is to sei,   596
þis worldes sinne · to don a-wey
And haue merci · on vs alle

þe same lomb · hit is to minne,
To don a-wei · þis worldes synne   600
   To þe we crie · and calle.

A prayer for
strength and
grace and peace.

Iesu for þi miht and grace
A-bate vr synnes · In veh a place
   þi pes mot on vs · falle.   604

¶ Whon he haþ vsed · he walkeþ riht

After the priest
has communi-
cated,

To Lauatorie · þer hit is diht
   For to wassche · his hende.

he washes again,
and says the
Post-communion,

So gostly · he comes a-geyn   608
Vn-to god · for-to preyen
   Sum special grace · hym sende
For al þe folk · þat þer wore,

and the people are
to kneel to the
end of the Mass,

Whuch þat he haþ · preyed fore,   612
   þat a Masse · may mende.
þen to knele · hit is best
Til hit cum · to Ite Missa est
   Be seid · in-to þe ende.   616

¶ þenne schul зe knele a-doun,
And sei a luytel Orisoun

and say a prayer
of Saint Ambrose,

   Riht on þis Maneere.
þe Orisoun is · of seynt Ambrose   620
þat he properly · in prose

which he made in
Latin prose,

   Made in his preyere.
þen to preye · is ful good tyme,
I con not wonder wel ryme   624
   On latin · зou to lere.

but I render it
into English verse,
as well as I can.

But noþeles · I wol assay
As neiз þe text · as euer I may.
   Herkne · and зe may heere.   628

¶ God þat diзed · vppon þe tre,

A prayer to our
Lord,

þat þe prest receyuede · bodile
   Vppon · þe Auter-ston ;
Graunt vs grace · whon we hennes go,   632

for inward peace
of conscience.

þat we may worþily · don al-so
   In vre concience · al on.

If we were judged
according to our
works we should
be banished from
His bliss.
After vr dedes · *and* we be demed,

From his blisse · we schal be flemed   636

   Out of þat worþli won.

God graunt vs grace · In wille *and* word

We may be worþi · to his bord,

   Vr lord lene vs · þat lon.   640

[Fol. 303 b., col. 3]
And pray also to
the Virgin, and
don't forget the
gospel after the
Mass:
ȝit prei vr ladi · as I ow telle

   þat ȝe forȝete not · þe god-spelle

     For þing · þat may bi-falle.

Tac a good entent · þer-to   644

Hit is · þe Inprincipio

   On latin · þat men calle.

A ȝer and fourti dayes · atte lest

For verbum caro factum est   648

an indulgence to
those who kiss
the ground, when
it is ended.
   To *pardoun* · haue ȝe schalle.

Mon or wo*m*mon · schal haue þis,

   þat kneles doun · þe eorþe to kis.

     For-þi · þenk on hit, alle.   652

Now I have
finished,
¶ Now haue I endet · so as is

   þe Maner · and þe Mede · of þe Mes :

and well pleased
I am.
   þer-of I am · ful bliþe

Ne more þer-of · to mele w*ith* mouþe.   656

I haue seid · as I couþe,

   I þonke god · fele siþe.

I think nothing
of my trouble,
if you profit by it;
Of my trauayle · is me nouȝt,

Wolde ȝe þenke hit · in ȝor þouȝt,   660

   And in þe chirche · hit kiþe,

but it is good to
know it, listen
who will.
þen were hit lykynge · of ȝor mynde

And gret cumfort · to Al Monkynde.

   Hose wol, lusten · and lyþe.   664

Still I have made
exception of three
things in the
mass-book;
ȝit is þer þreo þinges · on þe Bok,

Sikerly · þat I out-tok,

   And neuer dar make · in Mynde.

Hit was wel þouȝt · at my likynge,   668

I ches hit out · bi heuene kynge,

   þe toþer is ȝit bi-hynde,

But better þing · þen I haue told,

Herde ʒe neuere · of ʒong ne old 672

  On ground · þat men may fynde,

Saue fyue wordes · wiþ-outen drede,

þat no mon · but a prest schulde rede,

  Is comen · of cristen kynde. 676

God þat dyʒed · vppon þe Roode,

þat bouʒt vs · with his blessed blode

  Vp-on þe harde · tre,

ʒiue vs grace · boþe more and lasse, 680

þorw þe vertu · of þe Masse,

  Vr soules · mai saued be.

Fader *and* Sone · and Holigost

As þou art lord · of mihtes most, 684

  And sittes · In Trinite,

Whon we schal dye · no lengor dwelle,

Kep vs · from þe pyne of helle

  AMEN · For Charite. 688

but none has heard tell of better things than I have told,

except the words of consecration, which are for a priest alone.

A prayer to Christ,

for grace,

unto salvation.

A prayer to the holy Trinity against hell-torment.

APPENDIX V.

MERITA MISSÆ, BY LYDGATE.

(Cotton MS., Titus, A. xxvi, fol. 154.)

Prayer to the Creator for grace to instruct the laymen.

God of hewine, that shoope Erthe And heHe,

Ʒyf me grace svme word to teHe

To the lewde that can not rede,

But the pater noster and the Crede;   4

He bespeaks silence, even if they know as much as he does,

That I may teHe youe, or than I fare,

Houe ye shaH praye, whan and whare,

And thowgh ye can, as weHe as I,

for though a fool of a monk, what he says may be worth as much as a friar's tale.

To here my witte, hit is no foHye,   8

For sumtym is A foHe as good to here

As the word of A freer.

And there-fore, and it be youre wyHe,

Whan I speke, hould youe styH.   12

Devotions at bed-time,

At ewyn whane thoue to bedde shaH gone,

To god thi fadir thou make thy mone,

In manus tuas commendo, &c.

And loke thow sese in-to thi(1) honde

Lyf, sowHe, hows, and londe;   16

And say thi pater noste[r] stiHe,

And after thinke no man non iHe.

and midnight,

At mid nyght, Ʒif that thou maye,

Ris and to thi lord thow prayc   20

In worshippe of his passions aHe,

He had be nyght in cayface haHe.

. . . . (2)

What thou hast saide that orysone.   24

(1) thi *in* MS. *Read* his.
(2) *A line or lines left out in the MS.*

And at morowe whan thou dost wake,   *and at rising.*
Nowe is seson with the Cred thoue take.   *First the Creed,*
The nexte word after that thoue shalte nemen,
Aske thou the kyngdume of heuyne,   28   *then the Lord's Prayer,*
And for thy(1) sowHe the sam bone,
That hit be sawyd at the daye of dome.   *with intention for thy soul and body.*
And thowg thy body be of claye,
Set thow most ther-for and pray,   32   *[fol. 154 b.]*
That where in londe hit comyt or goo,
That hit be sawid fro sham or woo.
Bles the thanne, ȝif that thou maye,   *Then cross thyself, and away to church.*
And to the chyrche take the waye.   36
Whan thou comste to the holy place,   *At the door, take holy water,*
Caste holy water in thi face,
And pray to god that made vs aHe,   *with prayer for forgiveness of venial sins.*
Thi wenyaHe sennys mot fro the ffaH.   40
Than loke to the hy autere,   *Then pray to the reserved sacrament, hanging above the altar,*
And pray to hym that hangythe there,
Where in londe that thoue wende,
That he be at thi laste Ende.   44
Whan thoue haste asked that longithe to þe,
Wershipe Ewyr the Ternyte.   *and then worship the Trinity.*
And whan the preste rynget the beHe,   *When the priest rings the bell,*
Loke thou hold thy tong styHe.   48   *be silent,*
His wordis are of Swyche degre,
There faHythe no man to speke but he ;   *and hearken.*
And whan thou seyste the preste styHe,   *Mutual prayer of priest and people.*
Pray thou than with good wiHe,   52
Thou for hym, and he for the,
And that is a dede of charyte.
And whan the gospiHe shaHe be rede,   *Listen to the Gospel,*
Lestene as thoue were adred,   56
For Eury taHe of a kyng
Wold haue dredfuHe lestnyng ;

(1) MS. forthy

And what man saye it is not soo,

and be ready to
do battle for it.
[fol. 155]

Be redy to fyght or thou goo.   60

Than dare I say thou arte a knyght*e*,

That dare fyght in thi lordis right.

Pray for the
priest,
when he asks
your prayers after
the Offertory.

And he beddythe yove forto praye,

Loke that ye saye not naye,   64

But praye faste a-movng youe aHe,

That no temptacion on hym faHe ;

For he schaHe pray for youe styHe,

Hewyn blysse he bryng youe tyHe.   68

And for another
reason, pray when
the bell is rung at
the elevation,

And whan he ryngythe the cros-beHe,

Pray than for a nothyr skyHe,

That thow be wordy to see that syght,

That schaHe be in hys handis lyght.   72

And whan he restit hym vp on hyght,

kneeling,

Knele A-downe *with* aHe thy myght,

And ȝyf thoue aske any thyng,

Speke dredfuHy as to A kyng.   76

and casting thy-
self on the mercy
of our Lord.

And loke thoue aske no thyng of ryght,

But of his grace and of hys myght.

And ye wyHe a whyHe dueHe,

He illustrates his
meaning by an
example, of one
who has forfeited
house and land to
his earthly sove-
reign.

A good ensampiH I wiH youe teHe :   80

ȝyf thoue forfite hous and londe,

Hit faHythe into the kyngis honde.

That faHythe thoue in that Caas,

To put it into the kyngis grace.   84

And ȝif thoue make a sewte of ryght

Thoue getist it newer of grace nor gysthe.(1)

Than rede I the, nowght thou sewe of ryght,

But of hys gras and of hys myght.   88

[fol. 155 b.]

And namly the ȝifte of swyche A kyng,

That may so frely ȝif aHe thyng—

A kyng that mad bothe swne and mone,

Hit coste hym litiH to grant a bone.   92

(1) *Qu.* gyfte.—*Mr Brock.*

Lat thyn hart her-on dwelle,

Thare whylis I of the cecunde telle.

Whan he hathe that oste in honde,

    Loke thoue neythyr sette ne stoude, 96

But doo the reuernce that thou can,

In tokynyng that he is bothe god and man.

There is no twnge that can telle,

The rewerence that to hym selle. 100

And whan he partythe the oste on twoo,

Thynke on the sorow and on the woo,

That he suferde for thy sake,

Whan the Iewyse his vaynis brake ; 104

And how he dide for the weop

To his fader on olywete.

And ʒif thyne hert be good & kynde,

This loue thoue haue alle-waye in mynde. 108

And ʒif men the ypocryte calle,

Lat watyr owt of thyn eyine falle ;

For lasser loue schall none bee,

Thoue wepe for hym that wepte for the. 112

Of more loue maye no man telle,

Than deid for loue, and goon to helle,

Bynd thyn enmye, and bete hym downe,

And on thyn hed sete a crow[n]e. 116

His Erytage is so fre,

In thy myschefe shall ʒyef hit the.

His aungell, at his comandemente,

Thyne enmyece slayne and all to-rente. 120

Lat nowe no worlly thynge

This loue owt of thyne harte bryng.

And whan he is houʒelyed with that oste,

Pray than to the holy goste, 124

What sothen a wenture the be-falle,

ʒef that it be yower howʒell alle,

And ʒef ye be in cheryte,

ʒe be hoslyd as welle as he : 128

Side notes:

He goes on to speak of the second sacring, so called ;
(*Page* 110, *l.* 21)

and of the Fraction ;
(*Page* 112, *l.* 15)

and the emotion it is intended to arouse, despite sneers at hypocrisy,

with reflections on Christ's love and power.

[fol. 156]

When the priest is communicating,

pray that the mass may stand thee in stead of housel bread.
(*Page* 56, B. 597)

His loue and hys moche myght
3evythe youe hou3yĦ in that syght.
And aĦso 3e, that see him nought,
3yf ye loue hym in aĦ youre thowght,　　　　132
Whedyr ye Ryden or ye goone,
Lat youre loue on hym be oone.

The Rincing.
(Page 54, l. 576)
And whan the preste gothe to the lauatori,
Takeytħe it in no veyn glorye ;　　　　136
But thanke god *with* aĦ thy myght,
He 3ewythe the grace to se that syght.

Consideration
when mass is
ended.
For thow were wont whan thou ver yong,
Coweyte faste to see a kyng ;　　　　140
Than haste thoue sene that coste the no3t,
The kyng that aĦ thys world hathe wro3t,
The kyng that mad bothe day and nyght,(1)

. . . .

Here is given the
ensample of God-
frey of Bouillon;
Ther may none Erthyly tovng teĦ,　　　　144
The victory that to hym ffeĦe,
Godfray whane Ieru3alem
And myche of hethenesse whythem.
He was the beste crystyn knyght,　　　　148
That Ewyr fawght in goddys Ryght.

[fol. 156 b.]
and Charles the
Great;
Charlys wane AĦ frawnce,
And cristende spayne *with*-owtyn stawnce.
Kyng he was and Emp*er*ouu*r*,　　　　152
Of aĦ cristyndome he bare the fflou*ur*,
And Euyr-more he had in mynde
God that mad aĦ man-kynde.

and Arthur,
Arto*ur* com aftyr fuĦ sonne,　　　　156
And conqueryde into gretie Rome.
He was the beste, I ondyr-stonde,
That Euyr was kyng in Inglonde.

who bore about
an image of the
Virgin and Child,
He bare portred far and nere　　　　160
Owyr lady and her sonne dere,

(1) A line or lines wanting.—Not shown in the MS.

And whan he was in any care,
He prayd to the Image euyr mare ;
And as fayne he wolde hys mas here,   164
As any preste or any freer.

and prayed to it
In time of need,
and was always
fain to hear mass.

Take ensampyll of swyche blode,
And not of folys that can no goode,
That wylle not to the sacrament,   168
Doo Rewerence with good Entent.

Take them for
example, and not
ignorant de-
pravers of the
sacrament,

I dar well say that pryd gothe beforen,
And schame comythe aftyr, and blawythe horne.
Whan they wollde worshype wyne,   172
They ar schamyd, and all here kynne.

who bring shame
on themselves
and their kin-
dred,

They fare in chyrche as a lyone strong,
And meke in feld as any lomb.
ʒif Enemys com to any coste,   176
There wold I se hem blow her boste,
And in her othyr(1) beste araye,
Here long suerde and here lavncegaye.

Lions in church
and lambs in
battle,

where he would
rather see them in
pomp and circum-
stance, if need
were,

And ʒif ye will wyn the flouʊr,   180
Clothe hym in hys cotte armowyre,
And so thoue may wyrchyp wyne,
& chewe pryd withoutyn syne.

[fol. 157]

but still without
pride.

In Envye they may be allsoo,   184
That no man schould be-for hem goo.
Be svyche men, I ondyr-stonde,
May be the sawacyon of all a londe !

Warning against
the envious,
they want pre-
cedence,
and are first to
run away.

Schameles and brethelis—(that nowt thee   188
May do) all a contre fle.
And, thou I klype the, prowde knapys,
That make in holy chyrche Iapis,

As to the jeeter,
he thous him,

For he that wyll with Enymyes Fyght,   192
Wyll worshyp god with all hys myght.
Ther a man maye en-sampyll see,
Who wyll fyght and who wyll fle.

and so end his
warlike exam-
ples :

(1) *Read* alther-best

Tho newyr Enemys com newyr in llonde,   196

but all have to
fight manfully
against the flesh
and the devil.
Thow ned the to fyght, I vndeyrstonde,

With youre flesche, and with the fende,

That Eueryday hyt wyłł ʒow schende.

God that mad more and lasse,   200

A prayer for
grace,
ʒif vs grace to here masse,

And so to Fyght, and to praye,

and salvation at
the last day.
That we be sawyd at domys daye.   203

A M E N.

Explicit meryta mysse.

NOTES AND ILLUSTRATIONS.

THE FOUR TEXTS.

Page 1. *Mass-book.* This from very early times was the English name of the *Missale.* "Missal" is comparatively modern, and in all likelihood was never in ordinary use as long as the mass-book itself was a service book of the Church of England. By the Canons of Ælfric (xx), the mass-priest before he was ordained (gehadod) was to have for his spiritual work, amongst other holy books, "pistol-boc. godspel-boc *and* mæsse-boc."(1) The "mæsse-boc" also occurs in a similar enumeration(2) in Ælfric's Pastoral Epistle (xLIV); and in a list of the ornaments of the church at Sherburn,(3) which must be very nearly of the same date, and is written at the end of the York Minster (Xth century) Gospels, from which the Old English Bidding Prayer (*page 62*) is taken, we find "twa *Cristes* bec (*Gospels*), *and* i. aspiciens(4)

---

(1) Thorpe, *Ancient Laws*, II, 350. The epistles and gospels, the Calendar, the Grayle, &c. were not at first collected in a *Missale completum* or *plenarium*, such as is the modern missal, which embodies the parts of the service, assigned to priest, deacon, sub-deacon, and people. Muratori had never heard of any service-book as early as the eleventh century, "*in quo universus iste sacrorum apparatus coagmentatus et per ordinem distributus legatur,*" and hence he suggests a doubt as to the introduction of solitary masses before that time.—Maskell, *Mon. Rit.*, I, p. cxxxv ; Daniel, *Cod. Liturg.* I, 27.

(2) Thorpe, *Ancient Laws*, II, 384.

(3) King Athelstane gave the manor of Sherburne (*in Elmete*) to the see of York in the year 959, which may explain this entry in the York Minster Gospels.

(4) Before the days of title-pages books were often designated by the first words,—in inventories we often find the first words of the second folio for their better identification—and it is, therefore, not improbable that the *Aspiciens* may have been the Antiphoner or Anthem-book, which, as we find in Lyndwood—*Lib.* 3, *Tit.* 27. *Ut parochiani* (z)—contained not only anthems, but also the hymns, responds, &c., of the canonical Hours. The first respond of the nocturns, or first office of the first Sunday in Advent, begins "*Aspiciens a longe ;*" and Amalarius (*De Ordine Antiphonarii, cap.* 8. De officio, *Aspiciens a longe*) notes that these words "currunt per omne tempus adventus Domini in nocturnali officio, et matutinali, ac vespertinali,"

and i. ad te lcuaui(1) *and* ii. pistol bec. *and* i. mæsseboc." In the thirteenth century we have the Ormulum (*White*):—

> Icc hafe sammnedd o þiss boc
> þa Goddspelless neh alle,
> þatt sinndenn o þe messeboc
> Inn all þe ȝer att messe.—Ded. 29-32.

And in Havelock the Dane (*Skeat*)—

> A wol fair cloth bringen he dede,
> And þer-on leyde þe messebok,
> The caliz, and þe pateyn ok.—ll. 185-7.

It would be easy to multiply examples from wills and inventories down to the reformation ; the following are among the latest : John Lord Scrope of Bolton in 1494 leaves his "masse booke imprented" to his chaplain ;(2) and there were in the chantry of St Blase in York Minster in the year 1520 "ij mes bowkes, on of parchment, & ye oder of prynt."(3)

Our last example must be from a book of churchwardens' accounts(4) for the first year of Queen Mary, as that brings us down to the last reign in which Latin service-books were bought out of the church-rate :—1533 "Item paid for a Masse boke. vis. viiid."

P. 2. *Title.*   There is not a contemporary title to any of the six manuscripts. *Præmia missæ* has been written at the beginning of the Corpus MS. (Text C.) in a later hand, either from the mention of the "medes" of the mass (*line* 13), or from this being the name of another book often mentioned in wills and inventories of the XVth century, but of a very different character.

Mr Turnbull in his "Visions of Tundale" (1843) headed the fragment from the Advocates Library in Edinburgh as "The Mass" (our MS. A.), but the name here given more fully conveys the purpose of this "devocioun" (*page* 60, F. 351), which is now for the first time printed at length.

A poem with the title "De Meritis Missæ" is printed by Mr Wright from the Douce MS. among "The Poems of John Audelay" (*Percy Society*, 1844), parts of which however are much older than the "blynd Awdlay," as will be pointed out in the notes on the

---

(1) *Ad te levavi* are in like manner the first words (Ps. (123) cxxii, 1) of the *office* of the first Sunday in Advent ; and this book may have been the Grayle, which according to Lyndwood—*u. s.* (a)—contained not only the *Gradalia*, but also the *Officia*, and the other things "quæ ad chorum spectant in missæ solemnis decantatione."—See Durandi *Rationale*, 6, i, 25. " *Graduarius* dictus est a *gradualibus*, quæ in eo continentur ; qui a pluribus *officiarius* nuncupatur, ab *officiis*, seu *introitibus*, quæ ibi continentur."

(2) *Testamenta Eboracensia* (Surtees Society), III, 95. "Missall" also occurs in this collection (A.D. 1432) II, 21 ; and (A.D. 1436) II, 75.

(3) *York Fabric Rolls* (Raine), p. 278.

(4) Wing in Buckinghamshire.—*Archæologia*, XXXVI, 232.

piece from the Vernon MS. here printed (*page* 128). This poem was also called "Meritum Missæ" in the colophon of an early XVth century MS. in the British. Museum—*Harleian MS.* 3954, fol. 76.

It will be noticed that Lydgate's poem, printed Appendix V, is called "Merita Missæ" in the colophon, page 154.

P. 2, B. 1. *þo*, the midland form of the northern definite article "the," has invariably replaced it throughout this manuscript.

B. 2. *al ;* B. 3. *alle.* The distinction between *al* singular and *alle* plural is observed in this place, although not everywhere in this text. In the corresponding lines in text C., written some fifty or sixty years later in a Yorkshire monastery, we have *alle* in both these lines.

B. 4. *þat tyme.* Any time. Compare A. V., Dan. iii, 15 : "At what time."

B. 4. *wyrk*, C. *wyrke.* We still speak of an author's *works*, and critics, though perhaps disparagingly, of *playwrights.* Our forefathers used the verb also of literary labour :—

> Forthi me think almous(1) it isse,
> To wirke sum god thing on Inglisse.
> *English Metrical Homilies* (Small), p. 4.

B. 7. *Clerkes.* Learned men. This use of the word points to a time when book-learning was almost exclusively confined to the clergy, but it was by no means used only of clerics in holy orders :—

This wol Senek and other clerkes sayn.—C. T. 6766.

þo gan ore louerd prechi of clergie : and hardeliche forth stod : Mi clergie ne cometh nouȝt of me, ore louerd seide : ac of him þat me hidere sende.

Hou can he of clergie ? þis oþur seiden, : to schole neuere he ne wende.

> *Leben Jesu* (Horstmann), 874-6.

Compare A. V., St John vii, 15, 16 : "How knoweth this man letters, having never learned? Jesus answered them, and said, My doctrine is not mine, but his that sent me."

B. 8. *þo boke tellis.* This is a constantly recurring phrase ; and sometimes seems to have been used simply to fill up a line. We meet with it as early as the battle-song of Brunanburh :—Ðæs þe us secȝað béc. (*A.S. Chronicle*, A.D. 937, M.H.B. p. 386.)

Our MS. A. reads *yale bukes*, D. reads *olde bokus ;* and it is not at all unlikely that the later MSS. may here, as in other places, have preserved the reading of the original, which may have been altered by a scribe who was not used to the northern *-es* of the verb in the third person plural.

---

(1) An alms, or charitable work.

P. 2, B. 10. *messe herynge.* When this treatise was written the people
were expected to answer the priest much more than was afterwards enjoined; (1) but as time went on,—and this phrase may
not have been without its influence—the people's part became less
and less, until the mass became an exclusively clerical service. I
subjoin an extract, which very plainly bears this out, from that
very rare book "An Introductorie for to learne to speke French
trewly" by Giles Dewes, or du Guez, which was printed in 1532
or 1533, and reprinted by the French Government in the volume
with Palsgrave's Éclaircissement in 1872. This Giles was "school-
master for the French tongue to the Lady Mary," afterwards
Queen of England, and claims to have taught her father, King
Henry VIII. The French editor supposes the dialogues from
which I quote to have been written(2) in 1527, in which year the
princess was thirteen years of age, and if, as is not unlikely, they
represent actual conversations, a most intelligent pupil. Spite of
the many years he had lived in this country, the gallicisms of the
English translation betray the country of the author.

"Communycation betwene the Lady Mary and her amner, of
thexposytion of the masse" (*Ed.* Génin, p. 1063-4):

I haue good memory, maistre Amnere [*monsieur l'Aumosnier*],
how ye sayd one day that we ought nat to pray at masse, but
rather onely to here and harken, and dyd prove it by that one say
comuuely : I go here masse, which my lorde the President fortify-
ing sayd that we be nat bounde by the lawe to saye, but onely
to here, is it nat true ?

Ye, verely, madame.

Wherfore than sayth the preest after the offytorie,(3) in hym
tourning [*en soi tournant*] to the people, pray for me, etc. and our
Lorde, at his passyon sayd to his discyples, watch and pray, that
ye entre nat in temptation, with that that if our Lorde wolde nat
our prayers, why had he made the *Paternoster.*

Certaynely, madame, that whiche I shewed you was nat onely
but for to shew you how you ought to maintene you at the masse,
specyally unto that that one monysshe you for to pray.

In my God, I can nat se what we shall do at the masse, if we
pray nat.

Ye shall thynke to the mystery of the masse and shall herken
the wordes that the preest say,

Yee, and what shall do they which understande it nat.

They shall behold, and shall here, and thynke, and by that they
shall understande."

---

(1) *Ante,* p. 16, C. 86 ; p. 24, B. 274 ; p. 46, B. 488, where C., a revised
and adapted text, qualifies the answer "loud *or still.*"

(2) Introduction by M. Génin, p. 17.

(3) *Ante,* p. 24, l. 265 ; p. 100, l. 19, &c.

P. 2, B. 11. *þo fift parte.* Compare Audelay's Poems (*Percy Society*),
   p. 73.

> Both saynt Barnard and saynt Bede
> Sayne the masse is of so gret mede,
>   That no mon mend hit may,
> Weder that be(1) were hold or ȝong,
> He myȝt tel with no tung
>   Thaȝ he myȝt leve fore ay.
>
> *Ne exponere habit* (sic) *opus,*
> Half the medis of the masse,
>   Into his last day.
> Were he never so wise of art,
> He schuld fayle the V. part
>   Of the soth to say.

In the Vernon text (Appendix IV, page 132, lines 149—154),
which is itself older than Audelay's time, and either was borrowed
from by him very largely, or represents the older original which
was used for both MSS., we have the same notion, except that
there we have " þe tenþe part," and it is attributed to St Ambrose.

Another version of this MS. (Harleian MS. 3954) claims St
Augustine as its authority—the fourth name we find mentioned,—
but specifies " þe fyfte part." It is added to give an opportunity
of verbal comparison :—

> Sent austyn howso rede ryth,
> þe messe is so mych of myth,
>   þat no man telle may,
> Qweþer he be old or ȝong,
> He may not telle *with* tong,
>   þou he myth leuyn ay.
>
> Ne for to tellyn expres
> Half þe medys of þe mes
>   On-tyl hys laste day,
> Coude he neuer so mekyl of art,
> He xuld faylyn þe fyfte part
>   Of þe soþe to say.—fol. 74 *b*—75.

B. 13. *pardoun*—that is, indulgence or remission of punishment
in purgatory. Many examples of mediæval indulgences have
been printed. One occurs in the Treatise now printed from the
Vernon MS. (page 146, lines 647—652), for kissing the ground
at the gospel at the end of mass, and I here add another published
in a paper fly-leaf—in itself curious as an early example of English
block-printing—which I found stitched on to the vellum (*fol.* 44 *b*)
of the MS. York Horæ, in the Minster Library, elsewhere mentioned. The paper has no water-mark ; size, $5 \times 3\frac{1}{4}$ inches. Above

---

(1) *Read* " he."—ED.

is a shield with the cross and crown of thorns, and the instruments of the passion. On the stem of the cross is the pierced heart, and drops of blood falling from the right side into a chalice. The whole is rudely colonred. The words ECCE HOMO fill up the space outside the lower quarters of the shield, and below are the words :—

Who sum*euer* deuontely
beboildith thes armys(1) of
criste haith vj^m vii^o lv. y[*eres*]. (6755 years.)

In a printed York Horæ (*York Minster Library*, XI, O, 28), *fol.* 69 *b*, we have a rubric, specifying a somewhat similar indulgence, which justifies the conjectural expansion of y*eres* :—

¶ To all the*m* that afore this ymage of pyte denoutly saye .v. Paternosters .v. Aues and a credo . pyteously beholdynge these arme*s*(1) of cristes passion are grau*n*ted .xxxiiM vii hondred. and .vi. yeres of pardon (32706 years).

P. 2, C. 1—6. These half-dozen lines, compared with the Museum MS. above, will show the very numerous smaller differences between Northumbrian and the dialect of the midland scribe :— The *or* þe, þo; maste, *most;* gudness, *godnesse;* haly, *holy;* many falde, *mony folde;* talde, *told.* As they occur I shall draw attention to the variation, or rather the retention of the northern forms, where, as I point out in the Introduction, it leads me to infer that both texts were founded on a northern original.

'C. 4. *gone wyrke.* MS. D. "*gune.*" See also the York Hours of the Cross, p. 84, l. 40, and p. 86, l. 54 and 57. This is the preterite of ginne (A.S. gynnan), to begin, and is often used merely as an auxiliary.

"Ful long time gon he dwelle."—*Ante* (Vernon), p. 136, l. 295.

" þer er þe wordes of þe gospelle
þat Crist til his disciples gun telle."—P. C. 4699-700.

"The gost, that from the fader gan proceed."—C. T. 12255.

C. 10. þe *profet* of *the messe.* Here the thorn letter (þ) and " th " are used in writing the same word. In fact, before the date of this MS. the use of the thorn letter was beginning to be less frequent, and especially, if I am not mistaken, among scribes who were more in the habit of writing Latin. I noticed its absence in a long English document, copied into Archbishop Thoresby's Register in the preceding century.(2)

---

(1) In these quotations *arms* is used in the heraldic sense, but we find Chaucer putting a blasphemous oath into the mouth of the Sompnour (C. T. 6415) by the bodily arms of Incarnate God.

(2) In the *Primer in Latin and Englishe*, John Waylande, 1655, we have a very late example of a printed *thorn* in the *Benedicite*, fol. D 1 :—" Moistures, and þe hore frostes prayse ye oure lorde," and then " The earth," six verses farther on.

P. 2, C. 12. *crafte.* It may be that towards the middle of the fifteenth century, when this MS. was written, *wit* (B. 12 *above*) was beginning to bear the sense in which we now use it, and that *craft* seemed to the Cistercian copyist to be more suitable to the dignity of the subject. Though in the Aȝenbite (*page* 35) we find "wycked creft," it had not sunk down to the "crooked wisdom" with which we now connect it.

Craft or *cræft* (A.S.), like the Icelandic *kraptr* or *kraftr*, and the German *kraft*, was simply power, and it took some centuries before the process of degradation, which Archbishop Trench so well describes, took effect in this word, and it came to suggest that the powers of the mind had been used for evil, and to imply a purpose of fraud and deception.

Compare :—Sunnan cræftas (*the sun's powers*) : Wið þære sawle cræfta ænne (*with one of the faculties of the soul*).—Boethii, Cons. Phil. A.S. ab Ælfredo, *quoted* Bosworth, s.v.

> þy prayer may hys pyte byte,
> þat mercy schal hyr crafteȝ kyþe.
>
> > *Alliterative Poems* (Morris), p. 11, l. 355-6.
>
> I schal, þurgh craft þat ich kan, keuer(1) ȝou, i hope.
>
> > *William of Palerne,* 635.

See B. 371. "men of craft" (*skill, art*), craftsmen, artisans; and see Cursor Mundi, 86, where craft is used specially of versifying :—

> "Off suilk an suld ȝe mater take,
> Crafty þat can rimes make."

P. 3, E. 5. The blundering way in which the MS. of text E. is written has been noted in the Introduction. The first displacement occurs in this place. After line 4 in the MS. there follow the lines here numbered 39—48, as printed in the right order for the sake of comparison.

F. 4. *techeth ;* F. 8. *fyndest.* The reader will here and elsewhere observe the southern *-est* and *-eth* of the verb in this text.

F. 9. *Whiles the prest maketh hym boune.* This refers to the *Præparatio Missæ,* or the *Orationes dicendæ a sacerdote ante missam,* which are found under this or some similar rubric in many manuscript and most printed missals. These prayers were to be said by the priest before he began to "take his vestments on."

boune—ready, from búinn, pp. of the Old Norse búa, to make ready, and also in modern Icelandic use (Cleasby-Vigfusson, búa, II, γ) to pack [? *bind*] in bundles.

"I am boune" (*paratus sum*), Ps. (119) cxviii, 60.

"They busked *and* made them bowne."—*Percy Folio* (Hales & Furnivall), I, 91, *l.* 9.

For another use of this word, *ante,* p. 70, *l.* 7, and the note there.

---

(1) Keuer, *cure.*

P. 3, F. 10. *Vpon thi knees*, in the plural. "The men of this countray knele upon one knee whan they here masse, but the frenche men knele upon bothe." — Palsgrave, *Éclaircissement*, p. 599 (*Ed.* Génin). Mr Furnivall pointed out this quotation to me, and I have not elsewhere met with any mention of kneeling on one knee in church. If our author had written twenty years later, it might have been taken as one of the proverbial sayings he often uses as his examples. We might in that case have understood it as contrasting the progress of the reformation in the two countries, but it cannot have been intended to express the growing impatience at the encroachments of the Roman Curia. In 1530 the doctrinal side of the dispute with Rome had hardly become a question of national interest, so that we must accept what he says as a simple statement of fact, and few men can have had more ample opportunities of observation than Palsgrave himself (1). But however else the difference between the two countries may be accounted for, the one knee of our forefathers is no more to be attributed to any ecclesiastical authority than the sitting and lounging of some of their descendants can be laid to the want of rubrics directing them to kneel. We find the plural in B. 53 and 150 ; and in Myrc (E. E. T. S. ed. *Peacock*) :—

> " No non [*query* mon] in chyrche stonde schal,
> Ny lene to pyler ny to wal,
> But fayre on kneus þey shule hem sette,
> Knelynge doun vp-on the flette."(2)—ll. 270-3.

This direction is more strongly expressed in the "*Constitutions of Masonry*" (Ed. *Halliwell*, 1844) when the directions how to behave in church appear to have been transferred from Myrk for the most part without alteration ; but where Myrc (l. 283) bids the parish preest

> " Teche hem eft to knele downe sone,"

an interpolation exhorts the mason

> " On bothe thy knen down thou falle,
> For hyse love that bowȝht us alle."—*l.* 635-6.

---

(1) He tells us in his title-page he was "*Angloys, natyf de Londres, et gradue de Paris.*" He first took his bachelor's degree at Cambridge, and then went to Paris, and there studied some years before being admitted Master of Arts. We find him again in that country in 1514, when he attended the Princess Mary, whom he had been commanded by her brother Henry VIII "to instruct in the frenche tonge," when she was contracted in marriage to Louis XIII, and he returned with her after the King's death. He was a prebendary of St Paul's from 1514, and was also Rector of St Dunstan's-in-the-East on the presentation of Archbishop Cranmer from 1543 until 1544, when he died.

(2) *Flette.* Floor of the church, the "*in plano*" of the Latin rubrics, "Clived my saule to þe flet." (*Adhæsit pavimento anima mea*) Ps. (119) cxviii, 25.

The Constitutions also point out the difference between kneeling on one or both knees : in the directions how to behave " byfore a lorde " without any loss of self-respect (1) :—

> " Twyes or thryes, withoute doute,
>   To that lorde thou moste lowte ;
>   With thy ry3th kne let hyt be do,
>   Thyn owne worschepe thou save so " (l. 699—702).

So too in " The Boke of Curtasye " printed by Mr Furnivall in the Babees Book, from a Sloane MS., A.D. 1460.

> " Be curtayse to god, and knele doun
>   On bothe knees with grete deuocioun.
>   To mon þou shalle knele opon þe toñ,
>   þe toþer to þy self þou hald aloñ."—p. 304, l. 163-6.

I add one more direction from the Festyvall (W. de Worde, 1515), because it was given to the people in church at bidding the bedes on Sunday :—" Ye shall knele downe on your knees / and lyfte up your hertes makynge your prayers to almighty god, For the good state," &c.

In two places I find *kne*, but it by no means follows that kneeling on one knee is intended. One is in the Vernon MS., *ante*, p. 134, l. 215 ; the other in Lydgate's Vertue of the Masse—

> " ¶ Entryng the chirche, withe al humylite,
>   To here masse at morwe at yowre risyng
>   Dispose yowre self, knelyng on kne,
>   For to be there atte begynnyng.
>   Fro the tyme of his Revestyng,
>   Departe nat till he have doo :
>   To alle thy werkis [*Qu.* werk is] grete furtheryng
>   To abyde the ende of Inprincipio."
>
> Stanza IV, MS. Harl. 2251, fol. 179.(2)

P. 3, F. 12. *The whiles he doth on his westemente.* It has been pointed out in the introduction that the original of this treatise was written with reference to a foreign Use. It will be seen that the texts C. and E. simply leave out the lines (B. 33—40) which assume that the priest is already vested for mass, except the chasuble, before he comes to the altar. In this text the prayer, which, according to the other texts, is to be said at the Office, is transferred to the beginning, and prefaced by a dozen lines of original composition,

---

(1) These lines are also found in a poem, " Urbanitatis," in Mr Furnivall's *Babees Book* (p. 13).

(2) This piece of Lydgate's is one of the *Fugitive Poetical Tracts*, printed for private circulation by Mr Huth, from a unique copy of W. de Worde's edition, in the Cambridge University Library. There are many variations from this manuscript—e. g. amongst others in this stanza " knelynge on your knee," and in the seventh line it adds " it shall be." See *post*, p. 167 *nn*.

in order to adapt it to the English custom of the priest " don-
ning" his vestments before the people at the beginning of mass,
except when he was officiating at the high altar of some cathedral
or collegiate church, and, perhaps also, the altars of some of the
more important parish churches.

The rubrics of the mass-book, portesse, &c., and the Regulæ,
Consuetudinaria, or by whatever name, the orders for conducting
the services in the church of England, according to the several
Uses before the reformation, were drawn up with reference to the
mother-church ; and the modifications necessary to adapt them to
parish churches, for the most part were dependent on custom.
Although there are differences on other points, the following is the
rule, expressed in the same words, according to the use of Sarum
and York, "Dum tertia cantatur executor officii et sui ministri ad
missam dicendam se induant ; " and the Bangor rubric is the same
with merely verbal variations. The subsequent directions prove
that this vesting was not at the altar. According to the rubric
of the Hereford missal (Ed. Henderson, p. 113, 136), the priest
puts on the vestments at the altar. The alb and amice are alone
mentioned as being put on ; but the mention of them, as being
the first put on, implies the rest, and the rubric at the end of
mass specifies the alternative of the priest taking off his vestments
before going from the altar to the vestry.

This vesting at the altar, although an exception in the case of
cathedrals, was in all probability the general practice when distinctive liturgical vestments were first used.(1) In ordinary
parish churches, and also in most chapels in houses and castles of
the great, for whom these devotions were originally written and
had need to be adapted, it must of necessity have continued to be
the rule, for comparatively few old churches in this country were
provided with vestries, and when we do meet with them, except
in perpendicular churches, the style of architecture proves that
they are almost always later than the church itself. The existing
rule in the church of Rome appears to be that the vestments of
cardinals and bishops only, except in the case of certain other
prelates when they celebrate pontifically, should be placed on the
altar, those of bishops in the middle, and of others at the gospel
end (in cornu evangelii).(2) Other priests take their vestments

(1) Different forms of the old Ordo Romanus make mention of vestries,
but it is not unreasonable to assume that vestments were in use before vestries were wanted ; and the survival of the custom of taking the vestments
from off the altar in the case of bishops, and the reference to it in the old
statutes of religious orders, point to its early origin. Nor is this the only
case, though it is one of very trifling importance, where the ceremonial of
bishops, and more especially of the pope, and the more tenacious adherence of
mediæval monks and other regulars to their ancient usages, serve to illustrate
the practice, and not unfrequently the doctrine, of the early Church.

(2) This no doubt is in accordance with ancient custom, and we still find

from the altar upon sufferance only, when there is no vestry. This was forbidden by a decree of the Congregation of Rites (7th July, 1612), but the old practice maintained its ground in many cases, and De Vert (vol. ii, p. 388) mentions that in 1701 he had seen the vestments left on the altar from mass to mass.

At all events, it seems to have been assumed in this country (see, for example, Vernon MS., p. 134, l. 214; p. 136, l. 286; and extracts, post, p. 167) that the priest would ordinarily vest before the people; and not only were the churches provided with chests or coffers "pro vestimentis conservandis," but also the several chapels and side-altar for their separate use. A few examples may be given from the publications of the Surtees Society, Test. Ebor. vol. i, p. 183 (edited by Canon Raine). Richard de Dalton, barber of York, A.D. 1392, leaves to the high altar of the church of Holy Trinity in Miklegate, York, "unam cistam ferro ligatam pro custodiendis ornamentis dicti altaris." Vol. ii, p. 75, we have "Richard Shirburn squyer" of Mitton in Craven, A.D. 1436, bewitting (bequeathing) to the altar of St Nicholas in the "parysh kirke of Mitton," service books, vestments, altar-cloths, chalice, paxbrede, other ornaments "and a kiste for to keep all this gere in, with the appurtenance that langes to the same auter." In the York Fabric Rolls, the same editor has printed several inventories, from which it appears there was, A.D. 1360, at the altar of St John of Beverley in York Minster "una cista pro vestimentis reponendis" (p. 288); and at that of St Paulinus and St Chad, A.D. 1378, "una archa de Flaundres pro vestimentis reponendis in eadem, precii 13s. 4d.; unum armoriolum ligneum similiter pro iisdem, precii, 4s." (p. 300).

The inventories of cathedral and other churches afford many other examples of chests and coffers for vestments, not kept in vestries, but I have not met with any reference in liturgical treatises to the fact of vestments being kept in aumbries below the altars. I therefore add some quotations which bear upon it. In the year 1435, Richard Russell, Citizen and Merchant of York, amongst other bequests to his parish church, the now demolished Church of St John's in Hungate, leaves a wooden altar with an aumbry below.(1) He directs "quod unum altare fiat bene et

remnants of it, where perhaps they might be least expected. According to the rubric of the English Coronation Service "the archbishop goeth to the altar and puts on his cope," which is shown (Sandford's *History of the Coronation of James II.*) in the Plate of the "Prospect of the Inside of the Collegiate Church of St Peter in Westminster, as it appeared before the grand proceeding entered," placed ready on the middle of the altar. And so too as to the "*cornu euangelii*," the Lutheran ministers in Denmark and Norway not only wear the chasuble at the administration of the communion, but they still take it from the northern part of the altar.

(1) He leaves another wooden altar to the church after the fashion of this one. In the same collection of wills we have Dan John Raventhorp,

effectualiter de tabulis, in parte boreali dictæ ecclesiæ, coram yma-
ginibus Beatæ Mariæ et Sanctæ Annæ, et subtus idem altare
unum almariolum pro libris et vestimentis iidem altari pertinenti-
bus fideliter conservandis" (*Test. Ebor.* II, 53). The testator's
care for the faithful conservation of his bequests was not uncalled
for. We find among other presentments made as to York Minster
in 1472, that it was feared a certain vestment belonging to the
altar of the Blessed Virgin would suffer from damp "quia jacens
per longum tempus subtus altare."—*York Fabric Rolls*, 252. Not
to refer to other mediæval examples, it may be sufficient to quote
from Thiers, *Dissertations sur les Autels*, Paris, 1688, who speaks
in terms of condemnation of the practice, as if still existing, " de
reserrer les ornements et les livres nécessaires pour la célébration
des mystéres divins, sous les autels dans les armoires" (p. 34).
He quotes the recent synodal instructions of M. Godeau, bishop of
Vence, forbidding any aumbries in altars, and refers to the earlier
constitution of a provincial council(1) at Tholouse in 1590, which
follows:—" Fenestra in altari nulla sit, foramenve nullum, ut quod
Christi sacrosancto corpori sustinendo fuerit dedicatum, hinc nihil
aliud, omnino inseratur."

P. 3, F. 12, *westemente.* The use of *w* points to the late date of this MS.
Robert Calverley of Calverley, Esquier, A.D. 1498, bequeaths to the
church of Calverley " ij sewtes of westiments, one of qwhit for the
festes of our Lady, a noder of blake for Requiem."—*Test. Ebor.* IV,
157-8. Inventory, York Minster, A.D. 1543, " Altare nomiuis
Jhesu in the rudde loft . . . . sex westementes, one of blake
welwet" (*York Fabric Rolls*, 301). St Wilfrid's altar: " . . . . one
vestment of whitt satten *with* floures; one westement of witt
damask with birdes" (*ib.* 304).

Vestment is used in various senses—I. Any single vestment,
but more especially the chasuble; II. The complete set of mass-
vestments worn by priest, deacon, or subdeacon. The synodical
constitution of Walter Grey, Archbishop of York, A.D. 1250, require
the parishioners(2) to find " Missale vestimentum (*the* principal

---

priest of the chapel of St Martin in Aldwerk (York), leaving, A.D. 1432, to
the said chapel " Vestimentum cum altari ligneo."—*Test. Ebor.* II, 28. These
bequests were the deliberate acts of men who, to judge from their wills, were
not likely to offend against any established rule; and this I point out because
other examples, which I quoted some years ago in an incidental mention of
the use of wooden altars before the reformation (*Contemporary Review*,
vol. III., Oct. 1866, p. 261), were characterized by one of my critics as
" exceptional irregularities," and " make shift expedients."

(1) Labb. & Coss. XV, col. 1403, A. I have not been able to verify the
reference to the constitution of the bishop of Vence. M. Godeau was consecrated in 1636.—*Gallia Christiana*, XIII, 311.

(2) There is an ordination of the dean and chapter of York on the same
subject for the churches of their jurisdiction; and a similar constitution was
made for the province of Canterbury at the council at Merton, A.D. 1305.

mass-vestment) ipsius ecclesiæ principale, viz. casula, alba munda, amictus, stola, manipulus, zona, cum tribus towellis; corporalia; et alia vestimenta pro diacono et subdiacono honesta juxta facultates parochianorum et ecclesiæ." In this sense vestment was still used by Bishop Bonner, in his visitation, 1554 (2 Mariæ) :— " Articles concerning the church and ornaments of the same . . . . Whether the things underwritten (which are to be found at the cost of the parishioners) be in the church ; . . . . a principal vestment with chesuble, a vestment for the deacon and subdeacon " (Cardwell, *Doc. Ann.* (1844), p. 151). III. A suit of vestments, as in the extract from the will in the last paragraph, included a complete set for priest, deacon, and subdeacon. I give an instance where it occurs in the inventory of the ornaments of York Minster, A.D. 1510, with an explanation : " VESTIMENTA ALBA. Una secta, viz., pro presbitero, diacono, et subdiacono " (*York Fabric Rolls*, 232).

Vestment in the text is no doubt used for the principal or priest's vestment, consisting, as we have seen above, of chasuble, alb, amice, stole, maniple (or *fanon*), and girdle.

I add two extracts from unpublished manuscripts as to the vesting of the priest.

The first is from Lydgate's Vertue of the Masse (quoted above, page 163), where the several vestments are mentioned in the order which they are put on :—

" ¶ The morallisacioun of þᵉ prist whan he gothe to masse.(1)

¶ Vpon his hede. an Amyte. the prist hathe,
Whiche is a signe. tokene(2) of figure,
Outwarde a shewyng. grounded on the faithe.
The large Awbe.(3) by record of scripture
In rightwisnes. perpetually to endure ;
The longe girdelle. clennesse and chastite ;
Rounde on the Arme. the phanon dothe assure
Al sobrenes knet.(4) withe humilite.

¶ The stole also strecchyng on lengthe
Is of doctours. saithe the angels doctryne,
Amonge heretiks. to stonde in strengthe
Fro cristes lawe. neuer to declyne.
The Chesible(5) above. withe charite fyne,
As phebus, in his mydday spiere ;
Holdithe euer his cours. in the Right lyne
To strecche oute. his beames cliere.

---

(1) Interpretatio misse—W. de Worde.   (2) and a—W. de W.
  (3) largeable—W. de W.   (4) knytte—W. de W.
            (5) Chesuble—W. de W.

¶ A prist made stronge. with*e* this armure
A fore the Awtier. as cristis champiouñ
Shal stonde vpright. make no discomfiture,
Owre thre enemyes. venquysshe and bere downe
The flessh*e* the world. Sathan the felle dragouñ.
First to begynne. or he further passe
With*e* contrite. and lowe confessiouñ,
And so procede. devoutly to the masse."—MS. Harl. 2251, fol. 181.

The other is from Langforde's *Meditacyons for goostly exercyse in þe tyme of þe Masse*, written in the time of Henry VII, and now in the Bodleian Library (A. Wood, MS. 9), but here the putting on of the amice, alb, and girdle is not "improved upon : "—
"now ou*r* Intent ys. to move soolles. to þe devotyon of þe masse. *and* to the lovyng Remem*b*rance of þe **Passyon of Cryst***e*.
Now frome hensforthe furst reid þe titles *and* so aft*er*, þe Medytatyons.

When þe fanell*e* ys put on þe Lefte hand
Remember þe roips wit*h* þe whiche. þe knyghte*s* dyd bynd ou*r* Sauy*oures* hand*es*. when þa*i* dyd Leyd hym fro Tyrant to Tyrant.

When þe stoole ys cast ouer hys necke *and* crossyd on þe breist.
Haue medytatyon of þe bosteous roipys. wherwit*h* þe turmentors dyd drawe hys blyssyd body on þe crosse so sore. þat alle hys Ioynt*tes* was dyssoluyd. *and* hys Scenowys *And* vaynys alle to brast.

When þe pr*e*st castyth on hys ouermest vestment, callyd A chesible.
Remember þe Purpule Mantell*e* wherin they dyd cloith*e* ou*r* Sauy*our* in grett scorne, *and* howe þe*i* crovnyd *and* Septuryd hym wit*h* A Rode. *and* bete *and* mokyd hym. saing haile kyng of Iewys. spyttyng vnreu*er*ently in hys moost blyssyd faice."—*Bodleian MS.*, A. Wood, 17. fol. 7.

P. 4, B. 16. *Sacrament.* Sacrament is here used in its larger sense, for though the eucharist or sacrament of the altar was ministered in the mass,(1) the mass itself was not one of the seven, especially called, sacraments.

B. 17. *Ane.* The northern *ane* is here retained by the midland copyist on account of the rhyme, though at other times he has altered it to the injury of the sense; e. g. *ll.* 425 and 426 into ave [*Maria*], and *l.* 561 into ay (*ever, always*). E reads *on* and changes *name* to nome.
It may be noticed that, as *ll.* 229 and 231, 269 and 270, &c., the consonance of *m* and *n* was sufficient for the rhyme.

---

(1) "Sacramentum eucharistiæ non conficitur nisi in missa."—J. de Burgo, *Pupilla Oculi* (1510), fol. 12, B.

As to the substantive use of *one* in making a quotation, cf. Chaucer, *The Persones Tale;* Secunda pars penitentiæ :—" Witnesse on, seint Jame thapostil, that saith."

And the authorised version, Heb. ii, 6 : " For one in a certain place testified."

P. 4, B. 18. *Dam.* Dam, Damp, Dane, Dan, Daun ; Fr. *Dom*, O.F. *dam, danz, damp,* from Lat. *dominus* (*o* changed into *a*, as in *dame* from *domina*).

This title of respect, which latterly in France was specially given to Benedictines, was in England used of all ranks, lay and cleric, from the king to the handicraftsman, as witness Chaucer :—

" Lo hier the wise kyng daun Salamon."—C. T. 5617.
" Lok of Egipt the king, daun Pharao."—C. T. 16619.
" Wherfor, sir monk, damp Piers, by your name."—C. T. 16278.
" My lord the monk, quod he, be mery of chere,

. . . .

Whether schal I calle you my lord dan Johan,
Or daun Thomas, or elles dan Albon ? "—C. T. 15410-16.
" Unto a smyth, men clepith daun Gerveys,
That in his forge smythed plowh-harneys."—C. T. 3759-60.

B. 18. *Jeremy.* See the Introduction, and note, page 172.
B. 19. *a religyus.* C. and F. omit the article, but religious is constantly used as a substantive of men or women, who were bound by a private religion, or the rule(1) of a monastic or other order, in contradistinction to the lay-folk and clergy bound only by their christian profession, or their ordination vows.

" And syth yt ys so in seculers, moche more yt ys blamefull in relygyous."—*Myroure* (E. E. T. S.) 63.

" . . . . . ' þe dede of povert na mercy has

. . . .

Ne til na religiouse, ne til na seculere
For dede over al men has powere."—P. C. 1880, 88 and 89.

See " Bidding Prayer," *ante,* p. 68, l. 18. By the Act 4 Henry IV, c. 12 (1402), it was provided, sec. 5, that in every case of appropriation from thenceforth " a secular person be ordained vicar perpetual," and, sec. 6, "that no religious be in any wise made vicar in any church so appropriated, or to be appropriated by any means in time to come."

" . . priests, as well religious as other, have taken wives and married themselves."—*Proclamation against marriage of priests,* 16 Nov. 13 Henry 8 (1531).

B. 22. *No ianglyng make.* In Early English remains we meet with

---

(1) Thus we find mention of trespasses against God and against "the religion."—*Myroure,* p. 153.

frequent mention of jangling or chattering in church, and we find the phrase in use down to the reformation.

> " ȝyf þou euer ianglyst at messe
> Yn þe cherche wyþ more or lesse,
> And lettyst men of here preyers,
> For hem perel soþely þou berys ;
> þe halyday þou holdest nat ryȝt,
> And lettyst to wurschyp god almyȝt."

Robert of Brunne, Handlyng Synne, 1004-9.

> " When þou in kirk makes ianglyng
> Or thynkes in vayn anythyng ;
> Be it with-outen, be it with-in,
> Yhit it es a veniel syn."

Hampole, Pricke of Conscience, ll. 3478-81.

> " Whanne þou sittist(1) in þe chirche þi beedis þou schalt bidde ;
> Make þou no iangelynge to freende nor to sibbe."

Babees Book, p. 37, l. 25.

> " Auyse you wel also / for ony thinge
> The chirche of prayer / is hous and place
> Beware therfore / of clappe or Iangelynge
> For in the chirche / it is ful grete trespaas
> And a token of suche / as lackyth grace
> There be ye demure / and kepe ye scilence
> And serue ye god / with al your diligence."

Caxton's Book of Curtesye, ll. 78-84.

> " Whether any do use to commune, jangle, or talk in the church at the time of divine service ? "—Articles of Enquiry, 1547. *Cardwell*, Doc. Ann., p. 29.

See also the Ayenbite of Inwyt, p. 20, l. 215, and the Vernon MS., *ante*, p. 136, l. 281, and the note there.

P. 4, B. 23. *grett saumple.* Mediæval homilies and treatises intended for popular instruction were very commonly interspersed with legendary tales and " pleasant gestes," sometimes of a character which would rather scandalize a modern audience; but at all events so far as intention went,(2) not unlike the stories which

---

(1) It is hardly necessary to observe that sitting did not imply our sitting posture :

> "Alle men þat þis chaunce sees
> Sitteþ dowyn upp on oure knees."

Handlyng Synne, 950-1.

(2) No doubt they were intended to serve a moral purpose. The Knight of La Tour-Landry—and no stories would more offend modern propriety—thought "a man aught to lerne his doughters with good ensaumples."—*Ed.* Wright, E. E. T. S., p. 2. The name is given to our Lord's sayings :

> "Ore louerd wende a boute and prechede þat folk, and seide him ansaumples fale."—*Leben Jesu* (Horstman), l. 94.

And His parables are so called, *Alliterative Poems* (Morris), p. 15, l. 499.

in the present day are introduced in sermons under the name of anecdotes, though perhaps they may sometimes have been published a dozen times. They were often noted in the margin "exemplum," "narracio," &c., as in the Vernon MS., *ante*, p. 140, l. 438. In the note there will be given several versions of the same story, which are curious, not only in the philological point of view, but also as illustrating the absolute freedom which the writers allowed themselves when dealing with persons, place, and circumstances.

P. 4, B. 26. *messe here.* See note, p. 158.

B. 27. *When þo preste saies he, or if he singe.* The first "he" is not in the other text, and is evidently a mistake. "Say or sing" is constantly used with reference to the two ways of performing mass, saying without note, or singing according to the notation, which was often added in the MSS., and in service books, when they came to be printed. The alternative words are still retained in the rubrics of the Book of Common Prayer. Robert of Brunne speaks of "reading" in reference to the whole service, or perhaps of the lessons in the hours, and the epistle and gospel in the mass, as "read" is used in this treatise (B. 153), and in the English Prayer Book, of the Epistle and Gospel.

> " And þat day [*Sunday*] þow owest and shal
> For to here þy seruyse al,
> Matyns, messe here, to rede or syngg,
> Euery deyl to þe endyngg."—H. S. 821-4.

He may here be referring to the layman's part in the service— and the frequent bequests of mass-books and portesses by mediæval wills, both by and to laymen, and even ladies, show that more were able to read them than we are apt to suppose. He seems however to be speaking to men of all orders :—

> " How dur oþer prestys or clerkys
> Or þou lewede man, þat day worche,
> Whan þat day ys halewede yn holy chyrche ? "—H. S. 832-4.

Compare Archbishop Thoresby's Catechism (A.D. 1357) on the third (*fourth*) Commandment :—

> "**The third is,** that we sall hald and halowe oure holiday,
> The Sononday, *and* all other that falles to the yhere,
> That er ordayned to halowe thurgh halikirk,
> In whilk daies al folke lered and lawid
> awe to gyf tham godely to goddes service.
> To here it *and* say it, aftir thaire state is,
> In Worship of god almighten *and* of his gode halowes."(1)

In the *Myroure* there is a chapter, " What profyt is in the songe

---

(1) *Thoresby's Register*, fol. 296.—See *ante*, p. 118.

of diuyne servyse, more than in the saynge without note."—*Ed.*
E. E. T. S., p. 9.(1)

P. 4, B. 30. *prayere.* It will be observed that this word is here a
dissyllable, as in French. In the next century it would seem to
have been fully naturalized, and to have acquired the English
accent, and scanned as a monosyllable, if we may assume that the
alteration in C. 30 was made to suit the metre.

C. 18. *Saynte Jerome.* There does not appear to be anything in
the extant writings of St Jerome, or the spurious pieces, printed
as such with his works, which could be made to stand for this
quotation; but apart from this consideration, and supposing my
conjecture, as to Archdeacon Jeremiah being the author, to be as
far from the mark as it very possibly may be, it is still most
probable that the "Jeremy" of texts A. and B. is the true reading.
It would be much more likely for a scribe, who had never heard
of a "Dan Jeremy," to change it to St Jerome, upon whom so
many mediæval quotations are fathered, than for the well-known
name of Jerome to be changed into Jeremy; and we may observe
that the description, as a "devout man" and "a religious," would
have seemed especially applicable to this father, who was not
only known as one of the four Latin doctors, but also distinguished
in the Middle Ages as the "perfectus monachus."

P. 5, E. 24. *hely.* It was a great interest to Archbishop Whately to
trace the concatenation of ideas which led to manifest blunders;
and many amusing stories used to be current in Oxford of the
expedients he adopted to extract them from the men themselves
when his acuteness was at fault. I doubt whether even he could
have made anything out of some of the blunders of the puzzle-
headed scrivener of this text; and though I cannot pretend to say
what he meant by *hely*, I think I can guess why he avoided(2)
the word *ill*, which we find in the other MSS., except when, as in
lines 192, 272, and 529, the rhyme was too strong for him—not
because the old Norse "ill" (*Icel.* Illr; *M.G.* ubils; *A.S.* yfel;
Germ. übel), which came over with the Danish invasion, had
not found its way from the northern to his west-midland dialect,
and he did not know the meaning—but because he did know the
meaning, and looked upon it as a word of ill omen, and therefore
was unwilling to use it. I have not had an opportunity of
examining the MS. and observing whether in the places he writes
it, he has "*signed away*" the ill-luck, but I have noticed in other

---

(1) In the heading of the chapter (p. 23), it is "songe wythoute note."
(2) In line 373, he writes *heuy.* In line 51, speaking of confession, he
utterly destroys the sense, and instead of
          "Knowe to God that þai are ille",
writes—
          "Know to God þat harowd helle".

MSS. that when writing this very word *ill*, the names of the Evil-one,(1) certain sins, or curses, and so forth, the scribe has often added a small cross (2) for this purpose.

P. 6, B. 31-2. *know—draw.* Compare Hampole :

> " All es contende in þis tretice here
> þat I haf drawen out of bokes sere,
> After I had in þam understandyng
> Alle if I be of symple kunnyng."—*P. C.* 9577-80.

> " þarfor þis buke es on ynglese drawen
> Of sere maters, þat er unknawen
> Til laude men þat er unkunnand."—*P. C.* 336-8.

And the Ormulum :

> " Ich hafe wennd intill Ennglissh
> goddspelles hallge lare.
> Affter þat little witt tatt me.
> min drihhtin hafeþþ lenedd."—ll. 13—16.

B. 33. *auter al dight.* We find in Myrk an account of what was required in the fifteenth century :—

> " Fyrst se, prest, as I þe mynne,
> þat þow be out of dedly synne ;
> þyn auter þenne þou do dyȝt,
> þat hyt be after thy myȝt.
> Se þe cloþes þat þey be clene,
> And also halowet alle by-dene,
> Wyth þre towayles (3) and no lasse
> Hule þyn auter at thy masse ;
> Al oþer thynge þow knowest wel,
> What þe nedeth euery del.
> Loke þat þy candel (4) of wax hyt be,

---

(1) " Some vse when they here the fende named in play or in wrathe to say Ave maria; that lyke as he ioyeth of the vycyouse namynge of his owne name, so is he rebuked by namynge of thys holy name maria."—*Myroure*, p. 78.

(2) See example, *ante*, p. 118, l. 8. Cf. Lindisfarne Gloss., Jo. viii, 48.

(3) This counts the corporas. Durandi, *Rat.* 4, xxix, 1 & 7.

(4) It was directed by a provincial constitution of Archbishop Reynold, in a council at Oxford in 1322, "Accendantur duæ candelæ vel ad minus una." Unlike the direction in this place, we often find pictures where the light is in the hand of the minister; *e. g.* the woodcut frontispiece of W. de Worde's *Vertue of the Masse.*

The " Novum Registrum Ecclesiæ Lincolniensis," or the Statutes given by Bishop Alnwick for Lincoln Cathedral in 1440, lately printed by Bishop Wordsworth, the present occupant of that see (see an article in the *Quarterly Review*, January, 1871, vol. cxxx. 225), contain minute directions for the treasurer as to the number of candles to be provided according to the season, as for example :—"in festis novem lectionum . . . . invenire debet unum cereum super cornu altaris versus aquilonem et duos super parva candelabra

> And set hyre, so þat þow hyre se,
> On þe lyfte halfe (1) of þyn autere,
> And loke algate ho brenne clere,
> Wayte þat ho brenne in alle wyse
> Tyl þow haue do þat seruyse."—ll. 1865—1880.

The illuminations of manuscripts, and the woodcuts in early printed service-books, enable us to form a very accurate idea of a mediæval altar. In some cases, and more particularly in later examples, besides the paten and chalice, we may notice a cross or candlesticks or the pax-brede; and there are sometimes costers or curtains running on rods at the north and south sides of the altar. There is marked absence (2) of the numerous ornaments which may be seen on modern altars. Indeed, to judge from the manner in which they are spoken of in the following extract—the author being a Roman catholic clergyman—it would seem that their more general adoption was quite recent. He tells us that the altars of the Roman basilicas, " unencumbered with tabernacles, reliquaries, statues, or flower-pots, support a cross and six candle-sticks; furniture which is sufficient without doubt for all the purposes of solemnity, and yet may be endured even by a puritan. The other ornaments, or rather superfluities, which are too often to be observed on the altars of Catholic churches, owe their introduction to the fond devotion of nuns or nun-like friars, and may be tolerated in their conventual oratories, as the toys and playthings of that harmless race, but never allowed to disfigure the simplicity of parochial churches and cathedrals."—*Tour through Italy*, by Rev. John Chetwode Eustace, 4to, 1813, I., p. 373.

---

ante altare, qui ardere debent ad utrasque vesperas, completorium, matutinas et missas. . . . In diebus feriatis tantum unum cereum inveniat super altare; ad vesperas, completorium, et ad missas, duos super candelabra parva."

(1) That is, on the right hand, looking east, as in the old rubrics and ritual expositors. The right and left of the modern Roman rubrics refer to the right and left of the crucifix on the altar. See Maskell, A. E. L. 19. The more usual way of distinguishing the sides and ends of the altar in the Church of England before the reformation was north and south, as in the Eastern Church, and as still retained in the rubric of the Book of Common Prayer. See also p. 16, B. 156, and the note there; p. 54, B. 579, &c.

(2) The learned Benedictine, Abbot Gerbert, in his Disquisitions (Tom. I., p. 199), after discussing reliquaries, crosses, and candlesticks as ornaments upon altars, draws attention to the illuminations of the St Blas Missal (sæc. ix.), as showing the altar "planum quidem ac omnibus hactenus recensitis ornamentis destitutum, vestitum tamen." This vesting is not after the scanty fashion of later times, but, as may be observed in examples reaching down to the Reformation, was such as is described in the *Voyages Liturgiques* (p. 79, 80) at the cathedral of Augers about the beginning of the last century. " Les autels selon l'ancien usage . . . . . sont a nud, et ne sont couverts de quoi que ce soit ; de sorte que ce n'est qu'un moment avant d'y dire la Messe, qu'on y met les nappes, qui débordent comme celle qu'on met sur un table ou l'on dine, et il n'y a point de parement."

P. 6, B. 34. *reuysht right*—not as yet with all the vestments worn at mass, but, as may be gathered from the two following lines, and the thirteenth-century Rouen rubric quoted in the next note, p. 178, with amice, alb, girdle, maniple and stole, but without the chasuble. The fact that this was still the practice at Rouen at the end of the seventeenth century confirms the explanation here given ; and it is curious in itself as an instance of established custom holding its own, when the written law was silent, for the rubric there quoted had disappeared from the MS. missal of the next century, and was not inserted in the printed missal of 1497, which is the only one I have had opportunity to examine. In the description of the ceremonies at Rouen, in the *Voyages Liturgiques*,(1)—and unless I have overlooked it, there is no mention of the practice anywhere else(2) — it is mentioned (p. 328) that, during tierce, the priest who was to celebrate mass, the deacon and subdeacon, were " *revétus comme pour la messe, excepté la chasuble et les tuniques ;* " and (p. 361) that the priest who was to celebrate high mass on Sundays was, before tierce, " *revétu d'aube, d'étole et de manipule.*"

B. 35—38. The marginal note shows the sense in which I had understood this passage, and which I still conceive to be the meaning ; namely, that the priest was already vested for mass, except the chasuble, and took that, the " overmost vestment," from off the north end or north(3) part of the western side or front of the altar, and, stepping backward from the footspace of the altar, put it on over his head above the alb and other vestments which he had already put on according to a French local use.

I had not intended to prolong this note beyond a reference to my authorities for including this in the number of places in this treatise, which have led me to the conclusion that the original was written with reference to the Rouen use. But it so happens that the text has had the honour of an anticipatory criticism,

---

(1) *Voyages Liturgiques de France* par le Sieur de Moleon (*Lebrun des Marettes*), Paris, 1718. The journeys appear to have been made before 1698, see p. ix, p. xii, and 319.

(2) At Orleans the priest had formerly said the psalm *Judica* (*ante*, p. 90, l. 14) in his alb and stole before putting on his chasuble.—*Voyages Liturg.* 200.

At private masses the Cluniacs vested at the altar, the vestments and mass-book being brought from the vestry by a *conversus* or novice ; but they did not put on the chasuble until after confession.—Udalricus, *De Antiquis Clun. Monast. Consuetudinibus*, L. I., c. 30, quoted by Martene, *De Antiquis Monachorum Ritibus*, Lib. II., c. vi., 17, 18.

(3) The "south auter nook " (*cornu*) had been already occupied by the mass-book (p. 10, B. 87) when the altar was dight. The custom of taking the vestments from the north end at the beginning of the service is still retained in Scandinavian churches, and (when they are taken from the altar by simple priests) in Roman also.—See p. 164, *n.* 2.

the corrected proofs of the earlier sheets of this work having come
into the hands of Mr Scudamore when he was engaged in the
preparation of the second edition of his *Notitia Eucharistica*, which
has just been published. He does not accept my gloss in the
margin; but with the text before him, he cuts the knot (p. 116) by
a conjectural reading which suits his own rendering of the passage,
and argues that it is to be understood of spreading the corporas.

Mr Scudamore very courteously challenges me to a discussion on the question he has raised. First, then, as to this
alteration. In line 38, for "him" he reads "it."—"does it upon
IT." Now, if there were any authority in the manuscript for this
correction, it would at once settle the question in the sense for
which he contends, but there is none whatever. I had myself
copied it "hĩ" from the MS. some twenty years ago. Mr Brock,
whose accuracy is well known to the members of the E. E. T.
Society, had written it "him," in the copy which he made for this
edition, marking the expanded contraction in italic, and he left
it unaltered when he read the proof with the original. I had
therefore very little doubt myself, but I was unwilling to allow
the reading to stand if there could be any doubt as to its correctness, and referred the point to my friend Mr Thompson,(1) who,
with his usual kindness, answered my letter at once. He writes,
"the MS. has hĩ, which can stand only for *him;*" and from his
judgment as to the reading of a manuscript there is no appeal.

But, assuming that Mr Scudamore's is the only tenable explanation, there was no occasion for him to correct the text. Towards
the close of the xivth century, when the Museum manuscript was
written, "*him*" was still sometimes used in the dative, as "*his*"
was then, and down to the time of King James' translation of the
Bible, the genitive of the neuter "*hit.*" The "him" of the MS.
might therefore have been taken to refer to the altar, and "hit"
to the corporas, if this way of construing the line had been consistent with the remainder of the passage. For, apart from any
other consideration, I am inclined to think that a closer examination of the text will convince Mr Scudamore he is mistaken in his
explanation. He glosses "comes oback" (l. 37) as of the priest
"walking backwards" in order to spread the corporas on the altar,
and offers no explanation of the other half of the line—"a litel
doune;"—but if the "clothe" of the text had been the corporas,
or the altar-cloth, the priest would not have moved away from the
altar in order to spread it; rather in that case he would have
spread it on the altar before descending the altar-step for the confession.

Perhaps Mr Scudamore might not have found the same difficulty
if his attention had been directed to the mediæval ritual of the

---

(1) E. Maunde Thompson, Esq., MSS. Department, British Museum.

Church in France when the several provinces maintained the Gallican independence from Roman centralization ; or if he had known that "cloth" was used in early English for any garment, and especially for a vestment such as the purple robe with which the soldiers mocked our Lord, or the chasuble of the priest in the mass which was explained to symbolize it.(1)

In the present day we no longer use *cloth* in the singular in this sense, and when we use it in the plural we distinguish it both by the pronunciation and the spelling. Johnson explains *cloth*, plural cloths (*th* sounded), as "anything woven for dress or covering ; " and this definition holds good either of a whole piece or a portion when used as for an altar-cloth, table-cloth, neck-cloth, horse-cloth, &c. We also use the plural, spelt *clothes*, and as Johnson notes, pronounced "clo's," for clothing in general, or bed-coverings, but we no longer employ the singular for a single garment, as in the following examples.(1)

"Rochet, clothe, *Supara*."—*Prompt. Parv.* 435.

"I wold I had thy smock and every cloth."

Chaucer, *C. T.* 7215.

"He dede on cursing as a cloþ." ("*Induit maledictionem sicut vestimentum*.") Ps. (109) cviii., 17, in *Lollard Doctrines* (Camden Soc.), p. 24.

"An wif, þatt wass þurrh blodess flod
Well ner all brohht to dæþe,
Þurrh þatt ȝho ran (2) uppo hiss claþ,
Wass hal off hire unnhæle."

Ormulum, II., ll. 15516-9.

"touchide his cloth." "*vestimentum*" (Wyclif). Mar. v., 27.
"touchide the hem of his cloth." "*vestimenti ejus*" (Wyclif). Lu. viii., 44.

"Therefore Ihesus wente oute, beringe a crowne of thornes and a clothe of purpur." "*purpureum vestimentum*" (Wycliff). Jo. xix., 5.

"On my cloiþ þei castiden lott."—Wyclif, *Sermons* (Arnold), II., 127.

"Þo iewys kesten at þe dys
Qweþer xuld han hys cloth.

Poems (Furnivall), p. 248, l. 156-7.

The "Illusus induitur veste purpurarum " of the Hours of the Cross (*ante*, p. 85, l. 30) is rendered in the midland prose version,

---

(1) "The expressions (without example, so far as I know) of 'a cloth,' and 'a chasuble cloth,' for 'chasuble.' "—Mr Scudamore, *Notitia Eucharistica* (1875), p. 116.

(2) ran, *touched*, reinen (A.S. hrinan, *perf*. hran), to touch. Cf. Vulg. "*et tetigit vestimentum ejus*." S. Marc. v., 27.

printed by Mr Maskell (*Mon. Rit.* II., 50),—"He is skorned and clothid with the cloth of purpure."

I will only add a quotation given by Dr Morris (*Pricke of Conscience*, p. 313) from MS. Harl. 4196 :

> " þe purper clath þat he in stode,
> Was hardened all with his awin blode."

The so-called " Book of Ceremonies," which appears to have been considered in the southern convocation of 1539-40, but not allowed by the royal authority,(1) explains :—" The overvesture or chesible, as touching the mysterye signifieth the purple mantill that pylats souldyours put uppon crist after that they had scurged hym."(2)

These quotations will be sufficient to prove that " cloth " might very well have been here used of the chasuble as explained by the gloss in text E. (l. 39), but I am able to bring forward an example of the name of *cloth* being applied to the chasuble in a formal document, which, though of later date than our text, nevertheless goes to prove the earlier *usus loquendi*. On the 4th May, 1547, the Archbishop of York was informed of an intended Royal visitation, and the injunctions of the Royal commissioners are recorded in the register of the Dean and Chapter of York in October, 1547. *Inter alia* to the clergy of the minster : " For th' avoyding diuersitie of apparell of the clergie in tyme of theire service, it is injoined that the *pre*bends, vicars chorall, and all other ministers in this church shall not hereafter weare, occupy, or use in the chore or ellswher any clothe, cope, or other nesture above their surplises in any wyse differing [*from*] th' uniforme kind of apparell used most universallie through this realme, but shall utterlie ley awaie & forsake for ever the said clothe copes & use them no more."(3)

Assuming, therefore, that by *cloth* we are to understand *chasuble*, the ceremony here described may very fairly be included amongst the places where the original treatise agrees with the Rouen use. In the MS. missal, according to the use of that Church, described by Martene as having been written at latest in the thirteenth century, there is the following rubric after those referring to the putting on of the other vestments and the lighting

---

(1) This mystical signification was very common among mediæval expositors, *e.g.* William of Gouda :—" Induit casulam cogitans quod milites pylati, ipsum deridentes. tanquam volentem regnare, purpuream vestem induerunt."—*De Expositione Missæ*, Coloniæ [sæc. xv., s. a.] sig. A., ij *b*. Cf. the last of the Meditations quoted, *ante*, p. 168.

(2) MS. Cotton. Cleopat., E. v., f. 269 [277] *b*. This MS. is No. CIX. of the Appendix of Records and Originals to Strype's Ecclesiastical Memorials, but unfortunately there are many inaccuracies. In this place (p. 285) he prints, " The overvisor or chesible."

(3) *Acta Decani et Capituli Eboracensis*, 1543—1558, fol. 47 *a*. There are no stops in the original.

of the altar:—"*Postea accensis luminaribus, accipiat casulam cum duabus manibus, et stans ante altare, induat se, dicens:* Indue me," &c.(1) Let him take the chasuble with both hands [*take in both his hands a cloth*], and standing before the altar [*coming back a little down*], let him put it upon him [*does it upon him all above.*] Cf. text B, ll. 35—38.

P. 6, B. 35. *hende.* The midland scribe has in this place, as in line 284, retained *hende,* the northern plural of hand (*Icel.* hönd, *pl.* hendr), on account of the rhyme. The northern author appears to have used *handes* in the plural as well as *hende,* as in line 58 (rhyming to *standes*), where the scribe has copied both words as he found them, but in lines 39, 40, he has altered them into the midland *stondes, hondes.*

B. 36. *ende.* In the present day the end of a common table, of the oblong shape of later mediæval altars, would generally be understood to mean the narrower side; but we must not explain end in this place by our modern usage. So far as I have observed, end was never so used by any early writer when speaking of an English altar, but invariably, as here and in the following extracts, of the north or south part of the western side.

First, from the *Meditacyons* already quoted, p. 168:—

"Beholde in A solemne masse þat ys songe by þe Bushoppe or Priest. Reuesteid commyng owt of þe reuestre. whiche ys A holly plaice, wiþ liȝtes on eiche syde wiþ Deacan *and* subdeacan goyng A fore vnto þe mydes of þe Avter. *and* þer kysse þe sayme. After to go to þe Ryght cornar of þe Avter / And þen *after* to goo / to þe Lefte end of þe Avter / *and* þer the Gospelle ys rede. at þe last to returne Agayn to þe ryght end of þe Avter. The Qweyre Afore

---

(1) Martene *De Ritibus* (Antverpiæ, 1763), p. 229; Lib. I., c. iv., Art. 12, Ordo. 26. This rubric does not occur in the later MSS. given by Martene, nor in the earliest printed Rouen Missal, but (p. 238, Ordo. 34) he gives a MS. missal, "ecclesiæ Lehonensis" (St Pol de Léon), in which we have a similar rubric, except that it reads "*induat se illa;*" and in the Paris Missal of 1542 I find the rubric with the same variation. We may trace a survival of the older practice of vesting at the altar (*ante,* p. 163-5) in the chasuble being put on at the altar, although the other vestments may not have been. The old statutes of the Carthusians, given in Martene (u. s., Ordo. 25), direct the priest to vest in the church when the convent is not present, but when it is, then in the vestry, except that the chasuble is then always to be put on out of the vestry, "*casula tamen semper foris induitur.*" At Chalons, according to an old missal given in Martene (u. s., p. 127, art. 1), it seems that the chasuble was not put on until after the psalm *judica,* &c. (*ante,* p. 90, l. 20); but, nevertheless, the rubrics of the different French missals for the most part contemplate the putting on of all the vestments at once either at the altar or in the vestry. Unlike the Carthusians, as mentioned above, vesting at the altar was the rule of the Cluniacs at private masses, the vestments being carried from the sacristy with the mass-book to the altar by a *conversus* or novice. Udalricus *quoted,* Martene, *Monach. Rit.* 2, vi. 17.

and In þe meyne tyme Ioyfully synging.   Alle *þes* bene greytt
mysteryes. *and* doith signyfye grett Secrettes. of þe commyng off
our Sauyou*r*.   Furst," &c.   (fol. 2 *b*, 3.)

In the Order of Consecration of Nuns, printed by Mr Maskell
(*Mon. Rit.*, II. 309), it is directed that the virgins that shall then
profess, after being conducted up the quire, " addressyng theym
streight to the ryght (*south*) ende of the aulter, they shall lay
vppon it in order theyr veyles, rynges, and scrolles of theyr
professyon."   Then (*ib.*, p. 318) after they have subscripted their
professions, and prostrated themselves, there is the following
rubric: " ¶ And then shall the vergyns arryse : and go wyth the
bisshop unto the ryghte ende of the aulter.   And there they shall
take theyr veyles frome the aulter," &c.

My last quotations shall be from Becon, a scurrilous and
offensive writer, but he nevertheless is a good authority for the
usus loquendi during and before the time of the reformation :—

"Ye take up your mass-book, and away ye go to the other end
of the altar, to read the gospel."—*Displaying of the Popish Mass*,
Works, Cambridge, 1844, III., 264.   And again after the ablutions,
"taking up your book in your hand, ye come again to the altar's
end."—*Ib.*, p. 282. (1)

P. 6, B. 40. *haldes to god up bothe his hondes*—" holdyng up bothe my
handes. *a joinctes mains.*"—Palsgrave, 836 *b*.   The "*junctis manibus*" of the Latin rubrics.

> In the cherche thou knele adoun
> With good hert and devocion
> Hold up thi hondes then.—Audelay, p. 79.

B. 42. *meke him for his synne.*   Meke is used here of the spiritual
humbling of self which befits the conscience of sin, as by Hampole :—

> "For a man excuses noght his unkunning,
> þat his wittes uses noght in leryng,
> Namly, of þat at hym fel to knaw
> þat might meke his hert and make it law."
>   *P. C.* 169—172.

> "Lord mekyll þou mekede the for oure sake
> þat come fra so heghe oure kynde to take."
>   Nassyngton, *Religious Pieces* (Perry), p. 62, 1. 122-3.

> " All forr nohht uss haffde Crist
> Utlesedd fra þe defell
> 3iff þatt we nolldenn mekenn uss
> To follȝhenn Cristess lare."—*Ormulum*, 13948-51.

---

(1) Cf. B. 574-9, *ante*, p. 54.

Mæke seems also to be used like "humilio" and "humiliatio," of actual bowing or "louting."

"He mekyt(1) to þat mighty and with mowthe said."
Destruction of Troy, l. 952.
Cf. Vernon MS. p. 133, l. 188—190.

P. 6, B. 43, 44. *þare, mare*—retained for the rhyme. See *þere* two lines lower down and two lines above ; and *more*, l. 126.

B. 44. *mare*, of *quality* rather than *quantity*, as we now use *more*.

B. 45. *So dos þo clerk.* Here we have the northern third person plural *dos*, and *clerk* no doubt was written clerkes, as in Hampole :

"þir clerkes sayes,"—*P. C.* 8829,

but the midland scribe altered it into the singular, unless perhaps it was *folk* in the original, though in either case he betrays himself in his *hom* and *hor* of the next line, and the unchanged *þai* of line 48.

It will be noticed that the priest confesses to "all the folk" (l. 43), and there is no doubt that all the folk joined in the prayer for him, and then in the confession, at least as many as were able to do so—hence the "loude or stille "of line 52. Thus it was the "*litterati*" rather than the "clerici" specially so called, or the "clerks" in its larger sense (*see note*, p. 157)—those who "upon the book could know it" (C. 31, 83), rather than only the ministering "clerk" (*ante*, p. 54, B. 578)—who were required to "answer with good will" (C. 86). The "respondeant clerici," or "respondeant ministri," were comparatively modern rubrics, and it will be observed that all these texts (see page 8, B. 63) are alike in suggesting the use of the Confiteor.

In the first half of the fifteenth century English children, besides the Pater-noster, Ave-Maria, and other devotions, including the "Matthew, Mark, Luke, and John"—still handed on by tradition in many an old-fashioned cottage—were taught the *Confiteor* and *Misereatur*, as we learn from the "Boke of Curtasye" (Sloane MS. 1986), printed by Mr Furnivall in the Babees Book (page 303, ll. 153-4) :—

"To shryue þe in general þou schalle lere
þy Confiteor and misereatur in fere."

The *Misereatur* was the prayer of the people for the priest, and of the priest for the people (*ante*, p. 92, l. 1—4), after their several "general confessions" before mass, said by the people *in fere*, that is, in companionship, or saying together ; and said by the priest alone.

---

(1) Here the note (p. 490) suggests *mefyt*, which is explained as "*moved*" in the glossary. Cf. μετάνοια and *metanea* in Greek and early middle-age Latin rubrical directions for genuflection or bowing.

P. 6, B. 50. *lered & lewed*—

> "And wel bird,(1) ever ilk man
> Lof God after that he kan,
> Lered men with rihtwis lare,
> And laued folk wit rihtwis fare,
> Prestes wit matines and wit messe,
> And laued men wiht rihtwisnes,
> Clerk wit lare of Godes worde."
>
> *Metrical Homilies* (Small), p. 2.

B. 52. *" loud or stille "*—

> " Bot alle þas þat redes it, loud or stille,
> Or heres it be red with gode wille."
>
> Hampole, *P. C.* 9607-8.

B. 53, 54. *knese—sese.* Under correction I am disposed to include this among the places where the rhyme has led to the
retention of northern forms, which I bring forward in the
Introduction as an argument for the northern origin of this
treatise. My own study of northern English, as a living language,
for the last five-and-twenty years, quite apart from all Dr Morris
has taught us of the grammar, leaves no doubt as to " thou sees "
being very good northern, but I do not know enough of our old
midland forms to be sure that it may not also be midland.

B. 57-8. The retention of the northern rhymes *standes, handes,* has
already been noticed (*note,* B. 38), but it is curious to see that the
scribe has written " *hold* " here, though he has left the northern
" *haldes* " in line 40 when altering the rhymes.

B. 59, 60. *Eke to pater and aue.* In the margin I suggest that we
read *an* for the *and* in the MS., for otherwise we should have
the verb transitive *eke (to add)* without an object ; and the drift
of the rubric would be to add the creed to the Paternoster and
Ave, rather than to add an Ave to the Pater. In either case the
use of the Ave is spoken of as if it were a well-known devotion ;
and we learn from Roman Catholic authors, who have gone most
carefully into the subject,(2) that the earliest mention of it to be

---

(1) Bird. " Læt nu, Johan, forr þuss birrþ uss
      Ille rihhtwisnesse fillenn."

      Ormulum (Matt. iii, 15), 10665-6.

Bosworth does not give A.S. byrð (beran, *to bear*) in the sense of " it behoves," as it afterwards came to mean, as here, of that which is *borne* to us
as fitting. Cf. *Icel.* beer (bera, *portare*), *oportet.*

(2) Merati, *Additiones ad Gavanti Commentarium,* Venet. 1788, III.,
124. " Addere enim lubet, quod nullus eorum scriptorum, qui hortati sunt
fideles ad persoluendas quasdam pias preces, de Salutatione Angelica nullum
verbum potulerunt (*protulerunt*) ; et concilia usque ad Sæculum XI. (*XII.*),
necnon patres, symboli tantum et orationis Dominicæ meminerunt quæ a
populis disci, et quotidie recitari hortabuntur." The mention of the *eleventh,*
instead of the *twelfth* century, is evidently a misprint, for he afterwards says:

met with, either in treatises on prayer or acts of councils, occurs about the year 1200 in the synodical constitutions of Odo, Bishop of Paris ;(1) and from Dr Rock, that "in the year 1237 we light on the first formal mention of the Hail Mary in England."(2) We find in Mabillon(3) that it was prescribed in the diocese of Rouen in the year 1246, and that from that time forth the use of the angelic salutation as a prayer became almost a universal rule.

If, therefore, this mention of the Ave were any part of the original French, it would be almost fatal to my suggestion that it was written about the middle of the twelfth century ; but from internal evidence in the text itself, especially as compared with the later recensions, I am disposed to think that these two lines are an interpolation of a subsequent scribe, or at all events only an after-thought of the translator.

It will be observed that in this couplet the lines are of three accents(4) only, whereas all the other rubrics are in lines of four accents. It will be also observed that this is the only place where the Ave Maria is referred to in this text, except in lines 424 and 425, where *aue* is an evident mistake of a scribe who was not used to the northern "ane" (= *one*), and to whom the use of the Ave as a devotion was a matter of course. The Ave, &c., is added as a side-note at lines 82 and 620, and also at line 298, where the text specifies the Paternoster only, and MS. E., which represents the unadapted translation, omits this note. And not only is there this absence of the Ave-Maria in the body of this text, but we find the use of the Paternoster everywhere(5) enjoined without the Ave, when if the Ave were found in the original, it would naturally have been retained by the translator.

In the MSS. of the adapted and later form, the Ave is mentioned in all the places above quoted, except that none of them make the mistake in lines 424 and 425 ; and instead of the two lines in this place, which are an interpolation, or at all events a break in the

---

—"Inter preces igitur populo præscriptas hæc oratio. *Ave Maria, etc.,* primum invenitur apud Odonem de Suliaco Episcopum Parisiensem in suis statutis anno 1195."

(1) "X. Exhortentur populum semper presbyteri ad dicendam orationem dominicam et Credo in Deum et salutationem Beatæ Virginis."—Labb. & Coss. X., col. 1806, A. No date is given, but Odo de Suliaco (*De Sully*) was Bishop of Paris from 1197 to 1208, or, according to Mabillon, from 1196, so that Merati was wrong in his date, unless this is another misprint.

(2) *Church of our Fathers*, III., 318. See what may perhaps be a tacit reference to the recent introduction of the Ave, *ante*, p. 139, ll. 413-15.

(3) *Acta Sanctorum, O. S. B.*, Præfat. in Sæc. v., § cxxi.

(4) In text C., ll. 225-6 (p. 38), is a couplet with three accents, where its absence in the older texts proves the interpolation.

(5) B. 152, 262, 398, 480. It will be noticed that text C. (line 218) leaves out the line (B. 398) as to saying the paternoster, and instead inserts the note, Paternoster, Ave Maria, et cetera.

metre, the adapter has altered the rubric after the confiteor in the
exercise of his revising function.(1)

These variations in the mention of the Ave in the English
translation go very far to justify my suggestion as to the silence
of the original, and I take this assumption not in itself as a proof,
for there could be no proof short of MS. authority, but still for
what it is worth in arriving at a conjecture as to the date.

The English Ave-Maria as given in Myrk is as follows :—

> " Hail be þow, mary, fulle of grace ·
> God is wyþ þe in euery place ;
> I-blessed be þow of alle wymmen,
> And þe fruyt of þy wombe Ihesus. Amen."—ll. 422-5.

And I add the English from the *Primer in Latin and English*,
John Wayland, 1555, as it may be interesting from being the last
form in which it was put forth by authority in a service-book of
the Church of England :—

" Hayle mary full of grace, oure Lorde is with thee. blessed be
thou among women, and blessed be the fruite of thy wombe
Jesus. Amen."—Sig. B. ii.

The Festyvall explains the addition of the two last words :—
" Furdermore as for the salutacyon of our lady pope Urban(2) and
pope Johan to all being in clene lyfe that in the ende of the Aue
maria saye these wordes Ihesus. Amen. as oft as they saye it, they
haue graunted of pardon lxxxiiii dayes."—fol. 159 b.

As now used in the Church of Rome, there is a further addition
of a prayer to the blessed Virgin (" Sancta Maria, Mater Dei, ora
pro nobis peccatoribus nunc et in hora mortis nostræ "), which
was first authorised by Pope Pius V. by bull dated 7th July, 1568.

P. 6, C. 31-2. This text, written as it was for Rievaulx Abbey, would have
found many of the Cistercians who were able to understand the
Latin of the mass. Other adaptations of this text to the use of a
" religious " house will be pointed out in their place.

   C. 33. It will have been noticed that texts A, C, and D, omit the
reference in B to the foreign use as to vesting, and together with
it the explanation of the mutual confessions of priest and people,

---

(1) C. 55-6. Where A reads :—

> " when þu þi confiteor þus has done
> Pater noster and ave sey fast þer on."

and D :—

> " When thu thus thi confiteor has done
> Pater and aue fast pray one."

See F. 61-2, page 15, for another reading where the Ave is not mentioned.
These variations will weigh with those of my readers who are in the habit of
collating MSS. in deciding whether or no the original text has been tampered
with in this place.

(2) The addition appears to have been made by Pope Urban IV. between
the years 1261 and 1264.

and the general absolution of the priest. They here again follow the course of the original, as does text F, after the more complete adaptation to English uses, which has been already pointed out, page 163-4.

P. 7, E. 32. The more modern "*turn*" replaces the older "*draw*."

E. 34. *re-wesshut* might have been supposed to be a reminiscence of the old French participle *revestut*, if it were not for the curious upsilonism, so to call it, of this text; witness in the next few lines takus, hongus, komus, lytul, knelun, stondus, hondus, beginnus, synnus, askut, lerud, kneus, seus, jountly, &c.

E. 36. *A chesepull cloth.* Mr Scudamore asks, "May not 'chesepull' be simply a clerical error for 'corporal'?"(1) Even if I did not suppose that this reading had arisen from cloth having been glossed chasuble—rightly, as I venture to think I have proved (p. 177-8)—and the gloss being inserted in the line when the MS. came to be copied, I should be inclined to answer decidedly not. The writer of this MS. has abundantly proved that he was both ignorant and puzzle-headed, but when the words are the names of ornaments so well known, he can hardly have mistaken one for the other.—Certainly both begin with c, have a p in the middle, and end with l—at least the latinized form of corporas does;(2) but I find no example of that form before the fifteenth century, and chesepull was no doubt meant for chasuble, as for example,—the *Promptorium Parvulorum* (p. 73), " Chesypylle, *Casula ;*"—and the *Catholicon in Lingua materna*, or *Catholicon Anglicum*, quoted in Mr Way's note, p. 73, *n.* 4, " A chesabylle, *casula, infula, planeta.*"

E. 51. The harrowing of hell by our Lord was a constant topic in the popular religious writings of the middle ages, and was often represented in miracle plays and pageants, but it will be seen that its introduction here, instead of the acknowledgment of sin, is wholly out of place. See a suggestion as to the reason, page 172.

F. 40. *marketh*—evidently a mistake for meketh, see page 180.

P. 8, B. 63. *confiteor*—see note B. 42 ; page 180.

B. 64. *were als gode saie þis þer-for.* The translator does not suggest that it would be better for those who did not know the meaning of the Latin to use the English form of confession, possibly because it seems to have been a received opinion that there was a quasi-sacramental benefit in the Latin,—one of the three so-called sacred languages—though not " understanded of the people." A similar feeling seems to have been present to the mind

(1) *Notitia Eucharistica*, p. 116.
(2) Corporas has the authority of the first English Book of Common Prayer (1549), and continued in use after the reformation until the old tradition had died out, and corporal was more generally adopted from the Latin rubrics and foreign Roman Catholic authorities.

of the author of the Myroure of our Ladye. He translates the
service of the Brigettine nuns of Syon, as he had ' asked and had
license of the bishop to draw such things into English to their
gostly comfort and profit,' but he cautions them that the "lokynge
on the englyshe whyle the latyn ys redde ys to be understonde of
them that have sayde theyre mattyns or redde theyr legende
before. For else I wolde not counsell them to leve the herynge
of the latyn for entendaunce of the englysshe." (1)

P. 8, B. 65—82. The many forms of general confession before mass,
first by the priest to the people, and then by the people to the
priest, which were in use in the Western Church in the middle
ages, are very much alike.(2) The later ones, and in this they
are like the existing Roman missal, have a greater number of
saints mentioned by name, but there do not appear to have been
any variations of doctrinal or ritual significance. I must, however, bespeak the patience of my reader whilst I point out certain
verbal variations in the form here given, where it agees in two
distinctive points with the Rouen use of the twelfth century, and
differs from English and other contemporary uses, and from the
later Rouen Missal. It is only by the accumulation of small
coincidences that, in the absence of any direct evidence, I can
hope to make good the suggestion I have made in the Introduction, that the original of this treatise was adapted to the Rouen
use, and that it was written not later than the twelfth century.

The first of these points is the manner in which the sins are
specified. I will give the Rouen form as printed by Martene from
a MS. of the thirteenth century(3) inserting the English of our text ;
and then, by way of contrast, the English and some other uses,
which I think will be sufficient, without further remark, to prove
the coincidence in this instance.

ROUEN (XIII. Cent.). Confiteor Deo cæli (*I know to God full of
might*) et Beatæ Mariæ Virgini (*and to His mother maiden bright*), et
omnibus sanctis ejus (*and to all hallows* [the whole host of saints]

---

(1) *Myroure*, fol. xxxv (Ed. E. E. T. S., p. 71). This very rare book,
almost indispensably necessary to every one who desires to understand the
history of the religion of this country, has been reprinted by this society
under the editorship of Rev. J. H. Blunt, who has added very much to its value
by his own notes and other illustrative matter. The foliation of Fawkes' edition
(1530) is shewn in the margin, and it is much to be wished that care were
taken to do this in all reprints. Otherwise they are incomplete, and far less
available for the purpose of verifying references.

(2) See the York form, *ante*, 90, ll. 25—29. When said by the people the
vobis fratres—in some forms, "*fratres et sorores*"—was changed into "*tibi,
pater*."

(3) *De Ritibus*, Tom. I., Lib. I, c. iv., art. xii., Ord. 26, a MS. from the
Monastery of Fécamp,—"ad usum ecclesiæ Rotomagensis;" see also Ord. 37,
a MS. also of the Rouen use from the Monastery of St Ouen.

here), et tibi, pater (*and to thee, ghostly father*), quia ego miser peccator peccavi nimis (*have sinned largely*) contra legem Dei, cogitatione (*in thought*) locutione (*in speech*), tactu, visu (*in delight*), verbo mente et opere (*in word and work*) et in cunctis alus vitiis meis malis (*in many sins sere*), Deus, mea culpa (*I am to wite*(1)), mea maxima culpa (*and worthy to blame*).

SARUM.(2) " . . . . nimis cogitatione, locutione, et opere, mea culpa."

YORK.(3) "nimis corde, ore, opere, omissione, mea culpa."

ROUEN. (*Missale Rothomag.* folio, 1497), " cogitatione, locutione, opere, omissione."

MISSALE ROMANUM (Sæc. XIII—1570, &c.), " cogitatione, verbo, et opere."

PARIS (ed. 1542). " cogitatione, opere, omissione."

MISSEL DE PARIS, 1739. " cogitatione verbo et opere."

The other point of coincidence turns upon a single word—" Ideo deprecor TE " in the Latin, "Therefore I pray THEE" in the English—and all the more marked because the " te " is found in the two MSS. of the Rouen use, given by Martene, which have the confession (the one described as " old," the other of the thirteenth century), and in none of the other uses given by him,(4) and because it was afterwards omitted at Rouen, as we know from the printed Rouen Missal appearing without it.

But I must draw attention to the text, when it will be seen that I am relying upon the reading of Text C (line 46), which is not found in our oldest MS. Text B, but nevertheless most probably represents the reading of the original, and that for the following reason. An English scribe, whether a common scrivener, or a religious in a conventual scriptorium, must have been familiar with the Sarum " Precor Sanctam Mariam," or if in the northern province, with the "Ideo precor gloriosam Dei genetricem" of

---

(1) See note on l. 72, p. 189.

(2) *Missale Sarum*, Burntisland, 1861, col. 580. The Sarum and Ebor uses, and the modern Roman Missal, are printed in parallel columns, Maskell, A. E. L., 10.

(3) *Ante*, p. 90, l. 26. The Hereford Missal does not give the Confiteor at length, simply " Confiteor, &c."—*Missale Hereford* (Henderson), p. 114. Mr Maskell (u. s.) gives Bangor as the Sarum in the part here quoted.

(4) I find two similar forms in MSS. In a twelfth-century English MS. (*Cotton, Tiberius*, A iii., fol. 107 *b*), under the rubric (fol. 104 *b*) " *Votiva laus in veneratione Sanctæ Mariæ virginis*," there is a *Confiteor* where the prayer is addressed to the Virgin in the same direct manner :—" Ideo precor te, sanctissima Dei genetrix Maria, omnesque sanctos."

The other example is in Mabillon's *Voyage Litteraire* (Tom. I., p. 121), where we find the like personal address—not only to the Virgin, but also to the saints—in the *Confiteor* of the " *Ordo Vallis Scholarum*," from a MS. of the thirteenth century, " *Ideo precor te, pia virgo Maria, et vos omnes sancti Dei, et vos fratres.*" The printed Paris Missal of 1491 is the same with the addition of " *et Sanctæ.*"

the York use; and if the original had been "I pray Saint Mary" as in Text B, it is hardly likely that he would have introduced the personal pronoun, to which he was not accustomed; whilst on the other hand it is very conceivable that with the Anglican form in his head, a scribe might very naturally have written "Saint" instead of "thee," to which he was not accustomed.

I may add another fact which makes in the same direction. MS. C was written for Rievaulx Abbey, which was a Cistercian house, and as the Cistercian Order was specially devoted to the blessed Virgin Mary, it might have been that the more direct personal address was adopted out of greater devotion; but so far from this, it so happens that they retained the older form of confession given below, where the prayer is not directed to the Virgin or any saints.(1)

P. 8, B. 67. *alle halouse here*—E. 45 has "dere" (dear), and it is not improbable that when this MS. was written here (*host, army*) was becoming obsolete. Cp. the Te Deum : "Te martyrum candidatus laudat exercitus," and the Latin proper preface for Christmastide : "cum omni militia cœlestis exercitus."

B. 71. *sere*. Here again E gets rid of the unfamiliar word, but the meaning is preserved in "*of diverse manere.*"

Sere, *separate, sundry, divers*, was peculiar to the northern parts of England, or rather the Danelagh, and we at once trace its derivation in the Icelandic sér, the dative, singular and plural, of the reflexive pronoun (= Lat. *sibi*), and so *for oneself, separately, singly.*(2)

"All ser *annd* all an oþer."—*Ormulum*, 18678.

"For she ys cursede yn stedes sere
Foure tymes yn þe ȝere."—*Handlyng Synne*, 2029-30.

"Here have I shewed on a general manere
þe ioyes of heven, many and sere."

Hampole, *P. C.* 7873-4.

---

(1) "Confiteor deo et beate marie & omnibus sanctis et vobis fratres qu*ia* peccavi nimis cogitatione locutione & opere, mea culpa. Ideo precor vos orate pro me."—*Missale ad usum Cisterciensis ordinis* (Iohan. Petit, Paris, 1516), fol. 82. The missal from which I copy this (*York Minster Library*, XL, P. 3), although printed in France, must have been in use in this country in the reign of Henry VIII., as the name of Becket, and the title of Pope, are everywhere erased.

(2) Cleasby-Vigfusson, s. v. It may be explained, for the sake of those who have not paid attention to the subject, that the Icelandic is referred to, not as if any words in our language had travelled to us through Iceland, but because Icelandic has been less affected by change than the modern Danish or Norsk, and therefore may be taken to be a better representation of the old Danish, or the language of the several swarms of Northmen who migrated to Iceland, or settled on the eastern side of this country in the course of successive Danish invasions.

" Of seven manere of blisses sere."—*Ib.* 8168.
" Iesu þat boghte me dere
Iesu ioyne þi lufe in my thoghte
Swa þat þay neuer be sere."
Religious Pieces (Perry), p. 74, l. 62-4.

P. 8, B. 72. *I am to wite.*—Wite, *blame,* from the A.S. *witan,* to blame, to punish, and this from *wite,* a fine, punishment.

" Ne felle nohht i wite."—*Orm.,* 3295.

" Ꝥe wite is hise."—*Gen. & Ex.,* 2035.

" wite him nouȝt þat it wrouȝt · he would haue do beter,
ȝif is wille in eny weiȝes · wold him haue serued."
William of Palerne (Skeat), 5525-6.

" And but I do, sires, let me have the wyte."
Chaucer, *C. T.* 12881.

" Wharfore I am mare þan Iudas to wyte."
Nassyntôn, 302 ; *Religious Pieces* (Perry), 67.

" If thow wayte streyghtly oure synnes." [*Si iniquitates observavetis,* Ps. (130) cxxix., 3.] *Myroure,* 144.

" I laye the wyte on him : *je luy impute la faute.*"—Palsgrave, 605.

" I WYTE, I blame or put one in fault : *Je encoulpe* [inculpo], or *je reprouche.* Why wyte you me, and I am not to blame : *pour quoy mencoulpez vous et je ne suis pas a blasmer.*"—Palsgrave, 783.

In the phrases " lay the weight," " bear the weight," *wite* is the more usual pronunciation in the East Riding, and no doubt more etymologically correct than weight (*onus*), for which I at first mistook it.

B. 74-5. *mary—haly.* Cf. the assonance, B. 474-5.

C. 46. *I praye the, marye.* See before, p. 187.

P. 9, F. 44. *dere.* See note, p. 188, B. 67.

F. 44—60. The Confiteor is here brought to the same metre, as the body of the treatise—but not without injury to the sense, l. 46, 52.

F. 54. It will be observed that although the word is changed, the assonance or vowel rhyme of the original is preserved in l. 54.

P. 10, B. 81. *grace and forgyuenes.* An example of the use of the French word and its English equivalent, as elsewhere in these devotions, and in the Book of Common Prayer.

B. 82. The note as to Pater Ave, and Credo, is a marginal addition to the text. In the later Text C. (l. 56) the direction to say a Paternoster and Ave is an integral part of the text, as it is in MSS. A. and D. ; but it will be observed that the creed, which is twice referred to in the original (B. 61, 83), is not specified. I have elsewhere (p. 183) mentioned the inference I draw from these facts.

P. 10, B. 86. *bigynnes office of messe.* Here again I find an exact grammatical coincidence with the Rouen rubric of the twelfth century,
which was omitted in the texts, when they were adapted for
English use.

ROUEN. "Tunc incipiat officium missæ."

SARUM. "In dextro cornu altaris cum deacono et subdiacono
officium missæ prosequatur."

EBOR. "Et in dextro cornu altaris dicat officium."

HEREFORD. "Deinde incipiatur officium missæ."

MISS. ROM. "Deinde celebrans signans se signo crucis incipit
introitum."

The *officium missæ* was an anthem at the beginning of the mass,
after the *præparatio* was finished, and varied according to the day.
It was so called in many French and all the English uses, and in
the Mozarabic liturgy ; *Ingressa* in the Ambrosian ; and, as in the
rubric above given, *Introitus* in the Roman missal. It was
retained in the first English Book of Common Prayer (1549) ;
and, curious to say, the rubric introduces the alternative of the
Roman name. "Then shall the clerks sing in English, for the
office or introit (as they call it), a psalm appointed for that day."
I have not noticed a variation in any English service-book, except the Sarum portesse of 1555, where this anthem is called
"Introitus" in the Mass "De cruce," perhaps from being taken
bodily from a foreign source ; though in the Mass "In commemoratione Sanctæ Trinitatis," "De quinque Vulneribus," "De beata
Mariâ," and other Masses, the Anglican "officium" is retained.

B. 87. "*standes turnande his boke.*" This too may have been suggested by the Rouen rubric in this place, "postea aperiat librum,"
as the English uses have no corresponding direction.(1) It may
however simply mean, as I have glossed in the margin, that the
priest, having ended the preparatory office, for which the Mass-
book was not required, and being about to begin the altar service,
here found his places. The existing Roman rubric directs that the
priest, before saying any part of the offices "signacula ordinat ad
ea quæ dicturus est."

B. 88. *south ender syde.* So all the English uses : "In dextro cornu
altaris." *Sarum, Ebor, Bangor.* "Ad dextram cornu altaris."
Hereford.(2) The modern Roman rubric is the same in effect, the
right end of the altar looking east, being named left, in reference
to the Crucifix upon it, looking west : "ad cornu sinistrum, id est,
epistolæ."(3)

The priest who said Mass, the *executor officii* of the Anglican
rubrics, began at the south end, "fitted his book" to the north

---

(1) There is however a rubric to the same effect in several of the early
French uses : in the printed Paris missal of 1542, &c.

(2) Maskell, A. E. L., 18, 19.　　　(3) *Ritus Celeb. Miss.*, iv. 2.

end or gospel horn at the gospel (l. 156), and flitted it again to
the south end after rinsing the chalice (l. 580). The Sarum
rubric as to the several positions was as follows: "Sciendum est
autem quod quicquid a sacerdote dicitur ante epistolam in dextro
cornu altaris expleatur: præter inceptionem Gloria in excelsis.
Similiter fiat post perceptionem sacramenti. Cætera omnia in
medio altaris expleantur, nisi forte diaconus defuerit. Tunc enim
in sinistro cornu altaris legatur evangelium."(1)

P. 10, B. 89. *stondande.* Here we have *stond* for the northern *stand*,
but, as the lines immediately above and below, the northern *-ande*
of the participle is retained.

The layman was to " stand up upon his feet " (l. 84) when he had
finished the creed, which a previous rubric had directed him to
say "kneeling on his knees before he rose" (ll. 53 and 61), and
to continue standing until the end of the *Gloria in excelsis*, when
he was to kneel (l. 150). He is also in this text directed to stand
at the offertory (l. 245), whilst saying the Lord's Prayer at the
lavatory (l. 261), and after the rinsing of the chalice (ll. 577 and
600), but it will be observed there is no corresponding direction
in the corresponding places in the later MSS., except E, which
represents the older form of the treatise.(2)

B. 91, &c. This prayer occupied the time between the office and
the Epistle, except when the *Gloria in excelsis* was sung. It will
be observed that in the order of mass (*ante*, p. 93-4) there is no
corresponding prayer, the litany which was anciently used in this
place being represented only by the *Kyrie eleison*—Lord, have
mercy—which is the response in the Greek liturgies, as *Domine
Miserere* in the Milanese and other Latin litanies.

Other survivals from an Eastern source in Dan Jeremy's treatise,
are elsewhere pointed out, and it is curious to remark that this
prayer has very much the same character as the Eirenica or
prayers in a responsive form, like western litanies, for all estates
in the church, which are still said in this place,(3) except that, as
also in the mass (p. 92, l. 25), the ministering clergy had first prayed
for themselves to be cleansed from all defilement (ἀπὸ πάσης
κηλῖδος), whereas here the prayer for the priest is (B. 96—100) a
part of the people's prayer

(1) *Miss. Sar.*, Burntisland, 1861, col. 589.
(2) See note, p. 193, on C. 58 ; and Vernon (*ante*, p. 134), l. 215, an older
MS., where the layman is directed to stand.
(3) Goar. *Euchol.*, p. 64, and his notes (62), p. 123, and (2) p. 46. He
there mentions that the like were used in the Latin churches until the ninth
century, and gives the litany which was used in the Ambrosian office. Bona
(*Rer. Liturg.* 2, iv. 3) adds that this was used at Milan on the Sundays in
Lent; and there is still a direction to that effect: "loco *Gloria in excelsis*
dicuntur preces."—*Rub. Gen. juxta ritum Ambrosianum*, Mediolani, 1842,
§ 15.

P. 10, B. 95. Cf. prayer for priest, Vernon, *ante*, p. 133, ll. 192—208 ; and Lydgate, p. 149, l. 52.

C. 51. *grete mede.* It is difficult to account for this reading instead of "Manhede." The Cistercian scribe must have been familiar with the many pleadings of our Lord's incarnation in mediæval devotions.

C. 56. *fast thereon.* The corresponding line, F. 61 (p. 15), is "folweth soon."

> Cf. "After þat, fast at hande
> Comes þe tyme of offrande."—B. 241-2.

Where C. 102 has "*nere*," and F. 82 has "*nei.*"

> "Als fast as euer þat he has done,
> Loke þat þou be redy sone,"—B. 310-1.

> "Praye faste among you all."
>
> Lydgate, *ante*, p. 150, l. 65.

> "Beholde this prophete called Jeremye,
> Be a visioune so hevenly and divyne,
> Toke a chalice, and fast gan hym hye
> To presse out licour out of the rede vyne."
>
> Lydgate, *Minor Poems* (Percy Soc.), p. 98.

The employment of fast, as in the above examples, to express nearness of time, enables us to trace the connection between its opposite senses of immovability, and rapid movement.

The first we find exclusively used in cognate languages, and in the earlier stage of English (*Icel.* fastr ; *Germ.* fest ; *A.S.* fæst), —fast (*fixed, immovable*) as a post.

The other afterwards came to be also used as we too now use it —fast (*swift*) as the (1) post:

> "We mowen nought, although we had it sworn,
> It overtake, it slyt away so fast."—C. T., 12609-10.

The nearness of place may have been an intermediate step to nearness of time ; (2) as for example :

> "And þar es þe mount of calvery
> And þe sepulcre of Crist fast þarby."
>
> Hampole, *P. C.*, 5187-8.(3)

---

(1) "My days are swifter than a post."—Job, ix, 25.

(2) Compare the use of *hard :* "Naboth had a vineyard hard by the palace of Ahab."—1 Kings, xxi, 1.

"Trouble is hard at hand."—Ps. (P. B. V.) xxii, 11.

"Indeed, my Lord, it followed hard upon."—*Hamlet,* i, 2.

(3) Cf. "Abide here fast by my maidens."—Ruth, ii, 8.   "The ungodly cometh on so fast."—Ps. (P. B. V.) lv, 3.

"Who finds the heifer dead, and bleeding fresh,
And sees fast by a butcher with an axe,
But will suspect 'twas he that made the slaughter."

Henry VI, Part II, iii, 2.

And it is easy to see how the sense of quick succession of time, once fully established, passed into that of quick movement necessary to ensure it.(1)

P. 10, C. 58. *sayinge.* This form of the participle, instead of *sayand*, is an indication of the late date at which the original must have been modified.(2) In addition to the introduction of the Ave into the text, this and the other later MSS. leave out the direction to stand during the prayer, which is clearly supposed to be the rule in B. 84 and 89. The custom of standing at prayer, although not to the extent required by the Nicene canon, lingered on in the west at least till the thirteenth century; and there were traces of it at Orleans in the seventeenth. It may be that the change is to be attributed to the growth of the feeling—which we may trace in the modification of the rubrics, as, for example, the substitution of *clerici* or *ministri* for *populus*—that the appointed services were exclusively a clerical function, and that kneeling was the posture for the private devotions of the people.

P. 11, E. 90. *seyande.* The southern *sey* for *say*, with the northern participial ending.

P. 12, B. 97-8. Compare the prayer for the presbyters in the Apostolical Constitutions: " ὅπως ὁ κύριος ῥύσηται αὐτοὺς ἀπὸ παντὸς ἀτόπου καὶ πονηροῦ πράγματος."—Lib. viii, c. 10. Ed. Le Clerc, p. 397.

B. 99. *fulfille þis sacrament.* In the cautels which are to be found in the mass-books according to the several English uses are minute provisions for cases of a priest dying, or otherwise failing to complete the mass he had begun.

B. 100. *clene hert.* Cf. " puris mentibus," *ante*, p. 92, l. 27.

gode entent. Cf. C. 21, gude entent, where this MS. reads " gode tent." Entent may perhaps refer to the intention of the priest, as held to be necessary to the validity of sacraments in the church of Rome.(3) It was used for intention, as in the Myroure, Pt II, ch. xxiii, of "dressing" the entent in saying or singing holy service :—
" The fyfte thynge that longeth to the dew maner of saynge of denyne seruice is to take hede to what entente ye say yt . . . . yf the entente be good, the dede is good, and yf thentente be yuel, the dede ys yuel." (4)

It was also often used of attention :
" I entended to them and gaue them answeres."
Myroure, p. 48.

---

(1) Richardson (*s. v.*) rejects the "Welsh *Ffest,* properus, festinus," as the original of this word in the latter signification, and suggests that it is "a consequential application of *fast,* close. He comes *fast* behind, i.e. close behind ; to attain which closeness (suppose in a race) *speed* was exerted."

(2) Compare B. 375-6, where we have the participle *rynsande,* and the verbal substantive *rinsynge.*

(3) Aquin. *Summ.* III, lxiv, 8 & 10. *Concil. Trident.* vii, De Sacramentis, can. xi.   (4) *Myroure,* E. E. T. S., p. 60.

"Remembre the eke in your inward entent
Melchisedech that offred brede and wyne."
Lydgate, Minor Poems, p. 95.

"but take to theym entent
"Withe blythe vysage, and spiryt diligent."
Babees Book, p. 3, l. 69-70.

"And euer when he clepithe, wayte redy & entende."
id., p. 180, l. 936.

Hampole uses it to render "diligentia":

"And þarfor says Saynt Bernard right:
Si diligenter consideres . . . .
If þow wille, he says, ententyfly se."—P. C. 619—624.

Chaucer uses it of endeavour :—

"Wel oughte we to do al oure entente
Lest that the fend thurgh ydelnesse us hente."
C. T. 11934-5.

P. 12, B. 102. "is." The MS. here retains the northern is of the second person singular, which E. and F. change into art and ert.

B. 103. to þi modir, that is, to her honour, and that of all saints. Cf. "in honore tuo et beatæ Mariæ et omnium sanctorum tuorum." —Ante, p. 98, ll. 30-1.

B. 104. bi-dene. So the Ormulum of Job losing his children in addition to other trials :—

"Annd off, þatt he forrlæs his streon
Onn an daȝȝ all bidene."—ll. 4792-3.

And Hampole of removing mountains and the earth besides :—

"þai salle mow remowe at þair wille,
Ilka mountayne, and ilka hille,
þat ever was in þe world sene,
And if þai wild, alle þe erth bidene."—P. C. 7965-8.

B. 105. heres. The midland scribe here retains the northern -s of the third person plural. E. changes to the midland -n; and F. to the southern -eth.

B. 105-6. hele—wele in F. become "helihe" and "welihe."

B. 108. fremd, which is still in daily use as a north-country word, becomes "frend" in F.; and "halouse" becomes "seyntes."

B. 108. bi ony kynde. By, or in respect to, any relationship, natural or spiritual. Cf. the "secundum quodlibet" of the schoolmen.

It will be noticed that this use of the preposition seems to have been strange to the scribe (E. 108), who writes "or any kynde," but Chaucer uses it exactly as in the text :—

"Of what hous be ye, by your father kyn."—C. T. 15417.

And we still speak of relationships "by the father's or the mother's side."

P. 12, B. 112. *soules passed away.* E. reads " passe *and,*" and suggests what may perhaps have been the reading of the northern original " passand," and that prayer was made at this place for the dying and not for the dead. Cf. the many prayers for a passing soul in Primers and Horæ, and the direction to toll the passing bell, " when any is passing out of this life."—Canons (1604), lxvii.(1)

C. 66. *ille wild.* Qu. ill-willed, malevolent.

C. 71. *And to þe, moder, maiden clene.* It will be observed that in punctuating the text I had put a comma after þe, as if þe had been a personal pronoun (*thee*), as it is in the invocation of the blessed Virgin, C. 46, and elsewhere in this MS., C. 94, &c. As a matter of fact such direct forms of address are not uncommon, but on looking at this place again, I think that " þe " must be merely a dialectic variation of the possessive. Two lines above, we have " þe honour," where " þe " is as unquestionably used in this sense as the " thy " and " þy " of ten lines lower down. It may be noted as an illustration of the uncertainty of the spelling of this date that we have these three forms of the same word written a dozen lines (þe, thy, þy), and a fourth, þi (l. 59), within twenty lines farther back.

P. 14, B. 115. *On hegh-festis.* See rubrics, *Miss. Sarum.*, col. 3, 383; *Ebor.* (Henderson), 166 ; and *Manipulus Curatorum*, 1510, fol. 34.

F. reads *On Sunday.* Sunday, as we gather from the laws, both secular and ecclesiastical, before the Conquest, was held in especial reverence in the Church of England. We find Robert of Brunne giving a very marked expression to this feeling in the following passage, which is one of the many additions he makes to the original in translating the *Manuel des Pechiez* :—

> " Of al þe festys þat yn holy chyrche are,
> Holy sunday men oughte to spare ;
> Holy sunday ys byfore alle fre
> þat euere ȝyt were, or euere shal be.
> For the pope may þurghe hys powere
> Turne þe halydays yn þe ȝere
> How as he wyl, at hys owne wyl,
> But þe sunday shal stande styl.
> þe halydays þat yn hernyst are
> In ȝole he may sette hem þare,
> And of þe ȝole euery feste
> May he sette yn herueste.
> But, he may, þurghe no resun
> þe sunday putte vp no dowun ;
> þarfore þe Sunday specyaly
> Ys hyest to halew, and most wurþy."
>
> *Handlyng Synne*, ll. 805—820.

(1) Mabillon (*Acta Sanctorum*, O. S. B., Præf. in Sæc. I, § 103) proves from Bede, &c., the antiquity of the English custom of ringing a peal after death, as also directed in this canon.

P. 14, B. 116. *men singes or sayes.* I do not include this among the places
where the midland scribe had retained the northern forms of the
original text. Sayes is not necessarily the third person plural to
agree with men in the plural; for the indefinite *men* was used as
if singular like the German *mann* and the French *on.* And see
note, p. 171.

B. 117. *Gloria in excelsis.* See *ante,* p. 94, ll. 6—19.

B. 118. *es.* The midland scribe elsewhere writes *is,* but retains the
northern *es* to rhyme with *mes.*

B. 119. *Ioy* is used to render *gloria* here, and throughout the hymn;
in the *Gloria Patri* in the York Hours of the Cross (p. 82, l. 7),
and so in many other places,(1) which is all the more curious, as
the French *joie* (from the Latin *gaudium,* or rather *gaudia*) does
not appear to have been used in this sense.

The word occurs as we now use joy in l. 561, and in the York
Bidding Prayer, p. 71, l. 30, and Hampole uses it of the joys of
heaven :

"Alle manere of ioyes er in þat stede."—P. C. 7813.

B. 120. This is one of the lines with which the hymn is farced
(*stuffed*), as it was called in this country ; or *brodé,* as the French
ritualists called it. It will be noticed that there is also a farsure
in the Apostles' Creed (p. 20). There were similar additions to
the Latin of the mass in the *Kyries,* the *Sanctus,* the *Pax,* the *Agnus
Dei,* and the *Ite,* &c., and these interpolations were sometimes of
the most incongruous character. The rubric of the Sarum Missal
(col. 585) directed that this canticle should be sung "*cum sua
farsura*" at the principal mass (*in choro*). At the reform of the
Roman Missal in 1570, *farsuræ* were altogether abolished by
authority of Pope Pius V.

Martene (2) mentions that the epistle in some French churches
had been "barbara voce .... farcita." The barbarous French of
which he gives a specimen is merely the old French of the time ;
and this farce was most probably a relic of an older custom of
translating the portions of holy scripture read in the service into
the vulgar tongue. He says that he has heard that Archbishop
Le Tellier had abrogated the practice as it had existed in certain
parishes in the diocese of Rheims. I have happened to meet
with the text of his *Ordonnance,* dated at his *chateau* at Louvois,
the 5th October, 1686. The custom, whatever may have been
its former extent, appears to have been confined to St Stephen's
day, two deacons singing the epistle alternately in Latin and

---

(1) "Thou sittist on goddis riȝt side in the ioie of the fadir."—*Te Deum,*
Maskell, M. R., II, 14.

"To knowe the ioye of the endeles trinity."—*Collect for Trinity Sunday,*
[*ante,* p. 94, l. 27], *ib.* II, 28.

(2) *De Ant. Eccles. Rit.,* I, p. 102. See also III, 39, and III, 35, where
he speaks of the "ornatura seu farcitura prophetiæ."

French to a peculiar chant. It is asserted that the barbarous French text was a subject of laughter to all who were present; and the archbishop most expressly (*très expressement*) forbids the ceremony: "*le chant nous en ayant paru extraordinaire et la traduction ridicule.*"(1)

P. 14, B. 120. *myrthe* was used in a sense less hilarious than the present use of mirth.

> "Faines in Laverd, and glades in quert
> And mirþes, alle rightwise of hert."—Ps. (32) xxxi, 11.

> "Ffor þan salle haly kyrk þat tyde,
> In heven be new gloryfyde,
> And won ay þare with God alle-myghty
> In ioy, and myrthe, and melody."—P. C. 8815-8.

> " For I am lord of blis,
> Ouer alle this warld, i-wis,
> My myrth is most of alle."
>
> *Towneley Mysteries*, p. 3.

B. 122. *of gode wille.* The *bonæ voluntatis* of the Vulgate.

B. 124. *bisyly.* This is given by Dr Morris as an instance where "we have retained the southern orthography with the northern pronunciation." (2) Although we retain the word, we should hardly use it as it was used in the text.

> " *Custodi sollicite animam tuam* (3)
> þat es on Inglis in þis manere,
> He seys, kepe þi saul bysily here."—P. C. 5807-9.

And Hampole, in his *Virtues of the name of Jesus:*—"Tharefore joye sall noghte faile vnto hym þat couates besyly for to lufe hym in whaym angells ȝernys for to be-halde."—*Prose Treatises* (Perry), p. 4.

" Ye ought inwardly sorow for the defaulte and besely to kepe in mynde."—*Myroure*, p. 68.

" Business" too was used rather of the diligence or earnestness than of the matter in hand.

> " For about worldisshe thynges þai here travaile
> Ful bysily, þat at þe last sal fayle ;
> Bot wald þai do half swilk bysines
> About gudes of heven, þar al gode es,
> þai suld haf alle þat gude es þare,
> þat never sal faille, bot last ever mare."—P. C. 1066—1071.

" Make me according to my busyness
Partaker of thy crown and glory endless."
> *Prymer*, 1543, *ap* Maskell, M. R., II, p. xviii.

---

(1) *Annales Archéologiques*, 1850, p. 160. See *post*, p. 210.
(2) *Ayenbite*, p. viii.
(3) Deut. iv, 9, where the A. V., "Keep thy soul diligently."

P. 14, B. 125. *Als worthi es.* "Adoramus te *Glorificant agnum cives, quem digniter almi*" is a farse to this verse of the hymn, as it is found in an antiphoner of St Gregory of the eleventh century.(1)

B. 125-6. *es—les.* As he could not alter both words, the rhyme has compelled the midland scribe to retain the northern *-es* of the second person.

B. 126. *makes.* The northern *-es* in the first person plural.

B. 127-8. *grace—hase.* Here too we find the northern *has* in the second person, with the *a* long, as in *father,* and sounded as it is still spoken in the East Riding, and rhyming to *grace*, which it will be noticed retains its French pronunciation. Cf. grase, York Bidding Prayer, p. 69, l. 11, and C. T. 15242, where it rhymes to Thopas.

B. 128. *of al þi grace.* The *of* looks as if suggested by *de* in the French original. The Latin of this farse is as follows: "Benedicimus te, *Per quem omne sanctum et benedictio conceditur.*" (2)

B. 132. *comly* was used not as now more commonly only of becomingness of person, but also of character or actions.

> "tweire schead as mon haueð ba of god & of uuel, of cumelich & of uncumelich."—*Hali Meidenhad* (Cockayne), p. 25.

> "that him cumly grette" (*greeted*).
> > *Metrical Homilies* (Small), p. 140.

So Shakspeare:

> "This is a happier and more comely time."
> > *Coriolanus*, iv, 2.

> "Know you not, master, to some kind of men
> Their graces serve them, but as enemies?
> O what a world is this, when what is comely,
> Envenoms him that bears it."—*As you like it*, ii, 3.

Cf. A. V., 1 Cor. vii, 35, "that which is comely;" and O.Fr. *convenant, convenient.*

B. 134. *þi fadir fre,* that is, of spontaneous bounty.

> "*Quod gratis accepistis, gratis date.*
> He says, þat þat yhe haf of grace fre
> And frely resayved, frely gyf yhe." (3)—P. C. 5963-5.

> "Thou, mayde and moder, daughter of thi sone,
>
> . . . .
>
> Assembled is in the, magnificence
> With mercy, goodness, and with such pitee,
> That thou that art the soune of excellence
> Not oonly helpest hem that prayen the,

_____

(1) Georgius, *Liturg.*, III, 522.
(2) Bona, *Rer. Liturg.*, II, iv, 6.
(3) St Matt. x, 8. Cf. A. V., "Freely ye have received, freely give."

· But often time of thy benignite,
Ful freely, er that men thin help biseche,
Thou gost biforn, and art her lyfes leche."

C. T. 11964—11984.

Compare the prayer of Saint Bernard in Dante :
"Vergine madre, figlia del tuo Figlio

* * * * *

La tua benignità non pur soccorre
A chi dimanda, ma molte fiate
Liberamente al dimandar precorre."

Paradiso, xxxiii. 1—18.

P. 14, B. 135. *þou þat wostis þo worlds synne.* "Qui tollis peccata
mundi." Here again we have the northern *-s* in the second
person. I do not find the verb *wost,* but no doubt it is to worst,
to defeat. Cf. the pronunciation of *wust, woosted,* for worst,
worsted. The A.S. *wyrsian* appears to have been used only as
an intransitive, to worsen or become worse; but in the Ormulum
we have *wersen* as a verb active :—

"ȝeff aniȝ mann uss eggeþþ
To don ohht orr to spekenn ohht
Off ifell *annd* off sinne,
To werrsenn *annd* to niþþrenn uss
Biforenn Godess (1) ehne."—ll. 11842-6.

B. 136. *more & mynne.* Cf. l. 126, "more & les" for another form
of this tag so often used to eke out a line.

"From þon læston oð þone mæstan," or some similar expression,
is often used to give emphasis to our ancient English laws : e. g.
Ecclesiastical Institutes, xxii.—Thorpe, ii, 418.

B. 138. *in þis time.* Cf. "now in the time of this mortal life."—
Collect, First Sunday in Advent.

B. 139. The rhyme accounts for *hande* not being altered by the midland scribe. See note, p. 179, and contrast *none, alone, most,* and
gost in the next four lines, which admitted of a ready change.

B. 140. The MS. quoted above (p. 196) from Georgius here inserts
"nostris tu parce ruinis."

B. 143. The following are prayers for the mediation of the Blessed
Virgin from the York Horæ.

" ¶ A prayer to our lady. [fol. 161]

O Blessyd lady moder of Jesu & virgin immaculate, that
arte (2) welle of comforte, and moder of mercy, senguler

---

(1) *ehne,* eyes. Cf. *ante,* p. 151, l. 110, and *Myroure,* p. 249 : "teres
ranne oute of the vyrgyns eyne."

(2) This "*art*" and the "*hath*" of the next prayer illustrate the remark
elsewhere made, as to the affectation of southern forms in the York service-
books when they came to be printed.

helper to all that trust to the, be now gracyous lady medyatrice
& meane unto thi blyssed sone our saviour Jesu for me, that by
thyn intercessions I may obtayne my desires ever to be your
seruaunt in all humilite. And by the helpe & socour of all holy
saintes hereafterr in perpetual ioy euer to lyue with the. Amen."

"¶ To our lady. [fol. 170 b]

Blessyd marye, virgin of nazareth,
      And moder to the myghty lorde of grace.
That his people saued hath with his deth
      From the paynes of the infernall place,
      Now blessyd lady, knele before his face
And praye to hym my soule to saue from losse
      Whiche with his blode hath bought us on the crosse."

P. 14, C. 83-6. *If þou of letter kan—answere þereto with gude will.*
. It will be observed that in this text, the *Gloria in excelsis* is left
out. It is assumed, as in ll. 347-8, p. 56, that the reader will
join in the responses; and the rehearsal of the Paternoster is
enjoined only when he neither knows the service, nor can read it.
In a Cistercian abbey there will have been many who " of letters
could," that is, who understood Latin.(1)

This distinction is drawn in a thirteenth century manuscript,
which Martene quotes when speaking of the part taken by the
congregation in this part of the mass. " Literates (' *litterati* ')
said the same words as the priest, but he with a loud and they
with a low (*depressa*) voice. The unlearned (*laici*) prayed in
their mother tongue, every one according to his knowledge." (2)
Cassander quotes a canon of a council at Orleans,(3) which required
not only clerks and "religious" women (*Deo dicatæ virgines*) to
answer the priest, but also all the people with one voice (*consona
voce*). And we find that the laity in this country from very early
times took part in the service of the church, for at the end of the
seventh century they were not allowed to read the lessons in
church, nor to say the *Alleluia*, but only the psalms and the
responses (*responsoria*), without the *Alleluia*.(4)

It is very evident, however, that in France, even when the
language had but little diverged from the Latin, and still more in
this country, · where the "vulgar tongue" would have afforded
them no assistance, there could have been very few of the laity

(1) We still use *literate* in this sense in contrast with graduate candidates
for holy orders, the xxxivth Canon requiring that no one shall be admitted
who has not " taken some degree of school, or at the least, except he be able
to yield an account of his faith in Latin."

(2) " Ut scribit Anonymus Turonensis in suo M. S. Speculo Ecclesiæ."—
Martene *de Rit.* I, 133.

(3) *Liturgica (s. l.* v. *a*—? Colon. 1561), fol. 43 *b.*

(4) Archbishop Theodore's *Penitential*, II, i, 10, Haddan and Stubbs,
Councils, III, 191.

whose knowledge of the language would have enabled them to join in the Latin services. Still, as we may gather from the allusions to this custom in this and other places in our text, it was expected of them that they would do so, if and when they could ; and in the Vernon MS. (*ante,* p. 130, l. 86) this is laid down in so many words :

> " As þe prest seiþ his preyere
> So schulde vche mon þat him gon here
> And þei wuste what hit ware."

As we have seen above (page 158) this theory had died out before the reformation. A modern authority on these points, M. Romsée, Professor of Sacred Rites in the Diocesan Seminary of Liége, explains the existing rule in the Church of Rome. Speaking of the priests turning to the people at this part of the mass (*ante,* p. 94, l. 20), and bidding them " Dominus vobiscum," and of the answer " Et cum spiritu tuo," he says that it was formerly " made by all the people, but now is made more conveniently and more reverently (*convenientius et reverentius*) by the server only in the name of all." (1)

P. 15, E. 121. " *to tell.*" He did not understand the northern *till.*

E. 140. The upsilonism of this MS. has been pointed out, p. 185. Here the scribe writes " help us " (help*us*) with a contraction, as if he took it for the third person singular. .

E. 141. *name.* This mistake of the scribe arose no doubt from the northern original reading *nane,* which the midland scribe of text B has altered into *none.* Both have altered *al ane* in the next line ; but our scribe with his usual blundering has altered the northern *wonand,* which B reads unchanged in line 145, into *wonnying.*

P. 16, B. 149. After the *Gloria in excelsis,* or, when that was not used, after the *Kyrie,* followed the greeting of the people, mentioned in the note on C. 83 (p. 200), and then the collect, with the epistle and gospel.

B. 150. *Knele doun on þi knese sone.* This direction to kneel may be noticed in reference to the change from the ancient custom of standing at prayer which has been already mentioned (page 193). It would seem that towards the end of the seventeenth century, when Martene wrote his great work on the Rites of the Church, the people had returned to the practice of standing during the collect, unless perhaps he means that they sat in his time. He says that formerly the people knelt at the collect, on the deacon's bidding " Flectamus genua." He quotes from a sermon by St Cæsarius, who was bishop of Arles in the sixth century : "I beseech you, dearest brethren, and exhort that whenever prayer is made

(1) *Opera Liturgica,* Leodii, 1818, cum Approbatione et Permissione, Tom. IV, 105.

at the altar by the clergy, or prayer is bidden by the deacon, that ye bow down faithfully not only your hearts, but also your bodies. For often, as in duty bound, I diligently give heed, and when the deacon exclaims, let us bend our knees, I behold the greatest part standing as straight as pillars."(1)

P. 16, B. 151. *þi pater-noster reherce al-waie.* It will be observed that the later form which was adapted, not only for the English rite, but also, as I suppose, for the use of a "religious" house, here contemplates the rehearsing of pater-nosters by those only who were not literates (see C. 90 and note, p. 216); but the direction given here, and in lines 261, 398, and 601, was no doubt in accordance with the practice of the laity in general, at least until the Ave Maria became part of the accustomed devotions.(2) In the Excerpts (VI) of Egbert, Archbishop of York (A.D. 735—766), the canons under King Edgar (xvii & xxii), the teaching of the Pater-noster and the Creed is strongly enjoined; and in the "Ecclesiastical Institutes" (xxii) all are admonished from the least to the greatest to learn them, and it is added that in these two sayings (*cwydum*) is the foundation of all Christian belief, and that unless any one can sing them both, and so believe as is therein said, and often pray (*gebidde*) therewith, he cannot well be a Christian.(3) And we find from incidental notices that the pater-noster was so used. In the Festival there is a version of the story of Saint Austin of England and the women that jangled at mass,(4) and there it is said that Pope Gregory "came to the wymen and asked of them what they had sayd all the masse tyme, and they sayd our pater noster,"(5) that being evidently what they were expected to say. A string or "pair" of beads,(6) was

(1) De Ant. Eccl. Rit. I, 133.
(2) In Myrc (XV Cent.) the priest is directed to enquire in confession:
"Const þow þi pater and þyn aue
And þy crede now telle þow me."—ll. 917-18.
And the parish priest is enjoined:
"þow moste teche hem mare
þat when þey doth to chyrche fare,
þenne bydde hem leue here mony wordes
Here ydel speche, and nyce bordes
And put away alle vanyte
And say here pater-noster & here aue."—ll. 264-9.
(3) Thorpe, II, 418. The Ecclesiastical Institutes here quoted, though translated into English, and most probably of some authority in this country, were written by Bishop Theodulf of Orleans, who flourished about A.D. 797.— Haddan and Stubbs, *Councils*, I, p. xiii.
(4) *Ante*, p. 136-9.
(5) *Festyvall* (1515). In Dedicatione ecclesie, *fol.* 154 *b.*
(6) So Chaucer of the prioress:
"Of smal coral aboute her arme sche baar
A peire of bedes gaudid al with grene."—C. T. 158-9.

called a " paternoster "(1). We find the name so used in the earlier part of the thirteenth century in the " Lutel soth Sermun." It speaks of proud young maidens and warns against illicit love :

" Hwanne heo to chirche comeþ
to þe haliday
Heo biholdeth wadekin.
mid swiþe gled eye.
Atom his hire *pater noster* (2)

And so in Latin : "Unum par bedus de laumbre." " Unum par bedys de corall." *Test. Ebor*, I, 271. Beads were also called *orationes*, "unum par orationum de auro," *ib*. 213 ; and *preecs*, "meas preces de curalle," *ib*. 252 ; and *preeulæ*, "par precularum de gagate." *Wills & Inventories* (Surtees Soc.), I, 87.

(1) See Maskell, M. R. II, p. xlviii, where he quotes from Nicolas, *Testamentæ Vetusta*, I, 147, " a pair of paternosters of coral " in the will of Eleanor of Gloucester, A.D. 1399. *Patenôtre* is the French, and Littré gives an example in the thirteenth century : " Une femme qui tenoit unes paternostres en sa main." —*Miracles, St Loys*, p. 131.

(2) This is from the Cotton MS. *Calig*. A ix. fol. 249. Dr Morris gives a second text (Jesus Coll. Oxon. MS. 29) from a MS. of the latter part of the same (xiii) century :

At hom is hire *pater* noster ;

which leaves us in no doubt as to the contraction in the Cotton MS. being rightly expanded. At all events it is open to any one to form his own conclusion with an exact knowledge of the reading of the MS., and this is the advantage of the rule of our society which requires all contractions to be shown in italic. In Guest's *English Rhythms*, II, 330, the last lines are given thus :

" Atorn his hire primur ; biloken is hire teye."
" Run away from is her primer—lock'd up in her scrip."

I recollect to have noted them some years ago, when I first read Dr Guest's most interesting and learned work, and until I again met with them in Dr Morris's book, I accepted them as an example of the use of "primur" some hundred and fifty years earlier than I had elsewhere met with any mention of this English service-book. I have not been on the look out for it, and therefore my recollection must be taken only for what it is worth, but I do not recollect to have met with an instance of paternoster being used for a pair of beads in any earlier English manuscript.

Spelman had explained the word "beltidum " occurring in the tenth canon of the provincial council of Canterbury, held at Celchyth in the year 816, as if it meant a *rosary :*—"æt VII beltidum, pater noster pro eo cantetur" (H. & S. *Councils*, III, 584). Mabillon (*Acta Sanct*. O. S. B. Præfat. in Sæc. V. § 125), whilst exploding the notion that Venerable Bede was the inventor of rosaries, and that they were called "bedes" after him, does not doubt that the words "beltidum paternoster " meant a certain number of paternosters, though he agrees with Du Cange that the Rosary, which in great part consists of Ave Marias, was a later invention.

Johnson (*Canons*, (A.C.L.) I, 307) and Dr Lingard (*Anglo-Saxon Church*, II, 69) take the same view as to the belt of paternosters, but Professor Stubbs with his usual happy insight suggests that the word is derived " from *Bel* (A.S.), a bell, and *Tid*. (A.S.), time," and explains it " in reference to the seven canonical hours (*tidum*) at which the prayer bell rang."—*Councils*, III, 585.

biloken(1) in hire teye."(2)

Old English Miscellany (Dr Morris), E. E. T. S. (1872), p. 190.

Her paternoster at home and locked away in her coffer was a proof to the preacher that it was not her prayers or bidding her bedes that she thought about—

> " Masses and matines,
>   ne kepeþ heo nouht."

And the way in which it is said would seem to prove that the saying of paternosters would have been a sufficient minimum.

As to substitution of paternoster for prescribed prayers, see C. 87—90, and the note, p. 216.

P. 16, B. 153. *gospel rede.* Read in contradistinction to the said or sung of the preceding line, referring to the rest of the mass. Both epistle and gospel afterwards came to be sung, but the rubrics of the English uses, and also of the Rouen MS. elsewhere quoted, agree as to reading them ; and we find Amalarius in the ninth century pointing out the distinction : " Lectio dicitur quia non cantatur ut psalmus vel hymnus, sed legitur tantum. Illic enim modulatio, hic sola pronunciatio quæritur."(3)

B. 154. *stonde vp þen.* " The people all standing up " has always been the attitude in which the gospel has been heard, and a rubric or direction to this effect was almost, if not always, the only indication that the presence of the people was contemplated by mediæval ritualists and rubricians, so exclusively were they concerned with the ceremonies of the altar and the motions of the officiating clergy.

As might be expected, this point is not passed over in books intended for popular instruction—

> " And when the gospel me rede schal,
>   Fayne thou stonde up fro the wal,
>   And blesse the fayre, ȝep that thou conne,
>   When *gloria tibi* is begonne."
>
> *Constitutions of Masonry,* 629-32.

---

(1) *biloken.* So *Castel off loue* (Weymouth), 992 :

" Hit is in his cofre bi-loke so fast."

" This is the hand, which, with a vow contract,
    Was fast belock'd in thine."—*Measure for Measure,* V, 1.

(2) " Teye, of a cofyr or forcer. Teca, thecarium."—P. P. 487. Old Wykehamists will remember the "toys" at Winchester, even if recent reforms have improved them away.

(3) *De Eccles. Officiis.* III, ii. The following rubric in the Book of Common Prayer was struck out at the revision in 1661 : "and to the end the people may the better hear in such places where they do sing, then shall the lessons be sung in a plain tune, after the manner of distinct reading : and likewise the epistle and gospel."

Cf. Myrk, 278, &c.; Vernon, *ante*, p. 140, l. 425.

P. 16, B. 155. *flyttes his boke.* The reason given in the Micrologus (c. ix) is that there might be more room at the south part of the altar, where the oblations were always placed. When the oblations were made by the people in kind (but they never did so(1) until after the gospel had been read) the additional room would have been necessary, "ad suscipiendas oblationes."

When this custom had become obsolete the flitting of the book was required by the change of position of the priest still prescribed by the Latin rubrics; but this ceremony was abolished at the reformation. By the first Book of Edward VI the priest was directed to stand "afore the midst of the altar;" and by the second book "at the north side;" but under the rubrics of 1540 some of the clergy continued to remove the book from the right to the left part of the table ;(2) and in the time of Queen Elizabeth Bishop Parkhurst (of Norwich) at the Primary Visitation (1561) prohibits "shifting of ye boke."(3)

It will be observed that the reading of the epistle and gospel only at the altar is here specified as usual at low masses, or in parish churches, &c. At capitular masses, according to the Sarum use, they were read from a pulpit, or at the step(4) of the quire, according to the day; at Durham from an eagle on the north side; and elsewhere in these positions, or from the rood-loft, &c., according to local use.

B. 156. *north.* It does not seem that the points of the compass were ever employed in the rubrics of the Roman Missal, the Ordo Romanus, or other distinctively Roman ritual formularies; but it was the usage of the Church of England before the reformation, and the revisers of the prayer book in 1552, having occasion to specify a side of the Lord's table, very naturally reverted to it. In the present text, besides this place, we have "south altar nook," in lines 88 and 579. In the rubrics of Anglican, as of other missals, right and left are for the most part used, but in both the Sarum and York missals are examples of *pars australis*, or *aqui-*

---

(1) At Rouen, immediately after the epistle the sub-deacon brought the chalice and paten from the vestry and placed them at the south part of the altar where the missal had stood, and not on the credence table, the deacon having moved the missal to make room for them (*Voyage Liturg.*, 364), and a similar rite was observed at Tours.—*Ib.* 124.

(2) Bucer. *Censura, Script. Anglic.*, fol. Basil, 1577, p. 494. Bishop Ridley's *Injunctions*, 1550, Cardwell, *Doc. Ann.* I, p. 93, l. 13.

(3) Quarto, London, John Day, *s. a.* § 4.

(4) "*Ad gradum chori,*" probably from a lectrinum (*lectern*) which is elsewhere spoken of in the rubric. Martene (*De Ant. Rit.* I, 136), quoting from the Chronicle of Monte Cassino, mentions that the Abbot Desiderius placed a "gradum ligneum" without the quire, for reading the lessons at night, and the epistles and gospels at the masses of the principal festivals.

lonaris.(1) This practice may very probably have come to us,
like other peculiarities, through the ancient Gallican church from
the East. At all events the parts of the church and the sides of
the altar were in early times and are still distinguished in the
East according to the four quarters of the heavens. Goar uses
βορεῖον κλίτος or μέρος, and νοτεῖον μέρος (*north and south side or
part*) as the appropriate terminology in the description of the
church of a Greek monastery.(2) We find the phrases διὰ τοῦ
βορείου κλίτους, διὰ τοῦ βορείου μέρους,(3) and πρὸς ἀνατολὰς,
πρὸς δυσμὰς (4)—*towards the east, towards the west*—in the rubrics
of the Greek church ; and a similar use of north and south in the
rubrics of the Syriac *Ordo Communis*.(5) The early use of this
language in the East may also be inferred from its being found at
the present day among the Christians of St Thomas, in reference
to the parts of the altar, which we learn from Mr Howard's translation of their vernacular liturgy.(6)

P. 16, B. 157-9. *a cross vpon þo letter.* The custom of the reader,
whether celebrant or deacon, signing the book with sign of the
cross at the place where the gospel begun appears to have been
general, and is very commonly specified in rubrics.

So Lydgate's *Virtue of the Mass* :

"The gospel begynnethe withe tokene of tav.(7)
The booke first crossed and after the forhede."

Harl. MS. 2251, fol. 182*b*.

---

(1) *Miss. Sar.* Burntisland, col. 253, 255, 350. *Miss. Ebor.* (Ed. Henderson), p. 84, 204.
(2) *Euchologion*, p. 13 ; cf. n. 30, p. 31.
(3) Goar, *Euchol.* 4. 73. Εὐχολόγιον τὸ Μέγα, Venice (the modern Greek
Prayer Book), 1854, 4. 55.
(4) Goar, *u. s.* 67, 5. The modern Euchologion, 47, 6.
(5) Renaudot. *Liturg. Orient.*, 1716, II, 13. 24.
(6) *Christians of St Thomas and their Liturgies*, by Rev. G. B. Howard,
B.A., 1864, p. 195, 197-8. It may be observed that Archbishop Menezes (of
Goa) in his high-handed attempt to obliterate primitive usages among the
native Christians, that were not in accordance with the latest Roman ritual,
with which alone he was acquainted—a course Renaudot very strongly re-
probates,—allowed this Eastern peculiarity to remain in one of the rubrics
of their ancient liturgy, as castigated by him at the Synod of Diamper in the
year 1599.—*Liturgia Malabarico-Menessiana*, Raulin ; *Historia Ecclesiæ
Malabaricæ*, Romæ, 1745, p. 301.
(7) Ezekiel, IX, 4. "Set a mark upon their foreheads," where the
Hebrew תָו, a mark, is rendered σημεῖον by the LXX ; left untranslated by
Aquila and Theodoteon, Θαῦ ; and in the Vulgate, "signa thau super frontes ;"
and Douay "mark Thau." Tertullian (*Adv. Marc.* III, 22) quotes this as
"Da signa Thau in frontibus virorum," and goes on to apply it as a prophecy
of the cross which Christians should "print upon their brow." There is much
curious learning on this point in Vitringa (*Sacr. Observat.* II, 15), where he
gives extracts from Origen, St Jerome, and others.
    In the old Hebrew or Samaritan alphabet, the tau was cruciform, and it

P. 16, B. 158. *with his thoume.* The signing of the text of the gospel appears to have been general, but there was considerable diversity in the rubrics directing it. Many of the old uses are silent as to manner. The use of the thumb is prescribed in some cases, and of fingers (in the plural) in others. It will be seen (*page* 98) that the York MS. has no rubric on the point, nor have the printed editions. The Sarum rubric is as follows: " faciat signum super librum, deinde in sua fronte, et postea in pectore cum pollice."(1) The Hereford rubric specifies the thumb, without any mention of the breast, and the modern Roman and the Ambrosian (*ed.* 1849) agree in specifying the thumb, but add the signing of the mouth.(2)

The varying numbers of fingers and other particularities in making the sign of the cross by the celebrant at other places in the mass are directed by rubrics, but it will be sufficient to mention the manner of making the sign of the "large cross" by the laity, which is elsewhere (B. 176) enjoined in this treatise.

It was the first lesson taught a child at school.(3) The earliest notices of the manner of making the cross was with one finger, but in the seventh or eighth century it had become usual to use three. In our own country we find Ælfric prescribing this custom in his homily on the Exaltation of the Cross :(4) " þeah þe mon waſſge wundorlice mid handa ne bið hit þeah bletsung buta he wyrce tacn þære halgan rode . . . Mid þrym fingrum man sceall senian *and* bletsian for þære halgan þrynnesse." (*Though a man wave wonderfully with hand, yet is not blessing unless he make the token of the holy rood. With three fingers should one sign and bless for the Holy Trinity.*) In the Eastern Church the thumb and the two next fingers are used, the other two being doubled into the palm of the hand, as we see in old painted glass, seals, and illuminations; and the cross is made from the forehead to the breast, and then from the right to the left shoulder, and crosses on parts of the person or detached objects were made in the same

---

was the received opinion in the middle ages that the tau of the prophet was the sign of the cross, and this is very frequently brought forward in the mystical application of the ceremonies of the mass, and specially in reference to the T of the Te igitur, which the priest appears at one time to have kissed, as afterwards the rubrics required him to kiss the altar.—*Ante*, p. 104. Cf. "A sine of tau T make ȝe þer."—*Cursor Mundi*, 6078.

(1) *Miss. Sar.* col. 13.

(2) Gavanti notes this signing of the mouth as not being directed in the old *Ordo Romanus*, but refers to the *Gemma Animæ* as mentioning it. This treatise was written by Honorius of Autun in the twelfth century.

(3) *Boke of Curtasye.* Babees Book, p. 303, l. 144. St Chrysostom had exhorted Christians to teach their children from their earliest years to seal their foreheads (i. e. make the sign of the cross) with their hand.—*In Epist.* I, *ad Cor.* Hom. xii. Ed. Ben. Tom. X, p. 108 B.

(4) *Legends of the Holy Rood* (Morris), E. E. T. S., p. 105.

direction. Dr Rock(1) tells us, "Up to the middle of the fifteenth century the same method was likewise employed throughout the Latin church."(2) It may be observed that this cross is prescribed for the priest in the rubric of the York use (*ante*, p. 112, l. 6-9). In the twelfth century we find a pope giving a mystical reason for it ;(3) but modern Roman Catholics use the open hand, and make the cross from left to right ; and so much importance appears to have been attached to the change in the church of Rome, that we find that at the Council of Diamper (A.D. 1599) Menezes, Archbishop of Goa, made a canon,(4) abrogating the ancient custom which the Portuguese Missionaries found amongst the native Christians of St Thomas, and claiming a mystical significance for the new rule.(5)

---

(1) *Hierurgia*, II, 530.

(2) In the *Myroure* (*ed.* Blunt, E. E. T. S., p. 80) we find the nuns of Syon had adopted the change : " And then ye blysse you wyth the sygne of the holy crosse. to chase a waye the fende with all hys dysceytes. For as Crisostome sayth. where euer the fendes se the sygne of the crosse they flye away dredyng yt as a staffe that they are beten wyth all. And in thys blyss-ynge ye begynne wyth youre honde at the hedde downewarde. & then to the lyfte syde. and after to the righte syde. in token. & byleue *that* our lorde Iesu cryste came downe from the hed. *that* is from the father in to erthe. by his holy incarnacion. & from the erthe in to the lyfte syde *that* is hel. by hys bytter passyon. & from thense vnto his fathers ryght syde by his glorous asconcion."

(3) " Est autem signum crucis tribus digitis expimendum, quia sub invo-catione Trinitatis imprimitur, de qua dicit Propheta : Quis appendit tribus digitis morem terræ (Esaiæ. XL [12]), ita quod a superiori descendat ad in-ferius et a dextrâ transeat ad sinistram, quia Christus de cœlo descendit in terram, et a Judæis transivit ad Gentes."—Innocentii III, *De Sacro Altaris Mysterio*, Lib. II, c. xliv.

(4) "CCXXXVII. Cupiens Synodus Montanam hancce Ecclesiam om-nibus conformare consuetudinibus Latinæ necnon Sanctæ Matris Ecclesiæ Romanæ ; cui perfectam detulit obedientiam, cum probe sciat juxta morem ipsius signum crucis et benedictionem a læva ad dexteram partem duci, ita ut dum proferuntur ea verba : *In nomine Patris et Filii et Spiritus Sancti,* prius contacto capite manus per pectus deducatur ad ventrem ; deinde trans-versim, crucem perficiendo ab humero siuistro ad dexterum transferatur, id quod mystica significatione non caret ; significat enim virtute crucis Christi Filii Dei, ac Domini nostri, a læva reproborum translatos esse ad dexteram partem quæ est electorum ; præcipit, ut in instruendis pueris reliquisque, ipsis insinuetur modus se signandi cruce. qui adhibetur in ecclesia Latina, atque adeo abrogetur modus inversus, quo se signant in hac diœcesi ducendo manum ab humero dextro ad sinistrum."—*Synodi Diamperitanæ Actio* VIII, Decre-tum XXXVII. Raulin, p. 245.

(5) Nowhere perhaps in the present day are the Latin and Greek rites brought into sharper contact than at Warsaw, but an incident came under the writer's observation in that city in 1859, from which we may infer that there is not this same rigid intolerance of a difference in unimportant points in the Eastern Church.

The present emperor, Alexander II, had come into Poland on his tour of

P. 16, B. 162. *gods son of heuen.* Here "*of heaven*" must not be understood as if it were *heavenly.* The phrase in the text occurs in Thoresby's Catechism (*fol.* 295*b*) in stating the truth of conception of our Lord ; in the Festyval (W. de Worde, 1515, fol. 4), when Pope Gregory showed the host "turned into reed flesshe and blode bledynge" to the doubting woman, "and she cryed and sayd, Lorde I crye the mercy. I beleue yt thou arte veray god and man and goddes sone of heuen in fourme of breed ; " and in other places. It points to our Lord as " He that came down from heaven ; " "of heofnu," *Lindisfarne ;* " of heofne," *Rushworth ;* " de cœlo," *Vulgate.* Jo. iii, 13. " *Of*" was constantly used as a preposition of motion in the earlier monuments of our language : " stefn of heofnum cuoeð," *Lindis. ;* " stemn of heofnune cweþende," *Rushw. ;* " vox de cœlis dicens," *Vulg.* Matt. iii, 17. " þis wæs ȝefohten siþþan he of East-Englum com " (*after he came from East Anglia*).—*A.S. Chronicle,* A.D. 658, M.H.B., p. 316.

We still find an instance of the same use in the Authorized Version : " Come they not hence, even of your lusts."—Jam. iv, 1. And in the Book of Common Prayer : " O God, the Father, of heaven, have mercy upon us "—the " Pater, de cœlis,(1) Deus, miserere nobis " of the Latin litany.

---

inspection. He had not been in the cathedral since he had been there when a boy with his father upon occasion of his being crowned King of Poland, and since then there had been the Polish Revolution and the Crimean war. It was not therefore without significance when it was announced that he intended to present himself at the cathedral. At the appointed time he was received with great pomp by all the chief Roman Catholic ecclesiastics, the heads of religious orders, and a large number of clergy in the presence of the principal Polish nobility and high Russian officials. When he presented himself at the great western door, and was met by the clergy in procession, he crossed himself with the Latin cross, and long before he reached the step of the altar, near which I happened to be standing, the fact was passed from mouth to mouth, and I was told it with great excitement by those who were near me. I must own that until then I had never heard of the difference between the Latin and Greek cross, but a Roman Catholic friend soon explained it to me, and indeed one did not need to be a liturgiologist to enter into the hopeful augury, which the emperor's Polish subjects drew from this condescension to their religious feelings, their hopes too soon to be doomed to disappointment by the abortive attempt at revolution in 1861.

(1) The thought and the phrase may probably be traced to Solomon's prayer at the dedication of the temple ; "Hear thou from thy dwelling place, even from heaven, and when thou hearest forgive." " Exaudi . . . de cœlis." —*Vulg.,* 2 Chron. vi, 21. The comma which our printers have inserted (" Father, from heaven ") has not been sufficient in all cases to prevent those who do not know the source of the words of the petition, or the earlier force of the preposition, from the inaccuracy of reading and explaining the " Of heaven " in this place as " heavenly," though they might plead the example of the Authorized Version, which has used " heavenly " in a somewhat similar connection, " How much more shall your heavenly Father give the Holy Spirit," ὁ ἐξ οὐρανοῦ δώσει—(Lu. xi, 13). Here the *Bishop's Bible* had " of heaven

P. 16, B. 163. *reders. herers.* Cf. the prayer for grace to the curate
and all pastors in the York Bidding Prayer (p. 69, l. 1). And
notice that in that prayer, and in the corresponding place in later
forms, we have "techers " and "sugettes." Perhaps it is not far-
fetched to see in the "readers" and "hearers" of our text the
consideration for the layman, which is throughout its special
feature.

B. 163-6. Whether the translator found in this place a reference to
the rule of the diocese of Rouen, as to reading the gospel in French
immediately after the deacon had finished it in Latin,(1) or
whether he himself was one of those churchmen, who sought to
silence objectors by removing stumbling-blocks and correcting
abuses,—and we hear of many such in the highest stations in the
church before the reformation, until the party who would yield
nothing and learn nothing gained a triumph for a time by the
passing of the Act *de Hæretico comburendo*—or however else we
may account for it, a tone of dissatisfaction at the existing practice
in England is very evident in these lines.

For an example of a very different spirit in the thirteenth and
fourteenth centuries,(2) we have no need to go farther than the

---

give," and seems to have succeeded better in giving the force of the original
by keeping more closely to it. This has also been done in the old English
Versions, *Lindisfarne* "of heofnum," and *Rushworth* "of heofne," and also in
the *Rhemish* "from heaven," by following the *Vulgate*, "pater vester de cœlo
dabit."

(1) I cannot produce any authority for this being the practice at Rouen at the
date of our MS., but I think I may be justified in assuming that it was so,
because I find (*Voyages Liturgiques*, p. 418) that it was the rule of that diocese
at the close of the eighteenth century ; and it is most improbable that a
practice which was so exceptional, if not unique, in France, should have been
introduced at any intermediate date. Grancolas, who was a contemporary of
the author of the *Voyages*, mentions in his *Liturgie Ancienne* (p. 53) that the
reading of the gospel in Latin and French was directed in some old manuscript
rituals at Soissons and Tours, in a way which is quite inconsistent with his
having known that, when he wrote, it was the practice elsewhere in France.
De Vert, who wrote much about the same time (*Cérémonies*, III, 155), speaks
of the gospels having been explained *formerly ;* and in his Letter to M. Jurieu,
1 May, 1690 (*id. IV*, 362), answers his objection as to the gospel being read in
Latin, so that the people could understand nothing, " Ce n'est pas la faute de
l'Eglise si tous n'entendent pas le latin, et elle a eu de tres bonnes raisons pour
conserver son ancienne langue." The practice was adopted—though not the
rule at present—many years afterwards, when the public exercise of Christian
worship was re-established after the excesses of the first Revolution. At all
events, immediately after the Restoration in 1814 it was remarked that in
churches at Paris both Epistle and Gospel were read in French from the pulpit
before the Nicene creed, at the principal mass, on Sundays and holy days.

(2) There is no reference to the reading of the gospel in English in the
constitution of Archbishop Peckham, passed in provincial council at Lambeth
in 1281, as to the instruction of the lay-people, and known by its first words
Ignorantia sacerdotum ; where, if still enjoined, it would in all likelihood have

Vernon MS., in the Appendix (p. 140, l. 425-48), and there is no doubt that the Latin gospels continued to be read without translation down to the Reformation.(1) It recognizes the fact that there were laymen that were "none clerkes" who would have liked "to wite what þe prest seeþ " at the gospel ; but the writer appears to have proved to his own satisfaction that its true power still availed them, though they failed to understand it. We may well believe that there were parish priests, like Chaucer's " pore persoun of a toun,"

"That Cristes gospel truly wolde preche ; "

but we cannot doubt that there was a general neglect to observe, and at all events no attempt to enforce what in Anglo-Saxon times had been the written rule of the Church of England, as to the gospel in English. This had most probably fallen through after the Conquest in consequence of the intrusion into the Church of England of prelates who knew nothing of English, and, many of them, showed a contemptuous indifference towards the English clergy and laity, over whom they had been promoted.

It has been said, as by Dr Lingard,(2) that in the Anglo-Saxon Church the epistle and gospel were read in English, but if it is intended that they were read in set form, like the reading of the epistle and gospel in Latin and Greek when the Pope celebrates pontifically, or as they were read in the eighteenth century, at the Benedictine Monasteries of Monte Cassino, and St Denys in France, I have nowhere met with any contemporary authority for this opinion. On the other hand, the authorities usually brought for-

---

been mentioned ; nor in the similar instructions put forth in the convocation of York in 1357, and quoted as Archbishop Thoresby's Catechism.

(1) This seems very evident from the absolute absence of any contemporary mention or allusion, and still more from the manner in which the reading the epistle and gospel "in the vulgar " is mentioned in a letter to the Duke of Norfolk, printed in *Original Letters* (Ed. Ellis), 3rd Series, II, 192. The year is not given, but is probably 1531, and if I might venture to offer another conjecture, where the learned editor has been silent, it was written by Thomas Boleyn, Earl of Wiltshire, who was the Duke's son-in-law, and had been sent on an embassy to the Pope and the Emperor, accompanied by Cranmer and others, in the year 1530. He is describing the Protestant mass at Nuremburg, very much as we find it soon afterwards in the " *Ordnung der Messe, wie die soll gehalten werden* " of the " *Nürnbergische Kirchenordnung* " of 1533 :— "The Preest in vestmentes after oure manner, singith everi thing in Latine," "as we use, omitting suffrages. The Epistel he readith in Latin. In the " "meane time the sub Deacon goeth into the pulpite and readeth to the people " "after the Epistle in their vulgare ; after thei peruse other thinges as our prestes " "doo. Than the Preeste redith softly the Gospell in Latine. In the meane " "space the Deacon goeth into the pulpite and readith aloude the Gospell in " "the Almaigne tung." (*)

(2) *Anglo-Saxon Church*, I, 307.

(*) See also *England in the Reign of King Henry VIII.* (Ed. Cowper), E. E. T. S., p. 137, l. 1285.

ward seem to have had, or, perhaps, to have been obeyed as
having had, a more definite purpose than generally, "to enforce
the duty of preaching," as has been supposed.(1)

The so-called Excerpts of Egbert, Archbishop of York (A.D. 732
—766), require priests on holidays and Sundays to preach the
gospel to the people.(2) The Canons of Ælfric are more precise.
They require the mass-priest on Sundays and Mass-days to tell to
the people the sense of the gospel in English (þæs godspelles
angyt on Englisc þam folce), and concerning the Pater-noster and
the creed also, the oftenest that he can :(3) and, as a matter of
fact, the oldest sermons and homilies that have come down to us
are almost invariably on the gospel of the day. The same may be
noticed in the sermons of the next few centuries, which have been
edited by Dr Morris and others ; and at a later date Wyclif in his
sermons observed the same rule.

In the thirteenth century Ormin wrote the *Ormulum*, which, as
explained by himself in the dedication, is first a paraphrase of the
gospels, and then an exposition of their meaning for the use of
those who were bound to preach it to the people :—

> " Icc hafe sammnedd o þiss boc
>   þa Goddspelless neh alle,
> þatt sinndenn o þe messeboc
>   Inn all þe ȝer att messe.
> *Annd* aȝȝ affterr þe Goddspell stannt
>   þatt tatt te Goddspell meneþþ,
> þatt mann birrþ spellenn to þe follc
>   Off þeȝȝre sawle nede" (*Ded.* 29—36).

And he then goes on to explain,

> " Whi icc till Ennglissh hafe wennd
>   Goddspelless hallȝhe lare " (*Ded.* 113-14).

But his reasons, though well worth reading, are too long to insert
here.

In the next century we have the author of the Metrical Homilies,
edited by Mr Small, written for " lered and laued bathe," though
in one of them he inserts the Latin poem on the " Signa ante
judicium," which, as pointed out by the editor (*Introduction*, p. vi.),
a rubric directs the preacher to omit, " quando legit Anglicum
coram laycis." He thus explains his purpose :—

> The faur godspellers us shawes
>   Cristes dedes and his sawes.

---

(1) Maskell, A. E. L., p. 49.

(2) "III. Ut omnibus festis et diebus dominicis unusquisque sacerdos
evangelium Christi prædicet populo."—*Excerptiones Egberti;* Thorpe,
Ancient Laws, II, 98. " Closer examination shows the *Excerptiones Egberti*
not to be Egbert's at all."—Haddan and Stubbs, *Councils,* III, 403.

(3) *Thorpe,* Ancient Laws, II, 350-1.

Al faur a(1) talle thay telle,
Bot seer saues er in thair spelle,
And of thair spel in kirk at messe,
Er leszouns red bathe mar and lesse,
For at euer ilke messe we rede
Of Cristes wordes and his dede.
Forthi tha godspells that always
Er red in kirc on sundays,
Opon Inglis wil Ic undo,
Yef God wil gif me grace tharto,
For namlic on the sonnenday,
Comes lawed men thair bede to say
To the kirc, an for to lere
Gostlic lare that thar thai here,
For als gret mister(2) haf thay,
To wit quat the godspel wil say
Als lered men, for bathe er bouht
Wit Cristes blod, and sal be broht
Til henenis blis ful menskelie ;(3)
Yef thai lef her rihtwislie,
For wil Ic on Inglis schau,
And ger our laued brether knawe
Quat alle tha godspelles saies
That falles tille the sunnendayes
That thai mai her and hald in hert
Thinge that thaim til God mai ert.(4)

English Metrical Homilies (Small), p. 4—5.

These and similar collections were mainly intended for the
assistance of preachers,(5) but in the latter part of the fourteenth
and in the fifteenth centuries arose the practice, necessarily confined to the educated classes, of following the epistles and gospels
in an English translation ; and we find sometimes the four gospels,
and sometimes the whole of the New Testament with tables for

---

(1) one.—See note p. 215, B. 173.
(2) need.
(3) humanely, kindly.
(4) provoke. Cf. Heb. x, 24.
(5) This was the professed object of the Festyvale, as set forth by Myrc in
the " Prologus," except that it was drawn from the Golden Legend instead of
Holy Writ. " Myn owne symple understandinge feleth well how it fareth by
other that ben (*) in the same degre, and hauen charge of soules and holden to
teche theyr paryshens of all the pryncypal feestes that come in the yere.
" ¶ But for many excuse them for defaut of bokes and also by symplenes of
connynge. Therefore in helpe of suche clerkes this treatyse is drawen out of
(Legenda Aurea) *that* he that lust to studye therin, he shall fynde redy therin
of all the pryncypall feestes of the yere of everyone a shorte sermon nedeful
for them to teche, and for other to lerne."—W. de Worde, 1515, fol. 2.
(*) " By myne owne febul letture y fele how Yt fareth by othur yt bene."—Caxton.

finding the portions appointed to be read at mass. I give the
rubric of the table from a MS. belonging to my friend Mr Davies-
Cooke of Owston, Yorkshire, and Gwysaney, which is interesting
from its historical associations. It was part of the Llannerch
library, which he inherited through the Davies of that place and
of Gwysaney, Co. Flint, from Sir Edward Ffitton, to whom it was
given by Henry, eighth Earl of Northumberland, who has received
it from Lord Burghley, as appears by the unfortunate earl's(1)
autograph.(2)

"Ere bigynneþ a rule þat telliþ in whiche chapitris of þe bible(3)
ye may finde þe lessones pistlis *and* gospelis þat ben red in þe
chirche after þe usse of salisbury, marked wiþ lettris of þe a b c at
þe begynnyng of þe chapitris, towardis þe myddil or ende after þe
ordre as þe lettris stonde in the abc : first ben sett sundaies *and*
ferials togidre, And aftre þat þe sanctorum. þe propre *and* comonn
togidre of al þe ʒeer. And þanne last þe commemoraciones þat is
clepid þe tempral of al þe ʒeer. ffirst is writen a clause of the bigyn-
nynge of þe pistle or gospel : *and* a clause of the endinge þerof also.

þe I Sunday   romans xiii   d we knowen ende lord iesu crist.
in aduent.   M\[^t]. xxi   a whanne iesus end in hiʒe þingis."

After the invention of printing the epistles and gospels were
printed either separately,(4) or as an addition to the primer.(5)

No alteration was made in the manner of celebrating mass in
the reign of Henry VIII, but by the injunctions issued immedi-
ately on the accession of Edward VI, it was directed, "21. Also,

---

(1) Henry Percy, eighth Earl of Northumberland, having been committed
to the Tower as a favourer of Mary Queen of Scots, "was found dead in his
bed, shot by a pistol, 21st June, 1583, as alleged, by his own hand."
(2) Inscription in MS. :
"This booke was given me by The Lorde Burghley highe Treasurer of Eng-
lande the fourtenth of Januarie anno dni 1574.
                                   Northûberlãd.
And after gyven by the same hari Erelle northumbarland to Sʳ. Edwarde
ffitton of Gawsworth his Cosyn.
                                   ff[*rancis*] ffitton."
This MS. is small (5 × 3½) but beautifully written in the fifteenth century.
There are two quartos in the British Museum, MS. Harl. 1712, 9½ × 7½; and
MS. Harl. 1029, 9 × 7. In Maskell, *Mon. Rit.* I, p. lv, two similar MSS. are
mentioned in the King's Library.
(3) One of the MSS. quoted by Mr Maskell here reads "bible new lawe,"
or New Testament.
(4) *Title.* "Here be gynneth the Pytles and Gospels, of every Sonday
and holy daye of the yere."—*Colophon.* "¶ Imprinted at London by me
Robert Redman dwelling at the signe of the George next of St Dunstons
Church."
(5) "The Prymer in Englysh and Latyn, after the Use of Sarum, set out
at length with manye goodly prayers, &c., with the Epystels and Gospels on
every Sonday and holye daye in the Yeare."—London. Thomas Petyt [1543].

In the time of high mass within every church, he that saith or singeth the same shall read or cause to be read the Epistle and Gospel of that mass in English and not in Latin, in the pulpit, or in such convenient place, as the people may hear the same."(1)

For many years it has been very general among the Roman Catholics in this country to read the Epistle and Gospel in English, after they have been read in the Latin, at the principal mass on Sundays and holy-days, but this change has not prevailed at Rome or in other parts of Italy, or in other Roman Catholic countries.

P. 16, B. 168. *or els hit rede.* See the blessing, or rather the prayer of the priest for the gospeller and his prayer for himself in the York Mass, *ante,* p. 96, l. 18-24. I add the directions for the reader from the *Myroure,* which are dictated by a not less devout spirit, and would be very serviceable both to themselves and to their hearers in the case of many readers in the present day. " ¶ They also that rede in the Couente. ought so bysely to ouerse (2) theyr lesson before. & to vnderstonde yt; that they may poynte yt(3) as it oughte to be poynted. & rede. yt sauourly & openly to *the* vnderstondinge of the here[r]s. And *that* may they not do; but yf they vnderstonde yt. & sauoure yt fyrste themselfe."(4)

B. 169. *swete* is used of God, and especially in addressing our Lord, as in the Prymer rendering of the *Ave verum,* or Prayer at the elevation :—" O dulcis, O pie, O Jesu, fili marie." " O swete, O holy, O Jesu sonne of Marye." *Primer.* 1555. " O most dere lorde *and* saviour, swete Jhesu, I beseche," &c. *York Horæ,* fol. 140 *b.*

B. 170. *oure bale wold bete.* Cf. Vernon, *ante,* p. 129, l. 35.

> " Jesu, Jesu, my hony swete,
> My herte, my comfortynge,
> Jesu all my bales þou bete,
> And to þi blysse me brynge."
>
> *Religious Pieces* (Perry), p. 74, l. 69-72.

B. 173. *on a manere.* One contrasted with "anoþer" in l. 174. F. changes the northern " a " (= one) into the southern " o.", but the midland scribe lets it stand, possibly because he understood it as the indefinite article, as " a " is used in line 19.
See note B. 17, page 168.

> " Fader and sun and haligast,
> That anfald(5) God es ay stedfast ;
> Worthi driht in trinite,
> A God, a might in persons iii."
>
> *English Metrical Homilies* (Small), p. 1.

---

(1) Cardwell, *Doc. Annals,* I, 13.
(2) *Ouerse,* look over.
(3) " *Mind your stops,*" as here glossed by Mr Blunt.
(4) *Myroure,* E. E. T. S. (*ed.* Blunt), p. 67.
(5) Anfald, *simplex.* Cf. manifald, *multiplex.*

"God and man bothe in a person."

Registrum, Thoresby, fol. 295 *b*.

P. 16, B. 174. *bos*, where E. has the longer equivalent be-howus, the impersonal construction being preserved in both. Cf. the Thornton MS. (*Religious Pieces*, Perry, p. 8),

"And þis sacrement bus haue thre thynges."

The English of Archbishop Thoresby's catechism, from which this is taken, reads "behoues haue," and the Latin original "cuius tres sunt partes."

C. 85-7. It is assumed that the reader may be able to read the Latin, and this variation from the earlier text is accounted for, as elsewhere remarked, by the fact that this MS. was written for a religious house.

C. 88. Cf. the various reading of D. in the foot-note. I have glossed this in the margin as if it referred to the substitution of paternosters by those who knew no more, but perhaps the reference is to the reading from a book, instead of "cunning without book," as directed in B. 625, C. 370, p. 58.

C. 89-90. In a monastery there would be lay-brethren and novices, and perhaps professed brethren, not in holy orders, who could neither read the services from a book, nor say them without book, and in their case the repetition (*rehearsal*) of paternosters, as at a later date, of ave-marias and paternosters,(1) was held to be equivalent. Thus from St Francis' Testament, "Our dyvyne seruice the clerkis saide as other clerkis, and the lay bretherne said ther pater noster."(2) We find a similar rule in respect to the laity who were members of gilds, as, for example, the Gild of St Katherine at Norwich: "At *the* Dirige, euery brother and sister *that* is letterede shul seyn, for *the* soule of *the* dede, placebo and dirige, in the place wher he shul comen togeder; and euery brother and sister *that* bene nought letterede, shul seyn for *the* soule of *the* dede, xx. sythes, *the* pater noster *with* Aue maria."(3)

Penance also was commuted for paternosters when the penitent could not fast and had neither money nor "letters." Thus in the Poenitential of Archbishop Egbert of York: "LXI. An dæges fæsten man mæg mid anum peniȝe alysan: oððe mid twam hund sealmum. . . . And ȝif se man sealm-sang ne conne. þonne sinȝe

---

(1) In the fifteenth century the following was the rule for the sisters of Syon:—"*Of the servise of sustres unlettred.*" "They than kan not rede schal say dayly in stede of matens fourty paternostres, with as many aues, and oo crede; and for eche euensonge as many : . . . . . for our lady masse fyftene paternostres, with as many aues, and oo crede."—*Additions to the Rules*, Aungier's *Syon Monastery*, Appendix, p. 364.

(2) *Monumenta Franciscana* (Brewer), p. 54.

(3) Ordinances of the Gild, as returned in obedience to the writ of Richard II in 1388.—Toulmin Smith, *English Gilds*, p. 20. See the very interesting introduction to her father's work by Miss Lucy Toulmin Smith, p. xxix.

he for anes dæges fæsten. L. Pater noster. *and* swa oft hine on
corꝺan astrecce."(1)   A man may discharge a fast of one day with
one penny, or with two hundred psalms.   And if the man knows
not psalm-song, then let him sing for one day's fast fifty paternosters, and as often prostrate himself on the ground.

An indulgence of two thousand years was granted for saying
the prayer "*Domine Jesu qui hanc sacratissimam carnem,*" between
the elevation and the last Agnus Dei (*ante,* p. 106—112); and in
Wyclif's Apology we find it said that in the pope's bull granting
this indulgence that provision was made for the unlearned: "Also
putting to ouer (*adding thereto*) for lewid men, þat can not þis
orisoun, þat þei schal haue as mikel or more indulgencis for þe pr.
nr. as oft as þei sey it, and as gret charite and mekenes deseruing
indulgens."(2)

P. 16, C. 91.   This abridged reference to the gospel takes the place of
lines 152—174 in the older forms, which were not very pertinent
to the English rite when the gospel was read only in Latin.   See
note, p. 210.

P. 17, E. 155.   We may account for this variation in this text in order
to adapt it to the case of the mass-book being "flitted" by the
clerk, or the gospel being read elsewhere than at the altar.

P. 18, B. 176. *A large cros on þe þou make.*   At B. 159, we have the
cross by the priest, here the layman is directed to make the large
cross, which is described, note, p. 207-8.   And so Myrc, ll. 280-1 :

> "And blesse feyre as þey conne
> Whenne gloria tibi is begun."

In the "Additions to the Rules" of the sisters of Sion it is
directed "The *prose* or *sequence* ended, they schal turne to the
auter, so enclynynge at the *gloria tibi, Domine,* whan the preste
enclynethe, makyng a token of the crosse in ther forehedes, and
upon ther brestes, as the maner is."(3)   In a MS. missal of the

---

(1) Thorpe's *Ancient Laws,* II, 222.   A similar provision is included
among the Fragments of Archbishop Theodore : " De iis qui jejunare non possunt, nec habent unde redimere possint," which whether actually his work or
not is of very ancient date.—Thorpe, *u. s.* 69.   Cf. Haddan and Stubbs,
Councils, III, 212.

(2) *Wycliffe's Apology* (Todd), Camden Society, p. 8.   In the note, p. 122,
Dr Todd quotes the rubric to this prayer in the Sarum Horæ (Regnault, Paris,
1536).   "¶. Our holy father pope Bonifacius sextus hath graunted to all them
that say deuoutly thys prayer folowynge between the eleuacyon of our lorde
et the. iij. Agnus dei. x. thousande yeres of pardon."   This, as remarked by
the learned editor, differs from the apology and other authority quoted by him
in assigning *ten* thousand years to this indulgence.   He also explains that by
Boniface VI, is meant the pope, usually styled Boniface VIII (A.D. 1294—1303),
Boniface VI, who reigned only sixteen days, and Boniface VII, who was an
Anti-pope, not being counted.

(3) Aungier, p. 327 ; and see Amalarius, *De Eccles. Officiis,* III, 17.

monastery of St Denys "in Francia" of the eighth century, the
following prayer is given : " *Quando se signant.* Crucis vivivicæ
signo muni, Domine, omnes sensus meos ad audienda verba sancti
Evangelii, corde credenda, et opere complenda."(1)

P. 18, B. 180. *a sothfast god.* The scribe here, as in line 173, does not
alter the northern " a," as it has been altered in text E, and he has
altered it elsewhere.(2)

> " Ƿrifald   on   tal   *and*   a   on   nome
> trinus   in   numero   et   unus   in   nomine."

[Interlinear] *Anglo-Saxon Ritual* (Surtees Society), p. 111.

> " þe myght of þe Fader almyghty,
> þe witte of þe Son alwytty,
> And þe gudnes of þe Haligast,
> A Godde and Lord of myght[es] mast."

> Hampole, P. C. 1—4.

> " A Lord God of myghteʒ maste
> Fader, and Son, and Haly Gaste.
> Fadir, for thou ert almyhty,
> Sone, for þou ert all wytty(3)
> Haly Gaste, for thow all wyll
> That gud es and nathynge yll.
> A God and ane Lord in threhed,
> And thre persons yn anehede."

> Nassington, *Religious Pieces* (Perry), p. 57, l. 1—8.

And *Metrical Homilies*, quoted above, page 212.

—*Sothfast,* true, very.

> " Sothfast God and sothfast man."—P. C. 8658.

Cf. " Very God and very man " of the Athanasian Creed.

—*of mightes most.*

> " Dominus virtutum nobiscum."
> " Laverd of mightes with us es he."

> Ps. (46) xlv, 8.

> " Laudate eum, omnes virtutes ejus."
> " Alle his mightes him love yhe."

> Ps. (148) cxlviii, 2.

---

(1) Martene, *Antiq. Rit.* I, 188.
(2) Note (B. 17), p. 168.
(3) This special ascription of wisdom to our Lord is very often met with,
and is probably founded on 1 Cor. i. 24. I add a few lines, illustrating the
sense in which it was used from a very beautiful prayer to Christ in one of the
Early English Poems edited for the Philological Society by Mr Furnivall
> " I can no more but trust to the,
> In whom ys alle wysdom an wyt ;
> And thou wost what ys best for me,
> For alle thyng in thy syʒt ys pyt."
Early English Poems. Berlin, 1862, p. 141, l. 104-7.

P. 18, B. 182. *ioy*, that is *glory*. See before, p. 196. By an unwritten tradition "Glory be to thee, O Lord" continues to be used in the Church of England after giving out the gospel.

B. 184. *þat dere þe boght*. Cf. Ac. xx, 28, "which he hath purchased with his own blood."

> " And der mankind on rode boht."—*Eng. Met. Hom.* p. 4.

> " God þat boght þam dere."—Hampole, P. C. 3292.

B. 187. *Ihesu myne*. The MS. is very indistinct here owing to an erasure, but Mr Thompson pointed out very clearly that it does read " myne."

> Cf. "Swete iesu, louerd myn."—*Hymn.* MS. Harl. 2253.(1)

B. 190. *þo gode to chese and leeue þo ille*. Cf. Isaiah, vii, 15, 16. " . . . . refuse the evil and choose the good;" and Thoresby's Catechism on the fifth virtue, *Prudentia :*

> " it kennes us to knaw the gode fra the yuel,
> and al-so to sundir the tane fra the tothir,
> for to leue that is yuel, and take to the gode,
> and of twa gode thinges to chese the better."—Fol. 297.

> " Til wham (*man*) he (*God*) has gyven witte and skille
> For to knaw bothe gude and ille,
> And fre will to chese, als he vouches save,
> Gude or ille whether he wil have ;
>
> . . . .
> Whar-for þat man may be halden wode,
> þat cheses þe ille and leves þe gode."
>
> Hampole, P. C. 91—100.

B. 195-6. *Som-where bisyde, when hit is done,*
þou make a cros, and kys it sone.

The *Ordo Romanus* notices the custom of the people crossing themselves at the end of the gospel in the following terms :— " Perlecto evangelio, iterum se signo sanctæ crucis populus munire festinat."(2) Durandus also specifies this as one of the places where the cross ought to be made,(3) and Romsée refers to it as a peculiarity of the Carmelites.(4) I am not able to cite any contemporary mention of the particular observance enjoined in the

---

(1) *Quoted*, Guest's English Rythms, I, 296.

(2) Cassander, *Ordo Romanus*, Colon. 1561, fol. 5. Mabillon, *Mus. Ital.* II, 46. Le Brun, in a note (*Tom. I, p.* 117), quotes Remigius of Auxerre, as using the same words.

(3) " Sane regulariter in omnibus evangelicis verbis debemus facere signum crucis, ut in fine evangelii, symboli, dominicæ orationis," &c. *Rationale*, 5, ii, 15.

(4) " Hunc ritum in suam liturgiam invexerunt Carmelitæ, nam celebrans, lecto evangelio et missali osculato, se cruce signat in omni missa, quæ non est de *Requiem*."—Tom. IV, p. 135.

text, but it was explained to a Roman Catholic friend of mine, whom I had asked to make the inquiry, that "they used to make a cross on their book, if they had one, and if not, on their hand, and kiss it;"(1) and this explanation is confirmed by a passage in Becon, whose evidence I quote as having been a parish priest (Vicar of Brenzett in Kent) in the reign of Henry VIII, when the old ceremonial was intact, but only as to facts, which he mentions incidentally, and which were not matter in controversy. I cannot, however, quote this writer—and I may have occasion to quote him again—without once for all utterly disclaiming any sympathy whatever with the tone or tenor of his disgraceful attacks upon the adherents to the Church of Rome, which were characterized by an unusual grossness, even in times when unseemly allusions and unchristian invective were too common on both sides of the controversy. He says,(2) ". . . . ye rehearse a few Latin sentences out of the gospel, which neither ye for the most part, nor yet the simple people understand. And, notwithstanding, the silly, simple, sheepish souls solemnly stand up(3) and give good ear, as though they should hear some notable thing, and go home the better instructed; but all in vain, for they learn nothing. Only when ye rehearse the name of Jesus, they learn to make solemn courtesy; and so, a piece of the gospel being once read, they stroke themselves on the head, and kiss the nail of their right thumb, and sit down again as wise as they were afore."(4) In Myrc (l. 282) there is no direction of this kind:

> " And whenne þe gospel is I-done
> Teche him eft to knele down sone."

---

(1) My correspondent, who forwarded me this information, had himself been for many years the priest of an hereditary English Roman Catholic congregation, but he had never seen anything but the ordinary crossing. I asked another Roman Catholic clergyman, and he had formerly noticed something of the kind; and a country gentleman, who is several years their senior, told me it was common enough when he was a boy; but that, except in the case of one or two old family servants, and some of the Irish reapers who come over at harvest time, he had not seen it for a good many years.

(2) Thomas Becon, *Displaying of the Popish Mass*, Works, Cambridge, 1844, III, 257. He wrote this piece in Germany, where he had succeeded in making good his retreat, with the professed intention of persuading those of the clergy, who had conformed on the accession of Queen Mary, to throw up their preferment. His scurrilous violence is much more likely to have had a contrary effect, and the only excuse for him, and that is no excuse for his gross obscenity—judging of that only from what has been allowed to remain in the expurgate edition of the Parker Society—is that when he wrote it, he had only just escaped the stake by being accidentally released from the Tower in mistake for another prisoner.

(3) Cf. Lydgate, *ante*, p. 149, l. 56:
> " Lestene as thou were adred."

(4) In the Vernon MS. mention is made of another observance at the gospel after mass. See *ante*, p. 146, l. 650, and the note there.

In the Mozarabic liturgy the people answered *Amen*, which seems to carry a very early sound with it. In the York Horæ (*fol.* 4) there is the following rubric and prayer:—" ¶ *This prayer following ought to be said at mass whan the priest hath sayd the gospell.* Per hec sancta euangelica dicta deleantur uniuersa delicta."(1)

In the absence of any suggestion as to the origin of the practice mentioned in the text, and the similar observances referred to in this note, it has occurred to me that they may not impossibly be a maimed and expiring survival of a custom which would seem to have been universal in the church, and, we may well believe, to have taken its rise in the more demonstrative gratitude and reverence of the earlier Christians for the good news of the gospel. The *Ordo Romanus* describes the deacon, after he had read the gospel, as giving the book to the subdeacon, who thereupon held it before his breast above his chasuble ("*planetam*") to be kissed first by the bishop and clergy, and then by the people—"*universo clero necnon et populo.*"(2) In the thirteenth century, Pope Honorius III, under pain of excommunication, forbid the gospel to be presented to any layman to be kissed,(3) except a prince who had been anointed. Merati, in his disquisitions on the modern Roman missal at this place, mentions that Pope Paul III, in the year 1549, at the request of the King of Poland, indulged his queen, who had not been crowned, with this privilege of the kiss.(4) In the Eastern church there has been no similar exclusion of the laity ; and all, without exception, take part in the ceremonial kissing of the gospels on those occasions when it is enjoined to the clergy. In Russia the gospels, or rather the gorgeous and often jewelled binding, is kissed by all, from the Tzar to the private soldier and the monjic ; or,—if in the case of very large congregations, not by every one—apparently by all who present themselves, or are beckoned forward by the attendant clergy. In Greek churches the same rule is observed, and in the church in London Wall, the priest, as directed in the rubric,(5) may be seen

(1) The priest, after the gospel was read, according to the York use (*ante*, p. 98), said, " Benedictus qui venit in nomine Domini." Nothing is prescribed in the other English uses, but in the Roman mass, the server says : " Laus tibi, Christo."

(2) *Ordo Romanus*, Mabillon, *Museum Italicum*, II, 46.

(3) See the rubric of the York use, *ante*, p. 98, l. 16.

(4) *In Gavantum, Rub. Missæ Rom.* 2, IV, 2. Pope Benedict XIV gives the later rule of the Church of Rome, which restricts the kiss to the pope, cardinals, and bishops, and adds that it is allowed to princes, " ex tolerantia." —*De Missæ Sacrificio*, Sec. I, § 143.

(5) See the rubric ἐις τὸν ὄρθρον (*Euchologion*, 9 ; *Goar*, 9), as to the accustomed kiss of the gospels, ὁ ἀσπασμὸς τοῦ ἁγίου 'Ευαγγελίου παρὰ τῶν ἀδελφῶν συνήθως. In the Greek church *Orthros* (*Matins*) invariably precedes the liturgy, strictly so called, i. e. the order of Holy Communion. In this office the gospel is read by the priest standing at the south side of the altar facing north ; in the liturgy it is read by the deacon, if there be one.

coming into the nave, and the gospels are kissed by men, women, and children of the congregation. Renaudot quotes the rule of the Coptic liturgy, that the people should follow the example of the priests and kiss the book of the gospels when it was brought to them, after having been read [*in the ancient Coptic version*] and translated [*into the vernacular Arabic*].(1)

P. 18, B. 197. *som tyme.* Cf. Lydgate's *Vertue of the Masse;* MS. Harl. 2251, fol. 182 *b*:

"¶ Credo in solempne dayes.

¶ The gospel redde. a Cred after he saythe
 Solempne dayes. for a remembraunce
Of .xij. articles. that longithe to our faith*e*
 The whiche we are bounde to live(2) in oure creaunce."

A list of these solemn days is given in the rubrics, which vary slightly, according to the different uses. This mention of the creed shows that these devotions were intended for those who could hear mass daily, and not only on Sundays and the principal holy-days.

B. 202. *tellis*—viz. B. 241, of the Offertory.

C. 100. It will be noticed that the later texts omit the prayer during the gospel, and the cross after it.

P. 19, F. 75. *sayenge.* The modern form of the participle instead of the -*and* of the older texts.

P. 20, B. 204. *þin englyshe crede.* The creed to be said by the layman is the Apostles' Creed, or " þe lesse crede," as it was called,(3) "that each man is bound to can and to say,"(4) which was used in common prayer at prime and compline, and in private devotions. The Nicene Creed, the symbolum patrum or mæssecreda,(5) was used in the mass at this place. It will be observed that the distinction is drawn in this treatise, B. 198.

B. 208. *And alle of noght.* Cf. Hampole :

 " First whan God made al thyng of noght,
  Of the foulest matere man he wroghte,
  þat was, of erthe.'—*P. C.* 372-4.

B. 209-10. These two lines are written as one in the MS.

B. 210. *al onely.* Cf. alone, B. 142.

---

(1) *Liturg. Orient.,* I, 211.
(2) live, *for* bileve. A.S. gelyfan, *to believe.* W. de Worde prints "be-leue." See note, p. 163.
(3) *Old English Homilies* (Morris), First Series, p. 217.
(4) *Myroure,* 311.
(5) *The Canons of Ælfric,* IV, Thorpe, *Ancient Laws,* II, 345. " The Masse Crede," *Myroure,* 311. See *ante*, p. 98, l. 13.

P. 20, B. 213. *gast* preserves its northern(1) form to rhyme with *chast*, which did not admit of alteration, and similarly in B. 68 *gastly* is left unaltered, either *per incuriam* or to preserve the assonance to *largely*. The midland scribe does write *gost*, B. *ll.* 233, 275, &c.

B. 213-16. Cf. " He lighted doun ful mekeli
　　　　　Into the maiden wamb of Mary."
　　　　　　　　　　English Met. Homilies (Small), 12.

　　" And born of a mayden cleene
　　　　Bicause a man, in meekenes moost."
　　　　　　　　Songs to Virgin (Furnivall), p. 101, l. 11-12.

B. 217. *pounce pilat.* Ponce, which still lingers in our cottages, stood its ground in the Apostle's Creed in the daily service of the Prayer Books of Edward VI, Elizabeth, and until the last review in 1661, when it was changed to Pontius ; (2) and this is the more to be remarked as Pontius had been the rendering of the Nicene Creed from 1549. Perhaps some new-fangled classicist will protest against Pilate, and propose a further change to the Latin Pontius Pilatus in full.

B. 219. Cf. " And þei diden him upon þe rode,
　　　　　And he bougt *wit* his blissed blood.
　　　　　And sithen he went to helle
　　　　　þe fiendis power for to felle."
　　　　　　　　MS. York Minster Library, XVII, 12, fol. 63 *b.*

" And specially for þe haly crose, þat god was done opon." *Ante,* p. 68, l. 12.

B. 223. *Vp he rose in flesshe and felle*—

Compare : " In soule oonli þou went to helle,
　　　　　And took þens þi part, it was good riȝt,
　　　　　But up þou roos in fleish and in felle,
　　　　　þe þrid day bi godli myȝt."
　　　　　　　　Hymns to the Virgin, &c. (Furnivall), p. 102.

The *fell* may have been specified in these and other instances, with reference to the vision of the resurrection of dry bones in the prophet Ezekiel, " I will . . . . cover you with skin " (ch. xxxvii. 6). Or, perhaps, it may have been in reference to the place in Job, " Thou hast clothed me with skin and flesh " (ch. x. 11), that our forefathers may have so generally specified the skin in proof of a true human body.

---

　　(1) " Þai salle þair God apertly se,
　　　And alle þe þre parsons in trinite,
　　　Þe Fader, and Son, and Haly-gaste
　　　Þat sight salle be þair ioy maste."—P. C. 8651-4.
　(2) See Black-letter Prayer-Book of 1636, photozincographed 1870, p. 60. I happen to have a Prayer-Book of 1638, which has Pontius in this place; but there was no lawful authority for the change.

Thus to begin with an extract from the celebrated passage in Ælfric's Paschal Homily:—"Se lichama soþlice ðe Crist, on ðrowode, wæs ȝeboren of Marian flæsce, mit blode *and* mid bannm, mid felle *and* mid sinum, on menniscum limum, mid ȝe-sceadwisre sawle ȝeliff ært," &c. The body, truly, that Christ suf-fered in, was born of the flesh of Mary, with blood and with bones, with skin and with sinews, in the limbs of a man, animated with a reasonable soul. So again (of our Lord):—

"Man in felle and flesche was he."
> *English Metrical Homilies* (Small), 109.

"And alswa he ordaynd man to dwelle
And to lyf in erthe, in flesshe and felle."—P. C. 81-2.

"Bot þe ryche man saule feled in helle(1)
Payne, als he had bene in flesshe and felle."—P. C. 3076-7.

"Oft y crie merci, of mylse (*mercy*) thou art welle,
Alle buen false that bueth mad bothe of fleysche ant felle,
Levedi suete, thou us shild from the pine of helle,
Bring us the joie that no tongue hit may of telle."
> *Lyrical Poetry* (Wright), 102.

It will be observed that E. reads *Vp he ros as fel*.—When this was written, *fell* may have begun to be restricted, as now, to the skins of beasts; and the scribe, to get out of one seeming impro-priety, and unable to find another rhyme, blundered, as usual, into describing our Lord as *fell* · not to say anything of his utter dis-regard of the metre.

P. 20, B. 225. *stegh*—which we still have in the north, in the sense of mounting up, and more particularly by the help of a *stee* or ladder, appears to have been as strange to the southern scribe, as *fel* in line 223; and he blunders again into confounding the Resurrec-tion and the Ascension.

B. 226. *pouste*, from the O.F. *poesté*, Lat. *potestas*.

"For Ic am man under pouste,
And Ic haf knihtes under me."
> *English Met. Hom.* [Matt. viii, 9] (Small), 127.

It was also written, *pausty*.

"he þat giues me pausty."
> *Cursor Mundi* (Morris), Fairfax, MS. 4371.

B. 229, 231. *deme—ben*. Cf. the rhymes *synn* and *hym* (B. 269, 270), *temptacionem* and *amen* (B. 488-9).
B. 232. *In adam sede*.

"þens schalt þou come us alle to deeme
Boþe quik and dede of adams sede."
> *Hymns* (Furnivall), p. 102, l. 29, 30.

---

(1) Cf. Appendix, p. 135, l. 269.

P. 20, B. 235-6. *And so I trow that housel es bothe flesshe and blode.* This is, perhaps, in itself the most noteworthy passage in the treatise, regarded as a literary curiosity, and it, moreover, furnishes a note of time,(1) from which we may infer that the French original was not earlier than the twelfth century.

We at once see that the author has understood the "sanctorum" of the creed as neuter,(2) instead of masculine. In so doing, he has gone against the whole current of ecclesiastical tradition— "*Credo in . . . . sanctorum communionem*"—"I believe in . . . . the communion of saints." However contrary this may be to the principle of sound criticism universally professed, if not uniformly practised, at the present time, the forcing of any meaning which could be drawn from words, without reference to the context, or the subject matter to which they referred, would in those days have been regarded as a legitimate exercise of scholastic ingenuity, or mystical profoundness.

Dr Newman notices the absence of the "dogma of the real presence"(3) from all the creeds, and supposes that "the omission is owing to the ancient *disciplina arcani*, which withheld the sacred mystery from catechumens and heathen, to whom the creed was known." However this may be, we may fully admit the fact that the creeds are silent as to the doctrine ; and this makes it all the more curious that the exigencies of controversy, concerning the sacrament of the supper of the Lord, should have led to an article of the creed being pressed into service in support—or at least as a statement—of the doctrine, that "flesh and blood" were both present under each of the two species of bread and wine.

---

(1) This opinion was not formally accepted before the council of Constance in 1415 ; but it was generally received in the twelfth century, and was held to justify the withdrawal of the cup from the laity and afterwards from the clergy also, except the priest who was celebrating mass. We do not meet with it in the time of the Berengarian controversy, but we find it thus stated by Anselm in the end of the eleventh century, "*In utraque specie totum Christum sumi ;*" and by Peter Lombard in the middle of the next century, "*Integrum Christum esse in altari sub utraque specie.*" The council of Constance defined "*integrum Christi corpus et sanguinem tam sub specie panis quam sub specie vini veraciter contineri ;*" and the terms finally adopted in the creed of Pius IV, as now prescribed and professed under oath in the Church of Rome, are as follows : "*sub altera tantum specie totum atque integrum Christum verumque sacramentum sumi.*"

(2) "*Sancta*" occurs in an *Ordo Romanus* of the consecrated host. (Mabillon, *Iter Ital.* II, p. xxxix.) Unless, perhaps, we are to understand *evangelia*, we find a similar use in the Laws of King Cnut, "XXXVI. *Si quis falsum juramentum super sancta jurabit.*" Ἅγια in the Greek Liturgies is used of the holy gifts after consecration, as it is also used of them before consecration, when placed in set form and ceremony upon the altar. For this last use of *sanctum* and *sancta*, see Martene *De Rit. Antiq.* I, 197, 213, &c.

(3) *Grammar of Assent*, p. 141.

In the trilingual creed, printed by Dr Heurtley, to which he assigns the date of A.D. 1125,(1) this article is thus given :—

"Ic gelefe on . . . . . Halegan hiniennesse.
Jeo crei . . . . . La communiun des scintes choses ;
Credo in . . . . . Sanctorum communionem,"

where the insertion of "choses" points to a similar application.

There is a third and, so far as I know, among the many extant versions of the Apostles' Creed, and the varying paraphrases of this particular article, the only(2) other example of a gloss in a similar sense—and this embodying a farther development(3) of the doctrine—in Pierce the Ploughman's Crede.(4) The first two

---

(1) *Harmonia Symbolica*, Oxford, 1858, p. 91-3.

(2) At the end of the Royal MS. (17 B. xvii), from which our B-text is printed, there is written, or rather scrawled, on a blank leaf (p. 263-4), the creed in English in a very unformed hand of the xvth century. This article is paraphrased as follows ; but it will be seen that it is rather an incomplete enumeration of the seven sacraments, often specified under this head, as being the inheritance of the saints, than an application of the article to the sacrament of the altar ; and, moreover, it does not touch the particular point of the presence of the body and blood under the same species: " I beleue in sacrament of hooly chyrch a ʒift of the fadur & of the son & of the hooly goost thre persones in o godhead I beleue also in hooly chirch ordrynge us I byleue in þe sacrament of goddis flesche & his blood þat he shedde on the blissid rood tre for me and for alle man kynd."

Compare Dan Michel's *Ayenbite of Inwyt* (Morris), p. 14. " And ine þise article / byeþ onderstonde / þe zeve sacremens / þet byeþ ine holy cherche." Also Thoresby's Catechism. on this article :—

" That is comunyng and felaured of all cristen folke,
    that comunes togedir in the sacrements
    and in othir hali thinges that falles til hali kirke."

Durandus gives the following as an alternative exposition : "Vel præcipio sanctorum communionem, i. e. panem benedictionis de quo dicitur, Crede et manducasto."—*Rat.* 4, xxv, 26.

(3) The text asserts the presence of the body and blood of Christ, which were sundered by His death : the *Crede* speaks of Christ Himself in the oneness of His person and the fulness of His bodily nature, in which He suffered.

(4) This was a satirical attack on the friars, written quite at the end of the fourteenth century by an avowed favourer of Wyclif; and it is so very common to read history backwards—and especially the history of doctrine— that this definite statement of his belief may, perhaps, come most unexpectedly upon some of those who are familiar with the opinions of later reformers, and know that this very point afterwards became one of the great battle-grounds with the Church of Rome. But we must recollect that in the fourteenth century it was practical abuses and not points of doctrine which in the first instance gave rise to opposition, and even afterwards, at least in respect to the doctrine of the eucharist, it was not the presence that was in dispute, so much as the scholastic explanations which were put forward to account for it, and the logical consequences which were supposed to be involved in it.

lines of my quotation were among those left out, without any indication of the fact,(1) when the Crede was printed in the last
year of the reign of Edward VI, and so dealt with, no doubt, because they were inconsistent with the doctrine of the forty-two
articles then in force. Thanks to the practised sagacity(2) of Mr
Skeat, they have been recovered, and were for the first time printed,
when he edited the Crede for this Society.

> "And in þe sacrement(3) also · þat soþfast God on(4) is,
> Fullich his fleche & his blode · þat for vs deþe þolede.—
> And þouȝ þis flaterynge freres · wyln for her pride,

---

(1) Not only were these lines suppressed, but there was the further dis-
honesty of inserting others, printed unsuspectingly by previous editors, which
Mr Skeat proves to be forged, by their absence from the MSS., and also by
their failure in the laws of alliterative verse, though "the imitation of style
and spelling is very ingenious."—Mr Skeat's Preface, p. xviii.

(2) See his Preface, § 3—5.

(3) If we read *sacrament* in the singular, we must understand it of the
"form of bread;" for the notion of separating the thing signified from the
sign, and placing it in the "ordinance," was not mooted until some hundred
and fifty years after the Crede was written. *Sacremens* in the plural, the
reading of what Mr Skeat considers his best MS., was, perhaps, intended to
express the received opinion of the time that the "whole" presence was "*sub
utraque specie.*"

(4) Mr Skeat in his note here pointed out that "on" is often used in the
sense of "in;" and explained this place :—

"And I believe in the sacrament too, that the very God is *in* both flesh
and blood fully."

But "on" is also *one*, as in this very poem (*line* 4) :—

> "Alle in on godhed endles dwelleþ,"

and Mr Skeat now agrees with me that it is used here in this sense, and not
as the preposition. No great stress can be laid on the fact, that "in" already
occurs in this line, for nothing can exceed the uncertainty of spelling in MSS.
of this date (see note, p. 195) ; but the manner in which "one" is used in the
common places of contemporary divinity in treating of the change effected
by consecration, would seem to be conclusive as to the meaning being as
follows :—

And in the sacrament also [*I believe*] that very (*or* verily) God is one—
not two, the separate flesh and blood, but one—fully flesh and blood.

Quotations, in this sense, ranging from the twelfth century downward,
might easily be multiplied to any extent ; but I confine myself to two, which
have not been elsewhere printed.

The one from the Vernon MS., *ante*, p. 144, ll. 587-8,

> "God þat on the Rode was slon
> Þe two [i. e. *flesh and blood*, l. 581] and he beoþ boþe on."

The other is from the Latin original of Archbishop Thoresby's Catechism,
"Eucharistia est unum corpus Christi ; et illud, si digne sumatur, sumenti
proficit ad vitam æternam ; si indigne sumatur, ædificat ad gehennam."—
Thoresby's Register, fol. 298 *b*—*ante*, p. 119.

Disputen of þis deyte(1) · as dotardes schulden,
þe more þe matere is moved · þe masedere(2) hy worþen."
Pierce the Ploughman's Crede (Skeat), ll. 822-6.

P. 20, C. 101. *ay whil*, for *a whil*, one while, at one time, sometimes.
See B. 197, *som tyme;* F. 81, *whiles.* One while is used in this
sense by the "Translators to the Reader" of the authorized version
of the Bible: "One while through oversight, another while
through ignorance."

P. 21, E. 223. *fel.* See note, p. 223, B. 223.

P. 22, B. 239. *flesshe.* E. 239. *flesche.* No doubt that in the original
we should find *fles* rhyming with *forgyfnes* (l. 237). *Fles* or
flesse was the northern form of *flesh*, as we still hear it in the East
Riding.

    B. 241. *fast.* See note, p. 192, C. 56.

       hande, not altered, as elsewhere, into *hond*, that it might still
rhyme with *offrande*.

    B. 242. *tyme of offrande.* This may mean either the time at which
the layman might make his offering ; or—perhaps more probably—
that part of the mass which was called the offrande or the offertory.
This, as explained by the ritualists,(3) began at that point in the
service after the creed, or if the creed was not said, after the
gospel, when the priest turned to the faithful—in earlier times

---

(1) *deity.* The dispute here referred to was probably in reference to the
hypostatic union, or the inseparable conjunction of the divine and human
natures in the one Christ, by which the conjoint presence of the flesh and
blood was explained. Aquinas propounded his explanation under the name
of *concomitance*, which term was first used by him, and has since been adopted
by the Council of Trent in framing the authorized explanation of the Church
of Rome.—11 Oct., 1551, Sess. XIII, *De Eucharistia*, c. iii.

In the *Complaint of the Ploughman*, there is also a statement of this doctrine, not, however, in connection with the creed, but followed by a very direct
reference to the Wycliffite objection to the theory of transubstantiation :—

    "On our Lords body I doe not lie,
      I say sooth through true rede,
    His flesh and blood through his misterie
      Is there in the forme of brede.

    " How it is there, it needeth not strive,
      Whether it be subget or accident,
    But as Christ was when he was on live
      So he is there verament."
              Political Poems and Songs (Wright), I, 341.

(2) "more in a maze, more confused."—*Mr Skeat's note.*

(3) Officium quod nos dicimus *offerenda*, ab illo loco inchoatur ubi sacerdos
dicit, *Dominus vobiscum :* Et finitur ubi excelsa voce dicit, *Per omnia sæcula
sæculorum.*—Amalarii *de Eccles. Offic.* Lib. 3, c. 19. *Ed.* Migne, 1128 A. These
words are repeated, Honor. Augustodun. *Sacramentarium*, c. 85. *Ed.* Migne,
790 A.

catechumens and heathens were first dismissed(1)—and greeted them with the accustomed salutation, "The Lord be with you."(2) It extended to the end of the prayers for the acceptance of the gifts—the *secreta* or *super oblata*—and was followed by the preface. Here too in this country, unlike the Roman rule, was the sermon, when there was one during the celebration of mass.(3) The sermon in that case on Sundays in parish churches included the bidding prayers, before the preaching or sermon, as we now restrict the term.

P. 22, B. 243. *leeue.* As this occurs in a rubric, it seems more natural to suppose that it directs a definite act rather than permits what, from the very use of the phrase, would have been regarded as a failure to do what ought to have been done :—and this all the more, when we take it in connection with the " as þe lyst," explained in the next note. I have therefore assumed in the margin that *leeue* is used as a neuter verb, to remain (*remanere*), rather than in the active sense, to leave (*relinquere*),(4) as we find it used, *to let alone, to leave undone,* with a suggestion of neglect, as in Chaucer's matchless picture of the " pore parsoun " :—

> " Wyd was his parisch, and houses fer asundur,
> But he lafte not for reyn ne thondur,
> In siknesse ne in meschief to visite
> The ferrest in his parissche, moche and lite."—C. T. 493-6.

It is evident that the intransitive use of this verb was beginning to be obsolete in the fifteenth century, for E omits it altogether, and F changes it to *lete.* C retains it as *leve,* and the word again occurs in the same sense (C 356), but there written as *lyve ;* and we have it also, *ante,* p. 120, l. 13, in the determination that no material bread or wine *remained* (leved) on the altar after the saying of the sacramental words.(5)

---

(1) In the Eastern Church the proclamation for the departure of the catechumens is made to this day at this place, and the form is found in all the Greek liturgies. In that of St James the purpose of the exclusion is more fully indicated, as it specifies the uninitiated, and those who are " not able to join in prayer with us," and the so-called Clementine liturgy adds " the hetorodox." St Justin and St Chrysostom speak of this discipline, and it is curious to know that it was practised in Germany in the last century at the coronations of the Emperors, the ambassadors of other than Roman Catholic powers and the Protestant Electors withdrawing from the ceremony at this time.—See note on B 280, *secreta.*

(2) *Ante,* p. 102, l. 9.

(3) The rule according to the Church of Rome was, and is, that sermons in the mass should follow the gospel. See note, *post,* under Bidding Prayer, p. 62.

(4) It is used as a verb transitive, *ante,* B. 190, and *note,* p. 219.

(5) Cf. " Thus leeveth not of the breed but oonli the licnesse." Freer Daw Topias, *Political Poems and Songs* (Wright), II, 108.

See also Wyclif's *Works* (Arnold), III, 400.

We do not find *læfan* as neuter in Bosworth, but it would not
be difficult to multiply examples in later English,—for instance, in
the Ormulum :—

> "*Annd* siþþenn shallt tu makenn ʒunnc(1)
> To fode þatt tær lefeþþ."—8663-4.

> "Leef we now here."
> > *William of Palerne* (Skeat), 1836.

> "There fore þey schule wyth water & wyn
> Clanse here mowþ that noʒt leue þer In."
> > Myrc, *Instructions*, 258-9.

> "My godis that leves aftir my dettis paid."—Will of Sir John
Hedlam of Nunthorpe, Knight, A.D. 1461.—*Test. Ebor.* (Raine),
II, 247.

P. 22, B. 243. *wheþer þe lyst.* The free-will character of the people's alms
at the time of Holy Communion was always maintained in theory.
Thus we may notice that in our Vernon MS., though very strong
pressure is put upon the layman, he was nevertheless reminded
that he was not "þer-to in dette."(2) Whatever we may think
in this last instance, Dan Jeremy's whole tone proves that he was
sincere when he leaves it to his readers to offer or not as they list.
Unlike many mediæval tales and treatises on the mass, his first
thought seems to have been, as he expresses it in the next line,
that the laymen should know "how they should pray;" and,
whether we agree with or protest against his doctrine—a question
which I conceive to be wholly out of place in the publications of
this Society—we may well believe that the main purpose of his
treatise was the spiritual edification of better instructed worshippers, rather than the extortion of more bountiful mass-pennies,
which was the fruitful theme of contemporary satirists.

It is not very probable that our author had any acquaintance
with the writings of Justin Martyr, and it may admit of question
whether the phrase employed by him in this place and that here
quoted from the Mozarabic liturgy were derived from a common
scource ; but—more especially in connection with the fact of the
general resemblance of the Mozarabic and Gallican liturgies, and
the suggestion elsewhere made that there are traces in this treatise
of the Eastern origin of the Gallican liturgy—it is curious to note
the similarity of expression. The phrase in St Justin to which I
refer is found in his description of the Christian Eucharist. He is

---

(1) ʒunnc. *dual dative,* = σφωίν, for you twain. "*tibi autem et filio tuo
facies postea.*"—3 Reg. xvii. 13.

(2) *Ante,* p. 142, l. 515. So too in the Description of the ordering of
Princely and Knightly Funerals (*Book of Precedence,* Furnivall, 1869, p. 36),
though the offering of the chief mourners, &c., is prescribed, others are then
"to offer that will."—See also p. 242, and note (4), p. 235.

speaking of the collection for the sick and needy from those who were prosperous, and adds this farther condition, "being willing" —Βουλόμενοι.(1) The Mozarabic rubric after the oblation of the host and chalice is as follows: "Let the priest turn to the people; and let them make their offering if they should be willing —'si voluerit'—and let the choir say the 'Sacrificium'" or anthem answering to the offertory of the Roman and Anglican use.(2)

It will be noticed that the impersonal construction—lyst. *libet*(3) —is retained in C and E; C writing *luste*. As was the tendency of later English in respect to this and other impersonals, F has changed þe *lyst*, into the personal, *thu list*.

P. 22, B. 243. *Offer or leeue wheþer þe lyst.*—No part of the service of the mass presents more marked variations in the different uses, diocesan, provincial, and monastic, than the offertory. This, as I conceive, may be accounted for in churches of the Roman communion by the gradual shifting of the central point of the oblatory action from the oblation of the bread and wine—tho new sacrifice of the Sarum form of presentation(4)—to the recital of the words of institution or moment of consecration. It might be interesting to trace the mutual action of dogma upon ritual and of ritual upon dogma in this instance, but it would be too large a subject to enter upon in this place, even if it were possible to discuss it without touching on points which have been the subject of doctrinal controversy, and therefore, according to the view which the

---

(1) *Apologia* I, c. 67—Ed. Ben., 83 E.

(2) *Missale Mozarabes*, Rom. 1755, p. 3, l. 28. This is in the rubric for the first Sunday in Advent, which in other places is more full than that for the Ordinary of the Mass. The corresponding rubric there is: "*Postea offerat populus.*" Lesley in his note on this place explains that the offerers went up singly and made their offering to the priest (p. 223). He blessed them in the form, "*Centuplum accipies et vitam æternam possideas in regno Dei;*" and they then kissed his stole and made way for others.

(3) As an example of the curious analogy that may often be observed in different languages it may be noted that the substantives formed from these two verbs, *lust* and *libido*, have both gone off *in malum sensum.*

(4) "Acceptum sit omnipotenti Deo, hoc sacrificium novum."—*Sarum.* "Acceptum sit sacrificium istud omnipotenti Deo."—*Ebor.* Cf. "Et novi testamenti novam docuit oblationem, quam ecclesia ab apostolis accipiens, in universo mundo, offert Deo."—Iren. *adv. Hæres*, IV. c. 32.

In case any of my readers should turn to Maskell's "*Ancient Liturgy of the Church of England*"—which is still the most available, as until the publication of the Burntisland edition of the Sarum, and Dr Henderson's editions of the York and Hereford Missals, it was the only book on this subject within the reach of the student at a distance from our great libraries,— I may mention that by a curious misprint at page 56 the words here quoted from the Sarum use are altogether omitted; nor had Mr Maskell's attention been called to it, until I happened to point it out to him a few years ago when we met at the Bodleian Library, where the means of verification were abundantly at hand and were at once resorted to.

writer has taken of the duties as an editor for a mixed society,
ought to have no place in the publications of the E. E. T. Society.

The offering by the layman in the mass at the period of our
manuscript occupied so prominent a place in the church life of
our forefathers, and is so intimately connected with our subject,
that even at the price of a long note it may be convenient to
give some account of it.

The rubrics of the mass of the several English uses are altogether silent on this point, nor—perhaps because the lay offering
was every day passing before men's eyes—do we meet with any
detailed description in contemporary authorities, but numerous
incidental notices bring the ceremony very distinctly before us.

Except at coronations, ordinations, the consecration of nuns,
and special services when the mass was celebrated by a bishop, it
had ceased to be the custom in this country to offer bread and
wine.(1) The money-offerings of the people were received after
the offertory had been sung.(2) and the bread had been taken

---

(1) The bread and wine were "found at the cost and charges" of the
clergy. It was a very common provision in wills directing masses to be said
for the testator, that the priest should find bread, wine, and wax; and in the
Novum Registrum, or Revised Statutes of Lincoln Cathedral, already quoted,
p. 173, it is provided (*p.* 26) that the treasurer should find wine, water, hosts,
and candles for all the altars of the Church, and for the communion of the
faithful at Easter.

The waferer's was an established trade; and in the inventory of the stock
of a general shopkeeper at Kirton-in-Lindsay, forfeited to the king on his
suicide in 1519, we find singing-bread among the unnumbered sundries, in
company with nails, girdles, lace-points, &c. (Letter from Mr Peacock in
Gentleman's Magazine, April, 1864, p. 501-2.) The wafers were made in
irons called *singing-irons*. In 1429 Annas Wells of York leaves "tria instrumenta ferri vocata syngyngirons, ij alia instrumenta ferri pro pane ad
eucharistiam ordinando."—Canon Raine, *York Fabric Rolls*, Glossary, 353.

In 1371 the chamberlain of York Minster charges under the head of
Variæ Expensæ, "In iiij. m. wafris, 7s. 4d." (*Fabric Rolls*, p. 124). In 1375
"Pro iiii. m. wafers emptis pro choro, 7s. 8d." (*ib.* p. 127). There is a corresponding entry in 1551 : "For ij thowsaund singing breade spent this half
yeare, 16d." (*ib.* p. 136). The rubric then directed "that the bread prepared
for the communion be made through all this realm after one sort and fashion;
that is to say, unleavened and round as it was afore, but without all manner
of print, and somewhat more thicker and larger than it was, so that it may
be aptly divided in divers pieces."

(2) See Chaucer on the Pardoner :

> "Well coude he rede a lessoun or a storye
> And altherbest he sang an offertorie ;
> For wel wyst he, when that song was songe,
> He most preche, and wel affyle his tunge,
> To wynne silver, as he right wel cowde ;
> Therfore he sang ful meriely and lowde."—C. T. 711-16.

Lydgate in his *Vertue of the Masse*, quoted above, page 163, treats of the
Offertory in a very different spirit :

from the paten and laid upon the corporas, and the chalice "made," that is, after water had been mixed with the wine.(1)

It is not improbable that at the first all the brethren offered their gift at the altar, founding it on our Lord's words in the Sermon on the Mount.(2) The Apostolical Constitutions, though spurious and of no ecclesiastical authority, may nevertheless be accepted as reflecting with considerable accuracy the practice and tone of feeling in the third century, as they undoubtedly in-

---

¶ The offeratory next comyng   [fol. 182 b.]

¶ Interpretacioun . who wisely can aduerte
The offeratory . is named of offeryng
As whan a man . offrithe to god his hert
Richest(*) oblacioun . rekene by writyng
And for Melchisedeche . bothe prist and kyng
Gaf brede and wyne . to Abraham for victory
Whiche oblacioun . in figure by remembryng
Iche day at masse . seyde is the offeratory

¶ Tokenyng of Ihesu oure saviour and oure lorde
Ayen oure fieblenes . and Impotens
Last on the Awfer . callid goddis borde
His body his bloode . of most Reuerence
We to receyve it . withe diewe diligence
In forme of breede and wyne for a memory
Figurithe . that the lamb chief of Innocence
Offred vp his body . grounde of the offeratory.

                    MS. Harl. 2254, fol. 182 b—183.

See also *Langforde's Meditations*, quoted above, page 168 :

"At þe offertory when þe prest doith taik þe Chalice and holde yt vp and formys þe Oblatyon.

Haue medytatyon how our Lord þe Sauyour of Alle mankynd, most wyllfully offerd hym selff . to hys Eternalle father to be þe sacrifyce and oblacyon for mans Redemptyon and offer your selff to hym Agayn bothe body and soolle . whiche he so dere bowght. Rendryng in recognycyon of the same to hys grayce . by devoute Medytatyon . alle þe thankes off your harte . þat yt wolld lyke hys goodness to be þe ravmsom for your trespas and synnes."—Bodleian MS. A. Wood, 17, fol. 10-11.

(1) This we may gather from English authorities, but it was expressly laid down in the rubrics of several French uses ; e.g. in that of Evreux. The priest elevated the chalice with the wine and water, and the paten upon it, and the bread thereupon, and after the prayer *Suscipe* (cf. the York form, *ante*, p. 98, l. 29) he placed the bread on the corporas, and took the paten for the offerings, and after the offering said over the people : " Centuplum accipiatis, et vitam æternam possideatis." See MS. xiv. Cent.—Martene, I, 232.

(2) St Matt. v. 23-4. On the eve of the Reformation in this country bishops only appear to have laid their gift on the altar. See *post*, p. 238. Cf. the custom at Basle, *post*, p. 243.

(*) Cf. Bishop Heber's Epiphany Hymn:
    "Vainly we offer each ample oblation,
      Vainly with gifts would His favour secure :
      Richer by far is the heart's adoration,
      Dearer to God are the prayers of the poor."

fluenced them afterwards ; and they speak of the brethren offering
their "sacrifices, that is, their offerings (τὰς θυσίας ὑμῶν ἤτοι
προσφορὰς), to the bishop, either by themselves or by the
deacons."(1)   As the ceremonial of the Divine Service was elaborated, the distinction between the layman and the ecclesiastic
was more rigidly marked, and in the course of time restrictions,
which were more or less generally observed, were imposed by synods
and councils.   About the middle of the fourth century it was prescribed at Laodicea (*Can.* 44) that women should not enter the
sanctuary,(2) and (*Can.* 19) that only priests and deacons(3)
should enter the sanctuary and communicate.   But at the end of
this century (A.D. 390) this rule was not observed at Constantinople,
at least in [respect to the Emperor, as we know from the
account which Theodoret gives of the admission of Theodosius to
communion at Milan, by St Ambrose, after he had been excommunicated by him.   When he brought his gifts to the holy table,
as was the custom, he was going to remain within the rails, to
receive the Divine sacraments, "but the great Ambrose taught
him a lesson as to the distinction of places," that within was for
priests alone, and that "the purple made emperors, not priests,"
and the emperor thereupon in all good part explained that it was
not out of arrogance that he had remained within the rails, but
because he knew it to be the custom at Constantinople.(4)

---

(1) *Constit. Apost.* II, c. xxvii.   Martene in the *Voyage Litteraire de
deux Religieux Benedictins* describes an incident in a parish church near
Basle, which proves not only that the more simple practice of an earlier age
had survived to the beginning of the eighteenth century, but also that the
rule as to the exclusion of women was not of more force in the diocese
of Basle than, as we shall see, it was in this country.   He says (Vol. I, Partie
2, p. 141-2) : "Nous entendîmes ensuite la messe paroissiale, et nous remar-
quâmes que les hommes y étaient séparez des femmes, les hommes à la droite,
les femmes à la gauche, et qu'ils demeurerent à genoux durant toute la messe.
A l'offertoire une fille tenant un enfant nouvellement baptisé commença à
l'offrande suivie de toutes les femmes; elles mirent leur offrande sur l'autel
dû côté de l'épitre et firent le tour de l'autel."(*)

(2) Θυσιαστήριον, properly altar : but the altar itself was more generally
spoken of by the Greek fathers as the Holy Table, as it is still in the rubrics
of the Greek Church.

(3) Ἱερατικόι, which (*Can.* 24) is explained as including priests and
deacons.

(4) Theodoreti *Eccles. Hist.* V, 18, *Ed.* Gaisford, p. 439-40.   At the
Trullan or Quinisext Council of Constantinople, A.D. 692, the rule as to exclusion of laymen from the sanctuary was again ordained (*Can.* 69), but with
an exception in favour of the emperor "when he desired to bring gifts to his
Maker."   Nothing is said as to his communicating, but it would seem that
the custom of his going within the sanctuary survived from the time of

(*) It is not a little curious in connection with this laying on the altar of their offerings
by lay people by their own hands to find individual offerers spoken of as "*singuli sacri-
ficantes*" in the rubric of a MS. Missal for the diocese of Basle of the tenth century.—
Martene, I, 215 b.

Similar regulations became general in the West. An Ordo Romanus which reaches back to before the eighth century describes the reception of the gifts in kind from the laity, who remained in their appointed places according to their degree, whilst the clergy went about the church.(1) Cardinal Bona(2) quotes a capitular of Charles the Great, ordaining that they should offer on every Lord's day, and that their oblation should be received outside the rails or chancel skreen, "*foris septa*."(3) Theodulph of Orleans, about the same time, applied the rule of exclusion to women only. This capitular, being translated into English in the tenth century, may be supposed to have had a certain amount of authority in this country ;(4) but whether the exclusion of women from the altar ever obtained in the Church of England, or not, there can be no doubt there was no objection to women going up to the altar to offer at the date of our manuscript. Chaucer's Wife of Bath will occur to many of my readers :

" In al the parisshe wyf ne was ther noon.
   That to the offryng beforn hire schulde goon,

Theodosius till the extinction of the Byzantine empire. I find an account of the ceremonial in Codinus "*de Officiis magnæ Ecclesiæ et Aulæ Constantinopolitanæ*," and he wrote a few years only before the city was taken by the Turks. He says that when the emperor was prepared for communion, he went within the Bema, laid aside his diadem, received the portion of our Lord's body from the patriarch into his own hands, and himself put the cup to his own lips, like the priests. [*The bread sopped in the chalice was given to laymen into their mouths with a spoon.*]—*Hist. Byzant. Scriptores*, Venet. 1729, XVIII, 108.

(1) Ordo I, *Mus. Ital.* II, 10. See also Ordo II, *ib.* p. 47, Ordo III, p. 57. In a later Ordo (Ordo VI, p. 74), we find the bishop conducted to the place where the faithful, whether men or women, offered their oblations, and the deacon giving his hand, in which he held the chalice, for them to kiss after they had made them.

It is curious to notice that the revisers of the second book of Common Prayer in the reign of Edward VI, in preventing the people from coming up to the altar to offer their alms, should have sanctioned the adoption of the earlier and distinctively Roman practice of going about the seats to receive them. This practice has of late years become very general among the protestant dissenters, as well as in the Roman Catholic congregations in this country.

(2) *Rer. Liturg.*, 2, ix, 1.

(3) This is explained by a paralled constitution of Herald, Archbishop of Tours, quoted here by Bona :—" Ut populus extra cancellos stet ; ejus oblatio extra cancellos recipiatur."

(4) " VI. Ut fœminæ ad altare in celebratione non accedant. Eac we beodaՀ þæt þæm tidum þe mæsse-preost mæssan singe þæt nan wif ne ᵹenealæce þam weofode, ac standen on hyra stedum, and þe mæsse-preost þær æt hiom onfó þære ofrunge, þe hiᵹ Gode ofrian wyllaՀ."—Thorpe, *Ancient Laws*, II, 406. *We also command at what times the mass-priest mass sings, that no woman draw near the altar, but let them stand in their places, and the mass-priest there from them receive the offerings which they to God offer will.*

And if ther dide, certeyn so wroth was sche
That sche was thanne ont of alle charite."(1)

The constitutions of Theodulph, as referred to above, enjoin that
all Christian men should on Sunday morning come with their
offerings to the celebration of mass.(2) The authorities here
quoted prove that up to the reformation the offerers used to come
up to the altar, upon the celebrant giving them a signal by turning round; perhaps, if they were slow in coming forward, by
asking for his offering;(3) or by coming down the altar step,
attended, if it was high mass, by deacon and subdeacon; or, in a
small church, by the parish clerk. The offerings were placed in
the hand of the celebrant, or in the paten held by the deacon, or
in a bason, held by the clerk or by laymen(4) of estate standing
on the left side of the priest. The offerers went up, first men and
then women, in the order of precedence, according to their
"degree"—two and two, if mourners at funerals, members of
gilds in procession, &c.—and after kissing the paten in the hands
of the deacon,(5) or the hand of the celebrant, and, if a bishop,
receiving his blessing, they returned to their places.

---

(1) C. T. 451-4. See also examples of women offering in this country,
p. 238, in the diocese of Basle, p. 234. The *vetulones* at Milan are a witness
to this day of the ancient discipline.
    The knight of La Tour-Landry, speaking to his daughters of the great
worth of humility, tells them of "sum amonges women that of that gret pride
. . . . . . be envyeusis whiche shalle goo furst up on the offerande, for to
haue most of the vayne glorie of the worlde."—*Knight of La Tour-Landry*,
Wright, E. E. T. S., 1868, p. 150.
    Cf. Chaucer, The Persone's Tale. *De superbia.* "And yit is ther a
prive spice of pride that . . . . . . desireth to sitte above him, or to go above
him in the way, or kisse the pax, or ben encensed, or gon to the offringe
beforn his neighbore."
    (2) ". . . on morȝenne mid heora offrunȝum cuman to þære mæssan
symbelnysse."—Thorpe, A. L. II, 420.
    (3) See Vernon MS., *ante*, p. 142, l. 510.
    (4) Pope Pius V. forbid this giving of the paten to kiss (*Merati in
Gavanti*, Par. II, Tit. VII, Obs. xxi.), and it was afterwards forbidden by the
3rd Provincial Council of Milan, held under Cardinal Carlo Borrhomeo in
1574, "*Ne patena, cum oblatio fit, ... fidelibus ad osculum præbeatur.*"
—*Decreta*, Mediolani, 1574, p. 58. At Rouen, however, both in the cathedral
and parish churches, the forbidden practice continued to be observed—and
the description given of the ceremony in the eighteenth century might very
well have served for that in an English mediæval church. "Aux grandes
fêtes le célebrant avec le diacre et le soûdiacre descend au bas de l'autel, et
donne a baiser la patene. C'est le soûdiacre qui reçoit les offrandes, et qui
les porte sur l'autel."—*Voyages Liturgiques*, p. 366.
    (5) "Item the heire of the saide estate, after he hath offrede, shall stand
upon the lifte side of the preste receyving the offering of the swerde . . . . . .
    Item ij men of worship to stonde on the same side of the preste, holding a
bason with therin for the offering."—*Booke of Precedence*, Furnivall, E. E. T. S.,
1870 (*Ordering of a Funerall for a noble person in Hen. VII time*), p. 31.

The following extracts, which range from the coronation of the king to the "enterring of the dede corps" of a brother of a "Poor man's gild," will, without further explanation, give sufficient —perhaps those of my readers, who do not feel an interest in the small details of the lives of our forefathers, may think a more than sufficient—insight into this part of the layman's mass, and the accustomed payments in respect to it.

I have already referred to the Vernon MS. (*ante*, p. 142, ll. 509 —516), where we have the priest turning to the layman, who places the mass-penny in his hand (l. 522). In the tale of the vision of the widow at Caudlemas, we have the lady, who was the Virgin Mary, with her "great company of fair maidens" going to offer, and the details of the vision no doubt were in accordance with the practice of the time, the thirteenth or fourteenth century.

> "An tua clerkes scho saw comande
> In surplices wit serges berande
> And after thaim reuested rathe
> Com suddeken and deken bathe,
> And Crist him selven com thar nest,
> Reuested als a masse prest.
>
> . . . .
> And quen thai com til thair offerande,
> This lenedy yed with serge in hande,
> And ofered first als comly quene,
> And efter hir other bidene.
> This wif satte ay stille, als hir thoht,
> For offer hir candel wald scho noht.
> The prest abade bifor the auter
> Bot scho no wald noht cum him ner."(1)

The English rubrics of "the Order of Consecration of Nuns," given by Mr Maskell, present us with an example of the survival to the sixteenth century of the offering of the oblations of bread and wine by the people : "Every virgyn shall haue a long sudary or towell uppon both hir handys, and in the ryght hande she shall haue a patine with an host : and in the left hande a cruette wyth wine. And then commyng by ordre to offer, they shall shyft the hoste fromme theyr patines to the patine that the deacon holdeth,(2) and then delyuer theyr cruetteys to the bisshop, kyssyng hys hand : whereof the bisshop shall some deale put into the chalice whych

---

(1) *English Metrical Homilies,* Small, p. 161.

(2) This agrees with the Sarum Pontifical, but the York Pontifical here reads "in patenam quam tenebit episcopus vel ejus diaconus." *Ed.* Henderson, p. 169 : and so the Exeter Pontifical, *ed.* Barnes, p. 122. According to the modern Roman Pontifical a lighted candle takes the place of the ancient oblations.

is preparede for theym after theyr communion." Then followed
the "offeryng of other folkys."(1)

The corresponding rubrics at Coronations, Ordinations, &c., are
to be found in Mr Maskell's Monumenta and in the Anglican
pontificals which have been subsequently printed. I give an
extract from the "Device for the Coronation of King Henry VII."
because it is in English: "Whiles that ['the offertory, *Intende
voci'*] is in singing, the king crouned shalbe ladd .... to the
high aulter .... and the cardinal having his face to the
Quer, as the observaunce at thoffering is, the king shall offer an
obley of bred laid upon the patent of Saint Edward his chalice,
with the which obley after consecrate the king shalbe houselled,
also he shal offre in a cruet of gold wyne which he shal vse in the
said chalice after he is housilled, and aswell the said patent with
the obley as the cruet with wyne shall be delyuered unto hym by
the gospellar at the tyme of his offering."(2)

To this I may add an extract as to the offertory at his (Henry
VII.) "burial at Westminster." "The Archbishop of Canterbury
came from the altar to the second step of the said altar where he
received the offerings in manner following. The chief mourner.
.... Then came the bishops and Abbots and offered in
their order, the bishops going to the altar and there making their
offerings, and the Abbots going to the Archbishop, kissing his
hand and taking his blessing. After whom came the lords and
barons, making their offerings every man in his degree ....."(3)

Mr Toulmin Smith's Ordinances of English Gilds do not indeed
furnish us with any additional information as to the ceremonial at
the altar, but they supply contemporary evidence as to the uni-
versality of the custom of making offerings in the mass. In the
gild of St George the Martyr at Bishop's Lynn, begun A.D. 1374, it
was ordained "þat eucryche brothir and sister þat longes to þe
ffraternite shal be redy atte þe general day, atte hous þat is assigned
for þe fraternite for to gone ij. and ij. togedre worshipfully to þe
chirche, *with* þe Aldirman for to heren masse and euensonge, and
atte general messe to offre in worship of þe holy martir and at
messe of Requiem, ilk for hem þat ben deed, vp þe payne of *di lib.*
wax."(4) In the gild of St Katerine, Norwich, the amount of the
offering was prescribed: "and at *that* messe euery brother and
sister shall offeren an halfpenny."(5) The Carpenters' gild in the
same city were to go together in procession with their candle and
torches into the minster of the Trinity "and offeren es vp at þe

---

(1) Maskell, *Monumenta Ritualia*, II, 327.
(2) *Rutland Papers*, Camden Society, 1842, p. 21.
(3) Leland's *Collectanea*, Hearne, 1774, IV, 306-8. See *post*, particulars
as the offerings at the burial of noblemen, p. 242, and members of gilds, p. 243.
(4) Toulmin Smith's *English Gilds*, E. E. T. S., 1870, p. 76.
(5) *ib.* p. 19.

heye auter and heren þe heye messe and everi offerin an halpeny atte messe."(1) In the gild of St John Baptist, at Oxeburgh in the county of Norfolk, the alderman was to offer a penny at the mass, and each brother and sister was to give a farthing "in the worship of Seint Johan."(2)

The Northumberland Household Book and the Privy Purse expenses supply us with information as to the offerings of persons of a higher rank ; and though they are of a later date than the examples already quoted, and later than any of our texts, yet as these payments were very probably regulated by custom, which had not changed in the meantime, they may serve for the purpose of comparison.

"The ii^{de} day of July [1502] for the Queenes offring in the colleage of Windesore at high masse there. v s."(3)

"Item for thoffering of the Quene upon Christmas day [1502] v s. and for her howselle the same day xx d. Summa vj s. viij d."(4)

---

(1) ib. p. 38. Thiers, in his *Traité des Superstitions* (Tom. II, p. 519), speaks of large wax candles hung about with pieces of money, being still presented in his day.   (2) ib. p. 122.

(3) *Privy Purse Expenses of Elizabeth of York*, Nicolas, p. 27.

(4) ib. p. 89, *howselle*, that is the housel-bread or host. A sum was paid on each occasion of communicating independently of what may have been given at the offertory. See other examples collected by Sir H. Nicolas, page 202. The queen appears to have communicated three times in the year, Easter-day, All Saints, and Christmas-day, and paid the same sum on each occasion. At Easter (p. 1) there was a farther payment of xlvj s. viij d. "for hir pardon," the "schrift-silver" of Daw Topias (*post*, p. 241), or the "pro confessione" of Bishop Chrodegang (*post*, p. 240). Sir Harris is at a loss to account for so large a sum as ten shillings being allowed to buffoons for their howsel, but this last item may serve to explain it. At Easter, 1530, there is a payment in Henry VIII. Privy Purse Expenses (p. 41) "paid to Thom the Jester for his howsill, and for his leveray Cote. xxv s," where the coat accounts for the larger sum. In 1497 six shillings and eight pence was paid "for the kings [*Henry VII.*] offering at his Housillyng."

"Taking his rights," was also used in the same sense. In 1538, "Item for the Kingis offeringe this Sonday at takyng his rights in the mornyng vi s. viij d." (*Privy Purse, Henry VIII.*, p. 371).

In 1531 there is a payment of ten shillings each to three of the King's servants, "ayent Easter for to take their rights" (p. 121), a similar sum having been paid at the previous Easter, where it is entered "for ther howsell x s a pece " (*p.* 38).

In the Northumberland Household Book we find the same phrase used— "Item. My Lordis Offeringe accustomede yerely upon Ester-Evyn when his Lordshipp takyth his Rights—iiij d."

"Item. My Ladis Offeringe accustomede yerely upon Estur-Evyn when hir Ladischipe taketh hir Rights if sche be at my Lords fyndynge and not at hir owen—iiij d."

"Item My Lorde usith and accustomyth yerly to caus to be delyverid to his Lordschippis Childeren that be of Aege to take there Rights for them to offer upon Easter even after ii d to every of them."—p. 334-5.

On the 16th June, 1531, twenty shillings was paid for the king's

---

"Taking their housel" was also used :—

> "But for as moche as man and wife
> Shulde shewe her paroche prest her lyf
> Onys a yeer, as seith the book(*)
> Er eny wight his housle toke."

Romaunt of Rose, Chaucer's *Works*, Morris, VI, 194-5, l. 6385-8.

This payment for the housel was objected to by the Lollards :

> "Non licet offerre in acceptione corporis Christi."

Fasciculi Zizaniorum, 375.

Mabillon dates these money payments from the eighth century, though he does not consider they became universal until the twelfth. He quotes from the Rule of Chrodegang, Bishop of Metz, *c.* 42, " Si aliquis uni sacerdoti pro missa sua vel pro confessione ; aut clerico pro psalmis et hymnis, seu pro se ipso vel pro quolibet caro suo, aut vivente aut mortuo, aliquid in eleemosyna dare voluerit ; hoc sacerdos vel clericus a tribuente excipiat et exinde quod voluerit faciat."—*Præfat. in Acta Sanctorum, O. S. B.* Sæc. III, § 42. In this country the money offerings appear to have become the property of the individual priest, or of the body to which he belonged, except in the case of appropriate churches when the vicar was required to account for the whole, or a proportion of them.

On this point it may be interesting to quote from *Jacke Uplande*, a satire written about A.D. 1400, against abuses in the church and specially against the friars;—an answer by Friar Dan Topias, whose real name was John of Walsingham ;—and Jack Upland's rejoinder, as they very strikingly illustrate the tone of feeling at this time on these points. Jack asks :

> "Freer, when thou receivest a penie
> for to say a masse,
> Whether sellest thou Gods bodie for that penie,
> or thy praier, or else thy travell ?
> If thou saiest thou wolt not travell
> for to say the masse but for the penie,
> that certes if this be sooth,
> then thou lovest too little meed for thy soule ;
> and if thou sellest Gods bodie, other (*or*) thy prayer ;
> then it is very simonie,
> and art become a chapman worse than Judas,
> that sold it for thirtie pence."

Jacke Uplande. Political Poems, Wright, II, 23-4.

Daw Topias replies :

> "Jak, thou seist (*sayest*) with symonye
> The seuen sacramentes we sellen,
> And preien for no men
> but ȝif thei willen paien.
> God wote, Jakke, thou sparist
> here the sothe,
> And, er we departen us asoundre
> it shal wel be shewid.
> But oon is the sacrament
> that we han to dispensen

(*) See *ante* page 121.

offering at Windsor; and the same day he gave "to Coristars in Wyndesor in Rewarde. vj *s.* viii *d.*"(1)

On Easter day, 1537, the Princess (*afterwards* Queen) Mary, then in her twenty-second year, offered "at high mass, iii *s.* ix *d.*" (2); and in November of the same year we find, "Delyuered to my Ladys grace for her offring for xiii dayes, every day xii *d.* at Hampton Court and Windesor at the quenes masses. xiii *s.*"(3)

In the Northumberland Household Book, which was begun in 1512, we have an account of "his lordship and my lady's offerings accustomed" which extend over several pages. The following may serve as examples:

"Item My Lords offeringe accustomede upon Ester-Day yerely when his Lordschip is at home at the High Mass, if my Lorde kepe chapell—xii *d.*"

"My ladys" offering on the same occasion was eightpence; and "my lorde useth and accustometh upon Ester-day yerely when his Lordship is at home, if my Lord keep chapel, to cause to be delyuered to my Lords eldest son. the Lord Percy and to every of

---

> off penaunce to the peple
> when nede askith.
> I trowe it be thi paroche priest
> Jacke, that thou menest,
> that nyl not hosel his parischens
> til the peny be paied,
> ne assoilen hem of her synne
> withouten schrift silver."—*ib.* p. 45-6.

Jack in his rejoinder, after retorting that "oure gentil Jhesu" and his apostles

> "were the best prestes
> that ever rose on grounde;
> and the best messes song,"

answers the jibe against the secular clergy.

> "Dawe, thou spekest proudely,
> apeching oure prestes;
> but of oon thing I am certen,
> thai ben less evil than ȝe.
> For alle if thai synne oft,
> As it well knowen,
> ȝet the ground that thai have
> is playnly Cristis religion.
> And thouȝ thai straye oft therefro,
> ȝit mow thai com to grace.
> Bot ȝe han left that grounde.
> . . . .
> Bot I prayse nother prestes ne thee,
> for ȝour assent in symonye."—*ib.* p. 46-7.

(1) *Privy Purse Expenses, Henry VIII.,* Nicolas, 140.
(2) *Privy Purse Expenses, Princess Mary,* Madden, p. 24.
(3) *Ib.* p. 45. Queen Jane Seymour had died on the 13th of October.

my yonge Masters my Lords yonger sonnes After j *d.* every of
them for them to offer the said Ester-day in the chapel at the Hye
Mas—iij *d.*"(1)   Candles were offered at Candlemas and certain
other festivals, and there was a custom of garnishing them with
pieces of money, as Thiers tells us was practised in France.(2)
" Item my Lordis offeringe uppon Candilmas-Daie yerely to be sett
in his Lordschippis candill to offer at the High Mas when his
Lordschipp is at home V Groits for the V Joyes of our Lady—xx *d.*"
My Lady's offering was three groats ; my Lord's son and heir, Lord
Percy, two pence ; and " for every of my yonge masters my Lords
yonge sonnes to be set in the candells afore the offeringe j *d.* for
aither of them—iiij *d.*"   " Item. My Lordis offeringe accustomede
yerly upon Saint Blayes Day to be sett in his Lordschipps Candill
to offer at Hye Mas of his Lordschyp Kepe Chapell—iiij *d.*"(3)

On the marriage (February, 1548-9) of the Lady Barbara,
daughter of James Earl of Arran, and Duke of Chatellerault, Regent
and heir-presumptive to the crown of Scotland, we find the following entry in the Treasurer's accounts :—

" Item. gevin to the Lady Barbara to offir, the day of hir mariage.
xxij *s.* vi *d* " [*Scots*].(4)

The offerings at funeral masses were the subject of very definite
regulations, not indeed enforced by any law of the Church, but
not the less binding from the force of opinion.   In " *The manner
at the offering at the Interment of noble-men,*" as set forth at length
in the Book of Precedence, edited for this Society by Mr Furnivall,
we find specific directions as to the order and amount of the offerings.   There were to be three masses, the first in the morning, of
our Lady, the second mass of the Trinity, and at each certain
offerings are prescribed.   The third mass was of Requiem, and
that was sung by the noblest prelate *pontificalibus.*   The chief
mourners offer for the mass-penny vij *s.* viiij *d.*, " then all the other
to offer that will, the greatest estates to offer first, next after the
executors.   The offering don, the sermon to begin."(5)

The funerals of members of craft and other gilds were equally
the subject of regulation with those which were ordered by the
heralds ; and their offerings, to say the least, were as large in
proportion.   We have seen that a groat appears to have been the

---

(1) *The Earl of Northumberland's Household Book*, edited by Bishop
Percy, 1827, pp. 335-6.

(2) See note, before, p. 239.   (3) *ib.* p. 333.

(4) Preface, Lauder's *Minor Poems*, Furnivall, E. E. T. S., 1870, p. vii.

(5) *Book of Precedence*, p. 34-6.   " The number of mourners according to
the degree of the defunct " is also prescribed :—The King to have xv ; a
Duke, xiij ; a Marquis, xl ; an Earl, ix ; a Baron, vij ; and a Knight to have
v.   The first English marquisate was created in 1386, and this fixes the earliest possible date for these regulations, but they are probably much later, though
no doubt founded on established custom.

customary payment for a mass by high personages of the blood royal, in the sixteenth century, one penny was the sum paid by gilds and members of gilds in the fourteenth century. By the ordinances of the carpenters' gild at Norwich, which have been already quoted, on the death of a member, all were to be "at his messe of requiem from gynnyng to þe ending, and everi offerin a ferthing, and ȝeuen an halpeny to clmes for þe soul. And eueri broþer and sister ȝeuen a peny to do seyn a messe for þe soule and for alle þe bretherin soulis and sistrin of þis gilde, and alle cristen soulis."(1)

In the gild of St Katherine every member was to offer a halfpenny at the mass, and give a halfpenny for almes, "and for a messe to be songen for the soule of the deed, a peny."(2)

In these and other similar examples the payments by members were not for a single mass, provided by the joint payment of the whole fraternity; but the penny of each member was in payment for a separate mass. In the case of the Poor Men's gild at Norwich, each member did not pay the penny for a mass. All were required to be present at the "enteryng of þe dede corps" and to offer "at his messe," but it was ordained that they should give "xxx d for xxx messes singing, for the soule and for alle cristen soules."(3)

The offering in the time of mass, or "mass-penny," which in theory at least was always at "will,"(4) and the offering for the housel,(5) must be distinguished from the stipulated honorarium for masses with any specified application to be said at the desire, or on the behalf, of particular persons, living or dead. A specific payment was made in that case, although it had been forbidden at a legantine council at York in 1195, and the priest was allowed to receive the mass-penny only—"hoc duntaxat, quod offeretur in missa, recipiat." (6)

In the Privy Purse Expenses of Elizabeth, queen of Henry VII., in August, 1502, the queen being then sick at Woodstock, we find a payment "to fyve preestes for V masses doon before our lady at Northampton. xx d."(7) Sixteen years later we find her nephew, the Earl of Devon, in like manner paying his groat. 3 Jan., 10 Henry 8. "To a priest for singing mass before my lord 4 d." 13 Feb. "To a priest for singing a mass before my lord in Powles Church, London, 4 d.", and on this occasion my lord's offering appears to have been of the like amount.(8)

As may be supposed, very numerous bequests, and directions to executors for the procuring of masses, occur in mediæval wills. I quote that of John Burningham, Treasurer of York Minster and Provost of Beverley, who died in 1457, because it directs that the

---

(1) *English Gilds*, 38.   (2) *ib.* p. 20.   (3) *ib.* p. 41.
(4) Above, p. 230.   (5) Above, p. 239.   (6) Wilkins, I, 501.
(7) *Privy Purse Expenses of Elizabeth of York* (Nicolas), p. 37.
(8) State Papers, Henry VIII, Vol. III, No. 152 (iii).

masses should be celebrated with the matin and vesper offices of
the dead : " Item volo quod mille missæ de Requiem cum Placebo,
Dirige, et Commendacione, citius quo fieri poterit post mortem
meam, celebrentur pro salute animæ meæ, et animarum . . . . . :
et quod quilibet presbiter secularis vel regularis, ut prædicitur,
dicens placebo, Dirige, cum Commendatione et missa habeat iiij *d.*
Summa xvj *li.* xiij *s.* iiij *d.*"(1)

P. 22, B. 244. *stondes.* The northern *-es* of the second person remains,
although the *a,* as in many other places, has been *midlandized*
into *o.*(2)   The layman, according to the rubrics of this text,
had been standing from the beginning of the gospel (B. 177), and
continued to do so, throughout the offertory, until the priest
began the *secreta* (B. 281). It will be noticed that the later
texts C and F omit this reference to standing.   See note, p. 193,
on C 58.

B. 246. *god to paye.*   Here the verb " to pay " is used in its primary
signification.   The Old French *payer* comes from the Latin *pacare*
(pax, pacis), to make peace, to pacify, and was used in the same
sense, and also, to satisfy, and then because payment satisfies a
debt, to pay.

Littré does not notice the obsolete use, but he quotes from a
psalter of the thirteenth century, where we at once recognize it :

" Par ton commandement est la mers troblée et par ton commandement sera païe " [? Ps. (89) lxxxviii, 10].

In English we find it constantly used :

" Thi voyage mai noht pai me
Bot ef thou do that I bid the."

E. M. H., Small, 54.

---

(1) *Test. Ebor.,* Raine, II, 204.   It may be curious to compare the above
with a similar provision for masses by the late Cardinal Antonelli, who died
on the 6th Nov. 1876.   A translation of his will appeared in the *Times* (Dec.
7, 1876), whilst these notes were passing through the press : " During the
eight days following my death, I order that a hundred masses a day be celebrated with the alms of 30 sous(*) for each mass.   A part of these masses
shall be caused to be celebrated by the Mendicant Friars."

The payments for masses—the *pretium* of Lyndwood, and *retribution* of
later French writers—are now designated *eleemosyna,* and the amount is fixed
by the bishop.—Bened xiv, *Dr Synodo Diœcesana.* Lib. v. c. 9.   Dens,
Theolog., Dublin, 1832, VIII, 135.   As explained in this last-quoted Manual,
no priest, secular or regular, can exact more than the sum so fixed.   They
may receive more, or ask less, but this last may sometimes be forbidden "*ne
hinc consuetudo introducatur minus dandi in præjudicium aliorum.*"

(2) The scribe has not altered the northern *stand,* B 84, 261, 303, 507,
nor at line 593, in which last place it was necessary to the rhyme.

(*) Thirty sous, or *soldi,* is comparatively a much smaller payment than the four pence
of the York dignitary.   We may measure it by this fact—Canon Raine tells us in his note
that the south-west tower of the minster probably owes its erection in a great degree to
his bequest of £50 "ad usum ecclesiæ Eboracensis ;" and fifty pounds would be as nothing
for such a purpose in the present day.

Hampole, quoting St Bernard, ". . ut possit aut non placere deo aut displicere," translates:

> "Swa þat outher þan may it noght
> Pay God almighty, þat es swa wroght,
> Or peraunter it hym myspaye."—*P. C.*, 2560-2.

"For nouther is trouth. (*faith*) worth withouten gode werkes
Ne ne werk withouten trouth mai pai god almighten."

Archbishop Thoresby's *Catechism*, fol. 297.

In the Promptorium we find neither the verb nor the substantive in this sense (p. 377), "PAY or payment, *Solucio*"; "PAYYD, of dette, *Solutus*"; but we have "PAYYD, and quemed or plesyd, *Placatus*." And the various reading in our MS. D at the foot of the page(1) would seem to point out that the use of the word, except in the sense of payment, had already become obsolete at the beginning of the sixteenth century; in addition to which I may mention that Palsgrave (p. 651) gives a whole column of uses of "I paye," and does not notice either appeasing or pleasing, though (p. 433) he gives "I apay" as "*contenter*."

P. 22, B. 247—260. It will be observed that this devotion at the offering occurs in a shortened form in the Vernon MS., *ante*, p. 142, l. 524, "God þat was in Bethlem bore," &c. The first part of both forms are evidently taken from the same English original, but this would seem to have kept nearer to it, and the alterations in the Vernon MS. to have been made to adapt it to the requirements of the metre.

I have not been able to trace this prayer any farther either in Latin or French, but it will be noticed that it has a certain resemblance to parts of the mediæval Epiphany sequence. We have, as recorded in the gospel, the threefold gift(2) (ll. 248-9):

> "Huic magi munera deferunt præclara
> Aurum simul thus et myrrham."

Then the "*wyssing*" them home to their country (ll. 251-2), an

---

(1) The fragment in the Advocate's Library, Edinburgh, our MS. A, reads "pey." Mr Turnbull, in his Visions of Tundale and other fragments, printed "prey," but I mention that as no impeachment of his accuracy, for it is the only variation I was able to discover on a careful collation with the transcript which my friend Mr Raven had made for me. That it was a misprint which had escaped notice I am able to state on the best authority, for I wrote to him to look again at the MS., and he asked the late Mr Cosmo Innes, and he, with his usual readiness to help forward every kind of antiquarian enquiry, came out of court with him, examined the MS., and certified to the correctness of the transcript.

(2) Sequentia in die Epiphaniæ, *Miss. Ebor* (Henderson), I, 32; *Miss. Sar*, Burntisland, 1861, col. 85. There is no sequence for the Epiphany in the Missale Romanum.

addition to the gospel history, mentioned in the apochryphal gospel I, *Infancy*, iii, 3 :

> "Magi sibi stella micante prævia
> Pergunt alacres itinera patriam
> Quæ eos ducebant ad propriam."

The prayer for personal needs in ll. 253—460 may perhaps have
been suggested by the last part of the sequence(1) :

> "Omnis nunc caterva tinnulum jungat laudibus, organi pneuma,
> Mystice offerens Regi regum Christo munera preciosa,
> Poscens ut per orbem regna omnia protegat in sæcula sempiterna."

P. 22, B. 248. There is no occasion to enter upon the legend of the three
kings, but it may be acceptable to those who are interested in the
devotions of our forefathers to have before them the "Collects to
the Three Kings at Coleyn," as they are to be found in the Horæ,
both of Sarum and York.

"Oratio ad tres reges.

Rex Iaspar, rex Melchior, Rex Balthasar rogo vos per singula
nomina; rogo vos per Sanctam Trinitatem ; rogo per regem
regum, quem vagientem in cunis videre meruistis: ut compaciamini
tribulationum mearum hodie, et intercedite pro me ad dominum :
cuius desiderio exules facti estis: et sicut vos per angelicam
annunciationem de reditu ab Herode eripuit: ita me hodie libe-
rare dignetur ab omnibus inimicis meis visibilibus et invisibilibus :
a subitanea et improvisa morte, et ab omni mala confusione, mala
fama, et omni periculo corporis et animæ.   Amen.

Versus.   Reges Tharsis et insulæ munera offerent.
Responsorium.   Reges Arabum et Saba dona adducent.

Oratio.

Deus illuminator omnium gentium da populis tuis perpetua
pace gaudere : et illud lumen splendidum infunde cordibus
nostris quod trium magorum mentibus inspirasti dominum nostrum
Iesum Christum, Qui. tecum vivit [*et regnat in unitate Spiritus
Sancti, Deus.   Amen*].

¶ Alia oratio ad tres Reges.

> Trium regum, trium munus,
> Christus honor, Deus unus,
> Unus in essentia.

---

(1) Cf. the "Benedictio populi" in the Mass for Epiphany-eve in the
Gothico-Gallican Missal :

"Esto tuæ familiæ ipse lux itineris, qui stella indice clarificatus es Rex
salutis."—Forbes, *Ancient Liturgics of the Gallican Church*, Burntisland,
1855, p. 53.

Trina dona(1) tres signentur ;(2)
Rex in auro, Deus thure,
    Myrrha mortalitas.
Colunt reges propter Regem,
Summi reges servent gregem,
    Coloni Coloniæ.
Nos in fide sumus rivi
Ilii sunt fontes primitivi
    Gentium primitiæ.
Tu nos ab hac, Christe, valle
Duc ad vitam, recte calle,
    Per horum suffragia,
Ubi patris, ubi nati, tui.
Et amoris sacri frui
    Mereamur gloria.

Versiculus: Vidimus stellam ejus in oriente

Responsorium: Et venimus cum muneribus adorare dominum.

---

(1) *Dona.* Abl. Sing.—"Volo quod fiat generalis dona sive distributio . .
pauperibus."—Maigne D'Arnis, *Lexicon,* s. v.

(2) *signentur.* This is also the reading of the *Sarum Horæ,* Paris, Vostre,
1507. Cf. *servent* four lines below. This signification of the threefold gift
was thus explained by Pope Leo the Great : "Thus Deo, myrrham homini,
aurum offerunt regi, scienter divinam humanamque naturam in unitate venerantes."—*Serm.* xxxi, 2.

Cf. a hymn from a xiii century MS.—Mone, *Lateinische Hymnen,* I, 80 :

> "Jus in auro regium,
>   Thure sacerdotium,
>   Myrrha munus tertium
>   Mortis in indicium."

Also the *Latin Hymns of the Anglo-Saxon Church,* Surtees Society, *ed.*
Stephenson :

> "soþne hi andettan and god
> Verum   fatentur   et Deum
>   lac   berende   rynelice.
> Munus ferendo mysticum."
>
>   *Hymnus Epiphaniæ ad Vesperam,* p. 48.

> "ferdan   tungel-witegan   þi hi gesawon
> I bant   Magi   quam viderunt
> steorran folgiende forstæppendne
> Stellam sequentes   præviam
>   leoht   hi sohton mid leohte
> Lumen requirunt   lumine
>   god hi andettan mid lace
> Deum   fatentur   munere."—*ad Matutinam,* p. 51-2.

Cf. also the Epiphany Sequence from which a quotation has been made
above :

"Huic Magi munera deferunt præclara, aurum, simul thus et myrrham
    Thure Deum prædicant, auro regem magnum, hominem mortalem myrrha."

Oratio.

Deus qui tres magos orientales Iaspar, Melchior, et Baltazar, ad tua cunabula ut te misticis venerarentur muneribus sine impedimento, stella duce, duxisti : Concede propitius. vt per horum trium regum pias intercessiones et merita commemorationum nobis famulis tuis tribuas : vt itinere quo ituri sumus celeritate, letitia gratia et pace, te ipso sole vero, vera stella, vera luminis luce, ad loca destinata in pace et salute et negocio bene peracte cum omni prosperitate salvi et sani redire valeamus. Qui vivis.

Et regnas deus.   Per omnia secula sæculorum.   Amen.(1)

These extracts will interest those of us who do not accept the " Romish doctrine concerning . . . invocation of saints "(2) mainly from a literary or antiquarian point of view. We must not, however, forget that they present only one aspect of the faith of our fathers, and I cannot forbear adding a " Devout Prayer " from the York Horæ—and there are many such in the old Service-books of the Church of England before the reformation—for I do not doubt that the devout spirit, in which it is conceived, will commend itself to the religious sympathies of " all who profess and call themselves Christians " :

" O most dear Lord and Saviour ; sweet Jesu, I beseech thy most courteous goodness and benign favour to be to me, most wretched creature, favourable, lord, keeper and defender ; and in all necessities and needs, to be my shield and protection against all mine enemies bodily and ghostly. Merciful Jesu, I have none other trust, hope, nor succour, but in Thee all-onely, my dear lord sweet Jesu, the which of thine infinite goodness made me, of nought, like unto thy most excellent image ; And when I was lost by my first father Adam's sin, with thy precious blood, dear lord, thou redeemedst me, and since then ever daily most graciously with thy gifts of grace most lovingly thou feedest me ; Grant me therefore most gracious lord and Saviour to dread thee and love thee above all things in this present life, and after, in joy and bliss without end. Sweet Jesu. Amen."(3)

P. 22, B. 249-50. *myrre, þirre.* The rhyme, as in other places, accounts for the midland scribe retaining the northern þir, which, as we shall

___

(1) *York Horæ*, fol. lxiiii *b*—lxv *b*. The hymn is printed without a break, as often in MSS.

(2) *The Thirty-nine Articles of Religion*, Art. 22.

(3) *York Horæ*, fol. clx *b*. For once I modernize the spelling.

For devotions of the same character, see *ante*, pp. 28, 30, 40, &c., and especially the " Questions to be asked of one near death " (*Myrc*, ed. *Peacock*, p. 64). " Believest thou fully that Christ died for thee, and that thou may never be saved but by the merit of Christ's passion, and then thank thereof God with thine heart as much as thou mayest. *He answereth.* Yea." See also similar questions, slightly varying in form, in the *Craft of Deyng* (dying), *Ratis Raving*, Lumby, E. E. T. S., 1870, p. 7.

see in the next note, has been more or less successfully displaced in texts E and F, and in the Vernon MS.(1)

P. 22, B. 250. *forsoke*, refused. The more modern usage of *forsake* suggests the notion of leaving, deserting, neglecting, and implies an already existing relation. This appears to be the sense in which the scribe in Text E understood it:

> "þou forsoke non of hem þere."—l. 250.

(*Thou didst not desert any of those that were there*); unless indeed he referred "hem þere" to the presents, in which case his rendering exactly reproduces his original.

The proper meaning is preserved in the Vernon MS. and Text F:

> "þou tok heore offryng of all þre."
> Vernon MS., p. 143, l. 527.

> "And thou forsoke not here presense."—F 92.
> (*And thou didst not refuse their gifts.*)

This sense of refusing, forbidding, resisting, is that of the word in Old English: A.S. "*forsacan*, to oppose, to refuse"; and this from A.S. "*sacan*,(2) to contend, to defend one's right." It is given as one of the senses in the *Promptorium*, p. 172: "For-sakyn, *Desero, relinquo, renuo.* Forsakyn, and denyyn'. *Abnego.* Forsakyn' and refusyn. *Abrenuncio, refuto, recuso.*"

In the Lindesfarne Gospels, of the Baptist forbidding our Lord to be baptized of him (Mat. iv. 14), we have: "foresoc *and* forehead hine." *Vulg.*, "*prohibebat eum.*" A.V. "forbad him."

> "For al þas men sal bere his (*anticrist*) merk
> þat sal forsake (*refuse*) to wirk Cristes werk."—*P. C.* 4405-6.

The old sense of forsake has survived in our marriage service, "forsaking all other, keep thee only unto her" or "him,"(3) where *forsake* is not the abandoning of any "ante-nuptial attachments" (though it has been so understood), but is used in the sense of rejecting and refusing.

---

(1) MS. A reads, "þu for soke none of þere;" and D, "And *th*ou for suke nane of *th*ir."

(2) In Cleasby-Vigfusson, we find the Icelandic *sága*, to fight. Mr Skeat in his *Mæso-Gothic Glossary*, p. 193, draws attention to the connection between the English *forsake* and the Gothic *sakan*, which is used by Ulfilas in rendering ἐμάχοντο, Jo. vi, 52; μάχεσθαι, 2 Tim. ii, 24; ἐπιτίμων, Mar. x, 13; ἐπιτίμησον, Lu. xix, 39.

(3) According to the use of Sarum and Hereford, the priest was required to ask questions, much as in the present prayer-book, from the man and the woman, the Sarum manual specifying in their mother tongue, the form being given in Latin. In the York form of spousals the priest not only asked the question, but the form was provided for him in English: "*Postea Sacerdos dicat ad virum cunctis audientibus in lingua materna sub hac forma:* .... and all other forsake for her, and holde the only to her to thy lyues ende."—*Manuale Ebor*, Henderson, 26.

P. 22, B. 250. *þirre. þir*, or sometimes *þer* (these), is a distinctively
northern form. It is akin to *þeir* and *þær*,(1) the Icelandic masculine and feminine plural of the personal (*third person*) pronoun, but
in later northern English it is found in all cases and genders, both
by itself and with a noun following. It occurs in the *Cursor
Mundi* of the very gifts of the three kings:

> "O þir þre gifts, sais sum bok
> At ans all thre he tok."—ll. 11507-8.

And so elsewhere,

> "þir kinges rides forth þair rade."—ll. 11427.

And very frequently in Hampole, and the Metrical Homilies:

> "þir er þe wordes of þe gospelle."—*P. C.* 4699.

> "þer er Barnard wordes þat says."—*P. C.* 2548.

> "þe whilk þir clerkes noght elles calles."—*P. C.* 1281.

> "Thir fair wimmen fal in sin."—*E. M. H.* p. 15.

> "þas ten er þir, þat I now rede."—*P. C.* 3400.

> "þir wordes aftir þe lettre er hard to here."—*P. C.* 6759.

> "þer ten puttes veniel syns away."—*P. C.* 3410.

> "Ilkan of þir es a dedly syn."—*P. C.* 3369.

> "Whaswa wil of þer four take hede."—*P. C.* 1830.

> "In þir seven er sere materes drawen."—*P. C.* 9545.

> "With þer he was first norished þar."—*P. C.* 461.

> "For als men heres þer clerkes say."—*P. C.* 3392.

> "For bale sal ger thir bernes blede."—*E. M. H.* p. 23.

B. 251. *wissed hom . . . home agayne*, showed them the way home
again (*by the star.* See above, p. 245-6). In the *Promptorium*
(p. 530) we have, "Wyssyn, or ledyn, *Dirige.*" A.S. wisan.
Icel. vísa—"vísa e-m til vegar, *to show one the road.*"—C-V. 717.
Germ. weisen—Einem den rechten Weg weisen.

Cf. "Swa him God wisode."—*Gen.* xxiv, 12.

> "*Annd* wissenn hemm, *annd* ʒemenn hemm
> Fra deofless *annd* fra sinness."—*Ormulum*, 11244-5.

> "And þe right way of lyf us wysse."—*P. C.* 9472.

> "And ʒif we wyl leve our synne,
> He wil wys us for to wyne
> To heven the rede way."
> <div align="right">Audelay, <i>ed.</i> Halliwell, p. 67.(2)</div>

---

(1) Mätzner, *Englische Grammatik*, I, 320. See Cleasby-Vigfusson, 733 a.
   (2) Cf. Vernon MS., *ante*, p. 129, l. 37, where "techeþ."

" Wische me the richt way till Sanct-Androes."

Lyndesay, *Sat.* 1929.

The variations in Texts E and F in the parallel passage prove that *wissed* had begun to lose the meaning above shown. It does not occur in Palsgrave.

P. 22, C. 104. The variation from the original text will be noticed here. The Vernon MS. (p. 142, l. 509) also refers in this place to the priest's washing his hands.

C. 112. *noon of þir.* I cannot account for the presence of *noon* in this place, and it is especially curious when joined to such a distinctively northern form as *þir. Oon* (l. 313) is equally anomalous in a northern text. We might have expected the northern forms *ane* and *nane.* [See Correction, p. 400.]

P. 23, F. 85. *whethere thu list.* Note the change from the impersonal to the personal use of list.

F. 92. *here presense,* their presents. Present (gift) had been introduced into the language long before the date of this MS. (*see* Richardson, *s. v.*), but the form in which it appears here would almost suggest, that a sort of confused idea of our Lord's presence with the Magi on their homeward journey was running in the scribe's head when he wrote it.

P. 24, B. 257. *for-done,* done away with, taken out of the way.

Cf. " For ofte sythes of þe day men falles
In syns, þat clerkes veniel calles,
Thurg werk, or worde, or thoght in vayn,
And ilka syn es worthy pain,
þe whilk most be fordone clenly,
Outher here or in purgatory."—*P. C.* 3496—3501.

" Here may men se how mykel is mercy
To fordo alle syn and foly."—*P. C.* 6322-3.

B. 259. *mys,* both here and in Text C, is used as a substantive, though it will be noticed that in Texts E and F it has become misdeeds as in our modern English.

Cf. ". . . seiδ & deδ so much mis."—*Ancren Riwle,* p. 86.

" And yhit when he had done mys,
And thurg syn was prived of blys."—*P. C.* 109-10.

" Als Innocentes þat never dyd mys."—*P. C.* 3289.

B. 261. *ʒit vp-standande.* According to this text the people had been standing from the beginning of the gospel (see B. 154, cf. B. 176, 245), and continued to stand until the priest said the *secreta* (see B. 281) ; but, as has been pointed (*ante,* p. 191, 193), the direction to stand appears to have been purposely left out in the more recent texts.

B. 262. *wasshande.* See before, Order of Mass, p. 100, l. 5.

The washing of the hands after the offertory is prescribed in all the English uses, and the Mozarabic and other western(1) liturgies, except the Ambrosian, in which however the celebrant, before the *Qui pridie (ante,* p. 106, l. 27), " *Accedit ad cornu epistolæ, ubi stans, ministro aquam fundente, lavat manus.*"(2)

The York rubric in this place, as usual, is less full than others. The priest either went to the *piscina,* or to the " altars end," where he was served "with basin, ewer, and towell."

P. 24, B. 263. *wasshing.* See *wasshande* in the line above, an example of the distinction between the participle present and the verbal sub- stantive, which we have lost, and which evidently was not familiar to the scribe of Text E.

B. 263-4.   . . . . . *þo preste wil loute*
             þe auter & sithen turne about.

See the Vernon MS., p. 143, ll. 533—542, and the York rubric, p. 100, l. 10. *Loute* is the *inclinatus* of this and other uses.

Becon, whose more offensive ribaldry I omit,(3) gives a fuller account of this and the next ceremony at the *Orate :* " After ye have washed your hands, ye return again to the altar, holding your hands before you . . . . and bowing yourselves . . . . ye make a cross upon the altar and kiss it . . . . , and then . . . . ye turn yourselves, looking down to the people and saying : *Orate pro me, fratres et sorores ;*(4) 'O pray for me, ye brethren and sistern ;' when many times there is nobody in the church but the boy that helpeth you to say mass ; and so making solemn courtesy . . . . ye return again to your accustomed pattering."(5)

B. 264. *with stille steuen.* It will be seen that in the York Order of Mass (*ante,* p. 100, l. 19) there is no mention of the "*still voice.*" The Durham and Hereford uses in this resembled the York, and. the rubric of the Sherborne Missal is simply " *Sacerdos conuertit ad populum.*" In the printed editions of the Sarum use we have " *tacita voce,*" but no doubt this change from singing or intoning (saying), was the universal practice in this country, and, as explained by the old ritualists, was intended to signify the spirit of humility in which the priest asked the prayers of the people. Durandus here

---

(1) Also in this place according to the Syro-Jacobite rite. Renaudot, II, 11.

(2) *Rubricæ Generales,* Mediolani, 1849, § 19. Gerbert, *Disquisitiones,* I, 330, mentions other peculiarities in German and French uses. See also *Voyages Liturgiques,* 56. *Voyage Litteraire,* II, 111.

(3) See note, p. 220.

(4) *Displaying of the Popish Mass,* Works, Camb., 1844, III, 365-6.

(5) " *Sorores* " does not occur in the old Monastic uses, nor in the present Roman Missal, but it retained its place in the Paris Missal until 1615, and the Metz Missal until 1642. There are other and significant variations in the forms of different uses and at different periods. See the York form, *ante,* p. 100, l. 20.

says "*voce aliquantulum elata*,(1) *ut oratio omnium auxilietur ei, quasi non præsumens quod solus possit tantum officium exequi:*"(2) and the rubrics of Continental uses for the "*still voice*" are sometimes varied by directions expressly pointing to this humble attitude of the mind ; in that of Verdun, "*humiliter dicere debet ;*"(3) Bayeux, "*dimissa et humili voce.*"(4) In a very early printed Benedictine Missal we have "*humili capitis inclinatione ;* " and in an early MS. Missal for the diocese of St Pol de Léon there is the following rubric : "*Hic sacerdos vertat se ad populum, dicendo submissa voce, manibusque junctis ante vultum neminem respiciendo.*"(5)

The existing rubric of the Roman Missal directs the priest to say the two words *orate fratres* in a voice somewhat louder (i. e. than the preceding prayer which he had said *secreto*), "*voce non nihil elata*," and to say the remaining words of the address secretly.(6)

P. 24. B. 267. *Take gode kepe.* Take good heed, pay close attention to. This phrase so exactly corresponds to the French *prendre garde*, that we might have taken it for a bald rendering of the French original, except that we find it in the *Story of Genesis and Exodus*, which is some fifty years older than the date I assume for the translation of our text :

"of godes bode he nam gode kepe " (l. 939).

Whether it came from the French or no we find the phrase was very general in the fourteenth century :

"Herbes and trese, þat þou sees spryng,
And take gude keep what þai forth bring."

Hampole, *P. C.* 646-7.

"If þou lene nedful besynes of actyf lyfe and be rekles, and take na kepe of thi werldly gudes."—Hampole, *English Prose Treatises* (Perry), p. 15.

"Takest thou no kepe that my sister hath lefte me aloone to serue."—Wyclif, Lu. x, 40.

"¶ & tak kep, for from hennes-forthward."
Chaucer's *Astrolabe*, Skeat, p. 4, l. 2.

"And or that Arcyte may take keep."—*C. T.* 2690.

---

(1) This is illustrated by the rubric of the Præmonstratensian Missal of the xiith century, "*Mediocriter, ut possit audiri.*" Le Brun. IV, 246.

(2) *Rationale*, 4, xxxii, 3.

(3) Mart., I, 213.   (4) Ed. 1501—Le Brun. IV, 241.   (5) Mart., I, 239.

(6) *Ritus Celeb. Missam*, VII, 7. The Mozarabic rite differs from other western uses in requiring the priest to sing the *Orate*, as follows : "Adjuvate me fratres in orationibus et orate pro me ad Deum." The musical intonation is given in the Missal, p. 224.

> "They ben so bare, I take no kepe
> Bot I wole have the fatte sheepe,
> Lat parish prestis have the lene
> I yeve not of her harme a bene!"

(False-Semblant in the person of a Friar-pardoner.)

Romaunt of Rose, Chaucer's *Works*, Morris, VI, 197, l. 6463-6.

The same phrase occurs again in our text, l. 305, and in both these places it is used very much as the πρόσχωμεν of the deacon in the Greek liturgy,(1) though it would be too far-fetched to class this amongst the survivals of the Ephesine rite in Gaul which may be traced in Dan Jeremy's treatise, and in the practice of the Gallican and Anglican churches.

P. 24, B. 268. *Knoc on þi brest.* The celebrant was directed to do this by the rubrics of all the English uses except York, at the prayer in the canon (*ante*, p. 110, l. 9) "*Nobis quoque;*" as does the Roman Missal, as also at the mention of sins in thought, word, and deed —"*percutit sibi pectus ter*"—in the confession (Ctr. the York use, *ante*, p. 90, l. 27); at the *Agnus Dei* (*ante*, p. 112, l. 21); and before he receives the communion. Hampole specifies this practice, which of course was suggested by the publican in the parable smiting upon his breast, as one of

> "ten thynges sere þat veniel syns fordus here.
>
> . . . .
>
> knocking of brest of man þat es meke,
> Last enoyntyng gyven to þe seke."—*P. C.* 3400-8.

At the reformation it was provided by the Book of Common Prayer, 1549, that "As touching kneeling, crossing, holding up of hands, knocking upon the breast, and other gestures, they may be used or left as every man's devotion serveth, without blame."

B. 270. *noght worth to pray for hymm.* There is a marked absence in Dan Jeremy of the tone of sacerdotal arrogance, which was common among his contemporaries; and what is here said does not necessarily imply any assumption of moral superiority, but may rather have been intended to enforce the humility which both the downcast mien of the priest and the smiting on the breast of the layman were intended not only to express, but also to suggest. Cf. the collect for 12th Sunday after Trinity—a very happy rendering of the Latin original:

> "Pour down upon us the abundance of thy mercy . . . . giving

---

(1) Πρόσχωμεν is one of the calls of the deacon to the people which the Syriac liturgies retain in the original Greek, or in characters intended to represent it, just as *Kyrie Eleison* was retained in the west.—See Renaudot, II, 20; Howard, *Christians of St Thomas*, 219(d). It appears as "*Proschume*" in the Armenian Liturgy of the Mechitarist (*Uniate*) monks.—*Liturgia Armena transportata in Italiano*, Venezia, 1826, p. 39. It occurs several times in the so-called Liturgy of St Chrysostom, and the use of it in the liturgy is referred in this father, *Hom.* xix, *in Act. Apost.*, Ed. Ben. I, 159 E, 160 A.

us those good things which we are not worthy to ask but through the merits and mediation," &c. "*Effunde super nos misericordiam tuam ut . . . adjicias quæ oratio non præsumit, Per,*" &c.

From among the many that might be collected, I add one other similar plea of unworthiness from the Alexandrian liturgy of St Gregory, where the priest (ὁ ἱερεὺς λέγει), in a litany after the consecration, but before the communion, prays for himself and other clergy—"That Thou wouldest accept us, who by Thy grace have been called to this ministry to Thee (πρὸς τὴν σὴν κεκλη-μένους διακονίαν), unworthy though we be. *The people say,* Lord have mercy."(1)

P. 24, B. 274. *Answere þo prest with þis in hie (à haute, à haute voix),* with a loud voice.(2) Elsewhere consequential changes in our MSS. enable us to trace changes in the manner of conducting the service; but this rubric for the people to answer aloud to the *Orate* or the "*Obsecratio ad populum*" is of additional interest as an indication of the date of the original treatise.(3) In the later texts C and F it has been omitted, so as not to clash with the altered practice of the people, and the confused reading of text E may not improbably be accounted for by supposing that the writer was not acquainted with a custom which at the first had been universal in the East and West.(4)

(1) Renaudot, *Liturg. Orient.*, 1716, I, 111.
(2) "þe angell answerd him in hy."—*Holy Rood*, Morris, p. 69, l. 277. "þan seyd þe aungel to hym an hy."—Bonaventura's *Meditations*, Cowper, l. 397.
(3) My position throughout is that the original French of our text was adapted to the Rouen use. I do not know how far the reader may follow the argument in a subsequent note, that the answer in the next line had survived from the Rouen use of the twelfth century,—and through the ante-Caroline Gallican church from the Ephesine rite,—but inasmuch as the answer of the people in the Rouen Missal of the middle of the thirteenth century is rubricated "*clerici respondeant*" (Mart. I, 229), it follows that our author in directing the people to answer aloud, if he did adapt his treatise to the existing use of Rouen, must have written before the date of this manuscript, though it does not follow that the change from *populus* to *clerici* may not have been made earlier, more especially as in gradual and local changes of custom, as this was, the change of rubrics follows, rather than causes them.
(4) This rite of the priests' asking the prayers of the people at the offertory —though most accordant with the spirit of our English prayer-book—was not retained in 1549, when the old service books of the Church of England were revised and translated into the mother tongue,—partly, it may be, because the answer of the people had come to be in dumb show,—and still more, in all probability, because from an objection to the Sarum answer which was then prescribed for the laity in both provinces (*see* p. 264), and which the greater number of the revisers must have themselves used in Henry's time. Although it still preserved the older phraseology "*sacrificium laudis,*" nevertheless, in the form printed in all the editions, it referred to the propitiatory view of the mass as an offering for sin—"*pro peccatis et offensionibus*"—which it was the declared object of the reformers to reject.

It may be said that the rubrics of the Eastern rite, as now used, do not assign this answer to the people. But that, by itself, is no proof that the people did not join at the first, for as a rule the rubrics refer only to the officiating clergy, and the people are not uniformly specified except in cases where, as in the *Ectene*, they respond to the deacon; and I think it will be admitted that the two examples, which I now bring forward, go very far to prove that, whatever later practice may have been, the original rule of Eastern Churches was that the people should answer with the deacon. The first is from the Liturgy of the Christians of St Thomas, as it was "expurgated" by Archbishop Menezes in accordance with the acts of the synod of Diamper,(1) where—in the most unlikely of all unlikely places—I find a rubric at this place, "*Illi respondent cum diacono;*" and it is not conceivable that these native Indian Christians should have practiced this rite, unless they had received it at the first with their liturgy; and still more inconceivable that the Portuguese Archbishop should have established it amongst them, when it was obsolete in the Church of Rome, and at the very time when he was forcing Roman peculiarities(2) upon them instead of primitive customs—a course, upon which a distinguished prelate of his own communion, the learned Renaudot, has remarked with not undeserved severity.

My other example is from the Liturgy of St Chrysostom according to the use of the Greek monks in the Basilian monasteries in Sicily and the lower parts of Italy. In this the priest calls upon "those on the right and left" (the *circumstantes* of the Latin rubrics), and they answer (καὶ αὐτοὶ ἀποκρίνονται) in the words of the angel from the Greek of St Luke (i, 35), to which I shall again refer in the next note.

In the West there is no difficulty in finding evidence as to the people's part in the writings of the earlier ritualists and the rubrics of different uses. For example, Amalarius speaks of their *singing* the answer;(3) and we find it rubricated "*Responsio*

---

(1) Raulin, *Hist. Eccles. Malabaricæ*, Romæ, 1745, p. 309. Both the rubric and the answer of the people appear to have been wanting in the MSS. used by Mr Howard for his translations in *The Christians of St Thomas and their Liturgies*, 1864, see p. 220. So also in Hough, *Christianity in India*, IV, 633, and Renaudot, II, 20.

(2) See before, p. 208.

(3) *De Ecclesiasticis Officiis*, iii, *c.* 19. Cf. "Acclamans autem populus orare debet ita."—Walden, *Doctrinale*, IV, *c.* 35. In the Capitular of Otto or Hetto, Bishop of Basle (811—836), we find it laid down that not only clerks and nuns should learn the answers to the priest, but also that the whole of the laity should answer together with them : "Tertio, intimandum est ut ad salutationes sacerdotales congruæ salutationes discantur, ubi non solum clerici, et Deo dicatæ, sacerdotali responsionem offerant, sed omnis plebs devota consona voce."—*Hettonis Capitulare*, iii. *Patrolog.*, Migne, CV, 763. See also the council, quoted from Cassander, *ante*, p. 200.

populi ;" " *Respondent circumstantes ;*"(1) " *Tunc dicatur a singulis ;*"(2) " *Deinde respondelur ei ab omnibus,*"(3) and so forth.(4)
It is beyond our purpose to enquire what doctrinal or other causes had been at work to bring about this ritual change, but as we are here more especially concerned with the devotions of the people, it may not be out of place to draw attention to the change which did take place. A comparison of fourteenth and fifteenth century manuscripts and the first printed missals brings out the fact that at latest before the end of the fourteenth century the people's part had been already assigned to the clerks in a great majority of cases.(5) The insertion of "*secrete,*" which is not found in any one of the known MSS., in all the printed editions of the York Missal, *ante,* p. 100, l. 24, is noteworthy as an onward step in the process of excluding the laity from a participation in the service, which has reached a further development in the existing rubric of the Roman missal, requiring the priest as an alternative to answer himself.(6)

P. 24, B. 275. *þo holi gost in þe light.* Text E here reads "into" for "in." This may very possibly be an old reading preserved in E, as old readings are elsewhere preserved in it, and it certainly scans better. By the help of the MSS. at the foot of the page, we may restore the next line :

þe hali gast into þe light,
And send his grace into þe right.

(1) MS. (*Sæc.* VIII.), Monasterii S. Dionysii in Francia. Mar. I, 189. *Circumstantes* must not be understood only of the ministers of the altar or of those present in the quire, but of the whole congregation. Cf. "*circumstantium*" in the canon of the mass, *ante,* p. 104, l. 28.
(2) Ex. MS. *Pontificali* (*Sæc.* XI), Salisburgensi (*Salzburg*), Mart. I, 208. So also in the so-called *Missa Illyrici,* or the Mass printed by M. Flacius Illyricus, " *Tunc respondeatur ei a singulis.*"—Mart. I, 184.
(3) Ex Missali Tullensi (*Toul*), *Sæc.* XIII, Mart. I, 234.
(4) There is no occasion to multiply examples, for there can be no doubt of the fact. I will only add the *dictum* of a Roman ritualist of the highest authority : " Populus respondere consueverat . . . . . Nunc nomine populi unus minister respondet."—Maldonati, *de Cæremoniis, cui accedunt adnotationes* F. A. Zaccaria, Romæ, 1781, Tom. II, pars II, p. cxiij.
(5) The reading of the printed editions of the Sarum use is " *Responsio clerici* (or *cleri*) *privatim,*" but the Sherburne Missal written towards the end of the fourteenth century—now one of the choicest treasures of the Duke of Northumberland at Alnwick Castle, and unrivalled as an example of English art—preserves what would seem to be the older reading of the Sarum use :— "*responsio populi*" (p. 362) : and we find the same rubric in the beautifully printed folio missal (*ed.* 1500, fol. 93) of the "*diocese*" of Lyons, which even in recent times has been known for its resistance to innovations.
(6) " *Minister, seu circumstantes respondent: alioquin ipse Sacerdos.* Suscipiat Dominus sacrificium de manibus tuis (*vel* meis) ad laudem et gloriam nominis sui, ad utilitatem quoque nostram, totiusque Ecclesiæ suæ sanctæ. *Sacerdos submissa voce dicit:* Amen."

This couplet, I have no doubt, was intended to represent the answer in the oldest of the Rouen Missals, printed by Martene : " *Spiritus Sanctus superveniet in te et virtus altissimi obumbrabit tibi,*"(1) which is the Vulgate rendering of the answer of the angel Gabriel to the Blessed Virgin at the Annunciation.(2)

As we shall see in the next note, the verb " light " in the text was made to do duty in another sense, when the second couplet, (lines 277-8) was interpolated, as I propose to show it was, but the following quotations prove that it was the word which would have naturally suggested itself to an English translator.

In the present treatise we have :

" He lyght in mary mayden chast " (B 215),

where E reads, as here, " he lyȝht in to."

" þer nys no shapper but God almyȝt
þat yn þe vyrgyne Mary lyȝt."—H. S. 577-8.

" Kyd he was of myȝtis moost
and sent adown þe holi goost
And liȝhtned into Virgin marie
wiþouten(3) wem of her body."

Tale of Ypotyse, York Minster MS., xvi, L. 12, fol. 63 *b.*

" The holy Gost shall light in the."

Townley Mysteries, p. 75.(4)

It is an example of the tenacity with which words, after the sense in which they were first used has been lost sight of, still live on in forms, and more especially in liturgical forms, and so reveal their origin, that this rendering of a twelfth century original should have held its own through all the transcriptions of the translation, with no support from any English use, and spite of its adaptation to that of Sarum.

And this survival of a foreign form in the popular devotions of our forefathers is all the more remarkable, if I am not wrong in supposing that the Rouen answer(5) of the twelfth century was

---

(1) Mart. I, 229—quoted *ante,* p. 186.   (2) St Luke, i, 35.

(3) MS. inserts " ony."

(4) Cf. the *Te Deum* in the *Book of Common Prayer :* " O Lord, let thy mercy lighten upon us."

(5) This answer is the only one in the earliest of the Rouen MSS. printed by Martene (I, 228).

It is given as an alternative in that of the fourteenth century (Mart. I, 229), with one the same as Sarum, as it is in a MS. Missal of the same century, according to the use of the monastery at Fécamp (Mart. I, 230).

It is one of several answers in an eighth century manuscript at St Denys, printed by Martene (I, 189) ; and is given by him as the answer at Beauvais (I, 143). With a form "sucipiat," &c. (something like the present Roman form, *ante,* p. 257, *n.* 6) joined on to it, it was the answer at Soissons (Mart, I, 220).

It is one of the answers mentioned by Amalarius in the ninth century (*De Eccles. Off.,* iii, 19). Le Brun (IV, 180) quotes it from the manual written for Charles the Bald. See also Bona, *Rerum Liturg.,* 2, ix, 6.

itself a survival from the old Gallican liturgy, and that too in a rite
where it shewed its Ephesine origin by its agreement with primitive use.

Many points of agreement between the Gallican and Eastern
liturgies have been enumerated by writers on these subjects; and,
indeed, there would be no difficulty in proving from existing
documents the continued use in France, England, and Western
Germany of certain rites; for example, bidding prayers—in which,
I may remark in passing, the laity took a prominent part. I must
admit that I have no direct proof that the answer in our text was
used in the Gallican liturgy(1) beyond the fact that it is found
both in French Missals from the eighth century downwards, as quoted
in the foot-note, p. 258, and in the ancient liturgies of the Eastern
Church, as pointed out in the note below;(2) and being thus found

---

(1) In coming to a conclusion as to the probabilities of the argument which
I here propose, it must not be forgotten that at the time when the Gallican
liturgy was discarded for the Roman Missal by a high-handed exercise of the
regal power, and indeed for some hundred and fifty or two hundred years afterwards, there was no such thing as a *Missale plenarium*, or service-book, which,
like the modern Roman Missal or the Book of Common Prayer, professed to
contain the whole of the office (*see* p. 155, *n.* 1); and consequently that the
people's part, if committed to writing at all, would not be found in the book
intended only for the priest, which is all that has come down to us.

See also the York order of mass, *ante*, p. 102, l. 21 and l. 23, where in
the MS. from which this is a transcript two answers, which we know were invariably made, have nevertheless not been inserted.

Even when Missals were written "*in longum*," and after they were printed,
the answer was often not included. The Hereford among English printed uses
furnishes an instance. Cf. Dr Henderson's reprint, p. 118.

(2) In the liturgy of St James (*ed.* Trollope, p. 59) we have the priest asking
those " on this side and on that "—ἔνθεν καὶ ἔνθεν—equivalent to the words in
the rubric of the Basilian use, already quoted, p. 256—"and they answer" in
the words of the angel as already quoted from St Luke, i, 35—see also in
Neale's *Tetralogia*, p. 95.

In the Venice editions of the liturgy of St Chrysostom (p. 56, *ed.* 1854),
as printed in his text by Goar (*ed.* 1649), p. 73, and by Neale, p. 64, we have
the same answer, but here and in the Benedictine edition of St Chrysostom it
is assigned to the priest, in answer to the deacon. Goar, however, note 113,
p. 133, points out that this is a " very great error of the scribes or printers,"
and so, no doubt, it was, unless perhaps a feeling on the part of some reviser
that the old use was inconsistent with the dignity of the priest had something
to do with the alteration. He quotes Greek ritualists, and ancient MSS., to
prove what the genuine reading really was. One of the MSS. is that referred
to above. He gives another, p. 94, which he found in the King's Library at
Paris, in which the priest addresses the deacon only : " Deacon, pray for me,"
and he answers as before.

This reading of the liturgy as now used, and for more than two hundred
years, in the Greek Church, is all the more worth noting at the present time,
when we are constantly meeting with quotations from the Venice text, or a
translation, as if it represented the use of the primitive Church without change
and without interpolation.

at both ends, as it were, and the connection between the two being well established as respects other rites, it does not seem an
unreasonable inference to assume that the use continued uninter-
rupted during the interval.

In fact, except on this supposition, it would be difficult to account
for its presence in the Gallican Church after the end of the eighth
century, for, everywhere but at Milan, the Roman Missal had been
forced by Charles the Great, and his father before him, upon those
of their subjects who had been used to the Ambrosian and Gallican
liturgies—and this answer cannot be traced to any Roman source.

And there is yet another consideration which tells in favour of
my suggestion that this answer did find its way into the diocesan
uses of the Gallican Church from the old Gallican liturgy—and that
is, the antecedent probability of the "Responsio populi" would in
some cases have remained unchanged. There is abundant documentary evidence that many of the clergy yielded a very reluctant
obedience to the edicts of the new Augustus for the regulation of
the public worship of his churches—*nostræ ecclesiæ* is the phrase
he uses. Their unwillingness to accept the new forms to which
they were not accustomed is the explanation which French
authorities give us of the peculiarities of the old liturgy which
were to be traced in local uses; and it is only natural to suppose,
as we know to have been the fact in other cases, that the old forms
would have lingered on more tenaciously in the devotions of the
laity, and if so, then most especially in respect to the answer in the
text, for at that time it was exclusively the function of the people.

P. 24, B. 275-8.   The answer to the Sarum Missal is as follows:

"Spiritus Sancti gratia illuminet cor tuum et labia tua, et
accipiat Dominus digne hoc sacrificium laudis de manibus tuis
pro(1) peccatis et offensionibus nostris."(2)

---

(1) Instead of these words "*pro peccatis et offensionibus nostris,*" we find
"*pro nostra omniumque salute*" in the later form of the MS. Rouen Missal of
the fourteenth century, and the folio edition of 1497, and I have little doubt
that an examination of the earlier MSS. of the Sarum use would prove that
this was the earlier reading.

We find these words in the monastic use at Durham (p. 263), which otherwise in the latter part of the people's answer was not altogether unlike the
Sarum. I have not had an opportunity of examining any MSS. earlier than
the latter part of the fourteenth century, but the reading of the later Sarum
Missals seems to involve an inaccuracy of language,—and here we are not
dealing with doctrine.

For sins and offences a sacrifice of praise (*sacrificium laudis*), or a eucharistic sacrifice, properly so called, can hardly be offered; but rather a sin-offer-
ing; whereas, according to the reading, I would say *preserved* at Rouen, if that
were not to beg the question, a sacrifice of praise and thanksgiving, without
any violence to the language, might well be offered for the salvation of ourselves and all men—"*pro nostra omniumque salute.*"

(2) *Miss. Sar.*, Burntisland, 1861, col. 595.

It has been pointed out in the last note that the first two lines
are, in fact, the answer of the Rouen use at the date of the original.
When, however, the treatise came to be copied by a scribe, who
knew nothing of the older answer, the mention of the Holy Ghost
and the occurrence of the word "light" would not unnaturally
suggest the "*Spiritus Sancti gratia,*" and the "*illuminet*" of the
alternative answer of the fourteenth century Rouen use, which
was well known in this country as the answer of the Sarum use ;
whilst the awkwardness of "in thee light," instead of "thee
light,"(1) would not have attracted attention in an uncritical age,
unless indeed we suppose the various reading in A and its abrupt
ending to be an attempt to escape from the difficulty. Be that as
it may, "thy heart and thy speaking," in line 277, would have
been at once accepted by the midland and southern scribes of the
province of Canterbury as a sufficient rendering of the Sarum "*cor
tuum et labia tua,*" even if not intended for it.

Now the different answers at this part of the mass furnish one
of the most distinguishing points of difference in the several
mediæval uses, and in a Northern work, as, with all respect to Dr
Morris' *dictum* as to the dialect, I suppose this to have been, we
might have naturally looked for a distinctively northern answer,
that is to say, according to the use of York ; or, if it had been
written in the diocese of Durham, then according to the use (2) of

(1) Notice the syntax of the verb light = *illumino.*
>
> And þet he fulle us mid his mihte
> And mid his halie gast us lihte.
>
> *O. E. Hom.* (Morris), p. 63, ll. 137-8.
>
> Þatt lihht tatt lihhteþþ iwhille mann
> Þatt lihhtedd iss onn erþe.—*Orm.* 19073-4.
> Light min eghen (*inlumina oculos meos*). Ps. (13) xii, 4.
> Jesu my herte with lufe þou lyghte.
> *Religious Pieces* (Perry), p. 73, l. 49.

Cf. A. V., St Luke, ii, 32 : "A light to lighten the gentiles."

(2) In the books which touch upon the subject it is uniformly assumed that
the Sarum use was adopted at Durham : and a friend of mine, who is perhaps
better informed than any other scholar in this country on the subject of the
"Cathedrals of England," in a new edition of one of his many works, repeated
the statement after I had suggested to him that it admitted of doubt.

I still venture to think that this opinion is founded on a mistake except in
so far that it is a fact that the York use did not extend to Durham, although
by old law of the Church the several dioceses of the province were required to
conform to the use of the metropolitical church, as parish churches were to the
use of the mother church.

In the middle ages the ecclesiastical superiority of the Archbishops of York
was regarded with great jealousy and repugnance by their most powerful and
highly privileged suffragans, the prince-bishops of the county-palatine. This
feeling extended to their clergy, and it was only so recently as the meeting of
the existing convocation of York that the writer was a witness to the extinction,
at the suggestion of the present Archbishop, of what was perhaps the last

the Church of Durham ; but in the four lines we cannot trace the
answer of the York Missal (*ante*, p. 100, ll. 23-5) ; nor, at least in
respect to the first two lines, is the text any nearer to the Durham
use. I quote from a fourteenth century MS., written for the Cathedral Church itself, and formerly belonging to the altar of St John
Baptist and St Margaret, which was one of the nine altars ranged
along the eastern wall beyond the high altar :

---

formal expression of it—the presentation of protests by proctors from the
diocese, when answering to their names at the preconization of the synod, and
their customary rejection by the president as "frivolous and impertinent."

This was a very harmless formality, though from the time the Bishoprick
of Durham had ceased to be a county-palatine, and the bishop was reduced to
the position of any other suffragan, it had lost what little pretext there might
have been for its original adoption. The manner in which the clergy of
Durham exhibited their feeling towards their metropolitan was not always
equally unobjectionable. In the *Northern Registers*, Raine, p. 398, we have
a mandate from Archbishop Zouche to his official at York giving a detailed
account, which would not bear translation, of certain clerks of the Bishop of
Durham, and others, as alleged with the consent of the said suffragan, coming
to York Minster on the 6th February, 1349, and there, at the doors of the
quire "*subtus imaginem crucifixi*," being guilty of certain filthy acts by way
of insult to him.

We can readily understand that the Benedictine monks who served the
cathedral were sharers in the general feeling ; and as respects the Ebor
Missal they would moreover be unwilling to adopt its forms and ceremonies,
were it only that they were in many respects different from the Monastic use
which was the rule of other houses of their order.

The general impression as to the Sarum use may be explained by the circumstance that the Monastic use, adhered to at Durham, and in fact the uses
of all the different orders, though differing among themselves, had much in
common with the Sarum use, which was itself the old Benedictine use of
Sherburne, as modified by St Osmund in the eleventh century.

The only Durham missal I have had an opportunity of examining is the
Harleian MS. here quoted. In one afternoon at the British Museum I could
not collate very much of it, but besides the variation at the *Orate*, which has
led to this note, I took note of numerous differences from the Sarum use,
which were convincing to me, that it could never have been intended for it—
not only were there verbal variations in the rubrics, and a different nomen-
clature of Sundays, &c. (*e. g.* named from Pentecost, as York and Rome,
instead of "after Trinity," as Sarum and many French diocesan uses), but the
appointed vestments and ceremonies at certain feasts, epistles and gospels of
certain ferials, other portions of scripture, *secreta*, &c., were often different.
The only reference to the Sarum use which I did meet with, was the citation of
it—and not without a certain subaudition of monastic superiority—as the use
of certain seculars. After a rubric "*in Cœna Domini*"—"Post evangelium
tot hostiæ ponantur ad consecrandum quot possunt fratribus sufficere ipso die
et in crastino ad communicandum"—in a following rubric is added :—"Secundum consuetudinem quorundam sæcularium ponantur a subdiacono tres
hostiæ ad sacrandum, quarum duæ reserventur in crastinum, una ad perci-
piendum a sacerdote, reliqua ut reponatur cum cruce in sepulchro,"—the words
from "ponantur" to "sepulchro" being the Sarum rubric *verbatim*. Cf. *Miss.
Sar.*, col. 303.

" *Respondeatur a circumstantibus*, Dominus sit in corde tuo et in labiis tuis et suscipiat sacrificium de ore tuo et de manibus tuis pro nostra omniumque salute."(1)

Here we have the "heart and speaking" of the text, but not "light" or any mention of the Holy Spirit; so that unless the translator took the old Rouen answer, and added the Durham to it —and this intentional combination of the two answers is not at all(2) impossible—we must adopt the suggestion that I have made that these two lines were interpolated by a scribe, who intended to adapt his copy of the original English translation to the answer above quoted from the Sarum missal.

Such interpolation would not prove a midland origin of the translation. But if I should appear to any of my readers to have failed in making good my suggestion that the first two lines represent the old Rouen answer (St Luke, i, 35); and they assume that the four lines of the text, as it now stands, were the work of the translator and intended as the rendering of the answer which was universal in the southern province,—even this assumption, although at first sight it may seem to do so, does not necessarily touch the theory I have advanced in the introduction.

The answer of the Sarum use even as a part of the prescribed order of mass was not peculiar to the southern province. We have seen (page 258, *n.* 5) that it was an alternative in the Rouen fourteenth-century missal; and though it does not appear in the earlier missal, it by no means follows that it had not been previously used in the Church. In that case Dan Jeremy—supposing he wrote in the twelfth century—might very well have adopted it; or, if not, it is very conceivable that the later answer might have been interpolated in the original treatise before it was translated.

But there is a still further, and—if the reader accepts my suggestion (p. 257) that the people had ceased to answer "on hie" when the translation was made—a complete answer to an objection that the Sarum form proves the midland origin of the translation, in the fact, that although the Caroline answer to the Orate held its own in the York Mass, and was used by the officiating clergy, down to the Reformation,—*secretè* though it were,(3)—the Sarum

---

(1) MS. Harl. 5289, fol. 280 *b.* "Liber Sancti Cuthberti ex procuratione domini Johannis prioris Dunolm" (Johannes Fossor, Prior 1342 —1374).

This was also the answer at the Benedictine monastery of Bec (Mart. I, 242): an alternative in the MS. mass, printed by M. Flacius Illyricus, which was written for the Benedictine monastery of Hornbach in the diocese of Metz (*ib.* 184); an alternative also in the Benedictine monastery of Stablo on the Recht (*ib.* 213); and in that of St Gregory in the diocese of Basle (*ib.* 216). Cf. the Cistercian answer, *post,* p. 264.

(2) Witness the Beauvais answer referred to, *ante,* p. 258, n. 5.

(3) See *ante,* p. 100.

answer, with verbal variations which are also to be found in the
Sarum printed Horæ, was introduced in the York printed Horæ,
for the use of those who were simply hearing mass, as follows:

"*Whan the preest turneth*(1) *after the lauatory.* Spiritus sancti
gratia illustret et illuminet cor tuum et labia tua et accipiat dominus hoc sacrificium de manibus tuis dignum pro peccatis et offensionibus nostris."(2)

P. 24, C. 127. *Swilke prayers I walde ʒe toke.* It will be observed that the
later text cuts out lines 267—272, and in these two next (l. 127-8)
alters the rubric as to answering the priest aloud into a direction
for a silent prayer, as has been already pointed out, p. 255. Even
if we had not the older text before us, a later hand might have
been detected in the use of ʒe, instead of þu, which is invariably
used in the earlier text, and elsewhere in this MS., e. g. C 93, 94,
102, 106, 224, &c.

C. 129-32. It serves to illustrate what is said, p. 257, as to the congregation having ceased to make answer to the priest in the
fifteenth century, that the prayer which is here retained in the text
does not follow the monastic use which was observed at Rievaulx,
for which monastery the MS. was written. I am able to give the
answer there used from a Cistercian Missal already quoted, p. 188,
which for the reason there given, we know was used in this country, and very possibly was used at Rievaulx or some other Cistercian house in Yorkshire: "Dominus sit in corde tuo et in labiis
tuis: suscipiatur de manibus tuis sacrificium istud: et orationes
tuæ ascendant in memoriam ante Deum pro nostra et totius populi
salute. Amen."(3)

MS. A, *n.* (1). þo *awter kyste.* This must be either a corrupt reading awkwardly embodying a gloss as to the "lowting" of the altar
being accompanied by a kiss; or else the altar is called awter-kyste,
much as sometimes in the present day we hear it called altar-
table.

The rubric in the York use (*ante*, p. 100, l. 15) would alone
justify the first suggestion; and the rubrics of all the other English uses in one form or another direct the priest to kiss the altar
before turning to the people.

In respect to the alternative suggestion, I remember the rough
handling I received from some of my critics, who seemingly had
not been at the pains to cast their eyes over the examples I had

---

(1) The southern *-eth* of the verb shows the inclination to adopt the
fashion of the court in language, as well as ritual. A similar forsaking of old
northern forms will be pointed out in the Bidding Prayer, No. V.

(2) *York Horæ*, fol. 13 *b.* Cf. the answer in the Sarum Mass, *ante*, p. 260.
See also the same rubric and answer with the same variations "*illustret et*"
and "*dignum*" in the *Sarum Horæ*, Paris, Vostre, 1507.

(3) *Missale ad usum Cisterciensis Ordinis*, Paris, Petit, 1516, fol. 82 *b.*

quoted, because I had spoken of wooden altars in England before
the Reformation, and it is not unlikely that the fact of wooden altars
being used to keep vestments may be equally new to them, and
therefore equally incredible.

But not to encumber this note with proofs as to the practice of
the Eastern Church, or the Church in Italy in earlier centuries, I
will simply refer to the documents quoted above, p. 165-6, which
are more nearly the date of the present MS.

I will only add in respect to the mention of *kiste* that this name
is of constant occurrence for the *cista*, the chest or "locker" for
keeping the vestments and other ornaments of the altar, and that,
apart from its being used as an aumbry, the altar was called *arca*
in the sixth century. Grancolas, in speaking of altars being sometimes made very much like a box (*à peu prés comme un cofre*),
quotes Gregory of Tours as speaking in this way of the altar of the
Holy Rood at Poitiers, which St Radegonde had caused to be built
—"At illa tumultum sentiens venientium, ad Sanctæ Crucis arcam
deportari poposcit."(1)

P. 25, E. 258. The "ȝernynges" in the older text may have led to this
    variation—cf. "desire," F. 100—or it may be to introduce the
    prayer for forgiveness.
E. 261-2. Notice the change in the ending of the participle.
E. 270. See note as to "noght worth," *ante*, p. 254, B. 270. *ioynud*,
    joined (*with*) or enjoined.
F. 100. *desire*, for "ȝernynge" of the older texts.

P. 26, B. 280. *his priuey prayers.* The *secretæ orationes* or *secretæ*(2) of
    the Roman and later Anglican rubrics, Order of mass, *ante*, p. 100,
    l. 26 ; " his secro," Vernon, *ante*, p. 143, l. 545. The *Myroure*, p. 328,
    explains : " But before the preface, the preste sayeth preuy prayers
    by hymselfe. whyche are called secretes. and tho prayers he endeth
    as he dothe other collectes. or orysons. tyll he cometh to these
    wordes. *Per omnia secula seculorum*, And these wordes he sayeth by
    note. and so begynneth the Preface. And therto ye aunswer.
    Amen. And so ye saye. *Amen*, vpon the prayers that he hathe
    prayed pryuely in the secretes."

    This prayer was also called *secreta parva*, to distinguish it from
    the canon, and Durandus(3) speaks of it as the *secretela* or *secretella*.
    Another name was *super oblata*, as in early sacramentaries, the
    Anglo-Saxon Ritual, p. 108 ; Archbishop Egbert's Pontifical, pp.
    51, 52, &c., and originally in the Ambrosian rite, though in the
    modernized rubrics it has been printed *super oblatam*.

---

(1) *Hist.* lib. 9, cap. 19.—Quoted Grancolas, *L'Ancien Sacramentaire de
l'Eglise. Tome II, Partie I, Paris, 1699, p. 39.
    (2) Also *secretum ;* e. g. *in Coronatione Regis.*—Maskell, *Monumenta*, III,
43, &c.
    (3) *Rationale*, 4, xxvii, 1.

These prayers, like the collect, epistle, gospel, &c., varied according to the day.(1)   They are invariably in the plural, and are not
private in the sense of being offered by the priest for himself.
There are many private in this last sense for use at the offertory
in old MSS., rubricated, *"pro semet ipso"; "ad beneplacitum";*
or *"apologia sacerdotis",* or *"presbyteri"*—almost always in the
first person singular.   They were not originally part of any established *"ordo,"*(2) but the reader may observe two in the York
Mass (*ante*, p. 98, ll. 29—32, and p. 100, ll. 11—14), and others
have been inserted in the Roman Missal in comparatively recent
times.

But though not private in this sense, there is no doubt they
have been said in silence, wherever the Roman rite has prevailed,
from the ninth or tenth century.(3)   Towards the end of the seventeenth century some of the French bishops made an effort to
re-establish what they maintained was the ancient practice, in
respect to this prayer, and the canon.   Bossuet put forth a revised
edition of the *Missale Meldense* for his own diocese (*Meaux*), in
conformity with his view of the requirements of public worship,
which led to an animated controversy.   It was maintained against
him that this prayer was called secret because it was said *secretè*,
and that it was said *secretè*, because it was *secreta* or *arcana;*(4)
but, as pointed out by De Vert, this was reasoning in a circle,(5)
and proved nothing.   Bossuet answered that the prayer was called
secreta either because it was offered over the bread and wine which
had been set apart (*secreta*) from the offerings of the people, or else
—which is much more probable, and was the view advocated by
Grancolas, De Vert, and others—because it was a part of the *Missa
fidelium*.   The faithful(6) were then *secreti* or by themselves apart

---

(1) They were not retained in the Book of Common Prayer at the
Reformation, and the only survival of this ancient devotion in the Church of
England is to be found in the Order of Coronation.   The Archbishop, after
receiving the bread and wine from the sovereign, and reverently placing them
upon the altar, says the prayer, altogether primitive in its character : " Bless,
O Lord, we beseech thee, these thy gifts," &c.   See Maskell, *Mon.* III, 43,
" *Munera, quæsumus, Domine, oblata sanctifica,*" &c.   Cf. (Egbert's *Pontifical*,
p. 104) the " *super oblata* " in the mass "*pro regibus in die Benedictionis.*"
(2) " Non ex aliqua ordine sed ex ecclesiastica consuetudine."   Ivonis
Carnotensis, *Micrologus*, c. xi.
(3) Cardinal Bona (*Rer. Liturg.* II, xiii, 1) gives his opinion that the
custom of saying the canon aloud in the Latin Church was put an end to in
the tenth century—and this is probably correct of the whole Church, as distinguished from exceptional practice of the ninth or even the eighth century.
(4) Martene (*Tom.* I, p. 143) brings forward this name as given to the
prayer in many old MSS.
(5) *Explication des Cérémonies*, 1719, I, 390.
(6) This prayer is called *Oratio plebis*, in the 6th canon of the First
Council of Lyons (A.D. 517), where *plebs* is used for the "chosen people," as

from the Catechumens and others, who up to that point had been allowed to join in the service; though, in accordance with the discipline of reserve in the early Church, they were not allowed to be present at the "mysteries," which therefore were properly *secreta* or *arcana*. This would explain why the canon was also called *secret* when it was still said aloud and the people answered Amen. It was called *secretum Missæ*(1) in this country as late as the twelfth century, though the name *secreta* had been very early applied κατ' ἐξόχην to the prayers we are now considering.

But there is one fact beyond dispute, which, as far as this prayer is concerned, is far more decisive than any *à priori* or etymological arguments in proving that it was not said in silence from the first throughout the West. In the Ambrosian rite, where, as already mentioned, it is called the *oratio super oblata* or *oblatam*, a rubric directs—or did direct(2)—the priest to say it *clara voce*, or, according to Gerbert,(3) *alta voce*, and it is impossible to suppose that this could have been changed from "*tacita voce*," unless we had some record of the innovation.

---

in the canon of the mass "*plebs tua sancta,*" *ante*, p. 108, l. 12. See Gran-colas, *Liturgie Ancienne et Moderne*, 1752, p. 92.

(1) In the *Consuetudinarium* of Sarum, compiled by St Osmund, and printed Maskell, A. E. L., 180. Also in the northern province, at the legantine Council held at York, A.D. 1195, Constit. 3.—Wilkins, I, 501.

(2) Martene, I, 173, from the edition of 1560. So also in the *Rubricæ Generales*, § 18. I have the Milan edition of 1849 before me, and the rubric there stands as I here quote it, but I do not know how far it may have been since altered. In the last edition of "*L'Ordinario della Messa secondo il Rito Ambrosiano, colla versione Italiana*" prefixed to the *Vero Penitente* of Diotallevi I find (p. 34) a note under "*per omnia sæcula sæculorum,*" explaining that "This ending of the secret" (*segrete*—the Roman instead of the Ambrosian name) "is said by the priest aloud ('*ad alta voce*') because the people confirm what he has said ('*con voce bassa*') with a low voice."

For more than a thousand years the Roman *curia* has directed its efforts against the peculiarities of the Ambrosian rite, and since the beginning of the sixteenth century it has been modified in many respects. The comparison of our texts discloses changes in the manner of the people's devotions in the middle ages, and it may not be without interest to give another example of the process in the present day. I need not remind the reader who has paid attention to liturgical questions that the rubric and prayer speaking of the breaking of the body of Christ has been the subject of much controversy among divines of the Roman communion, and it is therefore very significant that in this Italian *Lay-folks Mass-book* (p. 49) the prayer at the "Fraction" (cf. *ante*, p. 112, l. 15) beginning *Corpus tuum frangitur* is translated "*L'Ostia che si spezza,*" &c.

Early English writers in their books "for the lewed" had no scruple in reproducing the language of their rubrics. For example, Robert of Brunne :

". . . euery prest aftyr þe sacre
He parteþ þere Goddys body yn þre."—*H. S.* 7950-1.

(3) "*Oratio super oblata alta voce dicenda*, ut expresse habetur."—*Disquisitiones*, I, 332.

P. 26, B. 281. *Knele þou doun.* It will be observed that there is no corresponding direction in the later texts, for they assume that the people
are already kneeling, see note, p. 251. The Vernon MS., *ante,* p.
143, ll. 545-7, agrees with this in directing the layman to kneel at
the secret.

B. 282. *in blak wryten.* Cf. the mention of *rubrics,* ll. 57, 624.

B. 283-4. *amende, hende.* Here, as in l. 36, the northern plural is
retained on account of the rhyme.

B. 287—296. It will be observed that this prayer of the layman during the " *secrets* " is an echo of the priest's " *Orate,*" *ante,* p. 100,
ll. 20-3, in asking it—though the *meum pariter que vestrum* . . . .
sacrificium, in grammatical exactness and in the sense which, in
theory at least, was always maintained in the middle ages,(1) ought
to have been " (offered) *by* the priest and by us all," but has been
paraphrased "*for* the priest and for us all."

B. 288. *þis solempne sacrifice,* that is the oblation of the bread and
wine as a sacrifice of praise and thanksgiving. It may be that
some of my readers who connect the idea of an offering for sin
with the sacrifices of masses—and this whether they accept or
protest against the doctrine—may not be prepared for this application of the name of sacrifice to the unconsecrated gifts, but the
name is invariably used in every one of the many mediæval
orders of mass I have had an opportunity of examining (for one,
the York use, *ante,* p. 100, l. 4, l. 18, &c.) ; and the elaborate
ceremonial which was prescribed by the rubrics and other ritual
regulations of western churches, and which is still observed at the
" great entrance " in the East, bear witness to the special solemnity
which was associated with this rite, until in the West an increas-
ing and almost exclusive prominence, doctrinal and ceremonial,
was given to the subsequent blessing and consecration of the gifts.

B. 292. *þo sakring to se.* Sacring is properly the consecration or
blessing of the sacramental elements ("Sacryn or halwyn, *Con-
secro, sacro.*" PP. 440), but from the twelfth century onwards it
was so closely connected with the elevation, which men could see
—and the words of the canon they could not hear—that it was
used in popular language for the elevation of the host, and not
only for the elevation of the host when it was consecrated (*ante,*

---

(1) "A cunctis fidelibus, non solum viris sed et mulieribus sacrificium illud
laudis offertur, licet ab uno specialiter offerri sacerdote videatur."—Petri
Damiani *Dominus robiscum,* c. viii. Five hundred years later we have the
same idea, though not so well put, in the *Book of Ceremonies* (quoted above,
p. 178), " The priest is a common minister in the name and stead of the whole
congregation, and as the mouth of the same, not only rendreth thanks unto
God for Christ's death and passion, but also maketh the common prayer and
commendeth the people and their necessities in the same " (i. e. *the mass*)
"unto Almighty God."—Strype, *Memorials,* Appendix, p. 285. Cf. the words
of the canon, *ante,* p. 104, l. 30, "*qui tibi offerunt hoc sacrificium laudis.*"

p. 106, l. 32), but also when it was again elevated(1) at the end of the canon (*ante*, p. 110, l. 21), according to an ancient rite, corresponding with the elevation in the Eastern Church, when the priest in all the liturgies now extant cries out, Τὰ ἅγια τοῖς ἁγίοις (*Sancta sanctis*, Holy things for the holy).

In the rubric, B. 406, we find the more exact phrase, *levation to behold*, but no doubt the one above was what passed current among the people.

Cf. " All came this lady to behold
And all still vppon her gazinge
As people that behold the sacring."
Percy Folio, I, 161, l. 524-6.

P. 26, B. 293. *lyuen.* The change to the midland third person plural in -*en* adds a syllable to the line to the injury of the metre. Cf. the northern -*es* in C 139. In F 119, the northern *lyves* is retained, but the scribe not improbably in " *the lyues* " supposed he had the definite article and a plural substantive before him, instead of the plural of the verb and the older form of the relative (þe), which not improbably was the reading of the original text, elsewhere altered into þat.

Alle þat lyuen in gods name, as elsewhere, of Christ. Cf. "All they that do confess thy holy name."—B. C. P.

B. 294. Cf. " Mary Moder, meke and mylde
Fro schame and synne that ʒe us schyllde
For gret on grownd ʒe gone with childe,
Gabriele nuncio."
Christmas Carols, Halliwell, Percy Soc., p. 7.

B. 295. *hethen are past.* Cf. Hampole :
" Wharfor it semes þat mes syngyng
May titest þe saul out of payn bryng,
þat passes hethen in charite."—*P. C.* 3702-4.

hethen, though a northern word, has been left out in C, probably because obsolete in the middle of the fifteenth century, and is changed to *hensse* and *hennes* in E and F.

B. 300—302. The priest had gone to his book (B 279), which had

---

(1) Becon (*Reliques*, fol. 130 b) remarks upon the name of sacring being given to the elevation, and (*Displaying*, Works, III, 277) speaks of the minor elevation, as it came to be called after the first elevation had been established, being " called the second sacring." It was, in fact, the third elevation, at least according to those uses where the cup was elevated as in England, but was nevertheless spoken of by ritualists as the second, *e. g.* Grancolas (*Liturgie Ancienne et Moderne*, 1752, p. 143): "The custom of ringing a small bell at the second elevation, and at low mass of answering *Ave salus*, &c., which are spoken to Jesus Christ, whom men elevate (*qu'on élève*), is a remnant of the ancient discipline, and shows that at some time there had been this elevation only." So also, p. 135. But he calls this the third elevation, *e. g. ib.* p. 133.

been flitted to the north end of the altar before the gospel (B 155), in order to "look his privy prayers" (B 280), and now "after privy praying," that is, when he has finished the *secreta*, he removes him a little space to the midst of the altar,(1) and there begins the preface with *per omnia sæcula* (C 144), which was in fact the ending of the secreta, but being said aloud in the tone of the preface, was considered a part of it.

P. 26, B. 303. *Stande vp þou als men þe biddis.* The Eastern origin of the answer to the *Orate* has been pointed out (*page* 259), and although it is in itself a thing altogether indifferent, it may not be unacceptable to those who are interested in tracing the families, so to speak, of different liturgies, to draw attention to what seems to be a similar character in this direction to stand at this place instead of continuing to kneel, as was the later practice. In fact, the connection is better established by coincidences in these smaller matters, which are not likely to have been expressly borrowed, than by the similarity of rites or devotions which may very well have been adopted on the score of their importance.

It will be observed that there is no reference to this direction in texts C and F which were adapted to the practice in this country ; nor have I met with any trace of any such direction in any use of the Latin rite, and certainly not in any of the old English uses. But in the Greek liturgies, and the so-called liturgy of St Clement in the Apostolical Constitutions, and in almost all the oriental liturgies collected by Renaudot, there is to be found in this part of the service either the Στῶμεν καλῶς of the deacon, to which St Chrysostom refers,(2) or some similar direction to stand ; and, like the πρόσχωμεν (*ante*, p. 254)—curiously enough with reference to the survival of a custom once rooted in the traditions of the people—in many cases, as we learn from Renaudot,(3) the untranslated Greek words are reproduced more or less exactly in the vernacular liturgies of the Copts and Syrians, as we also find them in the liturgy of the native Christians of St Thomas.(4)

When therefore we take into account the Eastern origin of the Gallican liturgy and its influence upon the service of the Church, not only in France, but also in this country, and especially upon those parts of it in which the people were more directly concerned, it will not appear fanciful to suggest that in the direction of the text we may recognize an Eastern form cropping up through the

---

(1) Cf. " *Ut autem sacerdos finierit secretas, retrahat se contra medium altaris, dicens* Per omnia sæcula sæculorum."—*Lib. Usuum Cisterc.* c. 53, ap. Martene. IV, 61.

(2) *De Incomprehensibili Dei natura.* Hom. IV, § 5, *Ed. Ben.* I, 478 C. He also quotes these words, but in another part of the liturgy, Hom. II, in II Cor. i, 11, *Ed. Ben.* X, 435 D.

(3) *Liturg. Oriental.*, Tom. I, 225 ; Tom. II, 75.

(4) Howard, *Christians of St Thomas*, 206.

Roman order, if not in this country, when the translation was made, at least in France when the original was written, and this although—whatever date we may assign to Dan Jeremy—he must have lived several hundred years after the Roman had displaced the national liturgy.

As to the "bidding," the words might very well have been used, though no longer in the service books, or a signal might have called the worshippers to their feet, and we find this practice still existing in the diocese of Orleans, though noted as peculiar, so late as the end of the seventeenth century.(1)

P. 27, F. 113. *God rehersé.* This may have been written by mistake for *receive*, or it might perhaps have been suggested by the thought that Christ presents in heaven what the Church offers on earth.

F. 119. *the lyues*, see above on B. 293, page 269.

P. 28, B. 307. *Sursum corda*, see order of mass, *ante*, p. 102, l. 24.

B. 308, *At þo ende*, sc. of the preface, *ante*, p. 102, l. 25—p. 103, l. 6.

[he] *sayes* sanctus *thryese.* It will be noticed that E reads *he says* in this place, and though in that text, notwithstanding the want of intelligence of the scribe, or perhaps in consequence of it, many old readings have been preserved which have disappeared in the other more recent texts, on looking at it again I am inclined to think I was wrong in adopting this reading and inserting it conjecturally in the B text. "Sayes" is the northern form of the second person, singular and plural, and in the York bidding prayer (*ante*, p. 66, l. 17, and p. 67, l. 1) we find the people bidden to pray with this form, "Says a paternoster and ave." It is therefore not at all unlikely that *sayes* here is a direction to the people to say the *Sanctus*, though the midland scribe may not have altered it to the "*saye*" to which he was more accustomed, as he did four lines lower down, from supposing that it here referred to the priest.

Martene (I, 143) draws attention to the fact that anciently the people joined in singing the *Sanctus*, citing several councils to that effect. It was the rule in this country, as witness a rubric in Archbishop Egbert's Pontifical, "*Dicit omnis clericus et populus*, Sanctus, Sanctus, Sanctus,"(2) and we find it referred to in the *Meditacyons* elsewhere quoted: "So lyke wyse dispose yow to say with þe prest *Sanctus, Sanctus, Sanctus.*"(3) As in other cases, already noticed, the people appear to have ceased to join in the *Sanctus*, as time went on, and it was said by the priest alone, or sung by the choir to elaborate music. According to the Roman rite, the *Sanctus* is said by the priest "*voce mediocri*," which cor-

---

(1) "Tout le monde se leve à *sursum corda* par geste."— *Voyages Litur-giques en France*, 220.

(2) *Pontifical of Egbert, Archbishop of York* [A.D. 732—766], from a MS. of the tenth century, *ed.* Greenwell, p. 120.

(3) MS. Bodleian, A. Wood, 17, fol. 12, see p. 168.

responds to the "stille steven" of these rubrics, and the people
kneel.(1) In England the priest "spoke the *Sanctus* with a loud
voice,"(2) and, at least in the thirteenth century, the people stood,
though we gather from our later texts they subsequently ceased
to do so. At the *Sanctus* it became the custom in this country
from the thirteenth century onwards at public masses at the high
altar (capitular, conventual, or parish, as the case might be) to
ring a bell, often hung in a bell-cote above the chancel arch,
which was called the Sanctus bell, or sauce bell, in order to give
notice to those who were unable to be present that the canon, or
sacring, was about to begin.

　　Cf. Lydgate's *Vertue of the Masse* (above, p. 163), p. 12 :

¶ **The sanctus sunge thries.**　　　　[fol. 18]

¶ The olde prophete . holy Isaye
Sawe in hevene . a trone of dignite
Where Seraphyn songe . withe *euery* Ierarchie
Sanctus . sanctus . sanctus . before the Trinite
After preface rehersed . tymes thre
Withe *noyse* melodious . and *after* that osanna
Highe in excelsis . to-fore the mageste
Afore the sacryng . of oure gostly manna.

P. 28, B. 310. The later texts leave out the prayer, l. 314-27, which, it
will be observed, is founded on the invariable part of the preface
(p. 104, l. 4-10). In the German Messbüchlein there is a "*Layen
gebett zum* Sanctus," which is to be said when the priest begins
the canon, and the choir are singing the *Sanctus* and *Benedictus*,(3)
and though this overlapping of the several parts of the service was
forbidden by different councils, it is not improbable that it gave
rise to the directions in the text, unless indeed they may be
accounted for as a reminiscence at Rouen, of the *Collectio post
Sanctus* of the Gallican liturgy. The omission of all reference to
any prayer in this place, in our later texts, when they were adapted
for English use, is more or less in favour of this suggestion.

---

(1) De Vert, III, 215.　　　　　(2) Becon, *Displaying*, p. 266.
(3) Fol. 142. The Messbüchlein here quoted (Dilingen, 1573) is described
in the title-page as "Ein gar altes, aber vast nutzliches Büch" (*a very old,
but most profitable book*), and contains the Latin of the ordinary and canon
of the mass, with a translation, explanation of the ceremonies, and devotions
in very quaint old German ; and is interesting in reference to our present
treatise, as having had the same object in view. It was edited (*inn Truck
geben*) and dedicated to the Dean and chapter of Augsburg by Adam
Walasser. He speaks of himself as having lived twenty years at Dilingen,
but whether a layman or cleric it does not appear. He seems to have been
very zealous for the "long-wished-for 'restitution' of the true old catholic
faith," taking for his example Tauler, and "such like excellent gostly
teachers," whom he brings forward in his introduction to two treatises by
Luis de Granada, "*verteutscht*" by him and published in the following year.

P. 28, B. 320. Cf. " Louede and blessede ay mote þou be,
    And with all herte I thanke the
    Of all þat þou has done and wroghte."
     Religious Pieces, Perry, p. 60, Nassynton, l. 25-7.

B. 328. *When þis is sayde, knele þou doune.* Cf. Vernon, *ante*,
p. 143, l. 558-9 :

  " Bi-twene þe sanctus, and þe sakeryng,
   ʒe schal preye stondynge,"

where "sakeryng"(1) appears to be used not of the consecration
and elevation only, but of the whole canon ; for the Vernon MS.
would seem to agree with our present text, as (l. 563) it goes on
to say, " Seþþe schul ʒe kneel adoun."

Perhaps, however, this difference may be attributed to the
ritual being in a state of transition, the congregation standing
during the first part of the canon and kneeling afterwards ; whereas
at the first they stood throughout, as afterwards, and when our later
texts were written, they knelt throughout the whole of the canon.

B. 330—333. The prayer follows this division—from l. 336 to
l. 354 thanksgiving for mercies received, followed (l. 355—360) by
a prayer for grace ; and then the prayer for all estates of men
(l. 361—387), and everlasting life (l. 388—397).

It will be observed that this division corresponds with that
of the canon. First the priest (p. 124, l. 18) prays for the
acceptance of the gifts, already offered at the offertory—like the
Ἔτι προσφέρομεν of the Greek liturgies—on behalf of the whole
church ; for which he then prays, and for the members of it, with
a memento of the living. The memento of the dead comes after
the consecration (*page* 110, l. 3), and it will be observed that the
prayers in the text (B. 454) follow the same arrangement.

But though this devotion for the lay-folk corresponds with the
main divisions of the canon, its greater fulness and particularity
shows that it is not borrowed from it. On the contrary, like the
prayer in English to be said at the office,(2) it continued to supply
for individual worshippers that which was lost in the public worship of the church by the disuse of litanies—except indeed so far
as it was supplied in parish churches by the bidding prayers.
And we may further remark that in its resemblance to eastern
forms, where they differ from the Latin, it is suggestive of the
people's prayers, which under the different names, never ceased to
be an invariable feature of the Eucharistic office according to the
several Greek liturgies, rather than of the *preces*, still said each

---

(1) *Sacrament* was also used for the whole canon :
  "Next the secrete, after the offeratory
  The preface folwithe afore the sacrament."
    Lydgate, *Vertue of the Masse* (above, p. 163), *fol.* 183.
(2) B. 91—114, and note. p. 191.

year, according to the rubrics of the Roman missal, on Easter Eve, or at Milan on all the Sundays in Lent.

P. 28, B. 331. Here the northern *ilk a man* and *þan* are left for the rhyme. In lines 612-13 the rhyme allowed a change to the midland forms.

P. 29, E. 328. *all men* replaces *ilk a man*. F 128 the *ilk* becomes *eche*.

P. 30, B. 336. We now come to the canon, or still-mass,(1) which long before the time of Dan Jeremy had been said in silence, the earlier *disciplina arcani* having been extended from the heathen to the layman. The knowledge of the words was in some cases kept from him of express purpose,(2) and in all the prescribed gestures of the priest had to serve as the sufficient signal for his devotions.

Thus, for example, the rubricated headings of the Meditacyons already quoted from (p. 168, &c.) :

"From þe begynyng of þe Canon which ys when þe prest after þe Sanctus, and after þat he haith kyssyd þe Crucifix(3) on the masse book, dothe Inclyne A-fore þe Avter unto the sacring be done."—Fol. 12 *b*.

B. 339. *of more gode.* C reads *of mare* and F *of mi*. The southern scribe would seem to have written *mi* for the northern *ma* (mare) in the copy before him ; and *godnesse*, because the use of good, as a substantive, in the singular may have already become obsolete.

B. 342. *My lyue, my lymmes, þou has me lent.*

---

(1) The canon was also called "*swimesse*" in early English (2. O. E. *Homilies*, Morris, p. 97, 242), from *swigan* or *swigian*, to be silent ; *swiga*, silence.—Cf. σιγᾶν, σιγή.

In modern German "*stille Messe*" is used of low mass (Binterim, II, 3, 240), but in the sixteenth and earlier centuries it was used, as in English, of the canon. Thus in the Messbüchlein (*above*, p. 272, note) it is explained, "*Der Canon haisst auch die Stillmess, darumb dass alle ding darinn haimlich und still gelesen werden.*" Fol. 114 *b*. In a bidding prayer, used in the Benedictine Monastery of St Blaise in the Black Forest, and quoted by Gerbert (*the Abbot*) from a xivth century MS., the Canon is called "*die stille Meesse.*" —Disq. I, 369.

(2) See Vernon MS., *ante*, p. 146, l. 665—670, and the note there.

(3) The crucifixion was often the subject of an illumination before the canon ; and in earlier printed missals there was almost always a full page woodcut of a crucifix, or the initial of the *Te igitur* (*ante*, p. 104, and note on Tau, p. 206) was a crucifix.

This kissing of the crucifix in the mass-book does not appear to have been directed by the rubric of any English use, but Gerbert (*Disq.* I, 413) has collected a number of authorities on this point, and draws attention to the fact that old missals are often stained in this place from being kissed.

All the English uses required the priest to kiss the altar (see the Ebor rubric, *ante*, p. 104, l. 16). So too in the *Book of Ceremonies*—"the priest . . . . . inclining his body, maketh a cross upon the altar and kisseth it" (Strype, *Memorials*, App. p. 287).

Cf. " For men sal þan strayte acount yhelde
Of alle þair tyme of yhouthe and elde ;
Noght anly of ane or twa yhere,
Bot of alle þe tyme þat God þam lent."—*P. C.* 5644-7.

" And cryede ofte vpon cryste . for some socour hym to sende
If any lyfe were hem lente . in þis worlde lengur."
Chevelere Assigne, 111-12.

" Adam, for þou has left mi lare
And broken þe bode þat I bad are,
And mare wroght efter þi wife
þan after me þat lent þe life."
MS. Harl. 4296, fol. 77, quoted by Dr Morris, *P. C.* p. 304.

" Lent time " is habitually used—at least on the Yorkshire Wolds,
where this note is written—in the restricted sense of the days of
our age above the " three score years and ten " of the psalmist.
It will have been seen that our fore-fathers used *lent* of life and
time in general ; and not only so, but the same phrase is applied
to all the good gifts of God, and the right use of them is enforced
as being loans or trusts to be accounted for, when the Lord cometh
and reckoneth with his servants (*St Matt.* xxv. 19)—a thought
still borne witness to—often unconsciously, though, it may be—by
the modern use of the word " talents."

Cf. " Ich hafe wennd inntill Ennglissh
Goddspelless hallȝhe lare,
Affterr þatt little witt tatt me
Min Drihhtin hafeþþ lenedd."—*Orm. Dedic.* 13-16.

" Als he þat gret and myghty es,
Es halden to defende þam þat er les ;
And þe ryche þam mykel rychesus has,
To gyf þam þat here in povert gas ;
And men of laghe alswa to travayle
And to counsaile þam þat askes counsayle ;
And leches alswa, if þai wyse ware,
To hele þam þat er seke and sare ;
And maysters of þair science to ken
Namly þam, þat er unlered men ;
And prechours Goddes worde to preche,
And þe way of lyf other to teche.
þus es ilk man halden with gude entent,
To help other of þat God has þam lent."—*P. C.* 5938-51.

See *post,* note on *læne life*, p. 62, l. 4.

P. 30, B. 344. *of þi grace.* Cf. Collect, Seventh after Trinity, " of thy
great mercy," and elsewhere B. C. P.

B. 345. *sere.* Here the later C, though written by a northern scribe, reads "many," though (C. 42, 229, 258) elsewhere it has retained it. See note, p. 18

P. 30, B. 348. Cf.

    "For godes loue he þolede moche : þat deore him hadde iboȝt."

Lives of Saints, Furnivall, xvii, 77.

    C. 154. *When þe preste þe preface hes doone.* No *collectio post Sanctus*, as in B. 314—327.

P. 31, E. 334. *I wel owe.* Note the change to the personal form, and so F. 135.

P. 32, B. 354. *godes.* C here reads *gude* in the singular, where we may observe the *-e* is sounded, and the reference being to the one, gift of forgiveness, there can be no doubt this is the true reading. The scribe may have made the alteration from the "good gifts" of God being generally spoken of in the plural. See a passage in Hampole as to the several account which men must give, each for himself:

> "Men sal alswa yhelde rekkenynges sere
> Of al gudes þat God has gefen þam here,
> Als of gudes of kynde and gudes of graces,
> And gudes of hap þat men purchases."

And he then goes on to specify them—*P. C.* 5894, &c. See later in the *Myroure*, p. 68 : Lord "that is geuer of all gooddes"; and so in the Book of Common Prayer: "Almighty God, the giver of all good gifts."

> Cf. "Godes of Laverd to se leve I
> In þe land of livand nou."—Ps. (27) xxvi, 13.

B. 354-5. *moo, als-soo.* Manifestly an alteration of the midland scribe from the northern rhymes, ma, alswa, as in C.

> Cf. "And Thomas Alqwyn spekes alswa
> Of þis mater, and of other ma."—*P. C.* 3948-9.

> "Salle love God and thank him þare
> Of alle gudes, both les and mare."—*P. C.* 8305-6.

B. 360-1. *Wirk, Kirk.* Here the northern forms are retained for the rhyme.

B. 361. *state of holy kirk.* Cf. "Ye shulle bydde for tham, that the stat of Holy Cherche and of this Lond well maintanid." Bidding Prayer, Diocese of Worcester, A.D. 1349. *Forms of Bidding Prayer*, H. O. C.[oxe, now Bodley Librarian], Oxford, 1840, p. 12.

B. 362. It will be observed this alone of our five MSS. omits the mention of the Pope, and in so doing, as pointed out in the Introduction, supplies a note of time, which enables us to fix the date of the translation at a time when the see of Rome was vacant for some unusually lengthened interval.

P. 32, B. 362. Cf. "Ut domnum apostolicum et omnes gradus ecclesiæ . . . . . . Ut archiepiscopum(1) nostrum et omnem congregationem sibi commissam in sancta religione conservare digneris."—*Preces*, (Ebor.) *Horæ*, f. 94 *b*.

B. 365. *wele mayntenandc.* Cf. the prayer that the good Yorkshir hermit, Richard of Hampole, asks his readers to offer for him:

> "Pray for hym specially þat it dru,
> þat if he lyf, God safe hym harmles,
> And mayntene hys lyf in alle gudenes."—*P. C.* 9616-18.

And so, too, of the last Emperor of Rome:

> "þe whilk sal wele maynteyn his state,
> And þe empire, withouten debate,
> And it governe thurgh laghe and witte,
> Als lang als he sal hald itte."—*P. C.* 4091-4.

B. 366. *states.*

Cf. "that nane has power to do bot bishop allane
that has the state and the stede of Cristes apostels."

Archbishop Thoresby's *Catechism*, f. 296 *b*.

C. 183. Note that Queen is omitted. This enables us to fix the exact date of the MS.—See Introduction.

P. 34, B. 368. *Oure sib men.* In a prayer "*For all estates*" in the primer of 1555 "omnes consanguinitate ac familiaritate . . . nobis iunctos."

Wele-willandes. Cf. "omnibus benefactoribus nostris."—*Preces*, (Ebor.) *Horæ*, f. 95.

B. 369. *tenandes and seruandes.* This one of the indications of the class for whom these devotions were written, and this mention of those in a lower station shows the practically religious tone which Dan Jeremy seems everywhere to have desired to give to these devotions.

B. 371. The same remark applies to "Merchants," whom I have not found specially mentioned in other forms of devotion.

tilmen. Cf. Bidding prayer, p. 65, l. 7 ; p. 70, l. 1 ; p. 78, l. 32, where landtilland. "Bless the labourers pains and travails of all such as either till the earth, or exercise any other handicraft." —*Primer*, 1553, reprint, P.S. p. 460.

B. 374-5. *specialy, haly,* not altered to holy, as elsewhere in this text, on account of the rhyme.

B. 377. *sclaunder, myscounforth.* In the York Horæ (f. 184) is a prayer "for them that falleth in disclaunder, reprofe, or any maner of trybulatyons" ; and (f. 185) another "to thanke god of delyuerance out of trybulacyon or dysclaunder, reprofe, or other dysease, and that also he is broughte by goddes helpe to moche comforth."

---

(1) The Sarum form is "episcopos et abbates nostros," which I mention, as it may be useful in identifying the "use" of manuscripts.

P. 34, B. 377-9. *in stryue*, . . *prisonde*, . . *exilde*. Τοὺς ἐν φυλακαῖς, . . ἢ ἐν δίκαις, ἢ ἐν ἐξορίαις.—*Liturgy of St Mark*, Renaudot, I, 147; or Neale, *Tetralogia*, 113.

B. 378-9. *prisonde*, . . . *opon þe see*, . . . *exilde*. Μνήσθητι, Κύριε, πλεόντων, . . τῶν ἐν φυλακαῖς, . . καὶ ἐξορίαις.—*Liturgy of St James*, Trollope, p. 88, or Neale, *Tetralogia*, p. 151. Cf. the *preces* of the Ambrosian rite: "Pro navigantibus, . . in carceribus, . . in exsiliis constitutis."

B. 379. *deserit*. C. *disheryd*. To disherit, like the O.F. *déshériter*, was not only to disheir or disinherit and cut off from a future inheritance; but it was also to deprive of an actual possession.

Cf.　　　　　　　　"þat folk of Rome also
　　　　He (*Maximian*) fondede to deserie, and mony schames do,
　　　So þat þe deserites in to þis lond come
　　　To Constantyn, þe gode kyng, for defaute from Rome."
　　　　　　　　　　Robert of Gloucester, Hearne, 1810, p. 85.

"Also all thase that fals witnes beres or brynges forth rigthfull matrimon[y] to distrubill or any man or woman to deseryte of land or of rent, tenement or of any other catell."—*The grete cursing*, MS. Manual (Ebor), York Minster Library.

The disherited must have been a large class in times of rebellion, and other troubles so frequent in the middle ages;(1) and Dan Michel will have had ample justification for including "men and wifmen, and children deserited, and y-exiled "(2) among the miseries of war.

C. 188. *sugettes* replaces the "*tenants*" of other texts, in this which was written for a monastery, where the several members of the community had no tenants, though they had their servants and inferiors, and Rievaulx, like other abbeys, had large possessions.

The landed estates of the monks did not escape the mediæval satirists:

　　　"Sume say no masse in all a week
　　　　　Of deinties is her most food.
　　　　　They have lordships and bondmen;
　　　　This is a royall religion;
　　　　　Saint Benet made never none of hem
　　　　To have lordshipe of man ne toun.

　　　. . . . .

　　　　They ben clerkes, her courts they oversee,
　　　　　Her pore tenaunce fully they slite;
　　　　The higher that a man amerced be,
　　　　　The gladlier they woll it write."
　　　Complaint of Ploughman, Wright's *Political Poems*, I, 334-5.

---

(1) See a case of forfeited lands being restored to disherited nobles in 1268 on the payment of a fixed sum, which the clergy helped them to pay.—*Letters from Northern Registers*, Raine, pp. 17, 20.

(2) *Ayenbite of Inwyt*, Morris, p. 30.

P. 35, E. 376. *dysesud*, instead of *desheryd*, is not to be understood of mental disorder or bodily ailment.

Disease was used rather of perplexity, trouble and vexation of spirit, as in rubrics of prayers in the York Horæ : "Thys prayer followynge is for them that have labour in temptacyon, or have any other dyscase with gouernaunce of the people."(1)

Cf. "Dysese or greve. *Tedium, gravamen, calamitas, angustia.*"—*P.P.* 122.

In the Lollard paraphrase of Thoresby's Catechism (*fol.* 8) we find *disease* passing into its modern use : "þan visyte þy neyȝeboris þat arn bedreden, blynde & crokyd, & in oþer dysesys, & comfort fyrst here sowlys þat þey falle not in despayre ne grucchyngge agayn þeyre godys visitacioun."

F. 170. *bi tale*, for *alle* in the other texts. Except that "to" has been inserted, this reading would have improved the rythm after *alle* had ceased to be sounded as a dissyllable, and it may very well have been suggested by the enumeration of the several classes.

P. 36, B. 383. *to þi pay.* See note, *ante*, p. 244.

> Cf. " He preyed to god · his orison ·
> Wiþ a gret · deuocion
> þat hit mihte · ben him to pay
> þe masse þat he scholde · synge to-day."
> *Man of Suffolk*, Vernon MS., fol. 198.

B. 384. *Foly,* when first introduced from the French, seems to have had an ethical sense, which it no longer bears, though we may still trace it in our English Bible.(2) It was used of sin, and specially of sins of the flesh.

> " purgatory,
> Whar saules er clensed of alle foly."—*P.C.* 357.

> " For if a prest þat synges mes
> Be never swa ful of wykednes,
> þe sacrament þat es swa holy,
> May noght apayred be thurgh his foly."—*P.C.* 3688-91.

> " þe saule salle ay hate þe body
> Ffor þe body wroght þe foly."—*P.C.* 8477-8.

> "O tyme as he þuder wende : he dude ane folie
> þat manie to helle bringeþ : þe sinne of lecherie."
> *Lives of Saints*, Furnivall, p. 57, l. 3-4.

> "   ȝyf þou euere þat þou wystest
> A nouþer mannys wyfe kystest,
> Or ȝaue here ȝyft for þat enchesoun
> þat sum synne myghte be doun,

---

(1) Fol. 181. See also fol. 184, quoted before, p. 277.
(2) Gen. xxxiv, 7 ; Deut. xxii, 21 ; Ju. xix, 23, &c.

þan as yn þe, þou fallyst yn synne
ȝyf þou to foly wuldest here wynne."(1)

                    H. S. 2956—2961.

P. 36, B. 386. *lend.* As "*lendian,* to land." Icel. *lenda.* Hence,
probably because where men, who had migrated, came ashore
and were landed, they fixed their abode, it came to mean, to
abide, to stay.
    Cf. "Swa þatt he muȝhe lenndenn rihht
            To lande wiþþ hiss wille."—*Orm.* 2141-2.
    " That him in hel sa harde band,
        That neuer mar sal he wend
        Out of hel, bot ay thar lend."—*E. M. H.* p. 13.

B. 390-1. *þe weders . . . make gode and sesonable.* The "kindly
fruits of the earth " are specified in all the Latin *preces,* but I find
nothing of this in any of them except the Ambrosian, where we
have, " Pro aeris temperie ac fructu et fecundate terrarum ;"(2)
whereas in the Greek liturgies we have an almost verbal corre-
spondence. In that of St Mark, Τοὺς ὑετοὺς ἀγαθοὺς πλουσίως
κατάπεμψον. κ. τ. λ. ;(3) and in that of St Basil, Ἐυκράτους-καὶ
ἐπωφελεῖς τοὺς ἄερας ἡμῖν χάρισαι, ὄμβρους τῇ γῇ πρὸς καρπο-
φορίαν δώρησαι.(4)

B. 395-7. Cf. "Wharfor ilk man with hert stedfast,
            Suld seke þat lyfe þat ay salle laste."—*P. C.* 8137-8.
    " Til whilk ioyes þat has nan ende,
        God us bring when we hethen wende."—*P. C.* 9531-2.

P. 37, F. 183. *Grace euere-lastyng.* The sense of *lend* (above, p. 275)
may have become obsolete, and this may probably explain this
change, which appears to have been made with some vague
reference to the sound, but to the utter destruction of the force of
the original.

P. 38, B. 401. *A litel belle men oyse to ryng.* The form of this rubric
points to a time when the ringing of the bell at the elevation was
not prescribed by any general authority, but was adopted in
particular cases because some men (the indefinite *men,* ante, p. 196)

_____

(1) " Si vous vnqes dun donastes
        A autru femme, ou beisastes,
        Pur trere sun qeor a folie,
        Tant cum en vous est, le auez trahie."
                    Le Manuel des Pechiez, 3099—3102.
    (2) Cf. the Eirenica in the liturgy of St Chrysostom : Ὑπὲρ εὐκρασίας
ἀερων. εὐφορίας τῶν καρπῶν τῆς γῆς, κ. τ. λ. ; and the Alexandrian liturgy of
St Basil, Τοὺς ἄερας ἔγκρασον.— Renaudot, I, 87. So that of St James,
Εὐκρασίας ἀερων, ὄμβρων εἰρηνικῶν.—Trollope, 88; *Tetralogia,* 153.
    (3) Renaudot, I, 148 ; *Tetralogia,* 115.
    (4) Goar, 175.

used to do it ; (1) and this very well tallies with the date I have assumed for Dan Jeremy.

When it was that the bell began to be rung must of course depend upon the date assigned to the earliest elevation of the host at the words of consecration. This has been a matter much in dispute, but the best opinion seems to be that this ceremony was first practised, in France, in the latter part of the eleventh century, consequent on the Berengarian controversy, and then spread by degrees throughout the West, and was adopted at Rome, so that by the thirteenth century, except as regards the elevation of the chalice,(2) it had become universal in the Latin Church.(3)

It must be a mistake to say, as is often said, that it was instituted by Honorius III, A.D. 1219, though very possibly he may have been the first pope to give it formal recognition. In the constitution ascribed to him in the Decretale of Gregory IX. (Lib. III, Tit. xli, c. x.) he does indeed require the priests to instruct the people to bow themselves reverently (*ut se reverenter inclinet*) when the host is elevated (*cum in celebratione missarum salutaris hostia elevatur*), but the very words prove that he was referring to an existing practice.

A still earlier episcopal recognition of the bell is to be found in a constitution of William, Bishop of Paris,(4) in the year 1199, or according to other authorities the year 1202 or 1203. In this he expressly refers to the fact that the ceremony had already been prescribed elsewhere : "*Sicut alias statutum fuit, in celebratione missarum, quando corpus Christi elevatur, in ipsa elevatione vel paulo ante, campana pulsatur.*"

Now if the origin of the elevation has been right.y placed in the eleventh century, as seems most probable, the first adoption of the subsidiary ceremony cannot be placed much later than the beginning of the twelfth ; and it has been placed some forty or fifty years earlier.

---

(1) The more peremptory "*men is to rynge*" of Text C, and "*he wol*" of Text E, both written in the fifteenth century, are adapted to the different circumstances of the case, when the ringing of the bell instead of having at most the sanction of particular ordinaries, had meantime become an established custom of more than two hundred years standing.

(2) Fornici (*Institutiones Liturgicæ*, Romæ, 1825, P. I, c. xxix) mentions that the Carthusians even now elevate the host only.

(3) Archbishop Menezes enforced this ceremony in the case of the Christians of St Thomas (Raulin, p. 317), but it has not in every case been considered necessary to union with the Church of Rome, for, as instanced by Renaudot (*Liturg. Orient.*, II, 572), it was not added to the Maronite Missal, when it was revised by the Roman censors.

(4) This is the earliest quoted by Gerbert (*Disq.* I, 362), and the fact that, having the works of Bona, Mabillon, Martene, &c., before him, with his great research, and all the resources of the magnificent library of his rich Benedictine abbey, he has found no earlier, may justify us in assuming there is no earlier.

As the canon was said in silence, some signal would very soon have been found useful to call attention to the elevation, especially in the case of those of the congregation who were distant from the altar, or could not see the priest, and who might therefore have let the moment pass without observing it. If elsewhere, Normandy, the home of Lanfranc, was not likely to have been behindhand in adopting ceremonies designed to symbolize the triumph of opinions, which he had so great a share in shaping, and which marked the overthrow of the leader of the rival school of Tours—and therefore it is no violent hypothesis to assume that in the twelfth century, or rather towards the middle of it, the Jeremy of Rouen, of history —whether he was identical with the Dan Jeremy of our treatise or not—could not have been unacquainted with the ringing of the little bell,(1) and may very well have spoken of it in the terms here used, before as yet it had obtained the universal acceptance, which three centuries later enabled the revisers of his treatise, or that of his namesake, to use the more peremptory terms already pointed out (p. 281) in a foot-note.

A further circumstance points to the conclusion that the French original with this reference to the sacring bell was written before either it or the elevation had become the universal custom. The tone of lines 402—420, which the later texts omit, is altogether that of the argumentative appeal of a man who was fully persuaded in his own mind of the truth and importance of the tenet he was advocating, and yet was doubtful how far it might commend itself to the acceptance of his readers. And there is yet one other fact which points to the same conclusion as to the date of the original. There is no allusion to the inclination, which is di-

---

(1) For a very full account of ancient ecclesiastical hand-bells, and drawings of every variety of size, shape, and material, see Ellacombe, *History of Bells*, Ch. vi, pp. 297—387.

The ringing of the hand or sacring bell must be distinguished from the ringing of the church bells at the *Sanctus* and the elevation, which was intended for those who were unable to be present.

In the *Voyages Liturgiques* the observance of this practice at Rouen (p. 368) and Laon (p. 425) is mentioned as if it was not common at the end of the seventeenth century. However this may have been in France then, the writer well recollects that the custom has not died out in Italy or Malta; and at Malta on certain *festas*, not only were the church-bells rung, but patteraro-salutes, or salutes of petards, were fired from Forts St Elmo and St Angelo; and by a custom which had been continued from the time of the knights the castle-bell on the cavalier of St Angelo was tolled, by signal from the tower of the church at the moment of the elevation.

Attention was called to the circumstances by the courts martial on Captain Atchison and Lieutenant Dawson of the Royal Artillery, who were broke, in consequence of religious scruples as to participating in the ceremony, by giving the necessary orders. The military are now relieved from this necessity, and the Maltese clergy are allowed access to the forts, and employ their own people to fire the customary salutes and to ring the bell.

rected in C (l. 225-6) and F (l. 201-2), and which we have seen was ordained by a papal rescript in 1219.

P. 38, B. 404. Cf. "Goddes sun (son) and Godes sand (messenger)
    Com to les mankind of bande."—E. M. II. p. 6.

"To loose the bands of wickedness."—Is. lviii, 6.

"I have broken thy yoke and burst thy bands."—Jer. ii, 20.

B. 444-5. bandes, handes. Here the northern forms are retained, though the scribe elsewhere has changed them to hondes, l. 20, and bondes, l. 477.

B. 406-7. behalde, salde. Here again two northern rhymes, though ten lines below the scribe has written þou biholde.

B. 406. leuacioun. The elevation of the host after the recital of the words of consecration. See note, p. 281. It will be observed that in the York mass (ante, p. 106, l. 33) there is no rubric for this elevation, nor is there in any known manuscript or printed edition, except in the MS. at Sydney Sussex College (the MS. D of Dr Henderson's edition), which seems to have been a fancy revision of the York use according to that of Sarum, and was altogether disregarded when the York service-books were printed,(1) though we find prayers "At the elevation of our Lord" in the York Horæ, and, no doubt, the northern province followed the rule of the Latin Church in the adoption of this ceremony. The Sarum rubric is as follows:

"*Post hæc verba elevet eam super frontem ut possit a populo videri, et reverenter illam reponat ante calicem in modum crucis per eandem factæ.*" In many of the later editions, after hæc verba, there is added "*inclinat se sacerdos ad hostiam, et.*" After the reconciliation with Rome in the reign of Queen Mary there is a further addition, in the Missal, as printed in 1554,—for the first time in any service-book printed in England,—of the words "*et capite inclinato illam adoret.*"(2) I add the rubric of the Missale Romanum for comparison:

---

(1) The earliest printed Ebor Missal, of which there is a known copy, is the Rouen edition, Violette, 1509. A "missale pressum, 2° folio, mine" is specified in an inventory, in 1520, as being in the chapel of St Stephen in York Minster.— *York Fabric Rolls.* 301.

(2) This interpolation was not made in the Sarum Portesse, "*Londini,* 1555," now before me. The late Archdeacon Freeman pointed out (*Principles of Divine Service,* Introduction to Part II. § 8) the absence of this direction to adore the host from the uses of the English Church before the Reformation. He does not mention another peculiarity of the Anglican ritual, which continued to be prescribed by the rubrics in the time of Queen Mary, as it had before the reign of Edward VI, and that is the elevation or "heaving" of the host before the *Qui pridie* (p. 106, l. 27). After the modern elevation of the consecrated host had been fully established, this was carefully guarded against in the Roman use, and was prohibited by several provincial councils on the continent, as pointed out by Gerbert (*Disq.* I, 362-3), the reason assigned by that held at Frisingen in 1440 being lest the people "by adoring a host which

"*Prolatis verbis consecrationis, statim Hostiam consecratam genu-flexus adorat: surgit, ostendit populo, reponit super corporale, iterum adorat.*"

P. 38, B. 411. *euen.* Cf. the phrase "even-handed justice."

B. 412. Cf. "After ilk ane of þam has lyfed here."—*P. C.* 8749.

B. 416. Cf. "Ande þou mayst loue hym wyþ no greythe
But þou haue of hym gode feyþe,
þat ys to seye, to beleue hyt weyl.
Alle þat ys wryte of hym euery deyl—
Stedfast beleue, of loue hyt comes ;
And of beleue, loue men nomes,(1)
So ys þe toon wyþ þe touþer,
Wyþ stedfast beleue loue ys þe broþer.
To whom oghte þan oure loue be went
But to þe beleue of þys sacrament ?
þys oghte to beleue euery crysten man,
And lerne þe beleue of one þat kan,
þat þe brede þat sacrede ys
At þe auter ys Goddes flesshe—
Boþe flesshe and blode þer ys leyde
þurghe þe wurdes þat þe prest haþ seyde,—
þat lyȝte wyþ ynne þe vyrgyne Marye,
And on þe rode for vs wulde deye,
And fro deþ to lyue he ros
God and man, yn myȝt and los."—*H. S.* 9938-57.

B. 419. See B. 427, and cf. "Yf yt lyke yow, ȝe may say with dew reuerence to þe blyssyd body of our Lord. In þe furst Elevatyon, þis Lytylle oryson following, that is taken of the churche, wherfore yt ys of more Auctorytie—*Salve lux mundi* . . . . And lyke wyse to þe blyssyd blood of our Lord. In the secund Elevacyon at your pleasure yow may say þis *Ave* . . . ."—Langforde's *Medita-cyons* (*ante*, p. 168), fol. 13 *b*-14. Cf. also Lydgate's *Vertue of the Masse*.

"At the lifting vp of the holy sacrament
Seythe Ihesu mercy withe affeccioun,
Or say som other parfite oreysoun,
Like as ye have in custom deuoutly,
Or ellis saithe· this compilacioun
Whiche here is writen in order by and by."

MS. Harl. 2251, fol. 183 *b*.

See also Myrc, *Instructions*, l. 302-3 :

"Teche hem þus oþer sum oþere þinge
To say at the holy sakeryng."

had not been consecrated (*adorando hostiam non consecratam*) should com-mit idolatry."   (1) *Glossed*, "taketh."

These extracts, from among the many to the same effect, which might have been produced, will serve to show that however stringently the doctrine may have been enforced, there was a certain liberty of choice as to the prayers to be said, though as time went on, it may be noticed that a more dogmatic turn was given to the devotions. We have two English forms in our texts, and those given in Lydgate (*u. s.*), and the Latin ones in Text F, which are printed, p. 287, and in addition to these and very many others in books of devotion there is a great variety put forth with authority in books of hours and primers and rubricated, "At the leuacyon of our lord"; "In elevatione corporis Christi," and so forth. I add one from the primer of 1555, both because, appearing there, it is the latest put forth by public authority in this country, and because it appears to have been very generally used, being found in the Horæ of Sarum and York, and in collections intended for the laity in France and Germany(1):

"¶ In eleuatione corporis Christi.

Ave verum corpus natum
de Maria Virgine
Vere passum, immolatum
in cruce pro homine.
Cujus latus perforatum
unda(2) fluxit sanguine.
Esto nobis pregustatum
mortis in examine.
O dulcis, o pie,
O Jesu, fili Marie."

The English is printed on the left half of the page of the primer.

"¶ A prayer to be sayd at the eleucyon of the sacramente.

HAyle very bodye incarnate of a virgin nayled on a crosse and offered for mannes synne,

---

(1) Mone (*Lateinische Hymnen des Mittelalters*, I, 280) finds this prayer, in a xiv. century MS., from the Benedictine Monastery of Richenau, where it is noted that "Pope Innocent composed this salutation," and that "This prayer has three years indulgence from the lord Pope Leo." In a MS. Collection of Prayers, &c., from the Monastery at Sion (Harl. 955), to which Mr Maskell refers (*A. E. L.* 93), we find this prayer with the v. l. "*vero*," noticed in the next note, and the addition "*nobis peccatoribus quæsumus miserere, Amen*," but with a smaller amount of indulgence. It is rubricated "he that saith at the sakeryng tyme this prayere . . . . . he schall have CCC daies of pardon."—fol. 75 *b*-76.

(2) This is also the reading of the York Horæ. Some MSS. quoted by Martene and Mone read "*mero*"; others by Mone, as the Sion MS., above, read "*vero*," and he adds that three repetitions of the *Verum* is in reference to the Trinity and the three soundings of the bell at the elevation.

whose syde beeyng persed, bloude ran oute plenteouslye.
At the poynte of death, let us receiue the bodely.
O swete, O holy, O Jesu sonne of Marye."

P. 38, B. 420. *prayes.* Notice the northern *-es* of the third person plural.

    C. 221. *skille* becomes *resoune* in F, and E gets rid of it altogether.

    C. 225-6. This interpolation is noticed above, p. 283.

P. 39, E. 411. *feythe* replaces the *trouthe* of B.

    F. 205. The change is probably due to the northern *sere* of the other texts. See note, p. 188, B 71.

    B. 422. *with-outen drede*—probably with reference to the objections of those who scrupled at the doctrine of a veiled presence of the personal Christ on the altar, as contrasted with His spiritual presence in the heart of those who have duly received His body and blood. It will be seen that the former doctrine is not necessarily implied in the prayer in the present text.

P. 40, B. 424, 425. *aue,* see before, p. 183.

    B. 428—435. These lines are written in the MS. as under:

L oued be þou kyng & þanked be þou kyng
   & blessid be þou kyng iħesu al my ioying
   of alle þi gyftes gode þat for me spilt þi blode
and dyed opon þe rode
þou gyue me grace to sing þo song of þi louing.

Mr Furnivall, with his extensive knowledge of English manuscripts, at once saw, what I had failed to notice, that these lines ought to be arranged as they are now printed in the text. He explained their appearance in this shape in the MS. by the scribe finding three half lines vacant, when he had written the first three lines, and then writing the three next in the blank space.(1) The eighth and ninth lines were written in one, as was very common, and as had already been done in this MS. in the case of lines 209-10.

The prayer, as thus arranged, is a regular nine-line stanza, lines 1, 2, 4, and 5, and lines 3, 6, and 7 rhyming together, and lines 8 and 9 also rhyming together, but not necessarily, as in this example, rhyming also with lines 1, 2, 4 and 5.

----

(1) In MS. service-books, and especially when a prayer or lesson begins with an illumination, it is very common to find the first line of the text continued in what would otherwise have been a blank space at the end of the preceding rubric ; or for the rubric to be continued, sometimes for three or four lines, on the right hand side of the following text.

An example of the use of a blank space in the line before an illuminated capital may be noticed in the St Chad Gospels (about A. D. 700), printed by the Palæographic Society, Plate 20.

P. 40, B. 432. *ioying.*

> Cf. "Ihesu, my King and my ioiynge!
> Whi ne were y to þee led?
> Full weel y woot in al my ȝernynge,
> In al ioie, y schulde be fed.
> Ihesu! me brynge to þi woniynge,
> For þe blood þat þou hast bleed."
> *The Love of Jesus*, Hymns, *ed.* Furnivall, p. 28, l. 195—200.

P. 41, E. 421, 422. *any, on.* These readings confirm the restoration I have suggested in the corresponding lines of Text B.

F. 218. These two Latin prayers or hymns here follow in the manuscript. The first occurs in the MS. York Primer (*fol.* 27), elsewhere quoted, prefaced by the following most curious rubric, which ascribes it to our Lord Himself, as though jealous of the worship paid to the blessed Virgin :

"[F]uit quidam clericus in portibus Burgundie qui cotidie salutauit beatam mariam per hec uerba Aue. apparuit ei xps dicens, Tu salutas cotidie matrem meam et es amicus ei. Si salutaueritis me eris meus amicus. Tum clericus ait Domine si scire[m], hoc libenter dicerim. Tunc dedit ei dominus verba salutacionis." It also occurs as the five first verses of a longer prayer, in the York Horæ (*fol.* 62), next to the *Ave verum* (*ante,* p. 285).

The second, which is written as prose in the MS., is given by Mone (*Lateinishe Hymnen,* I, 271) as the first strophe in a longer hymn, in which, as here, the first half of each strophe is the salutation, and the last the prayer.

The first strophe is found by itself, as here, in a MS. of the fourteenth century at Mainz, and with the same reading "*pro redemptis.*" In the other MSS. noticed in Mone, the third line reads "*tu sacrata hostia.*"

(I.)

Aue ihesu christe, verbum patris, filius virginis, agnus dei, salus mundi, hostia sacra, verbum caro, fons pietatis.

Aue ihesu christe,(1) laus angelorum, gloria sanctorum, visio pacis, deitas integra, verus homo, flos et fructus virginis matris.

Aue ihesu christe,(1) splendor patris, princeps pacis, ianua celi, panis viuus, virginis partus, vas puritatis :(2)

Aue ihesu christe,(1) lumen celi, premium(3) mundi, gaudium nostrum, angelorum panis, cordis iubilus, rex & sponsus virginitatis :

Aue ihesu christe,(1) via dulcis, veritas summa, premium nostrum, caritas vera, fons amoris, pax, dulcedo, requies nostra, vita perhennis :

---

(1) MS. xpē.—*Mr Skeat.*   (2) deitatis.—*Ebor.*   (3) precium.—*Ebor.*

(II.)

Aue caro christi(1) cara,
inmolata crucis ara,
    pro redemptis hostia.
Morte tua nos amara
fac redemptos luce clara
    tecum frui gloria.

P. 42, B. 454. *stede.* B. 459 and 300, *place,* the *hora* of older liturgiologists. *Place* is still used in the same way in the Book of
Common Prayer, as, for example, in the Order for the Visitation of
the Sick : " *The Curate may end his exhortation in this place.*"
It will be observed that this place for the layman's prayer for his
"friends that are dead" corresponds to the second memento of the
canon, *ante,* p. 110, ll. 3—8.

Cf. " We suld pray, bathe loud and stille
    For al cristen saules : þus charite wille."—*P. C.* 3782-3.

B. 461. *here.* The mistake of the scribe, who did not know " er,"
which, as well as " es" or " is," was the northern third person
plural. The change in F is still more curious, and proves how
unintelligible the northern dialect must have been in other parts
of the kingdom. See the *vl.* in D, which is not improbably the
original reading.

C. 242. *sprede his armes on-brade.* See the rubric in the MS. York
mass (*ante,* p. 108, l. 10), directing the priest to stand with his
arms cross-wise at the oblation of the consecrated bread and cup in
remembrance of Christ, which immediately precedes the memento
for the dead. There is no reference to this ceremony in Texts B
and E, which represent the original, and this addition is made, as
the other variations in the later texts, in order to adapt Dan
Jeremy's treatise to the form of worship in this country. It does
not appear that the celebrant at Rouen did spread his arms " on-
brade," though this was done in other French dioceses in the
middle ages, and also at Orleans, and by several monastic orders
in the seventeenth century,(2) as noticed by the author of the
Voyages Liturgiques, who was himself a native of Rouen.(3)
This ceremony is prescribed by the rubrics(4) of the Ambrosian

---

(1) MS. xpī.—*Mr Skeat.*
(2) *Voyages Liturg.,* p. 200. Le Brun (*Explicat.* I, 242) mentions Lyons
and Sens.
(3) *Ib.,* p. xii. The author's name was *Jean Baptiste le Brun des
Marets,* but he published his work as *le Sieur de Moleon.*
(4) "Extensis brachiis in modum crucis."—*Rubricæ Generales* (1849),
§ 20. St Ambrose is described as praying in this posture at his last hour :
"Ab hora undecima diei usque ad illam horam qua emisit spiritum, expansis
manibus in modum crucis orabat."—Paulin. *Vit. Ambros.,* p. 12, quoted,

rite, and Fornici, Professor of Liturgy in the Seminary at Rome, mentions that it is still practised by the Carthusians,(1) Carmelites, and Dominicans. He also asserts that it was never used in the Roman Church ;(2) and there does not appear to be any mention of it in any Roman Ordo.(3) It was the universal rule in the Anglican Church, at all events until the end of the fifteenth century,(4) and it was one of the ceremonies of the mass which were most vehemently denounced at the time of the Reformation. The early Christians appear to have been in the habit of praying at all times in this posture,(5) but as it was used by the priest in the mass, as here in the text, it was with special reference to the mention of " the blessed passion " of our Lord (*ante*, p. 108, l. 13), and is explained in the Micrologus, to signify "*non tam mentis devotionem, quam Christi extensionem in cruce.*"(6)

It will be seen that the same explanation is given in the Vernon MS. (*ante*, p. 144, l. 589) :

> " After, þe prest his armes sprede he
> In tokenynge he dyed vppon þe tre
> For me and al mon-kunne."

And so the " Book of Ceremonies " :

> " After which" (the consecration) "the priest extendeth and stretcheth abroad his arms in form of a cross, declaring thereby that according to Christ's commandment, both he and the people

---

Bingham, 13, viii, 10 *n.*—Hence probably the retention of this ceremony at Milan in contrast to the use of the Church of Rome.

(1) The Carthusians merely retain the Grenoble use of the eleventh century—"*brachiis extensis extra corpus in modum crucis*"—which was followed as a matter of course when the order was founded at *La Grande Chartreuse* in that diocese.

(2) *Institutiones Liturgicæ* (1825), P. I, c. 30. So also Le Brun, I, 242.

(3) The rubric of the Roman Missal (*Rit. Celeb. Miss.* IX, i.) directs the priest to stand "*extensis manibus ante pectus*," and prevents his making a cross of himself ("*quasi de se crucem faciens*," as some of the French uses expressed it) by precise directions (V, i.), that in this spreading of the hands before the breast they must not be either higher or wider apart than the shoulders, "*quorum summitas humerorum altitudinem distantiamque non excedat.*"

(4) Every edition of the Sarum and Hereford uses, and all the known manuscripts of the Ebor use, contain rubrics directing the spreading of the arms *ad* or *in modum crucis*, or (Hereford) *crucifixi;* but this rubric is omitted in the printed Ebor Missal, possibly from a desire to conform to the Roman use in that spirit of deference to Rome, which was a marked characteristic of the northern province, and traceable, at all events in some degree, to a jealousy of the preponderance of the See of Canterbury.

(5) See extracts from the fathers collected by Bingham, 13, viii, 10.

(6) Cap. xvi, and so Durandus : "Sacerdos igitur hoc repræsentans, dicendo tam beatæ passionis, manus in modum crucis extendit, ut habitu corporis manuumque Christe extensionem in cruce repræsentet."—*Rationale*, 4, xliii, 3.

not only have the fresh remembrance of his passion but also of his resurrection and glorious ascension ; and proceedeth to the *second memento.*"(1)

So also the *Meditacyons (ante,* p. 168) : "þe *prest* immedyaitly *after* þe Sacryng spreides and splays hys armys A-broyde in man*er* of a crosse, sygnyfy*ing* þe *presse* of the Passyon of Cryst, þe wh*iche* ought to be remembryd in þe hart*is* of faithfulle Crysten People." —Fol. 17 *b.*

P. 42, C. 243. *sethen dres ꝺam in þe ferste stede.* The *vl.* in D plainly suggests the true reading—"*in* þair *ferste stede,*" so that the line will mean " then straightens them (*his arms*) in their first place or position, so as to be as they were." The previous motion, as ordered by the rubric, had been to cover the chalice with the corporas, and the priest now draws back, and with his arms straight before him, as when covering the elements, makes four crosses over them. This paraphrase of the Latin rubrics enables us to make some sense of dres ꝺam, or þaim (*them*), which, especially as " dresdam " in the MS., at first appeared hopeless. It will be observed that I assume " dress " here has what would seem to be its primitive sense of making straight, like *dresser* in old French. Cf. the Italian *drizzare* and *dirizzare,* and the Latin *directus.* The verb to dress is used in this sense by Wyclif : " And shrewed things shullen ben into dressid thingis." St Luke iii, 5. (" and the crooked shall be made straight." A. V.)

So also Chaucer in a passage of his description of two companies of knights, in the Knight's tale, which—in these days of volunteering for the able-bodied and the provision for military drill for boys in elementary schools under the Education code—hardly needs explanation, uses *dressing,* as it is still used in the army, of straightening bodies of troops formed in line :

" In two renges faire they hem dresse."—*C. T.* 2596.

C. 254. *sekirly.* It is not surprising to find the *serly* of the northern original changed into the equivalent *diuersli* of the southern text (F 232) ; but this change by a northern copyist, who retains the northern forms, when it does not even preserve the meaning, shows that in a hundred and fifty years *sere,* even in the north, had already become obsolescent. See note, p. 188, and F. 205, and cf. C. 104, where *sere* is changed into *many.* In C. 42 *sere* is retained from the necessities of the rhyme.

P. 44, B. 467, *hele.* Cf. " A covert from the tempest." Isaiah xxxii, 2. B. 474. *alle Cristen soules hely.* It will be observed elsewhere in this text that the northern *haly* has been changed into *holy,* as *ll.* 3, 4, 213, &c., or *holi,* as *ll.* 233, 234, &c., although *haly* has been retained on account of the rhyme in lines 75, 375. Here texts

---

(1) Strype's *Memorials,* Appendix, p. 288.

C, D, and F read *haly, holly* and *holi*, without reference to the rhyme, unless perhaps in C. 264, *mercy* was pronounced as in French. In this place, as in lines 74 and 75, it is merely assonant.(1) *Heli* is not a usual form of *holy ;* it occurred to me, as this is a prayer for the release of souls from the pains of purgatory, that *heli* in this place might have been derived from *helien*, to cover, and be used of the dwellers in the unseen world, in reference to their being(2) covered or hidden from sight, and the more so, as "holy souls" was used of the Saints in heaven,(3) and I had not found *holy* used of the souls in purgatory in any early English writers. I have, however, met with the following and other passages in the Life of Bishop Grant, who died in 1870, which show this use,—and not improbably the traditional use—of "holy," by members of the Roman Catholic communion in this country. "He wrote a pastoral regularly every year for the feast of All Souls. In one of his latest, after adducing every argument of faith to compel his flock to assist the sufferers in Purgatory by alms-deeds and masses, the bishop said, 'We could relate wonderful instances of the temporal blessings which have been showered down upon friends of the departed as the reward of masses obtained for them.' The pastoral was a powerful one, and produced a great effect on many souls. A firm of Catholic lawyers were particularly struck by the sentence we have quoted, and forthwith promised a certain number of masses to the Holy Souls, if a complicated suit in which they were engaged were successfully terminated. They gained it, and so much more happily than they could have anticipated, that the promised offering to the Holy Souls was proportionably increased."(4)

---

(1) Similar assonant or vowel rhymes may be observed, C. 46 and 47, marye, haly.
> " Over þi sothenesse and þi merci
> For thou mikled over al þi name hali."—Ps. (138) cxxxvii, 2.

In Hampole, we have *mercy* and *mighty :*
> " For all if God be ryghtwyse and mighty
> He is full of gudenes and mercy."—*P. C.* 1726-7.

(2) Cf. our *hell* and the Greek *ἅιδης, Hades,* and *hele,* l. 467, above.
> "A welle wel helid under a ston."—*Gen. & Ex.* 1636.
> "A (*one, the same*) rof shal hile us boþe."—*Havelok,* 2082.

(3) "Þa halgan sawla, þe on heofonum wuniað, gebiddað for us þe on eorðan wuniað."—Bibl. Bodl. MSS. Junii 99. *Sermo ad populum in Oct. Pentecost.* f. 107 (Cent XI.), quoted Soames, *Bampton Lecture,* 1830, p. 359.

(4) *Francis Grant, First Bishop of Southwark,* by G. Ramsay, 1874, p. 213. See also pp. 208-9. In a Spanish *Lay-folks Mass-book* I find a devotion to the blessed souls in Purgatory (*Devocion a las benditas animas del Purgatorio*), in which the worshipper prays, that " by their intercession (*por vuestra intercesion*), he may have grace to repent him of his sins, and after this life eternal glory."—*Oraciones para asister al santo Sacrificio de la Misa,* Mexico, 1825, p. 393.

Dr Newman also uses the same phrase—"When the saints leave this world, they are spared that torment, which the multitude of holy souls are allotted, between earth and heaven, death and allotted glory."(1)

Heli occurs in other pieces, where hali is the frequent form :

"Ðat heli luue, Ðat wise wil."—*Gen. and Ex.* 51.

"Ðor quiles it folgede heli wil."—*id.* 204.

"For þou mekled over al þi heli name"
"*magnificasti super nos nomen sanctum tuum.*"

Egerton MS. Ps. (138) cxxxvii, 2.

P. 44, B. 477. *bondes,* but the northern *bandes* has been retained, l. 404, where it was wanted for the rhyme.

B. 482. *per omnia secula (ante,* p. 110, l. 24). These words being said aloud after the silence of the Canon, served, as we have seen they did at the end of the *secreta,* as a signal to the people that another part of the service was reached. Cf. rubric in the Medytacyons (*ante,* p. 168) : " *When þe þrest begynnyth* per omnia secula seculorum *afore the* pater noster," *fol.* 18.

B. 483. *vpright,* according to the ancient posture for common prayer —*ante,* p. 191, 193. This direction is omitted in the later revised texts.

P. 45, F. 234. *Socoure,* instead of *hele* (cover, defence *rather than* health), which may have become obsolete in this sense when this text was written.

F. 236. *ifere.* The scribe, in ignorance of the northern *sere (ante,* p. 180), speaks of prayer for (*all*) others altogether, instead of for (*some*) others severally.

F. 238. *ido.* A form unknown in the north, and inserted, apparently, to get rid of *kid.*

P. 46, B. 487. *holde þe stille.* In the Eastern Church, and according to the old Gallican and Spanish uses, the Lord's Prayer was said by priest and people ; but from the time of Gregory it· became the Roman use(2) for the priest alone to say the prayer, and for the people, as here directed, to answer at the words " *sed libera.*"

B. 488. *bot answere at temptacionem.* This manner of saying the Lord's Prayer was continued at the Reformation, the people answering, "But deliver us from evil," except at the beginning of

---

(1) *Sermons on Various Occasions,* 1870, p. 91.

(2) The custom of the Latin Church is explained in the *Myroure,* p. 330: "After the sacrynge the preste sayeth the *Pater noster,* all a lowde *that* the people may here yt. & pray the same in theyr hartes. And therfore he begynneth wyth *Oremus,* That is to say. pray we. For in .this tyme ye oughte to here the preste & to pray *with* hym. Amongest the grekes the *Pater noster,* is songe there of the quier & of al the peple. But amongest vs *the* preste alone syngeth yt in the name of all."

matins and evensong, and at the beginning of the Holy Communion, when the Lord's Prayer was said by the priest alone.

In 1552, when the Lord's Prayer was inserted in the service after all had communicated, the priest was directed to say it, " *the people repeating after him every petition;* " and in 1662 the primitive practice was restored, in every place, where the Lord's Prayer occurs, a rubric directing—though to this day it is disobeyed in churches when it is said by the priest alone at the beginning of the Holy Communion—that the people shall repeat it with the priest after the Absolution at morning prayer, "and wheresoever else it is used in divine service."

P. 46, B. 490. *Ken.* This verb is not only(1) *to know,* but also(2) *to cause to know,* as here. See next note.

B. 491. *who con not þis,* who know not this. *Con, kun, can,* is said to be, like *novi* and οἶδα, the perfect of a verb which has lost its present. In Mœso-Gothic (Ulfilas) *kann* is the perfect of *kunnan* = γιγνώσκειν, εἰδέναι.

In Icelandic *kunna* has the meanings of *to know* (nosse) and *to be able* (posse); and so the A.S. *cunnan.* As remarked, Cleasby-Vigfusson, *s. v.* p. 358, in these old languages the two senses of *knowing how to do,* and *being able to do,* are expressed by the same form, as still in the Danish *kunde* and Swedish *kunna.* In later English and modern German a distinction is made: *ken* and *can; kennen* and *können.*

In Palsgrave (p. 474) we have, "I can, I maye, *Je puis,*" and "I can, I knowe, I wotte, *Je scay.*"

In our present text we have this verb (B. 625) in the sense of getting off by heart, or knowing out of book. In B. 339 we find it as an auxiliary verb with *know:* "then I con know," and absolutely (= *posse*) in B. 442 and 531.

In text C (line 82) we have *kan (nosse),* when F reads *can* with " of:" "If þou of letter kan," a common construction, as in the Chevelere Assigne, l. 313 :

" For now I kan of þe crafte · more þenne I kowthe."

Cf. "And he þat can oght, suld lere mare
To knaw alle þat hym nedeful ware."—*P. C.* 175-6.

---

(1)   " İ sall þe say
Wharby þou sall ken þe way."
Legends of the Holy Rood, p. 66, l. 140.

(2)   "And thaim the wai til heuin kenne."—*E. M. H.* p. 3.
" Godes worde,
That precheour bringes out of horde,
That kennes man the riht wai
Until that joi that lastes ai."—*E. M. H.* p. 106.
"And maysters of þair science (*es halden,* l. 5939), to ken,
Namly þam þat er unlered men."—*P. C.* 5946-7.

" þe laws wele better mai he cun."—*Holy Rood*, p. 93, l. 216.

" Til he the firste vers couthe al by rote."—*C. T.* 14933.

The verb has survived in this sense in one place in the authorised version, which as I have not seen noticed elsewhere, I may
mention, St Matt. xxvii, 65 : " Go your way, make it as sure as ye
can." ὡς οἴδατε. *Vulg.* " sicut scitis." *Rushworth*, " swa ge cun-
nun." *Lindisfarne*, " swæ gie wuton." *Wyclif*, " as ye kunnen."(1)

lewed men. This implies a reproof to those who did not answer ;
and would seem to point to the decay of the custom of the people's
responding, which has been noticed elsewhere (p. 158, 201, &c.).
When text C was written in the fifteenth century, the change had
so far advanced, that it was left to their choice (C. 274) to answer
" loud or still."

P. 46, B. 496. *þat is.* It is curious to notice the persistence of dialectic
forms. Though the " which art" of the Lord's Prayer has been
printed in our English Bibles and the Prayer Book for more than
three hundred years, there are very many cottages in the East
Riding where " *Our Father, that is in heaven,*" is the home-use, the
" *which art,*" or, too often, a meaningless " witchhard," being
confined to the school and the church, the fact being, that neither
word is to be found in the country-side vocabulary. Some years
ago, in a class of farm-servants, I heard one of them explaining to
a lad, who had asked him the meaning of *which art*, that it was
" old-fashioned for ' *that is,*' like a many places in the Bible."
The explanation was so much to the point that I did not remark
upon his incorrect philology at the moment, though it has been a
hint to me ever since not to neglect the explanation myself.

B. 506. *will saye.* After the Lord's Prayer the priest said—that is,
" *aperta voce,*" and not *secreto* as in the canon—the *Embolismus*, or
prayer inserted after the Lord's Prayer (p. 112, l. 1—5). This
said, he took the paten, and touching the host,(2) kissed the paten,
and crossed himself with it ; and he then said or sung the prayer,
Da propitius pacem (*ante*, p. 112, l. 6—14), after which followed
the Fraction (p. 112, l. 15), and then, according to the English
use—in this unlike the Roman rule—the Agnus before the Commixture (*ante*, p. 112, l. 25).

B. 508. *saies* agnus *thryse*, the quire singing it with him, " Then
folowyth. *Agnus dei*, sayde 'of the preste. & songe of the quier.

---

(1) We use cunning (*s.* and *adj.*), but in a bad sense. In the A. V. the
word is for the most part still used in a good sense, Ex. xxvi, 1, &c. ; Ps.
cxxxvii. " Let my right hand forget her cunning " ; but also in a bad sense :
Eph. iv, 14, "by the sleight of men and cunning craftiness." We also have
the p. p. in uncouth = *unknown*, and so *strange, odd.* Cf. " The tre of kun-
ning of good and of yuel."—(Wyclif), Gen. ii, 9.

(2) " *When þe prest taketh the pattenynn* and *towcheid þe Ooste* and
kyssed þe patteyn, Saing Da pacem &ca."—*Meditacyons* (*ante*, p. 168), fol. 19.

where oure lorde iesu criste is called the lambe of god the father."(1) Martene, quoting the *Liber Pontificalis*, tells us the Agnus was appointed by Pope Sergius I. (in the seventh century) to be sung by the clergy and people.(2)

Cf. Lydgate, *Vertue of the Masse (ante*, p. 163), fol. 165:

> "Of *agnus dei* at masse · bien saide thre
> The first tweyne · besekyng of mercy
> The thrid for peas · and vnite."

p. 112, l. 22-3. It will be noticed that I have inserted the *agnus* twice within brackets. In the MS. it occurs once only, as in other early manuscripts.(3) It does not occur in the Gelasian Sacramentary, and according to the Ambrosian rite, it is said only at masses for the dead.

P. 46, B. 509. *he spekis of pese*. See p. 112, l. 24. *Dona nobis pacem*. This change from *miserere nobis* was an innovation of the tenth century. It was not at first adopted at Rome, and not at all at the Church of the Lateran.(4)

C. 278. *at*. The sign of the infinitive and a distinctive northern form, though in the phrase *at do* (whence the modern *ado*, like the French *affaire* from *à faire*), it found its way southwards. It occurs in our quotation from Thoresby's Catechism, *ante*, p. 118, l. 6, and very often in Hampole:

> "For I hungerd and yhe me fedde,
> I thrested and at drynke yhe me bedde."—*P. C.* 6151-2.

P. 47, F. 252. The older texts enjoin that the Lord's Prayer only shall be said. This merely asserts that there is none better, which points to the introduction of other devotions. See before, p. 183.

P. 48, B. 510. Cf. *Book of Ceremonies:* "The minister taketh the kiss of peace from the blessed sacrament, and sendeth it to the people, saluting each other *in osculo Sancto*, as biddeth S. Paul: admonishing thereby of the fraternal and mutual peace and concord, which they ought to have, without which peace and concord, this communion or sacrament of common union is to them nothing profitable, but much damnable."(5)

B. 514. *pax wil kis*. This is probably an adaptation by the English translator to the existing practice in this country. When Dan Jeremy wrote, the *osculum oris*, or the actual kiss between the faithful, had not been superseded by the *osculum instrumenti*, or kissing the *osculatorium*, pax, or pax-brede, made of wood, metal,

---

(1) *Myroure*, p. 331.   (2) *De Ant. Eccles. Rit.*, I, 151.
(3) Gerbert, *Disq.*, I, 381. See Scudamore, *Notitia Eucharistica*, 1876, p 679. At Lyons in the eighteenth century the *Agnus Dei* was still said only once.—*Voyages Liturgiques*, 64, 65.
(4) Gerbert, *Disq.*, I, 381.   (5) Strype, *Memorials*, App., p. 289.

ivory, or glass. Binterim(1) supposes that the use of the pax originated in this country in the thirteenth century. The " *Osculatorium* " is mentioned, towards the middle of the thirteenth century, in a constitution of Walter Gray (1216 × 1255), Archbishop of York, as one of the ornaments of the parish church to be provided by the parishioners; but I find in an ordination of the Dean and Chapter of York, distributing the charges in the churches within their jurisdiction between the prebendary, the vicar and the parishioners, that the pax, " *tabula pro pace*," is mentioned as being found by the vicar, which carries it back to a somewhat earlier date.(2)   It continued in use in this country down to the reformation,(3) but Le Brun, writing in the last century, mentions that giving the pax had been almost everywhere given up in consequence of the quarrels for precedence to which the ceremony had given rise.(4)

The kiss of peace was originally the preliminary of the administration of the Communion, and is so explained in the earlier ritualists.   And so in the *Myroure*, p. 331 : " This salutacio of

---

(1) *Denkwürdigkeiten*, iv, 3, 487. In this he follows Le Brun, *Explicat*, I, 296. See Maskell, *Ancient Liturgy*, 117, and a work on the Ivories in the South Kensington Museum, by the same author. The book of the gospels was sometimes used instead of an ordinary *pax.—Rites of Durham*, p. 7. In Germany a cross was also used for the purpose.—*Messbüchlein*, fol. 164 *b.*

(2) Canon Raine (*York Fabric Rolls*, 164) mentions in a note that the date is not known, but that in 1317 there was a visitation at South Cave, and similar orders were laid down.

(3) " After the *Agnus* ye kiss the *pax* . . . . . . and while the boy or the parish clerk carrieth the pax about, ye yourselves alone eat up all and drink up all . . . . . Ye send them a piece of wood, or of glass, or of some metal to kiss, and in the mean season ye eat and drink up altogether."—Becon, *Displaying of the Popish Mass*, Works, III, 279.

" the peple of highe and lowe degre
Kysse the pax, a token of unite."
Lydgate, *Vertue of the Masse*, fol. 185 *b.*

Cf. the articles of visitation of Bishop Bonner in 1554, where also notice the " thre kyns loues " of our text (B 520) :

" Item. Whether there be a pax in the church, not only to put people in remembrance of the peace that Christ bequeathed to his disciples, but of that peace which Christ by his death purchased for the people, and also of that peace which Christ would have between God and man, man and man, and man to himself. And the said pax in the church to be kissed of the priest, and to be carried to the parishioners at mass-time in especial remembrance of the premisses."—Cardwell, *Doc. Ann.*, I, 150.

See also, Cardwell, *Doc. Ann.*, I, 68, an injunction in 1548, as to the *Pax*, so long as the ceremony should be used.

(4) *Explicat*, I, 296(2). Mr Peacock (Myrc, p. 74) quotes from Sir Thomas More : " How men fell at varyance for kissing of the pax, or goyng before in procession, or setting of their wiues pewes in the church." There is a similar allusion in Chaucer, quoted *ante*, p. 236, n. 1.

pece is sayde betwyxte *the* preste & the quier before the receyu-
ynge of *the* sacramente. in token that yt may not worthyly be
receyued. but in peace. and in charite. for his dwellynge place is
in peace." In the earliest known rubrics it was directed, " *Post
hœc communicat sacerdos cum ordinibus sacris, cum omni populo.*"(1)
In the Lyons Missal of 1500 (*fol.* 90) the rubric is as follows:
" *Hic datur pax ad recepiendum eucharistiam.*" In this country a
practice had grown up of howselling the people, out of mass-time
(*extra missam*), at their Easter Communion, or the rare occasions
when the communion was administered, but the old custom was
observed at coronations, the conferring of orders, the consecration
of nuns, and other similar functions.(2)

P. 48, B. 515. *Knele þou*, until the priest " had rinsing done," B 576.
    There is no corresponding direction in the later texts, for the
    people had not stood up. See note, p. 191.

B. 520-3. These four lines are rubricated in F, and ought to be
    so here, as they are no part of the prayer. Like l. 536—9, and
    l. 546—9, they are explanatory of its three parts, corresponding to
    the scholastic division of the three kinds of love.

B. 520. *charite.* Cf. Lydgate, on charity from the Epistle to the
    Corinthians:

> "¶ Without charite · availethe non almesse,
> To clothe the naked · nor hungry folk to feede,
> Visite the sike · or prisoners in distresse,
> Herborow the poore · [*nor*] none almesdede.
> If charite faile · your *journey*(3) may nat spede,
> Nor al these vertues · ȝif charite be wele(4) sought.
> Yowre pater noster · yowre Ave · nor your crede,
> Where charite failithe · profitethe litel or nought."(5)

B. 520. *thre kyns.* Cf. the threefold division in Bishop Ken's Even-
    ing Hymn:

> " That with the world, myself, and Thee,
> I, ere I sleep, at peace may be."

---

(1) Gerbert, *Monumenta*, I, 238. In the Eastern Church the kiss of peace
is given before the Anaphora, which answers to the Latin Canon.

(2) See Maskell's *Monumenta*, Henderson's *Ebor Pontifical*, &c. In the
Device for the Coronation of Henry VII (*Rutland Papers*, p. 22) is a detailed
description of the houselling. Whilst the quire were singing the *Agnus Dei*
the chief bishop was to bring the *pax* to the King and Queen, "sitting on their
seiges-roiall," and when they had kissed it they were to descend and go to the
high altar; and "after the Cardinal hath commoned his-self" the King and
Queen were to receive the sacrament after saying their *Confiteor*, a long towel
of silk being held before them.

(3) *journey*, W. de Worde; charite in the MS. See *ante*, p. 163, n. 2.

(4) wele; *query*, nat.   (5) *Vertue of the Masse*, f. 185.

Lydgate, instead of the inward peace, brings in the angels:

"This trebelle peas · in Bethlem first began,
When crist was borne · of grace it did falle:
The first peas · betwene god and man,
Atwene man and aungels · and men alle."
                                        Vertue of the Masse, f. 182.

This threefold division of the prayer for peace, if not derived
from the *Eirenica* of the Greek Liturgies, or from some common
source, which perhaps it would be too much to say, is at all
events to be found there. Cabasilas, in a passage quoted by
Goar,(1) points out the reference both to an outward peace as
respects our neighbours (πρὸς ἀλλήλους) and an inward peace as
respects ourselves (πρὸς ἡμᾶς αὐτούς); but it will be observed
that both in the liturgy of St Chrysostom and that of St Basil
a third peace (with God) is distinctly prayed for: first, the peace
of God (τοῦ Κυρίου) ; secondly, peace from above (τῆς ἄνωθεν) and
the salvation of our souls; and thirdly, peace of the whole world
and the "accord" (ἐνώσεως) of all.(2)

P. 48, C. 281. [þou]. The insertion of this word was a mistake.
    C. 296. *make me lowe,* make my love. Here *me* is the possessive,
    but in E and F *me* is the personal pronoun, the sentence having
    been altered. Cf. be, *prep.* for by, C 76, 339, our "because." A
    common Irishism uses *me* as in the text, "me father," "me
    mother," &c.

P. 49, E. 513. *word* = world. This is not a *lapsus,* but a dialectic form.
    Cf. "O worde," in the world. *Havelok,* 1349.

        "þat ys bot fantum of þis werde
        Als ȝe haf oft sene and herde."
                            Cursor Mundi (Fairfax MS.), 91-2.

        "Out of this word wen ȝe schal wynd."
                    Audeley, *Poems* (Halliwell), p. 81, also p. 80.

    A similar form occurs in a manuscript Manual of Hereford
    use.(3) "Wyth this gold ryng y þe wedde. gold *and* silver ich
    þe ȝeue. *and* with my bodi ich þe worshep. *and* with al my
    wordelych catel I þe honoure."
        Cf. "a man of discret witte and in wordly matters well ex-
    perienced." Sir T. More, *Utopia,* Arber, p. 15, "wordely," *ante,*
    p. 125, l. 31. "Wordly, *mundanus.*"—*P. P.* 522.

P. 50, B. 532. *prest.* The translator no doubt retained this word from
    his French original, and it very commonly occurs in fourteenth-
    century MSS., but it has not taken root in the language. To

---

(1) *Euchologion,* 1647, p. 123, n. 65.
(2) Goar, *ib.* 64, 159. The modern *Euchologion,* Venice, 1854, p. 16.
(3) Hereford Cathedral Library, P. iii, 4; *Fol.* 13 *b, col.* 2.

judge from the mistakes in C and E, and the change to *redi* in F, it had already become unusual in the fifteenth century.

P. 50, B. 532-5. Cf. the catechism : "labour truly . . . . to do my duty in that state of life to which it shall please God to call me."

B. 536-9. This, as noted above, ought to have been rubricated as in F.

B. 539. *bytwix my soule & my body.*

> "to what thyng þe saule has talent
> To þat þe body salle ay assent."—*P. C.* 8459-60.

> "In inward pees ther is eek of the herte
> Which callid is a pees of conscience.
> A pees set outward, which that doth avert
> To worldly tresors with too great diligence."

Lydgate, on *Prospect of Peace*, A.D. 1444 ; Wright's *Political Poems*, II, 210.

B. 544. Cf. Hampole :

> "þe body salle hate þe saule bi skylle
> Ffor þe saule here thoght ay þe ille ;
> þe saule salle ay hate þe body,
> Ffor þe body wroght þe foly ;
> And for-þi þat þe saule fyrst syn thoght
> And þe body it afterward wroght,
> And wyld noght leve, ne stand þere ogayne,
> Until þe ded þe body had slayne,
> þar-fore bath to-gydyr salle dwelle,
> With-outen ende in the pyne of helle."—*P. C.* 8475-84.

Cf. also Lydgate, *Vertue of the Masse*, fol. 185 :

> ¶ Be ware ye pristis . whan ye yowre masse syng
> That love and charite . be nat ferre absent
> O gostly peple . afore make goode Rekenyng
> That yowre conscience . and ye be of on assent
> Or ye receyve . the holy sacrament
> Envye and Rankour . that they be set aside
> And parfit charite . be ay withe yow present
> That grace to godward . may be youre souerayne guyde.

B. 542. *Of one acorde.* Again cf. Hampole :

> "þe thred blys, als men may in boke rede,
> Es veray acord and anehcade,
> þat þe saules salle have in heven to-gyder
> With þe bodyse, when þai com þider."—*P. C.* 8447-50.

C. 313. *oon.* A most singular form to occur in the MS. of a Yorkshire monastery, as has been already noticed, p. 251.

P. 51, E. 524. Two lines wanting in the MS.

P. 52, B. 546. The reading of the MS., in which it agrees with C, E,

and F, is shewn in the lower margin, but I have restored the text
to what appears to have been the original reading, and the reading
in D goes to prove that I was ustified in doing so. "Without
doubt," "without dread," "without lies," were tags, with which our
early English versifiers used to eke out their measure—sometimes
in the most incongruous connection(1)—and a scribe might very
well have thought that his author in writing "the third love is
without," had unintentionally left out "doubt," especially if he
himself was not familiar with the schoolmen's method of considering charity, first in respect to God; then as it was within—
"interna," the "privy" of our text—as towards ourselves; and
thirdly, "externa," or *without*, as regards our neighbour.(2)

P. 52, B. 561. *have ay ioy.* Cf. Hampole, *P. C.* 8609-12:

> "Ilk ane with other salle be knawen,
> And fele other mens ioy als þair awen;
> And mare ioy and blys moght never be,
> þan ilk ane salle þere on(3) other se."

We have already seen the mistake, which the scribe has made
from the ignorance of the northern *ane*, and we have here an
instance of a similar mistake in his having written "haue ay ioy"
(*have always joy*) instead of "have a ioy" one, the same or a common
joy, as in C. Hampole uses *a* and *ane* exactly in the same way:

> "þis acorde and anehede sall never ceese,
> But ever-mare last with rest and peese.
> And salle þai be alle ane in company,
> And als a saule and a body."—*P. C.* 8465-8.

P. 53, F. 302. *for-ȝectes.* It is a well-understood rule that in estimating
the value of various readings, the one which presents some difficulty on the surface is very probably the reading of the original;
and I am disposed to think that the rule applies to the hybrid
compound before us. Although its meaning is obvious (= out-
casts), I have not met with it in any early English work, nor do
I find it in dictionary or glossary—and, what is more to the point,
Mr Skeat tells me he does not know the word either—and it is
easy to understand that a scribe meeting with it in the copy
before him, and still more if writing from dictation in a scriptorium, would be very apt to write the "naue forget," as in C,
which seemed very natural at the end of a long enumeration,

---

(1) See, for example, *ante*, p. 82, l. 14.
(2) See the *Schema charitatis* as drawn out in the *Secunda Secundæ* of
Aquinas, *Quæst.* 23. Cf. foot-note, p. 296.
(3) I leave out the hyphen of the printed copy (þere-on), as I understand
the line to mean, that there is no greater joy than that which each one shall
there (in heaven) see in others—or himself find by seeing that of others. As
in our text, there shall be joy over the good of others.

rather than to write a word which was strange to him. And there is another reason which inclines me to think that in *forȝectes* we have the reading of the original. Dan Jeremy is very careful to bring their duty towards servants and tenants, neighbours and subjects (*inferiors*) before the dwellers in castles and great houses for whom his treatise was written. He was quite the man "nono to forget," and still less "the desolate and oppressed," for whom we pray in our English Litany. He might not have had a precedent in the established forms of the Latin Church, but, even if the thought had not been suggested by his large-hearted charity, he would have found the words(1) ready to his hand in the liturgy of the Eastern Church, which,—as we have already seen— whether coming to him more directly, or through the medium of the old Gallican liturgy—had so markedly influenced the form and wording of his devotions in other places.

Forȝectes is a participle used substantively, precisely as we find *abjects*. Cf. Ps. xxxv, 15. "The very abjects came together."— P. B. V. "The abjects gathered themselves together."—A. V.

"We are the queen's abjects and must obey."

Shaks. *Richard III*, I, 1.

P. 54, B. 575. *rynsande*. B. 576. *rinsynge*. In these two words we have an instance of the indifference with which *i* and *y* were used, and also of the distinction in the form of the verbal substantive and the participle which was then made, but now is lost in modern English by our using the same ending for both.

In the Promptorium (p. 434) and in Palsgrave (p. 691) *rinse* is given only with a cup or vessel, but *rincer* in modern French is used also of the hands, and so we find it in the A. V., Levit. xv, 11, 12. There is therefore no difficulty in understanding the rinsing in this place, like the *resincero* of the Sarum rubric, and the *rincer* and *rincure* of French writers on ritual of the priest's rinsing his fingers after receiving the communion ; and this in England from the earlier part of the thirteenth century onward involved the washing out of the chalice into which the wine was poured.

This rinsing is a different ceremony from the washing of the hands in the Vernon MS. (*ante*, p. 145, l. 605-7), though both ceremonies occur in the same part of the service, and both were conjoined in the later English uses.

There is no mention either of the rinsing of the text, or the washing of the hands in the MS. York Mass (*ante*, p. 116, l. 1), where I have inserted from the printed Sarum rubric(2) the words

_____

(1) Ὑπὲρ τῶν ἀπολειφθέντων   Goar, p. 42; and the *Euchologion* (of the present Greek Church), p. 21.

(2) "*Qua dicta* (the prayer after receiving) *eat sacerdos ad dextrum cornu altaris cum calice inter manus, digitis adhuc conjunctis sicut prius:*

which refer to the rinsing in order to mark the place where it occurred.

In the printed editions of the Ebor missal there are no corresponding directions, but the prayer is rubricated, "*Post primam ablutionem*," which implies the second ablution, and the attendant ceremony.(1)

Learned ritualists,(2) who have written on this subject, do not

---

et accedat subdiaconus, et infundat in calicem vinum et aquam; (not wine by itself) *et resinceret sacerdos manus suas ne aliquæ reliquiæ corporis vel sanguinis remaneant in digitis vel calice.*

Cum vero aliquis sacerdos debet bis celebrare in uno die, tunc ad primam missam non debet percipere ablutionem ullam, sed ponere in sacrario vel in vase mundo usque ad finem alterius missæ; et tunc sumatur utraque ablutio.

Post primam ablutionem dicitur hæc oratio:
Quod ore (*ante*, p. 116, l. 3—5).

Hic lauet digitos in concavitate calicis cum vino infuso a diacono: quo hausto, sequatur oratio:
Hæc nos (*ante*, p. 116, l. 6—8).

Deinde lavet manus.—Missale Sarum. Burntisland, 1861, col. 627-8.

(1) *Missale Ebor*, Henderson, 1874, p. 202.

(2) It is only fair to quote Fornici, as he takes a rather different view. His *Institutiones Liturgicæ*, both as a recent work, and from the fact of his being Professor of Liturgy in the *Seminarium Romanum*, is of considerable authority, and is the text-book in many other seminaries. He says (*Pars*, I, c. xxxi.), "The earlier Roman rituals, *Ordines Romani*, and their expositors, are silent as to the purification" [the name now used for the first ablution or rinsing of the chalice], "but we can hardly doubt that out of reverence to the sacrament, this rite was of old prescribed by the popes (*a summis pontificibus*), for we know that it was observed by priests in the twelfth century, and there is extant a decretal letter of Innocent III., on this subject, written to the clergy of St Peter's, Maguelonne, and recited, Chapter x., *de celeb. Missæ*," i. e. the chapter of the decretals of Gregory in the Canon Law so quoted.

I venture to think that if there was any such precept, it must have been singularly overlooked. In the tenth century the bishops enforced an altogether different rite (see *post*, p. 306), and Innocent III., in the book he wrote before he was pope, seems not to have known of it. After he was pope he did indeed sanction the rite as a rule in the document here cited (given at length, *post*, p. 305), but with an exception, which was altogether disallowed in later rubrics.

Another fact which makes against the probability of the rite having been prescribed by papal authority out of reverence for the sacrament before the twelfth century is this—that in the tenth *Ordo Romanus*, which is of that date, the pope is described as making the perfusion in the chalice and himself drinking it ("*perfusionem facit in calice et ipse sumit*"), not at every celebration, but only on a certain Friday in Lent, and at masses for the dead. —*Ordo* X, § 15. Mabillon, *Mus. Ital.*, II, 103.

If Fornici meant only that the rite was practiced by certain priests, or at certain masses in the twelfth century, no doubt he is justified in saying so, but in that case it is somewhat singular that he did not say the eleventh century, as to which it was no less true.

In the "Customs of Cluni," collected by Udalric in the latter part of that

assign an earlier date than the twelfth century for this ceremony, but it cannot be said to have become general in the West until the thirteenth century. I therefore subjoin evidence that a ceremonial rinsing was known at Rouen at the date when I assume the treatise to have been written, which may anticipate an objection that the reference to the practice was introduced by the translator, after it has become well established, and not by Dan Jeremy in the middle, or some years before the end, of the twelfth century.

In the *Liber de Ecclesiasticis Officiis* written by John Bishop of Avranches before 1070, when he was promoted to the Archbishoprick of Rouen, dedicated by him to Maurilius, his predecessor in that see, and professedly drawn from the metropolitan source, he says(1) that when all had communicated—and the communion was still administered in both kinds—the priest gave the chalice to the deacon(2) to cleanse and consume what remained (*diacono calicem ad mundandum et sumendum quod remansit, porrigat*) ; and an acolyte brought another chalice to the priest to clean his fingers (*alterum calicem sacerdoti ad mundandos digitos*). Dan Jeremy must have been familiar with this custom in the next century, for curious to say, though in the mean time it had been developed into an elaborate ceremony, the "rinsing" survived at Rouen (spite of the most precise directions clothed with the authority of the papal see) (3) down to the seventeenth century very much as it had been in the eleventh, though the priest no longer gave the chalice to the deacon, but himself cleansed it, and drank the wine of the first infusion, or the purification as it was called.

In the *Voyages Liturgiques*, the author, who was himself a son of the Church of Rouen,(4) draws attention to this exceptional custom, which he tells us was, when he wrote, still the rule at Chartres and Lyons, and among the Carthusians. The deacon poured the wine into the chalice, and "a boy gave the priest water to wash in a basin as at the *Lavabo*,(5) and emptied it into

century (Lib. I, c. xxx.), and edited by D'Achery in 1661 (*Spicileg.*, IV, 146), we have an account of the administration of the communion in both kinds, after which the priest drank what remained of the consecrated chalice, and also the wine with which he washed the chalice, when it was poured into it by the subdeacon for that purpose.

(1) Johannis Abrincensis Episc. *de Officiis Ecclesiasticis.* Rotomag. 1679, p. 24.

(2) See *post*, p. 306, the Greek rubric when there is no deacon

(3) In the Commentary on the mass, which Pope Benedict XIV. wrote before he was raised to the papacy in 1740, we find (I, § 340) it was held to be a sin in any priest to use water only contrary to the use of the Church and the Council of Trent. He also cites the direction of his predecessor Pius V. for the priest to drink the purification and (second) ablution from the same part of the chalice as he had drunk the blood.

(4) *Voyages Liturgiques*, p. xii. *L'Europe Savante*, Octobre, 1718, p. 163—200. (5) See *ante*, p. 100, l. 7.

the piscina, so that he was not obliged to drink the rinsing of his fingers."(1) As respects Rouen, he says, that in all the missals printed in the preceding century "there was only one purification, or ablution with wine, as at Lyons and among the Carthusians. The last ablution with water and wine was not then practised, and they did not oblige the priest to drink the rinsing of his fingers."(2)

In England the custom of pouring wine into the chalice, and of its being drunk by the priest—which, like the elevation of the host, most probably originated in the Berengarian controversy and the logical consequences of the dogma then formulated—appears to have been fully established before the end of the first quarter of the thirteenth century. I give my authorities for this statement somewhat in detail, as I am not able to refer to any work where this has been done, because the origin of customs may be a subject of interest to some members of our society, and because in this particular case the exact time may be very nearly arrived at.

The earliest notice of the practice in this country is a canon of a provincial council at Westminster in 1200, when in the case of a second celebration being necessary, it was ordained that nothing should be poured into the chalice after the priest had received at the first celebration, and that the washing (*lotura*) of his fingers should be drunk after the second celebration, unless a deacon or other fitting minister, or some young child (*vel alius minister honestus vel innocens aliquis*), were present at the first celebration who might drink the washing with a safe conscience.(3)

A few years later the practice received papal sanction, though still with the same exception. Innocent III., in his book *de Sacro Altaris Mysterio*,(4) which was written before his elevation to the papacy in 1198, had made no allusion to this ceremony. On the contrary, he speaks of the priest washing his hands after receiving the eucharist, and lays it down that the water used for this purpose ought to be poured out in a clean place(5) with all due

---

(1) *Voyages Liturgiques*, p. 230.   (2) *Ib.* 315.
(3) Wilkins, I, 505*. Johnson, *Canons*, II, 85.   (4) Lib. VI, c. viii.
(5) "*In locum mundum.*" This is the θαλασσίδιον of the Greek liturgists, and in the West was variously called, *lavacrum*, *lavatorium*, *piscina*, *sacrarium*, *locus reliquiarum*, &c. We find it referred to in the "*Canons under King Edgar*," Can. 38 (Thorpe, A. L. II, 252), and Udalric in his *Consuetudines* (L. II, c. xxx; *Spicileg.* IV, p. 140) speaks of two such, formed in the floor; one "cavea de laterititiis tegulis facta in proximo altaris," and another like it, but a little farther from the altar, for washing the hands. Elsewhere (*u. s.* p. 143, and L. III, c. xiv, p. 198) he calls this last *piscina*. After he was made bishop of Augsburg he directs that it should be made in the vestry or near the altar. "Locus in sacrario, aut juxta altare sit, ubi aqua effundi possit, quando vasa sacra abluuntur, et ubi vas nitidum cum aqua dependeat, ibique sacerdos manus lavet post communionem."—Gerbert, *Disq.*, I, 397-8. *Concilia*, Ed. Ven. XI, 1075.

There are still piscinas in the floor of two chapels in Lincoln Cathedral, and

honour (*debet in locum mundum diffundi honeste*), for greater reverence to so high a mystery. But in 1212 or 1213, in answer to the clergy of St Peter's, Maguelonne, which was then the see of a bishop, afterwards transferred to the neighbouring town of Montpellier, he wrote, "that the priest ought always to pour wine into the chalice, after he had taken the whole of the sacrament, except when he had to celebrate mass the same day, lest if in that case it chanced that he took the wine, it might be an impediment to the other celebration."(1)

Nine or ten years later, at the provincial council held at Oxford in 1222, a canon was passed, not forbidding, as hitherto, the rinsing of the chalice at a first celebration, but decreeing that the priest should not dare to drink of the wine which was poured into the chalice,(2) or poured over his fingers.(3)

The rubrics of the English uses carry out the provisions of this canon ;(4) but there does not appear to have been any definite rule

---

in some few churches in this country. Within the last few days (May 1877) I have had an opportunity of examining a so-called well, which has lately been uncovered in Beverley Minster, in the course of repairing the floor near the altar. It is circular, about two feet six in diameter, lined with ashlar, ten or twelve feet deep, and being "*ad dextrum* (south) *cornu*," probably served to drain off what was poured into a piscina in the floor.(*) From the remains found on clearing it out, it appears to have been filled with refuse and rubbish during the civil wars. Except during some time of desecration, it can hardly have been commonly used to draw water from, after the altar was in its present place ; but as it is supposed there may have been, as at York Minster, an earlier and smaller church, not extending so far to the East, the well may in that case have been either in a vestry—a not uncommon place for a draw-well—or altogether outside the church.

Double piscinas are not very uncommon, and there are examples of three. Viollet-le-duc (*Dictionnaire de l'Architecture Française*, VII, 189) considers that in France there were no piscinas (Qu. *in the wall?*) before the twelfth century, and that they never formed part of the original design—*en vue de concourir a l'ensemble de la structure*—before the thirteenth century. Mr Parker (*Glossary*, s. v.) is of opinion that there were no piscinas in this country earlier than the middle of the twelfth century.

(1) *Decret. Greg.*, Lib. III, Tit. XLI, c. v.

(2) "*Iterato calici vinum infusum.*" It was held that the wine which was poured into the chalice the second time broke the fast necessary for a celebrant, because it retained its natural substance, which that which had been consecrated did not.

(3) Lyndwood, 226 ; *id.* App. 2 ; Johnson, II, 105.

(4) The only rubric in the York printed Missals is quoted above, p. 302. The rubric from the printed Sarum Missal is given, *ante*, p. 302. A third ablution with water is directed in the Hereford Missal (Henderson, p. 134, or Maskell, A. E. L., p. 131, 133), in the Arbuthnott [MS. sæc. XVI†]

(*) A similar drain or well, about 3 feet deep, and 18 inches across, but lined with rubble walling, was found in the parish where this is written, when we were building the new church, and had to take down the font in the old one.

(†) It was written by James Sibbald, Vicar of Arbuthnot, in the diocese of St Andrew's. He died in 1507.

in France and Germany until nearly the end of the century ;(1) and about the middle of it Durandus still speaks(2) of the pouring the washings (*aqua perfusionis*) into a clean place in the same terms as Pope Honorius in his treatise, though he also alludes to their being drunk (*sumptio perfusionis*) by the priest.(3)

The other ceremony, of the priest's washing his hands "when he hath used," was of much earlier date. The sixth *Ordo Romanus*, which relates to an episcopal mass and is assigned to the tenth century, is generally referred to : "When all had communicated, the bishop being seated, three acolytes minister water for him to wash his hands."(4) This may have applied only in the case where a bishop was the celebrant, but there is strong evidence that the practice was general in the tenth century, in the fact that one of the articles of enquiry by the bishop in all the parishes of his diocese, as given by Regino in his collection, is this : "Whether there was a place(5) in the vestry, or near the altar, to pour the water when the chalice and paten were washed, and whether there was a vessel hanging there for the priest to wash his hands after receiving the body and blood of the Lord."(6) It is not said that this washing took place, as that described in the *Ordo Romanus*, in the course of the service, and before mass was ended : but it is probable that it did, both because the rinsing in aftertimes occurred in that place, and because in another of these articles of enquiry it was asked, "Whether, mass being ended, the priest himself consumes that which remained over of the body and blood of the Lord ; and if he has no deacon or subdeacon, whether with his own hand he washes and wipes the chalice and paten."(7)

Missal (Burntisland, 1864, p. 163), and in the Sarum Manual of 1554 (quoted *Miss. Sar.* 1861, col. 627). In the Hereford MS. Missal (Henderson *u. s.*) is a singular rubric after the priest has received and before he makes the infusion, "*signat se sanguine.*" In all of these, as in the Sarum, the priest washes his hands after the ablutions (*see* p. 306).

All the rubrics on this point are late, and so far as has come under my notice, none of those in a longer form are earlier than the fifteenth century.

In the Sherburne MS., p. 392 (*ante*, p. 257), which is of the latter part of the fourteenth century, the rubrics are as follows: "*Post perceptionem corporis et sanguinis Domini et post primam infusionem,* Quod ore," &c. "*Post digitorum lavationem infra calicem dic,* Hæc nos communio," &c.   Cf. *ante*, p. 116.

(1) Romsée, IV, 375.   (2) *Rationale,* 4 ; lv, 1.   (3) *Ib.* liv, 12.
(4) Mabillon, *Mus. Ital.,* II, 76.   (5) *Ante,* p. 304.
(6) *Inquisitio,* c. 8, *ap.* Reginonem.   *Ed.* Baluzius, Paris, 1671, p. 22.
(7) *Ib.,* c. 65, p. 27.   It is curious to note the close agreement of the terms of this inquiry with those of a rubric at the end of the liturgy of St Chrysostom, which we find in Goar, p. 86 : "The priest comes within the prothesis and consumes that which was left in the holy cup with attention and devotion, and washes the holy cup thrice . . . . But if there is a deacon, he does this." In that case the rubric adds that the priest goes into the vestry, and there takes off the vestments.

It may be remarked in passing that the inquiries here quoted from Regino

It has been already mentioned that this washing of the hands was retained in English uses after the rinsing of the chalice and the priest's fingers had been established. The celebrant either went to the lavatory or *piscina*, or else water was "ministered" to him for the purpose. It was not retained in the Roman rite except when high mass was celebrated by a bishop, and then with the addition of precautions against poison(1) in the same form(2) as that prescribed at the washing of hands by the bishop whilst vesting before mass.(3)

P. 54, B. 579. The people had been directed to kneel (B 515) when the pax was given and whilst the priest was "using," and they are now to stand during the communion or anthem for the day (*ante*, p. 116, l. 9), so called from having originally been sung whilst the people were communicating.(4) They were to kneel again during the post-common, as was the English name for the prayer after the communion, and then to remain on their knees till mass was done.

As has been remarked in other places, there is no corresponding direction in the later texts, for when they were written, the congregation knelt throughout.

B. 578-9. The priest had flitted it to the north altar-nook at the gospel, B 155-6, note, p. 205 ; but after the reception of the sacra-

---

go very far to prove that the drinking of a first ablution by the celebrant was as unknown in the tenth century in the Latin rite as it always has been in the Greek.

(1) The "assay" must not be supposed to be exclusively directed against "Italian art." It was rather an evidence of state and ceremony. In this country it belonged to none under an earl. See Mr Furnivall's *Babees Book*, p. 196. I extract the detailed account of the assay of the water to wash the lord's hands, there given in the *Boke of Curtasye*, p. 322-3 :

"Þo euwere thurgh towelle syles(*) clene,
His water into þo bassynge shene.
A qwyte cuppe of tre þer-by schalle be,
Þer-with þo water assay schalle he ;

. . . .

Þo cuppe he tase in honde also,
Þo keruer powres water þe cup into ;
The knyȝt to þo keruer haldes anon,
He says (*assays*) it, ar he more schalle don."

(2) "Ordine superius dicto." — *Cæremoniale Episcoporum* Innocentii Papæ X *auctoritate recognitum*, Romæ, 1651, Lib. II, c. viii. (p. 243).

(3) "Cum fuerint ante Episcopum genuflexi, infundunt pauculum aquæ super labio ipsius lancis, eamque præsente Episcopo degustant, tum aquam supposita lance super manus Episcopi infundunt."—*Ib.* p. 212.

(4) See Hefele, *Beiträge zur Liturgik*, II, 281.

(*) There is a query as to this word, and the Dutch *ziggen* is instanced in the note as meaning to strain. My acquaintance with East Riding Yorkshire will not prove what the meaning may have been in olden days; but I feel sure that there are very few dairies in this part of the country where any other word is used for straining; and not a few where strain in this sense would have to be explained.

ment, the remainder of the office was said at the south part of the
altar where it had begun. At high mass the book in this place
was flitted by the subdeacon, but here(1)—as the presence of a
deacon only is contemplated at most—by the clerk. According to
the Roman rubric, the book at high mass is removed by the
deacon, but ordinarily *"per ministrum."*

P. 54, B. 581. *office.* We have seen that the anthem at the beginning
of mass was so called, *ante,* p. 190, but it is here used of the whole
mass. The Gallican Liturgy is spoken of by Gregory of Tours(2)
at the *"dominicum officium;"* in the old Anglican rubrics *"executor
officii"* is used of the principal minister, where *celebrant* would be
the modern phrase; and this name was applied to the mass in the
Church of Rouen, by John of Avranches: "Ite, Missa . . . . .
officium finiat."(3)

B. 581. *saies forth more.* The prayers whilst communicating and
at the rinsing had been said by the priest *secreto.* He now says
forth, as here, or on high, as C 344, the Communion-anthem, the
Post-common (*ante,* p. 116, l. 10—18), and, though not specified
in the York MS., he turned to the people, and said, *"Dominus
vobiscum."*(4)

 Cf. Lydgate, *Vertue of the Masse* (*ante,* p. 163), f. 185 *b*:
 "At the postcomvne(5) · the prist dothe hym remewe
 On the Right side · seythe d*o*minus vobiscum."

C. 344. This text has been altered, as already remarked, *ante,*
p. 307, in order to omit the direction to stand. By comparing
this with text F, we may notice that when it was written in a
monastery, the alteration shows a more exact adaptation to the
service, being made by monks, who in many cases were priests,
and, when not, were constantly present at the mass.

P. 55, E. 569. *receyuande.* This is not improbably the original reading:
B. 597. *housel-brede.* When Dan Jeremy's treatise was translated
into English, the doctrine of transubstantiation had been long declared by authority, and our author (*ante,* p. 225) not only
accepted it, but that of concomitance also, though the name
"transubstantiation" was hardly in use in his day, and "concomitance" most certainly not until long afterwards. To speak of
bread after consecration was, however, not forbidden, as, for example, in the still unaltered canon of the mass (*ante,* p. 108, l. 18),
where we find the consecrated bread and the consecrated cup
specified as the constituent elements of the sacrifice.

---

(1) *"Ad dextrum cornu altaris subdiaconus librum portet."*—*Miss. Sar.*
col. 628, note.
(2) *Hist. Franc.* II, 23, quoted, Mone, *Messen,* 4.
(3) Io. Abrinc. *De Off. Eccles.* p. 26.
(4) *Miss. Sar.* 629. *Miss. Herford,* 135.
(5) *Ed.* W. de Worde—"Post comyn."

P. 56, B. 596-8. Cf. Vernon, *ante*, p. 131, l. 116-18, and the extracts in the notes there.

B. 600. *knele doun sone.* Cf. Vernon, *ante*, p. 145, l. 614-16.

B. 602-3. In the time of Dan Jeremy, the " Ite, missa est," was the end of the mass—the office was finished, and the people had licence to depart,(1) after receiving the blessing; and this was laid down in the old Rouen rubric—"*Et benedictione recepta, recedatur.*"(2) It was remarked that at Rouen the old use prevailed down to the eighteenth century,(3) but in this country, at least in the southern province, it became the custom to add the " In principio," and the people were exhorted to " abide the end " of it. See Vernon, *ante*, p. 146, l. 645, and the note there.

B. 604-5. *ite—hit be.* If this was intended as a rhyme to the ear, as well as to the eye, it would seem that our forefathers adopted the same insular pronunciation of the vowels in Latin as ourselves, or at least as we older men were taught when we were young.

B. 605. *or benedicamus.* Cf. *Myroure*, p. 332: " But before this blyssynge *the* deken sayeth. *Ite missa est,* that is. Go ye. masse ys done. Or else go ye. *the* hoste of the holy sacramente. is offerde & sente for you. & for al mankynde to *the* father of heuen. And therfore *the* quier thanketh god saynge. *Deo gracias,* And som tyme the masse is ended all w*ith* thankynges. that is w*ith.* *Benedicamus domino,* Blysse we *the* lorde. *Deo gracias,* Do we thankynges to god. But *Ite missa est,* was ordeyned to be saide to let the people knowe *tha*t masse was ended. & so to gyue them leue to go. by cause the lawe chargyth *tha*t they go not oute of *the* chyrche tyl masse be done. For when. *Ite missa est,* is sayde. and the preste hathe blyssed. then they may go."

B. 606. *messe al done.* I quote the phrase from a will printed by Canon Raine, nearly a century later than the date of our translation, not that it is uncommon, but because it may be interesting to the early English student to have his attention called to the will, as being the earliest will in English, that is extant in the registry at York, those of an older date in the case of the greater nobles being in French, and those of smaller people in Latin.

" In Dei nomine, Amen. vij day of marce in the yher of our lord MCCCLXXXIII, I Ion of Croxton of Yhorke, chaundeler, ordans & makes my testament(4) in this maner. First, I wyte and I com-

---

(1) " Cum ad celebrandas missas in Dei nomine convenit, populus non antea discedat ab ecclesia quam missa finiatur, et diaconus dicit: *Ite missa est.*" Theodori Arch. Cant. *Liber Pœnitentialis,* c. xlviii, 18.

(2) De Vert, I, 143. *Voyages Liturgiques,* 315.

(3) *Voy. Litur.,* 315, 370.

(4) In the latter part of his will, where he evidently uses his own words, he calls it by the more English name of " wytword," which, with the ī long, is not yet quite obsolete in the East Riding.

mend my saule to all myghty God & to our lady synto Mary &
to saynt Michaell Archangell & to all the halouse in heven, and my
body to my grauen in the mynster Garth be for the butres at the
charnell, by syde my childer." He bequeaths *inter alia* serges and
torches with all the particularity of his calling, and continues,
" Also I will that on the day of my byrying that ilk a pur man
that es at the kyrk dor present haue aue ob' when the messe es
done."(1)

P. 56, C. 348. *answerynge.* The answer to the priest's "Dominus vobiscum" was, "Et cum spiritu tuo," and though in an ordinary
congregation when this text was written their ceasing to answer
was by this time almost taken for granted, as we may see by the
alterations in the later texts, yet in a conventual church there
must have been many who were able to do so.

C. 351. *þou has saide Ite.* Here again is a variation which is due
to the MS. having been written in a monastery where there were
many deacons and priests, who from time to time took the
deacon's part. Text F reads "the prest," the priest saying the
Ite when there was no deacon.

P. 57, E. 582-3. *are—kare,* to avoid the northern *ere—were.*

P. 58, B. 610—613. *God be thonked of alle his workes.* This expansion
of the *Deo gratias*—the answer to the *Ite* of the deacon—may
very well have been suggested by the *Benedicite,* or Song of the
Three Children, which, according to the use of Rouen, Sarum, and
York (*not* Hereford), and the rubrics of other missals, including the
modern Roman, was said by the priest after mass.—*Ante,* p. 117.

B. 518-19. *blesse—hesse.* In the northern original this rhyme was
very possibly *blis, his.*
Cf. " in werld isse—ai fulle of blisse."—Ps. (90) lxxxix, 2.

B. 518. *In mynde of god,* that is, of our Lord. Cf. *Myroure,* p. 330,
" make the token of the crosse vpon you in mynde of oure lordes
passyon."

" Sen God was for us boght and sold."—*P. C.* 2725.

"The offeryng of Goddis body."—*P. C.* 3700.

So also the Grace before meat, *ante,* p. 69, and the Bidding
prayer, *ante,* p. 58, l. 12, " þe haly crose, þat god was done opon ; "
and the prayer to Christ, Vernon, *ante,* p. 147, l. 677 : " God þat
dyȝed vppon þe Roode." Any number of similar quotations
might easily be produced.

This manner of speaking may have served to familiarize our
forefathers with the fact of the Divinity of " the man Jesus Christ,"
—" very God and very man, but one Christ,"—but it did not preserve them from the most gross irreverence :

---

(1) *Test. Ebor.* I, 184-6, and note, p. 186.

> "Whan þei sittyn at þe ale,
> And tellen many a fals tale,
> þei sweryn falsch as þei were wode
> be godis fleisch and his blode."(1)

These blasphemies may have survived in the modern 'sdeath, and 'sblood, though I suspect they are used in fiction rather than in real life, and very possibly, when used, are not understood.

This would unquestionably be true in the case of "bairn," a very common interjection among the older—already almost the past—generation of cottagers in the East Riding, which I have often thought may have originally referred to "the holy Child Jesus," though used by them in utter unconsciousness of any meaning, and most certainly without any thought of irreverence, for otherwise, as the parish priest, I should not have heard it as often as I have in the mouths of God-fearing and devout old Christian men and women.

P. 58, B. 618. *I me blesse*, that is, seek for a blessing on himself from him whom he calls upon. This older use of *bless* as a reflexive verb is unusual, if not obsolete in the present day, but there is an example in the Authorized Version, Isaiah lxv. 16 : "He who blesseth himself in the earth, shall bless himself in the God of truth."

To bless, however, came to be used absolutely for making the sign of the cross :(2)

> "Blesce þe al abuten mid te eadie (*blessed*) rode tocne."
> *Ancren Riwle*, 290.

> "He wolde him blesci wiþ(3) þe deuel : his riȝt hond he gan forþ drawe
> þe deuel him nom þerbi anon : he ne miȝte him noȝt wawe."
> *St Edmund the Confessor*, Furnivall, l. 284-5.

> "blissed with ryght hand."—*Romans of Partenay*, 3417.

> "Aryse be tyme oute of thi bedde,
> And blysse þi brest & thi forhede."
> *Babees Book*, p. 17, l. 11, 12.

The rubrics of the canon of the mass in the San-Blas MS., of the ninth century, and the first, or one of the first, with ritual directions, or rubrics, as we now call them, furnish an early example of *benedico* being used for signing with the cross. "Hic solam oblationem benedicit." "Hic ambos signat, id est, oblationem et calicem."(4) "Hic ambos signat, id est, oblationes et calicem tribus vicibus singulis singulas faciens cruces."(5)

---

(1) MS. York Minster Library, XVI, L. 12, f. 65.
(2) See *ante*, p. 208, note 2.
(3) Wiþ, *against*. See *ante*, p. 63, l. 5, and note, p. 323.
(4) Gerbert, *Monumenta*, 1, 234.　　　(5) *Ib*. 236.

Another illustration of this is afforded by a mistake in the gloss of the Liudisfarne Gospels (St John viii. 48), where the Jews answer, "Nonne bene dicimus nos, quia Samaritanus es," the translator has understood *benedicimus* as one word, and has glossed it, "bloedsade ue usic *and* sægnade."

So closely connected were these ideas of blessing, and signing with the cross, that conversely *segnian* and *senian*, like the German *segnen*, were used of blessing. Thus Cædmon of our Creator :

> " þà segnade selfa drihten,
>
> scyppend ússer."—*Ed.* Bouterwek, 1385-6.

And Venerable Bede, quoted by Bosworth : "Nam hlaf and senode, *took bread and blessed.*"

P. 58, B. 619. *With my blessyng god sende me hesse.* "After Ite missa est. þe prest stondeith in þe mydes of þe Awter. *and* blyssyd þe people."—Langforde's *Meditacyons*, f. 25.

I have drawn attention to points of resemblance between this mass-book and the Eastern liturgy. Here at the end is another, which at the least is a very curious coincidence, as the Greek occurs precisely in the same place at the end of the liturgy, in the Εὐχὴ ὀπισθάμβωνος, in the Liturgy of St Chrysostom, or the prayer which was said by the priest behind(1) the ambo, or, as explained by Goar, in the midst of the people, which begins— Ὁ εὐλογῶν τοὺς εὐλογοῦντας σε, Κύριε, κ. τ. λ. (*O Lord, who blessest those that bless thee*).(2)

B. 622—629. It will be observed that E does not add anything in the way of *envoy*, as in these lines. MS. D also ends in the same place.

B. 625. *to con*, or *cun*, as in C, and as used to be the traditional pronunciation at Winchester, that is, to learn by heart, or *record*, as in F. So "Al . . . . . . coulde it by heart."—Becon, *Reliques*, f. 128 *b*. See *ante*, p. 293, and "to can" in quotation from the Myroure, p. 222.

C. 356. *lyve to paye.* *Lyve* in this place is the same verb we have, B 243, in the form *leeue*, and is employed as there in the sense of *remaining*, and not leaving the place where the worshipper was engaged in his devotions.

It will be observed that this, the Cistercian copy, here varies from the other texts, which allow the layman to "wend his way," or "go home his way," after a prayer of thanksgiving and blessing himself at the end of mass. The alteration may perhaps be accounted for by this text having been written after it had become

---

(1) This name bears witness to the so-called basilican arrangement of churches, according to which before the altar meant to the east of it.

(2) Goar, 85. This prayer is also in the Liturgy of St Basil, Goar, 179. There is a similar one in that of St James, beginning Εὐλόγητος ὁ Θεὸς ὁ εὐλογῶν.—Trollope, 117 ; *Tetralogia*, 211.

the custom to " abide the *In-principio*." More probably it was made, as we have seen in other places, to adapt the treatise to the use of the monks, who were not engaged about the altar, and heard mass in their places in the quire, for, unlike the layman, it was of obligation to them to remain for the office, which was said immediately after the conventual mass.

Grancolas, remarking upon the non-introduction of the last gospel at Lyons and among the Carthusians in the beginning of the last century, says that in those churches where it was said by the officiating priest the choir did not heed it (*n'y a point d'égard*), and often sung sext the while.(1)

In the Carthusian order the priest who had said mass himself began the office for the following hour after the *Ite, missa est*. This was merely the survival of the older use in a community which was especially tenacious of ancient forms.

In contrast to the requirement of the original, we may notice that the not remaining was already looked upon as a neglect in the latter part of the fourteenth century. Sloth in Piers the Plowman, Pass. v. 1. 417-18,(2) first lies a-bed in Lent,

" Tyl matynes and masse be do."

He then goes " to the freres,"(3) and owns that,

" Come I to *ite, missa est* · I holde me yserved."

P. 59, F. 345. *ribrusch.* Compared with B and E, this looks a very strange form, but- in Palsgrave (p. 263) we have " Robrisshe of a boke—rubriche."

F. 346. *record.* Cf. Rules of Syon Monastery. " *Of the offices of the*

---

(1) *La Liturgie Ancienne et Moderne,* 183. Cf. *Miss. Sar.* 629. " Statim post *Deo gratias* incipiatur in choro hora nona quando post missam dicitur. Sacerdos vero in redeundo dicat Evangelium, *In principio*."

(2) *Piers the Plowman,* Skeat, B Text, E. E. T. S., p. 79. Clarendon Press Series, p. 58.

(3) The parish mass was said before noon, but in Lent no regulars in religious houses, whether of monks or friars, were allowed to break their fast before vespers. The hour of mass was deferred until then, and Sloth takes advantage of the "evening mass,"(*) and goes to the Friars.

Cf. The Capitular of Theodulph, quoted above, p. 235, and in its English form printed by Thorpe, as the *Ecclesiastical Institutes:* " xxxix. *Ut Jejunium non solvatur ante Vesperas . . . . .* þat is riht þate æfter non-sange mon mæssan ȝehyre . and æfter þære mæssan his æfen-sang on þa tid." " It is right that after none-song mass be heard, and after the mass, even song at the time," that is, at the same time, for in Lent mass and vespers were said as a continuous service, "*sine campanarum pulsatione*," that is, without a fresh call to church. See *Ancient Laws,* II, 436, 437. Cf. Martene, I, 108. *Voyages Liturgiques,* 203, 216, 292. *Miss. Sar.* 356. *Miss. Ebor.* 125. Grancolas, *Liturgie,* 177.

(*) " Are you at leisure, holy father, now,
Or shall I come to you at evening mass?"
Romeo and Juliet, IV, 1.

Prechours. Eche of the prechours schal, be-syde the sermon day, haue thre hole days at lest oute of the qnyer to recorde hys sermon."—Aungier, *History of Syon Monastery*, p. 391.

P. 60, B. 626. *skille.* It is somewhat unaccountable to find this word, which appears to have been in such common use as in the sense of reason, miswritten *swilk* and *suche*, as it is in C and F, to the utter destruction of the sense. The mistake must have been made by a copyist before the recensions represented by C and F were made, the *suche* being probably a southern gloss of a northern blunder.

Cf. " and þat is skille."—Vernon, *ante*, p. 139, l. 405.

" Me thynk þan þat it es skille and right."—*P. C.* 2052.

" Alle thyng he ordaynd aftir is wille,
    In sere kyndes, for certayn skylle ;
    Whar-for þe creatours þat er dom,
    And na witt ne skille has, er bughsom."—*P. C.* 47-50.

" For to do gile ne wrang unto na man
    Bot to do that skill is unto ilk man."
                            Thoresby's *Catechism*, f. 297.

B. 628-9. The author has ended his treatise, and he repeats the two first lines much as the Q. E. D. of a theorem echoes the beginning. See another instance in Robert of Gloucester. He begins the prologue (page 1, line 1) :

" Engelond ys a wel god land, ich wene of eche lond best,"

and p. 8, end of prologue,

" war þorw me(1) may wyte
    þat Engelond ys lond best, as yt is y-write."

þen was used with the force of wherefore, or therefore, in the statement of a conclusion, as, for example, Hampole, after telling how to help soules in purgatory, paradise, and hell, winds up :

" þan availles almus, messe, and bedes,
    To þe saules þat er in alle þre stedes."—*P. C.* 2723-4.

F. 354, 356. *sey* = *say*, written as pronounced, a southern form in strong contrast with the north. In the southern pieces here printed we have the forms, *seiz, seþ, seyinge, seid* (*Glossary*), and Chaucer uses *seye* (C. T. 7209), *seith* (C. T. 177), *seyn* (C. T. 180), *seide* (C. T. 182). I have elsewhere (p. 197) quoted a remark of Dr Morris as to the southern orthography being retained with the northern pronunciation ; and we have an example of the reverse in the "*sez he*" of the illiterate, and the equally incorrect *seth*, which is very often to be heard in our churches, instead of *says*

---

(1) *Me*, men, indefinite.

and *saith* being sounded, as written and as of old, to rhyme with *pays*(1) and *faith*.(2)

P. 60, Grace, l. 4—*ayl.* "ayl" and "schal" are not a very good rhyme to the eye; but in the East Riding up to the present day *ale* (*pr.* yăl) and *shall* (*pr.* sal) are sounded exactly alike.

The Ancren Riwle, p. 44, provides "graces" before and after meat, and also before and after drink :—" Bitweone mete, hwo so drinken wule, sigge benedicite : 'Potum nostrum Filius Dei benedicat. In nomine Patris *et* Filii *et* Spiritus Sancte, Amen.' And blesceƋ (*sign the sign of the cross*), *and* a last siggeƋ, 'Adjutorium nostrum in nomine Domini, qui fecit celum *et* terram. Sit nomen Domini benedictum ex nunc et in secula. Benedicamus Domino. Deo gracias.'"

THE BIDDING PRAYERS.

The bidding prayers, according to the use of York, in all essential points were alike in their use and structure to those which were used in the southern province, though the earliest of those here given (p. 62) is some centuries earlier than any others which have hitherto been printed.

The bidding prayers (as suggested by the name) are not so much a form of prayer, as a bidding of the bedes or prayers of the people, calling aloud upon them to pray, and directing them what to pray for, or, as in after times, calling upon them to use certain specified devotions, with a required intention—Paternosters, and afterwards Paternosters and Aves, or Aves only.

They were used not only in this country, but in Western Germany and in France, where they held their ground as a part of the *prône* without interruption until the old Gallican Church was overthrown at the Revolution—the primitive custom of the priest speaking in the mother tongue being everywhere retained. As they were unknown at Rome, there can be little doubt as to the correctness of the received opinion that they are one of those customs which the Gallican Church received from the East—and very possibly one of those which our own Augustine adopted from the Church in Gaul when he gathered the English Use from those of Rome and Gaul in accordance with the

---

(1) "For þe life of þe saule mare him pays
  Þan þe dede (*death*), for þus himself says."—*P. C.* 1734-5.

(2) "For I nought hold him in good faith
  Curteis, that foule wordes saith."—*Romaunt of Rose.*

"The gospel redde, a Cred after he saythe
Of xii articles, that longithe to our faithe."
  Lydgate, quoted, *ante*, p. 222.

advice of Pope Gregory the Great. At all events, as the first of the forms here given is alone sufficient to prove, bidding the prayers of the people was practised in this country before the conquest.

This custom of bidding prayer was of high antiquity. We find an example in the so-called Apostolical Constitutions (VIII, 9), and the nineteenth canon of the Laodicæan Synod in the fourth century directs the use of prayer by the bidding of the deacon—διὰ προσφωνήσεως. But there is no occasion to enter upon the minute archæology of the bidding prayer, as it has been so fully treated by learned writers on the subject.(1) Certain resemblances to earlier forms will from time to time be pointed out in the notes; and it may be sufficient in this place to notice one marked variation from the earlier practice, which became the rule both in France and this country. As appears from the rubric in the liturgy of St James,(2) whatever may be its date; in the Apostolical Constitutions, which in the main may be taken as representing the practice of the primitive Church; in the homily of St Chrysostom, where he so vividly describes this portion of the Eucharistic office;(3) and in many(4) of the early documents of the Gallican Church, not only is the bidding prayer—the προσφώνησις, or κέλευσμα of the Greeks, the *admonitio* of the Council of Orleans—associated with the homiletic teaching of the people, but it always followed it. In the mediæval churches of the West the bidding prayers preceded the sermon or pastoral instruction, when there was any, and at other times was used by itself, though, when in mass time, always in that part of it where the sermon, if any, used to be preached.

The French ritualists of the seventeenth and eighteenth centuries are very full in their account of the *prône*, and the several forms are

---

(1) See *Forms of Bidding Prayer with Introduction and Notes*, Oxford, 1840. The initials appended to the preface will be recognized as those of the present most popular Bodley's Librarian, the Revd. H. O. Coxe, whose unvarying kindness in helping them in their researches on all sorts of subjects will have made him well known to successive generations of readers at the Bodleian. See also Bingham, Book xv, ch. 1, § 2 and 3; Scudamore, *Notitia Eucharistica*, 299—308.

(2) Μετὰ δὲ τὸ ἀναγνῶσαι καὶ διδάξαι.—Trollope, 41; *Tetralogia*, 41.

(3) Hom. ii, *de Obscur. Prophet.*, Ed. Ben., VI, 188.

(4) Perhaps the reference to the Bidding Prayer by Florus Magister may be an exception. He was a deacon or subdeacon in the Church of Lyons, and about A.D. 840 wrote *De Expositione Missæ*. In ch. xi, on the sequence that is to be observed in the several parts of the liturgy, he says: "præcedente lectione apostolorum (i. e. *the epistle*) et evangeliorum, præcedente etiam nonnunquam sermone et allocutione magistrorum." Here he certainly makes a distinction between the *sermo* and the *allocutio*, and it does not seem unlikely that the *allocutio magistrorum* may be what we should now call the sermon, and *sermo*, the προσφώνησις, or bidding of prayer preceding it. In the Paris ritual, corresponding to the manual of the old English uses, and quoted by Grancolas (*Liturgie Ancienne et Moderne*, 57), the *prône*, which included both bidding prayer and sermon, is described as the "*sermo*, quem parochus inter missarum solemnia habet ad populum."

given in rituals of different dioceses. Nor is there any difficulty in ascertaining what was the rule in this country before the reformation; though it so happens that owing to a misconception as to the place of the sermon in the mediæval Church of England—and the connection between the sermon and the bidding prayer has been already mentioned—the evidence of our authorities on this point has been overlooked.

According to the sixth *Ordo Romanus*,(1) and a modern rubric of the Roman missal,(2) the sermon is preached after the gospel and before the creed, when the creed is said. Hence several writers on this subject,(3) who in this, as in other instances, may perhaps have accepted the existing Roman rule as founded on the unchanged custom of the Church, have supposed that the rule applied to the Church of England before the reformation. As a matter of fact, our present rubric, according to which the sermon follows the gospel and creed,(4) is much nearer the Roman practice than that of our forefathers. According to a rubric in the Sarum manual, which in the absence of an Ebor rubric we may assume to represent the practice of the Anglican Church, the bidding prayers, which were rubricated "the bedes on the Sunday," "*preces dominicales*," "*preces pro*," or "*in diebus dominicis*," were to be said on Sundays in the procession(5) before mass in cathedral and collegiate churches; and in parish churches not in the procession, but after the gospel and offertory, before some altar in the church, or a pulpit for the purpose (*ad hoc constituto*).(6) The connection between the place of the sermon and the bidding prayer is recognised in the constitutions of Archbishop Arundel against Lollards, put forth in a provincial synod at Oxford in 1408, where it is directed that the preaching, as there allowed, should be at the time of the accustomed prayers (*una cum precibus consuetis*), which Lyndwood glosses,

---

(1) Mabillon, *Mus. Ital.* II, 73.

(2) *Rit. celeb. Missam*, VI, 6. This rubric was added at the revision of the missal by Clement VIII in 1604.

(3) "In parochial service after the gospel, the bidding prayer was said, and the sermon preached."—Rock, *Church of our Fathers*, IV, 192.

Maskell, A. E. L., 48; &c.

(4) Durandus tells us that after the gospel and the creed "*post illa*" followed the preaching to the people.—*Rationale*, 4, xxvi, 1.

(5) At Rouen the Archbishop preached in the procession before mass on Ash-Wednesday and five Sundays in the year. *Voyages Liturgiques*, 354. I cannot refer to any notice of the time when the sermon was preached in our English cathedrals, though it is not unlikely that, as in parish churches, it may have been in connection with the bidding prayer, and consequently, as at Rouen, in the procession before mass. In many, if not all, the cathedrals of the old foundation the *rota* of the preaching turns of the bishop, dignitaries, and canons dates back long before the Reformation. At York, probably from the circumstance that he was generally absent from the city, the Archbishop was set down once only, viz. on Good Friday.

(6) *Processionale ad usum insignis Ecclesiæ Sarisburiensis.* London, 1554, fol. 56. The whole rubric has now been printed by Dr Henderson in the York Manual for the Surtees Society, pp. 133-6.

"Those which are used to be made on Sundays after the offertory to the people."(1)

By "After the Offertory" we must not understand immediately after the anthem so called (page 98, line 22). The name, as already remarked (page 228), was not confined to the anthem, but extended to the whole of the oblatory action. The precise point where the bidding prayers and sermon were introduced in the parish mass on the Sundays was most probably at the place where the priest ordinarily asked the prayers of the people (page 100, line 19), or rather after having done so. This at least was the place where the *prône*, which included the bidding prayer and the sermon, continued to be said by some of the French clergy, as by others after the *secreta*, and before the preface, so late as the eighteenth century, the Roman rubric to the contrary notwithstanding.(2) This suggestion entirely tallies with the extracts as to the place of the sermon in this country, which I here insert, as I have ventured to differ as to the matter of fact from men whose research and candour give them every right to speak with authority on these subjects.

In a Sarum Pontifical, A.D. 1315 and 1329, in the office at the consecration of nuns after the gospel, creed, and offertory, and before the preface, occurs the rubric, "*Hic si placet, fiat sermo.*"(3)

In the order for the consecration of nuns, given by Bishop Fox to the nuns of St Mary, Winchester, and "probably written soon after 1500,"(4) there is an English rubric, after the postulants have made their offering (*ante*, p. 237) they stood in a row on the north side "to thofferyng of other forlkys be doon; whych offeryng ended, the sermone shal be sayde by the bishop, or such a clerc as he shall appoynt . . . . And the bisshop shall after thofferyng and sermone prosequute the masse unto *Pax Domini*, before the *Agnus Dei.*"(5)

---

(1) *Provinciale.* Lib. V, Tit. v, (o) p. 291, *ad populum*, for the priest did not so much pray, as pray (*bid*) the people to pray.

(2) De Vert, *Explication des Cérémonies de l'Eglise*, 1709, I, 18, 19. The author strongly animadverts upon this custom, but he adds that it is not always the fault of the parish priests, but often that of their Rituals, which placed the *prône* after the offering instead of after the gospel, where the Roman missal places the sermon. Bauldry (*Manuale Sacrarum Cæremoniarum*, P. 1, c. x, § 1) in the previous century had drawn attention to the disregard of the then recent Roman rubric, in placing the sermon after the offerings (*post oblata*), which is a clear proof of the prevalence of the custom. In fact, not only was it enjoined in diocesan rituals, as mentioned by De Vert, but the "*prône* after the offertory" seems to be mentioned as a matter of course in the constitutions of a provincial council at Tours in 1583 (Grancolas, *L'Ancien Sacramentaire*, II, P. 1, 781).

The modern rubrics of the Ambrosian rite require the sermon to follow the gospel (§ 17). The creed is not said in this place, but (§ 18) after the offering, and before the prayer *super oblata* (*ante*, p. 267). *Query*—Whether, as in other cases, there may not have been an adaptation to the Roman rite.

(3) *The York Pontifical*, Henderson, *Appendix*, p. 208.

(4) Maskell, *Monumenta Ritualia*, II, 307.

(5) *Ibid.* II, 327.

The same order was observed at funerals, as appears by an extract from the Book of Precedence, which I have already quoted, *ante*, p. 242 : "The offering don, the sermon to begin." That this was the custom also appears from the directions for the Venus soul-mass in the *Testament of Sqvyer Meldrum* :

> " Efter the Euangell and the Offertour,
> Throw all the Tempill gar proclame silence ;
> Than to the Pulpet gar ane Oratour
> Pas vp, and schaw, in oppin audience
> Solempnitlie, with ornate eloquence,
> At greit laser, the legend of my life,
> How I have stand in monie stalwart strife."(1)

Other examples might have been produced as to the place of the sermon in the mass at particular functions ; but Thomas of Walden in his *Doctrinale* clearly speaks as if the same rule were of universal application. After the prayer in the offertory, *Suscipe, Sancta Trinitas* (*ante*, p. 98, l. 29), he goes on to speak of the sermon, adding that the subject was preferably taken from those parts of the scriptures which were appointed for the preceding lessons (epistle, gospel, &c.) : " ¶ Acceditur demum ad prædicandum apertius populo dignam congruamque conversationem celebrationi futuræ ; et e divinis libris tractatus assumitur, his præcipue quos primæ lectiones habebant."(2)

There is a marked absence of rubrics in the York forms,(3) but we find from other rubrics that the priest turned to the people whilst bidding their prayers, and to the east at the psalms and prayers.(4) In respect to the attitude of the people, a change appears to have gone on similar to that which has already been noticed as having grown up at mass,(5) namely, from the earlier(6) attitude of standing to that of

---

(1) Sir David Lyndesay's *Works*, Ed. Fitzedward Hall, Part III, p. 371, l. 162-8. With this curious travesty of a Christian service, cf. *post*, the Venus-mass of Lydgate, himself a Benedictine monk.

(2) Tom. I, Tit. iv, Cap. xxxiii, Fo. lxxxi. (3) See a rubric, p. 70, l. 18.

(4) Coxe, *Forms of Bidding Prayer*, 18, 20, 22, &c. Becon, *Reliques of Rome*, fol. 234, quotes from the Festival—not the edition of Caxton, 1483, nor that of de Worde, 1515, and most probably from a MS.—a form of bidding the bedes on Sunday in parish churches, the following rubric : " *While the Priest is saying the aforesaid Orysons* [ante, p. 70-1] *he shall stand with his face eastward, and looke vnto the high altare. When he hath once done, he shal turne hym againe to the people, and speake vnto them on this manner.* Furthermore ye shal pray for al Christen soules," &c.

(5) Bearing in mind the custom of the early Church as to praying standing on Sundays and the canon (xx) of the First Council of Nice, it may be a question how far we may accept the so-called Clementine Liturgy as representing the practice of the primitive Church as to kneeling. In it after the expulsion of the penitents, and before bidding the prayers of the faithful, the deacon adds ὅσοι πιστοὶ κλινώμεν γόνυ (all we of the faithful let us bend the knee).—*Cons. Apost.*, VIII, ix.

(6) *Ante*, p. 191, 193, 201, 224, 270, 292, &c.

kneeling throughout the whole service. Perhaps, however, the later
directions are to be understood merely as directing the people to kneel,
when they came to the actual prayers, and this is the more likely to be
the case if, as is most probable, the practice in our cathedrals and
other churches, of the people standing until the Lord's Prayer, has been
handed down from before the Reformation.

It will be seen that there are no directions as to this point in any of
the York MS. forms; but in that from the printed manual (*ante*, p. 78,
l. 14) the people are bidden to "kneel down devoutly on their knees
and make a special prayer." The Worcester form (A.D. 1349) begins,
"Ye shulle stonde up and bydde your bedys,"(1) and then towards the
end, after prayers in Latin, the priest proceeds: "Ye shulle kneelen
doun and bydde for your fader sowl," &c.(2) The form in the Sarum
Missal (circa A.D. 1400), printed by Dr Henderson,(3) is to the same
effect, and so is that given by Wharton from an old written copy;(4)
but in the forms in the printed Festival (Caxton, 1483; W. de Worde,
1515), in the form given by Hearne, as used in the reign of Henry
VII,(5) and in another in the time of Henry VIII,(6) and in a form for
the Diocese of London, printed by Dr Henderson,(7) a direction to the
people to kneel down on their knees is given at the beginning, and the
direction is not repeated at the end, where it was at first inserted, and
then partially, in the fourteenth century.

The priest turned to the people, when speaking to them: he then
turned to the altar during the Latin devotions; and afterwards to the
people, when he again spoke to them in the mother tongue.(8)

As forms from the conquest to the reformation are given in the
text, it may be acceptable to some of my readers if I here add the
form of bidding prayer which, more than a thousand years after the
date of the earliest in the series, we still continue to use in York
Minster before the sermon:

"YE SHALL PRAY

"For Christ's Holy Catholic Church, that is, for the whole con-
"gregation of Christian people dispersed throughout the world, especi-
"ally for the Church of England and herein for our Most Gracious
"Sovereign Lady, Queen Victoria, the Prince of Wales, the Princess of

---

(1) Coxe, 11.
(2) *Ib.* 22. This is preceded by the rubric "*In lingua materna conversus
ad populum dicat.*"
(3) *York Manual*, Appendix, p. 220*.
(4) *Errors and Defects in* Bishop Burnet's *History of the Reformation*,
by Anthony Harmer, 1693, p. 68, 166.
(5) *Robert of Gloucester*, 1810, p. 682.   (6) Coxe, 51.
(7) *York Manual*, Appendix, 223*. "3e shall knell down on your kneis
and pray devoutle and mekle to the Fader, the Son, and the Holi Gost, thre
persons and o Gode."
(8) Sarum rubrics. Henderson, *York Manual*, p. 134-5. Worcester
rubrics (1349), Coxe, p. 22.

" Wales, and all the Royal Family, for the Ministers of God's Holy
" Word and Sacraments, particularly for William, Archbishop of this
" Province, The Dean and Chapter, and the other Members of this
" Metropolitical Church.

" For the Queen's most Honourable Privy Council [for the great
" Council of the Nation now assembled in Parliament] and for all the
" Nobility [the Judges of this Assize] and Magistrates of this Realm,
" particularly for the Lord Mayor, the Recorder, the Aldermen, and all
" that bear office in this ancient City. That all these in their respective
" stations may serve truly and painfully to the Glory of God, and the
" edifying and well-governing of His people, remembering the account
" which they must one day give.

" And that we may never want a supply of fit and able men duly
" qualified to serve God in Church and State, let us beg a blessing upon
" all schools of sound learning and religious education, more especially
" on the Universities of the United Kingdom.

" Also, ye shall pray for the Commons of the Realm, that they may
" live in the fear of God, in humble obedience to the Queen, and in
" brotherly charity one towards another.

" Finally, let us praise God for all those who are departed out of
" this life, in the faith of Christ, humbly beseeching Him to give us
" Grace, so to follow their good examples, that this life ended we may
" be with them received into his everlasting kingdom, through our
" Lord and Saviour Jesus Christ.

"OUR FATHER."

P. 62. *BIDDING PRAYER I.* This is the earliest of our York bidding
prayers, and it is believed to be the earliest example of the
bidding prayers in the Church of England which is known to
have come down to us. It is written at the end of the York
Gospels,(1) but by another and a later hand. I took advantage
of a visit from Mr Maunde Thompson to obtain his opinion, and
he puts it at early XI century, which quite agrees with the

---

(1) This is supposed to be "the very copy of the Evangelists upon which
every new officer of the Church took his oath from the year 900 downwards "
(Raine, *York Fabric Rolls,* 143). In the inventory of the jewels, &c., belonging to York Minster in 1510, it is described under the "TEXTUS EVANGELICI.
Unus textus ornatus cum argento non bene deaurato, super quem juramenta
Decani et aliarum dignitatum ac canonicorum in principio inseruntur" (*ib.*
323). It was lost for some time, "but soon after the Restoration, according
to an entry in the chapter books, it was restored" (*ib.* 357), at which time it
was most probably rebound in the present rough calf. Mr Thompson puts the
form of oath, mentioned in the inventory as above, at XIV century.

The text itself begins with St Jerome's preface and the Eusebian canons.
Before each gospel, except that of St John, is a full-page figure of the
evangelist without any of the evangelistic symbols. At the end, with other
documents and memoranda, are the Sherburn Inventory, elsewhere referred
to, and the Bidding Prayer here given.

internal evidence; and the Gospels at X century, but hardly at
the beginning of the century, which is the date traditionally
assigned to them. ·

Until after the text was printed off I was not aware, or rather,
not having the book to refer to, I had forgotten, that Dr Rock had
printed the bidding prayer in the *Church of our Fathers.* The
transcript which he used was not altogether correct; but the one
here given has had the advantage of being compared by Mr
Thompson, who read line 22 for me, and suggested the manner in
which I have filled up the hiatus, where there is a hole in the
vellum, and therefore the members of the E. E. T. Society will
not be displeased to find it here, even if it were not required for the
completion of our series.

P. 62, l. 4. *On þyssan lænan life.* I have drawn attention, *page
275,* to the manner in which the verb *lene* was used some centuries
later ;(1) and in this place there seems to be a similar ethical
subaudition in the use of the adjective *læne.* This is suggested
by the then customary tenure of limited estates in land, *læna* that
is, or loans lent or granted by a superior, subject to certain
services, for a term or during pleasure, and revocable in case of
default, the absolute property remaining to the granter, the conditional and precarious usufruct to the grantee.

Lán in Icelandic has also the meanings of *loan* and *fief;* and
the phrase Guðs lán, *a loan from God,* also occurs.—See Cleasby-
Vigfusson, *s. v.*

ll. 3—4. Cf. a prayer in MS. Cotton. Jul. A. II:

> " þæt ðu gemilsige me
> mihtig Drihten,
> heofena heah-kyning,
> and se halga Gast ;
> and gefylste me,
> Fæder ælmihtig,
> þæt ic þinne willan
> gewyrcean mæge,
> ær ic of ðysum hlænan
> lyfe gehweorfe."(2)

---

(1) Cf. Bidding Prayer II, p. 64, l. 13 : " that god len thaim grace."

(2) "That thou have mercy on me, mighty Lord, high King of heavens,
and the Holy Ghost ; and assist me, Father almighty, that I thy will may
perform, ere I from this meagre life depart." —*Select Monuments of the
Catholic Church in England before the Norman Conquest,* by Ebenezer
Thomson, 1849, p. 224-5.

For the reasons given above I should have been inclined to render *hlænan*
transitory or precarious, which last would suggest the holding of an estate at
will to those who are familiar with feudal tenures.

Cf. Heb. xiii, 14 : " For here have we no continuing city."

P. 62, l. 5. *gehealdan* . . . *wið*.

> Cf. " Heald me here-wæpnum
> wið unholdum."
> " *Guard me with war weapons*
> *against the unfavourable.*"
>
> Thomson, *u. s.* p. 160, 161.

gescyldan wið, &c. Cf. York *Horæ*, quoted above, p. 248,
" shelde . . . ayent all myn enemyes bodely & ghostly."

> " To shildenn þe wiþþ all hiss(1) laþ."—*Orm.* 11887.

—*wið*, *against.* It may seem at first sight as if *with* was used in
old English in a sense different from the English of the present
day ; but if I do not mistake, the seemingly contrary senses are
reducible to that of *contact* or *nearness*, the precise character
being inferred from the context. As, for example, we fought with
(*contended with*) the French at Waterloo, and we also fought with
(*confederate with*) them in the Crimea,—in the one case we were
at war *with* them, in the other we had made an alliance *with* them.

> Cf. " Warniaþ wiþ ælce gytsunge."
> (*Cavete ab omni avaritia.*) St Luke xii, 25.
>
> " He faught with Arcite."—C. T. 2641.
>
> " Go out, I pray thee, and fight with them."
> Judges ix, 38.
>
> " That angel should with angel war."
> Milton, P. L. VI, 92.

l. 7. *urne papan*, our pope. In later forms, the pope.

l. 8. *ealdorman*, from *ealdor*, elder, but with no more reference to age
than the feudal *Seigneur* from *senior*.

This title, which in later times was confined to the holders of
office in municipal corporations—either several under a mayor,
or one, himself the chief officer, as at Grantham—was given not
only to the high officer of state, next in authority to the king,
but also, as we shall see, to the head of a religious house or
brotherhood.(2)

At the date of our MS. the Danish earl had taken the place, at
least in the North, of the Anglian alderman, which makes it less
likely that we are to understand ealdorman of the secular
dignitary, though it is possible that the older name might have

---

(1) *Against all his enmity.*

(2) This title was also given in 1494, and may have been given earlier, to
the master—as the head of a gild was afterwards called—of the gild of St
Katherine at Stamford (*English Gilds*, Smith, E. E. T. S., 1870, p. 188) ;
and this was very probably the title of the masters of the gilds of St Helena
and St Mary, as Englished by Mr Toulmin Smith from the Latin of the
Ordinances of the fourteenth century.—*Ib.* 148, 149.

maintained its ground in the language of the church. It seems,
however, more natural to understand it, as I suggest in the
margin, of the senior of the minster clergy, more especially as it
occurs between the mention of the archbishop and those who
owed frith and friendship to the minster. The office of dean,
it must be remembered, had not as yet been founded at York;
and the following evidence appears to be sufficient that ealdorman
might have been used in this sense.

After the flight of Paulinus, St Aidan was sent from Iona,(1) and
from that time the discipline of the Scottish Culdees spread through
the whole of Northumbria ; and though no Culdee(2) was raised to
the See of York after St Chad resigned it in 669, the brethren of
York Minster " retained the name Colidæi or Culdees until the
time of Henry I."(3)

In the Irish rule of St Columba the head of the community is
styled senóra,(4) which is evidently derived from senior (alderman); and so also in the ecclesiastical laws of Wihtred, King of
Kent, made at a wittenagemot at Berghamstede (Bersted, near
Maidstone) in 696 :

"XVII. Mynstres aldor hine cænne in preostes canne."(5)
*Let the senior of a minster clear himself with a priest's clear-
ance.*(6)

Centuries later we find the use of this name for the superior of
a monastery in this country. Orm, speaking of the life of a monk,
says he must be

> " buhsum till hiss alderrmann
> þatt hafeþþ himm to gætenn."(7)

And so on the continent, at the offertory in the mass of a

---

(1) Bede. H. E. III, 3. Ed. Smith, p. 105-6.

(2) *Gille de*, or *Cele de*, servant or child of God, Latinized *Culdæi*,
Colidæi, and *Kelidei*.

(3) Raine, *Fasti Eboracenses*, I, 21. The common property was not
apportioned in separate prebends until the time of Archbishop Thomas I, in
1090. The brethren were thenceforward called canons. ·"Tunc . . . statuit
decanum, thesaurarium, cantorem."—Stubbs, *X Script.*, 1709.

(4) Haddan and Stubbs, *Councils*, II, 119. Mr Haddan (p. 121) is of
opinion that this was not written by St Columba himself, but the later
production of some Columbite monk. In either case it proves the use of the
name for the superior.

(5) Thorpe, A. L. I, 40. H. & S. *u. s.* III, 236.

(6) The *canne*, or solemn averment, was the form of defence observed by
all defendants. That of the priest is laid down in the next clause. "XVIII.
Preost hine clænsie, sylfæs soðe, in his halgum hrægle, ætforan wiofode, þus
cweðende : Ueritatem dico in Xpo non mentior. Swylce diacon hine clænsie.
*Let a priest clear himself by his own sooth, in his holy garment before the
altar, thus saying,* Veritatem dico in Christo, non mentior. *In like manner
let a deacon clear himself.*"—H. & S. and Thorpe, *u. s.*

(7) *Ormulum*, 6304-5.

Benedictine house (*Hornbach*), a prayer was offered, "pro seniore nostro et cuncta congregatione sancti Petri."(1)

P. 62, l. 9. *frið* and *freondscype*, most probably with reference to the system of frith-borh or frank-pledge, by which every one, laic or(2) cleric, within or without a borough was held to be "under borge"—the members of the same frith gild (gyldan, gegyldan or *congildones*) being mutually responsible in all breaches of the law.

The clergy of the Minster, with their tenants and dependents, would have very early formed such an association. They claimed many special privileges by charter from King Edward the Confessor and Archbishop Alfred, in respect to themselves and their lands wherever situate. Until within the last fifty years the liberty of St Peter was a separate jurisdiction, with its "Peter-prison," in the Minster yard, the dean being *custos rotulorum*. The justices of the peace were appointed by the crown to "hold sessions and act in a judicial manner for the towns and districts within the Liberty, as fully as the same are administered by the justices for the several ridings in Yorkshire."(3)

l. 10. *on feower healfe*, on the four parts or sides. We speak of "people coming from all quarters," without reference to any definite fourfold division; and our forefathers appear to have used *healf* in much the same sort of way, that is, if we assume the radical meaning(4) to have been half, and not side or part.

Cf. "On the foure halves of the hous about."—C. T. 3481.

"Sire Edward oure kyng, that ful ys of piete,
The Waleis(5) quarters send to is oune countre

---

(1) Martene, I, 184. In the so-called *Missa Illyrica*, ante, p. 263.

(2) In the "Canons enacted under King Edgar" it is assumed that priests are connected with gilds as universally as with a church, or ecclesiastical district (*scrift-scire*), in which they were the appointed confessors: "IX. And we enjoin that no priest deprive another of any of those things which appertain to him, neither in his minster, nor in his schrift-district, nor in his gildship (*gildscipe*), nor in any of the things appertaining to him."—Thorpe, A. L. II, 247.

The "Laws of King Ethelred" (lxii) admonish men "that they everywhere willingly maintain the 'grith' and 'frith' of God's churches."—Thorpe, A. L. I, 327.

(3) *Church of St Peter, York*, York, 1770, II, 247.

(4) Ulfilas renders μέρος by halba, 2 Cor. iii, 10; ix, 3, ἐν τούτῳ τῷ μέρει, "in thizai halbai," cf. our "behalf."

Our early versions render Matt. xx, 21, "ad dexteram," "on þine swiðran healfe."—*St Matthew, synoptically arranged* (Kemble and Hardwick), Cambridge, 1858; and Wyclif here, "riȝthalf" and "lefthalfe," and so the Heliand (Heine), 5563-4:

"an twa halba
Kristes an Kruci."

(5) Wallace was executed on Tower Hill, and his quarters were sent to Newcastle, Berwick, Perth, and Aberdeen.

Oᶇ four half to honge, huere myrour to be,
Theropon to thenche, that monie myghten se ant drede."
Political Songs, Wright, C. S., 1839, p. 213.

" þe vour gospelles þet holdeᵹ al Cristendom up a uour halues."
Ancren Riwle, p. 30.

"Fat bules um-sete me on al halves."—Ps. (22) xxi, 13.

P. 62, l. 10. *stowe*. In later forms "house." Cf. page 71, l. 12, and the ˮΑγιος οἶκος of the Greek Liturgies.

ll. 11, 12. This may perhaps be best explained by the practice of religious houses in this and foreign countries entering into agreements for certain stipulated privileges as to prayer and masses during life and after death, on behalf of the members of each other's communities. We find from the Revd. James Raine, D.D., the learned Durham antiquary, in his preface and notes to the Surtees Society's edition of the Liber Vitæ, that the monks of the cathedral church of Durham made agreements of this nature with their brethren at Canterbury, Winchester, Gloucester, Coventry, Westminster, Angers, Caen, Evreux, Fécamp, and other places; and he gives copies of conventions of this character in an appendix.(1) His son, Canon Raine of York, who is no less an authority in all that concerns the history of his own cathedral, is not aware of any documentary proof that York Minster ever issued letters of confraternity. It is, however, very possible that they may not have come down to us, and at all events we can easily conceive that mutual prayers of this character might have been offered without any formal agreement.

Cf. prayers at the offertory in the *Missa Illyrici :* "pro eleemosynariis nostris et pro his qui nostri memoriam in suis continuis orationibus habent." " Pro omnibus eleemosynas nobis facientibus, et pro his etiam qui se commendauerunt in nostras orationes, et qui nostram memoriam in suis orationibus habent."— Martene, I, 183.

l. 13. " There is ghostly kynrede thrughe fongynge of chyldren at the fonte stone."—*Festivale*, f. 167 *b*.

l. 14. *for ure gildan* and *gildsweostran*. From this it might seem that membership of a gild was referred to, simply because it was as general as the spiritual relationship contracted at the font, and that in this sense the words were equally applicable both to the clergy and the other worshippers who were present. It is, however, more probable that the reference is to some gild or gilds specially connected with the minster, other than the religious corporation of the *fraternitas*(2) *Kelideorum*, which was after-

---

(1) *Liber Vitæ Ecclesiæ Dunelmensis*, Surtees Society, 1841, p. xv, xvi, 135-7.

(2) Alcuin, the most illustrious of the non-residentiaries of the cathedral

wards superseded by that of the dean and chapter. The system of frith-bohr or frank-pledge, as mentioned above (p. 325), extended to the clergy of the minster and their tenants; and in this sense they were members of a frith-gild, but this separate mention of gilds seems rather to suggest the voluntary associations of a religious and social character which were contemporary with the old municipal organization, and continued to flourish long after it had fallen into decay.(1)

We have no evidence that there were any such gilds in York Minster at the date of the bidding prayer,(2) but on the parchment fly-leaves of the *Codex Exoniensis* in the custody of the dean and chapter of Exeter, and given by Bishop Leofric, who transferred his see from Crediton to that city in 1050, there are entries of several gilds in the county of Devon connected with the cathedral. There are given in Hickes' *Dissertatio Epistolaris* (pp. 18, 19), and though from seventy to a hundred years later than the present bidding prayer—Bishop Osbern there mentioned having held the see from 1073 to 1103—they enable us to form an opinion as to the character of the gilds here referred to. I am indebted to Archdeacon Woollcombe for copies of all the entries and for much valuable information on the subject, and by his kindness I am enabled to give a more correct copy of the first entry, which may serve as a sample of the whole:

"On cristes naman. *and sanctus* petrus ap*ostolus* an gildscipe is gegaderod on wudiberig-lande. *and* se *bisceop* Osbern. *and* þa canonicas ealle innan s*anctus* petrus minstre on excestre habbaðˇ underfangen þone ilcan geferscipe on broðˇervædˇdene gemænelice forðˇ mid oðˇrum gebroðˇrum. nu doðˇ hig æt ælc*um* heorðˇe to gecnawnisse þam canonicon anne penig to eastron ælce geare. *and* ealswa æt ælc*um* forðˇfarenu*m* gildan æt ælc*um* heorðˇe ænne penig to sawul-sceote. si hit bonda. si hit wif þe on þam gildscipe sindon. *and* þat sawul-gesceot scculon þa canonicas habban. *and* swilce þenisce don for hig swilce hig agon to donne.

and Ðis sindon heora name þe beoðˇ on þam gildscipe. Brihti. Wlnod. Ealdwine." &c.(3)

---

church of York, writing from the Frankish court to excuse his absence from the election of an archbishop, speaks of the minster clergy as "familia nostra." —*Opera*, Migne, I, 221.

(1) See Kemble's *Saxons in England*, I, 238-9, 251 ; and *English Gilds*, by the late Toulmin Smith, Esq., issued by this Society in 1870, and the valuable introduction by the loving hand of his daughter.

(2) The Gild of the Lord's Prayer in York, the ordinances of which were returned in obedience to the king's writ in the year 1388-9, found a chandelier with seven lights, in token of the seven supplications in the Lord's Prayer, which was hung in the Cathedral Church of York, and lighted on Sundays and Feast-days in honour of God Almighty, the maker of that prayer, of St Peter the glorious confessor, of St William, and all Saints.—*English Gilds*, 138.

(3) In the name of Christ and Saint Peter the Apostle, a gild is gathered

See p. 71, l. 11, " þe brether and sistirs of our moder Kerke, saynt Petyr house of ʒorke."

P. 62, l. 15. They are to pray for others, not only generally, but also to speed their prayers. Cf. a prayer for all conditions of men in the Liturgy of St Mark :

Τὰς δὲ εὐχὰς αὐτῶν . . . . πρόσδεξαι—Renaudot, I, 134.

l. 16. *seceð*, used in the sense of *coming to, visiting*.(1) This is retained in our authorized version, 2 Chron. i, 5, "And Solomon and all the congregation sought unto it" (sc. the brazen altar). Cf. Canons enacted under King Edgar : "XLV. And we læraðð þat man on rihtne timan tide singe. *and* preosta gehwile þonne his tid-sang on circan gesece." "*attend his canonical hours in the church.*"—Thorpe, A. L. II, 254.   And so in Chaucer :

"go seken halwes."—C. T. 6238 (go on pilgrimage).

"Seke us in þi hele" (*Visita nos in salutari tuo*).—Ps. (106) cv, 4.

We find this prayer for those who worship in the particular church in the Eastern Liturgies, but without the constant reference in it to their alms, which is a very prominent feature in the mediæval formularies.(2)   Cf. the bidding prayers in that of St Chrysostom :

"For this holy house ('Υπὲρ τοῦ ἁγίου οἴκου τούτου), and for those who seek unto it (εἰσιόντων ἐν αὐτῷ), with faith, and devotion, and the fear of God."—Goar, 74, 164.

l. 17. *during and after life*, giving and bequeathing.   Cf. the later forms, " þat gifes, or sends, or in testment wytes."—p. 71, l. 23.

l. 19-21. These blank lines are left for the insertion of names, or to suggest their recital to the priest who was bidding the prayers.   There is no similar provision in the later forms, but there can be no doubt that those who had sought the prayers of the Church continued to be mentioned by name in the bidding

---

in Woodbury, and the Bishop Osbern, and the canons all, in Saint Peter's minster at Exeter, have received that same society into brotherhood, in common henceforth with other brethren.   Wherefore do (*pay*) they for every hearth in acknowledgment to the canons, one penny at Easter each year, and also for every deceased member at every hearth one penny for soul-scot, be it husband, be it wife, who in the gild may be, and the soul-scot shall the canons have, and such services do for them, as they ought to do.   These are their names who are in the gild.   *Here follow eighteen names.*

(1) Cf. the " Canons enacted under King Edgar," Can. xv, "sece mid his ælmessan cirican gelome, *and* halige stowa mid his leohte gegreta," "frequently visit churches with his alms, and greet holy places with his light."—Thorpe, A. L. II, 282, 283.

The "Laws of King Ethelred" enjoin that men " frequently greet God's churches with light and with offerings" (*lacum*).—*Ib.* I, 326.

(2) Cf. p. 65, l. 3-6; p. 71, l. 18-27 ; p. 76, l. 10-21.

prayer. So late as in 1514 we find a payment to the curate of a parish church in the city of York for praying for the soules of a man and his wife "upon Sondays by hys bedcrolle in the pulpit,"(1) which very plainly points to the bidding prayer, or "preces pro diebus dominicis,"(2) which, as already mentioned, were said on Sundays and in parish churches in the pulpit.(3)

The bede-roll, like the older diptychs, contained the names of those who were to be prayed for. The *Liber Vitæ* of the Church of Durham, referred to above, p. 326, which was laid on the high altar(4) of that cathedral, down to the time of the Reformation, in order that the names might be recited from time to time, shows the manner in which benefactors to that church were commemorated. There can be no doubt that benefactors to the church of York received some such stated recognition. The mention of Therferth and the blank before us afford an example; and though I cannot refer to any similar record as to the church of York, we find an earlier instance in the case of the sister metropolitical church of Canterbury. In the ninth century Osuulf, Alderman, and Beornthryth his wife gave land with a prayer to be admitted to the fellowship of God's servants there, and those men who had given their lands to that church.(5)

P. 62, l. 22. *þor[fe]rþes.* I have already mentioned that I have to thank Mr Thompson for the way I have filled up this hole in the vellum. There is room for only two letters, and he showed me, what I had not noticed, that there was still the lower part of a long letter, which might have been "f," and that the remnant of a letter on the right hand side might very well have been an e, and that so the name might have been Thorferth.(6) He arrived at his conclusion in far less time than I have taken to tell it, though he was kind enough to point out to me the process; and I venture to mention it, as the lesson may be as useful to any of my readers, who may amuse themselves in making out mutilated manuscripts, as I have found it myself.

(1) *English Gilds*, p. 145.
(2) *Ante*, p. 75, l. 1. Cf. p. 64, 68.
(3) Lyndwood V, 5 (o), quoted *ante*, p. 318.
(4) In the "Rede Boke of Darbye," a MS. written about 1061, there is an addition to the first memento of the canon of the mass (*ante*, p. 104, l. 28), "omniumque . . . . quorum nomina super sanctum altare tuum scripta habentur."—Dr Henderson's *Preface, York Manual*, p. xxi, and see authorities there quoted.
(5) Kemble, *Cod. Diplom.* I, 292 (ccxxvi.).
(6) I have been at the pains to look through the names in the Liber Vitæ and other lists of about the date of our text; and I find, Thorthuarth, Thorberth, Thorbern, Thorth, and Theruerth, but no name except Thorferth that will answer the conditions of what was an unsolved riddle till Mr Thompson found the *mot de l'énigme*. Dr Rock (C. F. II, 358) prints "For for . . . erþer (forþfaeþer?) saule."

Who this Thorferth was I cannot pretend to say. I cannot find the mention of any such name in connection with the Minster. In the Saxon Chronicle, A.D. 911, we read of the army of the Northumbrians breaking the peace and overrunning Mercia. On their way homewards, among the thousands slain were "Ecwils cing and Healfden cing . . . . . . and Ðurferð hold." Under A.D. 921 there is mention of a "Thurferth eorl." Florence of Worcester refers the transactions there mentioned to the year 918, and also mentions "Danicus comes Thurferthus," but there is nothing to connect him with the north of Humber.

P. 62, l. 23. *fulluht underfengen.* The verb long continued to be used in this sense.

> "Cristendom his that sacrement
> That men her ferst fongeth."
> *Poems of William de Shoreham,* Wright, p. 8.

Fulluht in Myrc becomes "folowynge," and the verb "folowe." —*Instructions,* p. 6.

> Cf. "Pray fore men and women mo and lees,
> That Crystyndam han tane."—*Audelay,* p. 80.

l. 24. *fram adames dæge.* Prayer for all souls from the beginning of the world occurs in several of the eastern liturgies. In the *Oratio generalis* of the Syro-Jacobite *ordo,* translated by Renaudot, there is a similar mention of Adam: "Memoriam agimus . . . . . eorum qui nobiscum adstant et orant ; cum omnibus qui a sæculo tibi placuerunt ab Adamo ad hanc usque diem."— *Liturg. Orient.* II, 16-17.

P. 64. YORK BIDDING PRAYER II. This form is printed without alteration in the original punctuation or otherwise from Dr Henderson's transcript from Sir John Lawson's MS., which he had made for his edition of the York Manual, and most liberally placed at my disposal before his own work was published.

l. 5-6. Cf. the Liturgy of St Chrysostom : Ὑπὲρ εὐσταθείας τῶν ἁγίων τοῦ Θεοῦ ἐκκλησιῶν.—Goar, p. 64. The *al* seems to point to churches having been in the plural, as in the Greek. Stabilness is perhaps a better equivalent for εὐσταθεία than the stability of later forms.

l. 6. *pape.* The Latin form retained, as C 181 (the Rievaulx text), perhaps from the tendency of the northern dialect to retain or adopt the "*a.*" But see *person,* three lines lower down, and the corresponding place in the later forms, where the Latin form is equally retained,(1) contrary to what has long been the common spelling and pronunciation, possibly from some confused notion of a false analogy to *parishen* (parish, belonging to parish, parishi oner, or parish priest), *par'shen* (which is still heard), *parson.*

---

(1) Cf. popil (*populus*), l. 13.

P. 64, l. 6. *of Rome.* We may sometimes see the same thing when there was no question of a pope elsewhere, and therefore there may be no significance in this naming of Rome, though there certainly is in the mention of the *true* cardinals in the next form (p. 68, l. 11), but this was written during the schism, when the English in common with the Germans and other northern peoples adhered to the pope *at* Rome, whilst the Anti-pope at Avignon was acknowledged in France, Scotland, Spain, Sicily, &c. From 1400 to 1406 Boniface IX. and Innocent VII. were successively popes at Rome, and Benedict XIII. was pope at Avignon; and this manuscript, as pointed out by Dr Henderson (*York Manual,* Preface, p. xv.), was most probably written in 1403, as it contains a Paschal table, beginning with that year.

l. 9. *of religion.* In any regular order. See note, p. 168.

—*person.* Hence the MS. was for use in a parish church. The bidding prayer for the diocese of London, printed by Dr Henderson in the Appendix to the York Manual (p. 223), here reads: "for the patron and the parson of this chirche."

l. 13. *len,* grant, lend. See note, p. 322. Cf. Chaucer's *Boethius* (Morris), p. 139: "He (*God*) knoweþ what is couenable to euery wyȝt, and leneþ þat he wot is couenable to hem."

l. 14. *to tak or scheu.* This is not a prayer that the prelates should first take example themselves(1) and then show it to the people, which would have required *and,* not *or.* It is rather an instance of those alternative or re-duplicated expressions—either English and French, or an obsolete or obsolescent word and one marked with the current stamp—which were often introduced in forms for the people, when a word was likely to have been misunderstood, both before and after the Reformation. For example, within a few lines we have "lely and trwly," "bigged and edefied"; and in later bidding prayers, "maintened or uphalden," "honorde or wirchipt," "charge or cure," and so forth.

The prayer is to the same effect as that at the ordination of deacons, if it was not suggested by it, that they may have the grace, "bene vivendi aliis exemplum præbere." We find this in the eighth century in the Pontifical of Egbert, Archbishop of York.(2) The laying of one(3) hand of the bishop on the heads of the

---

(1) "Forthi bird yong men prid forsake
And of child Jesus bisen (*example*) take."—*E. M. H.* 110.
"Of me takeþ ensaumple alle:
Bicom noman þe deoueles thralle."
Legend of Pope Celestin, 586-7.
Cf. "Take, my brethren, the prophets .... for an example."—St James v, 10.

(2) *Ed.* Greenwell, p. 19. Cf. Collect *Pro Antistite, Miss. Ebor.* II, 174.

(3) "Solus episcopus qui eis benedicit manum super capita singulorum ponat."—*York Pontifical,* Henderson, p. 27; so also the form in Maskell,

deacons was substituted in later English uses for the older rite of
the laying on of the bishop's hands,(1) but the prayer itself is
found in every Latin ordinal, and is retained in the form for the
ordering of priests in the book of Common Prayer.(2)

Tak would therefore seem to be the older *tæcan, monstrare,
præbere.*(3) In the middle of the fifteenth century we find a
Lollard complaining that the gospels drawn into English by
worshipful Bede were "in many places of so old euglishe that
scant can anye englishe man reade them;"(4) and *tak* in this
place might very easily have been misunderstood fifty years
earlier, if it had not been for the addition of *show.*

P. 64, l. 21. *pes.* Cf. Liturgy of St Chrysostom: Δὸς αὐτοῖς, Κύριε,
εἰρηνικὸν τὸ βασίλειον, κ. τ. λ.—Goar, p. 78.

l. 23. *trwly.* An early instance of this use of *w* in a Northern MS.

P. 65, l. 1. Cf. ἔτι δεόμεθα ὑπὲρ τῶν . . . . κτητόρων.—Goar, p. 39.

l. 2. See note, p. 331.

l. 3—6. It is curious to find a corresponding enumeration in the
Æthiopic Liturgy, and, so far as I have observed, in that only of
the Eastern formularies: "Bless those who offer incense, and holy
bread and wine, and oil and ointment, and veils and books for
public service, and vessels for the temple; and may Christ our God
recompense them in the holy Jerusalem."—*Æthiopic Liturgies and
Hymns,* p. 18. Was there a common original?

l. 4. *towell.* It will be noticed that in the later forms (p. 71, l. 19;
p. 76, l. 12) "altar-cloth" has been added as an alternative
expression, upon the principle pointed out above (p. 331).

When the later forms were revised the word was probably
beginning to be understood in the sense in which we now

M. R. II, p. 192. "Manum super caput cujuslibet."—*Bishop Lacy's* (Exeter,
Cent XIV.) *Pontifical,* Ed. Barnes, p. 85.(*) I add the modern rubric of the
Church of Rome: "Solus Pontifex manum dexteram extendens, ponit super
caput cuilibet ordinando."—*Pontificale Romanum a Benedicto XIV, recognitum et castigatum,* Mechliniæ, 1862, p. 52.

(1) "Deinde solus episcopus qui eum benedicit manus super caput illius
ponat."—*Pontificale Ecgberthi,* S. S., p. 18. The old rite was brought back
at the Reformation: "*Then the Bishop laying his Hands severally upon the
Head of every one of them.*"—Rubric, the Ordering of Deacons.

(2) "That both by word and good example they may faithfully serve Thee
in this office to the glory of thy name and the edification of thy Church."

(3) "Ic þe mæg tæcan oðer þing." *I can teach thee another thing.*
Boethius quoted. Bosworth, *s. v.*
"he þonne tæceð him dædbote" (of the confessor assigning penance).—
Canons under King Edgar. Thorpe, A. L. II, 266, § 1.

(4) *A compendious old Treatise,* written about 1480, printed, Marburg,
1530, Arber's Reprints, 1871, *Rede me and be not wrothe,* &c., p. 175.

(*) The prayer above quoted is printed "*bene merendi,*" but I happen to have the
interleaved copy of the late Dr Oliver, a learned Roman Catholic clergyman, whose assist-.
ance Mr Barnes acknowledges in his preface, and he has corrected it "*bene vivendi.*"

exclusively use *towel*. Palsgrave (p. 282) gives only "towell to wype on—*touaylle;* " and so also in the Promptorium (p. 498) this is the only sense given.

The corresponding Latin form (*tualea*) occurs in the tenth *Ordo Romanus*(1) of the eleventh century as altar-cloth ; and so *tobalia*, in the next century.(2) *Tobalia* occurs in the twelfth *Ordo* as napkin,(3) table-cloth,(4) and altar-cloth.(5)

It may illustrate the change in the ordinary acceptation of the word in this country to mention that in the constitution of Arch-bishop Winchelsey, *Ut Parochiani*, A.D. 1305, there is specified among the necessary ornaments of the church, "Frontale ad magnum altare cum tribus(6) tuellis," for the three altar-cloths ;(7) and that Lyndwood, not much more than a hundred years later, glosses the three towels : "Two to be placed on the altar under the corporas : but the third will be for use at the lavatory to wipe the hands."(8)

The old English compound which towel appears to have dis-placed was weofod-sceat ;(9) but altar had been so fully naturalized that we can hardly class altar-cloth as a hybrid, and it has main-tained its place in common use to the present day, although the existing canon describes it, as now used in our churches, as "a carpet of silk or other decent stuff." (10)

---

(1) Mabillon, *Mus. Ital.* II, 102.
(2) *Ordo* xi, *u. s.* 162.
(3) *Ordo* xii, p. 198. *Italian*, Tovaglionino.
(4) *Ib.*, p. 202. *Italian*, Tovaglia. It is used in this sense in the " *Urbanitatis*," printed by Mr Furnivall in the Babees Book, p. 14 :
"Also kepe þy hondys faire & welle
Fro fylynge of the towelle."
Also as napkin, *Ib.*, p. 323, 326.
(5) *Ordo* xii, *u. s.* p. 205.
(6) The older illuminations show the cloth covering the altar on all four sides (*ante*, p. 174). Afterwards the altar-cloth appears to have been dis-tinguished from the frontal, as covering or hanging down only over the two narrower sides. In an inventory of the date of 1440 (Peacock's *Church Ornaments*, p. 184) we find—
"Item vi autere towells of lynen clothe . . . . "
"Item ii pendant towell of red silk . . . . and 2 black pendant towell of silke . . . . for the corners of the auter."
(7) See to the same effect a quotation from Myrc, *ante*, p. 173 ; and the corresponding constitution for the province of York, A.D. 1250.—*The York Pontifical*, Henderson, p. 371.
(8) *Provinciale*, Lib. III, Tit. xxvii, p. 252. In the *Novum Registrum*, or Body of Statutes for Lincoln Cathedral (A.D. 1440) already quoted, p. 173, we have in the same chapter (p. 25) "Manutergia sive tuelli," and (p. 26) "tuelli sive linteamina."
(9) It occurs in the *Canon of Ælfric*, XXII (Thorpe, A. L. II, 350), requiring the altar-cloths (*weofod-sceatas*) to be in good condition : and also in the Sherburn Inventory, *post*, p. 334.
(10) Canon (1604), LXXXII.

P. 65, l. 4. *anourment.* The constitution of Archbishop Winchelsey, A.D. 1305, *Ut parochiani* specifies the ornaments of the church and of the ministers thereof, and the rule according to which in the province of Canterbury they were to be provided by the parishioners, and rectors or vicars respectively.(1)   A decree to the same purpose was made by Archbishop Grey, some fifty years earlier, for the province of York,(2) and there was a corresponding ordination by the Dean and Chapter of York as to the churches in their jurisdiction.(3)

The many inventories that have been published of the ornaments of churches and of their plunder give abundant details of these ornaments ; but I add that of the Church of Sherburn, to which reference has already been made, p. 155, although it has been printed by Canon Raine,(4) as it is probably the oldest inventory of the kind which is extant :

"þis syndon þa cyrican madmas on Scirburnan · þœr synd twa *Cristes* bec · *and* ii · rodan · *and* i · aspiciens · *and* i · ad te leuaui · *and* ii · pistol bec · and i · mæsse boc · *and* i · ymener · *and* i · salter · and i · calic · *and* i · disc · *and* twa mæsse reaf · *and* iii messe hakelan · *and* ii weoued sceatas · *and* ii · ouer brædels · *and* iiii handbellan · *and* vi · hangende bellan." I venture to add my own translation, though I cannot be at all sure that I have been successful in my identification of several of the items ;—and in a matter of this kind, where there is any doubt, the dictionaries are of very little use:—These are the church ornaments at Shireburn: There are two Christ's books (*gospels*) ; and two crosses ; and one Aspiciens (*Antiphoner? ante,* p. 155) : and one Ad te levavi (*Grayle? ante,* p. 156) ; and two *Epistolaria ;* and one mass-book ; and one hymnal ; and one psalter ; and one chalice ; and one paten ;(5) and two(6) mass-vestments (*surplices or albs?*) ;

---

(1) *Lyndwood,* III, tit. xxvii.
(2) In the Register of Archbishop Gray, A.D. 1250, *York Pontifical,* Henderson, p. 371 ; but in Labb. & Coss., XI, col. 763, " incerto anno."
(3) York Fabric Rolls, 164.
(4) *Ib.,* 142.
(5) The " charger " of the A. V., St Mark, vi, 25 (or *discus* in the Vulgate), was rendered *disc* in our old English versions; and it would be curious to know whether our forefathers merely used the common name for the paten, or whether, as they adopted *calic* from the Latin *calix,* they borrowed an ecclesiastical name from the δισκος of the Greek rubrics. In the " *Danmarks og Norges Kirke-Ritual,*" the service-book of the Lutherans in Denmark and Norway, the "chalice and paten " are still " Kalk og Dish."
(6) There can be little doubt but that the " v fulle mæsse reaf " in the list of Bishop Leofric's gifts to his new cathedral at Exeter, where there is no mention of *hakelan* or other vestments for the priest,—like the *Missale vestimentum* of Archbishop Grey's constitution,—included all the vestments worn by the priest at mass (see *ante,* p. 167) ; but as there is no "full " in this case, and the *hakelan* follow, I am inclined to think we must take *mœsse*

and three(1) mass cloaks (*chasubles?*); and two altar-cloths; and two veils; and four hand-bells; and four hanging-bells.

---

reaf as intending only a part of the full mass-vestment of the priest,—other than the hakela—for in a country church there would not have been vestments for deacon and subdeacon as at Exeter,—and therefore most probably the albs or surplices which come within the name. Reaf by itself is simply a garment, and frequently occurs in Anglo-Saxon laws and canons of church vestments in general ; for example : the clergy were required at every synod to have " becc *and* reaf to godcundre þenunge" (*books and vestments for Divine Service*).— *Canons under King Edgar*, III, Thorpe, A. L. II, 244.

(1) In making this suggestion I must admit that the Icelandic dictionary gives (C-V, 425) *cope* as the meaning of the cognate "*messu-hökul*" ; and if it were simply a question of linguistic, and more especially of Scandinavian, learning, I should not venture to differ from this, our highest authority.

There are those who suppose that the chasuble was always the exclusive eucharistic vestment in the west; and in that case the name alone would exclude the cope. For myself I lay no stress upon the mention of *mæsse*.— The name of mass was not exclusively used of the office of the eucharistic sacrifice ; and both chasuble and cope were for centuries used at mass and other offices by the celebrant and the assistant ministers, priests, deacons, and subdeacons. But I assume that the specific difference of the two vestments was this : that the cope was open down the front; and the chasuble was made with an opening in the middle to put over the head.

In this it was like the Roman *pænula* (see Dictionary of Greek and Roman Antiquities, Smith, *s. v.*); and without entering into the question whether, as some tell us, the "*cloke*" that St Paul left at Troas was a mass-vestment, or whether he used it for winter warmth, it is enough for our present purpose that Ulfilas translated its Greek equivalent φελόνης or φαινόλης (2 Tim. iv, 13) by *hakul*. So much then we know of the use of the word in a kindred language before our forefathers called their church vestment *hakela*. No description has come down to us from those times, and we may therefore accept the evidence which is afforded as to its precise meaning by its use in cognate languages in the present day. Nor does it seem unreasonable to suppose that when the Icelanders and other northern peoples received their Christianity and eccl siastical organization from this country they adopted its English name with the *hakela* of the Anglo-Saxon Church. Now the name of the vestment which is worn by the Lutheran ministers in those countries at the administration of the Lord's Supper, is in Iceland *messu-hökul*, and in Denmark and Norway, *messehagel* or *hacke*—evidently allied to the *mæsse-hakelan* of our inventory—and the vestment so worn is not a cope, open in front, but a chasuble, with a cross on the front and back, put on over the head, not indeed of the ancient full shape, but like the modern Roman chasuble, cut away at the shoulders, as chasubles began to be, after the introduction of the elevation of the host, for greater convenience in the execution of this ceremony.

In the absence of more direct evidence it makes for the correctness of my suggestion of *hakela* not being intended of a vestment open in front, that Mount Heckla is so called from a kindred Icelandic word applied to the cloud which caps its summit,—an idea which we also find in an English poem :

"Uch hille hade a hatte, a myst-hakel huge "
    Sir Gawayne (about A.D. 1360), Ed. Morris, l. 2081.

P. 65, l. 5. *halybred.* See the revised formula, p. 71, l. 32. For a very complete account, see Scudamore, *Notitia Eucharistica*, 1876, p. 887—893. See also Mr Peacock's note, *Myrc*, p. 89; Gerbert, *Disq.* I, 406; Maskell, M. R., I, p. cclviii—cclxi.

I add from Audelay's Poems (p. 80) an extract showing the received opinion on this head:

> " And oche day thi masse thou here
> And take hale bred and hale watere
> Out of the prestis hond ;
> Soche grace God hath ȝif the,
> ȝif that thou dey sodenly
> Fore thi housil hit schal the stond."

From the following extract from Brunne's *Handlyng Synne* holy bread seems to have carried home(1) to those who did not hear mass:

> " þe seruyng man þat seruyþ yn þe ȝere
> Oweþ to come when he haþ leysere.
> ȝyf þou come noghte, algate y rede
> Ete noght ar þou haue holy brede,
> For to many þynges hyt may auale
> To soule helpe, or lyues trauayle.
> þy body ȝyf þan smartly endes
> Hyt ys for housyl aȝens þe fendes."—l. 835—842.

—— *gaf to this kirk to day.* Theirs (*Superstitions*, II, 518) mentions that in some French churches the bread which was given to be blessed, was presented at the offertory to the sound of trumpets, drums, fiddles, hautboys, and flutes, ornamented with banderoles and with liveried attendants.

l. 11. *has gane or sal ga.* It is curious to observe how this reproduces the τοὺς ἀποδημήσαντας ἡμῶν ἀδελφοὺς ἢ μέλλοντας ἀποδημεῖν ἐν παντὶ τόπῳ κατευόδωσον of the liturgy of St Mark, (2) in respect to actual and intending travellers, though the prayer is here confined to those who go on pilgrimage. See the use of " gode gates," *ante*, p. 69, l. 36 ; and p. 78, l. 32, where " pylgrim-ages " replaces it.

l. 12. *brigges and stretes.* In the Canons under King Edgar, the making of bridges over deep waters and foul ways is specified among the almsdeeds, by which in the way of *dædbota* or penances much may be redeemed—*mycel man mæg alysan.*(3) Centuries later we find giving money to the poor, or for bridges,

---

(1) It was also the use of Rouen, down to the last century, to bring home small bits of the *pain béni* for those who were not able to be present at mass.— *Voyages Liturg.*, p. 422.

(2) Renaudot, I, 138. Cf. Malan, *Coptic Liturgy*, p. 28.

(3) Canons XIII and XIV, Thorpe, A. L. II, 282.

or church-work, are classed together as ways of making restitution when those who have been wronged are not to be found.(1) Later still we have Cardinal Pole in 1557 in his visitation articles inquiring, "XXVI. Item, Whether any do withhold any money or goods bequeathed to the mending of the highways or other charitable deed ?"(2)

I add a reference to this practice, which puts it on its true footing, from "Christ's Own Complaint," printed by Mr Furnivall from an early fifteenth century MS. :

> " þe porre peple þou doist oppresse
> Wiþ sleitis and wilis ful manye also :
> þou makist chirchis, and doiste singe messe,
> And mendist weies, men on to go ;
> And sum men þee banne & summe blesse ;
> Which schal y heere of þeise two ?
> If þou wolt haue grace as þou doist gesse,(3)
> Lete al falsnes be fleemyd þee fro."(4)

P. 65, l. 22. *in dette.* Cf. St Matt. vi, 12 : " Forgive us our debts, as we forgive our debtors," where " debts " includes sins of omission and sins of commission. The "*debita*" of the schoolmen, the Latin of the Vulgate in this place, was used of *duties,* and it would seem that *debt* is here intended of *failures* in duty rather than of *breaches* of duty, though some sins of omission were counted as deadly sins, and some sins of commission were not so classed.

We have an example of "debt" in the sense of duty in Thoresby's Catechism (*fol.* 295), speaking of the neglect of the people by prelates and priests,

> " that er halden be dette for to lere thame,"

where the Latin is "*juxta debitum curæ instruere.*"

---

(1) *Old English Homilies,* Morris, I, 31.

(2) Cardwell, *Doc. Ann.* I, 207. In 1372 Johannes de Oggill bequeaths "*ponti de Shincliff Csolidos argenti,*" together with lights and gifts of money to monks and friars.— *Wills and Inventories* (Dr Raine), Surtees Society, I, 34. Another Ogle—Robertus Ogill, miles—in 1410 also leaves 100 shillings to mend broken bridges in Northumberland, and specially in his own domain, as his executors see fit (*ib.* p. 48) ; and similar examples might be produced to any extent.

We may trace the same feeling in the way in which the money received for discarded vestments and other ornaments in the second year of King Edward VI was disposed of—for example, Hamerton in Huntingdonshire : "which money [the churchwardens] declare upon their othes was bestowed in the repair of on great bridge in the towne."

(3) Gesse was probably beginning to have the sense in which it is now commonly used in *old* England. A MS. of some thirty or forty years later reads " as þou thenkis."

(4) *Political, Religious, and Love Poems,* E. E. T. S., 1866, p. 181.

It may be that "debt" is an allusion to the parable of the un-
merciful servant to whom his lord forgave the debt(1) of ten
thousand talents ; and that it is to be understood of venial sins as
contrasted with mortal sins.   In this case there is not the cross-
division of the former suggestion, for each of these classes of sin
excludes the other ; but I am not able to point to any contemporary
authority, where debt is used in this sense.

P. 65, l. 22. *in prison.*   If this stood by itself, there would be no
difficulty in explaining it of purgatory, especially in connection,
as it is, with the prayer for those in deadly sin, were it not that
this first part of the Bidding Prayer is otherwise exclusively for
the living, and that prayers for the dead and all souls in purgatory
are specially bidden afterwards, p. 66, l. 26—34.

This prayer for those in prison, is not inserted in the corresponding place in the other York forms, where prayers are bidden
for those in debt and deadly sin ; nor, so far as I have observed,
is it in any other.   In the later forms we have (p. 70, l. 7) "bun
in dette or in dedely syn ; " and in the Sarum form, printed by
Dr Henderson, we have "alle þilke þat liggeþ in dedly synne
y-bounde,"(2) and it is not impossible that a reference to bonds in
an older form, or the mention of debt in this, may have suggested
the "poor debtors," or other prisoners, to a scribe, who had learnt
that it was one of the corporal acts of mercy

"to help them that in prison er,"(3)

and who might not have been alive to any incongruity in this
intermingling of spiritual and temporal needs, which would hardly
have found a place in the carefully arranged devotions of an
earlier period.

l. 25.   The people are to say a Pater and an Ave instead of the
Lord's Prayer of the earlier form (p. 62, l. 12, &c.), and our existing use (p. 321).

P. 66, l. 13. *breder.*

Cf. the Austin friar to Pierce the Ploughman :

"And ȝif þou hast any good · & wilt þi-selfe helpen,
Helpe us hertliche þerwithe · & here I vndertake,
þou schalt ben broþer of our hous · & a boke habben
(At þe next chapitre) · clereliche ensealed ;
And þanne oure prouinciall · haþ power to assoilen
Alle sustren & breþeren · þat beþ of our order."—l. 324—9.

See also, as quoted by Mr Skeat in his note upon this place :

---

(1) St Matt. xviii, 27,—"debitum dimisit ei."—*Vulg.*
(2) *York Manual,* p. 221*. Cf. *ante,* p. 71, l. 7, and note, p. 341, "bun.'
(3) *Catechism,* Thoresby's Register, fol. 295. "I was in prison, and ye
came unto me."—St Matt. xxv, 36.

"Ye sayn me thus how that I am your brother
Ye, certes, quod the frere, trusteth wel ;
I took our dame the letter under oure sel."

C. T. 7707—10.

P. 66. l. 14. *sisters.* The three great minsters or collegiate churches, York, Beverley, and Ripon, are here specified. Southwell, which was within the diocese of York, is also mentioned in the other forms (pp. 71, 78). As to York, it has been already mentioned (*ante,* p. 326) that there is no record of any charters of fraternization at York Minster. I have seen it stated that there were *sisters* belonging to Beverley Minster ; but I can find no authority for the statement ; nor have I chanced to meet with any record of a foundation of this description in any English cathedral. At Rouen there were thirty canonesses, either spinsters or widows. In the seventeenth century their prebends were not worth above six francs, paid by the Archbishop ; and at three obits, which were the only services they were required to attend in the year, the Chapter made a distribution of a like sum amongst those present. Although the value was small, these prebends were sought after by persons in good circumstances, because they conferred the legal privileges of the Chapter, but it was supposed that formerly they were more valuable, and that these sisters had charge of and washed the church linen.(1)

l. 31. *kirk-3erde. Kirk-garth* is more common in Yorkshire in the present day, where *church-yard* has not displaced it ; but there is abundant evidence that *"yard"* was formerly in common use, were it only that at York, what in some cities is the cathedral close, for centuries has been called the Minster-yard.(2)

Cf. Ἔτι δεόμεθα ὑπὲρ ἀδελφῶν ἡμῶν τῶν ἐνθάδε εὐσεβῶς κειμένων καὶ ἀπανταχοῦ.—*Euchologion* (Venice, 1854), p. 18. It will be seen that in our next bidding prayer (p. 72, l. 24) "or in any other" is added. In the Greek there is no mention of purgatory.

P. 68. *BIDDING PRAYER III.* I have transcribed this from the Manual in York Minster Library (XVI. M. 4), carefully preserving the punctuation of the original, except as marked within brackets. The MS. is upon vellum, $10 \times 6\frac{1}{4}$, and in good condition, but has been rebound.(3) Mr Bond and Mr Thompson of the British

---

(1) *Voyages Liturgiques,* 374-5. The *Novum Registrum,* or collection of Statutes of Lincoln elsewhere quoted, require (p. 26) the treasurer to find a washer-man or washer-woman (*lotorem vel lotricem*), to wash the albs [which would seem to include the surplices], the hand-towels, and linen of the altars.

(2) "Garth" was also used. In 1383, John of Croxton wytes his body to be buried "in the Minster Garth."—*Test. Ebor.*, I, 185.

(3) It was lettered "Rituale," which is the name of the corresponding Roman service-book ; very much as I have found old English portesses bound and catalogued as "Breviaries," when, not unfrequently, as also in the case of Horæ, &c., they have not been described as "Missale," or "Missale Romanum."

Museum, who did me the favour to examine it in 1870, dated it 1440—1450, judging from the handwriting only. It would seem that, although the Bidding Prayer was here an integral part of the book, as it was afterwards of the printed edition, it was not considered as properly belonging to the manual, which ends with the following rubric : "**Explicit manuale secundum usum Ebora-censem**," which is followed without a break by *Deprecatio*, &c., as in line 1.

This form was intended for use in a parish church (l. 20), within the City of York (p. 69, l. 16-17) ; after 1396, when it was made a city and county in itself, and sheriffs were appointed instead of bailiffs ; and also (l. 11) after or during the schism of rival popes which began with the election at Avignon of Clement VII. in 1378. All these notes of time tally with the date assigned by the Museum authorities, as mentioned above, from an examination of the hand-writing.

P. 68, l. 7. *þe.* The thorn letter (þ) here and elsewhere in the manu-script is written very much as the wen (ƿ) was written, when the two characters were used together.

l. 11. *trewe cardinals.* "True" was most probably inserted at the time of the schism, when there were pope and anti-pope, and for some time those rival popes, each with his college of adherent cardinals, mutually denouncing and excommunicating the others. This schism, begun in 1378, was ended in 1429, by Clement VIII, who had been elected to succeed Benedict XIII, voluntarily renouncing the pontificate.(2)

—— *patriarck of ierusalem,* not mentioned in other northern forms, but commonly inserted in the Bidding Prayers of the southern province.

l. 12—14. Cf. Maundeville, "For wee ben clept cristene men aftre Criste oure fadre. And ȝif wee ben righte children of Crist, we oughte for to chalenge the heritage, that oure fadre lafte us, and do it out of hethen mennes hondes. But nowe pryde covetyse, and envye han so enflawmmed of the lordes of the world, that they are more besy for to disherite here neyghbores, more than for to chalenge or to conquere here righte heritage before seyd."(1)

P. 69, l. 9. *communers,* first mentioned.

l. 17-18. Before the passing of the municipal reform act the corpora-tion of York consisted of a Lord Mayor, twelve aldermen, two sheriffs, "the twenty-four," so-called, whether more or less than that number, being such as had passed the office of sheriff ; and seventy-two common-councilmen. Henry VIII. in 1518 granted a common council of forty-one, and this number was enlarged to seventy-two by Charles II. The sheriffs were three in number when first appointed in lieu of bailiffs by the charter of 19 Richard II.

---

(1) *Voiage and Travaile,* Hailiwell, p. 3.   (2) See note, p. 331.

It will be noticed that the corporation continues to be specified in the Bidding Prayer (*ante*, p. 320), still used in the Minster.

P. 69, l. 26. *in quart and heill.* Cf. the "health and wealth" of the Prayer Book.

> " A, Laverd, sauf make þou me ;
> A, Laverd, in quert to be."
>
> (*O Domine salvum me fac, O Domine bene prosperare.*)
>
> Ps. (118) cxvii, 25.

> " Keper of mi querte." (*Susceptor salutis meæ.*)
>
> Ps. (89) lxxxviii, 27.

> " For þai er swa wilde, when þai haf quert
> þat na drede þai can hald in hert."—*P. C.* 326-7.

> " Ihesu ! putte in-to myn herte
> þe memorie of þi pyne !
> In sijknes, and eek in qwarte
> þi loue be euere myne ! "
>
> *Hymns*, Furnivall, p. 27, l. 169—172.

Quart (more rarely *quert*) is explained by a reference to the O.F. *cuor, queor* or *queur* (Lat. *cor*) ; but, as it was used for the most part in the northern dialect, more especially at first, may it not be a northern form of the A.S. *heorte*, which came to be used in the sense good heart, good case, well-being and safety, when the other form, heart, was used in the more general sense ? Cf. Icel. *hjarta* ; Goth. *hairto*, Gr. καρδιά.

P. 70, l. 6. *in quart*, in good condition (*heart*) and safety. See last note.

l. 6, 7. *bun in dette or in dedely sin.* Cf. p. 65, l. 22, the note, p. 338, and the quotation there, from the Sarum Bidding Prayer, where we have "y-bounde."

It will be admitted that " bun " in this place is *bound*, and that it is not to be explained as *ready ;*(1) and so too in the phrase in

---

(1) *Ante*, p. 161. The nautical *bound*, as in " *bound* for New York," is explained by an authority to which, as a rule, I am always prepared to defer, as if *bun* or *bown (ready)* were " now corrupted into *bound*." But this phrase is used of a ship, not only when in port ready, or making ready for sea, but also at sea, as, for example, when hailed or hailing, with reference to the port, cruising-ground, or point of rendezvous, to which she is under engagement, or orders, to make her voyage, when it seems more natural to understand it of *bound*, the pp. of *bind*.

> Cf. " When the messes were don
> And homward were alle bon."(*)

It may be that the etymological significance of the word came to be lost sight of, and that it became associated with the notion of bonds and binding obligation. In the East Riding *bun* or *bown* is still in every day use, in the

(*) *Coronation of K. Arthur* (R. Brunne), quoted by Mr Furnivall, Preface, *Handlyng Synne*, p. xl.

the next page (p. 71, l. 28), "women bun with childer"—the "women labouring of child" of our English litany—it cannot be "*bun,*" ready or about to be delivered, for we have the corresponding phrase in the Bedes for the Sonday in the Festival "in our ladyes bonds,(1) and with child," and the meaning is still more clearly brought out by the form in a MS. Sarum Missal (about 1400), printed by Dr Henderson: "And for alle wymmen þat beth in oure lady byndes that God for his mercy so hem vnbynde as hit be best to lyf and to soule."(2)

P. 71, l. 13. *Suthwell.* The county of Nottingham was then within the diocese of York. Cf. *ante,* p. 66, l. 14, where the three great churches in Yorkshire only are mentioned.

l. 15. *godhede.* Goodness here, rather than Godhead.

> "Evrich thing mai losen his godhede
> Mid unmethe and mid over-dede."
>
> *Owl and Nightingale,* 351-2.

"þat is þe perfeccion and þe guodhedde."—*Ayenb.* 79.
Contra—"þat bifalleþ to Godes godhede
    As wel as to his manhede."—*Castel off Love,* 81-2.

l. 17. *maste to goddes louing,* ad majorem Dei gloriam. *Louing* may have been out of use in the sense of praise, when this Bidding Prayer was printed in the following century; for in the printed manual (*ante,* p. 78, l. 23) we have "plesure;" and so also "welfare" instead of *heill.*

l. 25. *kirkwarke,* or what in later times, as at York, was called the fabric fund. Philippa, Countess of March, in 1381, devises "al overaigne de mesme l'eglise (*Austin Canons at Bisham*), deux cent3 livres a tiel entent qe les priour et covent de la dite maison teignront solempement le jour de mon anniuersaire as tou3 jours."(3) John of Croxton of York in 1383, "wytes to Saynte Peter warke x s."(4) And so Robert Willoughby in 1433, wills "To þe kyrke-

---

sense of ready, and, if I do not mistake, often with a further sense of duty or necessity. I may illustrate this by the way in which the word was lately used by both parties to a quarrel I was able to make up. One said, "I'se bun (*ready*) to shake hands," and the other, "I'll own I'se bun (*bound*) to submit."

(1) This may be explained by a devotion in the York Horæ, f. clxxvi:

"¶. For women trauaylynge of chylde. **Ps.** Beatus [Ps. i, with Gloria Patri] ✠ Maria peperit *Christum.* ✠ Anna Mariam. ✠ Elizabeth iohannem. ✠ Cilina remigium. ✠ Sic me feliciter parere concedat *omnipotens* deus in perfecto maturitatis tempore. Amen. **De Sancta Maria. Anti-***phona.* Sub tuam protectionem confugimus, ubi infirmi acceperunt virtutem: propter hoc tibi psallimus dei genetrix virgo. **versus.** Sancta dei genetrix virgo semper Maria. **Reponsorium.** Intercede pro nobis ad dominum deum nostrum."

(2) *York Manual,* Surtees Society, p. 221.
(3) Nichol's *Royal Wills,* 99.   (4) *Test. Ebor.* I, 185.

werke xl.s."(1) In 1444, we have a legacy "Fabricæ ecclesiæ Cathedralis Eboracensis xl s."(2) In 1448, Johnson "laborer," leaves " Ad opus ecclesiæ meæ, xx s."(3)

P. 72, l. 3. *hayls*. This word is specially applicable to the use of the Ave Maria, which, as has been pointed out, p. 184, as used in the Church of England before the reformation, did not include any prayer.

Here for the first time we have the use of the *Ave* without the *Pater-noster*, as the use of it with the Pater-noster was an innovation on the older form. Cf. p. 61, ll. 7, 12, &c.

P. 74. BIDDING *PRAYER IV*. This form is written in a later hand, on a blank leaf at the end of MS. Manual, from which Form III is printed. It will be observed that it leaves out the Latin devotions of the priest and clerks, and is in other ways much shorter than the other forms.

l. 20. *nyde*. In the Festival the corresponding phrase is "that haue most nede and leste helpe." Cf. p. 72, l. 2, where the living who have need of prayer are mentioned.

In the Sarum Prymer of 1538, is " A prayer to God for them that be departed, hauyng none to praye for them. *Miserere quæsumus Domine Deus*. Haue mercy (we beseche the lorde god) thorough the precyous passyon of thy onely begotten sonne our lorde Jesu Christe, haue mercy on those soules that haue no intercessours unto the to haue them in remembraunce, whiche haue neyther hope nor comforte in theyr tormentes, but onely for that they be formyd after thy ymage and likenes, and insigned with the sygne of faythe, which eyther by neglygence of them that be lyuynge, or longe process of tyme, are forgotten of theyr frendes and posteryte. Spare them, lorde, and defende thy creacyon, neyther despyse thou the worke of thyne handes, but extende thy ryght hande on them, and delyuer them frome the dures of theyr paynes, and bryng them into the company of the celestyall cytezens, thorough thy excedyng greate mercyes, whiche are most excellent aboue all thy workes. Which lyuest and reygnest, god, worlde without ende. So be it."(4)

P. 75. YORK *BIDDING PRAYER V*, from the edition of 1510,(5) with

---

(1) *Test. Ebor.*, II, 41.   (2) *Id.* II, 93.   (3) *Id.* II, 121.
(4) Maskell, M. R. II, 174, and see the rest of the note there.
(5) This edition is in small quarto (9¼×7). The colophon (fol. 103 *b*) is as follows: "¶ Manuale insignis ecclesie **Eboracen***sis* impressum per **Wynandu***m* **de Worde** commorantem **london***ii* in vico nuncupato fletestrete sub intersignio solis: vel in cimiterio sancti pauli sub ymagine dive marie pietatis (pro **Johan***ne* gachet et **Jacobo ferrebouc sociis**). Finit Anno d*o*mini millesimo qui*n*ge*n*tesimo nono quarto ydus Februarii.
Sane hoc volumen digessit arte magister
Wynandus de worde incola londinii."
Dr Henderson (*York Missal*, II, 258) enumerates copies as known to be

the addition of marginal notes, but without any alteration in the
punctuation, the contractions only being expanded in Italic, and
the Latin broken into lines and paragraphs. A comparison with
the older manuscripts shows—and this may also be observed in
the printed Ebor *Horæ*, and north country wills, and formal documents from the latter part of the fourteenth century downwards(1)
—that the northern dialect had ceased to be intentionally used as
the written language of northern clerks, though the strangeness of
the southernizing process is betrayed by the overlooking of several
northern peculiarities, or rather northern peculiarities other than
those which have been adopted in the common tongue.

In addition to the usual substitution of more modern words for
those which had become obsolete or obsolescent the following
may be instanced as being more properly dialectic changes:

bones	*for*	banes	moste	*for*	maste
bretheren, broders	„	brether	shall	„	sal
cherche	„	kirk	sowles	„	saules
every	„	ilk	such	„	swilk
from	„	fra	their	„	þare
great	„	mykill	them	„	þame, þam
hathe (3 *sing.*)	„	hase, hafes	therafter	„	þarefter
helpe (*imperat.*)	„	helpes	where	„	whar
hertly	„	hartly	whiche	„	qwilk
holy	„	haly	whome	„	whame
londe	„	land	worke	„	warke

extant in the five following libraries—Bodleian (Z. 13, *Th. Seld.*); Ripon
Minster; St Cuthbert's College, Ushaw; Beresford Hope, Esq.; and Magdalen
College, Cambridge. That in the Ripon Library is very closely cut, but is
otherwise perfect, and was lent to me for the purpose of this edition by the
kindness of Dr Hugh McNeile, the then Dean of that cathedral.

Dr Henderson mentions another edition of the manual (Gachet, without
date) in Archbishop Marsh's Library, Dublin.

(1) In 1493, "I, Robert Calverley of Calverley, esquier, being in good mynd,
maketh my testament in this forme . . . . . to be beried in the church of
Calverley."—*Test. Ebor.*, IV, 157. In 1541, Sir Richard Towgall, a chantry-
priest at Gateshead, Durham, "to be buryed within the church of gatyshead,
where my father and mother doithe lye."—*Wills & Invent.*, S. S. I, 117.

1545. "I Thomas man*ers* whol of mynd *and* remembr*ance* maiketh this
my testament . . . to be buryd in the quere of the Churche of Holye Elande
[*Holy Island*], wher my *predecessors* doythe lye *with* soulle messe *and*
derege."—*Ib.* I, 122.

On the 13th April, 1513, the tower of St Mary's, Beverley, gave way
and fell through the roof in the time of service. It is commemorated by an
inscription carved on a beautiful oak skreen, not later than 1530, which, not
without the protest of Sir Gilbert Scott, who tempered the recent restoration,
has now ceased to ornament the church. The northern *saules* has held its
ground, though *church* has taken the place of *kirk*: "Pray God haue merce
of all the sawllys . . . . slayn at the fauling of thys ccherc."

On the other hand the *-s* in the singular and plural of the present tense and the *-and* of the participle retain their ground, though the southern *hath* has supplanted the older *has*, and the final *-s* has been discarded in the imperative. It will be noticed that the following are in the plural :

redys	singes	worshippes
gives	sendes	upholdes

Does (not *doth*) occurs in the singular ; and *land-tylland* remains unaltered.

P. 75, l. 9. *Trewe to the kynge.* As the specification of the "true" cardinals was due to the schism in the papacy (*note*, p. 340), there can be little doubt that this addition to the earlier forms must have dated from the Wars of the Roses.

l. 10. In 1534, when Henry VIII. finally broke with the pope, he directed his name and the word *pope* " to be utterly razed " out of all prayers, calendars, church books, &c. ; and he was thereafter designated simply as the " Bishop of Rome," in all acts of parliament and other formal documents. In the June of this year there was issued a special document, limiting this part of the bidding prayer, " word for word."

In 1542 the Upper House of the Convocation of Canterbury considered the question of correcting and reforming portesses, missals, and other books ; and the more complete rasing and abolishing of the names of the Roman pontiffs and Thomas Becket by all priests. It continued to be one of the questions at visitations down to the year 1547, "Whether they have put out of their church books this word *papa*, and the name and service of Thomas Becket."

The danger of arbitrary punishment was so great that the presence or absence of these proscribed names may be looked for as a proof of a manuscript or book being English, or, at least, of its having been in this country until the danger was past. Of the large number which I have examined, I have never seen a service book which did not shew at least a colourable obedience.(1) In the beautiful Sherborne missal,(2) of which, by the kindness of its noble owner, I have made a renewed examination after these pages had been sent to the press, I noticed that this obedience had been carried to a great extreme—possibly because in this case the danger was very great—unless indeed it was the vandal act of some prying visitor or king's commissioner thereto authorized, who was searching for a pretext to fill the royal exchequer or his own. The page containing the musical notes of

---

(1) See above, p. 102, ll. 11, 18 ; p. 104, l. 23 ; and (where one might not have expected to find it) in the Vernon MS., p. 136, l. 294 ; p. 137, l. 325, and p. 139, l. 389.

(2) Above, p. 257, *n.* ; 306, *n.*, &c.

the *Gloria in excelsis* (p. 359) is ornamented in the margin with a series of most exquisite miniatures of pope, cardinal, patriarch, archbishop, &c. ; which remain uninjured except that the tiara on the pope's head has been roughly defaced. The only other miniature which appears to have been subjected to maltreatment is one in the mass (p. 44), "Sancti t[ho]m[e] martiris" (*Dec.* 29), where in a miniature of the archbishop, in the initial D of the collect, the jewels on the front of the mitre appear to have been purposely washed off, though the form of mitre has been allowed to remain, and the face is uninjured.

P. 76, l. 2. *quene.* Elsewhere the omission of a prayer for the queen (C 183), or the pope (B 362), has furnished a note of time. Henry VIII. was married to Catharine of Arragon on the 3rd June, 1509. The manual from which this form is printed was finished(1) on the 10th February, 1510. His queen was therefore prayed for, and it will be observed that it is equally exact in not praying for royal children.(2)

l. 20. The print inserts " our lady," and reads *sayntes* for the *halouse* of the earlier text, p. 71, l. 27.

P. 78, l. 23. *plesure.* This change proves that the "*louing*" of the earlier form (p. 71, l. 17) was already losing its first sense of praise.

P. 80, l. 13. *Ye or I be bounde to pray for.* Cf. " pro quibus exorare jussi et debitores sumus."—*Missa pro animabus quibus tenentur,* Collect, *Miss. Ebor.,* II, 188.

This is expressed more fully in the Bidding Prayer for the Diocese of London (*MS. Harl.* 335), printed by Dr Henderson : "Also yee shall pray speciale for the soules for which ye have had any gode by yefte or by qwest, whereby that ye have your lyvynge and your sustenance."—*York Manual,* 225*.

THE YORK HOURS OF THE CROSS.

The Hours of the Cross must not be confounded with the older Office of the Cross,(3) or the *Cursus de Sancta Cruce,* mentioned by Udalric. They do not appear to be earlier than the beginning of the

---

(1) See the colophon, *ante,* p. 344, *n.*

(2) Cf. *ante,* p. 62, l. 8 : "þe kynges childer."

(3) The Cotton MS. Titus D. XXVII. contains Offices of the Trinity and the Cross. The date is 1012 × 1020. See description with the photograph, No. 60, of the plates of the Palæographic Society. Fol. 66—73 are devotions for those who desire to pray before the Crucified ("*si vis orare ante cruci- fixum*"), first *ad pedem dextram* ; then *ad pedem sinistrum,* and so on *ad dexteram manum—ad sinistram manum—ad os eius—in medio pectore—ad aures eius.*

fourteenth century. One MS. (Reichenau 82) claims Pope Benedict XII, who died in 1342, as having put them forth. Another XIV. Century MS. assigns them to his predecessor John XXII. A third manuscript of the same century, also quoted by Mone,(1) has the following metrical prologue :

> "Subscriptas horas edidit de Ihesu passione
> Egidius episcopus ex devotione,
> Trecentisque diebus indulgentiæ dotavit,
> Quos et apostolicus Iohannes confirmavit."

By whomsoever written they became very general in Western Europe, and this has led to many various readings of the text, which are noted in Mone. There are also several variations between the Ebor Text and the Sarum, for which the reader is referred to the Sarum *Horæ*, or to the transcript in Maskell's *Monumenta Ritualia*, II, p. xi—xviii.

Mone gives a curious Norman French translation of the xv century. There is an old Dutch translation in his *Niederländ. Volksliteratur*, p. 151, and an old High German translation in Hoffman's *Geschichte des Teutschen Kirchenliedes*, p. 192. Mr Maskell gives the anthems in Latin with an English metrical version from printed Sarum *Horæ* and *Primers* ;(2) and metrical and prose translations from early fifteenth century manuscripts.(3) Dr Morris also prints a metrical version, from a fourteenth century manuscript,(4) but none of them claim to be of the York use, or are written in the northern dialect.

The hours, here first printed, are taken from a manuscript Ebor *Horæ*—the only one that is known—in the York Minster Library (XVI, K, 6), which appears in the catalogue, and is lettered on the modern binding as "Liber Precum, Sæc. XV." It is on vellum, $8\frac{1}{2} \times 6\frac{1}{4}$, of 120 leaves, the first and last originally left blank, but some entries of births in the Pulleyn family between 1597 and 1616 have been made on the *verso* of fol. 1, in a contemporary hand. It has been noted on a fly-leaf by a former librarian that it had been compared with a MS. in the Bodleian of the date of 1420 ; and from the character of the handwriting and illuminations this date may very probably be rightly assigned to it.

It had not been noticed that the prayers are "after the use of York," but that I am right in assuming this, I have little doubt—not so much from the markedly northern dialect of the English portions, which alone would not have been sufficient, as from the fact that it

---

(1) *Lateinische Hymnen*, I, 108.
(2) *Monumenta Ritualia*, II, p. xi—xvii.
(3) *Ib.*, p. 37-8, 45, &c.
(4) *Legends of the Holy Rood*, E. E. T. S., 1871, p. 222-4. Dr Morris gives the reign of Edward III. as the date of the MS. ; or—with a query— the time of "Edward II. and Isabella." If this last suggestion be correct it places the date of these hours at the very beginning of the pontificate of John XXII, or in that of his predecessor ; and at all events proves their early introduction into this country.

agrees with the printed *Horæ* in the Minster Library (XI, O, 28), "*secundum usum Eborancen,*"(1) in places where it is peculiar—as, for example, the mention of *Archiepiscopus noster*—and that the Calendar, which is distinctively York,(2) was most probably written by or for some

(1) The known editions and copies of the York *Horæ* are :

I. Rouen, Bernard and Cousin, 4to, 1512.—Three, Sir H. Hoare; St Cuthbert's College, Ushaw ; and St John's College, Cambridge.

II. Rouen, 12mo, Nich le Roy, 1538—One, Cathedral Library, Lincoln.

III. London, 12mo, Wight, ? 1554 × 1558(*)—One, Magdalen College, Cambridge ; and Fragment, York Minster Library.

IV. Mr Dickinson in his *List of Printed Service Books*, 1850, mentions another York *Horæ :* "1556, 12mo, London, Emmanuel College." Mr Chapman, Fellow and Tutor of Emmanuel, to whose kindness I am indebted for the notice (III) of the York *Horæ* in the Pepysian Library of Magdalen College, has been unable to find any trace of this book in their library. We might have supposed that the copy at Magdalen had given rise to a confusion in Mr Dickinson's informant, especially as there is no notice of it in his list, except for the mention of the date of the Emmanuel copy and that no printer is specified.

V. An imperfect copy in York Minster Library (XI, O, 28). I have taken some pains to find the place and date of this edition, but without success. From the frequent use of "et," as the expansion of "&" in the English prayers, this last is evidently the work of a French or foreign printer; but beyond this, and the fact that it is not of any of the editions above specified, I have been able to discover nothing definite. There are full page woodcuts before each hour, and numerous elaborate initial letters. The pages are surrounded by borders of saints, and hunting and other secular subjects, of the same character as those often used by Paris and Rouen printers in the earlier part of the sixteenth century. Mr Bullen, with the kindness for which I have always had to thank the authorities of the British Museum, was good enough to collect all the many wood-cut bordered books in the library for the purpose of comparison, but they did not help us. Mr Reed in the Print Department also was kind enough to examine the book, and he did not know the wood-cut borders, and had never seen the Annunciation treated in the same way. It is of an extreme realistic type, a full page cut before the matins (*fol.* 20, *b*) : the blessed Virgin is seated, the angel kneels on one knee before her ; and a ray proceeds from the first person of the Trinity to her ear, down which the dove is flying, followed by an infant Christ, bearing his cross.

An attempt has been made to complete the book, by inserting leaves of the small English edition above mentioned (III), and writing other portions on some of the blank leaves bound up with it. By whoever this was done— probably in the reign of Elizabeth—the book bears the marks of after use, and, quite apart from bibliographical considerations, seems to have a melancholy interest as the cherished, though mutilated and proscribed, possession of some devout adherent to his old convictions. These may have exposed him, if not to persecution, which may have been too likely, still to many inconveniences and discomforts from penal laws which—and we may all be thankful for it—are now swept out of the statute-book.

(2) There is, however, the following entry—but in a later hand—at July 14 : "dies cuniculares incipiunt. F*estum* reliquiarum *cathedralis* lincoln."

(*) There is no date in the title-page, and the book ends with *Finis*, without farther colophon ; but I think I am justified in suggesting the reign of Queen Mary as the probable date, from a reference to the dates of other books printed by Wight, and from the fact that no service books of the Ebor use were printed in the last ten years of Henry VIII.

one connected with the parish of All Saints, Pavement, in the city of York, as at the Ides (15th) of May there is the following note: " Dedicacion*is ecclesie* omnium *Sanctorum super* pani [*mentum*] Ebor."

These hours in English are written consecutively at the beginning of the manuscript. The Latin is given from the same manuscript, where these hours are inserted in the hours of the Virgin, except the words within brackets, which have been added from the printed *Horæ.*

P. 82, l. 1—3. This was not repeated, as was that, l. 4—6, with the Gloria Patri, l. 7—9, at the subsequent hours. The Myroure gives the reason. It directs the nuns to begin the service with an *Ave-Maria*, and then proceeds: " ¶ When ye hane thus begonne wyth oure lady and founde comforte in hyr. ye begynne to desyre to prayse oure lorde god. But for ye fele youre selfe vnworthy so moche as to open youre mouthe therto. therfore ye pray hym to open your lyppes. to hys praysynge and saye. *Domine labea mea aperies.* that ys Lorde thow shalte open my lyppes. *Et os meum anunciabit* &c And my mouthe shall shew thy praysynge. Thys verse ys only sayde at mattyns. that ys the begynnynge of goddes seruyce. in token that the fyrste openynge of youre lyppes, or mouthe. shulde be to the praysynge of god. and all the day after, they shulde abyde open. and redy to the same. and be so occupyed and fylled therwyth, that nothynge contrary to hys praysynge myght enter in. ne do eny thynge wel. eny tyme of the day. *with*out hys helpe. as he sayeth hymselfe in hys gospel. *Sine me nichil potestis facere.* that ys. wythout me ye may do ryghte noughte. Therfore bothe at mattyns. and at begynnynge of eche houre. ye aske hys helpe. & saye. *Deus in adiutorium meum intende.* That ys. God take hede vnto my helpe."(1)

l. 1. *lyppis.* It is sometimes assumed that *-is* or *-ys* in the plural is a mark of Scotch or rather English across the border; but not only do we find it here in an unquestionably York MS., and page 84, l. 49, "panys;" but we have below, l. 17, "domis" in the genitive, and so very commonly in later northern MSS.(2)

l. 12. *wysdome.* See note (3), *ante*, p. 218, and C. T. 14883.

l. 14. *withouten les.* Not an unusual tag to help out a rhyme.

> Cf. "The swetnesse lasted, withouten lees,
>   Till that the body buryed wes."
> *Guy of Warwick*, Zupitza, 10695-6.

---

(1) Ed. Blunt, E. E. T. S., 1873, p. 81.
(2) I may illustrate this by an inscription on two pillars, in the nave of St Mary's, Beverley, within ten miles of the southern boundary of the North-Humber-land. On one, " Thes to pillors mad gud," and on the other, "wyffes. god reward thaym." The next pillar was made by the minstrels, and the fact is not only recorded by an inscription; but a group of five of them is carved on a corbel projecting from the pillar. See note, *ante*, p.344, *n*, for the date, where also may be seen the same grammatical form in the quotation from the rood-screen.

> " an angel him bad withoute lye :
> Dauid, go to Arabye
>   To þe mount Thabor blyue
> and bringe to Ierusalem withoute les
> þo þre ȝerdes þat Moyses
>   sette þere by his lyue ! "

Canticum de Creatione, Horstmann, *Anglia*, I, 997—1002.
See also *Towneley Mysteries*, p. 5, and *post*, p. 384.

P. 82, l. 16. *tyde.* Evidently written by mistake from line 13.

P. 84, l. 22—5. With this prayer to Christ, compare one to St Helen
in the MS. Hours (fol. 98 *b*), from which this is printed :

> " Seint elene j þe pray
>   To helpe me at my last day
> To sette þe crosse *and* his passiono
>   Betwix my synfull saule *and* dome
> Now *and* in þe houre of my dede
>   And bryng my saule to requied."

This was probably a local form, for St Helen (Helena), owing to
the received opinion that she there gave birth to the Emperor
Constantine, was the object of special devotion in the city of
York, where one of the churches is called by her name.

The following is taken from the order of the visitation of the
sick, given in Maskell.(1)

At the last the priest exhorts the dying man to set the cross
(*crucifix*) before him and say, " I wot wel thou are nouȝt my God,
but thou art imagened after him and makest me have more mind
of him after whom thou art imagened, Lord Fader of heuene, the
deth of oure Lord *Jesu* Crist, thi Sone, whiche is here imagened I
set betwene the and my euil dedis ; and the desert of *Jesu* Crist I
offre for that I should have deseruid and have nought.

" *Sey azen :* Lord the deth of oure Lorde *Jesu* the Sone wiche
was bore of Seinte Marie, moder and maiden, I sette betwene me
and thi wrath."

l. 37-8. This petition appears to be peculiar to York.

l. 38. *mistime.* As in the litany, " a subitanea et improvisa morte "
—" from . . . . . murder and sudden death." Cf. St Luke xxi,
34 : " Lest . . . that day come upon you unawares."

l. 45. *of dedly synne me to shryue.* At first *scrifan* was used of the
shrift-father, who received the confession and assigned the penance,
and *andettan* of the penitent opening his sin, as in the prescribed
form of confession, " Ic andetta Ælmihtigum Gode and minum
scrifte—*I confess to Almighty God and to my confessor.*"(2) Afterwards it was used, like the French *confesser*, of the penitent who

---

(1) *Monumenta Ritualia*, III, 357-8, and see *post*, p. 396.
(2) Canons under K. Edgar, *De Confessione*, 6. Thorpe, A. L. II, 262.

made the confession, and of the confessor who heard it, probably because it came to be held that, as the confessor shrove their sins from men after confession,(1) they shrove or rid themselves of their sins by confession. This explanation is favoured by a suggested explanation of the word,(2) and by the usual construction, as in the phrase before us, and as *ante*, p. 124, l. 10, "caste out with meke schrifte alle venym of sin."

I find, however, in Richardson (*s. v.*) that Ihre, who supposes that the word was received from the English preachers of the gospel, derives the Swedish *skrifta*—and if so, the English *shrift*— from *scribere*,(3) to write, because the penance required was given in writing; and Skinner also because the names of those confessing were written down. Dr Richardson pertinently remarks: "Neither of these reasons has introduced the word into the Italian or French," nor has it into the German, or any Romance language.(4) He adds that "Lye quotes three instances from the Anglo-Saxon version of Boethius where the Latin *curare* is rendered *scrifan*." He also refers to Somner, who is quoted in the note.

P. 84, l. 52. *fays*, the northern form in marked contrast with the southern "*foon*" (foes).

---

(1) Cf. Mannum heora dæda scrifan—*u. s.*, can. I, p. 260.

(2) Somner. *s.* SCRIFAN. Delictorum confessiones exigere ve audire, pœnitentias injungere; to bear confessions and enjoyne penance, to shrive. *Item.* putare, amputare, resecare; to prune, lop, or shrive trees.

(3) In Cleasby-Vigfusson the Icelandic *skript* is given, I, a drawing; II, a writ or scripture, and in these senses it may very well be derived from *scrifan* and that from the Latin *scribere*, as we are there told. We also there find that *skript* is, III, (*eccles.*) confession and penance, but though there is a common form of the word, or words in these different senses, it does not necessarily follow that they have the same derivation. Our heathen forefathers knew nothing of confession, and therefore could not have brought the name with them, when they settled in this country; and it seems not unreasonable to suppose, as suggested above in respect to the Swedish *skrifta*, that the Icelanders received *shrift* in the sense of *shrift*, when they received their Christianity from England.

(4) There can be no doubt that many foreign ecclesiastical terms were grafted into the language from the time of Saint Augustine, and the first Latin missionaries, as Christ, apostle, pope, bishop, priest, deacon, mass, chrism, &c., but then it will be noticed that every one of these examples was imported in the sense it had hitherto borne. On the other hand, in a far greater number of instances, and more especially where it was desirable that the new words should be "understanded of the people," they were rendered in the vulgar tongue, as Hælend (*Saviour*); hallows, fulluht (*baptism*); housel (*eucharist*); gospel, rood, weofod (*altar*); mæsse-reaf (*vestment*); hacele (*chasuble*); heofod-lin (*amice*); sang-boc (*psalter*); bletsing-boc (*benedictional*); ræding-boc (*lectionary*); spel-boc (*book of homilies*); tidsang (*canonical hours*); and so the names of the several hours—and if all these, and many more of the same kind, why not shrift, remission, or cutting off of sin; scrift-boc (*book of penances*); scrift-scir (*parish*), &c. ?

P. 86, l. 68—71. There is no English anthem for compline in the York Manuscript. I have supplied it from the Cambridge MS. printed by Mr Maskell.

l. 72—8. The English "Recommendation" is also wanting in the York MS. Horæ, and it not being found in Mr Maskell's MS., I give it from the Primer of 1543, as printed by him in his preface.

P. 87, l. 49—56. It will be noticed that the York MS. has the Latin *Antiphona ad completorium*, and the *Recommendatio*, which last rubric or title I have supplied from the York *Horæ* of 1536. The other Latin titles within brackets are from the printed *Horæ* in the York Minster Library described above, p. 348 (V).

l. 57—61. The verse, respond, and prayer were repeated at each hour, as appears from the printed editions, where we find the first words with an **ut supra**, except that of Rouen, 1536, which describes itself on the title-page as "*sine require*" (without any, *see above*), and gives them in full at each place.

APP. I. THE MASS—YORK USE.

The order of mass, p. 90—116, is taken from a vellum manuscript(1) of about A.D. 1425, in the York Minster Library (XVI, A. 9). It would not be within the scope of the E. E. T. S. to produce in detail the grounds of the opinion here advanced, and I cannot refer to any writer on these subjects who has made the same remark; but it appears to me in the first place that the York Use, as here given, and notwithstanding some later and easily recognized interpolations, was in the main the ancient Gregorian mass, according to the Roman rite of the eighth century; or rather that it was the use "secundum ritum sacri palatii,"(2) which with most absolute self-confidence was enforced by a high-handed exercise of royal supremacy in the dominions of

---

(1) The MS. B of the *York Missal*, edited for the Surtees Society by Dr Henderson, which has been published since these extracts were printed. See *post*, p. 354.

(2) This phrase is used by Leidradus, Archbishop of Lyons, in his *Epistola ad Carolum Magnum*. We have no evidence as to what may have been the earlier York use—whether it was that compiled for England by St Augustine, from those of Rome and Gaul, with, it may be, some British customs other than those to which he had been used ("*moribus nostris contraria*."—Bed. H. E. II, 2)—or whether it was a Scottish use, introduced by missionaries from Ioua—but, as elsewhere remarked with respect to the Gallican liturgy, we know that Charles did not altogether succeed in abolishing diocesan uses in Gaul; and it is not at all inconsistent with the suggestion in the text that some ancient usages may have survived at York.

Charles the Great ; (1)—and further, that it was very probably introduced at York(2) by Archbishop Eanbald II, at the instance of his old master Alcuin,(3)—who, though established at the Frank court, had not

(1) In confirmation of this I 'may quote the conclusions of the Abbé Duval in his Études Liturgiques in the *Observateur Catholique* 1859, Tome VII, 161 :

"Charlemagne à l'example de Pepin, son père, et à la prière du pape Etienne, réforma lui-même ou fit réformer par ses écrivains les anciennes liturgies de l'Église gallicane, en y introduisant des pièces nouvelles ou tirées des livres romains."

(2) As regards the southern province it had been decreed about fifty years before this (A.D. 747), by a provincial council at Clovesho (*Canon* XIII), that the Roman model—"*exemplar quod scriptum de Romana habemus ecclesia*"—should be adhered to in all the offices of religion. St Osmund established the Sarum use in the eleventh century ; and it would seem that there had been some intention of extending it beyond the Humber, in the latter part of the fifteenth century. Among other proofs may be mentioned a MS. of the Ebor Missal now in the Library of Sidney-Sussex College, Cambridge (*MS.* D of Dr Henderson's edition), which was apparently an attempt to assimilate the York use to that of Sarum. That it was abortive is evident from the fact that the changes introduced in it were not admitted in any of the editions of the Ebor Missal, when it came to be printed.

There are sufficient grounds for supposing that Henry VIII. intended, even if he did not carry out his intention, that "the whole realm should have but one use." This was carried out in the reign of his son ; and when the Book of Common Prayer was taken away in the time of Queen Mary, the convocation under Cardinal Pole in 1557 considered the question whether the Latin service books should not be "uniusmodi per totum regnum."—Cardwell, *Synodalia*, II, 453.

(3) See Alcuin—Epist. LV, *Opera*, Migne, I, 224, and Epist. LXV, *ib.* 254. The following is one of the *Orationes solemnes* for Good Friday in the York Missal :

"Oremus et pro Christianissimo *Imperatore* nostri ; ut Deus et Dominus noster subditas illi faciat omnes barbaras nationes, *et faciat sapere ea quæ recta sunt, atque contra inimicos catholicæ et apostolicæ Ecclesiæ triumphum largiatur victoriæ* ad nostram perpetuam pacem."—*York Missal*, Henderson, I, 103-4. According to this form the kings of England, centuries before the times of our own Empress of India, were prayed for in the northern province as emperor.

The old "imperatore," which is itself older than the "Holy Roman Empire" of Charles and his successors, was retained in the Sherborne missal (p. 206), but has been altered *secunda manu* into "rege" for the *King* of England, and this is the reading of the printed Sarum (*ed.* Burntisland, 326).

"Imperatore" remains in the Roman Missal, though it may be a question what emperor is now prayed for at the Vatican. The clause shewn in italics (et faciat . . . . victoriæ) is found in neither Rome nor Sarum, and is very suggestive of the incessant wars of the Franks against the Saxons and other heathen tribes, which were professedly carried on, not merely for the conquest of "barbarous nations," who were dangerous neighbours, but also for their conversion to Christianity, and their submission to papal authority.

See also the *Missa contra Paganos* in the Ebor MS. missals (*ed.* Henderson, II, 178), which is neither in the Roman, Sarum, or printed York missals.

relinquished his place in the cathedral church(1)—and, very possibly, partly in deference to Alcuin's royal scholar, whose influence, at all events in secular matters, was acknowledged a few years later, in Britain, north of Humber, even if his paramount dominion was not formally recognized.(2)

I follow the fashion of not retaining the mediæval spelling of the Latin of the following extracts, though I had been very careful to do so in making my transcript some years ago, when I had undertaken to edit the York Missal, if the Surtees Society did not take it in hand. My friend Dr Henderson has now edited it for the society, and relieved me from my engagement, to my great satisfaction, and very much to the greater advantage of liturgical students. They have now within their reach the most complete edition of any provincial use which has hitherto been published—the only one where the variations of the order of mass and the canon in the printed editions and every known manuscript are shewn in parallel columns, and that contains a comparative calendar and index of fixed feasts, so necessary in the identification of uses.

P. 94, l. 3. *Psalmus,*—The name applied otherwise than to the Psalms of the Psalter, and we also find it used of the Creeds.

P. 96, l. 18—24. These two prayers are peculiar to this use. With the last compare that in the same place in the Mosarabic Liturgy: "Conforta me, Rex sanctorum summum tenens principatum ; da sermonem rectum et benesonantem in os meum, ut placeam tibi et omnibus circumstantibus."(3)

l. 10. The following is the rubric which has been omitted in the text : "*Sicuti evidens habeatur et plena cognitio, qualiter orationes quas collectas vocamus terminandæ sint ; Prius notandum est, quod in eis quandoque dirigitur sermo ad Patrem : quandoque ad filium : quandoque ad Spiritum Sanctum : quandoque ad totam trinitatem. Sed quando ad patrem, iterum considerandum est, utrum ita dirigatur sermo ad Patrem, quod fiat mentio de filio et spiritu sancto, vel non. Et si in oratione, quæ ad patrem dirigitur, fiat mentio de filio, refert an fiat ante finalem partem, an in ipso fine ; et secundum has diversitates variabitur finis. Si vero oratio dirigitur ad Patrem absque mentione filii et spiritus Sancti, finietur sic :* Per Dominum nostrum Jesum Christum filium tuum : qui tecum vivit et regnat, in unitate spiritus sancti deus *et cetera ut hic* Concede nos famulos tuos [*quæsumus, Domine, Deus*].(4) Deus qui miro ordine.(5) *Si vero de Spiritu Sancto fiat mentio, dicetur :* In unitate ejusdem spiritus sancti deus, *et cetera, ut hic* Deus qui corda fidelium,(6) Ure igni

(1) Note, *ante*, p. 326-7.
(2) See Freeman, *Norman Conquest*, 1867, I, 39-40. Palgrave, I, 484.
(3) *Missale Mixtum*, ab A. Lesleo, S. J., 219, l. 78.
(4) Collect, Lady-mass before Advent.
(5) Collect, St Michael and all Angels.
(6) Collect Mass of the Holy Spirit.

Sancti Spiritus renes.(1)   *Si vero de Filio fiat mentio ante finalem partem, dicetur:* Per eundem Dominum nostrum Jesum Christum, *et cetera, ut hic,* Deus qui de beatæ mariæ.(2)   Largire nobis, clementissime.(3)   *Si vero in fine fit mentio de Filio, dicetur:* Qui tecum vivit et regnat, *ut potest videri in oratione de sancto stephano, cujus finis talis est,* Qui novit etiam pro persecutoribus exorare dominum nostrum Christum filium tuum, Qui tecum, *et cetera.*(4) *Item in oratione* Deus qui salutis.(5)   *Si vero ad filium dirigatur oratio sine mentione Spiritus sancti, ut hic,* Excita domine potentiam tuam et veni,(6) *et similiter in orationibus de adventu domini, dicetur:* Qui vivis et regnas cum Deo Patre [MS. patri] in unitate spiritus sancti deus.   *Si fiat mentio de spiritu sancto, dicetur:* Qui cum patre et eodem spiritu sancto vivis et regnas, *et cetera.   Item orationes ad patrem, in quibus mentionem de Trinitate facimus, sic concludimus:* In qua vivis et regnas deus, *sicut in hiis orationibus,* Omnipotens sempiterne deus qui dedisti,(7) Populum tuum, domine quæsumus.(8)   *Illas vero quas ad ipsam Trinitatem dirigimus sic finimus,* Qui vivis et regnas Deus; *similiter,* Placeat tibi Sancta trinitas.(9)

   "*Secundum autem Romanam ecclesiam*(10) *nullam orationem cum* Per eum qui venturus est judicare *concludimus, nisi quando fit exorcismus in quo diabolum per divinum judicium ut a creatura Dei recedat exorcizamus.   Nam in aliis orationibus, quas cum* Per Dnm nrm *concludimus, Patrem ut per amorem Filii sui nobis subveniat imploramus.   In exorcismis autem diabolum per Dei judicium, ut aufugiat, increpamus, in quo judicio se scit diabolus potentissime damnandus, cujus timore judicii concutitur.*"

   There is a shorter rule of a similar character, but without examples, in the Sarum Cautelæ Missæ.(11)

---

(1) Collect, *Missa contra tentationes carnis.*
(2) Collect, Lady-mass in Advent.
(3) Collect, St Mary Magdalene.   (4) Collect, St Stephen.
(5) Collect, Lady-mass in Epiphany-tide.
(6) Collect, First Sunday in Advent.   (7) Collect, Trinity Sunday.
(8) I am unable to find the collect which is here referred to. There are two collects with this beginning, viz. those for the Saturday in the Lent Ember week (*ed.* Henderson, I, 59), and for the Thursday after the second Sunday in Lent (*ib.* p. 63)—but in neither of them is there any mention of the Trinity, nor do they end as here laid down.
(9) Prayer said by priest after mass.—See *ante,* p. 117. This ends (*similiter*) in like manner as a collect, although itself not a collect in the sense of the rubric.
(10) This mention of Rome and that above, p. 94, l. 31, date back, if I am not wrong in my suggestion, p. 352, from the times when the Roman *Ordo* was established by law in the Frank dominions, and when as yet the principle of agreement with it was not taken for granted.
(11) *Miss. Sar.,* 651. See also *Pupilla Oculi,* f. xxii. and note, Maskell, A. E. L., p. 30-31. The Roman rule is given *Rub. Gen.,* ix, 17.

P. 96, l. 21. *Vicarius.* The mention of the Vicar gives a local colour to the MS. and proves that it was intended for use in York Minster itself. The printed editions read "*diaconus.*"

P. 98, l. 22. See note, p. 288, as to the use of the name *offertory* for the whole service until the *secreta;* p. 231—244, as to offerings of the laity, &c.; and p. 318-19 as to the place of the Bidding Prayers and sermon.

   l. 29. This, the personal prayer of the priest—"ego," "meis"—with a distinct reference to the propitiatory character of the oblation, was adopted in the course of time, as an integral part of the service. Ives, Bishop of Chartres, towards the end of the eleventh century, pointed out in the Micrologus that the Roman Ordo appointed no prayer to be used between the Offertory and the *Secreta.*(1)

P. 102, l. 11—19. The substance of this rubric is to be found in a letter from Pope Pelagius II. to the bishops of Germany and Gaul, which Baronius ascribes to the year 590. Its genuineness was questioned by Cardinal Bona, for reasons which I need not discuss; and I only refer to it because Muratori in his dissertation *De Rebus Liturgicis* states it to have been a forgery of Pseudo-Isidore in the time of Charles the Great ;(2) and because this origin would account for its being found in the York Mass, if the circumstances of its introduction into this country are such as I have supposed.

P. 106, l. 12. Eugenius, the first of his name, was pope from 655—658, and there has been no Eugenius the seventh. It will be observed that there are seven crosses from this place to the consecration of the chalice; but I am inclined to think that my other suggestion in the English is the more probable—and that "*septem*" refers to the seven words (line 2), "*genetricis Dei et Domini nostri Jesu Christi,*" which may have been interpolated before the time of St Gregory, and which a rubric in the Sidney-Sussex MS. directs the priest bowing down to address to her.(3)

   l. 25. *Alexander papa instituit.* This rubric is not found in the printed editions of the York Missal, nor have I noticed it among the rubrics of the different uses printed by Martene, or elsewhere. It would seem, however, that it is at least as old as the time of Durandus. His commentary on this part of the Canon

---

(1) "Romanus ordo nullam orationem instituit, post offerendam, ante secretam."—*Microl.* xi. See also what he says in the same chapter as to another prayer beginning, "*Suscipe, Sancta Trinitas,*" which is now inserted in the Roman Missal, not being "ex aliquo ordine, sed ex ecclesiastica consuetudine." See also Bellarmine, *De Missa,* II, *c.* xvii.

(2) *Liturgia Romana Vetus,* Venet., 1748, I, 66-7.

(3) *York Missal,* Henderson, I, 182, MS. D: "Hic parum inclinatus dicat ad istam septem verba sequentia."

(*Qui pridie*, &c.) appears to refer to this or some similar rubric :—
" Hæc verba dicitur Alexander Papa primus addidisse, ut præmissum est."(1)

P. 106, l. 30. *Hic tangat hostiam.* The Sarum rubrics before the words of
institution are as follows : " *Et postea elevet paululum*,(2) *dicens*,
tibi gratiaŝ agens, bene ✛ dixit, fregit, *Hic tangat hostiam dicens*,
deditque discipulis suis."(3)   This touching is not crossing, nor
was it to be understood of breaking the bread.   A rubric of the
Sarum manual of 1554 explains that some silly fellows ("*fatui*")
did so, but that the Church consecrates before breaking, and so
does otherwise than as Christ did—" sic aliter facit Ecclesia, quam
Christus fecit."(4)

P. 108, l. 8. *Feceritis.*   This, of course, with a change of tense, is the
" Hoc facite " of the Vulgate, and the τοῦτο ποιεῖτε of the Greek ;
and, therefore, whatever English verb would render those phrases
would equally render this.   I venture to say this here, because
my alternative rendering (" or offer ") has been objected to,—
mainly on controversial grounds,—and may be objected to again,
when the completed work is in the hands of the public.   Now, I
was well aware that the rendering of this phrase had been a
subject of controversy, but I had undertaken to give " a verbal
rendering," and as I thought that as a matter of grammatical construction it fairly admitted of both renderings, I did not attempt
to choose between them on doctrinal considerations, and therefore
gave them both ; and for so doing I have the example of the
authorized version, where the very phrase occurs, Numbers xxix,
39, in reference to sacrifices at the feast of tabernacles.   The
Hebrew is אֵלֶּה תַּעֲשׂוּ, and the Septuagint ταῦτα ποιήσετε.   The

Vulgate renders, " *Hæc offeretis*," and our translators, " These
things ye shall do," and in the margin, " or *offer*."

l. 10.   See note, *ante*, p. 288.

l. 16.   See note, *ante*, p. 290.

P. 112, l. 21.   See note, p. 295.

P. 116, l. 1.   The MS. contains no rubric for the formal rinsing of the
chalice and of the priest's hands, though no doubt the innovation
had been adopted at York when it was written.   See note, p. 301-7.

---

(1) *Rationale*, 4, lxi, 1.

(2) " *Hic elevet hostiam dicens*."—Sherborne Missal, p. 383.   See note as
to the prohibition of this elevation of the unconsecrated host, after the
practice of elevating the consecrated host had been established.—*Ante*, p. 283.

(3) *Miss. Sar.*, 618.   (4) *Ib.*

APPENDIX II.

P. 118, l. 8. When I drew attention (p. 173, *n.* 2) to this place and the reason for marking a cross, I had not noticed that Mr Way (P.P, p. li. *n.*) mentions the sign of the cross being found after certain words of ill omen in the Promptorium, thus: "Diabolus, the deuel. ✠ Demon, the deuel ✠."

P. 120, l. 13. *levyth.* See note, p. 312.

l. 33. *eventually burned.* Meanwhile he had succeeded in making his escape from the Tower into Wales. There is some uncertainty as to his movements during the intervening four years, but having been again committed to the Tower, he was brought before the Lords in parliament assembled on the 13th December, 1417, and sentenced not only to be burned as a traitor to God and "*heretic noterement approvee et adjuggee,*" but also to be hung as a traitor to the king and his realm. The sentence was carried into effect on the 18th December, when he was drawn on a hurdle to St Giles' Fields, and there hung in chains, and "burnt hanging"—*ars pendant*—in the terms of his sentence as recorded in the rolls of parliament.

P. 121, l. 6. "þerfore þenk ȝe, clene prestis, hou moche ȝe be holden to God, þat ȝaf ȝou power to sacre his owene preciouse body and blood of breed and wyn, whiche power he grauntid nevere to his owene modir ne aungel of hevene."—Wyclif, *Works*, III, p. 288-9.

l. 18. *goddes borde.* It has been frequently asserted in the controversial literature of the last few years—sometimes as a reproach, and sometimes to the praise of the revisers of the service books of the Church of England in 1548—that they then for the first time used the name of God's board, or the Lord's table, or the holy table, in relation to the sacrament of the Lord's Supper. Without going out of our own country, or referring to the writings of the fathers or to the Eastern liturgies, which men who undertake to write dogmatically on these subjects ought to know something about, the mere fact of the occurrence of this phrase in a book, up to that date, so largely used by the clergy as the Festival, is enough to prove the contrary.(1) Ælfric in his paschal homily speaks of Christ's "beod" (*board*). The old English homily for

---

(1) This mistake nevertheless appears to have passed unchallenged by my lords, episcopal and legal, and by the counsel engaged in the proceedings before the judicial committee of the Privy Council in the case of Martin *v.* Machonochie. See the shorthand writer's notes, 20th Nov. 1868. *Fourth Report of the Ritual Commission*, Folio, 1870, p. 229.

Easter-day of the twelfth century, edited by Dr Morris, exhorts "þat holie bord bugen and þat bred bruken"—*go to the holy board, and partake of the bread* ;(1) and farther on, " þanne muge we bicunneliche to godes bord ̇ougen, and his bode wurðliche bruken "—*then may we go meetly to God's board, and worthily partake of his body*.(2) In the early part of the fourteenth century we find the phrase in the Ayenbite very much in the same connection in respect to clerks in holy orders—bishops, priests, deacons, and subdeacons,—and Dan Michel explains it of the wyeued (*weofod*) or altar : " Yet eft hi ssolle by more clene / and more holy / uor þet hi serueþ at godes borde of his coupe / of his breade / and of his wyne / and of his mete . Godes table is þe wyeued . þe coupe is þe chalis. his bread and his wyn : þet is his propre bodi and his propre blod."(3)

In the quotation from Lydgate (*ante*, p. 233) he speaks of the " Altar, called God's board."

In Robert of Brunne's Langtoft(4) we have

" Richard at Godes bord His messe had and his rights."

But there is no need to multiply quotations, and I have noted a great many where the phrase is used in this connection ; for— instead of being never used—the wonder would have been that it had not been in every day use, when in the prayer used in our Church in the eighth century at the dedication of an altar, in the earliest York Pontifical, was as follows : " Presta ut in hac mensa sint tibi libamina accepta, sint grata, sint pinguia et Spiritus Sancti tui semper rore perfusa ; "(5) and the same words occur in the latest York Pontifical, in the sixteenth century, though meantime the words, " in honorem sancti *ill*," have crept in before the " consecramus."(6) Nor was it only in the service books, but we find the same things in the canon law of the Church. The Legantine Constitutions of Othobon, afterward Pope Adrian V, passed in a " *Concilium Anglicanum*," of both provinces decreed (*Tit.* III. *De Consecratione*) : " Domus Dei materiali subjecto non differens a privatis, per mysterium dedicationis invisibile fit templum domini, ad expiationem delictorum et divinam miseri-

---

(1) 2nd Series, p. 94. (2) *Ib*. 98.
(3) Dan Michel's *Ayenbite of Inwyt*, Morris, E. E. T. S., 1866, p. 235-6.
(4) *Langtoft's Chronicle*, Hearne, p. 182.
(5) Benedictio vel Consecratio Altaris, *Archbishop Egbert's Pontifical*, Greenwell, p. 40-1.
(6) *Archbishop Bainbridge's Pontifical*, Henderson, p. 328. There is a separate prayer for the " *Consecratio tabulæ*," or the stone slab which formed the top of the altar. The words quoted also occur in the more elaborated office for the consecration of an altar, according to the existing Roman pontifical of Pope Benedict XIV, where we have " in cujus (*sc.* Dei) honorem ac beatissimæ Virginis Mariæ et omnium Sanctorum."

cordiam implorandam : UT IN EA FIT MENSA,(1) in qua panis
vivus, qui de cœlo descendit pro vivorum et mortuorum suffragiis,
manducatur."

APPENDIX III.

This piece was copied for the Society by Mr George Parker of the
Bodleian, and he also read the proofs with the original. The manuscript from which it is taken is *Ashm.* 1286 :—" A handsome and
valuable quarto MS., consisting of 257 leaves of vellum, gilt at the
edges, written about the year 1400, in a fair text hand, in columns,
with fair margins, and adorned with frequent rubrics, and painted
capitals and borders. Begins with A treatise of The Love of God ; and
Ends with A special Confessyoun."(2) The MS. was very probably
written for a favourer of Lollard opinions, as it contains (*fol.* 32—108)
"þe Pore Caytyf." There is little to remark as to the dialect. It does
not appear to have been tampered with, and is midland, with some
southern forms, and (p. 122, l. 29) an instance of the northern participial
ending.

P. 127, l. 10. *I can seye* = eye can see. Cf. 1 Cor. ii, 9. The scribe
 may have been writing from dictation, and have understood " I
 can say "—*say* with the pronunciation *sey*, see p. 314.

Cf. Hampole's rendering of the Vulgate :

" Eghe moght never se, ne ere here,
Ne in-tylle mans hert come þe ioyes sere
þat God has ordaynd þare and dight
Tylle alle þat here lufes him ryghte."—*P. C.* 7793-6.

APPENDIX IV.

The celebrated Vernon manuscript of the Bodleian has supplied this
piece. It is No. 121 of Mr Halliwell's account of the manuscript. It
consists of 688 lines, and extends from *Fol.* 302, *b, col.* 1, to *Fol.* 303,
b, col. 3 ; and has been copied for the Society by Mr George Parker,
who had already copied Mr Skeat's A-text of Piers Plowman from
the same manuscript. I collated his copy with the manuscript—a
very unnecessary piece of trouble, as I had no occasion to make an

---

(1) The gloss of Johannes de Athonia (John Acton) is " *Mensa.* Id est
Altare."—Oxon. 1679, p. 83.
(2) *Catalogue of the Ashmolean MSS.*, W. H. Black, Oxford, 1845,
p. 1051.

alteration of a letter—and Mr Parker has since read the proofs with the MS.

The date of the Vernon MS. is about 1375, but I am disposed to think that the original must be at least a century older, and that our text is a confused and very fragmentary copy. There can be no doubt that it has been very much mutilated, were it only in the process of southernizing the northern dialect. The creed has been omitted (l. 484), though (l. 485—508) fragments of an "exposition" of the creed are retained. The lines which are reprinted, pp. 362, 363, have been repeated, probably from the combination of different copies; and very possibly the lesson and *exemplum*, which does not occur in Audelay or the Harleian MS. (l. 436—448), may have been a later insertion, with tacit reference to Wycliff's translation of the Bible, and Lollard dissatisfaction at the gospel being read in an unknown tongue.

The metre is that which was called "cowee" or *versus caudati*, of which we have already had an example in the confession in the Mass-book (p. 8). It was so called from having kowes, pendants or tails(1)— that is, shorter lines between the couplets,—which are "coupled" or rhyme together. In this piece we have the double cowee, or staves of twelve verses, four rhyming couplets of four feet or accents in each line, followed by a line of three accents. The two couples of cowes or tails are intended to rhyme together, except that (l. 469 and 559) the copyist in order to get rid of northern forms has broken the longer stave into the more common one of two of six lines each.(2) Although

---

(1) *Kowes* from the O.F. *coe* or *keue* (queue). The involved style of this piece fully justifies what Robert of Brunne says in the prologue to his Chronicle of the metre in the hands of the makers of his day. He explains the different principle upon which he has rendered his original :

> "In simple speche as I couthe,
> þat is lightest in mannes mouth
> I mad nought for no disours,
> Ne for no seggers no harpours ;
> Bot for the luf of simple meñ,
> þat strange Inglis cañ not keñ :
> . . . .
> I made it not for to be praysed,
> Bot at þe lewed meñ were aysed
> If it were made in ryme couwee,
> Or in strangere, or enterlace,
> þat rede Inglis, it ere inowe,
> þat couthe not haf coppled a kowe,
> þat outhere in couwee or in baston,
> Som suld haf ben fordon,
> So þat fele men þat it herde
> Suld not witte howe þat it ferde."

Hearne's Works (*reprint*), III, p. xcix.

(2) The northern -*ande* is retained in the tail-rhyme (l. 665), because if it had been altered to *suffrynge*, as the others, it would not have rhymed with *hande*.

written in rhyme, many of the lines show much of the old alliterative feeling, even if, as might be very possible, some of them were not adapted from an older poem in that metre. In its present form it was intended for recitation " in hall,"

> " Herkneþ hende · in halle " (l. 595) ;

and the hearers are called on to listen (l. 17, l. 557) ; and harken (l. 628) ; and are addressed as " sires " (l. 257, 383).

" Jon the blynd Awdlay,"(1) somewhat to the damage of his originality, borrows from this piece, or rather, in all likelihood, from a common original, more than two hundred lines out of the four hundred and fourteen of his poem " De meritis missæ ; quomodo debemus audire missam," which calls itself a sermon, and claims an indulgence for the hearers :

> " Alle that han herd this sermon
> A c. days of pardon
> Saynt Gregore grauntis ȝou this."(2)

It was edited from a Douce MS. [No. 302, *fol.* 10*b*-12] in the Bodleian for the Percy Society by Mr Halliwell.

Very much the same matter, though with a very great many various readings, is included in the unpublished *Meritum Missæ* of the Harleian MS. 3954.(3) This was also intended for recitation, and the audience is addressed as " Lordingis."

The Vernon MS. as here printed is patched together from the copies of at least two different scribes, who have altered the original according to their several dialects. As one instance, the lines already mentioned as having been repeated are here given for the sake of comparison :

> " Whon þat þou comest · þe chirche with-Inne
> And þou sest · þe prest bi-gynne
> Take his vestimens · on."—l. 212-14.

> " Whon ȝe come · þe Churche with-Inne
> And ȝe seo · þe prest bi-ginne
> Take · þe vestimens on."—ll. 284—86.

Here the Douce MS. reads :

> " Fro tyme the cherche ȝe ben within,
> And the prest he doth begyn
> His vestmentus to take on."(4)

---

(1) He was a chaplain in the monastery of Hagmon in Shropshire, and became blind and deaf. He wrote in the early part of the fifteenth century.

(2) *Poems of John Audelay*, Halliwell, 1844, p. 81.

(3) This is a fairly written MS., early in the XV century, on vellum, oblong small folio. It contains among other pieces Sir J. Mandeville's travels, with rough illustrations, Piers Plowman, &c.

(4) Audelay, *Poems*, ed. Halliwell, p. 75.

And the Harleian MS. 3954, *fol.* 75 :

> " Sun þou be þe chyrch wiþ in
> And þe prest wyl be-gyn
> þe vestement to tan."

But amidst the jumble of dialects, there is no difficulty in recog-
nising Northumbrian as having been the dialect of the original, the
northern forms being retained, when they rhymed with a word, which
did not readily admit of being changed ; and in one or two other
instances where the scribe appears to have let them pass *per incuriam.*
In fact it would be very easy to restore the northern forms in the text
as it stands. For example, in the two staves where we have the lines
here quoted,—and they would perhaps be more difficult than any, but
for the hint in the Harleian MS.—the rhyme-words of the four tails
in the first (l. 209—220) are *con* (take his vestimens), *on, non,* and
euerichon ; and the northern forms would be *can* (þe vestement to), *tan,*
nan, and *ever ilk an.* In the second (l. 281—292) we have the tail-
rhymes *mon, on, euerichon,* and *bigon ;* and we may restore *man, tan,*
everilcan, and *bigan.* Or in the first stave (l. 5—16), which does not
occur in the other MSS., the scribe has not altered the northern *tan,*
and the other tail-rhymes which, however, do not rhyme with it, are *on,*
ston, and *gon,* and no doubt were originally written *an, stan,* and *gan.*
In the second stave there is nothing so obviously characteristic in the
tail-rhymes ; and in the third (l. 29—40) we have four northern forms,
say, may, day, and *way*—probably because *may* did not admit of being
transliterated, for a few lines above (l. 23-4) we have *seye* and *preye*
rhyming together ; and lines 596-7 we have *sei* (say) and *wey* (way).(1)
And so too in the couplets : l. 104 we have the northern þou *gas,* in
the second person, unaltered to rhyme with *pas ;* and so l. 578, in the
phrase " gas hame," *gas* has most likely been retained by an oversight,
but *hame* because a rhyme to *schame* did not readily present itself ;—
and upon the same principle we may account for the northern first
person singular being retained in " I sees," because rhyming with
" *lees,*" l. 176-7.

P. 128, l. 11. *pris prayere.* Cf. William of Palerne, l. 161, where the
Romance is described as a " pris tale ; " and in Robert of
Gloucester, Hearne, I, 409 :

> " Vyfty hors of prys þe kyng of þe londe
> And vyfty þousand besans, he send hem by his sonde."

P. 129, l. 36. Audelay begins his poem by borrowing lines 17—47.
His reading here—

> " ʒef we wyl of our syn lete,"

very probably shows what the original must have read.

---

(1) In the same stave we have *wey* and *weye* in lines 125 and 136, where
in line 133 *way* has been retained when wanted for the rhyme.

P. 130, l. 80. *zor seruice say*, of the people ; and so pointing to a time before they had ceased to join aloud in the ervice. See p. 200, 256-7.

l. 86-8. Further on(1) we may see what was the feeling, when this was written, as to the gospel in the mother tongue. It has already been pointed out(2) that in the later texts we may trace a change as to the practice of the people answering aloud and joining in the prayers with the priest, when they "of the letter could," which is recognized here and in the original of our Mass-book. In fact, some years before the reformation, not the practice only, but the theory, of congregational worship had died out ;(3) and in the reign of Queen Mary, after the English service had been in use during the reign of Edward VI, not only were laymen not expected to take their part with the clergy in the prescribed office, if they chanced to understand it, but their being able to understand the language was looked upon as a hindrance to their devotions.

Dr John Christopherson, Dean of Norwich, writing in defence of the recent submission of the Church of England to the see of Rome, describes the jeer of the malcontents at Divine service in Latin. "But now, I warrant you, you must turn your tippet, and lay away your old mumpsimus, and shut up your portesse(4) and your mass-book too, and put away clean your purgatory masses."(5) "But many," he afterwards admits, "grudge and are offended that the masses and all other Divine Service is in Latin, so that when they be in the church, they do not understand what the priest saith."(6) For himself he says, "I have oftentime much marvelled at us Englishmen of late that we came to the church at the time of our English service to hear only and not to pray ourselves. . . . . When they come to church, and hear the priests, who saith common prayer for all the whole multitude, albeit they understand them not, yet if they be occupied in a godly prayer themselves, it is sufficient for them. And let them not so greatly pass for understanding what the priests say, but

(1) Page 140, l. 425—448, and note, p. 211.
(2) Notes, p. 201, 257, 310.
(3) See note, p. 158.
(4) Portesse, or *Portiforium*, the old Anglican service book corresponding to the Roman Breviary. The English name occurs in great variety of forms— portous, portuows, portowse, portuyse, portuas, portuasse, portas, portes, portess, portos, portose, portosse, portuary ; but the form here (*portesse*) seems to have become general towards the middle of the sixteenth century ; and in 1610 we have the translators of the Bible adopting it in their address "to the reader."
(5) *Exhortation to all men to take hede and beware of rebellion*, John Cawood, 1554, Sig. T iiij. b. I modernise the spelling in the quotations. Christopherson was made bishop of Chichester in 1557, and died Dec. 1558.
(6) *Ib.* Sig. X. iij.

travail themselves in fervent praying, and so shall they highly please God. Yea, and experience hath plainly taught us, that it is much better for them not to understand the common service of the church, because when they hear others praying in a loud voice, in the language that they understand, they are letted from prayer themselves, and so come they to such a slackness and negligence in praying, that at length, as we have well seen in these late days, in manner pray not at all."(1)

P. 130, l. 90. *holi. writ.* We must not suppose that the writer pretends to have inspired authority for his statements. Both "holy writ" and "holy scripture" are used in the present day exclusively of such books as may be accounted canonical in particular churches; but in the middle ages, as in line 95, of patristic and mediæval writers of recognized authority.(2) We find a like wider use in authorized Roman Catholic formularies of a later date, e. g. "*Sacri scriptores,*" in the Catechism of the Council of Trent (*Pars* II, c. IV, *q.* 5). Our old writers used it still more largely of legendary tales ;(3) and, curious to note, while on the one hand they included the writings of the fathers, genuine and suppositious alike, in the general name of holy writ, on the other hand we find our Lord and the inspired writers classed together as doctors of the Church :—

---

(1) *Exhortation to all men to take hede and beware of rebellion,* John Cawood, 1554, Sig. X. v.

(2) Thus we find good old Richard of Hampole prefaces his account of the seven joys of heaven and the seven "schendschepes" of hell with the statement that he shows them

    "Als es fonden in haly wrytt " (*P. C.* 8186),

and he thereupon names his authority :

    " Ffor Saint Austyn þat mykelle couth of clergy.
    Says in a sarmon þat he made openly."—*P. C.* 8207-8.

And so, too, Robert of Brunne :

    " Of holy wryt, þe englysh y toke
    Dialogus men clepyn þe boke."—*H. S.* 1364-5.

(3) The York Minster Library MS. of the tale of Ypotyse—the appearance of our Lord as a child, under this name, to the emperor Hadrian—begins thus (*fol.* 58) :—

    " Lystenes to me and ȝe may heere,
    All þat wil of wysdom leere,
    Of a tale of hooli writte.
    Seint iohñ þe apostil witnesseþ it."

The writer furnishes an example of the reckless manner in which the authority of a weighty name was constantly claimed. His authority when he began, as we have seen, was Saint John the Apostle, and he ends with Saint John the Baptist (*fol.* 69) :—

    " Seynt iohñ þe baptist
    þat went on erþe w*it* I*es*u crist
    þis tale wrote in latyn
    Clerkis to haue in pa*r*chemyn."

" After the text of Crist, and Powel, and Ion)
And of oure other doctours many oon."—Chaucer, *C. T.* 7229-30.

P. 131, l. 98. *mony a mede.* This refers to the virtues or *virtutes missæ*, which were also known as the medes of the mass or *merita missæ*, though *merita* and *mede* were often used of the mass in a less restricted sense.

These *virtutes* or *merita* were sayings ascribed to our Lord himself, the evangelists, apostles, and ancient fathers, and so assigned without any attempt at critical exactitude—not to say, with an absolute unconcern as to the merest semblance of probable truth. They attribute to the fact of hearing a mass a variety of advantages, spiritual and temporal, most calculated to work upon the hopes or fears, the selfishness or affections, of the ignorant and superstitious. I hope this will not seem prejudiced or uncharitable, for I am not one of those who can see nothing to admire—or to desiderate— in the religion of our forefathers. In forming a judgment as to their opinions or practice, I endeavour, so far as I know how, to do so from their point of view, with their means of information, and in their circumstances; but in respect to those who debited these fables—and in this I may include the great majority of the legends and tales of the mass—the conviction has forced itself upon me, that whilst there were many humble and holy men who had a single eye to the saving of souls and the honour of their Lord, there were others to whom, whatsoever else they may have believed as to the merits of the mass, not the least of its merits was this, that it gave occasion for the mass-penny of the layman.

It would be an incomplete illustration of this part of our subject if the reader were left without materials for forming his own opinion. I have met with a great diversity from various printed and unpublished manuscript sources, and it had occurred to me to print some of the pieces entire in the Appendix; but they had so little to recommend them either to an antiquary or a philologist, that I have taken my own patience and my readers' into account, and give only a few extracts, without including all of those under the names of " Austin, Ambrose, Barnard, and Bede," who are mentioned in the text.(1)

I begin with a few of the first items of the " Vertewis of the Mess," from a MS. of the Lowland Scotch dialect of the fifteenth century, edited for the society by Mr Lumby.

" Her begynnis the Vertewis of the mess, apprewyt be the haly wryt, baith be our lord Ihesu cristes wordes, and vthir haly sanctis and doctour's of þe cristyne faith. And fyrst and formist.

" Sanct paul sais that rycht as our lord Ihesu cryst is mar worthi and mar preciouss than ony vthir creatur that god maid,

(1) Line 95. The Harleian MS. gives the four names, " Ierome, ambroce, Bernard *and* bede," and adds, " And Austyn ou*er* hem Ichon."—*fol.* 74, *b.*

sa is þe mess mar worthi and mar preciouss than ony vthir oresone or sacrifice that may be said or maid in this erd.

" Item, sanct barnard sais, that It is mar spedfull, neidful, and profitable to the manis saul-heill to her mess, with clen hart and gud deuotioune, na for to gif for þe luf of god þe fee of sa mickle land as a man may ourgang quhill the mess is in doinge.

" Item, our lord Ihesu sais that quhat sum euer thing þat men with clen hart and gud deuocione askes at the mess in thar praieres It salbe grantyt thaim or elles bettir and mar prophitable thing, na thai ask hyme be mekill. Item, *quicquid orantes petitis* &c.

" Item, sanct Jerome sais that till here mess with clen hart and gud dewocioune garres the saulys that he prayes for feil na payne in purgatory quhil that mess is in doinge."(1)

Next I give the opening of Lydgate's " *Virtutes Missarum*" from the Harleian MS. 3954, *fol.* 76, *col.* 2, which, notwithstanding the similarity of name, is not to be confounded with his " Vertue of the Masse," above, p. 163.

" Augustinus in libro de ciuitate, de vij virtutibus missarum. illo die quo videtur corpus Christi, victus necessarius tribuitur. ignorata iuramenta delentur · leuia colloquia dimittuntur · lumen oculorum confortatur · morte subitania non moritur · et si quis subito decesserit, pro communicatione habetur.

" Lordyngis dygne an dere,
Lystyn & ȝe may here :
I wyl ȝou shywyn a medicyne,
þat xal ȝou sauyn fro helle pynne,
ȝyf ȝᵉ it vnderstonde aryth,
ȝe xul wel plecyn god al-myth.

Listen, Lords, and hear of a medicine that can save from hell.

Seynt austyn in hys boke tellys,
Quat man þat in erthe duellys,
And here a masse with god wyl
Qwat mede longyt þer tyl.

St Austin is cited as saying,

Quat man be clene out of synne
And here a masse quan it be gyne,
He xal hys fode [*enjoy*] þat day
Suffesantly I dar wel say.

that a mass heard by one shriven of sin,

ensures sufficient food,

And thour þᵉ virtu of þᵉ masse,
Lyth othys suoryn xul fro hym passe ;
Idel wordis xul gon a-way
And be for-ȝouyn I dar wel say.

freedom from oaths lightly sworn, and forgiveness of idle words,

þᵉ syth of hys eyn gryȝe
Xal be confortyd, I ȝou seyȝe :
ȝyf he so þis body in bred,
It xal hym saue fro sodeyn ded ;

strengthening of the eyes,

(1) *Ratis Raving*, E. E. T. S., 1870, p. 113.

and viaticum in
case of sudden
death.
And ʒyf he happe þat day to deyʒe,
He stant for houselyd, I ʒow seye.
þis wytnessyt seynt austyn

Witness St Austin
and Lydgate.
And ledgyt hem in latyn.
Xij vertuwys þere be mo
I xal hem tellyn or I goo."

The twelve virtues follow. I add the third and sixth, as they are
not often met with, and the sixth is a further example of apostolical
authority being claimed. The eighth is given, *post*, p. 371.

"Gregori*us* · tercia vi*r*tus est quicquid comedit in die mag*is*
co*n*uenit nature sue p*ost* audic*io*nem misse q*u*am an*te* .

　　　 " Sen gregory, þe good man,
　　　　The iij scyl telle can.
　　　　Q*u*at ma*n* here messe or he dyne,
　　　　It is a good medycyne ;
　　　　Hys mete xal ha*n* þᵉ more fysou*n*
　　　　Afterward be resou*n*."

"Paulus" vj*ta*. vi*r*tus est mulier pregnans que int*er*est misse
deuota · si parit illo die · pueru*m* parit s*i*ne magno dolore &
s*i*ne dampne .

　　　 " Sen poule seyt q*u*at woman wit*h* chylde
　　　　Here a masse wit*h* herte mylde
　　　　And happe to chylde þ*a*t day
　　　　Here neythyr(1) xal ha*n* no gret fray
　　　　And þᵉ mod*er* þᵉ soþᵉ to seyne
　　　　She xal ha*n* þᵉ lesse peyne
　　　　And þis is þᵉ vj scyl
　　　　To hery*n* messe wit*h* good wyl."

The medicinal effect which is vouched by St Gregory (III
Virtus) appears under the name of St Ambrose in the *Dicta
Sanctorum*, the opening lines of which are quoted, p. 370.

" Ambrosius dicit · Quicquid h*omo* comedit a*u*t bibit p*ost* missam) ·/
meli*us* ingerit *et* pr*o*dest ei plusquam Ante missam) q*u*antum

　　　 " Seynt Ambrose doctour · whyche Affermyd was
　　　　Oone of the foure · seythe As I shalle the telle
　　　　A man that ete or drynkethe · Aftyr mas
　　　　The mete or drynke dygestythe Alle so welle
　　　　And to hys body · As trewe as gospelle
　　　　Profytythe more · then) be fore mas to ete
　　　　Therfore here mas · or thou take drynke or mete."(2)

----

(1) Neither of them.
(2) Rawlinson MS. *Poetry*, 36, *fol.* 6*b*. The Virtewis from the Ratis Raving
MS. (l. 3940) agrees with this in ascribing this to St Ambrose : " Item, sanct
ambross sais that quhat eu*er* met or drink a p*er*sone tak *efter* mess perfites
hyme mar til hes heil and lang lyf, na It that he etes befor mess."

The case of the woman with child, which appears above under the name of St Paul, in these *Dicta* is assigned to St Chrysostom.

"Iohannes Crisostomus · Si contigerit nulierem (*mulierem*) parere die illa qua missam / Audierit Absque dolore magno pariet . /

"Iohn Crisostom · Doctoure of gret renowne,
Seythe yif hyt be so þat ony womane
Wythe child · to be delyuered were bowne
That day she here mas · yf hyt plese god whane
The chyld shalle be borne · wythe oute sorow thane.
Grete to þe pregnaunt · thys is a gret grace
Now here thy mas whyls þou hast tyme *and* space."(1)

The same collection also professes to give the Latin of St Austin as to the remission of the "light oaths" (perjury) and "idle words" of Lydgate (above, p. 367); and as to hearing mass standing a man instead of being houseled, or taking his "rights."

"Augustinus · Videntibus corpus *christi* in *prima* die lumen conseruatur oculorum et omnia Iuramenta / vana iocosa periuria vel · ignota remittur (*remittuntur*).

"Austyne þe famous doctour excelent.
Remembrythe the syghte · of Crystys bodye
That day hyt is sene · thy syghte verament
Conseruyd is · As lokynge wythe thyne Ie
An Alle veyne othes · pleyes *and* periurye.
Or vnknowyne synnes · relesyd bene they
Here mas · *and* þou mayst not mysspede in feye."

"Augustinus · Si quis semel missam Audierit deuote *prima* die morte subitanea non / morietur · Et si sine communione obierit per communicato habetur in ecclesia /

"The same Austyne seythe · As ye may heer se
A mas deuoutly herd · be eny man)
That same day · no sodene dethe shalle haue he
And yif he dye · wythe owte hys ryghtys than)
For hys howselle hyt is had · As I can).
Shewe you be wrytyng · As thys doctour wryte
Therfor here mas · *and* therto þou delyte."(2)

---

(1) Rawlinson MS. *Poetry*, 36, *fol.* 7.
(2) Ib. *fol.* 8. In a Latin *catena*, "De virtutibus missæ" (Bodl. MS. 832, *fol.* 168, *b*), the Latin of St Augustine is given in another form, but I need hardly say that the reader will search the "De Civitate" in vain for anything to justify it.

"Augustinus in *libro* de *civitate* dei de interessentibus in missis publicis seu priuatis digne et sine mortali peccato existentibus ista sequitur commoda vbi dicit. Quod illo die quo videtur corpus *Christi* victus necessarius tribuitur · ignorata iuramenta delentur · levia colloquia dimittuntur · lumen oculorum confortatur Morte subitania non morietur. Et siquis subito discescerit pro communicato habetur."

I now give the beginning of the Rawlinson MS., from which the above quotations have been made (Rawlinson MS. *Poetry*, 36), *ff*. 6—9.

" *Hec sunt Dicta sanctorum de virtute sacramenti Altaris · Ac ffructu et effectu Misse provt infra patet*.

" As dyuers doctours hathe wryt of the vertu
    In herynge of the mas · and eke of the syght
Off the blessid sacrament whyche dothe subdu
    Alle euylle thoughtis · comaundyng be hys myghte
The ylle Aungel of man) to be At hys Flyghte.
    Fro mannys sowle · that day he herythe a mas
And scthe hym) · that is · shalle be · And euyr was."

The *Dicta* as those above given follow in Latin and English, and the piece ends with the following Envoy:

" ¶ Now Frende · And þou canst vndyrstand ɪatyne
    Rede the textys · of Alle tho holy men)
Whyche been) A boue · þou mayst se here wryten)
    And yif þou vndyrstand · no latyne then)
Rede þe Inglysshe · of euery balad when)
    Thou wylt · vndyr euery texte As þei stand
And þen shalt þou those textys vndyrstand

¶ And yif þou hast bene slewfulle here be fore
    In heryng of mas · yyf þou rede welle þis
Hyt shalle stere the · to here mas euyr more
    And so done · in feythe þou mayst not mys
To plese god · and to purchas hevyne blys .
    To þe whyche blys · god send them) þat dayly
Wylle here A mas · And they may come therby."

Lydgate's Vertue of the Mass (above, p. 167) ends with fifteen stanzas, which are rubricated " The vertu of heryng of Masse after seynt Bernard," the several virtues being of the same character as those in the pieces above quoted, except that here he does not assign them in the same *ad libitum* fashion to inspired or patristic authority. There is no occasion to multiply quotations, but I add one stanza because I do not remember to have met elsewhere with a similar appeal to the sailor's desire for a fair wind.

Sailors have no foul winds,   " ¶ Masse herd aforne · the wynde is not contrary
        To Maryners that day · in theyr sailing.
the poor have needful food,   And althyng · that is necessarye
        God sent to poraile(1) · that day in theyr feedyng.

---

(1) "sendeth to preuayle."—W. de Worde. "poraile " may not have been familiar to the printer.

Wymmen also · that gon on travelyng,
Folke wel experte · have therof a pref,
That herde masse in the mornyng
Were delyuerd and felt(1) woo no myschef."

and women in
labour have good
deliverance.

MS. Harl. 2251, *fol.* 187, *b.*

P. 131, l. 105. *poynteþ hit uch a pas.* That is, not guides or directs
him, but notes and numbers each step. See the Prpmptorium
Parvulorum (p. 406), "Poynted or prykked, *punctatus.* Poyntel,
stilus."(2) *To prick* is still used in this sense in the north; as, for
example, "pricking the match," of keeping the score at cricket,
or "pricking the bricks," of counting them and marking a stroke
for each hundred.(3)

Cf. Lydgate's "Vertue of the Masse:"

"In goyng thyder · his steppis more and lesse
Bien of aungels · nombred and told."—MS. Harl. 2251, *fol.* 187.

And so too the Ratis Raving MS., above quoted: "Item, sanct
augustyne sais that the gud angell that kepis þe manis saul comptis
wp and wrytis al the steppis at a man makes to the mess, and fore
ilkane of thaim god sal reuard her or hyme."(4)

Lydgate (see above, p. 367) is not satisfied with the name of
St Austin, but assigns this virtue to an evangelist:

"**M**atheuus · viij^ua. vi*rtus* est q*uod* in e*un*do & redeu*n*do ad
ecclesia*m*, passus numerantur & deo renumerantur (*remu-
nerantur?*).

"Matheu tellyt þe viij scyl
þat we xulde tan hede þer tyl
Quait man in erthe here a messe
Angelis arn al redy dresse
To wrytyn hys steppus be on & on
Of al þe weye þat he hat gon
Boþin out & in as it is ryth
And presentyt þer with god al myth."

---

(1) "felt no myschefe."—W. de Worde.

(2) "His felaw had a staf typped with horn,
A payr of tablis al of yvory,
And a poyntel y-polischt fetisly,
And wroot the names alway as he stood,
Of alle folk that gaf him eny good,
Ascaunce that he wolde for hem preye."—*C. T.* 7322-7.

(3) In my under-graduate days it was the custom at some, perhaps all, of
the colleges at Oxford to prick a hole in the bill or list at the name of each
man as he passed into chapel. At Christ Church the student, whose turn it
was to do this, was called prickbill; and though the verger now "pricks" the
"bill," the name of "prick-bill" still survives and is given to the senior of
the students elected in the current year.

(4) *Ratis Raving*, p. 104, l. 3964.

In the Douce MS. there is a curious mistake :

" An angel payntus thi face,"

the scribe not knowing the French *pas*, or mistaking the *p* for an *f*, and so making *face* of it.(1)

P. 131, l. 107. *elde nouȝt.* The Ratis Raving MS. (above, p. 366) assigns this to St Austin : "Item, sancte augustine sais that for al the tyme þat a persone be at þe mess he standis in sted, and eildis nocht, bot haldis hym in the samyn ȝouthed he was in quhen he come to þe mess."(2)

l. 110. *not blynt.* See Lydgate, above, p. 367.

l. 112. *þorw him þat mihtes may.* The phrase is repeated, l. 136. In the Douce and Harleian MSS. we find in both places, " Forsooth I thee say,"(3) but I am inclined to think that our text preserves the original reading, and that the scribes substituted a common-place tag because this was of unusual occurrence. Line 553, we have " þat al mihtes may ; " in the Alliterative Poems (Morris), p. 55, l. 644, " þat myȝtes al weldez ;" and in our B-text, *ante*, p. 18, l. 180, we have God invoked, as " of mihtes most," and frequently in the Psalter as " Laverd of mightes " (*Dominus Virtutum*, Lord of hosts). In Ps. (103) cii, 21, we have " Blisses to Laverd, alle mightes his," from the Vulgate " *omnes virtutes ejus*," where our modern versions have " all ye his hosts." *Virtutes* is the rendering of the Vulgate, and *mæhto* of the Lindisfarne gospels, for δυνάμεις, the " mighty works " of the authorised version.(4) I think therefore we shall not be very far wrong, if we understand it thus—that mights may—either as having power to do mighty works, or that possesses and weilds all powers.

l. 117. *I þe fay.* " In the true faith of God's holy name." *Burial of the Dead*, B. C. P.

l. 121. *tray or tene.* This phrase is as old as Cædmon. He makes Hagar in the wilderness tell the angel that she had fled " tregan and teónan."(5) In the *Orison of our Lady*(6) we have,

---

(1) *Audelay's Poems*, p. 68. The Harleian MS., "An angel poynted every pas."

(2) *Ratis Raving*, p. 113, l. 3943.

(3) *Audelay's Poems*, p. 68 and 76. At p. 68, it is printed, "Soyle as I the say," but this must be a mistake of the transcriber for soþle, sothly, truly, or forsooth, as in the other places. MS. Harl. 3954, *fol.* 74, *b*, and *fol.* 75.

(4) St Matt. xi, 20, 21; xiii, 54, 58, &c. In St Luke vi, 5, we have both the *mihtes* and the *may :* "And ne mæhte ðer mæht ænige gewyrce." *Et non poterat ibi virtutem ullam facere.*" The *genyrce* would not have been necessary to the sense, but was required on account of *facere* and the inter-linear verbal translation.

Cf. " Prey him þat best may."—MS. Harl. 3954, *fol.* 76.

(5) *Cædmon*, Bouterwek, 2268.

(6) I. O. E. H., p. 193, l. 61.

" Muruhǯe moniuold wiǯ-ute teone and trie,"
rendered by Dr Morris "trouble or annoy."

In a poem on the times of Edward II. :

" Al þat whilom wes murthe is turned to treie and tene."(1)

The Harleian MS. here reads :

> " þi mete *and* þi drynk
> þou xal han wi*th* lesse swynk
> Wi*th*-outyn trey *and* tene."

And Audelay :

> " And both thi mete and thi drynke
> Thou schalt wyn with lasse swynk
> Without travayle or tene."

P. 131, l. 125—130. The precept is made to apply to a journey,(2) but this is most probably a corruption, from the scribe not having understood the *pass* (French, *passer*, *trespasser*) in the sense of departing this life. In the Harleian MS. (*fol. 75, b.*) we have,

> " þerfore it is god or þou passe
> Euery day to heryn a masse
> On morwyn ʒyf þou may.
> ʒif þou may not at morwyn
> Loke þou do at vndryn
> Or ell*is* at mydday."

The scribe of the Douce MS. (Audelay, p. 75) would also have seemed to have stumbled at "*pass :*"

> " Here-fore, serys, more and lasse,
> Evere day here ʒour masse
> On morowe ʒif ʒe may."

P. 132, l. 136. See above, l. 112.

l. 140. The doctrine of the Church has ever been that "the wickedness of the ministers hinders not the effect of the sacrament," but it is curious, and painful, to observe how many mediæval tales and legends expatiate on the benefit of masses said by priests of particular churches or at the altars of particular communities, more especially of mendicant orders, in whose interests they are written : but the distinction as to prayer, which is here drawn, ought not to be attributed to any such mercenary motive.

---

(1) *Political Songs*, Wright, p. 340, l. 380.

(2) According to the Ecclesiastical Institutes (xxiv, *De Die Dominica cautius celebranda*, Thorpe, *A. L.* II, 420) a man was allowed to travel by land or by water on Sundays, " on þa ʒerad þæt he his mæssan gehyre and his gebedu ne forlæte." The Latin of Theodulphus is " ut horum occasione missa et orationes non prætermittantur."

Cf. " Neþeles þe seluyn messe
          Ys noþer þe wurse, ne þo lesse ;
          þe sunne hys feyrnes neuer he tynes(1)
          þoghe hyt on þe muk-hepe shynes,
          But þe muk ys þe more stynkynge,
          þere þe sunne ys more shynyngge.
          Ne more hyt ys lore þe vertu
          Of þe messe, but mannys pru.
          þoghe þe prest be fals or frow
          þe messe ys euere gode ynow ;
          But þe preyere haþ no myȝt
          For hys lyfe ys nat clene dyȝt."—*H. S.* 2297—2308.(2)

And so Hampole of the unworthiness of the minister, and the
avail of the prayers of a righteous man :

      " Allswa a prest alle-if he be
          Synful and out of charite,
          He es Goddes minister and haly kirkes
          þat þe sacrament of þe auter wirkes,
          þe wilk es never-þe-les of myght,
          Alle-if þo prest here lyf noght right

          . . . .

          For in Goddes name he synges the mes,
          Under wham in order he es.
          But speciel prayers with gode entente,
          þat es made besyde þe sacramente,
          Of a gude prest er wele better
          þan of an ille, and to God swetter."—*P. C.* 3682—99.

P. 132, l. 141. *As Monk, Chanoun, Hermyte or Frere.*

      Cf. " As ane monkis, or ane frere."
                              Douce MS.—Audelay, p. 72.

          " As ony abot, chanoun, or frere."
                              Harleian MS., *fol.* 75, *b.*

These enumerations are not exhaustive, but they are all intended
to illustrate the position that the ministration of parish priests or
any others are not to be rejected for any supposed superiority of
another class.   This is in strong contrast with the line taken by
the friars—except in the care of the poor—if we are to judge

---

(1) *tynes*, glossed " lesyþ."—*H. S.*, ed. Furnivall, p. 4.
      (2) " Ne quidez mie ne purquant,
          Qe le sacrement fu meinz vaillant
          De eux, plus qe en bone gent ;
          Car de home ne prent enpirement
          Nient plus que pet le fimer
          Le solail qe sur li fiert cler."—*M. P.* 2685—90.

from the satires of the period. For example, the Romaunt of the Rose:

> "I recke not of poore men
> Her estate is not worth an hen."

But as to others:

> "I make hem trow both most and least,
> Her parish priest(1) is but a beast
> Ayent me and my company
> That shrewes been as great as I."—(*fol.* 139, *b.*)

P. 132, l. 161—172. This stanza in our MS. is very corrupt, and I find that in my side-notes I failed to catch what was most probably the meaning of the original. Audelay does not help us, for he reads very much as here, except that he ascribes this "virtue" to St Austin. The Harleian MS. reads the second line.

> "A. C. M. ȝyf þou wilt here,"

here being the adverb of place, and not *year*, as mistaken by the scribe of the Vernon text.

The meaning seems to be that whatever number of masses a man caused to be sung here on earth for several souls, each individual soul should have the benefit. He need have no doubt (*l.* 170) of his dole (mass-groat, *ante*, p. 243), but was to trust that each soul should have a mass, "all-whole," in contrast, that is, with two-faced or many faced masses (*missæ bifaciatæ, trifaciatæ*, or *multarum facierum*), for which more than one payment had been received, which though condemned as "a detestable abuse," would nevertheless seem to have been not uncommon, to judge from the censures directed against them, and the manner in which a resort to the practice is repudiated.(2)

P. 133, l. 169. *laste endynge*, i. e. of the mass. Cf. the Harleian MS. here—

> "þerfor quan þou art in kyrke
> Thynk þeron *and* be not erke
> On tyl þe last endyng.
> Have no dowte of þi dole
> Be trost þou hast a masse hole
> Thour help of heuene kyng."

The Vernon scribe, though he has let *sere* (l. 161) stand, has almost altogether obscured the meaning of the original in getting rid of the northern *kirk*, and by the change of person : first he speaks

---

(1) See as to the jealousy between the regulars or "religious," and the secular or parochial clergy, a quotation from Friar Dan Topias.—*Ante*, p. 241.

(2) "Non auctoritas ecclesiæ sed cupiditas ministrorum instituit."— "Tanquam detestabile reprobamus."

The question, "An sacerdos non potest per unam missam satisfacere duobus stipendiis?" is answered in the negative by Dens.—*De Sacrificio Missæ*, 0, Opera V, 377.

in his own person,—I rede (*advise*) ; then of himself and of other clerks in the mass—our *ending ;* and lastly he identifies himself and his hearers—our *doubt,* our *dole.*

P. 133, l. 176—180.   This apology is not in the Douce or the Harleian MSS., and the insertion, like the example of the adder (p. 379), would seem to have been due to the controversies which had arisen when the Vernon MS. was written.

l. 188. *Confiteor.*   See p. 6, B. 43 ; p. 90, l. 25.

l. 192. *for the prest pray.* See p. 10, B. 95, &c.

P. 134, l. 208. *syng of loue.* The song of praise here referred to is probably the *Gloria in excelsis.* See p. 14, B. 119.

l. 221. *þi drihten,* that is, a prayer beginning with *Domine.* We learn what this was from the York *Horæ* (*fol.* xiv.) : "¶ *Whan thou entrest into the chyrche saye thus:* Domine in multitudine misericordiæ tuæ introibo in domum tuam : adorabo ad templum sanctum tuum et confitebor nomini tuo. Domine deduc me in justitia tua propter inimicos meos : dirige in conspectu tuo viam meam."(1)

l. 222. *deore god almihten.* I am not able to identify the prayer here intended with the same certainty as the first. It may perhaps be the "*devout prayer*" from the York *Horæ,* "O most dear Lord," quoted above, p. 248; or a Latin prayer in the York *Horæ* (*fol.* lxx. *b*) : "Benignissime Domine Jesu Christe, respice super me miserum peccatorem oculis misericordiæ tuæ quibus respexisti Petrum in atrio, Mariam Magdalenam in convivio, et latronem in crucis patibulo. Concede mihi ut cum beato Petro peccata mea digne defleam ; et cum Maria Magdalena perfecte te diligam ; et cum latrone in cœlesti paradiso æternaliter te videam, Qui cum, &c. Amen."

l. 223. *And in Marie I me aseure,* that is, put me under the safe-guard of. The devotion here referred to may be the Anthem *de Sancta Maria,* which has been quoted above, p. 342(2), "Sub tuam protectionem confugimus," &c.

l. 232. *vnkuynde creature,* contrary to nature. Cf. " A deuoute prayer in Englyshe " in the York *Horæ* (*fol.* lxxxiiii. *b*) : "O glorious Jesu / o mekest Jesu / o moost swetest Jesu . . . . . I crye the mercy with herte contryte of my grete unkyndness that I haue had to the."

P. 135, l. 245—256. This prayer would seem to have been intended for clerks, or the people at the time when they took a more direct part in the mass.

l. 268. *But,* unless, and so Lydgate in his *Virtutes Missarum* uses *but* in this same connection.

---

(1) It will be observed that this is from Psalm v—part of the eighth verse with a transposition of the first words, and the whole of the ninth verse.

"*Quat* soule þat tyme he prey fore,
But it be endles for-lore,
As many as he wyl for calle,
þai xul be delyueryd alle
Out of peyne, resting
Qwyl þe messe is in seyzyng."(1)

P. 135, l. 272. *non hope of hele*, and so Hampole :

"Bot til þam þat er dampned for ay
Na gude dede avayle ne help may,
Nouther almus dede, prayer, ne messe."—*P. C.* 3706-8.

In the "Tale of the Falmouth Squires," printed for this society in Mr Furnivall's collection of *Political and Religious Poems* (1866), we have, not indeed the offensive illustration of the "ded dogge," but a father in the pains of hell warns his son (p. 100) :

"Thou take me never in thi prayer."—l. 230.

giving as a reason,

"For euer the lenger þu prayes for me,
My paynes shalle be more and more."—l. 233-4.

The received opinion was that the pleading of the church did not extend beyond purgatory. On the other hand we have the often-told story of Saint Gregory and his "gran vittoria,"(2) in having obtained the transfer to Paradise of the soul of the Emperor Trajan, "without singing of mass,"(3) though the legend tells us the pope was cautioned by an angel never again to pray for the release of a soul from hell.

The writer of *The Stacyons of Rome* appears to have thought it a much more simple matter. In describing the chapel of the *Scala cœli*, he says :—

"Who-so syngeþ masse yn þat chappelle
For any frend, he loseþ hym fro helle ;
He may hym brynge þorow purgatory, y-wys,
In-to þe blys of paradys.
Ther sowles abyde tylle domis day
In myche Ioye, as y ʒou say."(4)

In the MS. York *Horæ*, from which the *Hours of the Cross* are printed, there is a Latin prayer (*fol.* 83), which a rubric vouches as equally prevailing :—" *Cuilibet dicenti hanc oracionem, conceditur quod si esset in statu eterne dampnationis, deus transfert penam in purgatorii penam. Si vero fuerit in statu maxime purgatorii, deus*

---

(1) Harl. MS. 3954, f. 76. See above, p. 367.
(2) Dante, *Purgat.* x, 75, in the description of the sculptures on the marble bank of the first circle of purgatory.
(3) *Piers Plowman* (Skeat), C Text, p. 220, l. 85.
(4) *Poems*, 1866, Furnivall, p. 119, l. 172—176.

mutat hanc purgatorii penam et ipsum sine purgatorio ad eterna gaudia proculdubio perducat."

P. 136, l. 289. This story is told with some variations of St Austin of England, both in the Douce and Harleian MSS. Robert Brunne has a similar story of jangling women and the fiend in his *Handlyng Synne.*(1) He does not give a name to priest or deacon, but in the Book of the Knight of La Tour-Landry in Anjou,(2) of which the French original was written much about the same time as our Vernon MS., we find the claims of local saints(3) are recognized, and St Martin takes the place of the pope, and St Brice officiates as deacon instead of our English saint.

l. 310. *As God ʒaf him þe grace.*

"þan wyst þe prest þurghe þat syʒt
þat he was weyl wyþ Gode almyʒt."—*H. S.* 9306-7.

P. 137, l. 316. *race.* This word occurs as a verb active, as for example the damned in Hampole:

"þair awen flessch of-ryve and race."—*P. C.* 7379.

And Lydgate in his *Poem against self-love:*

"Lat every man doon his besy cure
To race out pride and set in first meeknesse."(4)

Chaucer in his *Boethius* uses *arace*(5) in the phrase to "arace cloutes out of clothes,"(6) and in the *Clerkes Tale:*

---

(1) Ed. Furnivall, p. 287, l. 2263, 9315. There is nothing to correspond in the French original.

(2) *Translation*, ed. Wright, E. E. T. S., p. 41.

(3) St Martin was Bishop of Tours, and was succeeded by St Brice (Britius) in that see towards the end of the fourth century.

(4) *Minor Poems*, Halliwell, Percy Soc., p. 162. Lydgate continues the horticultural metaphor—rooting out—planting in.

(5) We still have this verb in the compound form. Johnson gives "erase (Fr. *raser*), to destroy, to exscind;" and Richardson, "Lat. *eradere, erasum*, to scrape out." Both give the example of the heraldic "erased," which is used in contrast to "couped," but if the word in this sense were connected with shaving, whatever may be the case when used of making an erasure, its heraldic use would not in itself imply anything different from *couped*, whereas instead of the clean cut of the couped, it means jagged, as if the head or limb of the animal had been "plucked out," as in the quotation in Richardson. This explanation would have seemed enough to suggest that the primary meaning was to eradicate, to tear out by the roots; and, *pace* the lexicographers, that both *eradicate* and *erase* had a common derivation: *eradicate* coming direct from the Latin, and *erase* through the O. F. *erracher, aracher* (arracher); Lat. *exradicare, abradicare.* See Littré: *racine*, L. L. *radicula*, Lat. *radix, icis.* Palsgrave, as Leland above, seems to have kept this etymology in view: "I pull up by the roote, or pull out by vyolence. *Je arrache, arracher, jesrache,* or *araser*, and *je desracine.* Hercules, in his furye, pulled up gret tres by the rootes: *Hercules, en sa fureur, arracha les arbres hors de terre*, or *esracha*, or *desracina les arbres.*"—*L'Eclaircissement*, 670, *a.* (6) *Boethius*, Morris, E. E. T. S., p. 11, l. 195.

"The children from her arm they gonne arace."—*C. T.* 8979.

But the verb is here used intransitively, and in the next line as a verb active, and can hardly be the word which, with the same spelling, means "to tear," or "root out." It's meaning seems to be "to stretch;" and, although I cannot refer to other examples of this use of the word, it makes sense in both places, which "rooting out" most certainly does not; and I think it is justified by the use of kindred words.

Cf. Icel. *rekja*, part. *rakinn*, "to spread out, unfold, unwind, of cloth, a clew, thread, and the like" (C-V. 492); also "*rekkja*, to strain, stretch out."—*Ib.* 493.

M. G. *uf-rakjan*, which Ulfilas uses for ἐκτείνειν, *e. g.* "ufrakei þo handu þeina," "*stretch forth thy hand*."—St Luke vi, 10; and for ἐπισπᾶσθαι, "ni ufrakjai." Vulg. "*Non adducat præputium.*" A. V. "*Let him not become uncircumcised*" (lit. *be stretched*).—1 Cor. vii, 18.

A. S. "*ræcan*, to reach, extend, hold out, offer." Bosworth quotes "ræhte forð his hand," "*put out* (stretched forth) *his hand.*"—Gen. xxxviii, 28. Bouterwek(1) quotes, "to unrihte handum ræcean, *extendere ad iniquitatem manus suas.*"—Ps. (125) cxxiv, 4. See also the perfect "rauhte," in l. 348.

P. 137, l. 319. *marbel ston.* A touch of local colour, for according to this version of the legend the Church was at Rome.

l. 336. *I say* = saw.

"Twey wymmen Ianglede þere besyde,
Betwyx hem to, y say a fende."—*H. S.* 9279-80.

l. 338. *langare*, at a longer (greater) distance, further on.

St Augustine showed the pope where he saw the fiend sit, and, with a malediction at the mention of him, pointed to where the women sat, further off than the fiend.

The piece was intended for recitation, and was probably accompanied with a certain amount of action.

P. 140, l. 429. *To wite what þe prest seiþ.* See p. 211.

l. 445. *endauntes.* A reference to "the deaf adder, which refuseth to hear the voice of the charmer."—Ps. lviii, 4, 5.

Cf. "Als of a neddre def als-swa
þat stoppand es his eres twa,
þat noght sal here þe steven wicchand
Of hunter wichand wiseli in land."—Ps. (58) lvii, 5-6.

l. 446. This *exemplum* of the adder may probably have been added after the rise of the Lollard controversy as to the reading of scripture in an unknown tongue.

---

(1) *Cædmon*, II, 236.

It may be noticed that this stanza is not corrupted by frequent transcription of scribes who wrote in different dialects.

P. 141, l. 461—72. It will be noticed that the two last tails do not rhyme with the two first. The northern -es in the second person singular (*ledes*, l. 469) no doubt gave occasion to a southern scribe to make the change.

P. 142, l. 512. See as to the offertory p. 230—242.

l. 519. *catel encrease.* See on "virtues" of the mass, *ante*, p. 366.

l. 521. *þus seide.* See p. 22, and note, p. 245.

l. 522. *in his honde.* See note, p. 236-7.

P. 143, l. 537. *loute.* Note, p. 252

l. 545. *secre.* Note, p. 265.

l. 559. *stondynge*, altered from the northern *standand.* As time went on the people knelt during the canon. See p. 273.

P. 144, l. 571. *þe belle.* The ringing of a bell at the elevation was general when the original was written, if I have rightly placed the date in the thirteenth century. See *ante*, p. 280.

l. 572. *scorn.* The received doctrine as to transubstantiation or, more exactly, concomitance was not explicitly allowed by all the English schoolmen in the thirteenth century, and their opinions may possibly have been the occasion of this language. But the reference seems rather to those who gave offence by irreverent conduct than to theological dissidents. It does not look like an insertion with reference to the Lollards or Wycliffites, after enquiries had passed from the schools to the people, for what was objected against them was not so much a denial of the reality of the sacramental presence, as their assertion of the continued existence of the substance of the elements of the bread and wine.

l. 581, 582. *Flesch—blod.* This language, apart from lines 587-8, might have been written by one who did not accept the doctrine of concomitance, and may probably have come down from an earlier period. According to this doctrine the blood accompanies the body (hence the name), and the body is present in the chalice—*totus et integer Christus sub utraque specie.* The greater definiteness of later forms is very marked, "Lord in form of bread" (*ante*, p. 40, C. 237), and so forth.

l. 587-8. See before, p. 225.

l. 590. *spredes he,* "ad modum crucis," p. 108, l. 10, and note, p. 288.

P. 145, l. 605. *Whon he haþ vsed,* i. e. drunk of the chalice or communicated. The use of this verb in English, in the sense of drinking, seems to have been confined to the holy communion, not, however, invariably(1) of the consecrated elements. It was

(1) "Also he shall offre, in a cruet of gold, wyne, which he shall vse in

used in the twelfth century in France of common food and drink :
" les grosses viandes user ; " " del meillur vin usout (usait) que
l'un trover poeit."(1)

It has occurred to me that the English ecclesiastical use of this
word may have arisen from the Vulgate, 1 Tim. v, 23, " modico
vino utere, propter stomachum tuum "—" use a little wine for thy
stomach's sake ; " and that its employment for the communion of
the laity was a survival from the times before the overruling of
the command that all should drink of the cup. In the Promptorium

---

the said chalice, after he is housilled."—(Device for the Coronation of King
Henry VII.) Rutland Papers, S. S., p. 21.

Communion, sub utraque specie, was conceded to the kings of France at
their coronation, but it will be seen from this extract that in this country
there was no distinction of persons, and that the denial of the cup applied to
the king equally with others.

The change from the previous custom of the church, in formal abrogation
of our Lord's command, was very gradual, but it had become the rule in the
West by the end of the twelfth century. Still, as unconsecrated wine continued
to be given to the communicants in the chalice, the unlearned appear to have
remained in ignorance of it ; and in 1281, the date of Archbishop Peckham's
Lambeth constitutions, the administration of the communion under both kinds
was a practice in cathedrals and monasteries.—(Lyndwood, lib. 1, tit. 1, c.
Altissimus, p. 9.) It is there rehearsed that in other churches (minoribus
ecclesiis) it is permitted to the celebrant only to receive the cup (sanguinem
sub specie vini) ; and parish priests are required to instruct the simple folk
(simplices) that what is "given to them to drink in the chalice (in calice) is not
the sacrament, but wine without water (vinum purum), that they may the more
easily swallow the sacrament which they had received." The Roman missal
of 1570, which was decreed by the Council of Trent, directs the celebrant to
purify himself and the communicants (se, et eos qui communicarunt, puri-
ficans) ; but when it was revised for the first time in 1600, it was directed—
and this remains, if not the practice, still the rule according to the existing
missal, Rit. Celeb. Miss. x, 6—that the server should follow the priest bearing
a vessel (vas) with wine and water for their purification. Gavanti gives the
reason for adding the water : and the alteration from the calix of the mediæval
constitution to the vas of the modern rubric, is explained in the Annotations
issued by the Prince-Bishop of Augsburg, in 1612, to the clergy for the
purpose of introducing the Roman rule : " In order to avoid a scandal and an
error on the part of the people " (very probably as content in their ignorance
as our simple folk in 1281), " the ablution," as the purification is here called,
" is not to be given to the communicants according to the hitherto existing
custom, in a chalice, but in a silver goblet, not made like a chalice, or in a
glass drinking-cup, unlike those used at table."—Annotationes in quibus
regulæ Romano more rite celebrandi et ministrandi insinuantur. Dilingæ,
1612, p. 12. De communicantium Ablutione.

(1) Martyr de Saint Thomas de Cantorbéry, 93, 102, quoted Littré, s. v.
In the Manuel des Pechiez, we find a similar use in respect to the sacrament
of the altar :

" Ky le cors deu vodra vser
On le prestre qe le deit sacrer."
Roxburghe Club Edition, Furnivall, l. 7235-6.

we find it of communicating : "Vsyñ, in sacrament receyvynge, *Communico.*"(1)   And so in Joseph of Arimathie :

" He vsede of(2) Goddes bord ; "(3)

of communicating in both kinds, and this, when said of the celebrant, meant to the English translator(4) the whole action of the mass before (*devant*) those who heard it.

It is very constantly used in this sense, as in the *Myroure* (p. 331), " in tyme of *Agnus dei* & whyle the preste vsyth ; " and so in *Langforde's Meditacyons*, of this part of the mass, " from þe sacryng unto þe using be done."(5)   In the rubrics of the Hereford missal we find the same use in the Latin : "postquam dixerit orationes usque ad usum, antequam utatur, cantet vel dicat in audientia."(6)

In St Gregory's Trental we have the word used precisely as in the text :

" When þe preste hath don his masse
Vsed and his hondes washe,
Anoþur oryson he moste say
þat yn þe boke fynde he may
þe post-comen men don it call."—l. 225—9.(7)

But Myrc, in rendering the *Cautelæ Missæ*, employs " *use* " in the more restricted English sense of drinking only :

" ȝef any fly, gnat, or coppe.
Doun in to þe chalys droppe,
ȝef þow darst for castynge þere,
Vse hyt hol alle I-fere,
And ȝef þy herte do wyþstonde,
Take vp þe fulþe wyþ þyn honde,
And ouer the chalys wosche hyt wel
Twyes or thryes, as I þe telle,
And vse forth þe blod þenne,
And do þe fulþe for to brenne."—l. 1937—46.

P. 145, l. 614. *to knele hit is best.*   See a similar rule, B 600, and note as to the later practice of the people kneeling before the post-common, p. 307.

---

(1) P. P. 512.
(2) Of = *from off.* We may trace the use of "of" in this sense in the A. V., and, as it happens, in the same connection : "We have an altar, whereof they have no right to eat."—Heb. xiii, 10.
(3) E. E. T. S., 1871, ed. Skeat, p. 22, l. 660. Cf. the quotation from the Ayenbite, *ante*, p. 359.
(4) Mr Skeat gives the French of the original in his note, p. 65 : "Si fist deuant nous ichel saint sacrement."
(5) MS. Wood, 17, f. 24, *b.* See *ante*, p. 168.
(6) Ed. Henderson, p. 74.
(7) *Poems*, Furnivall, E. E. T. S., 1866, p. 91.

P. 146, l. 639. *bord*, of " the marriage supper of the Lamb."—Rev. xix, 9.

l. 645. *þe Inprincipio.* In principio are the two first words of the Gospel according to St John, here used for the gospel written in the first fourteen verses of the first chapter, which from the earliest times has been the gospel for Christmas-day throughout the West.(1) A superstitious belief in its specific efficacy led to a frequent resort to the hearing of this gospel in the Latin, which gave occasion to a canon which was passed in the year 1023 in a provincial council at Selingstad, or Seligenstadt, on the Main, above Frankfort, in the Diocese of Mainz: "Quidam etiam laicorum et maxime matronæ habent in consuitudine ut per singulos dies audiant evangelium *In principio erat verbum*, et missas peculiares, hoc est de S. Trinitate aut de S. Michaele; et ideo sancitum est in eodem concilio, ut hoc ulterius non fiat nisi suo tempore, et nisi aliquis fidelium audire velit, pro reverentia sanctæ Trinitatis, non pro aliqua divinatione ; et si voluerint ut sibi missæ cantentur, de eodem die audiant missas, vel pro salute vivorum, vel pro defunctis."(2)

Durandus mentions this gospel as being sometimes said at the end of mass ;(3) and according to the Sarum rubrics it was said by the priest *in redeundo,* whilst returning from the altar. There is no mention of this in the York or Hereford missals.

Martene finds no reference to this rite in the mediæval uses of the monastic orders, and the first mention of it, that he met with, was in an ordinary of the Monastery of Bursfeld,(4) which, as we find from Gerbert, was printed at Baden in the year 1608, nearly forty years after the insertion of the rule in the Roman Missal.(5) Gerbert appears to have found no trace of it in Germany, nor Grancolas, de Vert, Le Brun, or Lebrun des Marettes (*De Moleon*) in any French diocesan uses before the sixteenth century. In this country, however, the use of this gospel at the end of mass appears to have been the rule in the province of Canterbury in the year 1305, for in the provincial council held that year at Merton, it was decreed that no stipendiary or other priest should,

---

(1) St John, i, 1—16, is the Easter-gospel of the Eastern Church.

(2) Conc. Salegunstadiense, Can. x. The sixth canon decrees that "stultissimi presbyteri" shall not throw the corporas into a fire to put it out ; but Canon xiv. allows the resort to ordeal on a charge of adultery.

(3) "Quidam volentes dicere, finita missa, evangelium sancti Iohannis, vel aliud."—*Rationale,* 4, xxiv, 5. The practice, probably, like others of the more modern ceremonies, originated with the friars. Le Brun quotes from a Dominican missal of the thirteenth century, where this gospel occurs among the devotions which the priest used after mass, "ob suam ipsius peculiarem pietatem."—*Explicat.* I, 333. The ordinary of the Dominicans, A.D. 1254, specifies cases in which this gospel may be said by a celebrant when taking off his vestments.—*Ib.* n. (1).

(4) *De Ritibus,* IV, 63.   (5) *Disquisit.* I, 405.

without leave of the rector, on Sundays and festivals, or at funerals, begin to say his own mass until the gospel of the principal mass was ended (*post lectum evangelium majoris missæ*), which Lyndwood(1) glosses, "non ante solemnem missam finitam," and so shows that the canon did not refer to the gospel for the day.

The rule as to saying the gospel at the end was not inserted in the Roman missal until 1570. The rubric requires it to be said at the altar, but in France in the eighteenth century it was not said at all at Lyons, and in many other dioceses it was said, as in the later Sarum use, in returning from the altar.(2) The previous rule, as already mentioned,(3) had been that the people departed at the *Ita missa est*. It was decreed at the first council of Orleans in 511 that the people were not to depart until mass was ended, and that in the absence of the bishop they were to await the blessing of the priest.(4) Within a few years (A.D. 538) this rule was so far modified that laymen were required to await the blessing of the bishop, if present, and not to depart before the saying of the Lord's Prayer,(5) which in the Gallican Liturgy was said as in the Roman rite, before the communion, except that it was said by the people with the priest.(6)

P. 146, l. 651. *þe eorþe to kis.* Myrc advises this observance as a remedy against pride :

> " Agaynes pruyde wythouten les,
> þe forme remedy ys mekenes,
> Ofte to knele and erþe to kys,
> And knowlache wel þat erþe he is."—l. 1667-70.

Lydgate explains its meaning :

> "Ye devoute peple, which kepe one observance
> Mekely in chirche to kysse stone or tree,
> Erthe or iren, hathe in remembraunce
> What they doth meane and take the moralite ;
> Erthe is clere token of the humanyte
> Of Crist Ihesu ; the stone, the sepulcre ;
> The spere of stiele, the sharpe nayles thre
> Causide his fyve woundis, remembrid in scripture."

---

(1) *Provinciale, Lib.* 3, *Tit.* 23, p. 238 (*m*).
(2) Fornici mentions that even now the Carthusians have not adopted the modern practice.—*Instit. Liturg.*, Pars. I, c. xxxii.
(3) Notes, *ante*, p. 309, 313.
(4) Concil. Aurel. I. *Can.* xxvi. (*al.* xxviii.)
(5) Concil. Aurel. III, *Can.* xxix.
(6) The episcopal benediction here spoken of was given, not at the end of mass, but before the priest and people received the communion ; and this permission to depart points to the decay of the earlier discipline which forbid any to take part in the oblation who did not remain and communicate.

And he afterwards counsels this observance as in the text :

> "Yowre hertis ye lyft up into the est,
> And al your body and knees bowe adowne,
> Whan the prist seyth *Verbum caro factum est,*
> Withe al yowre inwarde contemplacioun,
> Youre mowthe ferst crosse with hyghe devocioun,
> Kissing the tokens rehersed here aforne,
> And ever hane mynde on Cristes passioun,
> Whiche for thy sake wered a crowne of thorne."(1)

The rubrics of the Sarum missal require the choir to genuflect and kiss the earth in the procession on Palm Sunday,(2) and the people to kiss their seats or the ground (*formulas vel terram*) when they rise from prostration after the solemn absolution on Ash Wednesday and Palm Sunday.(3)

A like rule obtained in parts of France in the beginning of the eighteenth century. At Vienne in Lent they kissed the ground at each of the hours ;(4) and at Orleans their seat.(5) The ordinary (*ordinarium*) of Rouen directed the clergy, on all the week days in Lent, to make a cross on their seat and kiss it.(6)

See *ante*, B 196, p. 18 ; and the note, p. 220.

P. 146, l. 657-8.

> Cf. "Iesu y þanke þe of þy grace
> þat þou hast lent me wyt and space
> þis yn englys for to drawe
> As holy men haue seyde yn sawe ;
> For lewede men hyt may auayle
> For hem y toke þys trauayle."—*H. S.* 11292-7.

l. 659-61.

> Cf. "For þis makyng I wille no mede,
> But gude prayere, when ȝe it rede.
> þerfore, ȝe lordes lewed,
> For wham I haf þis Inglis schewed,
> Prayes to God he gyf me grace,
> I travayled for your solace."
> *Robert of Brunne's Prologue,* Hearne (*reprint*), III, p. ci.

---

(1) Lydgate's *Minor Poems,* Halliwell, Percy Society, 1840, pp. 60, 61.
(2) *Miss. Sar.,* 261.   (3) *Ib.* 133, 300.
(4) *Voyages Liturg.* 19.   (5) *Ib.* 205.
(6) "Sur leur place." *Ib.* 314. This is explained, p. 396, where it is said, "Ils baisoient chacun leur *banc.*" At Frontevrauld the nuns kissed their seat (*leur siege*) both in Advent and Lent (*ib.* 109).

In this same work (p. 457) it is stated on the authority of a Syrian priest that the Eastern Christians, before receiving the holy communion, kiss their right hand on the ground ; but I do not remember to have met with any mention of this elsewhere.

The writer, we may observe, though quite alive to the pecuniary "vertue" of the mass (*ante*, p. 366), most likely did not belong to a mendicant order (*ante*, p. 132, l. 141), and not improbably was a secular priest. At all events neither he nor good old Robert Mannyng seem to adopt the mercenary system of the friar in the Sompnour's Tale :

> "Thomas, nought of your tresor I desire
> As for myself, but for that our covent
> To pray for you is ay so diligent."—*C. T.* 7556-8.

P. 146, l. 665. *þreo þinges.* The mention of the "fyue wordes" (l. 674) points to the consecration of the bread as one of these exceptions : the consecration of the cup is most probably a second; but the fragmentary condition of this piece prevents our being able to find out what the third may have been, so many points in the mass being left without any notice or explanation.

P. 147, l. 674. *fyue wordes*, viz. "Hoc est enim Corpus meum" (*ante*, p. 106, l. 32), which are our Lord's words as translated in the Vulgate, with the addition of "enim."(1)

l. 674. *þat no mon but a preste schulde rede.* This may be noted as an incidental evidence of the feeling of the time, but I forbear to discuss the causes, because it would be impossible to do so without trenching on the disputed territory of religious controversy. It is, however, very evident that the reserve(2) here so openly avowed, and evidently without any fear of giving offence, grew out of the practice of saying the canon in silence, which became general in the West in the ninth or tenth century,(3) with exceptions on certain occasions, which are still recognised in the Roman rubrics. Writers in the twelfth century attributed the change to a miraculous manifestation of divine wrath against some shepherds at the time when the canon was openly recited. It was believed(4) that they said the words of consecration over

---

(1) The Mozarabic omits "enim" and adds "quod pro vobis tradetur." The modern Ambrosian retains only the Roman form, but it used to add "quod pro multis confringetur," and this, Mabillon (*de Liturg. Gall.* p. [xix.]) says, was no doubt the Gallican form.

(2) It is curious to think that all this mystery should not have prevented, if it did not cause, the "*hocus pocus*" of the conjuror, which I must have heard scores of times in my younger days, without a notion on my part—and no doubt the performers shared in my ignorance—of the solemn words which gave rise to it.

(3) *Ante*, p. 266(3) ; p. 274.

(4) "Contingit ergo ut quodam tempore pastores panem super lapidem quendam ponerent, qui dum hujus secretæ verba proferrent, in carnem conversus est, et forsitan, transubstantiatus, ut sic loquar, in corpus Christi. In quos divinitus facta est acerrima vindicta. Nam ad unum omnes percussi sunt divino judicio cœlitus misso. Ex quo quidem facto statutum fuit, ut posthac tacite et submisse diceretur."—Belethi, *Rationale*, c. xliv.

some bread—or in other accounts(1) bread and wine, which were changed into flesh and blood; and that they were thereupon struck dead to a man. Pope Innocent III. lends no credence to this legend, but more reasonably explains that it arose from the rule, instead of the rule having originated in the miracle.(2)

We meet with a very striking instance of the prevalence of this feeling something like a hundred years later than the date of our MS. John Buschk, a Canon regular, and Prior of the Monastery at Sulta, was delegated to visit and reform monasteries both of men and women of different orders; and was very much mixed up with, if not in some sort at the head of the Brethren of Common Life.(3) Writing about the year 1470, he describes his having, when only " a simple brother, called a black friar to account for having preached at Zutphen that laymen ought not to have books in Dutch " (*Teutonicales*). In his very life-like account of his discussion with the Prior of the Dominican Convent, to which the friar belonged, he tells us that when he objected that laymen had mass-books and even the canon in Dutch (*Etiam cum canone in Teutonico*), he answered that he did not allow this, and that he had himself burnt the canon when he found some nuns with it in Dutch, but that this was no argument against all, learned and unlearned alike, having and reading books for the amendment of their lives and arousing their devout feelings.(4)

In the next century " Pope Pius V. forbade the use of vernacular translations of the office of the blessed Virgin ; "(5) but the most stringent exertion of the papal authority was reserved for the seventeenth century. As early as 1587 the whole missal was translated into French, and published by command of the Cardinals of Lorraine and of Guise, who were successively Archbishops of Rheims ; and several other editions followed, the Latin being either on the opposite page or in parallel columns— one by Archbishop de Harlay, of Rouen, which in 1650 was approved by the Assembly of the Clergy of France. But in 1661 Pope Alexander VII. issued a bull, at the instance, as was supposed, of Cardinal Mazarin, in which he sets forth that he had

---

(1) See *Gemma Animæ*, Lib. I, c. ciii. Cf. [Pseudo-]Alcuin, *De Divinis Officiis*, Ed. Froben., p. 502.

(2) De Sacro Altaris Mysterio, Lib. III, c. i.

(3) The *Fratres Vitæ Communis* took no vows, but lived according to the Augustinian rule. They flourished in the Netherlands and the neighbouring parts of Germany in the fourteenth and fifteenth centuries, occupying themselves, amongst other good works, in copying religious books, especially in the mother tongue, and were among the first to establish printing-presses in their brother-houses.

(4) Buschii *de Reformatione Monasteriorum*, Lib. II, c. xvii, Leibnitz ; *Scriptores Brunsvic.*, II, 927. See as to Nuns of Syon, *ante*, p. 186.

(5) Maskell, *M. R.*, II, p. liv.

heard with great sorrow that certain sons of perdition, to the ruin
of souls and in despite of the practice of the Church, had reached
such a height of madness as to turn the Latin missal into French,
and had dared to print and retail it without regard to state or
sex, "and had thus endeavoured to cast down and trample the
majesty of the most sacred rite embodied in the Latin words, and
by their rash attempt expose to the vulgar the dignity of the holy
mysteries." He thereupon declares his abhorrence and detestation
of this novelty, and for ever condemns, disallows, and interdicts
any missal in French by whomsoever written, or by whomsoever
hereafter to be written; forbids the printing, reading, or possession
under penalty of excommunication, and requires the surrender of
all copies to the ordinary or the inquisitor, in order to their being
burnt.(1)

---

(1) I give the bull at length, as, curiously enough, neither De Vert, nor Le
Brun, nor, so far as I have observed, any other of the French ritualists refer to
it. It is of course in the subsequent editions of the Bullarium, and I notice an
abstract in Pittoni's *Constitutiones Pontificiae*, Venet., 1740, I, 314, *No.* 925.

"Alexander Papa VII.

Ad futuram rei memoriam.

Ad aures nostras ingenti cum animi nostri mœrore pervenit, quod in Regno
Galliæ, quidam perditionis filii in perniciem animarum novitatibus
studentes, et Ecclesiasticas Sanctiones ac praxim contemnentes, ad eam nuper
vesaniam pervenerint, ut Missale Romanum Latino idiomate longo tot
sæculorum usu in Ecclesia probato conscriptum ad Gallicam vulgarem
linguam convertere, sicque conversum typis evulgare, et ad cujusvis Ordinis,
et sexus personas transmittere ausi fuerint, et ita Sacrosancti Ritus majestatem
Latinis vocibus comprehensam dejicere, et proterere, ac Sacrorum mysteriorum
dignitatem vulgo exponere temerario conatu tentaverint.

§ 1. Nos, quibus licet immeritis Vineæ Domini Sabaoth a Christo Salvatore
nostro plantatæ, ejusque pretioso Sanguine irrigatæ, cura demandata est, ut
spinarum hujusmodi, quibus illa obrueretur, obviemus incremento, earumque
quantum in Deo possumus, radices succidamus, quemadmodum novitatem
istam perpetui Ecclesiæ decoris deformatricem, inobedientiæ, temeritatis,
audaciæ, seditionis, schismatis, aliorumque plurium malorum facile produc-
tricem abhorremus, et detestamur.

§ 2. Ita Missale prædictum Gallico idiomate a quocumque conscriptum, vel
in posterum alias quomodolibet conscribendum et evulgandum Motu proprio,
et ex certa scientia, ac matura deliberatione nostris, perpetuo damnamus,
reprobamus, et interdicimus, ac pro damnato, reprobato, et interdicto haberi
volumus, ejusque impressionem, lectionem et retentionem universis, et singulis
utriusque sexus Christi fidelibus cujuscumque gradus, ordinis, conditionis,
dignitatis, honoris, et præeminentiæ, licet de illis specialis, et individua mentio
habenda foret existant, sub pœna excommunicationis latæ sententiæ ipso jure
incurrendæ perpetuo prohibemus.

§ 3. Mandantes quod statim quicumque illud habuerint, vel in futurum
quandocumque habebunt, realiter, et cum effectu exhibeant, et tradant locorum
Ordinariis, vel Inquisitoribus, qui nulla interposita mora exemplaria igne
comburant, et comburi faciant, in contrarium facientibus, non obstantibus
quibuscumque.

Datum Romæ apud S. Mariam Majorem sub Annulo Piscatoris, die 12

This vehement denunciation appears to have been ignored almost from the first. Translations of the ordinary of the mass and the missal were published with the authority of archbishops and bishops; and at the time of the revocation of the edict of Nantes distributed "by thousands" among the *Nouveaux convertis.*

In 1851 the Congregation of Rites forbid "the translating, printing, or publishing of the ordinary of the mass in the vulgar tongue;"(1) and this decision appears to have been more respected by the French clergy of the present day than the Pope's bull was by their Gallican predecessors. I find that in 1860 a translation of the missal was published by the Abbé Alix, with the approbation of the Archbishop of Bordeaux, with the following notice: "*Le tradacteur s'est conformé à la défence de la Congrégation des rites en ne traduisant pas le canon de la messe;*" and in several recent missals for the laity which I have had an opportunity of examining, I observe that other devotions are inserted *sans phrase* in place of the translation of the canon.

APPENDIX V.

This piece is from Cotton, Titus, A. xxvi, in the British Museum, a paper MS. of about 1470. Mr Brock copied it for the Society, and I read the proof with the manuscript. It is one of the many productions of that most copious poetaster, Dan John Lydgate, the monk of Bury. The scribe has added the title *Merita Missæ* at the end, but it must not be confounded with the *Vertue of the Masse* (*ante*, p. 163), nor with the *Virtutes Missarum* (*ante*, p. 367) of the same author, from which extracts have been given in the notes.

I here insert a fourth piece by Lydgate, being a Venus-Mass, or parody of the Mass addressed to Cupid, "the mighty god of love," which is complete to the end of the epistle. It is taken from MS. Fairfax, 16, in the Bodleian,(2) and Mr G. Parker has read the proof

---

Janu. 1661, Pontificatus Nostri Anno sexto."—*Bullarium Romanum*, Luxemburgi, 1727, VI, 138.

(1) *Dictionnaire des Décrets,* Migne, 1860, c. 1232, "Traduction." Here see also a less explicit answer as to the "abus général et invétéré, que les fideles aient entre les mains en latin et en français, non seulement l'Ecriture sainte et surtout le Nouveau Testament, mais encore l'ordinaire même de la messe littéralement traduit."

(2) This MS. also contains poems by Chaucer, Occleve, &c., and is dated "Anno 1450." On the first leaf is written:
"I bought this Att Gloucester 8 Sept. 1651.
ffairfax
intending to exchange it for a better booke.
Note y^t Joseph Holland hath another of these manuscripts."

with the manuscript. It is very curious as an illustration of the tone of feeling, which could sanction such dealing with holy things, and all the more curious when we remember it was the work of one who had taken the vows of a Benedictine,(1) and, as we gather from other pieces of his, was himself in priest's orders—nor is his choosing the subject less worthy of remark if, as may not be improbable, he borrowed from an Italian original.(2)

The several parts are indicated by rubrics in the manuscript, and I have added references to the corresponding places in the ordinary of the Mass.

[fol. 314]

¶ **Introibo.** *(Ante,* p. 90, l. 12.)

Wyth all myñ Hool Herte entere
    To fore the famous Riche Autere
    Of the myghty god of Love
Whiche that stondeth high above
In the Chapel / of Cytheron
I will wyth gret devocion
Go knele / and make sacrifyse
Lyke as the custom doth devyse
Afor that God / preye and wake
Of entent I may be take
To hys seruyse / and ther assure
As longe / as my lyf may dure
To cont[i]nue / as I best kan
Whil I lyve / to ben hys man

¶ **Confiteor.** *(Ante,* p. 90, l. 25.)

I am aknowe / and wot ryght' well
I speke pleynly as I fel
Touchynge / the grete tendyrnesse
Of my youthe and my symplesse
Of myn vnkonyng / and grene age
Wil lete me han noon avantage
To serue loue I kan so lyte
And yet myn hert / doth delyte
Of hys seruauntys for to here
By exaumple of hem / I myghte lere

---

(1) See a somewhat similar travesty by Lyndesay, *ante,* p. 319.

(2) There are hardly any poetic themes which the old monk has not handled, though whether in every case he has adorned them may well admit of question. Among his *Minor Poems* (Percy Society, p. 220) Mr Halliwell gives a "Lovers Complaint" in the person of a love-lorn maiden, beginning:

    "Allas! I woful creature
    Lyveng betwene hope and drede,
    How myght I the woe endure,
    In tendrenesse of wommanheede?"

To folowe the wey / of ther seruyse
Yif I hadde konnyng to devyse
That I myght' / a seruaunt be
A-mongys other in my degre
Havynge ful gret repentaunce
That I now) erste / me gan) avaunce
In loue court my-selfe to offre   [fol. 314 b]
And my seruyse / for to profre
ffor ffer of my tender youthe
Nouther be Est / nouther by Southe
Lyst Daunger / putte me a-bake
And dysdeyn) / to make wrake
Wolde hyndre me / in myn) entente
Of al this thyng / I me Repente
As my conscience / kan) recorde
I sey lowly Myserycorde.

¶ **Misereatur.** (*Ante,* p. 92, l. 1.)

By god of louys Ordynaunce
ffolkys / that haue repentaunce
Sorowful in herte / and no-thyng' lyght
Whiche ha nat spent hys tyme aryght'
But wastyd yt / in ydelnesse
Only for lake of lustynesse
In slep / slogardye / and slouthe
Of whom) / ys pyte / and gret routhe
But when / they repente hem) ageyn)
Of al ther tyme / spent in veyn)
The god of love / thorgh hys myght
Syth that Mercy / passeth ryght'
The mot acceptyd be to grace
And pute daunger out of place
This the wyl of Dame **Venus**
And of hyr Bisshoppe **Temvs**

¶ **Officium.** (*Ante,* p. 92, l. 33.)

In honour of the god Cupide
ffirst that he may be my guyde
In worshepe eke of the pryncesse   [fol. 315]
Whyche ys lady / and Maystresse
By grace they may / for me provyde
Humble of herte / devoyde of pryde
Envye and Rancour set asyde
With-oute chaunge / or doubilnesse

¶ In honour of the
ffirst that he

Ioye and welfare in euery tyde
Be yeve to hem / wherso they byde
And yive to hem grace / on) my dystresse
To have / pyte / of ther hyghnesse
ffor in what place / I go or ryde

¶ In honour ffirst that

¶ Kyrie. (*Ante,* p. 93, l. 33.)

Mercy ⁝ Mercy ⁝ contynuely ⁝ I crye
In gret disioynt ⁝ Vp-on) the poynt ⁝ to deye
ffor that pyte ⁝ ys vn-to me ⁝ contrayre
Daunger my ffo ⁝ dysdeyn) also ⁝ whylk tweye
Causen) myn) herte ⁝ of mortal smert ⁝ dyspeyre
ffor she ⁝ that ys ; fayrest y-wys ⁝ of ffayre
Hath gladnesse ⁝ of my syknesse . to pleye
Thus my trouble / double and double / doth repayre

¶ XPe.

Repeyreth ay ⁝ which nyght' nor day // ne cesseth nought'
Now hope / now dred / new pensyffhede / now thought'
Al thyse yfere / palen) myn) chere / and hewe
Yet to hyr grace ech hour' / and space / I ha besought'
Hyr' lyst nat here / ffor hyr daunger / doth ay renewe
Towardys me / for certys she / lyst nat rewe   [fol. 315 b]
Vp-on) my peyne ⁝ and thus / my cheyne ys wrought'
Which hath me / bounde / neuer to be founde / vntrewe

¶ Kyrie.

Vntrewe nay ⁝ to se / that day ⁝ ged forbede
Voyde slouthe / kepe my trouthe / in dede
Eve / and morowe / ffor Ioye or sorowe / I have behyght'
Til I sterve ⁝ euere to serve / hir womanhede
In erthe lyvynge / ther is no thyng / maketh me so lyght'
ffor I shal dye ⁝ ne but wer hir Mercye more than) ryght'
Off no decertys / but Mercy certys / my Iourne spede
Adieu al play ⁝ thus may I say / I woful wyght'

¶ Gloria in excelsis. (*Ante,* p. 94, l. 7.)

Worsshyppe to that lord above
That callyd ys / the god of love
Pes / to hys / seruantes euerychon)
Trewe of herte / stable as ston)
            That feythful be

To hertys trewe of ther corage
That lyst chaunge / for no Rage
But kep hem / in ther hestys stylle
In all mane*r* wedris ylle
    Pes concord and vnyte
God send hem / sone ther desyrs
And reles / of ther hoote ffyrs
That brenneth at her herte sore
And encresseth / more / and more
    This my prayere
And aftyr wynter / wyth hys shourys
God send hem counfort / of May flourys
Affter gret wynd / and stormys kene   [fol. 316]
The glade son*n*e / with bemys shene
    May appere
To yive hem lyght' / affter dyrknesse
Ioye eke *after* hevynesse
And after dool / and ther wepynge
To here / the somer foulys synge
    God yive grace
ffor ofte sythe men ha seyn
A ful bryght' day / after gret reyn
And tyl the storme / be leyd asyde
The herdys vnder bussh abyde.
    And taketh place
After also the dirke nyght'
Voyde / off the Mone / and sterre lyght'
And after nyghtys / dool and sorowe
ffolweth ofte a ful glade morowe
    Of Auenture
Now lorde that knowest hertys alle
Off louers / that for helpe calle
On her trouthe / of mercy rewe
Namly on swyche as be trewe
    Helpe to recure.
  Amen. (*Ante*, p. 94, l. 19.)

¶ **The Oryson**. (*Ante*, p. 94, l. 24. [fol. 316 b]
Most' myghty / and most dredful lord
That knowest / hertys fals and trewe
As wel ther thynkyng' as ther word
Bothe of lovers / olde and newe
Off pyte / and of mercy Rewe
On thy *ser*uaunt*es* / that be stable
And make ther Ioye / to Renewe
Swich as wyl neu*er* be chau*n*gable

¶ The Epystel in prose.   (*Ante*, p. 96, l. 14.)

ffrom) the party of the pore plentyff in love wyth many yers of
probacion professyd to be trewe / To all the holy ffraternite and Con-
frary : of the same bretherhede / And to alle hospytlerys and Relygious /
nat spottyd / nor mad foul wyth no cryme of Apostasye nouthyr
notyd nor atteynt with no double fface / of symulacion nor constreyned
countenaunce of ypocrysye / To alle swiche chose chyldre of stabylnesse
wyth-oute variaunce of corage / or of herte Ioye / Elthe / : and long
prosperyte / wyth perfeccion of perseueraunce / in ther trouthe
perpetually / tabyde // Experyence techeth / that pilgrymes / and
folkes custommable to vyage // Whan they vnderfange / any long /
weye wiche that ys laboryous // Somwhile off consuetude / and custom /
they vse a man) to Reste on) ther wey // Off entent to wype / and wasshe
away the soot of ther vysages // And sum also vsen to ley adoun
the hevy ffardellys of ther bake // ffor to alleggen) ther wery lemys of
[fol. 317] her grete berthene // And some outher vsen) to gadryn) wyne / And
some to drynken outher water or' wyn // of ther botell or Goordys to
asswage / the grete drylınesse of ther gredy thruste // And some of
hem somwhile Reknen and accounten / how myche they ha passyd / off
ther Iourne / And sodeynly tourne ageyn) ther bakkys towardys / som)
notable seteys Which they of newe / be partyd fro / And therwyth
al Recorden / and remembren hem / of Cytes / Castell / and touns
which they ha passyd by / and nat forgete / hylles / no valeys /
dygne / to be put in remembraunce of hyt / for a Memoryal / Some
entytlen hem / in smale bookes of Report / or in tabylys / to callen
hem to mynde / whan they sene her tyme / And som ought' callen to
mynde grete Ryuers and smale / And pereylles of the see that they ha
passyd by / And whan) they han alle accountyd / and ageyn Rebatyd /
the partyes passyd off her Iourne / Off nowe they take to hem force /
vigour / and strengthe / myghtyly Wyth-oute feyntyse / to performe /
and manly / to acomplysshe / the Resydue / and the remnaunt' of her
labour // And thus .I. in semblable wyse / al the tyme of my lyff' /
ffrom) my grene tendre youthe / And tyme that I hadde / yerys of
dyscrecion beynge / and contynuynge / as an Errynge pylgrym / in
the seruyse of the myghty and dredful god of loue / how many
perylous / passages / and wayes / that I ha passyd by // How ofte in
compleynynge I have setyndon // to wypen away the soot of myn)
[fol. 317, b] inportable labour' / And dronken ener among of my botell and Goordes
the bytter drynkes of drerynesse / And offte sythes assayed / to
casten adoun the inportable fardel / of myn heuy thoughtys / And
amongys al this thyn)gys // lookyd bakward to consydren / and sen
the fyn and the ende of my worthy bretheren / and predecessours in
love // that ha passyd the same pilgrymage / to-forn // And ther I ha
founden / and seyn the grete trouthe of Troylus / perseuerant' to hys
lyves ende // The trewe stable menyng of penalope / The clennesse / of
polycene // The kyndenesse off Dydo / quen of cartage / And rad also

ful often in my contemplatyff medytacions The holy legende of
Martyrs / of Cupydo / The secre trouthe of Trystram and ysoude And
the smale Gerdouns of woful Palamydes / All thyse / and an hondryd
Thousand mo callyd to mynde / me semeth / amonges all I am on) of
the most for-sake / And ferthest set behynde of grace / and moste
hyndred to the mercy of my lady dere / Nat-wyth-stondynge the grete
party of my pilgrymage / that I ha done But that I shal euere / for lyfe
or deth / contynue / and perseuere trewe to my lyves Ende ¶ Besech-
ynge ful lowly / to alle yow my brethere / vn-to whom) thys lytel Epystel
ys dyrect // That yt lyke yow / of pyte / amonge your / devout
obseruaunces to han me Recomendyd / with some Especial Memorye /
in your prayers / That yet or I dye / I may sum mercy / fynde / Or
that the god of love / Enspyre my ladyes herte of hys grace what I
endure for hyr sake.

P. 148, l. 10. *freer.* This is how our Benedictine answered the constant
attacks which the mendicant orders levelled at the monks, whom
they decried as "possessioners," or owners of landed estates. The
jealousies and rivalries of their several orders(1) supplied a fruitful
subject to the mediæval satirist, but they all combined to vilipend
the more ancient monastic bodies and the secular or parochial
clergy.

So—to give a single instance—the friar in Chaucer begging
for his house :

"Neither it needeth not for to be give
As to possessioneres that mow lyve,
Thanked be God, in wele and abundaunce."—*C. T.* 7303-5.

"These curates ben ful negligent and slowe
To grope tendurly a conscience."—*Ib.* 7398-9.

"The clenness and fastyng of us freres
Makith that Crist acceptith oure prayeres."—*Ib.* 7465-6.

"And therfor may ye seen that oure prayeres
(I speke of us, we mendeaunts we freres)
Ben to the hihe God mor acceptable
Than youres, with your festis at your table."—*Ib.* 7493-6.

---

(1) The white-friar in the Ploughman's Crede (l. 380—392) thus speaks
of the black and the grey friars :

"For ryȝt as Menoures · most ypocricie vseþ
Ryȝt so ben Prechers proude · purlyche in herte.
But, Cristen creatour · we Karmes first comen
Even in Elyes tyme · first of hem all.
. . . .
And þerfore, leue leel man · leeue þat ich sygge,
A masse of vs mene men · is of more mede
And passeth all praieres · of þies proude freers."

P. 148, l. 15. *sese into thi honde.* This is a translation of "*in manus tuas commendo spiritum meum* "—Ps. (31) xxx, 6—Lydgate not having made the change from the second to the third person, which was necessary to fit it into its present place. Its suitableness for the last devotion before going to rest has been recognized by its insertion in this place in many forms, as, for example, in the compline service of the nuns of Syon : "Another Responce, *In manus tuas,* I betake my sowlle lorde in to thy handes. Verse. *Redemisti,* Thow haste boughte me ageyne, lorde god of trouthe."(1)

These were also the words which the priest called on the dying man to say when he saw "that he neiheth (*neareth*) the deth "— "*And sai :* Into thi handes, Lord, I betake my soule, for thou God of treuthe bouʒtest me. *And sei it threis.*"(2)

In the form from the Landsdown MS. printed by Mr Peacock(3) this is to be said for him if the dying man cannot say it himself : "Thanne let the Curat desire the sick persone to saye In manus tuas *et cetera* withe a good stedfast mynde and yf that he canne, And yef he cannot let the Curat saye it for hym."

P. 149, l. 25. Cf. the corresponding directions in the Festyvale (*f.* 157 *b*) : "Than it is well done y^t of what degree or ordre or occupation thou be / saye dayly at the leest at thy rysynge . Paternoster . Ave maria . and a Credo / or elles fyue of eyther in remembraunce of ye passyon of our lorde / and the grete compassyon of our lady . Ex revelation*ibus* sancte brigite (and crosse(4) the in the foreheed . Hec hieronim*us*) And folowe thou Cryste . Augustin*us* . As moche as thou mayst / of whom thou takest thy name called a crysten man. And beware that thou bere not ye name voydely . And therewyth nourysse the worme of conscyence that neuer shall dye."

l. 32. *set, sc.* on knees. Cf. Primer, 1555, *sig.* ° i :

"¶ *How a man shal behaue him self in the morning whan he ryseth.*

¶ Whan thou risest in the mornyng loke that thou with all humbleness of mynde knele down, and lyftyng up thy hearte, thy handes, and thyne eies unto heaven unto god the father almightie, praye on thys maner."

l. 42. The pyx of ivory or metal, containing the reserved sacrament, was in this country hung by chains under a canopy in a vase

---

(1) *Myroure,* 168.   (2) Maskell, M. R. III, 357-8. *Ante,* p. 350.
(3) Myrc, p. 65. The *Rituale Romanum* also appoints these words to be said in the ear at the last (" *in exspiratione* "), but adds to the commendation of the psalmist a prayer to the Blessed Virgin : "Tu me ab hoste protege et hora mortis suscipe."

(4) It will be observed that *cross* here takes the place of the more usual *bless* of older forms.

above the altar. Dr Rock(1) says that "the first wooden or stone tabernacle resting on the altar seen in this land was put up in Queen Mary's reign."

In France the vessel in which the pyx was hung above the altar was generally in the shape of a dove. A provincial council at Thoulouse, A.D. 1590, required the reserved sacrament to be kept "tabernaculo ligneo non pensili,"(2) but it continued to be hung above the high altar at St Denys and other churches in France, until the first revolution ; and, when the writer was at Malta, was still so hung in St John's Church, Valetta.

P. 149, l. 47. *rynget the belle*, at the beginning of the service. The bell at the elevation is mentioned, line 69. Cf. Harding's Answer, " We have commonly seen the priest when he sped him to say his service, to ring the saunce (*Sanctus*) bell, and speak out aloud, *Paternoster ;* by which token the people were commanded silence, reverence, and devotion."(3)

l. 52. *Thou for hym and he for the.* See form of prayer, *ante*, p. 10. So late as the eighteenth century in the diocese of Rheims the priest turned to the west before the prayer *Aufer a nobis* (*ante*, p. 92, l. 25), and said " Orate pro me fratres, et ego pro vobis."(4) In connection with this, and the many instances where, as we have seen, eastern forms survived in the Gallican Church, it is curious to notice that in this part of the service the priest in the Syrian Jacobite service turned to the people and asked their prayers for the Lord's sake.(5)

l. 58. *dredfulle*, as usually in our older English, *feeling dread* not *dread inspiring.*

P. 150, l. 67. *stylle*, secretly, as in lines 17 and 48.—See note, p. 182, B. 52.

l. 86. *gysthe.* I have given Mr Brock's suggested reading (*gyfte*), but on looking at it again, I am not at all sure that we ought not to read *gysthe.* *Gift* in the form ʒ*ifte* occurs within two lines ; and though I do not find the word *gysthe*, we may very well suppose there may have been such a word. It would at all events complete the sense—You would get it neither of grace (the king's favour to you), nor gysthe (your own craving). In German we have the kindred word *geiz.* Boswell gives the verb *gytsian*, and *gytsung*, desire, craving ; and quotes from Boethius, " He ne mæg þa grundleasan gytsynge afyllan," *He cannot the boundless desires fill.*

(1) *Church of our Fathers*, IV, 208.
(2) P. 2, *c* v, 1—Labb & Coss, XV, 1379.
(3) Quoted Jewel's *Reply unto M. Harding's Answer*, Works, I, 292.
(4) Krazer *de Liturgiis*, Aug. Vindel., 1786, p. 385.
(5) Ordo communis liturgiæ secundum Ritum Syrorum Jacobitarum, Renaudot, *Liturg. Oriental.*, II, 2. According to the Latin rite the priest did not ask the prayers of the people until later in the service at the offertory. See *ante*, p. 100, l. 20.

P. 152, l. 151. *cristende spayne.* We have already seen the curious use which Lydgate made of his knowledge of heathen mythology,(1) and the way he here brings in the gestes of the trouvères is almost equally incongruous. Charles' success against the Saracen invaders of Spain was one of their chosen subjects, and as a matter of history he did extend his boundary across the north-east of Spain, from the Bidassoa to the mouth of the Ebro.

l. 153. *bare the Floure.* Cf.

> "Of alle þe clerkes of þat land; he bar þe flour."
> Celestin, l. 190, *Anglia,* p. 72.

> "Of Christendome he ber the prys."
> *Political Songs,* Wright, C. S. 246.

l. 160-1. *He bare portred far and nere.* Layamon describes the shield *Pridwen,* which Arthur hung from his neck, with this precious portrait :

> "He heng an his sweore !
>   ænne sceld deore.
>   his nome wes on Bruttisc !
>   Pridwen ihaten.
>   þer wes innen igrauen !
>   mid rede golde stauen.
>   an on-licnes deore !
>   of drihtenes moder."(2)

Nennius says that he bore the image of the Virgin on his shoulders (*super humeros suos*); and William of Malmesbury ascribes his single-handed prowess against nine hundred of the enemy at Badon Hill to this image which he had affixed (*armis suis*) to his armour.

Sir Gawayne also had the image of the Virgin on his shield.

"In the more half of his shelde hir ymage depaynted."(3)

P. 153, l. 179. *Lavncegaye,* a javelin which appears to have been very much like the *Assegay* of the Amakosa Caffres, and to have been thrown very much as they throw it. As our forefathers on actual service used crossbow, sword, battle-axe, or men-at-arms the lance, it is probable that lancegays were not such effective weapons as the seven assegais the Caffres used to carry for their whole armament in war time, before free-traders supplied them with fire-arms and gun-powder.

Cf. "And in his hand a lanncegay
A long sword by his side."—*C. T.* 15162-3.

---

(1) *Ante,* p. 167, l. 39, and pages 390—5.

(2) *Ed.* Madden, 1847, II, 464, l. 10—17. Sir Frederick Madden mentions in a note that the name *Pridwen* is said to be Welsh for *the fair form,* or *that which is white,* in allusion to this figure of the Virgin.

(3) *Sir Gawayne and the Green Knight,* ed. Morris, l. 649.

P. 153, l. 190. *thou I klype the.* This thouing him was the extreme of insult, and it may be worth noting that the very phrase is still used in this part of England with the same intention. I have been told of it more than once as a matter of complaint; and I will copy what I wrote some five-and-twenty years ago, which was probably the first time that I noticed it, after I had begun my collections for an East Riding vocabulary. A man who had forbidden his mother-in-law his house said to me: " I'll not deny it. I did thou her, and sorry I is to thou my wife(1) mother, but I says to her—Thou I calls thee, and I bids thee get thee out of my house, and never again set thy foot over my freshwood " (*threshold*). I may add that as a matter of course and in all good part he would have thou-d his wife, friends, children or servants, the plural being reserved for elders, betters, and strangers, according to the received etiquette of the country side.(2)

CORRECTIONS AND ADDITIONS
TO NOTES.

P. 182, B. 54. *sese.* I find that the presence of *-es* in the second person singular is in no respect decisive. Dr Morris gives it as characteristic of the West-Midland dialect of Lancashire and Cheshire—*Alliterative Poems*, 1869, Preface, p. xxiii. We meet also with the northern *-s* of the verb, with an occasional southern *-th* in Robert of Brunne's (East Midland) *Handlyng Synne*, as, for example :

> " þey been but as glemys
> þat yn þe þouʒt lepys
> A nyʒt whan þou slepys,
> þat you wakyng þenkes
> Before þy yʒen hyt blenkys."—l. 424-8.

> " þe deuyl hyt shewyþ."—l. 498.

> " Syttyþ dowyn upp on oure knees."—l. 951.

P. 214, 215. I omitted to notice the injunction put forth by Bishop Shaxton in the diocese of Salisbury in 1536 ; and most probably in other dioceses at the same time. It requires all having cures, every Sunday and holyday to recite and sincerely declare in the

---

(1) I preserve the *-s* in the verb, and the omission of the *-s* in the genitive, as characteristic both of the existing and of the early Northumbrian dialect.

(2) See a note by Mr Skeat as to corresponding use. *William of Palerne*, p. xli. Cf. " thou thou'st him some thrice."—Shaks. *Twelfth Night*, III, 2, &c.

pulpit at the high mass time in the English tongue both the
epistle and gospel of the day, if there be time thereto, or else one
of them at the least.(1)

P. 225 (2). "*Sancta*" had a larger signification than I here suppose.
It refers to certain relics, as it occurred in the oath tendered to
the canons of Chartres on their being received: "Sic vos Deus
adjuvet et hæc sancta."—*Voyages Liturgiques*, 227-8.

P. 248 (3). Maskell, M. R. III, 357, may also be referred to an
addition to Ratis Raving, but I return to this note because I have
since noticed that the question here quoted, or rather one to the
same purport in a service book printed at Venice in 1573, has
been formally condemned. I give an extract, so far as it refers
to this question, from the very rare "Index Librorum Expur-
gatorum Illustrissimi ac Reverendiss. D. D. Gasparis Quiroga,
Cardinalis et Archiep. Toletani Hispan. generalis Inquisitoris
iussu editus. De Consilio Supremi Senatus S. Generalis Inquisit."
Madriti 1584:

"*Ordo Baptizandi cum Modo visitandi*

Ex libro, qui inscribitur, Ordo baptizandi, cum Modo visitandi,
impresso Venetiis, anno 1575. *Fol. 34, ad medium deleantur illa
verba.* Credis non propriis meritis, sed Passionis domini nostri
Iesu Christi virtute & merito, ad gloriam peruenire?

Ibidem, paulo post, deleantur illa verba: Credis quod dominus
noster Iesus Christus pro nostra salute mortuus sit? & quod ex
propriis meritis, vel alio modo nullus possit saluari, nisi in merito
Passionis ipsius?"

P. 251, on C. 112. *noon.* I was at a loss to account for the apparent
anomaly of this form in a northern manuscript. I find another
example in the ordinances of the company of scriveners(2) of the

---

(1) Burnet's *Reformation*, Part II, Records, No. 59.
(2) The late Mr Davies, Town-clerk of York, who was a most careful
enquirer into all that concerned the antiquities of the city, gives many
interesting particulars as to this company—the *Escriveners de text, Scriptores,*
or Text-writers—in his work on "*the York Press,*" p. 3. He copies the bye-
laws in French of the date of Edward III, and the revised ordinances in
English, which appear to have been confirmed by the corporation in the latter
half of the fifteenth century.

As may be noticed in the extract here given, besides the text writers, the
company admitted to their membership,

I. The *Limners,* or *Enluminers,* who painted the miniatures, and did the
gilding, &c.

II. The *Notours,* who inserted the musical notes;

and, III, the *Turners* and *Flourishers,* who did the elaborate initial and
capital letters, and the floriated borders.

Mr Davies also mentions that the York bookbinders and booksellers
formed another company.

city of York, so that the occurrence of *noon* in this place was probably no more than an early instance of the southernizing tendency which became very marked at the end of the century.(1) "Noo priest having a competent salary, that is to say, vij marks or above, shall exercise the craft of text-writers, loiners, noters, tournours,(2) and florisshers for his singular prouffit and lucour, nor take noone apprentice, hired man, or othre servaunt into his service, nor make no bargains or covenantes to that intent,(3) under the pain of forfaitur of xiii *s.* iiij *d.*"

P. 338, on p. 65, l. 22. *in prison.* A passage in the Ancren Riwle (p. 126) shows that this place may be understood neither of purgatory nor a debtors' prison, as here suggested, but of the bondage of sin :

"We beoð alle ine prisune her, *and* owen God greate dettes of sunnen."

---

(1) See before, page 344.

(2) Cf. "Les lettres tourneures, ainsi nommées a cause de leurs figures rondes et tournantes seroirent dans les premieres impressions aux commencement des chapitres, comme elles avoient servi dans les manuscrits."—Lambinet, *Origine de l'Imprimerie,* Tome I, 295, quoted Davies, *York Press,* p. 5.

(3) I add a note—and it is the last—to this somewhat discursive illustration, because I think it cannot be without interest to the members of a society whose *raison d'être,* if not the production, is at all events in the first instance the printing of early manuscripts. It is a covenant, such as that contemplated in the ordinance, for a service-book, most probably for use in York Minster, as it is entered in the acts of the Chapter of York.

It is curious as showing the sum that was paid for writing and limning, and also that the size of the large or uncial letters, mentioned in the last note, was not left to the fancy of the turners, but was matter of definite stipulation.

The entry is dated the 26th August, 1346, and is here printed from Raine's Fabric Rolls, p. 165-6 :

"Comparuit Robertus Brekeling scriptor, et juravit se observare condicionem factam inter ipsum et dominum Johannem Forbor, viz., quod idem Robertus scribet unum psalterium cum calendario ad opus dicti domini Johannis, pro v s. et vi d. : et in eodem psalterio, de eadem litera, unum placebo et dirige cum ympnario et collectario pro iv s. iij d. Et idem Robertus luminabit omnes psalmos de grossis litoris aureis positis in coloribus, et omnes grossas literas de ympnario et collectario luminabit de auro et vermilione præter grossas literas duplicium festorum, quæ erunt sicut grossæ literæ aureæ sunt in psalterio. Et omnes literæ in principiis versuum erunt luminatæ de azuro et vermilione bonis, et omnes literæ in inceptione nocturnorum erunt grossæ literæ unciales(*) continentes v lineas, set *beatus vir*(†) et *dixit Dominus*(‡) continebunt vj vel vij lineas; et pro luminatione prædicta dabit v s. vi d., et ad colores, dabit pro auro xviii d. et ij s. pro una cloca et furura."

(*) As to these uncial or capital letters, see the last note.
(†) Psalm i. was the first for matins on Sunday.
(‡) Psalm (110) cix. was the first for vespers on Sunday.

GLOSSARY.

The letters A, B, C, D, E, and F refer to the lines of the Texts, p. 2
—60; B.P. to the Bidding Prayers, p. 61—80; H.C. to the Hours of
the Cross, p. 81—89; L to Lydgate's *Merita Missæ*, p. 148—154; P to
Appendix III, Preparation for communion, p. 122—127· V to the
Vernon MS., p. 128—147; and "p." to all other pages.

For abbreviations used in referring to quotations, see p. 469.

When two numbers have "/" between them, the first refers to the
page, the second to the line. A second number within ( ) refers to a
footnote on the line thus marked.

The * refers to a note on the line thus marked.

A, *interj.* Ah! P 124/31, 127/7.
— *indefinite article*, B 19; C 19.
— one contrasted with another,
B 173. *Note*, p. 215.
— one, of the Divine Unity, B 180.
Note, p. 215, 218.
— the same, the like, C 332. *Note*,
p. 216. Cf. "Two of a size,"
"Both of an age."
— one in number, B 157; B.P. 65/
25, 70/14; p. 360.
"For better es a dai dwelland
In thi porches ouer a thousand."
Ps. (84) lxxxiii, 10.
See ANE.

ABOUNE, above, B 38.
"Our Loverd in manhed sall þan sitt
Aboune þe synful."—P. C. 540-5.

A-CORDE, accord, harmony, B 541.
"þis acorde and anehede sall never
cease."—P. C. 8465.

AFT, afterwards, E 502. See EFT.

AFTER, AFTUR, after.
— of time, B 200, 241, 263.
— according as, B 8.
— in proportion to, B 412; V 146/
635.
"Efter þe workes þat þu has don."
P. C. 2455.
Cf. "Deal not with us after our sins,
neither reward us after our iniquities."—
Litany, B. C. P.

AGAYNE, *adv.* again, B 252, 579.
AGAYNES, *prep.* against, B 350.
AGHT, 3 *sing.* ought, B 167.
AGNUS, the anthem so called, B
508; p. 112/21.
AL, *adj.* all, B 2, 259, 260, 316.
Note, p. 157.
— *adverbially*, wholly, *omnino*, B
33, 210, 606.
ALKYN, ALKYNS, of all kinds, B
120, 256, 467, 589.
ALLE, *sing.* B 43; *dative*, C 2, 121,
122, 144.
— *pl.* 3*, 39, 251, 430, 456.
ALLE BIDENE, B 104. See BIDENE.
ALLE IF, *conj.* although, P 126/21.
ALMOUS, an alms, any work of
charity, an alms-deed, p. 157.
ALONE, B 142; where C, AL OON.
AL-ONELY, all one, only one, alone,
B 210.
ALS, also, B 124, 597.
"Myʒt *and* als bewté."
Alliterative Poems, Morris, 23/765.
—, as, B 54, 64, 85, 178, 303, 442,
562.
ALS-SO, also, B 25.
ALS SOO, B 355.
ALS SWA, also, C 25, 173.
ALTAR. See AUTER, WYVEDE.
ALWAYE, B 507.

AMENDE, *v. a.* to amend, to mend, B 259, 283; roads or bridges, B.P. 65/13. See MENDE.

AMENDMENT, B 188.

AMYTE, the amice, *amictus* or *galea*, and in O.E. *heued-line* = head-linen (*O.E. Homilies*, II, 163), the linen cloth, first put on the head, and then on the shoulders around the neck, whence sometimes called *humerale*, p. 167.

AN. See AND.

AN, one, C 252.

AND, if, B 447; V 130/88, 131/114; p. 370/15.
"We use many times and in the stead of if."—Palsgrave, 872 *b*.
"Yhit suld him thynk, and he toke kepe, His lyfe noghtbot als a dreme in slepe."
P. C. 8075-6.

ANE (*used substantively*), one, a man, B 17, 424, 425. *Note*, p. 168.

— *numeral*, one, p. 275/3.

— *adj.* any, p. 274/28.

ANEHEDE, *s.* unity, p. 218.

ANES, *gen. sing.* one time, once, p. 118/5.
Cf. "Bot ȝe most come to ȝour curatures (*curates*) be the comon lawe And schryve ȝoue sothely of ȝour synne at the lest enus a ȝere."
Audelay, p. 43.

ANOON, at (*one*) once, anon, P 126/21, 25.
"But herkneth me and stynteth but a lite, Which a miracle bifel anoon."
C. T. 2676-7.

AN OþER, one other (of the same kind), B 159.

ANOþER, one of another kind, B 174.

ANOURMENT, *ȝ.* ornament, B.P. 65/4, 71/20; [ornament, B.P. 76/13.]

ANSWERE, to answer, B 274.

APAYRE, APERE, *v. a.* to impair, O.F. *empeirer*, Lat. *impejorare*.

APECHING, *part. pres.* accusing, p. 241.
"I apeche, I accuse, *Jaccuse*."
Pals. 433.

APPEL, *s.* apple, V 141/488.

AR, 3 *pl.* B.P. 71/14. Cf. er, es. *See* ARE.

— *conj.* before, V 136/293. See ARE.

ARE, 2 *pl.* V 130/82.

— 3 *pl.* B 122.

— *adv.* just now, ere, of yore, p. 275/7. A.S. *œr*, Icel. *ár*, M.G. *air*.
"As I sayd are."—E. M. H. 77.

ARLY, early, C 303. See ARE.

ARTE, technical skill, B 12.

ARUN, 3 *pl.* are, E 290; where B are, C er, F ben.

ASCH, *v. a.* to ask, V 142/510 (rhymes with wasch).
"Kyndly þou asches."—M. A. 343.
"To worshyp me as I wylle asse."
Town. 58.

ASCHELER, Ashlar, stone worked square for the straight face of a wall, &c., V 138/364.

ASEURE, *v.* to assure, V 134/223.

ASKE, *v. a.* to ask, B 448.

ASSENT, *s.* B 542.

ASSOYLE, *v.* to absolve (of sin), to solve (a doubt), B 49.
"This is my drede, and ye, my bretheren twye
Assoileth me this questioun, I yow preye."—C. T. 9527-8.

ASTATE, *s.* estate, state of life, B 533.
"Men schulde wedde aftir here astaat."
C. T. 3229.
Cf. "All estates of men in thy holy church."—B. C. P.

AT, *sign of infinitive*, to, C 278*, p. 118/6. *Note*, p. 295.
"At midnight I ras to þe at shrive."
Ps. (119) cxviii, 62.

— *pron.* that, p. 371/18.
"To me be turnand dredand þe
And at knewe þi witnesses to se."
(*et qui noverunt testimonia tua*)
Ps. (119) cxviii, 79.

— *prep.* to, according to, *secundum*, V 132/137.
"We take our leave at lesse and more."
Sacrament, 966.

" this is nedeful at all that cristen liffes."
Abp. Thoresby's Catechism, *f.* 296, *b.*
" And scrued hym at all hys will."—
Met. Hom. 71.
Cf. Icel. "*At landslögum*, by the law
of the land."—C-V. 28, VI.

AT, *prep.* (of time) at, B 308, p. 118/6.

— *conj.* that, B.P. 66/11.
" bytwen þe payne of helle namly
And þe payne of purgatory
Es na difference bot at þe tane
Has ende, and þe tother has nane."
P. C. 2740-3.

— *conj.* when, "ut," V 138/377.
" þai come telle him þat ilk niȝt.
atte þai sulde on þe morne fiȝt."
Holy Rood, Morris, 109/41-2.

AUE, the Ave Maria, or Hail, Mary, B 60, 82; C 56.

— *instead of* ane, B 425. *Note*, p. 183.

AUMBRY, *s. almariolum*, a cupboard, p. 165-6.

AUOKET, advocate, B.P. 66/11.

AUTER, altar, B 33, 264.

— corners of, apparently of north and south sides, p. 333 (6).

AUTERCLOTHE, B.P. 76/12. AWTER-CLATHE, B.P. 71/20. *Note*, p. 332.

AUTER-END, B 36. *Note*, p. 159.

AUTER-MYDDIS, B 302.

AUTER-NOKE, the horn of the altar, or end of the west side; and sometimes of the narrow (north and south) sides of the altar, p. 333 (6). See ENDE.

— NORTH, B 156.

— SOUTH, B 88, 579.

AUTER-STON, V 145/631.

AUTERE, L 149/41.

A-WAY, B 517, "do away."

AWBE, the *alba* or alb, a white linen vestment, used also of the close fitting vestment worn by the officiants at mass, of black or other colour according to the suit, p. 167.

AWE, *v. impers.* and *pers.*
" For we awe to trow."
P. C. 2510.

AWEN, *poss.* own, B 403; C 336. But B 565, OWNE.

AWGHEN, *poss.* own, C 222.

AWTER. See AUTER.

AWTER-CLATHE, B.P. 71/20.

AWTER KYSTE, A 24/n. See *Note*, p. 264.

AWTIER, altar, p. 168/2; p. 165/21. See AUTER.

AY, *adv.* aye, always, for ever, B 111, 296, 501.

— *for* a, one, the same, B 561*.

— *for* a, one (of number), C 101, where ay whil, *for* a (*ane*) whil, one while, sometimes; *but* ay whils = ever whilst. S.e *Note*, p. 228.

— = a, one (of kind), B 561.

— ever, B 296. See EUERE.

AYE, ever, B.P. 69/2.

AYTHER, either one of two.
" And noght anly of ayther by þamself þan."—P. C. 5980.

— both of two (*uterque*), B 542, C 313. [E eyþur, F eythere.]
" Ayther worlde now waxes alde."
P. C. 1511.

AY-TO, ever until, until, B 481.

BALAD, O.F. *balade*, 1. a piece in verse divided into stanzas with the same refrain; 2. here used of the several stanzas which, as may be observed, p. 369, end with " here mas," &c. p. 370/19.

BALDLY, *adv.* boldly, confidently, V 131/119.

BALE, *s.* evil, woe. A.S. bealu, Icel. böl, B 170*, 141/489; V 131/35, 139/418.
" I mae unhale men al hale
And def men I bete of bale."
E. M. H. (Small), 35.

BALEFUL, *adj.* evil, B 404.

BANDES, *s.* bonds, B 404. Cf. BONDES, B 477.

BANES, bones, B.P. 72/23.

BASON, to receive the offerings, p. 236.

"bacyns pur l'autier d'argent susorrez."—Will of Edmund, Earl of March, 1380; Nichol, *Royal Wills*, 106.

Cf. "decent bason to be provided by the parish."—B. C. P.

BE, *prep.* by, B 528, 573; C 76, 339; V 138/358; H.C. 65/15; p. 337/28; 370/9; p. 371/28. Cf. our "be(*by*)-cause."

"If he be not promoted be thos forsaid parochinars."—*Wills and Inventories*, S. S. I, 118.

"Offrande of lof godes, and righte Sal worschip me, be day and night."
Ps. (50) xlix, 23.

— *imper.* be, B 182, 256; V 131/130.

— *subj.* be, B 6, 529, 605; C 330.

BE-COME, *perf.* became, B 216.

BEDE, prayer, F 8; V 130/64.

"þanne he hauede his bede seyd."
Havel. 1385.

BEDES, beads on which repeated bedes (or *prayers*) were told, p. 203(2).

BEDLEM, Bethlehem, C 109.

BEETE, V 141/489. See BETE.

BEHALDE, *v. a.* to behold, B 406; C 226.

BEHOUES, *imper.* B 521.

BELIUE, BELYUE, quickly, forthwith, H.C. 84/29; B 49.

"Bylyue," "ad tost" (aussi-tôt).—H. S. 8857.

Cf. our "Look alive!" = Look sharp!

BELLE, B 401; V 144/571; L 149/47. See CROS-BELLE, LITEL BELL.

BEN, *pp.* been, B 231, p. 121/10; 1 *pl.* P 126/30; 3 *pl.* F 116.

— *inf.* to be, P 126/26.

BENEDICAMUS, said at the end of mass, B 605, p. 117.

BEO, be, B 131/129. See BE.

BESY, diligent, P 123/23.

BESYNES, BESYNESSE, diligence, P 122/29; p. 253. See BUSYNES.

BETAKE, to commit, commend, p. 396/8.

"Yn-to þy keepyng y here (*her*) betake."
Bonaventura's *Meditations* (Ed. Cowper), 695.

"Here biteche I þe miue children alle þre."—*Havelok*, 384.

See SESE, TAK.

BETE, *v. a.* to better, to amend, to make amends for, to expiate, B 170. A.S. bétan, *amelior.*

BETHLEM, Bethlehem, B 247.

BI, *prep.* by, B 85, 108 [C be]. *Note*, p. 198.

BI, *imper.* be, B 181; but "be," B 182, and C 99.

BIDDIS, 3 *pers. of* BID, to ask, pray, command, 303.

"Byddyn, Mando ... Oro."—P. P. 35. Cf. the phrase "bid the bedes."

BI-DENE, BY-DENE, thereby (of time or place), at (*by*) once, together, besides, B 104. See *Note*, p. 194; p. 173; p. 237.

BIDS, 2 *sing.* B 448. See BIDDIS.

BIG, to build, B.P. 65/2.

BIGYNNE, *v. a.* and *n.* B 41.

BIHOLDE, *v. a.* B 417. See BEHALDE.

BILLE, a formal document, a letter, V 144/580.

Cf. A.V. "take thy bill." St Luke, xvi, 6.
"And whan sche of this bille hath taken heede,
Sche rent it al to cloutes atte laste."
C. T. 9826-7.

BINETHE, beneath, B 57.

BIRD, *impers.* ? *pret.* of bos (*or present*). Cf. Icel. ber, *oportet*, O-V. 60; bera, C. III; p. 331(1).
"we ne standenn nohht
Swa summ uss birrde standenn."
Orm. 11469-70.
"Thus was Crist offered for our hele,
Forthi bird us be til him lele,
Of us self bird us offerand mak."
E. M. H., 158.

BISET, *part.* bestowed, V 142/516.
"I in fewe yeeres
Haue spendid upon many diuers freres
Ful many a pound, yet fare I never the bet,
Certeyn my good have I almost byset."
C. T. 7531-4.

BISYDE, beside, besides, B 54, 195.

BISYLY, *adv.* diligently, earnestly, "*soigneusement*," B 124*, p. 197. See BUSYNES.

BLAK, *used substantively*, black, of the prayers, B 282.

BLAK LETTER, written in black and contrasted with rubric, B 440.

BLAME, *v.* to blame, B 73.

BLESSE, *v. a.* to bless, to praise, to confer a blessing on, B 124, "*benedicamus.*"

— *v. refl.* to bless, pray a blessing for oneself, to sign with sign of the cross. B 618; L 149/35. *Note*, p. 311.

"fingres .... þat tu þe mide blescest ant makest þe marke of þe deore rode." —*Seinte Marherete*, 13.

"Lifte up thyn handes and with thy fingres blysse."—*Lydgate*, M. P. 45.

"Then blysse you and go to bed."— *Myroure*, 169.

BLESSID, *pp.* blessod, B 429; where C, blessed.

BLESSYNG, *s.* blessing, signing with sign of the cross, B 619; where C, the northern *blissinge*.

BLIS, BLISSE, *s.* bliss, glory, B 323; V 146/636.

"Som sal noght deme, bot demed be
Til blis, als men of grete charite."
P. C. 6049-50.

"And yates of ai up-hafen be yhe
And king of blisse in-come sal he."
Ps. (24), xxiii, 7.

"And þair blisse turned þai ('*et muta-verunt gloriam suam*')
In likness of a kalfe ctand hai"
Ps. (106) cv, 20.

"Our perfect consummation and bliss."—B. C. P. *Burial Service*.

BLISSYNGE, C 366. See BLESSYNG.

BLODE, *s.* blood, B 236, 409; C 167; F. 145.

— used of persons of high qualities, or high breeding, L 153/166.

"Gaf he Sara, ðat faire blod."
G. and E. 1192.

"And stande lyke lusty bloudes
Adventuring lyfe and goodes."
Upcheering of the Mass, 1547.
Mr Huths' Reprints.

"These were 17 giants bold of blood."
Percy Folio, I, 97/181.

BLYNNE, *v. a. & n.* to cease from leave off, stop, V 144/586.

"ȝyf þy wraþþe þou wilt not blynne," glossed "leue."—H. S. 119/3738.

"ȝyf þou wylt of oþys blynne
þan wyl y pray for þy synne."
H. S. 25/747-8.

"Blinne fra wreth" (*desine ab ira*).
Ps. (37) xxxvi, 8.

BLYNT, *adj.* blind, V 131/110.

BLYSSE, to bless, C 365. See BLESSE.

BODILE, *adv.* of corporal reception of the sacrament of the altar, V 145/630.

BODY, B 303, 539.

BOGHT, redeemed (of Christ), B 184, 348.

BOKE, BOKES, *s.* book, B 3, 155, 202; C 17.

— a formal document, p. 338. See BUKE.

BONDES, bonds, bands, B 477. See "band."

BONE, petition, boon, V 130/64, 132/143; L 149/29, 150/92.

"Listes þe bon þat scho him bad."
C. M. 20590.

BORD, a table, a feast, V 146/639.

BORDE, GODDES, God's board, the Lord's table, 121/18, 233/20, 382/3. *Note*, p. 358.

BORNE, born (of birth), B 247.

BOS, *impers.* it behoves, B 174.

"For aligate buse me."—E. M. H. 80.
"Me bos telle."
Allit. Poems, Morris, 56/687.
"To do þi will I am redy
But þe bus teche me þo way."
Morris, *Holy Rood*, 65/127.

See *Note*, p. 216. See BIRD.

BOSTE, noise, boast, arrogance, strife, L 153/177.

"þan is þere chydyng and boste
þere is nat þe holy goste."
H. S. 62/1900-1.

BOT, *conj.* except, B 9.

— unless, without, B 201, 448.

"And but freres ben first y-set · at sopers & at festes,
þei wiln ben wonderly wroþ · ywis, as y trowe."
Ploughmans Crede, 21/554-5.

"What so ʒe doo, if ʒe gyfe all þat ʒe hafe un-to þe nedy, bot ʒe lufe þe name of Ihesu, ʒe trauelle in vayne."—Hampole, *English Prose*, Perry, 4.

BOT, but, B 171, 174, 202.

BOTHE, *numeral*, both, B 35, 284.

— *conj.* both, B 236.

BOUNE, ready, prepared, F 9. See BUN. See *Notes*, p. 161, 341.

"I am boune" (*paratus sum*).
Ps. (119) cxviii, 60.

Bow, *v. a.* to bow, B 585.

BOWNE, *adj.* p. 369/7. See BOUNE.

BRED, bread, B 500. See "housel."

BREDE, HOUSEL-, the consecrated bread ministered at Communion, B 597. See *Note*, p. 308.

BREDER, brethren in a religious corporation, brothers of natural relation, B.P. 66/13. See also BRETHER.

BREST, breast, B 268.

BRETHER, B.P. 66/28. See BREDER.

BREÞER (*the northern plural*), B 468; but later, C 257, brother; E, brodur.

BRIGGES, bridges, B.P. 65/12.

BRIGHT, *adj.* of B. V. M., B 66.

"Moder, quod sche, and mayde bright, Marie."—C. T. 5261.

BRING, *v. a.* B 397.

BROÞERE, *sing.* B 565. See BREÞER.

BRUKEN, *v. a.* to use, to partake of, p. 359/2; where of receiving the sacrament of the Lord's Supper. See USE.

BUKE, book, C 20 (but "Boke," C 17); B.P. 71/19.

BUN, *pp.* bound, ready, B.P. 70/7, —71/28. See *Note*, p. 341; cf. BOUNE.

John Percy, of Scarborough, in 1500, provides an obit

"for my saule and all my kyne saulez and goode doers, and in general for all these saulez for whom by any titell or reason I am bon to pray fore."—*Test. Ebor.* III, 184.

"The soules that we ben bound to pray for."—Hearne, *Robert of Gloucester*, p. 625.

"For all yes and oyer (*oþer*) yt we are bonded to pray for."—*Ib.* p. 682.

"Man! beþinke þee what / þou art From whens þou come, and whider þou art boun."
Poems, Furnivall, 167/110-11.

BURYELLES, *s. pl.* burial rites, burial, p. 121/12.

BUSYNES, *s.* diligence, of earnest, serious purpose. Cf. A. V., Rom. xii, 11, "not slothful in business." (τῇ σπουδῇ, Vulg. *sollicitudine*.) H.C. 86/77. See BISYLY, and *Note*, p. 197.

— the matter about which men are diligent.

BUT, unless, V 135/268. *Note*, p. 376.

"Hym byhoves knaw himself with inne."
P. C. 147.

BUT IF, unless, p. 121/12. See BOT.

"Forrþi þatt nohht ne meʒʒ ben don Allmahhtiʒ Godd toewenne But iff itt be wiþþ witt annd skil Annd luffsummlike forþed."
Orm. 1660-3.

BY, B 493. See ÞERBY; see BE.

BYFALLE, *v. i.* to happen, fall out, B 590.

BY-FORNE, *prep.* before, B 248.

"For þat I herd me bi-forne Micel snibbing þam amange."
Ps. (31) xxx, 14.

BYHOUES, *impers.* it behoves.

BYLYVE. See BELYVE.

BY-TWIX, betwixt, B 539.

CAN, *v. a.* to know by heart, p. 222. See CON.

— to know, absolutely, L 148/7.

"Swylk men had nede to lere Of other men þat can mare þan þay."
P. C. 155-6.

— of knowledge of a particular subject, C 83; F 64. See *Note*, p. 293.

— to can, to be able, V 141/475.

CANDEL, *s.* wax light on the altar, p. 173.

CARE, sorrow, distress, B 478; L 153/162.

"Care, thought—*chagrin*."—Pals. 202.

" Careful herte him ouȝhte come
þat þeucheþ vpon þe dredful dome."
C. L. 453-4.

" God sente on him sckenesse and care."
G. and E. 775.

" Elles suld þe hert, thurgh sorow and
care
Over-tyte fayle, warn some hope ware."
P. C. 7263-4.

" Kare com to his hert."
W. of P. 743.

Cf. " Be careful for nothing."—Phil.
iv, 6.

CATEL, CATELL, s. property, chat-
tels, V 142/519. O.F. catel.

" Catell in cofers."—Ploughm. Crede,
11/183.

" Wel can Senek and many philosopher
Bywaylen time, more than gold in
cofre.
For loss of catel may recovered be
But loss of tyme schendeth us, quod
he."—C. T. 4445-8.

— cattle, B.P. 79/1.

CAYFACE, Caiphas, L 148/22.

CERTENLY, without question, B
· 522.

CESE, v. i. to cease from, B 508,
548. See SESE.

CHALES, CHALYCE, CHALICE, s.
the chalice, B 399; B.P. 65/3,
71/19, 76/12.

CHANOUN, canon, V 132/141.

CHARGE, s. primarily load of a
carriage (Fr. charge, Ital. carica,
L.L. carricare, from carrus), care
or cure (of souls) undertaken,
B.P. 74/7, where "cure" is
used as an alternative; trust
conferred, B.P. 74/9.

" That have charche of ȝoure soule in
here kepyng."—Audelay, p. 43.
Cf. Moses "laid his hands upon"
Joshua " and gave him a charge."—
Num. xxvii, 25.
" Set the priests in their charges."—
2 Chron. xxx, 2.

CHARITE, CHARYTE, B 333, 511,
513, 519.

CHAST, chaste, B 215.

CHASTISE, v. a. to correct, restrain,
set right. O.F. chastier, Lat.
castigo. V 138/369.

CHAUNCE, s. that which falls out
unforseen, B 594.

" Be nat sorowful to do penaunce
Y am with þe yn euery chaunce."
H. S. 5367-8.

O.F. cheance, from cheoir, Lat.
cadere. [Cf. Germ. Fall, Zufall,
from fallen and accident, in the
sense of casualty, also from cado.]

CHAUNGE, v. a. to change, B 427.
" Vche day chawnge þyn ost."
Myrc, 60/1948.

CHERE, face, countenance; and so
of the welcome to a petitioner or
guest expressed by it. O.F.
chère, L.L. cara, Gr. κάρα, caput,
V 133/185.

" God haue merci on us and blesse us:
liȝtne he his chere on and haue mercy
on us." Ps. (67) lxviii, 1. Mask. M.R.
II, 17.
" His port, his chiere, and his figure
Bien ever present in my sighte."
Lydgate, M.P., 221.
Cf. Italian proverb: " La vivanda
vera E l'animo e la cera."—Vocab. della
Crusca, s. Vivanda.

CHESE, v. a. to choose, B 190.
" For to chesenn himm an folk
Off all mannkinn."
Orm. 11234-5.
" And þare-with he gaf hym a fre wille
For to chese, and for to halde
Gude or ille, wether he walde."
P. C. 78—80.

CHESEPULL, chasuble, E 36. Note,
p. 185.

CHESIBLE, chasuble, p. 167, 168.
Wyclif, Ex. xxv, 7, has chesiple,
where Vulg. and A.V. "ephod."
" Chesypylle, chesible, casula."
P.P. 73.
" Chesabyl.e, casula, infula., planeta."
Cath. Angl., ib.

CHEWE, v. to eschew, L 153/183.

CHILDE, sing. child, B 216; pl.
CHILDER (the· northern form), B
370; B.P. 69/7; B.P. 71/29.
" þe wande, he (' Salamon') says, of
disciplyne smert
Sal chace foly out of þe childes hert.
þerfor maysters som tym uses þe wand
þat has childer to lere undir þair hand."
P. C. 5878-82.

CHIRCHE, church, *kirke* of earlier forms, B.P. 75/9, 20, 26. See *Note*, p. 344.

CHOLLE, jowl, V 137/318.

CHOPPE, *v. a.* to strike, hit, *also to* chop, V 137/18

CHYLDE, *v. n.* to give birth to a child, p. 368/23.

CLANNESSE, V 135/251. See CLENNES.

CLENE, clean, pure chaste, B 94, 100, 103.
" And of chastite of virgyns clene
þat chast and haly av has bene."
P. C. 3828-9.

CLENLY, *adv.* sinlessly, B 383.

CLENNES, *s.* purity of life, B 15; C 15.

CLERE, *adj.* clear, of heart and conscience, B 94, 557.

CLERK, *s.* scholars, learned men, B 7, 173; V 140/435. *Note*, p. 157.
" He was a bysshope and ful gode clerk
þat shewe hys bokys of hys werk."
H. S. 8823-4.
" Euesque esteit et ben lettre,
Ce unt ces liures ben proue."
M. P. 6757-8.
" Bathe klerk and laued man."
" lered and laued bathe."
E. M. H. 4.
— of the minister or server to the priest in the mass, B 578.
— *pl.* the *clerici* or song-men, B 45. *Note*, p. 181.

CLERKES, in contradistinction to priests, B 362, 611; B.P. 64/10, 69/3, 75/26.

CLOTHE, garment, vestment, chasuble, B 36. *Note*, p. 177-8.
" clath." " On bak ne bed."
C. M., Cotton, 6799—6801.
" Hiss clap wass off ollfentess hær."
Orm. 3208.

CLOUT, *s.* a blow, V 137/321.

COME, *v.*, B 302.

COMEPELYN, *s.* compline, the last of the canonical day hours, H.C. 86/68.

COMLY, *adj.* (*from* come) comely, convenient, becoming, as applied to act, or circumstance, or per-

son, B 132. *Note*, p. 198. Cf. Fr. *convenant, convenable.*

CON, *v. a.* to know by heart, B 491.
— to get off by heart, B 265; *perf.* COUÞE, V. 140/451. See CAN. *Note*, p. 312.
— to be able, B 442, 531. See "may."
— *auxil.* B 339. See *Note*, p. 293.
— (= gone, C 4), B 4. See GONE.
" How þe Maudalan sore cone grete."
C.M. 189.

CONFORTED, *pp.* comforted, p. 367.

CONFORTH, *v. a.* to strengthen, comfort, B.P. 65/20.
" And gret comforth and solace it es to me."—P. C. 8877.
" Bot ogayne þat dred yhit might he
Thurgh hope of hert conforted be."
P. C. 1642-3.

CONSAYUED, *pp.* conceived, B 340.

CONTRE, a country, B 252.

CORAGE, heart, spirit, not merely of bravery in actual combat or bodily danger.
" He hathe no corage of a man truly
That seechith pleasaunce worshippe to despise."—*Poems*, Furnivall, 64/381.

CORNER, of altar. See AUTER.

COSTE, coast, border, frontier, not necessarily the sea-board; also of a country, L 153/176.
" This bethe the wordes of cristeninge
Bi thyse Englissche costes."
W. de Shoreham, P. S. p. 10.

COSTERS, curtains hung at the north and south sides of altar; from Fr. *coste* (côte), Lat. *costa*; side, p. 174.
" Cortinæ a lateribus altaris utrinque appendantur."—*Statuta Synodalia Eccles. Leodiensis* (A.D. 1287), xi. Martene & Durand, *Nov. Thes.* iv, 838.
" ii cortinæ pro lateribus altaris."
Inventory, Bp Hatfield, A.D. 1381.—
Wills & Invent., S.S. I, 37.

COUÞE, *pret.* of CON, to ken, V 140/ 451, 141/474.
— to can, be able, V 141/475. *Note*, p. 293.

CRAFT, CRAFTE, *s.* power, intellectual ability, skill, art, handicraft, B 371; C 12. *Note*, p. 161.

CRAVE, *v. a.* to crave, to ask, B 447, 512. A.S. *crafian*, Icel. *krefja.*

CREDE, creed, B 61, 197, 204, 423; V 140/451.

CRISTEN, *adj.* Christian, B 112, 456.
— *v. a.* to baptize, C 80.
— to convert to Christianity, bring within christendom, L 152/151.

CRISTENDAM, the profession of a Christian as undertaken in baptism; baptism, V 128/7; p. 330/19.

CRISTENDOM, baptism, B.P. 65/19, 71/31; p. 330/13.
"þe crystendome at hym he toke."
H. S. 7878.
"le gyu (*Jew*) deuient chrestien."
M. P. 6178.
"þe sacrament of eristendom."
Wyclif, *Works*, III, 285.

CRISTYNDOME, christendom, the aggregate of Christian nations, L 152/153.

CRISTYNMEN, Christian men, B.P. 74/10.

CROS, *s.* the Cross on Calvary, B 219.
— Sacrifice of the cross, H.C.82/20. Cf. "By thy Cross and Passion."
B.C.P.
— the sign of the cross, B 196.

CROS-BELLE, rung at the elevation of the host, L 150/69.

CROSE, *s.* cross, B.P. 68/12.
— *v. a.* to sign with the cross, p. 385/6.

CUMBRE, *v. a.* to overwhelm, V 139/412.
"And his sergant that cumbered was Wit parlesi (*palsy*), al had he rase."
E. M. H. 129.

CUN, *v. a.* C 370. See CON.

CURE, pastoral charge, B.P. 68/22, 74/8, 75/20.

CURET, CURATE, *s.* clerk having pastoral care, whether rector,

vicar, or stipendiary, B.P. 68/24; p. 121/14.
Cf. "Bishops and curates."
B. C. P.

CURTEYSE, courteous (of God), P 127/8.
"And God is curteys, and wul wele Forȝyue þe þy trespas euery dele."
H. S. 7334-5.
"Curtcis Crist."—*Plow. Crede*, 6/140.
— — (to God), 163/10.

DALTE, *pf.* of deal, to divide, distribute, V 130/74.

DAM, a title of respect, B 18; Dane, E 18. *Note*, p. 169.

DAY, B 207, 224; V 131/116.

DEBONERLY, *adv.*, Fr. *Débonnaire*, *de bon aire*, kindly (of superiors), mekely (of inferiors), P 126/15.
"To tellen to debonere men he sent me" (ad annunciandum mansuetis misit me).—Wyclif, Isaiah, lxi, 1.

DED, *adj.* dead, B 231.

DED, *s.* death, H.C. 84/28; p. 299/24.
"Ded es þe mast dred thing þat es."
P. C. 1666.

DEDE, *s.* death, F 214; V 129/58, p. 169; p. 350/16.

DEDE, *adj.* dead, B 455.

DEDE, *s.* action, deed, B 97*, 534*, 591. See DEYD.

DEED, *adj.* dead, B 219.

DEEDE, *s.* death, C 238. See DED, DEDE.

DEGRE, rank, station, B 332, 533.

DEKEN, deacon, B 153.

DEKNE, deacon, V 136/300.

DELE, *s.* part, portion, B 304*, 526*.

DELE, to deal with, V 135/274.

DELITE, *s.* delight, B 71.

DEME, *v. a.* to judge, B 229, 411; V 146/635.

DEORLICHE, dearly, V 135/254.

DERE, *adj.* dear, beloved, B 166, 468.
— *adj.* dear, of high price, costly, B 184, 348.

DERLY, *adv.* dearly, with feeling, with devotion, B 464.

"derely hym þonkeȝ."—*Sir Gaw.*, 1031.
"siþen hör diner watȝ dyȝt & derely serued."—*Ib.* 1559.

DESERIT, *pp.* dispossessed, deprived of property in possession or inheritance in expectation. *Note*, p. 278.—B 379. See DISHERITE.

DESESE, *v. a.* to disquiet, vex, trouble, E 376. *Note*, p. 279. See DYSEASE.

DETTE, IN, in duty bound, V 142/515.

— in debt, of unfulfilled spiritual requirements, B.P. 65/22, 70/8, 76/26. *Note*, p. 338, 401.

DEUOCION, DEUOCIOUN, DEUOCIOUNE, devotion, B 285, 329, 453.

DEUOCYON, C 14.

DEUOUTE, *adj.* devout, B 19.

DEYD, deed, H.C. 84/23 (*of good deed*); 24 (*of evil deeds*).

DIGHT, *pt.* made ready, arrayed, B 33.

"Abraham . . . diȝt his asse."
Wycliff, Gen. xxii, 3.
"Nothing diȝt with sour douȝ."
Ex. xii, 19.
"What kyn paynes in helle er dight."
P. C. 6432.

DISHERITE, *v. a.* to dispossess, p. 340.

DISHERYD, *pp.* C 199. See *Note*, p. 278. See DESERIT.

DIȜE, to die, V 130/72.

DO, *v. a.* B 24, 444.

— to offer, p. 357.

— *pp.* done, transacted, B 591. See DON.

— ON, to put on, don, F 12.

— OPON, to put on, B 38.

— OUT, to excommunicate, p. 118/8.

DOLE, portion, deal, V 133/170.

DON, DONE, *pp.* done, B 443.

— ended, B 194, 195, 606.

"Til al the noyse of the pepul was i-doo."
C. T. 2536.

DON, put to death, B 219, 408; B.P. 75/12; B 408.

"þou was ordained to be done to deed."
Nassynton, 232.

DOS, DOSE, 3 *plural*, do, B 16, 46; C 16; E 16.

— *3 pl.* B.P. 69/31.

DOUN, *adv.* down, B 281, 585.

DOUTE, *s.* doubt, fear, B 546, C 317.

DRAW, *v. a.* to render, translate, B 32. Also of original composition.

"In other Inglis was it drawin,
And turnid Ic haue it til ur awin
Language of the Northin lede,
That can na nother Inglis rede."
E. M. H. p. xxii.

DREDE, fear, dread, doubt, B 422.

"Redeth Senek, and redith eke Boece
Ther shuln ye se expresse, that no drede is,
That he is gentil that doth gentil deedes."—C. T. 6750-2.

— *v. a.* of godly fear, p. 248/31.

DREDFULLE, *adj.* respectful, feeling dread or respect, L 149/58.

[Love] "makeþ þe herte milde and dreduol."—*Ayenb.*, 144.

The later use is rather of inspiring dread, or worthy of respect, in which sense it was also used, p. 393/27.

"Dredefulle . *timidus, pavidus.*
Dredefulle and vggly. *Terribilis, horribilis.*"—P. P. 131.

"a best / þet com out of the ze . . . to meche dreduol."—*Ayenb.*, 14.

DREDFULLY, respectfully, "as to a kyng," L 150/76. Cf. "Most dread sovereign,"—Dedication, A. V.; and the use of φόβερος in Greek liturgies. "Most dread liege."—Shak. *Henry VIII*, v, 1. The notary in the Latin attestation of the French will of Edward the Black Prince, A.D. 1376, styles him "*princeps metuendus*" (Nichol, *Royal Wills*, 76); and *Metuendæ majestatis* is very common.

DRES, DRESS, *v. a.* to dress, straighten, set in order, direct, C 243; F 221; p. 371/27. *Note*, p. 290.

DRYUE, *pp.* driven, H.C. 84/28.
"þat neȝh is driue to þe deþ."
W. of P. 39/978.

DUNT, *s.* dint, blow, V 138/353.
"deaðes dunt," a death blow.—
A. R. 274, 366.

"And with hamers gyf swa gret dyntes
þat alle to powdre moght stryke hard
flyntes."—P. C. 7017-8.

DURST, *perfect of* DARE, B 447.

DYED, *perfect of* DIE, B 349.

DYSEASE, *s.* and *v.* of perplexity of
mind or vexation of spirit;
malaise, E 376; p. 277. *Note*,
p. 279.
"that ben in all disease."
(*qui in omni pressura sunt.*)
Wycl., II Cor. i, 5.

EFTER, *prep.* after, B.P. 69/12.

EFT-SONE, EFT SONE, *adv.* soon
after, again, forthwith, B 506;
F 253; p. 220.
"Bote a man, ore louerd seide,
Eft sone i bore beo,
He ne mai neuere for no þing
þe blisse of heouene seo."
Leben Jesu, 289-90.
"Alas! he seyd, what have y wroghte
þat y shulde euere hym (*God*) forsake
þat ys so redy me eft to take."
H. S. 252-4.

EKE, *v. a.* to add, to increase, B
60; E 192.
"And eke over al þi loof sal I."
"*Et adjiciam super omnem laudem tuam.*"
Ps. (71) lxx, 14.
"Eke mote Laverd over yhou."
Adjiciat Dominus super vos.
Ps. (115) cxiii, 14.
"to eke þair paynes."—P. C. 6817.
— *conj.*, p. 370/7; also, *insuper*,
"also, *aussi.*"—Pals. 877. Cf.
Germ. *auch.*

ELD, ELDE, *s.* age, 118/4; p. 275/2.

ELDE, *v. i.* to age, grow older, V
131/107.

ELDIRS, *gen. pl.* forelders, ancestors,
B.P. 66/29.

ELLIS, *adv.* otherwise, B 7, 87, 201.

ELS, *adv.* else, C 7.

ENCENTYNGE, inciting, excitement,
P 125/35.

ENCHESON, ENCHESOUN, *s.* cause,
occasion, motive, purpose, P 123/
18, p. 279. O.F. *achoison*, Lat.
occasio.

ENDAUNT, *v. a.* to charm, bewitch,
tame, V 140/445. O.F. *dompter.*
"*To dawnte*, blanditractare."—
Cath. Anglic. P.P. 115, where
Mr. Way quotes the reference in
Piers Plowman to the dove which
Mahomet had trained to come to
his ear for food:
"Thorugh his sotile wiltes
He daunted a dowve."
Ed. Skeat, B. xv. 392.

ENDE, AUTER-, the north or south
end of west side of altar, B 36.
Note, p. 179.
— LEFT, at which the gospel is
read, p. 179.
— *s.* end, B 240.
— *v. a.* to end, B 623.

ENDLES, *adj.* eternal, endless, B
211.

ENDYNG, *s.* hour of death, H.C.
84/25.
"bai sal finnde at his last endyng."
P. C. 2228.

ENGLISHE, B 32, 199, 495.

ENGLYS, E 199.

ENGLYSHE, B 204.

ENSAMPILL, ENSAUMPLE, example,
C 23; L 150/80.
— also in sense of advice, *Piers
Plowman*, Skeat, A, x, 106-7.

ENSENSE, *s.* incense, B 249.

ENTENT, intention of worshipper,
B 15, 416; L 153/169.
— intention of priest, B 100. *Note*,
p. 193.
— diligence, purpose, endeavour,
B 543; C 21; F 3. See TENT.

ENTENTLY, *adv.* diligently, "*diligenter*," 125/24.

EORÞE, earth, V 146/651.

ER, *conj.* ere, before that, V 130/75.
See ARE.
— 1 *pl.* are, H.C. 84/26.
— 3 *pl.* are, C 141, 202; p. 118/7.
"Tylle heven, whare alkyn ioyes er."
P. C. 7981.

ERE, 3 *pl.* are, B 588; H.C. 84/28.

EREN, *pl.* ears, B 585.

ERKE, *adj.* weary, 375/30.
"to calle to god for grace looke *thu*
neuer be irke."—*Sacrament*, 917.

ERLY, *adj.* early, B 532. See ARE.

ERT, ERTE, 2 *sing.* art, C 171; F
26.

ERTHE, earth, B 121, 207, 392.

ERTHLY, *adj.* earthly, B 161.

Es, 3 *pl.* are, B.P. 66/30; H.C.
82/8.

— 3 *sing.* is, B 235, 413.

-ES, *pl. of nouns,* B 7, 369, 454,
455, 456, 554.

-ES, 2 *pers. sing.* B 139, 245, 271,
303, 413. See -IS.

ESCHEWE, *v. a.* to eschew, shun,
B 535 [enchewo, F 282].

ESSE, 3 *sing.* is, B 462.

ETCHEWE, B 358. See ESCHEWE.

EUEN, evenly, impartially, in-
differently, B 411. *Note,* p. 284.

EUENE, *s.* smooth surface, V 138/
364.

EUENKYN, *adj.* of like kind, H.C.
72/22. Cf. "Even-cristen,"
fellow Christians.

EUERE, ever, C 142; for *ay* of B
and F.

EUERILK, EUERILKE, every, each
and all, B 526; C 297.

EXILDE, *pp.* exiled, B 379.

EYINE, *s. pl.* eyes, L 151/110. Cf.
Eyne, *Myroure,* 249; Eghen.
P.C. 575.

FADER, father, *acc.* B 205; *gen.* B
227, 468; B 468.

FADIR, *gen.* B 134, 139.

FADRE, *s.* father, B 68, 145.

FALL, *v. n.* to fall, L 149/82.
"Suffre al þat falliþ to him."
Wyclif, I, 346.

FALLYTHE, *impers.* L 149/50, 150/
83.
"Him falles serve himself that has na
swayn."—C. T. 4025.
"Fallyn or happyn. *Accidit, evenit.*"
P.P. 148.

FANELLE, *s.* the maniple, p. 168.

FARE, *adj.* fair, B.P. 68/8.

FARE, *v. i.* to fare, go, journey, B
441.

FAST, *adv. of place,* close, B 241.

—, FASTE, *adv. of time,* soon, B
310; C 56; L 150/65.

— *adj.* quick, rapid, V 137/311.

FAY, *s.* faith, V 131/117.
"For they nolde not forsake here trw
fay
An byleve on hys falsse lay."
Masonry, 520-1.

FAYN, FAYNE, *adv.* fain, V 133/
183; L 153/164. See "fyne."

FAYS, *pl.* foes, H.C. 84/52.
"And hethen men fra synne ras
That before was Criste faase."
E. M. II. 77.

FEL, *adj.* stern, fierce, E 223; V
136/287. *Note,* p. 233.
In a good sense.
"That the mayster be both wyse and
felle."
Masonry, Halliwell, 194; *ib.* 785.

FELAWES, fellows, companions, C
326.

FELE, many, V 128/9, 146/658.

FELICHYP, *s.* fellowship, company,
B.P. 68/8.

FELLE, *s.* skin, B 223; V 135/269.
Note, p. 223.

FELOUSE, *s.* fellows, equals, B 555.
See FELAWES.

FENDE, *s.* fiend, the devil, L 154/
198.

FER, *adv.* far, B 556.

FERDNES, *s.* fear, B 447.
"Thurg thretynges þat þai sal mak
And thurg þe ferdnes þat he sal tak."
P. C. 2230-1.

FERE, *s.* companionship. A.S.
fera, gefera, one journeying
(*faring*) with another, a com-
panion, p. 181. See F 236, and
Note, p. 292.
"Of o dysshe þey etyn yn fere."
Meditations on the Supper, 3/68.
"And whan assembled was this folk in
fere."—C. T. 4747.
See FARE.

FESTIS, holy days, B 115. O.F. *festes.*

FETE, *s.* feet, B 84, 577.

FIFT, fifth, B 11.

FLEMED, *pp.*; FLEME, *v. a.* to banish, V 146/636. A.S. Fleon, *v. n.* to flee. Flyman, *fugare,* to make to flee.

FLESSHE, *s.* flesh, B 223, 236, 239.

FLETTE, *s.* floor, p. 162.
"Clived mi saule to þe flet."
Adhæsit pavimento, Ps. (119) cxviii, 25.

FLYTTE, *v. a.* to remove (of priest or clerk removing book on altar), B 155, 579; also as *v. n.* of changing abode, or the shorter flights of a bird.

FOLK, *s.* the people or congregation, "*populus*" of old rubrics, B 43.

— *s.* the people, distinguished from rulers, B 367.

FOLKE, *s.* all Christian people, B.P. 65/24.

FOLOUSE, 3 *sing.* follows, B 199.

FOLY, *s.* foolishness, sin, uncleanness, B 384. See *Note,* p. 278.
"folye,
As ryot, nasard, stywes, and taverns."
C. T. 13880.

FOLYS, *s. plur.* fools, L. 153/167.

FONDYNGE, *s.* temptation, V 139/411. See FOUNDYNGE.

FOR, *conj.* B 7; P 126/12.

— *prep.* notwithstanding, B 12.

— for the sake of, B 79, 91.

— in behalf of, B 49.

FOR-DO, *v. a.* to do away with, to forgive, destroy, B 257*. Cf. "to do for." "fordon" occurs in the Egerton MS. of the E. E. Psalter for "*confundantur,*" Ps. (35) xxxiv, 4, where the Cottonian MS. reads "schent." *Note,* p. 251.

FORGETE, *v. a.* forget, B 194, 272.

FORGYFNES, FORGIUENES, FORGYFNESSE, forgiveness, B 81 110, 237.

FORLORNE, *pp.* utterly lost (of final perdition), C 240; H.C. 82/17.

FORME, *adj.* First of time and quality (*positive of* former, foremost), p. 384.
"Hit arn fettled in on forme, þe forme & þe leste."—A.P., 90/38.
"our forme fader Adam."—P.C., 483.

FORNE. See BY-FORNE.

FORSOKE, *pf.* refused, B 250. *Note,* p. 249.

FORTHE, forth, B 581.

FORTHE-AFTER, B 202.

FORÞI, for that, therefore, B 273, 334, 416.

FOR-TO, with purpose, B 218, 280.
Cf. "For this cause I raised thee up for to shew in thee my power."—Ex. ix, 15.
"For to do."—Acts iv, 28.

FORȝECTES, *part. used substantively,* rejected, abject, F 302. *Note,* p. 300.

FOUL, *s.* filth, V 138/362. A.S. *Fúl.*

FOUNDYNGE, *s.* temptation, B 504.

FRA, *prep.* from, 69/25.

FRAM, *prep.* from, F 20.

FRE, *adj.* noble, generous, frank, B 134. *Note,* p. 198.

— free, V 142/496.

FREMDE, not of kin, B 108.

FRENDES, friends, B 455, 555.

FRENDIS, B 559.

FRERE, friar, member of a begging order, V 132/141; p. 339.
"I speke of us, we mendeaunts, we freres."
C. T. 7494.

FRO, from, B 96, 505.

FROW, *adj.* light, loose (in conduct), p. 374/9.
"fals and mercuh and frouh" (of worldly love).—O.E.M. 94/44.

FROYTS, fruits, B 392. C, frute.

FUL, *adv.* full, fully, B 24.

— *adj.* full, B 65.

FULFILLE, FULFYLLE, *v. a.* to bring to full end, to complete the number, to satisfy, B 99; B 534.
"For God sal fulle-fylle alle þair lykyng."
P. C. 8497.

FULLUHT, cleansing (from sin), the sacrament of baptism, B.P. 62/23. Cf. fullere; Lat. *fullo*, one who cleanses or whitens cloth, a fuller.

"þatt borenn iss þurrh Hali3 Gast
þurrh fulluhht *annd* þurrh læfe."
Orm. 17300-1.

FURST, *adv.* first, E 490; V 134/236.
— *adj.* first, E 518; V 143/536.
— *s.* prince, E 543; where B, C, F, prince. Cf. Germ. *Fürst*.

FYNDE, *v. a.* to find, B 17.

FYNE, *adj.* fain, glad, B 561.
" Red letter in parchemin
Maketh a child good & fyne
Lettrys to loke & se."
Poems (Furnivall), p. 244, l. 12—14.
Cf. "My lips will be fain."
Ps. lxxi, 21, P. B. V.
See FAYN, *adv.*

FYSOUN, *s.* great plenty, p. 368/16. O.F. *fuison* (*foison*), Provenc. *fusion*, Lat. *fusio*, a pouring out (of abundance).

GA, to go; B.P. 65/11; gas, 2 *sing.* V 131/104; gas, 3 *pl.* p. 275; gane, *pp.*, B.P. 65/11. See Go.

GAF, *pret.* gave, B.P. 65/5.

GAINSTANDINGE, withstanding, B.P. 69/12, 76/9.

GAN, began, V 136/291. *Note*, p. 160. See GONE, GUN.

GANE, *pp.* See GA, GAS.

GAS. See GA.

GAST, GASTE, ghost, B 213; C 129, and *passim*. See GOST.

GASTLY, spiritual, B 68; C 40.

GATE, *s.* a way by which men go; a street; "fen of gates." *lutum platearum.* Ps. (18) xvii, 43. Journey which men go, B.P. 65/11, 69/36. See GA.

GEF, 3 *sing. subj.* give, B.P. 69/11. See GIF.

GENTYLLES, gentlefolk, B.P. 74/15. "Gentry, of norture and maners, *Comitas.* Gentry of awncetre [*ancestry*], *Ingenuitas*," P.P. 190.

GERTE, *pret. of* GAR, to cause, H.C. 84/43.
" And then gar him kisse the boke," of oath to suppliants for sanctuary at Beverley.—*Harl. MS.* 4292.
" Gar any man lose his wardly gudes."—*Great Cursing MS.,* *York Manual,* where the printed Manual reads "causeth . . . . . worldly goodes."
" Fra dede of synne to life of grace
That geres us fle the fendes trace."
E. M. H. 77.
" He gert thaim sit down."
E. M. H. 90.

GESSE, *v. i.* to suppose, P.P. 190. " *Estimo, arbitror, opinor,*" but Palsgrave, 591, "*je deuine,*" B 85, p. 337(3).

GIF, GIFE, *v. a.* to give, C 53, 347; B.P. 65/18. See GEF, GYF, GYUE, 3EUE.

GILT, *s.* guilt, of sins of omission, B 572.

GO, *v. n.* to go on foot, as opposed to riding, B 592; L 152/133. See GA, GOON.

GOANDE, B 592. See Go.

GODE, *adj.* good, B 21, 64, 192; C 77. See GUDE.
— *s.* the good, B 190, 321.
— *s.* good gift, benefit, grace, B 339; B.P. 71/24.
" Geuer of all goddes."—*Myroure,* 68.

GODES, *s.* goods, property, B 354.
" No mannys gode shalt you stele."
H. S. 66/2048.
"God 3eueþ ofte times to goode men goodes and myrþes."
Chaucer's Boethius, Morris, 132/7, 8.

GODHEDE, goodness, B.P. 71/15. *Note,* p. 342.

GODNESSE, *s.* goodness, B 1, 366; E 1. See GUDNES.

GOD SPELLE, *s.* Gospel, V 146/642.

GODYS, good gifts, F 151. See GODE.

GOLD, *s.* B 249.

GON, *inf.* to go, V 138/370.

GON, *pp.* gone, V 128/16, 137/346, 136/295, 137/325, 138/361. See GONE.

GONE, *pret.* did, 130/87; began, did, C 4. *Note,* p. 160.

GONNE, V 136/304. See GONE. *Note,* p. 160.

GOOD, *s.* (in singular) property, chattel, goods, B.P.V. 76/16; cf. B.P. iii, 71/24. See GODE.

GOON, going, L 151/114.

GOONE, 2 *pl. of* GO; *v. n.* to go, walk, in contrast with riding, L 152/133.

GOONGE, *s.* "preuy, *cloaca, latrina.*" PP. 203.—P 125/11.

GOSPEL, GOSPELLE, GOSPLE, the portion of the gospel appointed to be read at mass, B 153, 194; V 136/301.

GOST, *s.* ghost, B 233, 275. See GAST.

GOUVERNYNGE, *s.* governance, B 528.

GRACE, *s.* grace, B 106, 127, 160, 358, 458; B.P. 68/18; V 136/310.
— *s.* pardon, B 81; V 131/113; p. 391/30. See *Note,* p. 189.

GRAME, *v. a.* and *n.* to grieve, anger. *Subs.* O.T. 13331. A.S. *grama.*

GRANE, *v. n.* to groan, the reading in MS. Harl. for GRONE, V 137/325, where Audelay, p. 77, has GRAME.
" He is oft seke and ay granand."
P. C. 798.
"granen iþe eche grure of helle (*groan in the eternal horror of hell*)."— *Hali Maidenhad,* 47.

GRAS, *s,* grace, B.P. 74/8.

GRASE, *s.* grace, B.P. 69/11.

GRAUE, *s.* grave, B 220.

GRAUNT, *v.* to grant, B 258, 353, 460, 500.

GRETE, *adj.* great, O 23, 170; of storms, B 390, "great storm of wind;" of weighty examples, B 24; of men, B 372.

GRETT, *adj.* great, B 23.

GREUE, to grieve, V 137/335, 139/389.

GREYTHE, *s.* preparation, p. 284. Cf. A.S. "geræde, trappings, *phaleræ.*"
" Wen hit watȝ fettled & forged & to þe fulle grayþed."
Allit. Poems, p. 46, 343.

GRONE, *v.* to groan, *altered from* "grane," V 137/325. See GRANE, GRAME.

GUDE, *adj.* good, O 21, 28; *passim.*

GUDE, *s.* good gifts, gifts of grace, C 158, 173. *Note,* p. 276.
"Of al gudes þat God has gefen þam here Als of gudes of kynde (*nature*) and gudes of graces,
And gudes of hap þat men purchases."
P. C. 5895-7.

GUDE-FREND, *s.* benefactor, B.P. 72/22.

GUDES, *s.* goods (of commerce), B.P. 70/6.

GUDNES, goodness, C 1, 186. See GODNESSE.

GUN, began, H.C. 84/40, 86/54, 57; V 138/370, 382. See GAN, GONE.

GYF, *v. a.* give, E 81; B.P. 68/23.

GYFTES, gifts, B 430.

GYLT, guilt, B 356.

GYSTHE. See *note,* p. 397.

GYUE, *v. a.* to give, B 28, 81, 435, 450.

GYUYNGE, giving, B 347.

HACELA, a chasuble, p. 335.

HAFE, 1 *sing.* have, C 166.

HAFES, 3 *pl.* have, B.P. 69/10.

HALD, *v. a.* to hold, B 40 (haldes), B.P. 65/21.

HALD ON, *v. n.* to hold on, B.P. 65/7.

HALE, *adj.* whole, *integer,* 118/3.

HALOUSE, *s. pl.* saints, B 67, 75, 104.

HALY, *adj.* holy, B 75; C 3, *passim.*
— *adv.* wholly, C 166.
"Gifes noght the tendes haly with-outen any withdrawing."—*MS. York Manual.*

A mason, on the "werk of þe kyrk of Sanct Petyr" (*York Minster*), swore "upon þe boke *that* he sall trewli and bysyli at his power . . . hald and kepe haly all *the* poynts of *this* forsayde ordinance in all thynges *that* hym touches." — *York Fabric Rolls*, 183.

HALY BRED, holy bread or holy loaf, blessed with an appointed prayer and given to the people on Sundays and other holy days instead of the Sacrament, B.P. 65/5. *Note*, p. 336.

HALY DAYES, B 115.

HALY KYRKE, C 3, 180.

HALY MEN, C 4.

HAM, *acc.* them, F 97.

HAME, *s.* home, C 114.

HAN, 3 *pl.* have, V 132/148.

HANDE, hand, B 139, 241; V 144/568. See HENDE.

HANDES, *pl.* B 58, 405. See HENDE, HONDES.

HARDE, *pp.* heard, B.P. 70/12.

HAS, 1 *sing.* I have, B 443.

HAS, HASE, 2 *sing.* hast, B 83, 344, 438, 452; C 161, 162, 351.

HAUES, 2 *sing.* hast, H.C. 82/20.

HAW, to have, F 48, 56.

HE, *adj.* high, B.P. 70/2.

HE, *pron. pers.* B 20.

HEDDE, *perf.* had, V 129/42; V 137/344.

HEDE, *s.* heed, B 154.

HEDE, B 230. See MANHEDE.

HEF, *v. a.* to heave, raise, V 143/552.

"I þe messe hwon þe preost hefð up Godes licome."—*Ancren. Riwle*, 32.

"When sche hef hir heued heyer, sche perced þe selue heuene."
Chaucer, *Boethius*, Morris, 5/43.

HEGH, *adj.* high, B 115, 484.

HEGHEST, *superl.* highest, B 143.

HEGHLY, *adv.* B 101.

HEILL, *s.* health, of body or soul, B.P. 69/26, 71/17.

HELE, *s.* that which hides, covers, defends, B 467. *Note*, pp. 290, 292.

"Forthi thet Godd Naaman helid Toc thou gift, and sithen it heled."
E. M. H. 131.

— *s.* health, B 375. See SOULHELE.

— *v. a.* to heal, 275/32.

HELEFUL, healthful, B.P. 75/23.

HELLE, *s.* hell, B 221. *Note* 291(2).

HELPE, *s.* help, B 256, 294, &c.

HELY, holy, B 474.

"Seint Aeldrede of heli god mayde was and hende."—*Vernon MS., f.* 38.

HEM, *gen.* of them, E 150.

— *dat.* to them, F 233.

— *acc.* them, E 251.

HENDE, *pl.* (*northern*) hands, B 35; B 284; V 145/607. See HANDES.

— *adj.* handy, ready, courteous, V 144/595.

HEO, she, V 134/224, 140/441.

HER, their, E 363.

HERE, *v. a.* to hear, B.P. 82/10; C 61; B 459, 586.

— *adv.* here, B 203, 204.

— *s.* host, army, company, B 67; C 39. *Note*, p. 188.

"A mikell here off engglepeod" ("*a multitude of the heavenly host*").— (St Luke, ii, 13), *Ormulum*, 3370.

— *pron. poss.* their, F 163.

HEREN, 3 *pl.* hear, B 173.

HERERS, hearers, B 163.

HERIS, 2 *sing.* hearest, B 604.

HERKEN, *v. a.* to harken to, B 486.

HERKNYNGE, *s.* harkening, B 28.

HERT, *s.* heart, B 277, 304, 316.

HERWE, *v. a.* to harrow, to sack a stronghold, ravage a country, V 142/502.

HERYNGE, hearing, B 10.

HESSE, *poss.* his, B 619.

HETHEN, *adj.* heathen, 68/13; B.P. 75/13.

HETHEN, *adv.* hence, B 295; p. 280/27.

HETHYNG, mockery, scorn, H.C. 84/41.

HEUEN, *s.* heaven, B 207, 225. HEVENE, C 272.

HEUEÞ, V 143/540. See "hef."

HEW, *v. a.* to lift up, to raise, F 11.
"hewys hys handys on heghte."
M. A. 4156.

HEXTE, highest, V 130/68, 77.

HEYLFULL, *adj.* healthful, whole-some (of doctrine), B.P. 69/1.

HIE, *adj.* high, loud, B 274.
"þe angell answered him in hy."
Holy Rood, Morris, 69/278.
"þey brought hym to pylate and cryed an hy."—*Med. Soper.* 534.

HIGHT, *s.* heighth, loud voice, B 482.

HIR, *pr. poss.* her, B.P. 66/12.

HIS, *poss.* B 18.

HIT, *n.* it (the aspirate being preserved), B 24, 105, 272, 489; V 145/606, 615.

HOKER, scorn, V 144/578.

HOLD, HOLDE, *v. a.* to hold, B 58; B 445.

HOLI, *adv.* wholly, F 144. See HOLLY.

— *adj.* holy, B 233, 234, 568, 587.

— -WRIT. See WRIT.

HOLY, B 3, 4, 213; H.C. 82/20. See HALY.

HOLLY, *adv.* wholly, B 347.
"Alle holy oweþ þy shryfte be doun."
"*Ta confessiun deit estre enterre.*"
H. S. 11820.

— *adj.* holy, B 141; E 75.

HOLY WATER, L 149/38.

HOM, *pron. dat. pl.* them, to them, B 14, 46, 251, 386, 476. HORNE, L 153/171.

— *pron. acc. pl.* them, B 384, 477, 502.

HOM, HOME, *s.* home, B 252; F 332.

HONDES, *pl.* hands, B 40. See HENDE, HANDES.

HONOURE, *s.* honour, worship, B 380.
"Offred and honoured at þe hiȝe auter."
Sir Gawayne, 592.

HOOL, *adj.* whole, 125/21.

HOPE, *s.* B 273.

HOR, *pr. poss.* their, B 117; B 387, 476.

HORE, *pr. poss.* their, B 110, 198, 366, 464, 466, 477, 558; E 252, 462, 477. See ÞERE.

HORNE, *s.* horn, wind instrument, L 153/171.

HOSLED, *pp.* L151/128. HOUSELED, V 146/664. See HOUSEL.

HOU, *adv.* how, V 129/23, 29, 33.

— to think, consider, heed. A.S. *hogian,* Icel. *huga,* V 139/395.
"umbe þe bota ne huȝa𝖉—takes no heed of the amendment."
O. E. H. I, 113/3.
[To how is still used in the East Riding. I heard it for the first time in the phrase "Let us how it a while," and the expla-nation that was given on the instant—"studying how"—was perhaps more ready than etymo-logically correct.]

HOUSE, of York Minster, B.P. 71/12; of Beverley Minster, B.P. 71/12. See *Note,* p. 326.

HOUSEL, *s.* sacrifice, host of bread and wine, consecrated in the Eucharist. A.S. *Húsl.* M.G. *hunsl* (= θυσία, 1 Cor. x, 18, &c.; λατρεία, St John, xvi, 2), B 235. Here of the kind of bread, but the wine hallowed in the chalice is called húsl; Canons under King Edgar, xli.; Thorpe, A.L. II, 252.
"He bletsode hlaf and win to husle."
Canons of Ælfric, xxxvi.; Thorpe, A.L. II, 360.

HOUSEL, HOSEL, *v. a.* to housel, to administer the communion; *pass.* to receive the communion, V 131/118; p. 238, 241; p. 368/2.

HOUSEL-BREDE, *s.* the host, here the *viaticum,* B 597.
Cf. "Gange se preost syð𝖉an to þam Godes weofode mit þære husel-lafe þe he hadȝode on Ðunres-dæg."—*Ælfric's Canons,* xxxvi. (as to Good-Friday); Thorpe, A.L. 2359.
"Housil of Goddes body."
P. C. 3402.

How, *adv.* in what manner, B 26.

Howsilling, *s.* ministration or reception of the Eucharist, p. 239(4).

How3ell, *s. & v.* L 151/126. See Housel.

How3elyed, *pp.* houseled, L 151/ 123. See Housel.

Hus, *pro. pers.* us, B.P. 66/12.

Hy, *v. n.* to hie, H.C. 82/5.

Hym, probably a mistake for thyn, C 201.

— *dat.* to him, C 273, 274, 277.

— *acc.* him, C 364.

I *for* In, *prep.* V 131/117; V 137/ 320.

I, *s.* eye, 127/10.
"þat sight he sal se with gastly eghe."
P. C. 2234.

Ianglyng, Iangelynge, *s.* prating, chattering, B 22; C 22.
"Iangelyn, iaberyn, *Garrulo, blatero.*"
P. P. 256.
"Nay, quod the fox, but God give him meschaunce
That is so indiscret of governance,
That jangleth, whan he scholde holde his pees."—C. T. 12919-21.
"She jangleth like a jaye." *Elle jangle* or *cacquette comme ung jay.*—Pals.
"Whether any do use to commune, jangle or talk at the time of divine service."—*Articles of Enquiry,* 1547. Cardwell, D. A. 29/28.
"Sweet bells jangled out of tune."
Hamlet, III, 1.

Iape, *s.* jest, ribald joke, L 153/ 191. "Iape, *Nuga, Frivolum, scurrilitas,*" P. P. 257; where see Mr Way's note.

Iesu, *nom.* Jesus, H.C. 84/33, 86/ 54.

— Iesuys, *gen.*, H.C. 86/69; H.C. 84/36. See Ihesu.

I fere, together, in general, F 236. *Note,* 292. See Fere.

Ihesu, *nom.* B 315.

— *voc.* B 318, 322, 432, 446.

Ilk, Ilke, each, B 266, 331, 332, 421, 627; C 150, 151, &c.

Ilke an, Ilkane, each one, C 252, 327.

Ilk one, each one, B 463, 556.

Ille, *adj.* of actions, wicked, bad, B 24; B 376, 535; C 196, 306.

— of persons, B 51; p. 374/26.

— *s.* evil, B 190, 272, 544; C 315; V 134/210.
Icel. *Illr.*, U-V. 318. See *Note,* p. 172. See Ylle.

In, *prep.* of place, B 3.

— of motion, into, B 504.

Inquart, B.P. 69/26. See Quart.

Intil, *prep.* into, unto, B 32, 479.
"It suld frese and turn al in-til yse þar."
P. C. 6644.
See Til, Until.

Ioy, *s.* joy, B 114, 397; B.P. 71/30.
"He preched on sa fair maner,
That it was joi for to her."
E. M. H., 90.

— glory, B 119, 126, 128, 142, 146, 182; H.C. 84/29, 82/7. *Note,* p. 196.

Ioying, glorying, B 432. *Note,* p. 287.

Ioyntly, of the hands clasped in prayer, B 58.

Is, 2 *sing.* art, B 102, 496. *Note,* p. 294.

-is, 2 *sing. of verbs,* B 604. See -es.

-is, -ys, *plural of substantives,* B 98, 225, 558, 559.

I-sought, *pp.* sought out, discovered, V 132/148.

It, *shortened form of the neuter pronoun hit,* C 24, 61, 63, *passim.* See Hit.

I-whils, I whyls, whilst, B 245, 575. See Whiles.

I-wis, *adv.* truly, in truth. Cf. Germ. *gewiss,* V 136/288.

Kan, C 83. See Can and Con.

Kare, C 267. See Care.

Ken, *v. a.* to make to kan (know), to teach, to show, B 147, 490; V 141, 475; p. 275. See *Note,* p. 200, 293.

"I can fynde in a felde · or in a four-
longe an hare
Better than in *beatus vir* · or in *beati
omnes*
Construe oon clause wel · and kenne
it my parochienes."
       Sloth in *Piers the Plowman*,
       B, v, 424-6.
"Thaim I suld bathe lere and kenne."
       E. M. H. 85.

KEPE, *v. a.* to keep, to watch for,
B 189; B.P. 64/10, 68/21.
"Againe þe comyng of Ihesu Criste
To kepe him when he doun sal come."
       P. C. 5028-9.

KEPE, *s.* charge, care, heed, B 267,
305.

KEPE, *pp.* kept, F 171.

KEPED, KEPYD, *pp.* kept, B 363,
374; C 182, 194.

KEPTE, *pp.* kept, E 371.

KEUERE, *v. n.* to recover, V 131/
124.

KID, KIDDE, *perf. of* KITHE or
CUÐEN, *v. a.* to show, manifest,
B 471; C 467.
"þat so muche loue him kuiþe wolde."
       —— 590.
"Whatt gate þiss maȝȝ ben þatt tu
O Godess hallfe kiþesst."
       Orm. 2451-2.
"The kyndenesse þat myne eueue—
cristene · kidde me fernyere
Sixty sythes, I, sleuthe · haue forȝete
it sith."
     Piers the Plowman, B, v. 439-40.

KIRC, KIRK, KYRC, B 3, 234, 413.

KIRK WARKE, building or repara-
tion of churches, B.P. 71/25.
Note, p. 342.

KISTE. See KYSTE.

KLYPE, *v. a.* to call, L 153/190.
"And eek ye knowe wel, how that a jay
Can clepe Watte, as wel as can the
pope."—C. T. 644-5.

KNAPYS, *s.* knave, L 153/190. A.S.
Cnápa, cnáfa, son, boy; Icel.
knapi; Germ. *knabe.*
"þaȝe he be a sturn knape."
       Sir Gawayne, 2136.

KNAWE, to acknowledge, confess,
C 37. See KNOWE.

KNEES, *s. pl.* F 10.

KNELANDE, *part.* kneeling, B 53,
405.

KNELE, *v. n.* to kneel, B 150, 281,
328, 515, 600.

KNELEN, 3 *pl.* kneel, B 39.

KNELLE, V 144/571.

KNESE, *plur.* knees, B 53, 150.

KNOC [on þi brest], B 268.

KNOW, KNOWE (*Novi*), B 31, 339.
(*Agnosco*), B 51, 65.
"Of these and of all other, as far as
god knawys me gyltye, I knawe my
selffe gylty."—*Form of Confession.*
Maskell, M.R. II, 281.

KUYNDE, *s.* kind, kin, nature, V
134/203. See KYNDE.
"þe body es dedly here thurgh kynde."
       P. C. 1717.

KUYNDELICH, *adv.* kindly, natural
to the kind, with natural affec-
tion, V 143/531.
"Bodily ded, þat is kyndely
Es twining betwene þe saule and þe
body."—P. C. 1686-7.
See UNKUYND.

KYD, *pp.* of cyðan.

KYNDE, *s.* kin, kind, relationship,
B 108.
— nature *as opposed to* grace, p.
276.
— *adj.* natural, kind (*pius*), L 151/
107.

KYNG, KYNGES, B 248, 428, 429.

KYNS, kinds, sorts, B 520; al
kyns, 106; alkyns, 120, 589.
See KYNDE.

KYRC, KYRKE, church, B 3; C 3.

KYS, *v. a.* to kiss, B 196.

KYSTE, *pp.* kissed, A 24, *n.* 1.
— *s. Cista*, kist, chest, p. 265.

KYþE, *v. a.* to make to know, V
128/18.

LÆNE, *adj.* lent, precarious, tran-
sitory, frail, lean, B.P. 62/4.
Cf. "lêhni fehu," *Heliand*, 1550.
See *Note*, p. 322.

LAGHE, *s.* law, p. 275/29, 277/13.

LARE, *s.* learning, the northern form of lore, teaching, V 130/79, 275/6, 22.

LARGELY, *adv.* greatly, B 69.

LASCH, *v. a.* and *n.* to loosen, give way, V 138/350. O.F. *lascher* (lâcher), to slacken.
"Lask his peynes."—Myrc, 1736.

LASSE, *adj.* less, V 128/4, 5.

LAST, *v. n.* to last, to endure, B 111, 296, 386, 479.

LAT, to let, permit, C 315. See LET.

LATE, *adj.* late, B 532.

LATEN, Latin, B 494.

LAUATORIE, a *piscina*, the ceremonial washing, V 145/606; L 152/135.

LAUDE, *adj.* lay, p. 173.

LAVNCEGAYE, javelin, assegay, L 153/179. *Note*, p. 398.

LAYDE, *pp.* laid, B 220.

LECHE, *s.* physician, P 125/20; p. 275.

LEDE, *v. a.* to lead, B 504.

— *v. n.* to be leader, V 130/62.

— *s.* people, V 141/473. A.S. *leod;* Germ. *Leute.*

LEEDE, *s.*, V 134/209. See LEDE, *s.*

LEES, V 133/176. See LES.

LEETE (INTO), to light on, come to, V 129/36. See LIGHT.

LEEUE, *v. a. pf.* LAFTE, to leave, to relinquish, to leave undone, B 190; p. 229.
"As touching kneeling, crossing, holding up of hands, knocking upon the breast, and other gestures, they may be used or left, as every man's devotion serveth."—*The Book of Common Prayer,* 1549.
"When he had left speaking."
St Luke, v, 4.
"Lest my father leave caring for the asses."—1 Sam. ix, 5.

— *v. n.* to remain, B 243. See *Note*, p. 230.

— *v. a.* to believe, p. 120/16, V 140/419.

LELE, *adj.* loyal, faithful, V 134/208, 136/280. O.F. *leal, leial, loyal.*

LELY, *adv.* loyally, obediently to law, B.P. 64/23, 69/28.

LEN, LENE, *v. a.* to grant, to lend, B.P. 64/13; V 146/640; p. 173/16. *Notes,* p. 275, 322.

LEND, LENDE, *v. n.* to go ashore, to abide, to last, B 386; H.C. 84/31. *Note,* p. 280.

LENE, *v. n.* to remain, V 136/291.

LENGE, *v. a.* and *n.* to lengthen, to remain, V 130/62.

LENT, *pp.* lent, B 342. *Note,* p. 275. See LON.
"þe gudes spendid þat God had þam lent."—P. C. 5993.
"Truly y desire as nout nothinge ellis, but þat y might geue to my Lorde his oune gode, þat he haþe lent me: þat is to sey my body, my tyme, and alle my wyttis."—Arundel MS., 197, *quoted,* Thomson's *Te Deum,* p. 54.

LEO, *s.* lee, shelter, defence, cover. A.S. *hleó.* Icel. *hlé* ("fara i hlé, to seek for shelter," C-V 270). V 130/62.
"of hleó sende" (*into banishment*).
Cædmon, 102.
"earmra hleó," *protector of the poor.*
Ib. 4104.
"in lee of leudeȝ."—*Sir Gaw.,* 27/849.
"We lurkede undyr lee."
M. A., 43/1446.

LERE, *s.* learning, that which is taught, doctrine, manner of teaching, B 174.

— *v. a.* to make to learn, to teach, V 133/186, 145/625; p. 337.

— to learn, F 1; p. 239.
"Bot nou er yong men sa bald, That thai will lere bathe yong and ald, For ar thai kann thaimselven ken, Wil thai wisdom lere other men."
E. M. H. 110.

LERED, learned, taught, B 50.

LERER, *s.* teacher, B 164.

LERING, *s.* teaching, B 172.

LES, *sing.* and *pl.* falsehood, H.C. 82/14. See *Note,* p. 349. A.S. *leas,* false,—*bútan leáse,* without concealment, deceit; whence "leasing," Ps. iv, 2; v, 6.

LESE, *v. a.* to loose, B 404; C 267.

"A, Loverd, lese mi saule" (*O Domine libera animam meam*).—Ps. (116), cxiv, 4.

LESSE, *adj.* less, B 44.

LET, to hinder, p. 170/5.

— LETE, LETTE, *v. a. & n.* to fail, let be, cease, omit, leave, F 85; V 132/139; p. 170/8.

"At Cristes lar will thai noht lete That sat mekeli at maisters fete."
E. M. H. 110.

"þan may he nat hys bedde lete."
H. S. 4260.

"þou lewede man knowest also What ys to lete, what ys to do."
H. S. 7414-15.

— to let, permit, B 544.

LETTER, THE LETTRE, LETTERS, literature, book learning, written matter; C 83; *Note*, p. 200. See CLERK.

"Mony excusun ham by defaute of bokus and sympulnes of letture."—*Festial*, *prefacio*, sig., A. ii.

"And alle þe toþer beþ þe better þat heren þys tale or reden þys lettyr."
H. S. 10074-5.

— the text, B 157.

— BLACK, in contrast to the rubrics, B 440.

— ENGLISHE, *query*, black-letter in contrast to rubric; *or* in English and not in French or Latin? B 199. Johanna de Walkyngham in 1346, bequeaths "psalterium meum cum littera grossa et quemdam librum scriptum littera anglicana."—*Test. Ebor.* I, 17.

LETTIR, the text, B 426.

LEUACIOUN, elevation of host, B 406.

LEUAND, *part.* living, H.C. 84/22.

LEUE, *adj.* dear, pleasing, B 166.

— *v. a.* to leave, p. 121/20; V 129/38; p. 299/23.

— *v. a.* to believe, p. 276.

— *v. n.* to remain, p. 120/13. See LYUE.

— *v. n.* to live, p. 159/8.

— *s.* leave, V 130/65.

LEWDE, lay, illiterate, 148/3.

"Whether þou be lered or þou be lewed."
P. C. 2444.

LEWED, *adj.* ignorant, lay, 'ιδιώτης, B 50, 173, 491; V 133/183, 186; 140/436; p. 385/30.

"This every lewed vicory or parsoun Can say, how ire engendreth homicide."
C. T. 7590-1.

See under PARISCHEN.

LEYN, *v. a.* to conceal, V 143/538.

LIGHT, *v. n.* to alight, to descend, B 275. Icel. *létta*. *Note*, p. 258.

Cf. A V. "Neither shall the sun light (πίσy) on them, nor any heat."—Rev. vii, 16.

— *v. a.* to lighten, *illumino*, p. 261.

LIȝTTELOKER, *compar.* lighter, p. 124/21.

"And ȝe shul lepe þe liȝtloker."
P. Plow. B. v., 578.

LIST, *v. n.* to like (*velle*), F 85. See LYST, *impers. libet.*

LITEL-BELL, a hand-bell, B 401. "Lytell bell, *sonnette, campane*," Pals. 239.

LITEL, *adj.* little, B 301.

LOG, *v. n.* to lug, V 138/350.

LOKE, *v. a.* to see, regard, look at, B 271, 280, 624.

— to look upon, B 413.

— *v. n.* to look to yourself, take care, B 198, 278, 311.

LOMER, *s.* illuminator of manuscripts, p. 401(3).

LON, *s.* loan, V 138/376; V 146/640. See LENE.

LONDE, *s.* land, B.P. 76/4, 5.

LORD, LORDE, B 211, 255.

— of lay hearers or readers, p. 385/30. See LORDYNG.

LORDYNGS. Used in addressing an audience, as now "Gentlemen," p. 367. See SIRES, note, p. 362. Cf. Jack Cade's "Fellow Kings." 2 *Henry* VI, IV, 2.

LORE, *pp.* lost, p. 374/7.

LORNE, *pp.* forlorn, F 216.

LOS, *s.* praise, p. 284. O.F. *los.* Provenç. *laus, lau.* Lat. *laus.*

"So schaltow gete god los."
V. of P. 5132.

"Hui perdra Charles de son los grant person (*portion*)."—Ronc. 59. "Jà n'i croistra vos los ne vos honors."—Couci, vii. (Littré).

LOVE, *s.* love, B 520, 522, &c. A.S. lufe. See LUF, LOW.

— *v. a.* to love, B 523, 527, 547.
"I sal love þe, Laverd."—*Diligam te Domine*; Ps. (18) xvii, 1.

"þe way of mekenes principaly,
And of drede, and luf of God almighty
þat may be cald þe way of wisdom."
P. C. 141-3.

A.S. *lufe,* love; *lufian,* to love.

— — *v. a.* to praise, B 123 (where Latin *Laudamus te*).

"Offrande of lof," *sacrificium laudis.*
Ps. (50) xlix, 23.

"In din of beme him love yhe;
Loves him in harpe and in sautre."
(*Laudate eum in sono tubæ*),
Ps. (152) cl, 3.

A.S. *lof,* praise; *lofian,* to praise. Cf. Germ. *loben;* and Portug. *louvar,* Ital. *lodare,* Lat. *laudare.* See LOS.

— *v. n.* to render praise, B. 169.

LOUED, *pp.* loved, B 567.

— *pp.* praised, B 428.

LOUH, *perf.* laughed, V 137/324.

LOUING, LOVYNGE, *s.* praise, B 278, 325; B 436; C 132; B.P. 64/16; B.P. 71/17. See *Note*, p. 342, 346. See LOWYNGE.

"loved his loving"
"laudaverunt laudem ejus."
P. C. 317, 321.

LOUTE, *v. a.* 1. to bow down to, to do reverence to, B 263; 2. to reverence, B 627.

"The first commandment charges us
and teches
That we leve ne loute nane false
goddys."
Thoresby's *Catechism, f.* 295 b.

"ymagis and crosses ben lowtid of men."
Pecock's *Repressor,* 562.

— *v. n.* to make obeisance, to kneel, V 133/189, 143/537; p. 163/5.

"lowting or bowing downe, or knel-

inge to images."—*Injunctions,* Archbishop (Lee) of York, 1536.

LOW, LOWE, *s.* love, C 296, F 356.

— *v. a.* to love, F 274, 294 (but *loue,* 298, 299, &c.).

LOWSE, *v. a.* to loosen, F 244.

LOWYNGE, *s.* praise, C 117. See LOUING.

LUF, *s.* love, C 307, 317.

— *v. a.* to love, C 298.

LUSTE, *impers.* it pleases, E 243. See LYST.

LUYTE, *adj.* little, V 144/585.

LUYTEL, *adj.* little, V 145/618.

LYF, *s.* life, B 240.

LYG, *v. a.* and *n.* to lie, to lay, B 593.

LYGHT, *v. n.* to alight, B 215. See LIGHT.

LYKE, *impers.* it pleases, p. 284.

LYKYNGE, *s.* enjoyment, E 343; where B, LYUYNGE.

LYMMES, limbs, B 342.

LYST, *impers.* it pleases, B 243; C (LISTE) 105; but F 85, as a *verb personal,* THU LIST.

LYþE, to hearken, V 128/17; V 146/664. Cf. Icel. *hlýða messu,* to hear mass, C-V 274.

"Helde þi nere (*aurem tuam*) to me and liþe."—Ps. (31) xxx, 3.

LYUE, *s.* life, B 342, 346, 357, 375; V 135/242; p. 119. See LYF.

LYUEN, 3 *pl.* live, B 293 (where C 139, LEVES).

LYUYNGE, living, B 346.

LYVE, *v. n.* to live, B 357.

— *s.* life. V 142/501.

— *v. n.* to remain, C 356. See LEVE, LEEUE.

MA, *compar.* more, C 153.

MAGESTE, majesty, B 227.

MAKE, to make, B 449; C 94.

MAKYNG, *s.* versifying, p. 385/28.

MAN, *s.* man, C 19; P 126/3. See MON.

MANERE, *s.* manner, way, B 25, 173, 177, 421.

MANHEDE, manhood, B 79, 230.

MANKYNDE, mankind, B 409.

MANY, *s.* a number, multitude, H.C. 84/48.

— *adj.* many, B 63. C 6, *passim.* See MONY.

MARCHANDES, traders, shopkeepers, B 371.

MARE, *adj.* greater, B 44, 126; V 130/85. *Note,* p. 184.

MARKETH, F 40, for MEKETH.

MASTE, *superl.* of MA, greatest, C 1.
"þou bethleem iuda,
þof þou be noght þe mast cite
þou es noght lest of dignite."
C. M., 11466/9.

MATIR, matter, subject, B 171.

MAWNDE, *s.* the maundy, *Cœna Domini,* or last passover with the Twelve, F 360. See Skeat, *Notes to Piers Plowman,* B XVI, 140, p. 379.

MAY, *pres. ind.* 1, 2 and 3 *pers. of* MOWE, to be able, to have might, *pollere.* B. 516, 550; V 132/136, 143/553. See MIHTES.
"And pray we God þat alle þyng may."
H. S. 952.

MAYDEN, *s.* maid, virgin, B 215.

MAYN, *s.* main, V 129/52; V 143/544. Cf. "with might and main."

MAYNTENANDE, *part.* maintaining, B 365.

MAYSTER, master in sense of gaining the mastery, V 130/59.

ME, *poss.* my, C 296.

MEDE, meed, reward, B 13, 466, 473; C 51.

MEEDE, V 128/20. See MEDE.

MEER, *s.* Mayor of Corporation, B.P. 69/17.

MEID, B.P. 69/30. See MEDE.

MEKE, to humble oneself, to genuflect, B 42; P. 126/15. *Note,* p. 180.

— to humiliate, to make humble, P. 126/2.

MEKENES, MEKENESSE, meekness (*Divine*), B 213; P 124/14.

MELE, *v.* to speak, V 146/656. Icel. *mæla.*
"vuldorgâst godes vordum mælde."
Cædmon, 2906.
"þe blod on his face con mele
when he hit schulde schewe, for schame."—*Sir Gaw.* 2503-4.
"Thane laughes syr Lottez and alle one loude meles."—M. A. 382.

MEN, *pl. of* MAN, B 39.

— *indefinitely,* as we now use *one* or *they* for want of it, B 116, 197, 303, 401; p. 251. Cf. the GERM. *man* and Fr. *on* (homo). In the A.V. *men* is used indefinitely, St John, xv, 6, "men gather them, and cast them into the fire;" where the nom. is not expressed in the Greek, and if it were, would hardly be ἄνθρωποι. Robert of Brunne uses both the Teutonic and the Romance:
"Men wete never what nede one has."
H. S. 9595.

MENDE, to mend, amend, B 238.

MENES, *gen. pl.* men's, B.P. 68/14.

MERCI, MERCIE, *s.* mercy, B 78, 273, 443, 446.

MERK, to mark, write, B 426.

MES, mass, B 92.

MESCHIEF, *s.* mischance, a coming short of purpose. O.F. *mes* (Lat. *minus*), and *chef,* head, p. 229/22.
"In siknesse ne in meschief to visite."
C. T. 495.
Cf. *Achever,* to bring to an end (head), to finish.

MESSE, mass, B 9, 291.

MICHILHEED, *s.* greatness, P. 125/27.

MIGHT, power, might, moral strength, B 188, 451.

MIGHTES, *pl.* powers, mights (*with* most), B 180; V 147/684; p. 218/15.

— (*with* may), V 131/112, 132/136, 143/553. See MAY.

MIKEL, *adj.* great, many; *adv.* much, very, B 160. See MYKEL.

MILDE, merciful, pitiful, B 213.

MINISTER, *s.* of the priest who celebrates mass, p. 374/17.

MINISTRE, *v.* to administer (the sacrament of the altar), P 123/29. See MYNISTRE, PARISCHYNS.

MINNE, to minish, lessen, V 145/599. See MYNNE.

MOCHE, *adj.* much, in sense of great, L 152/192.

"Gode of his myche mercy."—*Bidding Prayer, Dio. London.* Henderson, *York Manual,* 223*.

MOD, mood, V 137/329 (anger, 1 O.E.H. 67/215).

MODER, MODIR, MODRE, mother, B 66, 103, 148, 468.

MODERKIRKE, mother church, the cathedral church, B.P. 71/11.

MON, *s.* man, B 19, 146, 161, 211, 564, 612.

— *indef.* V 128/2. See MEN.

MONE, *auxil. v.* must, B 415. Icel. *muna* (older form), *mon,* shall, will. *Hodie,* E. Riding, *mun.*

"Bot he þat his wille til God wil sette, Grete mede þarfor mon he gette."
P. C. 95-6.

— *s.* complaint, moan, V 137/328; L 148/14.

MONK, V 132/141.

MONNES, *gen.* man's, B 266.

MONY, B 5, 70, 388. See MANY.

MOO, *for* MA, B 354.

MORE, *adj.* greater, B 126, 136, 146. See MA, MOST.

"A more maister wolde I beo."
Celestin, 147, *Anglia,* I, p. 71.

MORNETYDE, "*hora matutina,*" the morning, H.C. 82/13.

MOROWE, the morning, L 149/25.

MOST, *adj.* greatest, B 143, 180; P 124/13; V 130/59, 147/684. See MAST.

"For þys is one þe most synne þat any man may fallyn ynne."
H. S. 159-60.

MOT, *pres.* may, might, B 319, 571 (where C MOWGHT); V 145/604.

MOWNE, *subj.* might, P 127/12.

MYCHE, *adj.* much, great, P 124/15.

MYCHE, *adv.* much, P 124/21.

— *s.* great part, L 152/147.

MYDDIS, *s.* the middle, the midst, B 302.

MYGHT, strength, B 65, 528; H.C. 86/62.

MYKEL, *adv.* greatly, B 283, 441.

MYKILL, *adj.* great, B.P. 72/26.

MYLDE, mild, V 133/185.

MYN, *poss.* mine, B 533.

MYNDE, *s.* memory, memorial, B 185; B 618; V 128/22.

MYNE, *poss.* mine, after the substantive, B 187, 560.

MYNISTRE, *v. a.* to administer the sacrament, P 123/21. See MINISTRE.

MYNNE, *adj.* less, B 136. Icel. *minnr, minnst,* less, least; M.G. *mins.*

— *v. a.* to mind = remember, keep in mind; to remind, bring to mind; to make mention of, V 130/66, 133/193, 139/391, 141/456.

MYRK, *adj.* dark, B 415; H.C. 86/57.

MYRRE, myrrh, B 249.

MYRTHE, gladness, mirth, B 120. See *Note,* p. 197.

MYS, *s.* misdeed, B 259. *Note,* p. 251.

MYSCHEF, MYSCHEFE, L 151/118, p. 371/4. See MESCHIEF.

MYSCOUNFORTH, need of comforting, discomfiture, B 377. See CONFORTH.

MYSDEDE, misdeed, B 82, 501.

MYSTIME, to come unready, or when cut short in preparing, H.C. 84/38.

NA, *adj.* no, C 22.

NAME, *s.* name, B 179, 293.

— *v. a.* to name, call upon, B 133.

NAMELY, NAMLY, *adv.* especially. "*Precipue,*" P.P. 351, like the German *namentlich,* B 548; P 124/1; p. 275.

" For a man excuses noght his unken-
nyng,
þat his wittes uses noght in leryng,
Namly of þat at hym fel to knaw."
P. C. 169-71.
"And helpes sinful men biden,
But namlic helpes scho tha,
That turns noht thair lof hir fra."
E. M. H. 163-4.

NE, *conj.* nor, C 89; p. 121/6; P
122/12; p. 245/7.

— *adj.* no, none, p. 225/7.

NEDDRE, adder, viper, V 140/439.
M.G. *nadrs*, A.S. *nœdre*, Icel.
naðra.

NEDE, *s.* need, B 164, 260, 490.

NEDEFUL, necessary, B 537.

NEDLYNG, *adv.* of need, of necessity, B 521.

" þan nedly behoves be punyst syn."
P. C. 2864.

NEDLYNGES, C 292. See NEDLYNG.
This and other adverbs in the
same form, as *hardlings, mostlings*,
are still in general use in the
East Riding.

NEGHE, *adj.* nigh, H.C. 84/51.

NEGHTBUR, neighbour, B 547, 554.

NEIȜ, NEIH, to draw near to, P
122/23; p. 396/11.

NEMENE, to mention, V 138/361.

NEMPNE, *v. a.* to name, V 135/263.
A.S. *memnan*, Icel. *nemna*.

NEODEþ, *v. impers.* there is need,
V 140/422.

NERE, *adj.* near, B 400, 556.

NEUEN, *v.* to name, utter, give
utterance to, Icel. *nefna*, B 120,
132, 146, 161 (*of reading gospel*),
309, 497.

NEUER, *adj.* never, B 6.

NEWE, *adv.* now, B 172.

NEXT, B 57, 246, 345.

NEY, *adj.* near, F 195.

NIGHT, B 207.

NIS = ne is, is not, V 133/195.

NO, *adj.* B 22. [C na.]

NOGHT, *adv.* not, B 270, 415, 602;
H.C. 84/25.

NOGHT, *s.* nought, nothing, B 208.

NOKE, corner, nook, of the *cornu
altaris*, used of both ends (north
and south) of the west side of
the altar, and also of the north
and south sides, B 88, 156, 579.
See on END, p. 179. The modern
use of nook appears to be confined to a recess or re-entering
angle.

NOMELY, especially, B 615. See
NAMELY.

NON, no one, B 201, 250; F 252.

NOON, southernizing form of NANE,
none, C 112. See *Note*, p. 400-1.

NORTH, B 156.

NOþELESS, not the less, nevertheless, V 145/626.

NOY, *v. a.* to hurt, B 98.

" And if thei drynke any venym, it schal
not noye hem."—St Mark xvi, 18.

NYGHT, B 525. See NIGHT.

OBAC, *adv.* aback, B 37.

OBLEY, of bread; or OBLEY, the
host or wafer, p. 238.

" Þe paste of þe vble nat ne oghe
Be made of any maner of soure doghe."
H. S. 10098-9.

" Le uble ne est fermente
Qe le prestre ad sacre."
M. P. 7388-9.

OEN, ought, B 197. See OWE.

OF, *prep.* by, B 17, 141, 344, 610;
p. 121/5.

— from, B 162. *Note*, p. 209.

— for, B 339, 609, 614.

— by reason of (grace), 344 (godnesse), 352.

OFFER, *v. a.* B 243.

OFFERANDES, offerings, oblations,
B.P. 64/24, 69/29.

OFFERD, *perf.* offered, B 248.

OFFERTOUR, the offertory, the
anthem so called, p. 319/6. See
p. 98/23, p. 232(2).

OFFERYNGES, B.P. 78/25, where
Offerandes in the older forms.

OFFICE, *s.* " of messe," the *officium*
or anthem so called, the Roman
Introit. B 86. *Note*, p. 190.

OFFICE, the whole office or order of mass, B 581. *Note*, p. 308.

OFFRANDE, offertory, the anthem so called, B 242. *Note*, p. 228.

— offering, thing offered, B 253. Derived from the Latin *Offerenda* or French *Offrande*, and not from the northern participle. "Offryng, *offrende*."—Pals. 249.

OFT, B 193.

OLDE, old, B 370.

ON, one in number, E 180; F 78.

— one in substance, V 144/588. See A, ANE.

— AL ON, all one, all at one, at peace, V 145/634. Cf. "Lo, eche thing that is ooned (*united*) in himselve Is more strong than what it is to-skatrid."—C. T. 7550-1. Cf. B 541, of one a-corde.

— *prep.* in, B 173, 177, 421, 563.

ONY, any, B 471, 590.

OON, a southernizing form of ANE, one, the like, C 313. See *Note*, p. 400-1.

OPEN, *prep.* upon, B 159. See OPON.

OPPON, OPON, OPONE, *prep.* upon, B 36; B 227, 349, 378, 413, 436. See UPON.

OR (*of time*), ere, before, B 41, 48, 61, 508, 603. "We, or ever he come near are ready to kill him."—Ac. xxiii, 15.

— *conj.* or, B 151, 605; OR ELLIS, B 87.

— *poss.* our, H.C. 86/64.

ORDAYN, to ordain, of God's ordinance, B 393.

ORDEN, *v. a.* to ordain (of resolves of council), B.P. 69/12.

ORDINER, *s.* ordinary, having ordinary ecclesiastical jurisdiction, B.P. 64/12.

ORESOUN, orison, B 286.

ORISON, prayer, B 452; E 286, 448.

ORNAMENT, *s.* B.P. 76/13, replaces "anourment" of earlier forms.

OÞER, other, B 563. AN OÞER, B 159.

OTHER, *conj.* or, p. 240. See OUTHER.

— either, p. 171/31.

OTHERE, *acc. sing.* other, B 564.

OÞERWAYSE, otherwise, B 595.

OUERSE, *v. a.* to look over, p. 215(2).

OUNDRON, *s.* the hour of tierce, H.C. 84/40. See UNDERN.

OURE, *poss.* our, B 172, 256, 395.

OUTE OF, not in (charity), B 511.

OUTHER, either, *with* or, B 116.

— or. See OTHER.

OUT-TAKE, *v. a.* to except, make exception of, V 146/666. "He outtoke nothing but a tre." *Holy Rood*, Morris, 63/51.

OWE, *impers.* B 338.

— *personal*, owe, ought, P 122/14. See OEN, AGHT.

OWNE, *poss.* own, B 565. See AWEN.

OYN, one, F 209, 210.

OYSE, *v. a.* and *n.* to use, to be accustomed, B 401. "To mych to oys familiaritee Contempning bryngith." *Lancelot*, Skeat, 1701-2. "That (*wisdom*) God hauis giuen us for to spend In god oys til our liues end." E. M. H. 3.

PAI, *v. a.* to please, 245/6. See PAY.

PAPE, pope, C 181; B.P. 64/6*. *Note*, p. 330.

PARDONE, C 137. See PARDOUN.

PARDOUN, *s.* indulgence or remission of temporal punishment on earth and in purgatory, B 13, V 146/649.

PARECHEN, *s.* parishioner, B.P. 69/23.

PARELS, perils, B.P. 69/25.

PARFITE, perfect, B 521.

PARICHIN, parish, B.P. 71/29. "I Iohn hedworth esquier of haverton within the parishinge of the College

Kyrke of Chester in the strett."— *Wills and Invent.* S. S. I, 112.

PARISCHYNS, parishioners, B.P. 65/15.

"And also" [*ben accursed*] "alle the men of religion, whether they be monk or chanon, or frere of any ordre, that ministre or ȝeue any other mennes parichenes, either lered or lewed, any of these .iii. sacramentis . . . of houslyng, or of anoynting or elles of weddyng; but if thei have special leve ther to of hem that kepe the soules of the parishens."— *The Great Cursing, Manual. Sar.,* 1510, *ap.* Henderson, *Man. Ebor.* p. 91*.

PARLYMENT, parley, conversation, V 136/382.

PARSON, person (of Trinity), p. 223(1).
 Cf. "   in proper parsoun."
     P. C. 4958.

PART, PARTE, share, part, portion, B 11, 463, 542; B 542.

PAS, a pace, step, V 131/106. Fr. *pas.*

PASKES, Easter, p. 118/6.

PASSAND, *part. pres.* the passing souls, or "agonizantes" at the point of departure, E 112. *Note,* p. 195.

PASSE, *v. n.* to pass from this life, p. 373/16; from purgatory, B 477. Fr. *passer.*

— (*PASSE*), to give heed, to weigh, to take into consideration, p. 364/34.

"I peyse, I waye, *Je poise*" (Je pèse). —Pals. 655.

"It moste be considered, trusteth me, For gentil mercy aughte pass right."
     C. T. 3090-1.

"But I passe not at all," Ἀλλ' οὐδενὸς λόγον ποιοῦμαι.—Ἀc. xx, 24. (Genevan) Barker, 1607.

"As for these silken-coated slaves, I pass not;
It is to you, good people, that I speak."
    Shaks. 2 *Henry VI,* iv, 2.

" a stone of such a paise
That one of this times strongest men, with both hands, could not raise."
     Chapman, *Iliad.* xii.

Cf. Ital. *pesare,* " Se tu per tanto la precienza di Dio . . . . pesare vorrai." —*Boezio della Consolazione* de B. Varchi, Firenze, 1551, v, 6.

PASSED, *pp.* past, departed, deceased, B 112. Cf. Fr. *les trespassés.*

PASSYD, C 80. See PASSED.

PAST, *pp.* B 295.
"I passe, I dye, *Je trespasse.*"—Pals. See under TITTER.
"Disturb him not, let him pass peaceably."—2 *Henry VI,* iii, 3.

PATER, Pater-noster, the Lord's Prayer, B 60.

PATER-NOSTER, B 152, 261, 398, 423, 480, 485, 494, 574, 601.

PAX, the pax-brede, or *Osculatorium,* B 514. *Note,* p. 295.

PAY, PAYE, *v. a.* to appease, to please, to pay, B 246, 530; V 131/106; p. 379, 245/6. See *Note,* p. 244.

PAY, *s.* good pleasure, satisfaction, B 383.

PAYDE, *pp.* satisfied, "well-pleased," B 617.

— paid, bound by payment received, B 445.

PENAUNCE, penance, 121/11.

PENY, penny, of the offering at mass, V 142/515; p. 241, *n.* 6.
"The lord marques [*of Dorset*] being chief mourner . . . . . offered a piece of gold of ten shillings for the maspeny."—Funeral of K. Henry VIII, Strype, *Mem. Reform.* Orig. Edw. VI. p. 15.

PEREL, PERIL, *s.* peril, B 257, 345.

PERIS, *s. pl.* peers, B.P. 69/8.

PER OMNIA SECULA, the end of the *secreta,* or beginning of preface, p. 54.

— B 482; p. 102/11. *Note,* p. 270.

PERSON, rector of parish, *vulgo,* parson, B.P. 64/9, 68/20, 75/20. *Note,* p. 330. See PARSON.

PES, *s.* peace, C 320, 322.

PESE, *s.* peace, B 111, 121, 509, 510, 521, 549, 551.

PHANON, *s.* the maniple, p. 167.

PINE, torment. See PYNE.

PISTILLE, the portion of Scripture appointed for the epistle, C 85.

PITE, PYTE, pity, B 68; C 50.

PLACE, *s.* B 345, 459.

— in service, B 300; C 143. Cf. "stede," B 454. *Note*, p. 288.

PORAILLE, *s.* poor people, p. 370(1). Cf. Ital. *poveraglia.*

PORE, *adj.* poor, B 372.

PORTESSE, *s.* the *portiforium* of the Anglican and Gallican churches, a service book containing the Canonical Hours, and corresponding to the Roman Breviary, p. 194.

PORTRED, *pp. of* PORTRAY, used of sculpture as well as of painting, L 152/160.

POSTCOMVNE, POST-COMEN, the *Post*-communio (p. 117, 307), or Postcommon, and in older MSS. *ad complendum*, p. 308/22, 382/19.

POUNCE, Pontius, B 217. *Note*, p. 223.

POUSTE, power, B 226. *Note*, p. 224.

POYNT, *v. a.* to prick, to note, to number, V 131/105. *Note*, p. 371.

PRAIE, PRAY, PRAYE, to pray, B 29, 74, 244, 270, 271, 292, 464; V 143/556.

— used of saying the creed, V 140/453.

PRAIERES, prayers, B 254.

PRAYANDE, *part. pres.* praying, B 299.

PRAYERES, B 454.

PRAYERS, B 266, 279, 459.

PRAYDE, *pp.* prayed, B 616.

PRAYSED, *pp.* praised, B 5.

PREFACE, of the mass, C 154.

PRESENCE, *s.* presence, B 403; C 222; F 198.

PRESENSE, *s. pl.* presents, F 92*. *Note*, p. 251.

PRESENT, *used substantively*, of actual presence, or present time, B 569.

PREST, *adj.* ready, B 532.

"At all seasons prest and ready."
Roy's *Rede me*, Arber, p. 92.

PREST, *s.* priest, B 279, 289; V 134/206.

PRESTE, priest, B 27.

PREY, to pray (for), V 134/206.

PREYE, V 129/24. See PRAY.

PREYERS, prayers, V 122/20, 129/24.

PREYEÞ, 2 *plur. imperat.*, pray ye, V 143/544.

PRINCE, "of pese," B. 549.

PRIS, *adj.* precious, choice, V 128/11.

"Þe kinges price stede."
Chev. Ass. 279.

Cf. "Arthur was knyghtly and Charles of grete prys." — Lydgate to K. Henry IV. *Political Poems*, Wright II, 141.

PRISON, B.P. 65/22. See *Note*, p. 401.

PRISONDE, imprisoned, prisoners, B 378.

PRIUE, *adj.* private, secret, B 536.

PRIUELY, *adv.* B 313, 492.

PRIUETE, *s.* privacy, unheard by the people, B 29.

PRIUEY, *adj.* B 280.

— *adv.* "*secreto,*" B 299.

PROFER, *v. a.* to offer, B 254.

PROFET, *s.* benefit, B 10.

PRONE, PROSNE, *Præconium* or *Proœmium.* The bidding prayer and sermon, or other pastoral instruction in the mass of the Gallican Church, p. 316.

PROPIRLY, *adv.* B 538.

PROVINCIALL, the superior of an order within his province, p. 338.

PRU, *s.* profit, advantage. O.F. *prue.* p. 374/8.

"Vauntage—*preu, auantaige.*" — Pals. 284.

"Moche good do it you: *bon preu vous face.*"—Ib. 523.

"Þat turnd is til vr gretter pru."
C. M. 1442/25196.

"But þys ys for þyn owne prow
Þat I have teche the now."
Myrc. 548-9.

PURCHASE, *v. a.* to get, acquire otherwise than by birth—not merely of buying with a price. O.F. *pourchasser,* of eager pursuit. *"A pied sans chausses pourchassant sa vie de maison en maison."* — Commines, III, 4 (Littré): *Pour,* prefix in sense of thoroughness and *chasser,* to hunt. p. 276/26.

Cf. "purchase to themselves a good degree."—1 Tim. iii, 13.

"I purchase. I get the propertie or possessyon of a thyng. *Je pourchasse.*"—Pals. 670.

PURGATORY, B 472.

PURUAYDE, *pp.* provided, B 424. See VN-PURUAYED.

PURYFYING, churching of women after childbirth, B.P. 71/31.

PUT, *v. a.* to add, V 129/49. Cf. the phrase "put two and two together."

PYNE, *s.* punishment, pain, torment, B 472, 478.
"þus sal þai dyghe and heuen bliss tyne
And be putted til endeles pyne."
P. C. 2053-4.

— *v. n.* to pine, languish.

— *v. a.* to punish, torture. PYNED, *pp.* tormented (of our Lord's passion), B 217.
' Ki fu de la nette pucelle nee
E pur nus en croix pene."
M. P. 7241-2.

PYNEFUL, *adj.* painful, full of torment, F 214.

PYNSTAL, *s.* the place of execution. A.S. "*Stal, Steal, Stœl.* Stall, place, stead," H.C. 84/43.
" ʒyt aftyrwarde he lete hym slo
Wyþ ful vyle deþ and pynyng wo."
H. S. 9911-12.
" Si cruelment en croiz penez."
M. P. 7220.

PYTE, pity, B 77, 585.

QUART, *s.* good heart, well-being, B.P. 69/26, 70/6.
— *adj.* hearty, safe, prosperous. *Note,* p. 341.

QUENE, *s.* queen, B 364.

QUOD, *pret.* quoth, said; *cwæð,* *pret. of cweðan.*

QWEN, *adv.* when, H.C. 86/57.

QWHEN, *s.* queen, H.C. 82/11. [Otr. "Where" for Quire, A.D. 1519, *York Fabric Rolls,* 267.]

QWYK, *adj.* quick, alive, B 231.

RACE, *v. a.* to pull, to tear, V 137/ 317.
— *v. n.* to tear, V 137/316. See *Note,* p. 397.

RADDE, *pret. of* REDE, to read, V 136/302.

RADLI, *adj.* readily, vehemently, V 137/315.

RANSAKE, *v. a.* to make a thorough search. Icel. *rann-saka,* properly, to search a house, *rann,* house, C-V 483; V 124/7.
" Seli þat ransakes witnes hisse." *Beati qui scrutantur testimonia ejus.*—Ps. (119) cxviii, 2.

RATHE, early. A.S. *rhæð.*
" þou languissed for desyr of þi raþer fortune."—Chaucer, *Boethius,* 39/ 735.

RAUHTE, *perf. of* RECHE, to reach, lay hold of, lay violent hands on, V 138/348. See *Note,* p. 379.
" þe wilk reches fra þe begynnyng
Of mans lyfe until þe endyng."
P. C. 553-4.
"Ful semely aftur hire mete sche raught."—C. T. 136.
"þat what rink (*warrior*) so he rauʒt · he ros neuer after."
W. of P. 1193.
" And he raht til her at the laste
And droh the serge, and scho held fast."—E. M. H. 162.

RECHELESLY, *adv.* carelessly, negligently. A.S. *reccleas, rece,* to reck, take care for, P 128/8.
"Yhit sons and doghters þat unchastyd war
Sal accuse þair fadirs and modirs þar,
Forþi þait þai war rekles and slawe
To chasty þem and hald þem in awe."
P. C. 5544-7.

RECORDE, *v. a.* to con, get off by heart, F 346. O.F. *recorder*

RED, to advise, V 135/272. See REDE.

REDE, *v. a.* to read, to read without (*singing*) note, B 153 165 439; V 136/301.

— *absolutely*, of officiating clergy, B.P. 69/4, 75/26.

— to advise, B 245, 416; V 136/ 275; L 150/87, 439, "I rede þou rede."

REDER, *s.* reader, *lector*, B 163.

REDY, *adj.* ready, B 311, 352, 552.

REFRAYNINGE, restraining, B.P. 76/9.

REHERCE, *v. a.* to repeat, B 152, 193.

REISE, *v. a.* to raise, of the elevation, V 144/581.

"Ne Iesu was nat þe oble þat reysede was at the sacre." H. S. 339/10006/7.

"Quant le prestre en mains le teneit E al people mustreit Ceo qe il a la messe sacreit." M. P. 7272-4.

RELIGYUS, *s.* a man or woman bound by a private rule, B* 19. *Note*, p. 169. See under PARISCHYNS.

RELYGION, RELYGYON, *s.* the rule of an order or community, B.P. 68/18, 19; 75/18. See RELIGYUS.

RELYGIOUS, *adj.* according to the religion, religious, B.P. 75/19.

REM, *s.* realm B.P. 69/14. See REUME.

REMEMBER, *v. a.* to recal to mind, to put on record, p. 369/20.

REMOW, to remove, B 301.

"I am remewed fro þe citee." Chauc. *Boethius*, 19/441.

RESAYUE, *v. a.* to receive, B 287. RESCEYF, O 133. RESCEYUE, P 122/7. RESAYUED, *pp.* B 340. RESCEYVED, O 159.

RESCEYUYNGE, *s.* receiving (*of the sacrament*), P 122/2, 123/11.

RESOUN, *for* orison, B 286.

REST, B 551, of eternal rest, B 296.

RESTIT, *pret. Query*, rested, arrested, stayed, *or* raised, ele-

vated? O.F. *arrester*, Ital. *arrestare*, L 150/73. See REISE.

RESTRENING, restraining, B.P. 69/ 15. See REFRAYNINGE.

REUERENCE, reverence, B 402.

REUEST, *pp.* F 39. See REUYSHT.

REULE, to rule, B 277, 367.

REUME, *s.* realm, B.P. 64/18.

REUYSHT, *pp.* vested, O.F. *revestut*, *pp. of revestir*, of the putting on of ecclesiastical vestments by one already vested in his common clothes, whence also *revestry* for *vestry*, B 34.

REWE, to rue, to make to rue, to grieve, to be sorry for, to take pity, B 359; V 129/54, 136/280; p. 393/33.

"Alle daie he rewes," *tota die miseretur*, "is merciful."—Ps. (37) xxxvi, 26.

"Drihhtinn ræw off mann." *Orm.* 14326.

"Moysæs ræw off þatt follk." *Orm.* 14782.

See RUE UPON.

REWERENCE, *s.* reverence, L 151/ 100.

RE-WESSHUT, E 34. See REUYSHT. *Note*, p. 185.

REYGNE, realm, B.P. 74/11, 74/14. See REM, REUME, ROYALME.

RIBRUSCH, rubric, F 345. See *note*, p. 318.

RICHE, *adj.* rich, B 372.

RIGHT, *adj. of the right side*, B 227.

— *of sound mind*, B 343.

— *adv.* B 34, 276. See *note*, p. 257. RIGHT SO, B 253, 503. RIGHT SONE, B 607.

RIGHTS, taking, of receiving the holy communion, p. 239(4).

RIGHTWIS, *adj.* righteous, B 599.

RIGHTWISNESSE, righteousness, righteous judgment, B 367.

RINSYNGE, *s.* the ceremony of rinsing the chalice, the ablution, B 571. *Note*, p. 301-6.

ROBRIK, ROBRYK, rubric, B 57; B 624. See RIBRUSCH.

Rod, *s.* rood, H.C. 86/61.

Rode, *s.* rood, cross, but differing
in its use from that of "cross"
in this, that cross is used both
of the material and a transient
cross; whereas rood is used of a
material cross, or with reference
to the Cross of Calvary, "tacn
pære halgan rode," B 349, 434;
H.C. 84/47; "done on rode," B
408.

— *s.* rod, wand of office, p. 168.

Rogge, *v. a.* to lay violent hands
on, to pull at, to tug. Cf. Icel.
róg, strife, warfare, V 137/315.
Wild beasts " worow men belyve,
And rogg þam in sonder and ryve."
                        P. C. 1229-30.
See Rauhte, and cf. Icel. *rögg*,
and the phrase "synd rögg af
ser," C-V 507.

Roode, cross (of Calvary), V 147/
677. See Rode.

Roos, *s.* praise, boast, V 141/468.
Icel. *hrós.*
" Ne be nat proude þoghe þou weel dows
Yn þyn herte to make a rous."
                        H. S. 5159-60,
where glossed "boste."

Ros, *pret.* B 410. See Ryse.
"All idell ȝellp *and* idell ros."
                        Orm. 4910.

Royalme, realm, B.P. 75/8. See
Reyne.

Rue upon, to take pity on, P 126/
11. See Rew.

Ryde, *v. n.* to ride, contrasted
with to go (*on foot*), B 592; L
152/133. See Go.

Ryme, to compose in metre, V
145/624.

Ryng, to ring, B 401.

Rynsande, *part. pres.* rinsing, B
570.

Ryse, to rise, B 61.

-s, 1 *sing.*, V 137/177.
-s, 2 *sing.*, B 139, 245, 393, 413, 443,
448; V 131/104. See *Note*, p. 399.
-s, *plural of verbs*, B 16, 47, 105, 116.
Sackles, without cause, guiltless,
H.C. 82/15. See Sake.

Sacrament, generally of the
whole office of mass, B 16, 99.

— the sacrament of the altar, L.
153/168.

— consecrated host, B 568.

— also used particularly of the
consecration as distinguished
from the sacrifice or oblation of
the unconsecrated gifts, B 417.

— of the canon, p. 273(1).

— to receive, P 122/3.

— to minister (*administer*), P 123/
21, 29. See Parischyns.

Sacre, to consecrate, p. 121/6. *Note*,
p. 268.

Sacrifice, B 288*, where used of
the offering of the unconsecrated
gifts. See *Note*, p. 268.

Sacrynge, consecration, C 219.
" A prest sacriþ Goddis body and
maketh breed and wyn turne into
Cristis flesch and his blood bi vertue of
his ordre and Goddis wordis."—Wyc-
lif, *Works*, Arnold, III. 285.
" Of ancient times all the bishops of
Scotland were sacred, and confirmed
by the Archbishop of York."—4 *Inst.*
(Coke), 346.

Sadli, *adv.* gravely, soberly, H.C.
86/71.
" But teche hem alle to leue sadde."
                        Myrc, 260 (of "*solid belief*").

Saide, *pp.* said, B 600.

Saie, *v. a.* to say, to say aloud
(the creed, pater-noster, agnus),
B 197, 198, 484, 508. *Note*, p.
171.

Saies, 3 *sing.* says, B 27. Saith,
p. 315(1).

Sake, cause (in the cause of, be-
cause of), B 456. A.S. *sacu*,
trial, cause, sake; Icel. *söc*, gen.
sakar, a charge, the crime (*crimen*),
M.G. *sakjo* (μάχη, 2 Tim. ii, 23).
" In her senvolle sake."
                        Shoreham, 66/4.
" Withouten skil sake or any" (*sine
causa*).—Ps. iii, 8.
" Sle þu man wiþ-outen sake."
                        C. M. 6833.
See Sackless.

Sakering, *s.* consecration, V 143/

558, where used for the whole Canon Missæ.

SAKRING, *s.* consecration, B 292, 400.

— elevation, B 292. See *Note*, p. 268.

"Sacryng or levation."—Becon, Display, *Works*, III, 276.

SALDE, *pp.* sold, B 407.

SALL, shall, H.C. 82/2. SALLE, C 61. See SHAL, SCHAL.

SANCTUS, B 308, 326; C 147; E 305, 323.

SARY, *adj.* sorry, B.P. 65/20.

SAT *for* SUTH, *conj.* since, F 267.

SAUE, *adj.* safe, B 449.

— *v. a.* to save, B. 218.

SAUMPLE, *s.* example, the "narratio," or forbesne of Old English sermons and tales, B 23.

SAUȝ, 3 *sing. perf.* saw, V 136/308. See SEȝE.

SAY, *perf. of* SEE, *v. a.* saw, V 137/336.

"And whan þou say hem sette in þe court."—Chauc. *Boet.* 37/958.

"Of saul herde þei wel þe steuen But nouȝt þei say þat coom fro heuen." C. M. 19643-4.

"Nay I say him nat here wirche Syn Satirday."—C. T. 3664.

"His Godhed may not be sayne With no fleschle eyne." Audelay, p. 45.

SAY, *v. a.* to say, B 222, 281; V 129/31, 132/160. See SAIE, SAYE, SAIDE, SEI, SEY, SEþ.

SAY OR SING, B 27. *Note*, p. 171.

SAYANDE, B 298, 481.

SAYDE, *perf. of* SAY, B 200, 438.

SAYE, B 177, 245, 261; C 271. See SAY.

SAYES, 2 *sing.* sayest, B 286.

— 3 *sing.* or *plur.* B 116. See *Note*, p. 196.

SAYING, *s.* that which is said, B 582.

SAYN, *v. a.* to sign (with the sign of the cross), V 143/541. *Note*, p. 207. SAYNANDE, *part. pres.* B 399.

SAYNT, saint, B 74; B.P. 78/17, 18.

SCHELD, *v. a.* to shield, H.C. 84/52. Cf. B.P. 62/5. See SHIELD.

SCHENDE, *v. a.* to put to shame, disgrace, ruin, A.S. *scendan*, L 154/199. See SENCHYP.

"Be I not schent withouten ende" (*confundar in eternum*).—*Te Deum*, Maskell, M. R. II, 14.

SCHEU, *v. a.* to show, B.P. 64/14.

SCHEWE, *v. a.* to eschew, C 236.

SCHOP, *perf.* created, V 135/250.

"The king that al this world scheop." O. & N. 79/25.

See SHOOPE.

SCHRIFT-SILVER, the money paid to the schrift-father or confessor, p. 241, *n.* 8. See p. 239(4).

SCHRIFTE, *s.* confession, P 124/10. See SHRIFT.

SCHRIUE, *used absolutely*, to confess, V 135/243.

— OF, to rid, clear (by confession), V 133/190, 134/227. See *Note*, p. 350-1.

SCLAUNDER, B 377, "*scandalum*," shame, evil fame, matter of reproach.

"No sclaunder is to hem."—Ps. (119) cxviii, 165. *Prymer*, Maskell, M. R. II, 170. *Non est in illis scandalum.*

"In þam in na shame." E. E. *Psalter*, S. S.

"If any . . . repreve another of her contre, or kynrede, or of any other sclaunderouse fortune or chaunce fallen at any time."—*Addition to Rules, Syon*, Aungier, 259.

SCOURGED, *pp.* B 408.

SCYL, *s.* reason, p. 368/13, 371/24. See SKILL.

SE, *v. a.* to see, B 178, 292.

— *pp.* seen, V 131/111, 115.

SECRE, the *secreta*, or prayer *super-oblata*, V 143/545. See *Note*, p. 266.

SECUNDE, *adj.* second, B 536.

SEDE, *s.* seed, offspring, B 232.

"Abrahame and his sæde."

"To Abraham and his seed." St. Luke, i, 55.

SEE, *s.* sea, B 378.

SEES, 1 *sing. northern,* I see, V 133/177.

SEI, *v. a.* to say, V 144/596. SEID, SEIDE, V 142/52, 146/657. SEI-ENDE, F 262. See SEY.

SEIDEN, 3 *pl. perf.* said, V 138/378.

SEIþ, SEITH, 3 *sing.* saith, F 321; V 141/478. See SEþ, *Note,* p. 314.

SEIZ, 3 *sing.* sees, V 137/323.

SEKE, *adj.* sick, B 378.

SEKIRLY, surely, securely, C 254, where probably by mistake.
"For þai salle be þare syker and cer-taine."—P. C. 8559.

SELLE, L 151/100, perhaps for ·FELLE. See FALL.

SELUE, *adj.* same, B 563.

— self, B 142, 557, 562.

SEN, since, C 160. See SYN, also SYTH, SETTHE, SITHEN, &c.
"For sen Crist, als I sayd befor, had dred
Of þe ded, thurg kynd of his manhede."
P. C. 2212-3.

SENCHYP, disgrace, punishment, from SCHENDE (*which see*), rather than from *senchen* (A.S. *sencan*), to make to sink, B.P. 69/14.
"Our shenshyp and oure shame."·
H. S. 256/8251.
"For þai suld have þan þe mare shen-shepe,
· And þe mare sorow."—P. C. 381-2.
"Til bair grete shenshepe and repruve."
P. C. 6221.
"And yhit seven schendsschepes wille I neven
þat er even contrary tylle þa seven"
(*blisses*).—P. C. 8181-2.
"Ffor þai salle on nathyng have me-neyng,
Bot anely on þair awen wicked lyfyng,
And on þair sorow with-outen eude
And on þair wrechedness þat salle þam schende."—P. C. 8371-4.

SENDE, to send, B 260, 276. SENT, B 343.

SEO, 2 *pl.* ye see, V 136/285.

SERE, several, separate, B 70, 345, 420, 469; E 70; C 42; V 128/12, 132/161; p. 173/6, 10; p. 276. See *Notes,* p. 188, 275.

SERGE, *s.* (*cierge*), large wax candle, to be set on pricks, B.P. 71/26.
"ilk serge contenand two pouds of wax."—Will of Richard Shirburn, 1436; *Test. Ebor.* II, 75.

SERLY, *adv.* diversely, B 465. See SERE.

SERMON, *s.* a discourse not delivered in church, p. 362/14.

— (SARMON), a sermon, a homily, p. 365(2).

SERUANDES, servants, B 554.

SERUE, to serve, B 543.

SERUICE, SERUYCE, *s.* service, B 287, applied to the whole office of mass.
"Ad missam, de quocunque fiat ser-vitium."—*Miss. Sar.* 386.

— of life-long obedience to God, B 387.

— of the priest's part in worship, B 580; C 346; B 580.

— of the layman's part in worship, V 129/23.

SERWE, *s.* sorrow, V 137/326, 337.

SERYS, p. 273/24. See SIRES.

SES, 3 *sing. of* SESE, C 280; F 256.

SESE, *v. n.* to cease, V 142/518. See CESE.

— *v. a.* to seize, yield the posses-sion of, commend, L 148/15.
"I put in possession, *Je saisis,*"
Pals. 673.
"Sesyn or ȝeue sesyn in lond or oþer godys, *Sesino.*"—P. P. 454.

— 2 *sing. of* SEE, thou soest, B 54.

SESONABLE, seasonable, B 390.

SEST, *pp.* ended, B 602. See SESE.

SET, *v. a.* to insert, B 425.

— yet, L 149/32.

SEþ, 3 *sing.* saith, V 143/548. See SEIþ.

SETHEN, afterwards, then, C 144. See SITHEN.

SEþþE, then, afterwards, V 134/217, 237, 143/549, 144/563, 567.

SETTE, to set (of kneeling on the knees), F 10; p. 162.
"Sytteþ dowyn vpp on oure knees."
H. S. 951.

SETTE, to sit (on seat), L 151/96.

SETTHE, since, F 138.

SETTIS, 3 *sing.* he sets, B 23.

SEUER, *v. n.* to separate, part company, B 396.

SEWE, to make suit for, L 150/87.

SEY, to say, F 252; F 354, 356; V 129/23. See SEI. SEYE, P 124/35, 126/6, 127/10; V 129/23. See SEÞ. I-SEID, *pp.*, V 141/476. SEID, *perf.*, V 142/521. *Note*, p. 314-15.

SEYINGE, the saying, p. 120/15.

SEYS, 2 *sing.* seest, C 213.

SEӡE, 1 *sing. perf.* I saw, V 138/356.

SHAD, *perf.* shed, B 409.

SHAL, shall, B 357, 448.

— 2 *sing.* shalt, B 402, 453.

SHAME, *s.*, B 294.

SHAPPER, shaper, Creator, p. 258. Icel. *Skapari*, used only of the Creator, C-V 538. See SHOOPE.

SHEW, *v. a.* "*anuncio,*" to make known, shew forth, p. 439/17.

Cf. A.V. "Ye do shew the Lord's death till he come."—1 Cor. xi, 26.

SHILD, to shield, protect, B 505.

"Fra whilk payne and sorow God us shilde."—P. C. 9471.

See SCHELD.

SHOOPE, *perf. of* SHAPE, to shape, form, create, A.S. *scyppan, scóp;* Icel. *Skapa, skóp;* M.G. *ga-skapjan, gaskop* (Marc, xiii, 19); Germ. *schaffen, schuf,* L 148/1. See SHAPPER, SCHOP.

"He þatt all þiss weorelld shop."
Orm. 3678.

SHRIFT, SHRYFT, *s.* absolution or confession, B 597; P. 121/10.

SHRYUE, *v. a.* to confess sin with an accusative of the person opening his sin, the persons to whom confession is made in the dative, and the sin governed by of, as, the priest shrives him of his sins to all the folk. See B 43-4.

"And ga to þe prest hym to shrife
And tak his penaunce in his life."
P. C. 3508-9.

SHRYUE, to absolve of sin (of the priest), B 35.

"þe preost me walde eskien on esterdai hwa me scriue."—O. E. H. p. 25.

SHRYVEN, *pp.* absolved upon confession. See SCHRIUE and *Note*, p. 350-1.

SHULD, should, B 622. SHULDE, B 21, 244.

SIB, *adj.* related, of natural or spiritual relationship (godsybbas, B.P. 62/13), B 108.

SIBMEN, relations, kinsmen, B 368, 469, 553.

SIGGE, to speak, V 138/356, 139/383.

SIKIRLY, surely, securely, C 297. See SEKIRLY, SYKERLY.

SING, *v. a.* B 435. See SAY.

SIRES, sirs, V 135/257. Cf. "Sirs," Acts xxvii, 10, 21, 25.

SISTERS, B 469.

SITE, *v. n.* to sit, V 137/336. SITEN, *perf.* V 138/378

SITHE, F 322. See SITHEN.

SITHEN, since then, afterwards, B 159, 264, 307, 408, 490.

SITT, *v. n.* to sit, B 593. See SETTE.

— *v. n.* to abide, B 415.

SKILL, *s.* skill, discernment, reason, a reason, cause. A.S. *scylan,* to divide, separate; Icel. *skilja,* to cut, part. "The original sense, viz. *to cut,* Lat. *secare,* appears in Gothic *skilja,* a butcher," C-V 546.—B 626; C 221; V 139/405; p. 299. See *Note*, p. 214.

SKILWISE, *adj.* reasonable, p. 118/9.

SMALLE, *adj.* small, B 372.

SO, B 235, 558.

SOCOURE, *s.* succour, B 102, 260.

SODAN, *a.* sudden, B 594.

SOLEMPNE, solemn, B 288.

SOM, some, B 197.

SOM-WHERE, somewhere, B 195.

SONDRY, sundry, B 420.

SONE, the sun, H.C. 86/57.

— *s.* son, H.C. 84/22.

— soon, B 84, 150, 196, 258, 577.

SOTHE, truth, B 222.

SOTHEN, sudden, L 151/125.

SOTHFAST, true, faithful, B 180.

SOUERANLY, *adv.* supremely, above all things, B 527, 530. SOUE-RENLY, B 523.

SOUERAYNE, *s.* supreme lord, B 102.

SOUEREYNE, *adj.* sovereign, superior, supreme, of dominion, P 125/15.

— supremely salutary, P 123/14, 126/13.

-SOUHT, I-, sought, V 132/148.

SOUL, B 105, 221. SOULES, B 112, 295, 456.

SOULDE, should, C 11, 21.

SOUL-HELE, soul's health, B 105.

SOUTH AUTER NOKE, the south or epistle end, B 579. *Note,* p. 205-6.

SPACE, of time, B 188.

— of place, B 301.

SPECIALY, B 374.

SPED, *pp.* helped forward, prospered, B.P. 70/12, 76/30.

SPEDE, *v. n.* to speed, to succeed, B 62, 158.

SPEKE, to speak, B 20; C 20.

SPEKING, *s.* speaking, B 277.

SPELLE, to tell, to teach, V 142/508.

SPENDE, *v. a.* to spend (of time), B 622.

SPICERIE, fragrant spices, H.C. 86/70.

"Spyce, *espices.* a kynde, *espece.*"—Pals. Lat. *species.* Cf. Fr. *épicier,* grocer. Ital. *speziale,* druggist.

SPILLE, to spoil, destroy, cast away, kill, B 545.

"Welthes (*man's*) lif trobles and droves And the saul of man may lightly spille."
P. C. 1319-20.

SPILT, 2 *sing. perf.* spilledst, B 433.

SPIRITIS, spirits, B 98.

STANDANDE, *part. pres.* standing, B 261.

STANDE, to stand, B 84, 507, 593.

— UP, B 303. See STONDE.

STATE, condition, B 361.

— "degre," B 332.

— rank, B 366.

STAWNCE, L 152/151; *Query,* a stop, a pause? Cf. F, *stance;* Ital. *stanza,* a stop, halt, from Latin *stare.* "*La stance* (strophe) *était ainsi dite parce que c'est une sorte d'arrêt,*" Littré.

STEDE, place. See *Note,* p. 288; B 454, 596.

"To I find stete to Laverd."
"Donec inveniam locum domino."
Ps. (131) cxxxii, 4.

STEERE, *v. a.* to stir, 123/14.

STEGH, *pf.* went up, A.S. *stigan. Note,* p. 224; B 225.

STERVE, *v. n.* to die. "Steruyn *idem quod* Deyyn," PP. 474.—p. 392/31. Cf. Germ. *sterben.*

STERYNGE, *s.* stirring, 125/35.

STEUEN, *s.* voice, *stefen,* O.G. *stæfn* (stemn) B 265, 312. STEUENEN, H.C 82/10. STEVEN, C 271 *passim.*

STIFFELOKER, *adv. compar.* more stiffly, firmly, P 123/34.

STILLE, silent, B 52, 265, 312.

— motionless, B 487, 507.

STONDE, *v. n.* to stand, B 39, 445.

STONEY, *v. a.* to bewilder as by a flash of lightning, to stun, V 138/354. O.F. *estonner (étonner).* Lat. *attono.* L.L. *extono.*

Cf. A.V. "The king was astonied."— Dan. iii, 24.

STORNE, probably for TORNE, to turn, 24/A(1).

STRETES, streets, B.P. 65/12.

STRYUE, strife, B 377.

STUNT, *v. n.* to stint, stop, stop short, stand still, V 138/354.

"Heo ne stunteþ neuere."
C. L. 894.

STUR, *v. a.* to stir, disturb, V 140/427.

SUBGETTES, SUBGETS, *s.* Persons committed to the charge of a spiritual pastor, B.P. 75/22, 23, 24, 75/24.

SUCCHE, such, F 191, 203. See SWILK.

SUE, to follow, to ensue.

SUGETE, *s.* feudal or other subordinate, an inferior, B 554.

"Selle no parte of thyne heritage vnto thy bettyr, but for the lesse pryce selle yt to thy subiecte."—*Proverbys, Poems,* Furnivall, E. E. T. S. 1866, p. 32.

SUGETTES, of those placed under pastoral teaching, B.P. 69/2.

SULOKER, *adv. compar.* (?) surloker, more surely, P 124/21.

SUNNE, *s.* sin, V 129/31, 130/70. See SYNNE, V 129/38.

SUSTEND, *pp.* sustained, B.P. 65/5.

SWA, so, C 329.

"And þarfor ligges þou sorowand swa Bot say to me and I sall ga."
H. R. 63/29-30.

SWETE, *adj.* sweet, B 325, 449; F 191.

— *as substantive,* B 169.

SWILK, SWILKE (*northern*), such, B 394, 418, 457, 566; C 127, 214.

SWYNK, to work, labour, V 131/119.

SWYTHE, quickly, forthwith, F 124.
"This mai ran tille hir moder swithe."
E. M. H. 39.
"Yhouthede passes swithe."
P. C. 5713.

SYDE, *s.* side, B 227.

SYKERLY, surely, securely, B 526. See SIKERLY.

SYLE, to strain, p. 307(1).

SYN, since, B 171, 341. See SEN.

SYNFUL, sinful, B 462.

SYNGYNGE, *s.* singing, B 9.

SYNN, SYNNE, *s.* sin, B 46, 55; V 129/38.

SYTH, thereafter, then, E 337. See SEÞÞE.

T. þ.

TAK, *v. a.* to show, B.P. 64/14. *Note,* p. 331.

TAKE, to give, B 21, 175, 305.
"And till ȝoure moder he toke þat tide Bath þe west and þe south syde."
Holy Rood, Morris, 63/57-8.
"He took Scrapion's lad the sacrament

in his hand." 'ἐπέδωκεν τῷ παιδαρίω.—*Apology Private Mass,* 1562, printed P. S. 1850, p. 28.

"Þo ten pownd y take þe here."
H. S. 5761.

TAKE, to take, B 138, 419.

— receive (*of sacrament*), p. 118/11, 239(4).
"un-worthile haue i husel tane."
C. M. 1555/28303.

TAKEN, *pp.* H.C. 82/13. See TAN.

TALDE, *pp.* told, C 9.

TALE, *s.* the act of telling or counting, that which is told, the number, a story, F 170. A.S. tellan, *numerare.* "Tale of mi daies," "*numerus dierum,*" Ps. (39) xxxviii, 5. Cf. A.V. "I may tell all my bones," Ps. xxii, 17. "Tale of bricks," Ex. v, 8.
"swa many sternes smale, þat na man may þam telle bi tale."
P. C. 7705-6.

See *Note,* p. 279.

TAN, TANE, *pp.* taken, B.P. 68/22; H.C. 86/65; V 128/7.

TARYINGE, tarrying, B 334, 582.

TECHER, spiritual master, B.P. 69/1.

TELLE, to tell, B 8, 13, 25; C 13. TOLDE (*perfect*), B 9. TALDE, C 9. See TALE.

TEMPTACIONS, B 96; B 488.

TENANDES, tenants, B 369.

TENDES, tithes (tenths), B.P. 64/24, 69/29, 78/25. See TIGEÐINGE, 62/16.
"Abram gaf him ðe tigðe del."
G. and E. 895.

TENE, injury, V 131/121. A.S. teona.
"Ne do ic þe nænne teonan." "*I do thee no wrong.*"—St. Matt. xx, 13.
"To wrekenn hire tene" (to avenge her vexation).—*Orm.* 19900.

TENT, heed, attention, intention, B 21, 175; V 130/73, 137/341, 139/384. See ENTENT.
"And men þarto toke mekill entent."
H. R. 82/708.
"Now to the helme will I hent And to my ship tent."
Towneley, 31.

TEXT, the words of the spoken or written original as distinguished from comment, paraphrase, or translation, V 145/627; p. 366/1, 370/16.

ÞAI, *nom.* they, B 11, 48, 51.

ÞAIRE, *pron. poss.* their, B 12, &c.

ÞAM, *dative,* to them, C 255.

ÞAME, THAME, *dat.* to them, C 14, 265.

— *acc.* C 265, 266.

THAN, ÞAN, then, B 330; C 2, 30, 143, 219, 283; D 37/(3).

— than, *in comparisons,* C 158. See THEN.

THANK, THANKE, ÞANK, *v. a.* to thank, B 127; C 361, 362. THANKED, 357, 358, 359. See THONK.

THANNE, then, F 195.

ÞARE, there, of place, B 43. See ÞERE.

ÞAT, *demons.,* B 8, 147.

— *conj.* that, B 22, 395.

— *relative sing.* that, who, whom, which, B 105, 247, 382, 502; C 4, 75, 109, 202.

— *for* then, C 125.

ÞATE, *rel. accus.* whom, B 4, 93, 107, 465.

ÞAUH, though, V 135/261.

ÞAY, THAY, *nom.* they, C 11, 331; F 151.

ÞE, THE, *definite article,* C.E. and F *passim.* See Þo.

— THE, *pron. pers.* thee, B 275, 276; F 48. See ÞU, ÞOU.

— *pron. poss.* C 69, 71. See ÞI, ÞY. *Note,* p. 195.

THE, *pron. rel.* who, F 119. See *Note,* p. 269.

ÞEI, they, V 141/475*.

ÞEIʒ, though, V 132/154.

ÞEN, therefore, *ergo,* B 628.

— then (of time), *tunc,* B 35, 265, 269, 281, 306, 400.

— when, *quum,* B 279.

— than, *quam,* B 146, 339, 595; V 147/671.

ÞENK, to think, B 184, 269, 361.

-ÞENK, ME-, methinks, B 164. See THYNKE, THOUGHT.

ÞENNE, then, P 123/1. See ÞEN.

ÞER, there, *before verb substantive,* B 379; V 141/477; V 146/665.

— *adv.* where, V 140/439, 446.

ÞER-BY, thereby, together with, B 493.

ÞERE, there, of place, B 41 (cf. "ÞARE," B 43), 514.

— *pron. poss.* their, C 78, 185, 265, 266. See HORE.

ÞERETO, ÞERTO, thereto, B 23, 292, 445; C 23; F 3.

ÞERFOR, ÞERFORE, for (*instead of*) that, F 64; C 36.

ÞERFORE, therefore, for reason of this, B 53, 540. See FORÞI.

ÞER-WITH, therewith, B 423.

ÞIES, *pl.* these, them, F 151, 177. See ÞIS.

ÞESTERNES, darkness, V 142/503.

"And heffness lihht bishineþþ all
    Mannkinne þessterrnesse."
                 Orm. 18851-2.

ÞEÞIN, thence, Icel. *þaðan* or *þeðan,* B 229.

"For swa pured and fyned never gold was
   Als þai sal be, ar þai þeþen pas."
                P. C. 2720-1.

ÞI, *pron. poss.* (*before consonant*), B 271, 454, 455, 458. ÞIN, *before vowel or aspirate,* B 101, 204, 380. ÞINE, *acc.* B 198.

ÞING, *sing.* thing, B 1. ÞINGE (? *pl.*), B 505.

ÞIR, ÞIRRE, they, of them, to them, them. See *Note,* p. 250; C 112; B 250.

ÞIS, THIS, *sing.* this, B 2, 16 *passim;* C 173.

ÞIS, THIS, *pl.* these, them, C 200; V 136/305. See ÞIES.

Þo, *def. art.* (Midland), the, B 1. *Note,* p. 157.

ÞOF, though (*still pronounced* thöf *in the East Riding*), B 426.

THOGHT, ÞOGHT, *s.* thought, B 71, 97, 193; C 65.

THOLE, to suffer, to make to suffer, F 214; p. 276/4. Þolede, p. 276.

Þonk, Þonke, Thonk, *v. a.* to thank, B 330, 338, 355, 613, 614. Þonked, 610, 611, 612. See Thank.

Þoo, these, those, B 170.

"I sal blis to þoo þat blissen þe." (Wyclif) Gen. xii, 3.

Thorght, *for* through the, B 148.

Þou, B 244, 448. See "Thu."

Thoume, thumb, B 158.

Þow, thou, B 453. See Þou, Thu.

Thre, three, B 248, 251.

Threhed, Trinity, p. 218.

Thryd, Thrid, third, B 224, 546.

Thryes, thrice, C 280. Thryese, B 308.

Thu, thou, F 76, 85, 92, 97, 107, 127, 203. Þu, F 191.

Thurgh, through, B 213, 226.

Þus, thus, B 20, 327.

Thyng, B 256. See Thing.

Thynke, to think, C 180. See Thenk.

Til, *conj.* until, B 153, 263.

— *prep.* to, B 43, 380, 389, 394, 397, 472, 563, 580; B.P. 64/24.

— *of motion,* to, B 225, 302. See To, In-til.

Tilmen, tillers of the ground, husbandmen, B 370.

"Kaym a tylman." *Cant. de Creatione*, 478.

Tille, *prep.* to, B 594.

-Tille, Þere-, thereto, C 92.

Titter, *compar. of* Tite, soon, Icel. *titt*, neut. of *tiðr*, frequently used adverbially = at once, with all speed, "sooner" is substituted for it, P.P. 76/31; B.P. 70/12.

"Alle men sal þan tite upryse." P. C. 4979.

"Wharfor it seemes þat mes syngyng May titest þe saul out of payn bryng þat passes hethin in charite." P. C. 3702-4.

To, *prep.* to, B 107, 112, 403, &c.; C 200.

To, unto, B 387; P 124/27.

— according to, in proportion to, B 527, 533.

— for, B.P. 71/17; to goddes louing, B 255; to þi louing, B 380; "to þi worship," V 146/539; V 146/649. Cf. our "to thy honour and glory."

— *before infinitive,* B 386, 401, 527, &c.

— *conj.* until, B 194, 302, 399; C 91.

— *intensive prefix.* See To-rente.

— *adv.* too.

Togge, *v. a.* to tug, V 137/314.

Tok, *perf. of* take, gave, paid, V 137/341. See Take.

— received, V 143/527.

Torche, *s.* torch, Lat. *intorticium*, candles made of wax and rosin and twisted together, B.P. 71/26; B.P. 76/19.

Anthony St Quintin of Harpham, in the East Riding, A.D. 1443-4, leaves 50 pounds of wax and rosyn for four torches to be burnt about his body on the day of his burial.—*Test Ebor.* II, 95. In the churchwardens' accounts of Yatton, Somerset, I find charged in 1467, "Item, payd for wex & rosyn. xxs."

At line 1176, *Brun de la Montaigne*, a xiv Century MS. edited for the Société des anciens Textes Francais (1875), by M. P. Meyer, we have "En. iiij. c. torti fu li feus alumés," which points to the Latin derivation (*tortus, pp.* twisted) more directly than the "*torse*" in xiv Cent. examples quoted by Littré.

To-rente, *pp.* rent to pieces, L 151/120.

"To-rendeð þe olde pilche, *renaeth the old cloak.*"—A. R. 362.

Tournour, one who puts in the capitals in the spaces left by the text-writers, often (*see* F 1, p. 287/16) not filled in, p. 401(2).

Towayl, altar-cloth, p. 173; howselling-cloth, p. 297(2).

Towell, a cloth, a table or altar-cloth, as distinct from the corporas, a napkin, a towel. *Note*, p. 332; B.P. 65/4. Edward the Black Prince, by his will A.D. 1370, leaves to our Lady's chapel, Undercroft in Canterbury Cathedral, "deux vetementz sengles, cest assavoir, aube, amyt, chesyble, estole, et fanon avec towaill convenables a chacun des ditz vestementz."— Nichols' *Royal Wills*, p. 71.

Traueling, of women in labour, B.P. 71/32.

Tray, vexation, trouble, sorrow, A.S. *trega*, loss. See *Note*, p. 372; V 131/121.

Tre, Tree, *s.* tree, timber, wood, p. 384.

— of the cross of Calvary, V 141/490, 144/591, 147/479.

Trespas, *v. a.* to trespass against, B 502.

Trespasse, *s.* trespas, transgression, B 476.

Tretys, treatise, V 128/1.

Trouthe, Trouþe, *s.* faith, belief, B 414; V 141/471.
"To helpe oure trouthe thurghe þat þat we see a thyng and trowes anoþer."
—Of the Supper of the Lord, *Mirror of St Edmund, Religious Pieces*, Perry, p. 42.

Trow, to believe, to trust, B 205, 212, 233, 414.

Turne, to turn, B 264, 388, 558. Turnande, *part. pres.* B 87.

Twyese, twice, B 309.

-Tyde, Morne-, morningtide, H.C. 82/13.

Tyllande, tilling, B.P. 70/1. See Tilmen.

Tyme, *s.* theme, subject, P. 124/36.
"Tyme of a sermonde, *thesme*."
Pals. 281.

— *s.* time, B 30.

Vche, each, V 129/30.

Ver, 2 *sing.* were, wast, L 152/130.

Verray, *adj.* very, true, V 131/109.

Vertu, virtue, power, effect, B 6, 9, 570.
"Forthi schaued Crist thar, hou Jowes That wald noht trow on his uertues, Suld ga for thar wantrauth til pine."
E. M. H. 128.
"Not in worde, but in vertue."
(1 Cor. iv, 20) *Myroure*, 67.

Vestment. See Westement, *Note*, p. 166-7, and under Towell.

Vm, *prep.* A.S. *ymb*, about, after, B 624 (governing While).

Vmwhile, sometime, C 369. Cf. Icel. *Um, Umb, prep.* around, during; "*um tima, um stund*, for a while, C-V 649; B 1.

Vncel, unblessed, wicked; A.S. *sel*, blessed, happy; Icel. *sæll*; Germ. *selig.*—V 138/381.

Uncuþ, *pp.* unknown, *hence*, strange.

Vnderfange, *v. a.* to undertake, p. 394/11.

Vnderne, Vndryn, A.S. *Undern*, the third hour, tierce, 9 A.M. V 131/129; p. 373/20.

Undo, *v. a.* to translate, to explain, p. 211/9.

Ungod, *adj.* not good, H.C. 84/49.

Vnkuynde, unnatural, V 134/232, and *Note*, p. 376.

Vn-puruayde, unprovided, B 424.

Vnspede, hindrance, disadvantage, C 88.

Vnstable, B 390.

Vntil, Vntille, *prep.* to, unto, B 121, 169, 471. See Til.

Vp, *adv.* up, from the posture of kneeling, B 303.

Up-haldes, upholds, B.P. 65/2.

Vpon, upon, B 31; B 157. See Open, Opon.

Vp-right, *adj.* upright, erect, B 483.

Vp-standande, *part.* standing up, B 261. See "Stande vp."

Vse, to use, of the priest communicating, V 145/605; of drinking the unconsecrated wine after receiving the host, p. 238/13. See *Note*, p. 380-2.

W for U, C 296, lowe (love), L 150/91, 151/99, 100.
Cf. "I beqwthe my saule to God Almighty."—(A.D. 1444) *Test. Ebor.* II, 106.
— for V. See REWERENCE, REW-ESHUT, WESTEMENT, &c.

WANE, *pret. of* win, won, L 152/150.
"For what þing willam wan a-day wiþ his bowe."—W. of P. 190.

WAR, *adj.* ware, P 123/7; "*cautus*," P.P. 516; A.S. *wær*, ware, wary.
"Wha-swa wille thynk ay on þis manere And be war, and make hym redy here."—P. C. 2674-5.

WARE, 3 *sing.* were, V 130/88.

WARLY, *adv.* warily, P 126/27.

WAS, 2 *sing.* wast, B 247.

WASSHANDE, *part.* washing, B 262.

WASSHING, *s.* washing, B 263.

WATE, *v. a.* to know, C 88.
"*And* Crist wass æþ to witenn þatt Forr Crist wât alle þingess." *Orm.* 19673-4.
"All-if þai wat þat þai sal be safe." P. C. 5372.

WEDERS, *s. pl.* winds, showers, B 390.
"For God ordains here, als es his wille Sere variaunce for certayn skille Of þe tyms and wedirs and sesons In taken of þe worldes condicions." P. C. 1422-5.
"Wedyr, *idem quod* storm, *nimbus pro-cella*."—P. P. 520.
"And wurð ðis weder sone al stille." (*of the plague of hail*, Ex. ix, 22.) G. & E. 3059.
"As wedre vpon erbe" (*as the small rain vpon the tender herb*).—Deut. xxxii, 2.
"To wakan wederez so wylde þe wyndez he callez."—E. E. A. P. 64/948.

WEILLFARE, welfare, B.P. 69/13.

WEL, *adv.* well, B 233, 360. See WELE.

WELCOME, B 181.

WELDING, wielding, ruling, V 139/401.

WELE, *s.* wealth, well-being, B 106; C 74; E 106; where F 30, welthe. Cf. HELE, health.
— *adv.* well, B 305, 365, 338, 527. See WEL.

WELE-WILLANDES, well wishers, B 368.

WELL, a spring (not necessarily with the notion of being sunk), H.C. 86/59.
Cf. "A well of water, springing up." St John, iv, 14.

WENDE, to wend, turn, return. A.S. *wendan*, Icel. *venda*, M.G. vandjan.—B 609; p. 280/11.
"Bot tylle þe blys of heven mon þai wende And have þare þair lyking with-outen ends."—P. C. 7518-19.
— to translate, p. 212/29, 275/21.

WENE, *v. a.* to ween, to think, to hope, V 140/419.

WENYAL, *adj.* venial, L 149/40.

WEOFOD-SCEATTAS, altar (*sheets*) cloths, p. 333, 334.

WEOLE, *s.* well being, well doing, V 134/205.

WERE, *subjunctive*, B 595.
— *s.* war, variance, B 589.
"Engel wirð a-gen him cam Als it were wopnede here, Redi to silden (*shield*) him fro were." G. & E. 1786-8.
"his croun bere Wele, and in pees with-outen were." P. C. 4087-8.
"þarfoe þat tyme was mykyl þro And oft was boþe werre and wo." H. S. 10569-70.

WERK, *s.* work, B 72. WERKES, B 363, 610.

WERLD, world, A.S. *weorold*, Icel. *veröld*, *pl.* WERLES, "werld of werles," H.C. 84/31.
"In werlde of werlde and in ai." "*In æternum et in sæculum sæculi.*" Ps. (9) ix, 6.

WERLDE, world, C 2. See WERLD, WORD.

WESTEMENTE, vestment, especially the chasuble, F. 12, where probably for the complete mass vestment. See *Note*, p. 166, and under TOWELL.

WEUEDE, altar, A.S. *weofod.* "Æt þæs weofodes sidan," Lev. i, 11.
— V 143/537.
"Godes table is þe woyeued."
Ayenbite, 236.
"Mi hende betwix un-derandes wasche I sal;
And um-ga, Laverd, þi weved."
(*Circumibo altare tuum.*)
Ps. (26), xxv, 6.

WHAS, whose, B.P. 72/23.

WHAT-SO, whatsoever, B 444.

WHAT TIME, V 140/452.

WHEN, *of time,* B 27, 29, 33.
— *conditional,* insomuch as, in so far as, B 31.

WHEN-SO, whensoever, B 116.

WHEþER, whether, whichever, B 243.
"And fre wille to chese, als he vouches save,
Gode or ille whether he wil have."
P. C. 92-3.

WHI, *adv.* why, B 24.

WHILE, *s.* while, time, "*momentum,*" P. P. 524.—B 624; C 101, where "Ay whil," *for* a (*ane*) whil, one while, sometime. See *Note*, p. 228; *but* "ay whiles" = always, whilst.
"Ay whiles he es in dedly syn,
His help vailles noght, bot es in vayne."
P. C. 3645-6.

WHILES, WHILS, "the whiles," whilst, B 357, 487; F 12.
"And do here penaunce whilles we lyf may."—P. C. 3930.
"Whilles þe days of þi youthe sal last."
P. C. 5715.

See I-WHILS, UMWHILE.
— at times, sometimes, F 81.

WHILK, WHILKE, which, B 538; C 309; p. 118/4.

WHO, those who, B 491.

WHOSE, whoso, whosoever, V 141/ 466, 144/578.

WHYLS, "I whyls," whilst, B 245. See WHILES.

WHYTHEM, with hem, therewith, L 152/147.

WICKED, *adj.* B 505.

WIDE, *adj.* B 225.

WIGHT, *s.* "*creatura,*" person or thing, p. 240, *n.* 5. A.S. *wiht;* Cœd. *viht;* Ulf. *vaiht, vaihts;* Icel. *vættr.* There is something derogatory in the modern use of *wight,* as of *wicht* in German, but there was nothing of the kind in Early English.
"Who saved Daniel in thorrible cave,
That every wight, sauf he, mayster or knave,
Was with the lioun frete or he asterte
No wight but God, that he bar in his herte."
C. T. 4893-6, and cf. l. 4908, 4921,15598.
"Melusine, the fair swete wyght."
W. of P. 3992.
"If giftts thou receyue of any wyght
well ponder their degree:
A kynde pore mans harty rewarde
is worth the other three."
Babees Book, 102/733-6.

WIL, WILLE, 2 *sing.* to will (*velle*), B 284, 442, 444; L 154/199.

WOLD, WOLDE, wished, B 470.

-WILD, ILLE-, having ill will, malevolent, C 66.

-WILLANDS, WELE-, well wishers, B 368. *Note,* p. 277.

WILLE, *s.* will (*voluntas*), B 122, 189, 360, 499.

WIRCHIP, *v. a.* B.P. 71/18. See WORSHIP.

WIRK, to work, B 360 (wyrke, C 179).

WISDAM, WISDAME, wisdom, B 143, 450.

WISE, mode, manner, B 335.

WISSE, to guide, teach, B 251. *Note,* p. 250.

WIT, WITT, WITTE, wisdom. *Note,* p. 161.—B 12, 343, 450; p. 270.

WITE, blame, B 72. *Note,* p. 189.

WITH, with, against. *Note,* p. 323;

B 140, 145, 273; C. 156; H.C. 62/5; p. 311(3).

WITHOUTEN, *prep.* without, B 114, 240, 582.

— *adj.* outward, B 546. *Note*, p. 299-300.

WITTE. See WIT, wisdom, p. 277/13.

WOD, *adj.* mad, V 137/330.

WOLD, would, B 244, 446.

WOLDE. See WIL.

WON, *s.* wont, accustomed dwelling, V 146/637.

WONAND, *part.* dwelling, B 145.

WONDER THING, miracle, V 138/365.

WONDYS, wounds, H.C. 84/27.

WONE, *v. n.* to dwell, V 143/530.

WONYNGE, *part.* dwelling, altered from "wonand," V 143/562.

WORCHE, *v. a.* to work, F 157. See WIRK, B 189.

WORD, *s.* world, E 513. *Note*, p. 298. See WERLD.

—, WORDE, *s.* word, B 72, 181, 189, 509.

WORDELY, *adj.* worldly, P 125/31. See WORD.

WORDY [? worðy], *adj.* worthy, L 150/71.

WORLD, WORLDE, world, B 137, 396. See WERLD, WORD, WORDELI.

WORSHIP, *s.* honour, B 16, 380.

WORSHIP, *v. a.* (of God), B 125; B 125, 337.

— to shew honour to a church by gifts, B.P. 76/11. WORSHIPPED, B.P. 76/15. See WIRCHIP.

"And worschyp þys stede (*church*) whyl þat we lyue."—H. S. 278/8966.

WORTH, WORTHE, WORþI, WORTHI, *adj.* worthy, precious, B 73, 125, 270; P 124/16, 23. WORTHIEST, B 629.

WORþLI, *adj.* worthy, of worth, V 146/637.

WORTHYEST, B 1. See WORTH.

WOSTIS, 2 *sing.* B 135, 137, thou

worstest. See *Note*, p. 199. Cf. the phonetic spelling: "Item a vestment of black woosted."— Lincolnshire Inventory, A.D. 1440, Peacock's *Church Furniture*, p. 182.

WOUNDES, WOUNDIS, wounds, B 225, 598; B 225.

WRAKE, *s.* vengeance, B 137.

"So cam on werlde wreche and wrake."
          G. and E. 552.

See WREKE.

WRECCHE, wretch, wicked man, P 126/12.

WRECCHIDNESSE, misery, P 123/2.

WRECHED, wretched, B 80.

WREKE, *v. a.* to avenge, take vengeance for, V 139/395.

-WRIT, HOLI-, religious works of authority, not of Holy Scripture alone. *Note*, p. 365; V 130/90.

WROGHT, WROUʒT, *pp.* worked, made, B 206; of the Divine inspiration of the gospel, V 140/432.

WRY, to accuse, "*accuso*," H.C. 84/35.

"With ham bothe i-wreiid was
And in the ditement was i-pilt."
        Political Songs, Wright, 198.

WRYTE, WRYTEN, *pp.* written, B 204*, 246, 282; F 8.

WYLD, *perf. of* WYLL, would, p. 299/23.

WYLL, to will, almost an auxiliary, L 154/199. See WILLE.

WYMMEN, women, B 369.

WYRK, WYRCHE, *v.* to work with head or hand, B 4; C 4. See *Note*, p. 157.

WYSE, *s.* manner, B 583. See WISE.

WYST, 2 *sing. pret.* thou knewest, B 244.

WYTE, to blame, C 44. See WITE.

— *v. a.* to know, p. 119/15.

WYTT, WYTTE, wisdom, E 12; B.P. 74/12.

WYTTE, *v. a.* to bequeath, H.C. 86/55.

"I bewitt my saule to Gode."—Will,
A.D. 1436. *Test. Ebor.* II, 75.
"I Witt to Kirkly kirke in Cleveland my
blew damask goun to make a vestment of."—Will, A.D. 1454, *ib.* 175.

WYTWORD, *s.* a will, testamentary
disposition, p. 309 (4).

YHERE, *s.* year, p. 118/5.
YLLE, *adj.* evil, C 24. See ILLE.
YOVE, *pp.* given, p. 292/4.
— YS, *plural affix. Note,* p. 349(2).
YUEL, *adj.* evil, B 98. See EUIL.
ȜAF, *v. a.* gave, V 136/310.

ȜE, ye, B.P. 64/1, 66/17, &c.
ȜERDE, *s.* rod, wand, p. 350/5.
ȜERNYNGE, yearning, desire, B
258, 529.
ȜET, yet, F 330.
ȜEUE, to give, F 3.
ȜEW, *v. a.* give, F 60, 323. See
GIVE.
-ȜEWNESS, FOR-, forgiveness, F 316.
ȜIT, ȜITTE, yet still, moreover (ἔτι),
further, A.S. *Ȝyt,* B 11, 261; B
411, 607; C 11.
ȜUT, yet, F 149.

INDEX.

TABLE OF ABBREVIATIONS.

A. E. L., Maskell's Ancient Liturgy of the Church of England. Second edition, 1846.
A. L., Ancient Laws and Institutes of England (ed. B. Thorpe), 8vo, 1840.
A. P., Alliterative Poems, E. E. T. S., Morris.
A. R., Ancren Riwle, C. S. Morton.
A. S., Boswell's Anglo-Saxon Dictionary.
Aungier, History of Syon Monastery, by G. J. Aungier.
A. V., Authorized Version of Holy Bible.
Ayenb., Dan Michel's Ayenbite of Inwyt, E. E. T. S., Morris.
B. C. P., Book of Common Prayer, 1662.
Becon, Works, Parker Society, 1844.
Bing., Bingham's Antiquities of the Christian Church, 8vo, 1834.
Bint., Binterim, Denkwürdigkeiten der Christ - Katholischen Kirche. Mainz, 1825—1831.
Bona, Opera Omnia, Antverp., 1694.
Cædmon, von K. W. Bouterwek, 1849.
C. L., Castel off Loue, ed. Weymouth.
C. M., Cursor Mundi, E. E. T. S., Morris.
C. S., Camden Society's Publications.
C. T., Chaucer, Canterbury Tales, ed. Wright.
C-V., Icelandic-English Dictionary, by R. Cleasby and G. Vigfusson, 1874.
Doc. Ann., Cardwell, Documentary Annals, 1844.
Durandi. *See* Rationale.
E. E. H., Early English Homilies, E. E. T. S., Morris.
E. M. H., English Metrical Homilies, small, 1862.
Euchol., Εὐχολόγιον τὸ Μέγα, Venice, 1854.
F. Z., Fasciculi Zizaniorum, Rolls Series, Shirley.
G. & E., Genesis and Exodus, E. E. T. S., Morris.
Gavant., Thesaurus Sacrorum Rituum, Autore B. Gavanto cum additionibus Merati, Venet., 1788.

Gaw., Sir Gawayne and the Green Knight, E. E. T. S., Morris.

Gerbert., Monumenta Veteris Liturgiæ Alemanicæ, Typis San-Blasianis, 1777.

Goar., Εὐχολόγιον sive Rituale Græcum., Paris, 1647.

H. R., Legends of the Holy Rood, E. E. T. S., Morris.

H. & S., Haddan and Stubbs Councils and Ecclesiastical Documents.

H. S., Robert of Brunne's Handlyng Synne, Roxburghe Club, Furnivall.

Howard, Christians of St Thomas and their Liturgies, 1864.

Ib., Ibidem, in the same volume, book or chapter.

Id., Idem, the same work or the same author.

Le Brun., Explicatio Missæ, Latine reddita, Venet., 1770.

Lydg. M. P., Lydgate's Minor Poems, Percy Society, Halliwell.

Lynd., Lyndwood, Provinciale, Oxon, 1679.

M. A., Morte Arthure, E. E. T. S., Perry.

M. C., Manipulus Curatorum, Argentorat., 1487.

M. F., Monumenta Franciscana, Rolls Series, Brewer.

M. G., Skeat, Mæso-Gothic Glossary, 1868.

M. P., Manuel des Pechiez, by William of Waddington, Furnivall. See H. S.

M. R., Maskell, Monumenta Ritualia Ecclesiæ Anglicanæ, 1846-7.

Man. Ebor., Manuale et Processionale Ebor., S. S., Henderson.

Mart., Martene de antiquis Ecclesiæ Ritibus, Antverp., 1763.

Masonry, Constitutions of Masonry, Halliwell, 1844.

Miss. Ebor., Missale ad usum Ebor., S. S., Henderson.

Miss. Hereford., Missale ad usum Herford., Henderson, 1874.

Miss. Moz., Missale dictum Mozarabes, ab Alex. Lesleo, Romæ, 1755.

Miss. Rom., Missale Romanum, corrected by Urban VIII., 1634

Miss. Sar., Missale ad usum Sarum. [Dickinson], Burntisland.

Mus. Ital., Mabillon, Museum Italicum, Paris, 1724.

Myr., Our Ladyes Myroure, E. E. T. S., Blunt.

O. E. H., Old English Homilies, E. E. T. S., Morris.

O. & N., The Owl and the Nightingale, Percy Society, Wright.

Orm., Ormulum, White, 1852.

Pals., L'Eclaircissement de la Langue Française, par Jean Palsgrave, Paris, 1852.

P. B. V., Prayer Book Version of Psalms.

P. P., Promptorium Parvulorum, C. S., Way.

P. S., Parker Society Publications.

Provinc. See Lyndwood.

Ps., Early English Psalter, S. S., Stevenson.

Ps. Where the Vulgate is quoted, the number, according to the Hebrew and A. V., is placed in a parenthesis.

Rationale, Durandi Rationale Divinorum Officiorum, Lugdun., 1538.

Renaudot, Liturgiarum Orientalium Collectio, Paris, 1716.

Sacrament, The Play of the Sacrament, W[hitley] S[tokes], 1862.

Shoreham, The Religious Poems of William de Shoreham, Percy Society, 1849, Wright.

S. S., Surtees Society Publications.

Tet., Neale, Tetralogia Liturgica.

Test. Ebor., Testamenta Eboracensia, S. S., Raine.

T. M., Towneley Mysteries, S. S.

Ulf., Ulfilas, von M. Heyne, 1874.

V., Vulgate Version of Holy Bible.

Voy. Litt., Voyage Litteraire de deux Religieux Benedictins, Paris, 1717-24.

Voy. Liturg., Voyages Liturgiques de France, par le Sieur de Moleon (*Le Brun des Marettes*), Paris, 1718.

W. of P., William of Palerne, E. E. T. S., Skeat.

Wyclif, Works, Ed. Arnold, 1869.

ERRATA.

p. 82, l. 19, *after* þe *insert* a comma.

p. 101, l. 4 from bottom, *for* say his *read* say the

p. 156, l. 7, *for* Havelock *read* Havelok

„ l. 20, *for* 1533 *read* 1553

p. 165, l. 11, *for* side-altar *read* side-altars

p. 168, l. 11, *for* MS. 9 *read* MS. 17

p. 169, l. 21, *for* C. and F. *read* C. and E.

p. 174, l. 12, *for* marked *read* a marked

p. 180, l. 9, *for* subscripted *read* subscribed

p. 183, *note*, l. 1, *after* oratio *delete* full stop.

p. 186, l. 3 from bottom, *for* cæli *read* cœli

p. 187, l. 4, *for* alus *read* aliis

p. 192, l. 26, *after* a post *add* (1).

„ l. 32, *for* (2) *read* (3).

p. 197, last line, *for* p. xviii. *read* p. xvii.

p. 203, l. 4, *for* Hwanne *read* Hwenne

„ *note* (2), l. 10, *for* is hire teye. *read* in hire teye

p. 205, l. 13, *for* 1540 *read* 1549

p. 209, l. 3, *for* of conception *read* of the conception

p. 236, l. 13, *for* (4) *read* (5).

„ l. 18, *for* (5) *read* (4).

p. 255, *note* (4), l. 6, *delete* because

p. 283, l. 1, *for* and which we have seen *read* and as we have seen

p. 339, l. 11, *after* Beverley Minster *add*, I find it stated in the *Book of the Provost of Beverley* (a MS. dated 1410, now the property of Mr Crust of Beverley), fol. 1, that the collegiate church was re-founded by St John of Beverley for divers ministers, including "*sanctimoniales virgines.*"

p. 353, *note* (3), l. 16, *add*, It was ordered by Pope Pius IX, in 1861, that the Emperor should no longer be prayed for, "ob sublatum Romanorum imperium," though the words of the prayer were to be retained in the missal.

p. 360, *note* (1), *for* Athonia *read* Athona

p. 413, *add* -ES, 3 *plur.*, B 16, 44, 46, 105, 164 ; F 119. See *Page* lx.

p. 423, *add* LOVE, *v. a.*, to love, B 451.

CLAY AND TAYLOR, PRINTERS, BUNGAY.

[*To be added to* Meditations, *Original Series*, 1875, *No.* 60.]

NOTE

TO THE

"MEDITATIONS ON THE SUPPER OF OUR LORD AND THE HOURS OF THE PASSION."

Early English Text Society, 1875, Original Series, No. 60.

WHEN Robert Manning's translation of the *Meditations of our Lord* was published in 1875, only two manuscript copies of the Poem were known to be in existence, one in the British Museum, the other in the Bodleian Library. On my return to England a month ago, Miss Toulmin Smith informed me that she had discovered another copy in a MS. volume belonging to the *Bedford Library*, and made arrangements for me to examine it to see whether this copy differed materially from that already published.

Leaves 1 to 175 inclusive of the MS. contain the *Cursor Mundi* in English as far as the Final Judgment. Into the body of the *Cursor* the copyist has worked the *Meditations* as an integral part of that poem. If the reader will turn to Dr Morris's edition of the *Cursor*, Part III, p. 855, he will find the Trinity MS. (l. 14914) reads—

> For to suffere peynes grym
> Monnes soule to haue to him
> Of þe passioun speke we here
> Hoy he vs bouȝte ihesu dere
> Secundum euangelium

Where the Bedford MS. reads (leaf cxix, col. 2)—

Fforto Soffre paynis grim
Manis Soule to haue to hym
Here begynneth þe meditation of
þe pascion of Crist & of þe
Lamentation of oure Lady Saint
Mary þat Sche made for her
Son when Sche Se hym
torment among þe Iewis which
Was compiled of bonaventure
a gode clerk & a Cardinall of Rome
& þe meditacions of all þe houris of þe day.

After going through this new MS. of the *Meditations,* I do not think there is much cause for regret that we did not know of its existence earlier, as it is a much later copy [the MS. is dated on the back of leaf 216, "*primo* die Ianuare Anno dni M.cccc.xlij."] and very inferior to those in the British Museum and the Bodleian. It omits a large number of words, and transposes others, often for the worse, and leaves out lines 7 and 8, 165 and 166, 516 to 523 inclusive, 1041 and 1042, 1141 and 1142. The headings to the different meditations are also omitted.

On the other hand, we have two new lines which occur between ll. 652 and 653 of the printed edition. They are—

Beholde man þy lorde on þe rode
þere was no lym bote þat ran on blode

And the MS. probably gives more correct readings of the following lines than the Brit. Mus. MS. gives :—

214. So ȝiffe þe payne or endeles blis.

216. Is godson quik and not dede.

1101. þey schull in hell euermore a be lore

1102. Bote I hym to þis deth had I bore.

Lines 61-62, 251-252, 887-888, and 1093-1094 have been transposed. Some of the verbal differences may be noted here :—

In l. 50 we find "Seventyn & twey."

Ll. 63, 64. Her table was brode & ffoure quarter
þo maner of a chekyr

103. "wept ffast" for "ete faste"

108. Iudas Scariot þat is So bolde

150. Before his traytour ffete sitting
238. "Comforte" for "enformed"
268. Kitte her hertis & made hem bolde for "colde."
270. with handis wringing for "here hedys bowyng."
316. "Distempryd" for "dysturbled"
344. "day & night" for "gode and ryȝt."
367. "while" for "þyrwhylys"
410. "valay of distres" for "valey of dyrknes"
414. "blode clere" for "blody couloure"
477. "of Iangeling" for "eche a gadlyng"
502. "Schenschipe . . . hate" for "frenshepe . . . debate"
567. "punchyd" for "punged."
578. "Iewis" for "þeues"
608. "þe cros" for "þyn herte"
655. "nailis" for "veynes"
718. "Iohn beholde þy modir" for "beholde þy modyr, broþer"
744. "Anguyschyd" for "angred"
756. "swetyng" for "shyittyng"
850. "I am his modir" for "hys sory modyr."
944. "wroght" for "boȝt" [Better]
958. "Kist his hede" for "lyfte hyt"
974. "Wiped" for "swaþed"
1123. "ffadirs" for "fendys"

With lines 1029-1030 of the printed poem the following from the Bedford MS. may be compared :—

> ȝiff þou arise þe þrid day
> Truly I am comfort ffor euer & aye.

With the following extract from the MS. under examination I bring these few notes to a close :—

> Se now þe maner of þe crucifying
> Two laddirs be sett þe cros behynde
> and two enemyes vp fast þay clymbe
> With hamyrs & naylis scharpely swifft
> A Schort ladder hym pight

282075

þere as þe ffete Schorter were
Beholde þis Sight w*ith* rewly tere
Crist Ihesu his bodye vp stye
Be þe Schort laddir þe cros on hye
W*ith* oute nay he gan vp wende
And when he cam to þe ladder ende .
Towards þe cros his bak he layde
And his riall armys displayed
His ffeyre handis he oute streght
And to þe crucifiers hem right
And to his ffadir he caste his yen
And sayde here I am ffadir myn
Vnto þis cros þou mekist me
My ffor manhede I offre to þe
My breth*ers* & Sist*ers* þou hast made hem
Ffor my loue fadir be merciabill to he*m*
All olde Syn*n*is þou hem fforʒeffe
And grau*n*t þy blis w*ith* vs to lyue
Derworthy fadir saue all man kyn
Lo here I am offred for her Syn.

          Leaf cxxiiij, col. 2, and back.   Lines 628 to 652

                              J. M. COWPER.

Watling Street, Canterbury,
       Jan. 17, 1878.

CPSIA information can be obtained at www.ICGtesting.com
224677LV00011B/9/P

9 781164 050506